595

AT ISSUE:
POLITICS IN THE
WORLD ARENA

Second Edition

At Issue: Politics in the World Arena

Second Edition

STEVEN L. SPIEGEL, Editor
University of California, Los Angeles

St. Martin's Press
New York

To the memory of my father

ACKNOWLEDGMENTS

"Is United States Foreign Policy 'Imperialist' or 'Imperial'?" by Jerome Slater. Reprinted with permission from the *Political Science Quarterly* 91 (Spring 1976), 63–87.

"The Case for Nonintervention" by Melvin Gurtov. From *The United States Against the Third World* by Melvin Gurtov. Published in 1974 by Praeger Publishers, New York. Excerpted and reprinted by permission.

"The Universalization of Ethnicity: Peoples in the Boiling Pot" by Nathan Glazer. From *Encounter*, February 1975, pp. 8–17, © 1975 by Encounter Ltd. Reprinted by permission.

"Ambush at Kamikaze Pass" by Tom Engelhardt. From *Bulletin of Concerned Asian Scholars*, Winter-Spring, 1971, pp. 65–84. Copyright © and permission by Tom Engelhardt.

"The United States in Opposition" by Daniel P. Moynihan. This article originally appeared in *Commentary*, March 1975 (59:3), pp. 31–44. Reprinted from *Commentary*, by permission; copyright © 1975 by the American Jewish Committee.

"The United States and the Third World: A Basis for Accommodation" by Tom Farer. Excerpted by permission from *Foreign Affairs*, October 1975. Copyright 1975 by Council on Foreign Relations, Inc.

"The Strategy of Terrorism" by David Fromkin. Excerpted by permission from *Foreign Affairs*, July 1975. Copyright 1975 by Council on Foreign Relations, Inc.

"Is Peace Possible in the Middle East?" by Walter Laqueur. This article originally appeared in *Commentary*, March 1976, pp. 28–33. Reprinted from *Commentary*, by permission; copyright © 1976 by the American Jewish Committee.

"The Soviet Union, China and the West in Southern Africa" by Colin Legum. Excerpted from *Foreign Affairs*, July 1976. Copyright 1976 by Council on Foreign Relations, Inc.

"U.S. Imperialists, Old and New" by Penny Lernoux. Originally published in *The Nation*, April 3, 1976, pp. 391–397. Reprinted by permission.

"Appeasement and Détente" by Theodore Draper. Reprinted from *Commentary*, by permission. Copyright © 1976 by Theodore Draper. A revised version of this article will be published in *Defending America* by Basic Books, Inc., in April 1977.

"Détente is in the Eye of the Beholder" by Roger Morris. © 1976 by The New York Times Company. Reprinted by permission.

Preface

This second edition of *At Issue,* like the first, seeks to provide a selection of the most useful and interesting articles on the major political, economic, and social issues that are current in international affairs: among them, racial and ethnic conflict, the balance of power, the world crisis in energy and food production, the future possibilities of world order, and the crisis of foreign policy-making institutions. My aim has been to give the reader a sense of the complexities and dynamics of present-day world politics while also providing background on specific questions. Though the problems encountered by Americans in formulating and conducting foreign policy have not been stressed exclusively, I have generally oriented the volume to the dilemmas faced by the United States. The book is therefore designed to be useful for courses in American foreign policy as well as world politics.

The articles presented here were chosen after extensive investigation in the major journals and periodicals that are concerned with international affairs. Over three hundred potential selections were examined; the preferences and reactions of my students counted heavily in the final choice. Among the criteria were readability, the extent to which articles informed students and might be relevant to a variety of international problems, how well they represented a broad spectrum of ideological and national views, and how well they might withstand the constant change of events. Despite efforts to meet this last criterion, however, any book on politics in the world arena is bound to date rapidly; in fact, fewer than half a dozen of the readings from the first edition have been retained in this new one.

I am grateful to many who have provided needed advice and assistance. I am especially indebted to dozens of colleagues around the country who have used the first edition and generously taken the trouble to send me their suggestions for improving it. From its beginnings this book has been a collaborative effort with my students in world politics and American foreign policy at UCLA, and once again their encouragement and vigorous participation have made the project an exciting one. Dana Markiewicz struggled through the long hours of search and reexamination with energy, good cheer, and perceptive analysis. Carol Becker's enthusiasm and personal involvement was an inspiration, which constantly invited the exploration of new perspectives and fresh approaches. Her tireless efforts were much appreciated. As always, I am deeply grateful for the ideas, understanding, and partnership which my wife Fredi provides, and I wish to thank Mira, Nina, and Avishalom for keeping out of the piles of xeroxed papers and heaps of magazines which cluttered the house while this edition was being prepared.

The subjects discussed in this volume represent some of the most important questions now before the statesmen of the world, and many of the articles present grim alternatives and disturbing analyses. On the other hand, humor, or at least an appreciation of irony, seems to me sometimes almost the only possible response to the vicissitudes of world politics, and I trust that an occasional touch of humor in this volume will not be mistaken for levity. Above all, I hope that the reader's experience with this book will help to make the study of international politics both intellectually rewarding and enjoyable.

Steven L. Spiegel

Contents

Prologue

The purpose of this volume is twofold: to identify the crucial developments in international politics with which American foreign policy must deal and to explore several major issues which will necessitate careful and painful decisions in the years ahead. The selected readings are designed to provide material for discussion and debate in the hope that a new American approach to the rest of the world will in fact emerge. Such an approach should be less devoted to ideological abstractions and simple contrasts between weakness and strength or internationalism and isolationism, and more inclined to recognize and respect the distinct cultures in which the peoples of the world exist.

This book is divided into four parts. The first, "The Conflict of Peoples," examines the nature and causes of current international conflicts—between great and small, satisfied and dissatisfied nations. The role of ethnic differences in causing conflict is stressed, but the effects of economic gaps between rich and poor and conflicting great power aims are considered as well. We also examine the turmoil in the Third World which has led to a growing crisis between north and south and a diverse set of responses to the affluent West by nations that feel disadvantaged—responses that range from the strategy of terrorism to economic challenges raised by countries dependent on the export of a single commodity (e.g., copper, coffee).

The second part, "The Burden of the Strong," concentrates on the problems of the relations between the major powers. We assess the relations between the United States and the Soviet Union, the effect of China and its sometimes unfathomable domestic politics on the global balance of power, the role of both the Western European states and Japan as allies of the United States and their potential increased function in the world power balance, and the future of great-power relations within Europe and Asia. We also consider the role of armaments—especially nuclear weapons—in their effect on the balance of power between the United States and the Soviet Union and among less powerful nations that are members of the international system.

The third part, "The Crises of Institutions," deals with the problems that plague political institutions on all levels of global society. The European unity movement, the ineffectuality of the United Nations, and the impact of multinational corporations are considered here. Is the European unity movement stagnating, and if so, what does that mean for the future of America's relations with Europe? Similarly, the withering United Nations will either be revived or it will not play an effective role in an increasingly complex international environment. At the opposite extreme, multinational corporations—those semiprivate

1

and semisovereign agencies which have become progressively more influential in international affairs—probably will continue to grow in prominence. Their role will be explored in this section.

In part three we focus on the nation-state, paying special attention to the United States. We explore organizational constraints and bureaucratic procedures which, some argue, cause governments to act in seemingly irrational ways. In particular, we examine the sorrowful decisions of the Vietnam War and the dubious practices of the U.S. Central Intelligence Agency—two cases in which unquestioned bureaucratic procedures and organizational constraints contributed to serious errors in American foreign policy making.

Finally, in the fourth part, "The Problems of the Future," we consider the promise and pitfalls of technological development, with special attention to population growth, the energy crisis, the food supply, and the environment, and to their possible effects on rich and poor nations alike. As new technologies have developed, enabling people of different cultures to come in closer contact with each other through faster means of travel and communication, many hoped for a comparable increase in international understanding and cooperation. History, however, has moved in another direction, as various groups have made use of improved global communications for harmful ends. The transistor radio thereby becomes a vehicle for whipping the masses into frenzied hatred, the jet airplane an instrument for destruction and a focus for terrorist activities, the oil well a symbol of exploitation or blackmail.

It is ironic indeed that while the superpowers have reached a nuclear standoff, the number of human beings killed in local upheavals has increased at an accelerating rate. The atomic bombs dropped on Hiroshima and Nagasaki killed or wounded approximately 220,000 Japanese; but as many as three million people were killed in the 1971 war for independence of Bangladesh, more than two million in the unsuccessful effort against the Nigerian government to establish an independent state of Biafra, and hundreds of thousands in Indochina during the prolonged conflict in that area. On the one hand, a technology of ever greater destructiveness has made the great powers cautious. On the other hand, weaker states and groups have improved their capacity to engage in traditional types of conflict.

It is evident that future challenges to American foreign policy will be severe. Yet it should also be apparent that the increasing sophistication of our technology offers new opportunities for cooperation as well as conflict. In our opening selection Richard Holbrooke deals with the mood of the United States shortly before James Earle Carter brought his politics of compassion to the Oval Office. Holbrooke cautions against a proliferation of criticism and a diffusion of pessimism as he notes the sense of drift in American policy, but calls for a time of calm. As we turn to the many dilemmas confronting American foreign policy, it is well to remember with Holbrooke the resilience of American institutions after 200 years—including the capacity to withstand the tragedy of the terrible years of Vietnam and Watergate.

Introduction

A Sense of Drift,
A Time for Calm

Richard Holbrooke

For 12 years, . . . one issue—Vietnam—provided a relatively simple litmus test for everyone. People were placed with relative ease on a single-band spectrum from hawk to dove; and individuals moved along it, invariably from right to left, as the war ran into increasing difficulties and growing opposition at home.

Many thought that the battle lines shaped during those years of hard and divisive national debate would continue in the post–Vietnam era. Had they survived intact, the debate would have been relatively clear-cut, easier to understand and follow, than has in fact been the case. But that did not happen.

The sides are no longer clearly drawn. Indeed, the confusion is often so great that one cannot even tell which side of certain debates some of our highest leaders favor. One week President [Ford] seems to side with those fearful that America has become militarily inferior to the Soviet Union. The next week, he asserts that America remains "second to none." His uncertain trumpet is matched by others, including his secretary of state, whose private gloom over the decline of the West is exhibited only rarely in public, where he sticks for the most part to statements that if America will only regain its national consensus and follow its commander in chief, it will again be the most powerful nation on earth. Critics argue that we are getting weaker and must take decisive action to regain clear-cut supremacy. Others assail us for continuing the arrogance of power, of insensitivity to the new realities.

That these are the most difficult questions our nation must face is obvious. But the answers are neither obvious nor, ultimately, empirically derivable. They must come, in fact, out of the confusion of the national debate, and we must understand in advance that the answers will not be definitive.

There is among some observers a feeling that the very casualness of our process argues against hope, presents a case for despair and a pessimistic outcome. Thus we hear James Reston, for example, constantly lament the fact that "Washington" is dealing with "the politics of the problem," not with the problem itself. Yet the distinction is largely misguided; politics *is* the problem but also the opportunity, indeed, the essence of the nation's strength as a democracy.

ODD CONVERGENCE

As America enters its third century, we find an odd conjunction in American political life—a convergence of two different critiques of America: the Vietnam-based, guilt-ridden anguish of the left, and the striking emergence, in the last year, of a new pessimism within what is often called the neoconservatives. Each group inadvertently reinforces the other, and adds to our national sense of drift and uncertainty.

Vast differences, of course, exist between the two groups here described, and it is for this reason that one must assume, and hope, that their present conjunction is inadvertent and temporary. Increasingly, the left has looked on the state as an enemy, a force that must be weakened since it cannot be captured. The conservatives on the other hand now see strong state power as their potential ally, and view what they regard as its erosion as a grave threat. These are not straw men; they are the focus of the debate. Both approaches are equally misguided.

Liberals, predictably, will find themselves in the middle of this overly simplified spectrum. Their present anguish is by now well documented. It stems primarily from Vietnam, but many other issues merged over recent years to reinforce the lessons of that ugly war. The roll call of policies which liberals advocated and which turned out to be corrupt is almost too long to list.

A few key elements of this view of America as a corrupting influence in the world should be mentioned, however, if only to remind us of just how sad our recent string of revelations has been. Beyond Vietnam they include: Cambodia, Chile, Bangladesh, Burundi, Angola, Cyprus, FBI and CIA abuses and excesses, Watergate, Lockheed and other improper business practices overseas, ITT, and assassination attempts. Each revelation was an essential part of the process of redefining our past and rethinking our future; those who argue that the revelations themselves are wrong are missing the deeper significance of what they call an "orgy of self-destruction." It is essential to understand our past in order to reshape our future.

But the left's critique of America's role in the world has taken on some ominous overtones. There are those who now accept the proposition that because America has done some evil things, America itself is an evil force in the world. The theological overtones are disturbing, of course, but so is the ease with which some people can now embrace extreme extrapolations.

But even more fundamental is the abuse of reason which is involved in such black-and-white views of foreign policy. At its best, foreign policy is often a choice between the lesser of two evils. And many policy issues come down to a choice between conflicting positive principles—when, for example, the principle of non-intervention in the internal affairs of another country conflicts with a concern for human rights.

These conflicts must be resolved in ways that do not seem immoral or unreasonable to most people. That this so often has not always been the case does not mean that our nation is itself evil or incapable of finding a better foreign policy. It does mean that we have been badly led. Thus, in their sweeping horror at the consequences of the use of power, in their willingness to assume the worst about their own country, in their disillusionment with the bright, liberal rhetoric of the Kennedy years, the left critique—at least at its anguished worst—is a cul de sac, a dead end, which could lead to isolation from the rest of the nation.

This potential isolation is by no means a sure thing. Relatively few people want to cut themselves off entirely. What looks like a group is in fact a spectrum, a range of opinions. While some people are falling off the end, many are climbing back on. . . .

THE NEW PESSIMISTS

The left has recently been met more than half-way by some people who are not even perceived of as a group. Some of them have been called neoconservatives, but they have now become, in fact, "the new pessimists"—although they would presumably resist the description.

The new pessimists tend to see their worst fears about the decline of American power coming true. Many of them predicted that if the United States abandoned its commitments to the South Vietnamese government of Nguyen Van Thieu, it would mark the end of American leadership in the world. In the congressional votes on such issues as Turkish aid and Angola, they find grim evidence that they were right. In the assaults and revelations of the press—including for some even Watergate—they see signs of the collapse of essential authority. In the growth of Soviet military power, they see the greatest imaginable threat to America's survival.

A remarkable example of this sort of thinking was Norman Podhoretz' lead article in the April [1976] issue of *Commentary,* which he edits, dramatically titled, "Making the World Safe for Communism." But other examples abound; the verbal similarities between the left and right pessimists symbolize the strange covergence that is taking place. Bruce Russett, an opponent of the war, and Henry Brandon, reflecting in part the outlook of Henry Kissinger, write of "The Retreat of American Power." Henry Steele Commager calls his latest collection of essays, simply: "The Defeat of America." *Commentary* runs an entire issue under the theme, "A Failure of Nerve?" Richard Rosecrance edits a collection of essays by leading American and European observers with the odd and wholly inaccurate title, "America as an Ordinary Country."

C. L. Sulzberger, writing in *The New York Times* from London, describes a decline in American prestige overseas exceeding "by far what most Americans imagine to be the case." Many Americans, wrote Stanley Karnow in *Newsweek International,* were reluctantly conceding General de Gaulle's cruel description of the United States as a nation that had gone from "infancy to decadence without attaining maturity." Daniel Patrick Moynihan, having lately left his bully pulpit at the United Nations, has described democracy as a "recessive form of government, like monarchies used to be—something the world is moving from, rather than to." James Schlesinger has written that "The West is clearly in disarray, and within a few years could actually be at bay." And *U.S. News and World Report* ran a special cover story asking, "Is Democracy Dying?" Their "upbeat" answer, in effect: "Not Yet."

The message of the new pessimists varies, and sooner or later they usually make some rhetorical bow in the direction of traditional American pride. Politics requires even pessimists to express some faith in their country, but there is an underlying gloom which can be summarized as follows:

> The presidency is so important as an institution that we must be ready even to accept specific errors of presidents, such as Vietnam or Watergate, in the national interest.

> Public debate and congressional involvement in foreign policy are dangerous, if not downright immoral. Congress, in particular, is a body whose involvement in foreign policy is by and large an unwarranted interference.

> The true measure of a nation's strength is its international reach and influence. Domestic issues may come and go, but the nation is measured primarily by its international standing.

> That standing is in turn measured by the amount of disposable power—military power—that a country can apply.

> The hard give-and-take of the democratic process, at least when it intrudes into foreign policy, is somewhat distasteful. The press in particular is an adversary, increasingly seen as a threat to democracy rather than one of its main attributes.

Every one of the arguments cited above has, in my opinion, some validity; none comes solely from thin air or overheated imagination. Congress *is* a mess, often shallow and ineffectual. The press *is* a mixed bag, ranging from outstanding through irrelevant to just plain awful and irresponsible. Public debate on foreign policy issues *does* make implementation of policy more constrained, more chaotic, and more difficult. And military power *is,* without question, a vital ingredient of our policy.

Furthermore, the nation *is* clearly drifting. Its leaders have failed us far too often in recent years, the bright promises of their television rhetoric dimmed by poor performance and shallow deceits. Public relations has replaced policies: imagery has succeeded where imagination has failed. This failure of leadership goes far beyond weakness in the Oval Office, and encompasses Congress and the press, business and labor. It is not surprising that every survey of the people shows that confidence in institutions—virtually all institutions with the possible exception of the Supreme Court—is at an all-time low.

WHO ARE THE NEW PESSIMISTS?

What are we to make of this extraordinary conjunction of the new pessimism of the conservatives with the older, Vietnam-based, guilt-ridden pessimism of the liberals? Is it temporary, an accidental meeting of different groups with different objectives, momentarily joined in common dismay with the situation we confront? Or is it rather, in Winston Churchill's phrase from another time, the "end of the beginning" of our magnificent history? Daniel Bell, for one, is not sure. After writing that "The American century lasted scarcely 30 years, [and] foundered on the shoals of Vietnam," he concludes on a hopeful note: "Of all the gifts bestowed on this country at its founding, the one that alone remains as the element of American exceptionalism is the constitutional system. . . ." If that remains, says Bell—referring to the "common respect for the framework of law, and the acceptance of outcomes under due process"—then the United States may remain "humanized among nations." It is a thoughtful and sober yet hopeful conclusion, one that I share. Unfortunately, it is not shared by many of the new pessimists, or the left, still confused by the recent past.

Recently I talked with a distinguished American political scientist, now spending a year in Paris. "What are you doing?" I asked. "Oh," he replied, "I spend most of my time explaining to French editors and professors that America is not finished in the world." "But why do they think that?" I asked. "Because Kissinger keeps telling it to them in private," he replied.

What an extraordinary thought. Kissinger would deny it, of course, but think of it a moment: The U.S. secretary of state as a leading spokesman for the theory that America is in retreat.

It is true?

Lately, Kissinger's sensitive antennae have begun to tell him that too many people have heard him lament the future of civilization, that he has been *too* gloomy, and that his message is not consistent with the demands of the presidential campaign. Accordingly, he has begun to swing around again, and in his public statements he has begun to extol our virtues and our strengths.[1] But his recent repositioning seems more tactical than thoughtful; for a long time it has been no secret that Kissinger is desperately concerned about the fate of this country, and that his own personal political difficulties have heightened his gloom.

So, despite recent public adjustments, Kissinger must be understood as a key to the new pessimism. Normally, no single person could have such a pivotal role, but Kissinger remains unique, a man with continuing influence among academicians and intellectuals, journalists and foreign leaders. Even in his decline, Kissinger's voice is by far the most powerful and important in this country today on foreign policy; raised now in private frustration against his own country's recent course and his own growing troubles, it is being listened to overseas.

Kissinger's behavior is, to my mind, strange for a secretary of state. He has confused his own troubles with those of the republic. But even if his assessments were true, which I do not believe to be the case, Kissinger should not make the kinds of statements that he has recently been making in private. If Kissinger believes that the American era is over, crushed beneath the weight of our unwieldy processes that he does not believe in, he is hardly the best man to represent our nation internationally, no matter how skilled he is as a negotiator.

But Kissinger stays on, convinced that if our decline is under way, then he is the man best equipped to get the best deal for us before it is too late. One may be pardoned, I hope, for questioning both assumptions.

Kissinger is not alone in his views. But curiously, the two men in public life who have taken positions most close to his, in overall, historic terms, have been such bitter personal rivals for power and attention that the unlikely trio has gone so far unremarked. I refer, of course, to Daniel Patrick Moynihan and James Schlesinger. While in the government, both men were thorns in Kissinger's bureaucratic side. Each sought access to the president, and a role in the formulation of American policy which exceeded Kissinger's desires. What Kissinger wanted, as we all know, was maximum control over the processes and policies of the executive branch, and minimum interference from Congress. Neither Moynihan nor Schlesinger was willing to concede the game to Kissinger, and thus, while each was still in service, Kissinger fought them regularly, raged against them behind their backs, and intrigued against them at every opportunity. In the case of Schlesinger, Kissinger succeeded too well, and now finds himself facing a new secretary of defense who is less knowledgeable about technical defense issues, yet more potent politically—that is, a man who knows less and can get more. In Moynihan's case, Kissinger helped make Moynihan a minor folk hero.

But my point does not concern their differences, which were often overadvertised by the press and are, in any case, no longer a factor in the formulation of policy. The critical conjunction does not concern their disagreement on the Soviet Backfire bomber, or what Kissinger and Moynihan say about each other.

Rather, it is the common conviction all three seem to share that America's strength has been shattered by the erosion of unity at the center, by the excessive interference of Congress, by the attacks of the press, by our weakness in standing up to our critics overseas, and by an unchecked growth of Soviet power.

To all three men, and to others who share their views, the fault seems to lie in a lessening of central authority, in a weakening of the strength of the institutions, far more than a *weakness* in our leaders. Listening to them, I fear that I hear them saying, between the lines, "The fault is in the people, who, egged on by Congress and the press, are losing faith in their institutions." They don't say, as I would, "Perhaps the fault is in the quality of leadership."

The quality of leadership—no wonder people shy away from the issue. After all, it is hard enough to judge such matters generations later, even for historians who can argue heatedly over the nature and quality of, say, Franklin Roosevelt's leadership. Impossible, then, to deal with a comparison between today's pygmies and the giants of our mythic memory. Yet it is hard to believe that they, or their subordinates, will measure up to the men of earlier times.

I do not mean to sound nostalgic, but I fear we are in the hands of a pygmy generation, and that instinctively people know it. The last of the great figures of World War II and the cold war have departed the active scene, replaced by their staff aides, special assistants, and cautious bureaucrats. In business, faceless organization men have taken over huge, self-perpetuating corporations. In journalism, a more confusing picture, worthy of more detailed analysis, has emerged, for the press can no longer hide behind its traditional shield as a mere observer—it has become a participant, and to some a very special object of hate and blame. Its dominant force now is television, its guiding lights a new set of values; success is show biz. In Congress, the collapse of the rigid old baronies was necessary, but nothing coherent has come forward to replace them yet; instead, chaos under decent and ineffectual leaders has been the trend. And in labor, the dinosaurs hang on, immensely powerful, but without vision.

EASY ANSWERS

To some, the answers to America's present malaise are simple. They call for more unity behind the president—simply because he is president, right or wrong; increased defense spending, to counter the growth of the Soviet military; and ways to restrain the press, that unruly and sensation-seeking adolescent who keeps printing the wrong thing at the wrong time.

In particular, lately, a growing number of critics of the so-called "neoconservative" school are concentrating their fire on the "media," blaming it for, or crediting it with—take your pick—far more than it really deserves. If the news is bad, the press is increasingly blamed for bringing it to us, for twisting it into a negative mold.

No matter what the excesses and errors of the press, this argument strikes me as a refuge for people who are no longer willing to present their case openly, to let it ride or fall on how it is judged by the people. The role of the press and television is critical in America today, but it is not the villain some have made it out to be.

What is really going on? Our internal debates have been so bitter that it is hard to look at the real strength of the nation.

Not that this task is easy. Disputes rage these days over almost every measurement of our national strength, especially in comparison to that of the Soviet Union. Who is spending more on defense? Who has the greater strategic weapons capability? Who has more natural resources? Who produces more steel? Food? Doctors? Who gained and who lost in Angola? In the Middle East?

I do not propose to address each one of these difficult questions here. But it is important never to lose sight of some basic facts about our nation's real strengths—strengths so immense that they have carried us through the traumas of the last decade; strengths which are still there, waiting to be rekindled by new and better leaders.

First, to start with Schlesinger's own definition of power, we remain, by a considerable margin, the most powerful nation on earth militarily. While Schlesinger would admit this, he would maintain that the trend is disturbing. But our strategic nuclear striking power is more than enough to deter an attack by any rational decision-maker, and no amount of power can deter an attack by an irrational leader.

But I would question the very measurement of power as partially outmoded. America must remain a strong power militarily, but what we have learned in recent years is that other kinds of power are growing rapidly in importance—economic power, resource and energy power, food power. To maintain enough strength to influence events as we need to, we need all these kinds of power—and fortunately we do, to a degree that is still unmatched in the history of the world, *except by our own recent past.*

Economically, the United States enters its third century still in a clear world leadership role. At the end of a world war in which everyone else paid devastating costs, we were totally dominant, and that hegemonial era, of course, has ended. America's importance in the world economy has declined in relative terms, but we remain first. Our share of world GNP, 39 per cent in 1950, is down to 27 per cent now—still a huge percentage. The dollar has grown in importance, and there is every likelihood that it will remain the dominant currency for at least the next decade.[2] In short, if we no longer make all the rules in the economic world, we remain the unquestioned leader.

Is this a bad thing, a sign of decline? Hardly. The nearly absolute position of dominance that followed the 1944 Bretton Woods agreements had to end, and indeed our own enlightened policies of foreign aid to Europe and Japan encouraged and hastened the process. The problems we now deal with in the economic sphere are to a considerable extent problems of success. That does not lessen their importance—but it should at least put the situation in perspective.

What the present situation requires has been expressed by Marina v.N. Whitman as follows: ". . . to find the political will to modify our own short-term economic interests to the requirements of an international economic order which we no longer control." We must use our natural strengths, she concludes, to replace "leadership based on hegemony with leadership based on persuasion and compromise." While the task will be difficult, it is within reach; Whitman points out, "there is no acceptable alternative."[3]

As for energy and natural resources, the emphasis has been, rightly, on our growing dependence on foreign sources. But we should, once again, not forget that solutions or at least reductions in the size of our problems are within our reach, and that the United States has been hurt less than any other importing country by the five-fold increase in the price of oil since 1973. Our comparative advantage, ironically, increased in many ways during this period.

Then there is food. It is by now well-known that we have become the breadbasket of the world. The United States and Canada will probably export, for example, a total of 94 million metric tons of grain in 1976. Of the seven major regions of the world, only one other, Australia-New Zealand, will be a wheat exporter. The rest of the world will be net importers, and the second biggest importer of all will probably be the Soviet Union.

This is a relatively new development. Prior to World War II all geographic regions except Western Europe were net exporters. The two worst performances in this area have been in Asia and the Soviet Union. In fact, the Russian performance in agriculture is appalling, and must be taken into account when trying to measure how the two powers compare. And as for the rest of the world, the worldwide movement outside North America from export to import status has been a one-way street: no country has gone against this trend in the last two decades. Here, surely, is an area where we must take the lead internationally, demanding certain performance levels and reserve systems, while still dealing with farmers' concerns at home.

If we remain the strongest nation militarily, economically, and in terms of resources and food, why do some Americans fear that history now favors the Russians?

The answer, of course, takes us right back to where we started, not with our strengths but our divisions. Kissinger and many others feel that such sights as the congressional rejection of aid to Angola are an invitation to the Soviet Union to begin knocking on the next door, perhaps Rhodesia or Zambia. Or that Castro, emboldened by Angola, will try his hand again. Or that the Israelis will conclude that we would no longer stand by them in a showdown. In short, that our word is no longer good; that, in Podhoretz' prophecy, we are witnessing the beginning of "Finlandization from within."

There is a serious conceptual trap which is implicit in these theories of America's decline. They are derived in large part from the concept that *perceptions* of power and national will are just as important as actual national strength itself—and that the world perceives our resolve and will as eroded.

But from what evidence would one deduce the erosion of American will or strength? In fact, the people who profess the greatest concern with that erosion are the same people who most regularly proclaim it; they are the heralds of the very thing they most lament.

This approach is difficult to deal with because it confuses objectives and values. Was Angola, for example, of real importance to the United States? Not really—and anyway, we could have sought relations with the MPLA. Yet the Russians were there, and we were caught again in the old and cruel trap—if Moscow is on one side, we must be on the other, as indeed we have been for many years. The result, in this case, was accentuated by Kissinger's public behavior. Knowing in advance that the Congress would reject any request for aid in Angola, Kissinger nonetheless made major public statements that the vote was critical, and if it failed, then we would be seen around the world as having measurably weakened. How unskillful to draw attention to a certain impending defeat! What priorities and values lie behind such odd action? I confess to some uncertainty as to whether or not Kissinger did it because he wanted to emphasize the importance of the vote and perhaps turn it around, or because he and the president wanted to lay responsibility for the inevitable MPLA triumph in Angola at Congress' feet. In either case, it is not the sort of thing that a person seeking to maximize his strength would do—to choose a losing battle and then raise the ante just before defeat. Angola, however, followed a recurring pattern.

HISTORY DOES NOT FAVOR MOSCOW

In any case, history does not favor the Russians. In a dreadful decade for America, they have made few inroads internationally—and have been set back themselves in some areas. They have seen their side gain for the first time in Africa just now, but they have lost in the Arab world since 1972, when Sadat kicked them out of Egypt. They have made gains in South Asia, in India, but have not turned Communist Vietnam or half-crazed Cambodia into part of their orbit. Their bitter conflict with China continues. In Western Europe, they have watched Rumania follow Yugoslavia into nearly independent status, and have been unable to keep control over the Communist parties of Italy and France. In Portugal, the situation, once so bright, has dimmed. Their leadership is old and uninspired, their system destructively rigid. "A process of degeneration has set in," says Zbigniew Brzezinski, although "it has not yet reached critical proportions."

Some scholars viewing the twin difficulties of the two greatest powers, have concluded that there is something systemically wrong with the way governments and institutions deal with the problems of the modern world. But I suspect that the differences between the two systems are so vast that they will respond differently to future challenges.

We are living in a peculiar moment, almost suspended between Vietnam and Watergate on the one hand, and the election of a president on the other. For the first time we have an appointed president. We have been going through a relentless and grueling re-examination of ourselves, a period of self-revelation and public exposure that might have caused a revolution in a country less strong than ours. But to sweep the problems away, or to deny them, or to punish those who draw attention to them, would be unwise and still more divisive. What is vitally important is that we learn from our mistakes and our past, but not give up our dreams and values as a nation.

That we have fallen far short of those dreams and values we all know. But they are worthy goals, and worth pursuing still. The nation is still strong, far stronger than its critics of either liberal or conservative persuasion realize. It can survive everything but its own defeatism. We must take counsel of our fears, but not be governed by them.

We still possess, in addition to the sheer measurable elements of power already mentioned, an enormous force that we cannot use these days, but that I hope will once again, someday, be part of our "arsenal"—the basic moral force that exists in the principles of our system of government—a force eroded in recent years under leaders who apparently did not really believe in them.

Implicit in the beliefs and attitudes of some of our recent leaders is the feeling that we can only be strong by not being ourselves; that surely is the domestic equivalent of one of the most unfortunate phrases from the Vietnam war, that "We had to destroy the town in order to save it."

I end, then, not with a prediction—for the world is too uncertain for that—but with an expression of personal hope: that this slum of a decade we have lived through will end, and that we will regain our self-confidence and self-esteem; that we will recognize that we do not need to dominate the world in order to live safely in it, still the most powerful nation on earth. And above all, we must retain our belief in the exceptional nature of our system of democracy. That is our ultimate source of strength.

NOTES

[1] In Phoenix, Arizona, for example, on April 16, Kissinger sounded oddly like the man he was attacking, Ronald Reagan. But rhetoric makes strange bedfellows.

[2] See Richard N. Cooper, "The Future of the Dollar," FOREIGN POLICY 11.

[3] Marina v.N. Whitman, "Leadership without Hegemony," FOREIGN POLICY 20, p. 160.

PART
I
The Conflict of Peoples

The first part of this volume concentrates on the conflicts of peoples: disputes between nations or groups in close proximity who are thrust into conflict by economic, ideological, social, or ethnic divergence; and disputes between strong and weak powers over differences in military strength and wealth. All of these articles focus on deeply held attitudes of hostility among peoples, but each has a different perspective on the origins of international conflicts.

The first two articles in the opening section of this part deal with the record of the United States in foreign affairs: Is the United States an imperialistic power? Should it continually intervene in the affairs of others? Jerome Slater in "Is United States Policy 'Imperialist' or 'Imperial'?" examines the radical critique of American foreign policy and finds it lacking. He asks, "If the United States is an 'imperial' power, where is its empire?" In examining the American position in the Third World, Slater finds a waning U.S. influence, little domination, and no control. This author assesses America's declining inclination toward military intervention and the inherent weaknesses of economic intervention. Melvin Gurtov, however, focuses on U.S. military interventions. In making "The Case for Nonintervention" he concentrates on the ideological consensus which, he believes, led American policymakers to expansionist interpretations of the national interest and distorted perceptions of developments in the Third World. But in arguing against a policy of intervention, Gurtov leaves the door open a bit by proposing conditions when intervention might be acceptable. Readers must consider the merits of these conditions. How would you deal with crises in southern Africa, Korea, the Middle East? What about threats to such non–Third World countries as Great Britain, Japan, West Germany, even Israel? Perhaps the conditions which Slater identifies are sufficient to account for the creeping caution in American policy; perhaps Gurtov's strictures must be followed or a tendency to activist intervention will be reinforced.

These first two articles develop the theme of the impact of national outlook and cultural divergence on the attitudes of particular groups toward their adversaries in other countries. Nathan Glazer in "The Universalization of Ethnicity" deals with the problems resulting from

15

the fact that ethnic identities are becoming less coincidental with national boundaries. Despite the popularity of Marxist doctrine around
the world, ethnicity is becoming a stronger basis for peoples' loyalty
than class. Thus we are faced with the curious situation that recent
technological improvements in communications and transportation
coincides with a period of "fragmentation," when people identify with
groups which constitute entities that are different from and often
smaller than their nation-state. Instead of causing cooperative impulses, the new world "disorder" has frequently led to intensified
conflict. Glazer deals in detail with the implications of these new conditions; we examine their repercussions throughout the remainder of
this volume.

As an example, Tom Engelhardt in "Ambush at Kamikaze Pass"
warns that their estrangement from one another may not consciously
be recognized by different peoples. Many American readers may view
Engelhardt's characterization with skepticism and be reluctant to accept the article's conclusions. But Engelhardt teaches an important
lesson: enmity need not be conscious; subliminal suspicion toward
those who look or act different from us may easily lead to conflict.
Engelhardt demonstrates how American cinema has reflected and per-
petuated prevailing American views of other peoples. Though his
article deals with the United States, it could be applied to other countries as well. For example, the Russian fear of peoples both to their west
and east, especially the Germans and the Chinese, is an often re-
counted theme in Soviet cinema. The Engelhardt article should
sharpen Americans' awareness of their prejudices.

In the next section we turn from the less often recognized conflicts
of ethnic bias and hostility to the more traditional and better-known
issue of the gap between have and have-not countries. Here the problems are exploitation, inequality, and economic development, as well as
perceived ethnic discrimination. The complaint of most Third World
countries was well presented by President Boumédienne of Algeria in a
United Nations General Assembly speech delivered in April 1974 when
he said, "The will to gain and cling to their position of dominance over
world resources has been the guiding principle in the behavior of the
major imperialist powers of the world." In their articles, Daniel Patrick
Moynihan and Tom Farer address themselves to the challenge of the
third world. In a piece written shortly before he became the U.S. delegate to the United Nations for a brief but controversial and vibrant
tenure, Moynihan examines "The United States in Opposition" to the
large majority of developing states. He claims Americans have failed to
understand the prevailing philosophy in the Third World, an outlook
heavily influenced by British socialism with an ironic, inherent
bias against economic development. According to Moynihan, this
philosophy favors redistribution of wealth rather than production.
Moynihan recommends a more activist policy in defense of American
values by calling for the defense of civil and political liberties and the
censure of those who preach but do not practice equity and justice. His

criticism (but not his latent optimism) is reinforced by the "Prime Minister's coup d'etat" of 1975 in India, by which India's Indira Gandhi suppressed her opponents and seized nearly dictatorial power.

Moynihan is inspiring in style and substance; by comparison, Farer is more sober in both regards. He explicitly rejects Moynihan's theoretical hypotheses and practical recommendations. Instead he advocates accommodation to legitimate demands as the essence of statesmanship rather than as a demonstration of weak will. Farer's premise is that the harshness of Third World rhetoric and the cohesiveness of the Third World is explainable not only in terms of economics, but more importantly, in wounded pride and sensitivities which result from these countries' continued relegation to inferior positions by countries of the developed world. He advocates a more accepting attitude, singling out American policy toward South Africa, the Arab-Israeli conflict, and questions of global wealth. Since Farer wrote his article, conditions have altered somewhat. In an African tour of April 1976, U.S. Secretary of State Henry Kissinger indicated a change in the U.S. position, oriented toward majority rule for Rhodesia and independence for Namibia—the southwest African territory controlled by South Africa.* In the Middle East, the Lebanese civil war has demonstrated the political and military weakness of the Palestine Liberation Organization (PLO), causing the Arab world to fall into even more than its accustomed disunity. The civil war has also raised questions anew concerning the soundness of a policy for resolving the Palestinian question before relations among Arab states have stabilized and without clear indications of a willingness by Palestinian leaders to normalize relations with Israel.

Moynihan and Farer present contrasting approaches for dealing with the Third World challenge. Readers will have to determine whether they favor Farer's approach to accommodation, Moynihan's defense of Western values, or some other course.

The other aspect of American reaction to the Third World is revealed by an examination of the actual turmoil occurring there. To illustrate this chaos we have selected four major problem areas— international terrorism, the Middle East, southern Africa and the Panama canal issue. Terrorism is the great symbol of frustration and alienation in the modern world. As Michael Walzer has pointed out, no longer do terrorists attack individuals they perceive as guilty of specific wrongs against a class, group, or state; rather, innocent victims are used as instruments for terrorists' political objectives.** In his article "The Strategy of Terrorism" David Fromkin argues that, lacking sufficient strength to achieve their aims, terrorists depend on the outraged over-reaction of the terrorized to accomplish their goals. The

*See the article by Colin Legum, "The Soviet Union, China and the West in Southern Africa."

**Michael Walzer, "The New Terrorists," *The New Republic,* August 30, 1975, pp. 12–14.

author's historical examples are instructive and his arguments impressive, yet his position is not uncontroversial. Spectacular counterattacks like the Israeli rescue mission at Uganda's Entebbe Airport on July 4, 1976, can raise morale at home and diminish terrorist stature abroad. Fromkin teaches us important lessons, and patience is one, but his message is tempered by the knowledge that most governments have been unprepared to adopt the full range of measures open to them to protect their citizens against terrorist raids. Yet, few can argue with his contention that "Terrorism wins only if you respond to it in the way that the terrorists want you to." The problem for governments is choosing the appropriate reaction.

Terrorism has been used more widely in the Arab-Israeli dispute than in any other recent international conflict. In our next article Walter Laqueur asks the tantalizing question, "Is Peace Possible in the Middle East?" Judging from his response, the answer is no. Laqueur identifies the many problems associated with the illusive solution of establishing a Palestinian state between Israel and Jordan. He also seeks to discredit several myths about Middle East peacemaking. Here his views are sobering, for he points out that even if lasting peace between Arabs and Israelis could be achieved (and he does not believe that it will), the Middle East would still be unstable because of the many conflicts among Arab states. The civil war in Lebanon, which began in 1975, is tragic testimony to the accuracy of these remarks and of the recurrence of ethnic conflict.

Ethnic hostility is also a central factor in the conflict in southern Africa. But despite facile attempts to link the Arab-Israeli and southern African disputes, the issues are totally divergent. Colin Legum, examining the role of "The Soviet Union, China and the West in Southern Africa," demonstrates one of the differences—the pattern of outside intrusion. He describes the rivalry between China and the Soviet Union for influence with the liberation movements of the area and the implicit alliance between the United States and China. He skillfully depicts these outside influences against the dynamics of the dispute itself. The trends and issues Legum assesses are crucial in helping us understand the complexities of this region—previously unknown to most Americans.

A slightly different view of the turmoil in the Third World is presented by Penny Lernoux in "Face-off in Panama: U.S. Imperialists, Old and New." Like Legum, Lernoux deals with a case of outside intrusion in a local area, yet here the question is not one of competition among great powers but of a great power in trouble. Lernoux shows how domestic disputes within Panama and the United States have produced a stalemate in discussions over a new treaty between the two countries. She points out that the issue has become a symbol of U.S. domination in Latin America in particular and the Third World as a whole, and she argues that unless the Panamanians acquire greater control over the territory within their borders, the political and economic losses for the United States will far outweigh any tactical military benefits.

The upheavals in all three of these regions—the Middle East, southern Africa, and Latin America—vitally affect the interests of the United States. How to react to these new challenges—to accommodate or confront; to pursue the defensive or the offensive; to compromise or stand firm—are critical questions that will confront American policy-makers in the next several years. Whatever solutions are offered, the turmoil in the Third World is likely to remain and to assume a variety of forms.

Imperialism and Intervention: The Dynamism of the Strong

1 Is United States Foreign Policy "Imperialist" or "Imperial"?

Jerome Slater

For most of the postwar period the dominant scholarly consensus on the United States role in international politics closely paralleled the image that policy makers themselves held: the United States was a defensive, status-quo power seeking to contain the revolutionary or simply imperialist expansionism of Soviet-led communism. The dominant critique of United States foreign policy operated well within this framework of assumptions; one common argument was that the United States had a tendency to overreach itself, to undertake commitments that excessively taxed its military and economic capabilities. The focus was on the *limits* of American power; critics never tired of quoting Sir Denis Brogan on "the illusions of American omnipotence."

RADICAL "IMPERIALIST" THEORIES

In a remarkably short time, this dominant image of the role the United States has played since World War II has shifted, at first only among radicals, but more recently—and more importantly—among a growing number of mainstream historians and political scientists. Since the early 1960s radical critics have seen the American role as imperialistic rather than defensive: a deliberate, planned, and generally quite successful effort at world domination under the pretext of the "containment" of a largely nonexistent communist military or political threat. The central goal of this domination usually is described in terms of the open-door policy—maintaining access on favorable terms to overseas raw materials, markets, and investment outlets for United States private capital. On behalf of the open-door policy the government, acting as an instrument of American corporate interests, has consistently sought to preserve a capitalist status quo around the world, covertly or overtly employing the vast range of power at its disposal to crush all incipient or actual threats. Even the policy makers, it is argued, do not "really" believe the threat to be communism per se—witness the growing normalization of relations with an increasingly status-quo Soviet Union and even China!—but rather revolution, socialism, or even simply nationalism, for truly socialist or nationalist regimes would close off their economies to United States penetration and domination. Radical critics, then, see economic self-aggrandizement at the heart of American imperialism, although some point to the Wilsonian crusading idealist tradition—the mission to bring the blessings of capitalist freedom and democracy to the rest of the world—as a separate but complementary historical force that only serves to deepen and legitimize the American expansionist drive.[1]

Implicitly or explicitly, United States expansionism is seen as analogous in both motivation and consequences to nineteenth-century European colonialism. Outright military invasion and occupation (except as a last resort) is no longer feasible in the era of modern nationalism, countervailing Soviet power, and potential domestic opposition, the argument runs, so neoimperialism has developed new, more subtle methods. Through its vast economic power—the billions of dollars invested in the Third World by American-controlled multinational corporations; United States government control of economic assistance to underdeveloped countries, either directly in its bilateral programs or indirectly through its domination of the major international financial institutions; the dependence of Third World countries on American markets for their exports of raw materials and commodities and imports of manufactured goods and modern technology; the centrality of the dollar in the world monetary system, etc.—the United States works to keep the rest of the world conservative, capitalist, and docile. As Harry Magdoff, one of the most influential theorists of neoimperialism puts it: "Colonialism, considered as the direct application of military and political force, was essential to reshape the social and economic institutions of many of the dependent countries to the needs of the metropolitan centres. Once this reshaping had been accomplished economic forces—the international price, marketing, and financial systems—were by themselves sufficient to perpetuate and indeed intensify the relationship of dominance. . . ."[2]

In any case, economic power is supplemented by close American ties with conservative local elites, whose own continued status and power is dependent on United States support—the politicians; the bureaucrats; and especially the forces of repression, the military and the police, who are trained, financed, equipped, and frequently led by American "advisors." At a more subtle or insidious level, there is the power of "cultural imperialism," the central role of the United States in the world communications network and mass media, which provides the means to shape popular images and aspirations in ways consistent with the maintenance of world capitalism and United States domination.

If more forceful action is necessary to prevent undesirable change and shore up cooperative client governments, the argument continues, the CIA is always available to provide information, advice, propaganda, subsidies, bribes, weapons, private armies, and a whole repertoire of "dirty tricks," including coups d'etats and/or the murder of particularly stubborn recalcitrants. And if all else fails, direct military action, facilitated by the worldwide network of United States bases and troop deployments, can shore up the empire at its weakest points, as in Lebanon, the Dominican Republic, and Indochina.

Such is the power of neoimperialism, then, that outright colonial occupation and rule is not merely impractical, but it is unnecessary, for the same ends can be attained equally if not even more effectively, precisely because of the more subtle, insidious, unrecognized nature of the new methods of domination and exploitation: *only imperfect amateurish imperialism needs weapons; professional imperialism is based on structural rather than direct violence.*[3] Indeed, not only are the methods of neoimperialism more effective, but the scope of its domain is greater than even the most extensive of the territorial empires of the past, for modern imperialism "knows no frontiers," "extends its net over the whole planet"; "the empire is everywhere."[4] So goes the radical, neo-Marxist critique of United States foreign policy.

NONRADICAL "IMPERIAL" THEORIES

Somewhat unexpectedly, in the last decade or so important aspects of this radical analysis have been accepted by an increasing number of nonradical, non-Marxist students of United States foreign policy, and even by some conservatives. Though it is not accurate to describe the overall United States world role as *imperialist* or *imperialistic*, they argue, it is accurate to describe it as *imperial*. No analyst thus far has thoroughly and systematically contrasted the concept of an "imperial" role with an "imperialist" one, but it seems clear that at least four important distinctions usually are implied. First, imperial policies are seen to be primarily a function of the structure of the *international* rather than the *domestic* system, in particular, of course, the absence of international institutions capable of maintaining peace and performing other critical governmental functions. Second, an imperial policy or posture is not fundamentally economic in nature: it is neither motivated by economic gain, nor (as already suggested) is it structurally rooted in any particular socioeconomic system, such as "capitalism." Imperial relationships are concerned with power, either for its own sake or as an instrument of some larger, primarily noneconomic objective, such as "world order." For example, Robert W. Tucker argues that although United States postwar policy was initially motivated by a concern for national security defined in limited, defensive, traditional terms—the containment of Soviet expansionism and the maintenance of a balance of power in Europe—it later became generalized and diffused into the much broader objective of maintaining a world environment congenial to American values and institutions, which in turn required an activist, interventionist projection of American power overseas on a scale that could only be termed imperial.[5]

Third, writers describing the United States as an "imperial" power are usually less inclined (although they are often somewhat ambiguous on the matter) to attribute to policy makers a *conscious intent* to dominate, whatever their motivations, than those preferring the "imperialist" label. That is, the United States may play an imperial *role* without having an imperial *policy*. The focus is primarily on consequences, not intentions or motivations. The root cause of the American imperial role, or, alternatively, a conception of security so broad as to require imperial policies de facto, is simply power itself. *Any* great power in the present world system is irresistibly drawn toward imperial policies, argues Raymond Aron; only weak states with no alternatives adopt a conception of the national interest restricted to mere political survival.[6] In effect, goes the argument, interests and commitments of states naturally and inevitably expand as their power expands.[7]

The final significant distinction is that terms "imperialist" or "imperialistic" are invariably condemnatory and indicative of a radical disaffection with United States foreign policy, whereas this is not necessarily the case for "imperial." Indeed, if imperial policies are seen as deriving fundamentally from an anarchic international system, the emphasis is far more likely to be on the "responsibilities" than the "abuses" of power. For example, Aron argues that even if the American role in Europe during the postwar period could be accurately described as imperial, it was both right and desired by the people of Western Europe; and relatively conservative writers like George Liska and John Spanier call for a more open, self-conscious, unapologetic imperial role for the United States as the only alternative to global chaos.[8] Even Tucker, who until very recently has been a most forceful critic of the American imperial conception of its national interest, has now (because of the growing power of the Third World) begun to worry about who will maintain a semblance of world order.[9]

The distinctions between "imperialist" and "imperial" conceptions or models are important ones, but it is also of critical importance to take note of what they have in common: both are—indeed, *must*—be based on the premise, implied or explicit, that in the postwar era the extent of United States power and the nature of its behavior—whatever the causes, motivation, intentions, or effects—warrants comparison with the undoubted empires of the past, in particular the European colonial empires of the late nineteenth and early twentieth centuries. Even the mildest, least condemnatory, and most qualified conception of an American imperial, let alone imperialist role, cannot escape that connotation and still remain meaningful. Imperial implies *great* power, not merely unequal power; it implies the capacity to dominate or control other states, not merely to influence them; it implies an empire, not merely a sphere of influence.

How accurately does this central image of American hegemony or control fit the reality of postwar international politics? The remainder of this article will be devoted to examining the validity of the theories that have thus far been briefly summarized. The focus will be on American relations with the Third World, where surely the argument of American imperialism, if valid, must have its greatest force. The discussion will distinguish between radical, neo-Marxist, and nonradical, non-Marxist analyses of (a) the motivation or causes and (b) the consequences or effects of United States foreign policy.

MOTIVATIONS FOR "IMPERIAL" OR "IMPERIALIST" POLICY

We shall begin with a discussion of radical, neo-Marxist theories of the causes or motivations of American policy.[10] Is the open-door policy—unrestricted access to the economies of the Third World—structurally necessary to the survival of United States capitalism, or, more generally, to the health of the economy? Some contemporary neo-Marxists, most notably Gabriel Kolko,[11] do in fact so argue, following Lenin's earlier arguments about the crucial dependence of late monopoly capitalism on overseas economic imperialism. Consider first direct overseas investment. Although the figures vary, all recent analyses demonstrate that private overseas direct investment is only about 5 percent of total investment (i.e., 95 percent of United States direct investment is domestic), and the vast majority of that overseas investment is not in the Third World but in the advanced industrial societies of Western Europe, Japan, Canada, and Australia. The proportion of overseas investment in the Third World, then, is less than 2 percent of all United States investment, which would hardly seem critical.[12] Looked at from a different perspective, as of 1968 the income from corporate investment in the Third World was only 3–4 percent of the total income of United States corporations, and it was declining relative to income from investments in the industrial world.[13]

The figures for trade reveal the same nonessentiality of the Third World to the United States economy. Total American trade with the rest of the world is only about 7–8 percent of GNP and, once again, by far the largest and most rapidly growing proportion of that trade is not with the Third World but with the advanced countries.[14] Only in the case of strategic raw materials is the Third World *possibly* of critical importance to the American economy, and even here the situation is far from clear. For the moment the United States is increasingly dependent on overseas oil as well as other important raw materials such as copper, tin, and bauxite found in Third World countries. But (1) it is still the case that *most* of these raw materials are produced not in the Third World but in the developed countries; (2) mining the deep seabed is likely to soon further reduce United States dependence on Third World countries; and (3) pending that development most economists still argue that substitutes and alternatives to Third World raw materials, even oil, are now or soon will be available, at costs which are higher, but not so much higher as to make Third World importations more of a necessity than essentially a convenience.[15] In any case, it is only very recently that the United States has become dependent on strategic raw materials imports from the Third World countries to any significant degree, whatever the exact magnitude of that dependence might be now and in the future, and thus the matter is entirely irrelevant to the alleged structural necessity of the open-door policy in the past.

Even if the United States economy *was* structurally dependent on access to Third World markets, raw materials, or sources of investment, would it follow that imperial *control* of the Third World is a necessity? The radical argument depends on that assumption, although it is nearly always left implicit; that is, that the choice is the stark, all-or-nothing one of imperial domination or no access at all. When made explicit, though, the assumption is demonstratively preposterous. Indeed, there seems to be a clear *inverse* relationship between "imperialism" and prosperity in the postwar period. Though of course other factors have also played important roles, it is interesting to note that the least imperial countries have had the highest overall growth rates (Japan, West Germany, Canada, the Netherlands, the Scandinavian countries—all dependent in varying degrees on interstate trade and investment), while the most imperial have done least well (France and Britain in the 1940s and 1950s; Portugal, with the lowest per capita income in Europe for the entire postwar period). Nor should this be unexpected: it is not just that the maintenance of political and military imperial control is extremely costly when there is serious indigenous opposition, but also that states perceived by the nationalist and sensitive Third World countries as imperialist, whether accurately or not, are much more likely to suffer economic retaliation than those seen as quite harmless. In case of renewed Arab-Israeli conflict, for example, the Arabs are probably more likely to cut off oil shipments to the United States than to Japan. The radical assumption is best stood on its head: *only* efforts to gain imperialist economic control, to push against a door that is already open, would be likely to provoke nationalistic resentments intense enough to override economic rationality and close off American access to Third World products.

All this may be true, implicitly or explicitly concede some radical analysts, but policy makers, however inaccurately, *believe* that the health of the United States capitalist system requires an open door to the Third World economies and therefore direct political or economic control over them, and act accordingly, i.e., imperialistically.[16] While this is certainly a logical possibility and a neat theory-saver, the evidence is overwhelming that it is a wholly inaccurate description of how policy makers in fact have perceived American interests in the Third World. There is, after all, an enormous body of available material in the form of memoirs, official documents, and scholarly analyses on how American policy makers have defined the "external challenges" to the United States, in the Third World and elsewhere. It rather conclusively shows that genuine security fears; ideological anticommunism; expansionist idealism; or other political, strategic, or psychological factors have been at the roots of the United States postwar policies, including interventionalist or, if you will, "imperial" behavior.[17]

Still another variant of the neo-Marxist argument is that open-door imperialism in the Third World, while neither structurally necessary to the United States economy nor genuinely believed to be so by policy makers, *is* necessary to the largest, most powerful banks and corporations which in turn control foreign policy.[18] Both parts of this argument are quite unpersuasive. A number of scholars have demonstrated that, with the exception of the seven oil majors (to be examined below), the largest United States foreign banks and corporations are among those that are *least* dependent on the Third World, as the overwhelming proportion of their investment, sales, and profits come from the American domestic market, Europe, Japan, and Canada. And, more importantly, while it would be beyond the scope of this article to go into detail, no serious scholarship on the foreign policy-making process in the United States government supports the notion that it is controlled or in most cases even substantially influenced by the desires of "big business." Indeed, even in the case of those American-based multinational corporations which *do* have major investments in the Third World, most recent scholarship establishes that the distance between the corporations and the United States government is increasing, as both the policy makers and the corporations are coming to realize that, faced with growing nationalism, *no* interests— economic or political, private or public—are served by government involvement in corporate disputes with indigenous governments.[19]

The final variation of the neo-Marxist argument is at once the most sophisticated but also the least subject to empirical confirmation or refutation. It is not that corporations control foreign policy or that political leaders consciously seek to promote and protect corporate economic interests, but rather that all United States elites are products of American history, institutions, and class structures, and as such have internalized an overall ideology or *weltanschauung* that equates the maintenance of capitalism at home and its extension overseas—i.e., the open-door policy—with the preservation of the entire "American way of life."[20] The problem with this formulation, "sophisticated" as it may be, is that it is so broad as to be quite immune from normal tests of evidence. It is quite easy to show that American foreign policy makers since World War II have not usually defined their objectives in terms of the open-door policy, the preservation of capitalism, or, indeed, in economic terms of any kind, either in their public rhetoric or in their private correspondence, memoirs, or intragovernmental communications, but then it can be claimed that the policy makers were either concealing their "real" objectives or that their anticommunism and security fears were "ultimately," perhaps even unconsciously, rooted in the desire to preserve capitalism as an economic system.[21] Similarly, instances in which United States policy has been oriented toward the protection or promotion of American economic interests overseas are seized upon as irrefutable proof of the theory, whereas the far more numerous instances of United States passivity when confronted with economic nationalism are treated as signs of the growing subtlety of corporate capitalism, which is willing to let minor infractions on its imperial control go unchallenged in the interest of preserving "the system" as a whole.[22] Or, in another version, even intervention which is overwhelmingly counterproductive in economic terms, such as in Vietnam, is explained in terms of "the empire's" need to preserve the system as a whole by supporting even "the weakest links in the chain."[23] As others have pointed out, both in the context of examining this variant of neo-Marxist theory and in discussing the nature of scientific inquiry in general, a theory so broad that it is capable of "explaining" both A and its opposite B (intervention and nonintervention, intervention that is economically productive and intervention that is economically costly), a theory that rests not on the empirical evidence considered in its entirety but on assertion buttressed only by the selected evidence that fits, is no theory at all, but simply dogma.[24]

It is not the contention of this article that economic considerations, including if you will the maintenance of an open-door for products and investment capital, do not play a significant role in United States foreign policy, but only that such economic considerations have not been the central, dominant ones. Certainly it is obvious that the government has sought to promote trade and investment around the world and has often used its economic and political influence on behalf of such objectives. In so acting, political officials have been motivated by several factors: the belief that an open economic world is genuinely in the best interests of all states; the belief that it is beneficial to the United States economy; and the belief that one of the obligations of the government is to protect and promote the legitimate activities of its citizens abroad, at least as long as those activities do not conflict with larger policy objectives. But what is crucial are the *means* used on behalf of the open-door policy, that is, the *intensity* of the government's commitment to it or the *priority* that policy has relative to other foreign policy objectives.[25] Normally, the government has promoted the interests of private corporations by diplomacy only: verbal representations, exhortation, and bargaining. On some, but increasingly exceptional occasions, the government has gone further, making use of both positive and negative economic sanctions, through its bilateral assistance programs and its influence in international financial institutions, on behalf of private economic interests. On most occasions where the government has resorted to economic pressures, though, larger issues than mere nationalization of American property are perceived to be at stake, as in the case of economic and other actions by the United States against Cuba and the Allende government in Chile. Finally, there is *no* case in which it can persuasively be argued that Washington resorted to serious covert political action or the use of armed force on behalf of private economic interests as such. Apparent exceptions to this assertion, such as the CIA's role in the overthrow of Iran's Mossadegh following his nationalization of oil corporations in 1953, on closer inspection do not undermine the argument, for oil is the *one* foreign economic commodity perceived to be absolutely vital, not to private interests but to the United States economy as a whole. Indeed, what is particularly striking about the case of oil is that even *given* its critical importance, the government nonetheless has consistently subordinated easy and favorable access to it to other, noneconomic objectives: as many observers have pointed out, if economic rather than cold-war, ideological/moral, or domestic considerations dominated foreign policy, the United States stance in the Arab-Israeli crisis would have been very different over the last three decades.[26] So even in the single case in which one might *expect* to find economic considerations to be dominant, the reality has been different. That being so, it is hardly credible that the United States interventions in Guatemala in 1954 and the Dominican Republic in 1965 were motivated by, respectively, banana and sugar interests, rather than by ideological, cold-war, and even strategic considerations genuinely believed—whether accurately or not is irrelevant—by policy makers to be at stake in those countries.[27]

To summarize, while it is true that in a general way the United States seeks an open-door policy around the world, it is usually quite restrained—i.e., nonimperialistic—in the methods used to attain this goal. The more clearly it is that purely private rather than national economic interests are involved, the less likely it is that the government will take punitive actions against other states. To go even further, to the extent that *only* economic interests are involved, even where those interests are national rather than private in scope, the less likely it is that the government will resort to serious economic coercion, let alone armed force. Put differently, the more important the issue for the United States as a whole, as seen by policy makers, the more likely it is that economic considerations will be subordinated to noneconomic ones whenever they conflict, as in the past they have in the Middle East.

The argument that United States policy is motivated by noneconomic but still imperial pretensions is a far more serious one than the neo-Marxist theories. It is at once more sophisticated and less of an affront to common sense, and it does not suffer from the shoddy scholarship and ideological dogmatism that so frequently mar much of the radical literature. Quite the contrary; scholars of the deserved stature of Robert Tucker, Stanley Hoffmann, Richard Falk, and others have all described United States foreign policy in terms of its imperial nature. Certainly there can be no doubt that policy makers have often, even typically, described their objectives and policies in *rhetoric* that can fairly be called "imperial": the Truman Doctrine's universalist declaration that it was the policy of the United States "to support free peoples who are resisting attempted subjugation by armed minorities or by outside pressures," Kennedy on the United States as "the watchman on the wall of world freedom," Johnson on history "thrusting" the "responsibility" on the United States "to be guardians at the gate," and so on. Still, it is doubtful that this rhetoric accurately reflected the real, operational purposes of policy makers, for the more plausible interpretation of foreign policies since World War II suggests that the guiding motivation was to meet what was perceived as the quite specific challenge by communist forces in quite specific places. The United States has not in fact sought to preserve world freedom; it has not tried to suppress all revolution, let alone all social change; it has not even tried very hard to create or maintain an environment congenial to American institutions and values; and it has certainly not deliberately set out to dominate other nations; it has simply tried to prevent the spread of communism (whether wisely or not is not relevant here) to areas where communism was not already in power. It cannot be denied that the broadening of the goal of the containment of communism from Western Europe to the entire world, combined with the continuing strain of Wilsonian universalism in American thinking, made the United States (in Stanley Hoffmann's words) at least *"implicitly* imperialistic,"[28] but the weight of evidence suggests that the concrete day-to-day policies of the government were considerably more limited. Put differently, we may concede that America's ideological universalism was at least potentially imperial and at some level accurately reflected the genuine long-term hopes and aspirations of the postwar political leadership, but yet deny that such sweeping conceptions of the United States "responsibility," requiring a conscious or unconscious effort at benevolent world domination, were at the root of operational policies.

Yet, one hesitates to make too much of this argument. Even if it is correct that anticommunist security fears rather than broader aspirations lie at the root of United States policies, the globalization of those policies might still produce imperialism. Certainly it is hard to avoid the conclusion that meddling in the internal politics of far-away, relatively unimportant states such as Greece, the Congo, and Chile—not to mention Indochina!—reflects what might justly be labeled as an imperial mentality or conception of American security interests. So the more important argument of this article is that the notion of the United States as an imperial power exaggerates its actual *capacities* to control events around the world.

CONSEQUENCES OF UNITED STATES FOREIGN POLICY

What, then, of the *consequences* or *effects* of the postwar policies, whatever their causes, motivations, or intentions? Has the impact of United States power on the rest of the world, especially on the Third World where surely the impact must be greatest, been sufficiently extensive to justify describing it as "imperialism," "neoimperialism," "indirect imperialism," or "informal imperialism"? At least implicit in such descriptions and often quite explicit is the argument that the extension of American economic, political, and military power into the Third World has been on such a scale as to reduce those countries to a position not substantially different from the past when they were actually under military occupation and direct political rule. The consequences for the Third World, it is argued, are both economic exploitation and political subordination, just as in the past.

In the last decade or so, particularly in the literature on United States–Latin American relations, the theory (or theories) of "dependence" has become the dominant theme in radical writings. In their more sophisticated versions, dependence theories hold that Third World countries have become inextricably integrated in the world capitalist system, dominated in turn by United States capitalism, as producers of raw materials and consumers of manufactured products.

Because they are weak and economically undiversified, however, Third World countries are relegated to the "periphery" of the system, kept underdeveloped or impoverished by the low prices they receive for their exports, the high prices they must pay for their imports, and the onerous conditions which they are forced to accept in order to have access to foreign capital through either loans or investment. Although dependence may be partially a consequence of the deliberate exercise of power, it is more fundamentally a function of the capitalist structure. As long as world capitalism continues in its present form, the Third World cannot escape underdevelopment, for its "surplus production" will continue to be in effect appropriated for the benefit of the advanced capitalist societies. Under capitalism, then, underdevelopment is not a transitional stage to development but a permanent condition: "economic development and underdevelopment are the opposite faces of the same coin."[29]

Why do more Third World countries not rebel against this structural exploitation? Because, according to the dependence theorists, although Third World *people* as a whole suffer, the local political, business, and military *elites* benefit: their power, status, and wealth are directly linked to the preservation of the exisiting "system," i.e., investment and production by local subsidiaries of the giant multinational corporations; military assistance programs; CIA advice, support, and financing; and so on. Without this alliance between the elites of the center and the periphery, the entire structure of indirect capitalist control over the Third World would be impossible. Put differently, it is this mutually symbiotic alliance that is the functional equivalent of the direct military, political, and bureaucratic control structures of the older, colonialist versions of imperialism.[30]

ECONOMIC EXPLOITATION?

Let us examine this theory or argument, looking first at the question of whether the United States economically exploits the Third World. To begin with, what does the term "exploitation" at the nation-state level mean? It is remarkable how little effort has been made to systematically define the term in either the classical literature on imperialism or the more recent literature on neoimperialism. Standard dictionary definitions provide some clues, but do not take us too far. For example, *Webster's Third International* defines exploitation as "an unjust or improper use of another person for one's own profit or advantage"; *The American College Dictionary* defines the term as "to use selfishly for one's own ends." In the literature on imperialism, three possible usages seem most common. First, there is the deliberate use of power by one state to attain economic advantage *at the expense* of the victimized state. In this case there is *absolute* deprivation, or a zero-sum game, in which the exploiter's gains are the exploitee's losses; thus, in the absence of the exploitative relationship, the exploited state would be economically better off. There are, of course, many historical examples of imperialism as pure exploitation in the sense discussed here: the ancient slave empires, the plundering of the New World by the Spanish, and perhaps some of the more single-mindedly avaricious and brutal instances of nineteenth-century imperialism, such as Belgium's exploitation of the Congo. A number of radical writers today consider "neoimperialism" to be exploitative in this extreme sense.

Second, exploitation may be understood to mean the deliberate use of power by one state simply to maximize its economic advantages in exchange relationships with weaker states. In this case there is relative rather than absolute deprivation; it is a nonzero-sum game, for each side is economically better off than it would be in the absence of the relationship. However, we are justified in calling it exploitation since one side gains much more than the other as a direct result of the deliberate use of its power. Thus, there is a clear quality of "unfairness" about the relationship, however difficult it may be to give an operational meaning to that notion.[31] It will be noted that this usage includes the key concepts of "selfishness" (and therefore necessarily of "deliberateness") and "injustice," common to most dictionary definitions. Probably most nineteenth-century imperialism approximated this kind of exploitation. The colonies were better off in a purely economic sense than they would have been had they never been colonized, but the asymmetries of advantage were so great as to be justly characterized as exploitation; one thinks, for example, of the relative pittances given to the oil-producing states by the oil majors backed by their governments in the Middle East in the early decades of the twentieth century. It is important to reemphasize here that if we wish to distinguish "exploitation" from mere "inequality," surely a useful distinction to maintain, the asymmetries of advantage (a) must be *very* great, not merely somewhat unequal, and (b) must stem from the deliberate use of power by the stronger party.

Yet, it may be objected, what of cases in which the asymmetries of advantage are very great as a result of unconscious, unintended, but yet very real asymmetries of power? For example, it is often contended that the prices received by underdeveloped societies for their exports are at a much lower level relative to the prices they pay for their imports from industrial countries than they would be in a genuinely free, competitive open market based on pure supply and demand, rather than one structured in a variety of oligopolistic ways in favor of the advanced countries. If indeed the structural constraints, the rules of the game, are loaded, however unconsciously, something more than mere inequality would seem to be involved; yet to call it "exploitation" would violate our common-sense (and dictionary) understanding of exploitation as involving the conscious, deliberate use of power. Perhaps the best solution to this essentially philosophic problem is to stipulate that major inequities stemming from "the system" (structures of power, international customs and rules) should initially be understood as inequality only, but that if the workings and consequences of that system are subsequently made clear to the advantaged powers and yet they (now consciously) continue to rely on their greater power to resist changes, then the relationship indeed becomes exploitative.

We can now proceed directly to examine the charge that the United States, as the leading contemporary neoimperialist power, economically exploits the Third World. According to classic economic theory, free trade in an open international market is of mutal and equal benefit to rich and poor nations alike, because of the familiar principles of comparative advantage based on specialization and division of labor. However, in the real world international trade may not be truly open and based stricly on supply and demand, and the benefits may be unequally distributed. Until quite recently, it was widely accepted, even by non-Marxist and nonradical economists, that in fact the terms of trade were weighted against the Third World countries as a result of the deliberately or unconsciously exercised political and financial power of the industrialized world, for it was generally thought that at least since 1940 the prices of raw materials and other commodities exported by the Third World has steadily fallen relative to the price of manufactured goods they had no choice but to import from the industrialized world. In actual operation the international "free trade" system, it was usually conceded, had the same disadvantages as the domestic "free enterprise" system: where not all participants have equal political and economic power, the rich do disproportionately better than the poor, or even in more extreme formulations, the poor are actually *further* impoverished. The open-door policy or economic liberalism became, in the words of two sophisticated writers, simply "the ideology of a continuing American hegemony."[32]

In the last few years, however, the accuracy of this assessment has been called into question, as it has applied to the recent past, as well as to the present and the forseeable future. A recent study, for example, concluded that *even excluding oil from the calculation,* in the last twenty-five years the prices of raw materials exported by poor countries had risen at about the same rate as the prices of imported manufactures.[33] Steven Krasner has gone even further, arguing that the Third World countries have been relative *beneficiaries* of restrictive schemes imposed by the consuming states or their multinational corporations: "For most primary commodities, the actual prices are higher than those that would prevail in a free market. In terms of neoclassical concepts of value, *consuming states have been exploited by producing areas.*"[34] As for the present and forseeable future, there is a growing consensus that as a result of the increasing scarceness of certain key raw materials and the ability of producing states to form successful cartels, not only in oil but also in other commodities (copper, tin, bauxite, and apparently more on the way), the terms of trade will increasingly shift in favor of the Third World, or at least that part of the Third World fortunate enough to control major commodities or raw materials.

Does the direct corporate investment of advanced countries in the Third World constitute exploitation, in either the absolute or relative senses of the word? According to radical critics, foreign-owned subsidiaries of multinational corporations "decapitalize" the underdeveloped countries by taking out more in profits than they put in through investment; further block local growth and industrialization by buying up smaller local firms or driving them out of business through cutthroat competition; create sudden unemployment by ruthlessly closing local subsidiaries whenever worldwide profit maximization so dictates; remove key sectors of the economy from local control; create a domestic bourgeoisie whose self-interests are tied to foreign industry rather than indigenous growth; disrupt local cultural patterns and institutions and substitute in their place the crass materialism of the West; and, in general, integrate the economies, social structure, and political institutions of Third World countries into permanently subordinate peripheral positions in the world capitalist structure.[35] Among themselves, critics may disagree on whether these alleged consequences of foreign investment are intended and stem from the deliberate governmental strategies of the advanced countries to gain political and economic domination over the Third World, or whether they are the unintended, uncoordinated by-product of private corporate greed. But there is no disagreement that the Third World is exploited by foreign investment.

Other students of foreign investment see the matter quite differently. Foreign investment is said to clearly bring with it many positive benefits. Foreign companies have the capital and the skills initially lacking in underdeveloped countries to explore for, develop, produce, and market raw materials that would otherwise lie dormant for decades. In the course of doing so, they build transportation networks; employ large numbers of local people usually at wage rates much above host country norms; build housing, schools, and hospitals; and through taxation contribute much needed foreign currency. In the manufacturing area, multinational corporations provide the managerial skills, the infusion of advanced technology, and the access to world markets that the underdeveloped countries lack.

To be sure, the multinational corporations usually make profits, sometimes very high profits, but they also take risks—the political risks of nationalization, the economic risks of failure—and without the promise of high profits they simply would not invest at all. And it is wrong to conclude that a net economic loss—exploitation—has necessarily occurred at the point at which the outflow of profits exceeds the inflow of new capital investment, for the notion of "decapitalization" ignores the value of the economic infrastructure left in place and the transfer of technology, labor, and marketing skills which have or at least should have led to continuing, self-sustaining development.

Still, there are undoubtedly costs, as the critics have pointed out: the elimination of local competitors and the squeezing out of infant industries, the domination of key sectors of local economies by foreigners and the consequent difficulties of instituting national planning and economic controls when a substantial proportion of the economy is immune from such measures, the political and psychological resentments. Probably the balance of cost and advantage cannot be determined in general, but only on a case-by-case basis, depending on the indigenous context and the precise terms of the agreements negotiated between foreign investors and the host governments.[36]

What certainly is clear is that although there is considerable nationalistic rhetoric about the evils of foreign investment, most Third World countries continue to actively seek it. Nor can it be argued, á la the dependence theorists, that this simply reflects an alliance between local reactionaries and foreign exploiters, for in recent years even the most radical, nationalistic states (such as Cuba, Algeria, Peru, and even to some extent China) have sought increased foreign investment. To be sure, they have insisted on terms that do not unduly compromise national independence, but the fact that they can successfully do so certainly suggests a rather more evenly distributed balance of power between the multinational corporations and the Third World countries than the literature on "exploitation" implies.

Finally, even foreign aid is seen by many radicals as nothing more than another instrument of control and exploitation of the Third World by capitalist countries, particularly the United States. Here the argument is that economically the aid eventually comes to be a net burden on Third World economies: repayments on past loans mount higher and higher, until they exceed new inflows of assistance. Politically, it is argued, aid serves mainly to support reactionary dictatorships and local oligarchies who block real social change and balanced economic growth, and who serve as agents of United States imperial control in the Third World.

There is no doubt that for a number of Third World countries the annual inflow of new capital assistance is less than the outflow in the form of interest on past debts, but it is clearly fallacious to conclude that this *necessarily* demonstrates that aid is harmful, for if the previous aid has been used productively it will have generated new sources of wealth out of which interest on previous debt can be repaid. And it cannot be doubted that a number of countries have in fact achieved self-sustained growth in good part because of the infusion of major amounts of foreign aid; examples are Western Europe following the Marshall Plan, Turkey, Taiwan, Brazil, and South Korea. To be sure, most of the latter countries are indeed conservative and authoritarian, but it cannot be seriously argued that United States assistance created those conditions, as opposed to the quite different proposition that aid is more likely to go to safely pro-American and therefore usually conservative regimes. Aid, we may conclude, if efficiently used, promotes overall economic growth and thus cannot be considered exploitative; economic growth, however, by no means assures democracy, social change, or even equitable distribution of the fruits of growth, but these are matters determined by indigenous policies and practices only slightly or not at all subject to outside influence.[37]

We may now sum up. Taken as a whole, have the economic ties between the United States and the Third World been economically exploitative? It is obvious that the United States has enormous economic power; that this power has consequences for other, weaker states; that the consequences are sometimes though hardly invariably detrimental; and that while these detrimental consequences may frequently be the unintended result of sheer United States power, they are sometimes undeniably the result of deliberate, self-seeking polices on the part of the United States government. If by exploitation one means absolute deprivation, though, it is clear that the United States has not economically exploited the Third World, for the underdeveloped world as a whole has grown at a rate of 2 percent per annum *per capita* since 1945, and over 5 percent per annum per capita since 1960, rates which are historically very high, higher for example than the growth rates of the United States or the European countries during any comparable length of time prior to World War I.[38] To a substantial degree, this relatively high growth rate is attributable to the sharp increase of foreign aid, investment, and trade between the developing countries and the advanced industrial ones, primarily (at least until fairly recently) the United States.

Has there nonetheless been exploitation in the sense of *relative* deprivation? For most of the postwar period, it is true, the rich got richer faster than the poor got "richer" and thus the gap between them was growing (although it is likely that this trend has ended in the last few years). The most persuasive evidence, though, is that the growth rates of the rich had little or nothing to do with their "exploitation" of the Third World: the rich got richer because of an increase of both domestic productivity and of trade and investment among themselves, while the poor did not develop at higher rates because of their essentially indigenous problems: one-crop economies, high population rates, political instability, etc. To be sure, there can be absolutely no doubt that the rich countries, particularly the United States, *could* and (according to my values) *should* have done more, much more, to help the Third World countries develop. That is, the United States and other developed countries in their total economic relations with the Third World have been guided primarily by self-interest rather than by the desire to help the poor; had their priorities been different the Third World would be substantially better off today. Take the case of foreign aid as an illustration. Radicals have pointed out the variety of ways in which foreign aid is at least in part structured to promote access for private investment, subsidize American shipowners, promote, American export industries, and so on. The total effect of the various restrictions on the uses to which recipients may put bilateral United States assistance clearly lowers the real value of that assistance, but equally clearly it does not reduce that value to zero or even less. Foreign aid thus benefits, not exploits the recipients, although the benefits are not as great as they would be if the amounts were larger and unconstrained by restrictions designed to assist American industries. One may still conclude that the economic relationship between the United States and the Third World is deplorable but the problem is not exploitation, at least if understood in a reasonable sense, but rather neglect, indifference, and moral callousness. What the Third World needs from the United States and the rest of the developed countries is not less but more aid, trade, and private investment, though undoubtedly on better terms than in the past.[39]

POLITICAL CONTROL?

None of this analysis denies, of course, that economic power carries with it political leverage. But is this political leverage sufficient to give it political control over the Third World, as the "neoimperialist" or even simply "imperial" argument implies? The evidence from events in the real world, particularly during but not limited to the past few years, hardly suggests that this is the case.

If economic power carried with it considerable political control, one would expect that *at a minimum* such control would be sufficient for the imperial power to protect its major economic interests, particularly in areas of the world where its economic power is greatest. That is, the imperialist (or imperial) model would predict—*must* predict—that the United States could exert sufficient political control to at least preserve the position of its major multinational corporations in Latin America. And yet over the past decade there has been a wave of nationalization of United States corporations around the world in general—e.g., in Ceylon, Egypt, Indonesia, Algeria, Libya—but *particularly* in Latin America. The United States government has been nearly helpless to prevent these actions against its corporations and, with only several partial exceptions, has all but ceased to try. The International Petroleum Corporation (IPC) case in Peru is particularly instructive and historically significant. During the mid-1960s the liberal Peruvian government of Fernando Belaunde Terry began taking steps looking toward the nationalization of IPC, a subsidiary of Standard Oil of New Jersey. IPC, backed by the U.S. Embassy in Lima, strongly resisted, and from 1964–1966 Washington withheld economic assistance from Peru in an effort to force the Belaunde government to back down. In early 1968 Belaunde and IPC reached a compromise settlement, involving gradual nationalization, compensation, and a continued role for IPC in managing the oil fields, but the compromise outraged Peruvian nationalistic opinion, and shortly afterward a nationalist military coup overthrew Belaunde, and the new government immediately seized all properties of IPC. IPC, it will be noted, had annual revenues three times as large as Peru's entire GNP, and its payroll was 25 percent larger than that of the Peruvian government,[40] the sort of figures frequently cited to demonstrate the helplessness of Third World governments before the awesome economic power of multinational corporations. And yet, the Peruvian government simply marched several hundred troops into IPC properties and expropriated them without compensation! The Nixon administration subsequently tried to help the IPC gain compensation and apparently for a while informally slowed down assistance to Peru, although it refused to apply the Hickenlooper Amendment, which by law clearly applied to the case and would have required the immediate cessation of all economic assistance until IPC had been "promptly and effectively" compensated. In the face of Peruvian adamance, after a while even the half-hearted efforts of the Nixon government were dropped. The Peruvian government subsequently nationalized the huge and "powerful" Grace and

Cerro de Pasco United States-owned multinational corporations, as well as a number of smaller ones, and dramatically increased taxation and in other ways imposed restrictions on many others. Relatively little compensation has been forthcoming, and the United States government has remained on the sidelines.

The lesson of the Peruvian experience and the helplessness of both the corporations and the United States government has not been lost on other nationalistic Latin American regimes. In 1969 a Bolivian military regime abruptly expropriated the United States-owned Gulf Oil Corporation and "forced or frightened almost every sizable U.S. firm out of the country."[41] In 1971, the Allende regime in Chile expropriated without compensation the huge, American-owned Anaconda Companies; as in Peru "The efforts of the U.S. government to influence the process of providing compensation only strengthened Chilean intransigence,"[42] and once again the Nixon administration stopped short of applying the Hickenlooper Amendment.[43]

In the last few years, the wave of nationalization has rapidly spread. The Peronist regime in Argentina took a number of steps against United States corporations; even conservative regimes (such as Brazil) who otherwise welcome foreign investment are responding to popular nationalism and anti-Americanism by tightening controls over United States enterprises; and, most significantly of all, the Venezuelan government, which has been gradually gaining control over the oil industry in the past twenty years, will fully nationalize all foreign (mostly United States) oil corporations by 1976. Though the economic interests involved are enormous, and Venezuela is still the largest foreign supplier of imported oil, neither the affected corporations nor the United States government have sought to apply any pressure, but rather are passively accepting the inevitable.

It is now increasingly recognized that as the host countries gain in knowledge, confidence, and experience, and as European and Japanese multinational corporations seek to compete with American business for access to the Third World, the bargaining relationship between multinational corporations and indigenous governments is rapidly shifting in favor of the latter, with the United States government relatively powerless and increasingly disinclined to try to resist. The "dependencia" pattern, under which local elites collaborate with foreign investors against their own national interests, is rapidly disappearing and was probably always exaggerated anyway.[44] Without local allies, more direct action on the part of the "metropolitan" countries would be required; yet, armed force on behalf of private interests is practically out of the question in this day and age, and economic pressures can be relatively easily resisted by proud nationalist regimes and only worsen the situation for the multinational corporations. In the past few years it is clear that most corporations have come to grips with the new realities, seeking to adapt to rising nationalism as best they can, with no recourse to threats of economic retaliation or United States governmental assistance.[45]

Even short of outright nationalization, the terms of both trade and investment between the Third World and the advanced industrial world are rapidly shifting. The rise of OPEC in the Middle East is the most dramatic example, of course: in the 1920s host oil-producing countries received in taxation only about 10–15 percent of oil corporation profits on production; by the mid-1970s the general figure was over 80 percent and that of a far larger pie. Other raw materials producers are now seeking to form price cartels in emulation of OPEC, and while it is doubtful that any will achieve quite the fantastic success of the oil producers, the fact is that collaborative action to restrict production has led to dramatic price rises for Third World producers of bauxite, tin, copper, and other raw materials. Once again, the government has been powerless to prevent these developments, even though they inflict varying degrees of damage not only on United States-based multinational corporations but on the economy as a whole, and there are increasing indications that adaptation rather than coercive resistance will be the general American response.

Aside from the rapidly spreading adverse economic developments that the United States has been powerless to prevent, American political and military influence in the Third World has markedly declined in the last decade, nowhere more so than in Latin America, supposedly the stronghold of United States "neoimperialism," "hegemony," or "domination." Anti-American nationalism is at a peak, and the Latin American bloc is no longer a reliable ally of the United States in the United Nations or in other international organizations. In general Latin American support for overall United States international policies is at a postwar low. Most important, the United States has proven to be, perhaps if not quite powerless, then at least decreasingly powerful in preventing revolutionary social change in Latin America. The Cuban and Peruvian regimes have successfully resisted all pressures (serious and sustained in the former, half-hearted and transient in the latter), and other states "are advancing frankly towards socialization."[46]

CONCLUSION: IF THE UNITED STATES IS AN "IMPERIAL" POWER, WHERE IS ITS EMPIRE?

Obviously no one would wish to deny that the United States has enormous economic, political, and military power, and that this power must have a significant impact on other states, both intended and unintended. The question, however, is whether this power is so great as to warrant calling it either "imperialist" or "imperial." Even if these terms, or the notion of a United States "empire," are meant to be understood metaphorically rather than literally, we still must decide whether the metaphors are insightful and enlightening rather than misleading.

It seems reasonable to insist that the term "imperialism" (and all its usual variants) not be used as if it were synonymous with power and wealth as such, or alternatively as a mere name for the observable fact of the global expansion of American influence since World War II. Nor should imperialism be equated with *inequality* of power, per se, as some radical writers implicitly or even explicitly do. To define imperialism in such broad terms, or to treat such concepts as power, control, domination, and influence as if they were synonymous and all equal to imperialism, is simply to obscure highly significant distinctions that would only have to be reinvented if we wish to understand the real world.

Benjamin Cohen's definition of imperialism seems reasonably appropriate: "any relationship of effective domination or control, political or economic, direct or indirect, of one nation over another."[47] Such a definition clearly implies that great power is involved, not merely inequalities of power, and that the relationship is nearly wholly one-sided. However, it is possible to distinguish three different dimensions of power: *control,* defined as the invariable capacity to achieve objectives even in the face of opposition; *domination,* implying great power but falling somewhat short of outright control; and *influence,* meaning the capacity to *affect,* to a greater or lesser degree, the policies and behavior of other states. The term "imperialism" and all its usual variants should be limited to cases in which the power of one state over another is sufficient to establish control or at least a high degree of domination; it has no place where the relationship is simply one of influence, even of asymmetrical influence. Given the invariable connotation of the term "imperialism," the scope and degree of control must approximate the kind of control exercised by nineteenth-century European powers over their colonies. This should not prove objectionable, since most analysts describing the United States role as either "imperialist" or "imperial" in fact do equate, implicitly or explicitly, American power today—i.e., its capacity to control—with that of the nineteenth-century colonial powers.

Where in the world, even in the Third World, does the United States actually enjoy *control*? In Asia? In Africa? In the Middle East? A moment's reflection, without further argument, should suffice to reveal the very suggestion as being without foundation. Perhaps in Latin America, then? In which Latin American countries does the United States exercise control or domination: Argentina, Peru, Venezuela, Bolivia, Ecuador, Mexico? Hardly, for the United States has clearly been opposed to many significant policies and actions of those states and has been unable to affect them. What about Brazil and Chile since Allende, where the general drift of affairs is apparently pleasing to Washington? Even though covert actions did play *some* role in the establishment of military dictatorships in those countries, especially in Chile, the bulk of the evidence as well as plain common sense suggests that indigenous forces in such large and complex societies were surely far more important. What, then, about the Caribbean area? Here, indubitably, the United States has considerable leverage, though not control and only doubtfully even domination, except for some extreme cases, such as Cuba before Castro and the Dominican Republic in the 1960s. Certainly countries like Haiti, the Dominican Republic, Guatemala, Honduras, and Nicaragua *are* economically dependent on the United States and make it a practice to support American foreign policies; on the other hand, even leaving aside the rather dramatic Cuban case, other Caribbean countries (such as Panama, Jamaica, Trinidad and Tobago) have charted a clearly independent economic and political course and throughout the entire area anti-American nationalism is on the rise.

The growing acceptance of the "imperial" model or metaphor to the contrary notwithstanding, we may boldly but confidently conclude that the United States today does not "control" *any* country *anywhere*, and in only a slightly more qualified manner we may also reject the notion of United States "domination." That the United States has varying degrees of *influence* in the Third World is of course undeniable, but it is a declining influence, and limited in scope and effectiveness to only certain matters. As noted earlier, the United States has been all but powerless to stop rising nationalism and radicalism, as well as attacks on its interests and policies around the world. How does the United States today typically react to the nationalization of property, to dramatic increases in the prices of critical raw materials, to demands that it remove its military bases, to anti-American riots, to insults and contempt? On increasingly rare occasions with suspension of economic *assistance* to the offending state, more typically with mere diplomatic protest, and, increasingly, simply with silence—a sullen silence born of futility, perhaps, but significant precisely for that reason. "Imperialism" should be made of sterner stuff—and certainly it used to be.

Thanks to its growing wealth; the rapidly increasing availability of external aid, trade, and investment from sources other than the United States (Japan, Western Europe, the Soviet Union); and the increased domestic and external constraints on the use of military force, the Third World today is less vulnerable to United States power of any kind than at any time since World War II. The relationship cannot be plausibly described as "imperialist" or "imperial" at all, and only doubtfully and decreasingly as "dependent." It would be more accurate to see the relationship between the United States and the Third World in terms of *mutual* dependence, *mutual* power, and *mutual* vulnerability. To be sure, there are still considerable asymmetries of power—the United States has more *potential* power than the Third World, but it has become increasingly costly for it to actually employ that power. Still, so long as inequalities remain, we may expect the attacks on United States "imperialism" to continue, however inaccurate and misleading they in fact are, both because the shibboleth of "imperialism" provides a convenient myth to deflect attention from the indigenous problems of Third World countries and because inequality per se has become the real focus of Third World resentment of the advanced industrial societies.[48]

NOTES

[1] See especially William A. Williams, *The Tragedy of American Diplomacy* (New York, 1962); William A. Williams, *The Roots of the Modern American Empire* (New York, 1969); and N. Gordon Levin, Jr., *Woodrow Wilson and World Politics* (New York, 1968). Levin

summarizes his argument in this manner: "The needs of America's expanding capitalism were joined ideologically with a more universal vision of American service to suffering humanity and to world stability" (p. 148).

Other radicals point also to bureaucratic expansionism or the irresistible temptations to expansionism inherent in the "Imperial Presidency," but even when the thesis is broadened in these ways the core of the argument remains that of economic self-aggrandizement. See especially Richard J. Barnet, *The Roots of War* (New York, 1972), and Franz Schurmann, *The Logic of World Power* (New York, 1974).

²In Roger Owen and Bob Sutcliffe (eds.), *Studies in the Theory of Imperialism* (London, 1972), p. 164.

³Johan Galtung, "A Structural Theory of Imperialism," *Journal of Peace Research,* no. 3 (1971), p. 91 (italics in original).

⁴Claude Julien, *America's Empire* (New York, 1971), pp. 218, 262.

⁵For the most complete statement of Tucker's views, see his *Nation or Empire?* (Baltimore, 1968). For a similar view see Raymond Aron, *The Imperial Republic* (Englewood Cliffs, N. J., 1974).

⁶Aron, *The Imperial Republic.* Other important analysts seeing the United States as playing an unconscious, unintended imperial role include Townsend Hoopes, *The Devil and John Foster Dulles* (Boston, 1973), and Graham Allison, "Cool It: The Foreign Policy of Young America," *Foreign Policy,* Winter 1970–71.

⁷For an explicit statement of this position, see Robert W. Tucker, *The Radical Left and American Foreign Policy* (Baltimore, 1971), p. 73.

⁸See Spanier, *American Foreign Policy Since World War II* (New York, 1973), p. 238; Liska, *Imperial America* (Baltimore, 1967), and Liska, *War and Order* (Baltimore, 1968), *passim.*

⁹See Tucker's recent series of articles in *Commentary,* especially "A New International Order," February 1975.

¹⁰Some of the analysis of the radical, neo-Marxist theories in the ensuing section is not original, but simply a summary of what this author believes to be the most persuasive scholarship on the subject. It is included as a necessary part of the overall effort to systematically list, classify, and analyze the full range of arguments on the United States imperialist or imperial role.

¹¹See especially Gabriel Kolko, *The Politics of War* (New York, 1968), and Joyce Kolko and Gabriel Kolko, *The Limits of Power* (New York, 1972).

¹²Lincoln P. Bloomfield, *In Search of American Foreign Policy* (New York, 1974), p. 37.

¹³S. M. Miller et al., "Does the U.S. Economy Require Imperialism?" *Social Policy,* September/October 1970.

¹⁴Aron, *The Imperial Republic,* p. 164; Bloomfield, *In Search of American Foreign Policy,* p. 37.

¹⁵For a summary of some arguments see Benjamin J. Cohen, *The Question of Imperialism* (New York, 1973), chap. 4.

¹⁶See Julien, *America's Empire:* "There is a basic and complete agreement among U.S. [political and economic elites] . . . that the growing of the empire is indispensable to the preservation of American way of life" (p. 379). See Williams, *Tragedy of American Diplomacy,* for the most complete statement of this point of view.

¹⁷For example, see the recently declassified famous "NSC-68", a top-secret, intergovernmental document prepared by the secretarys of state and defense in 1950 to set forth the overall rationale for the United States containment policy. Throughout the report the emphasis is on the communist threat to democracy and freedom and the fundamental principles of Western civilization; no word is to be found about an "open door," the maintenance of capitalism, or, indeed, economic matters at all, except as related to the building of military and political strength. NSC-68 was published in full in *The Naval War College Review,* May/June 1975.

¹⁸The most complete statement of this view (which derives directly from Hobson's famous analysis of nineteenth-century European colonialism), is in Harry Magdoff, *The Age of Imperialism* (New York, 1969). See also the essays by James O'Connor and Paul A. Baran and Paul M. Sweezy in K. T. Fann and D. C. Hodges (eds.), *Readings in U.S. Imperialism* (Boston, 1971).

¹⁹The best evidence of this, of course, is the rapidly growing wave of nationalization of American private investments around the world, with the United States government

reaction rarely going beyond rather *pro forma* protest. This will be discussed in greater detail below.

[20]See Williams, *Tragedy of American Diplomacy,* for the most complete statement of this point of view.

[21]See Bernard S. Morris, *Imperialism and Revolution* (Bloomington, Ind., 1973), who writes that where one cannot find evidence of economic motivations, as in Vietnam, "the governing class may well have concealed its economic interests behind a cloud of ideological verbiage" (p. 36).

[22]For one among many examples of this approach see Anibal Quijano Obregon's essay in Julio Cotler and Richard R. Fagen (eds.), *Latin American and the United States* (Palo Alto, Calif., 1974). Quijano accounts for the recent examples of United States government nonintervention after American corporations in Latin America have been nationalized in these terms: "Since the principal imperialist state's policy is constrained by the new forces conditioning international politics, this state must now face situations in which the mere defense of the interests of each North American imperialist firm operating in these countries could aggravate the contradictions and the political-social conflicts within these countries. This, in turn, could threaten the very existence of capitalism as a mode of production in these countries, owing either to the flaring up of nationalism that derives from these readjustments of imperialist domination, or to the triumph of revolutionary, socialist social forces. In the face of these conditions, the principal imperialist state in the hemisphere finds itself obligated to accept, or at least tolerate and adjust to, the political currents that under the banner of nationalism seek to reduce the internal social tensions of some countries, and obligated, as well, to maintain capitalism by readjusting its methods of operation and the very conditions of imperialist exploitation" (p. 81–82).

[23]Timothy Harding in Fann and Hodges, *U. S. Imperialism,* p. 14. Harry Magdoff also makes use of the "weakest link" metaphor to argue that even in Vietnam economic considerations ultimately underlay United States policy (in Owen and Sutcliffe, *Theory of Imperialism,* p. 170).

[24]For similar conclusions about the neo-Marxist analyses see Tucker, *The Radical Left;* Cohen, *Question of Imperialism;* Robert Maddox, *The New Left and the Origins of the Cold War* (Princeton, N. J., 1973); James Kurth in Steven J. Rosen and James R. Kurth (eds.), *Testing Theories of Economic Imperialism* (Lexington, Mass., 1974); Ole R. Holsti, "The Study of International Politics Makes Strange Bedfellows," *American Political Science Review,* March 1974.

[25]See Tucker, *The Radical Left,* for a similar argument.

[26]Also, Peter Odell in *Oil and World Power* (London, 1970) has shown that in the late 1950s and early 1960s the United States government prevailed upon American oil corporations not to plot with Venezuelan rightists against the Betancourt regime, even though Betancourt had put into effect substantially higher taxation of oil profits; of greater apparent importance to the government was that the Betancourt regime was considered as a possible liberal alternative to Castroism and a model for the kind of government envisioned by the Alliance for Progress. Moreover, the United States government today is *discouraging* exploitation by American oil companies of the apparently oil-rich coastal waters between China and Taiwan and South Asia, in order to avoid political conflict with the Peking government. See *The New York Times,* September 5, 1975, and Selig S. Harrison, "Time Bomb in East Asia," *Foreign Policy,* Fall 1975.

[27]For discussion of the Guatemalan and Dominican interventions, see, respectively, Jerome Slater, *The OAS and the United States Foreign Policy* (Columbus, Ohio, 1967), and Jerome Slater, *Intervention and Negotiation; The United States and the Dominican Revolution* (New York, 1970).

[28]In Lynn H. Miller and Ronald W. Pruessen (eds.), *Reflection on the Cold War* (Philadelphia, 1974), p. 18 (italics added).

[29]Andre Gunder Frank, *Capitalism and Underdevelopment in Latin America* (New York, 1967), p. 9.

[30]The most complete and sophisticated statements of the dependence model are to be found in ibid.; Galtung, *"A Structural Theory of Imperialism";* Magdoff, *Age of Imperialism;* Osvaldo Sunkel in Yale H. Ferguson and Walter F. Weiker (eds.), *Continuing Issues in International Politics* (Los Angeles, 1973); Dale Johnson in James D. Cockroft et al., *Dependence and Underdevelopment* (New York, 1972).

[31]For discussions of exploitation in this sense, see Klaus Knorr, *Power and Wealth* (New York, 1973), p. 12, and Barrington Moore, Jr., *Reflections on the Causes of Human Misery* (Boston, 1970), pp. 53–54.

[32]David P. Calleo and Benjamin M. Rowland, *America and the World Political Economy* (Bloomington, Ind., 1973), p. 242.

[33]As reported in *The New York Times,* May 29, 1975.

[34]"Trade in Raw Materials," in Rosen and Kurth, *Testing Theories of Economic Imperialism,* p. 195 (italics added).

[35]For major criticisms of foreign investment see Frank, *Capitalism;* Sunkel in Ferguson and Weiker, *Continuing Issues in International Politics;* Crockroft et al., *Dependence and Underdevelopment;* Richard J. Barnet and Ronald E. Muller, *Global Reach* (New York, 1974).

[36]For the most balanced, sophisticated treatments of the impact of foreign investment in the Third World, see Louis Turner, *Multinational Companies and the Third World* (New York, 1973); Raymond Vernon, *Sovereignty at Bay* (New York, 1971); A. Kapoor and Phillip D. Grub (eds.), *The Multinational Enterprise in Transition* (Princeton, N. J., 1972); Charles P. Kindleberger, *American Business Abroad* (New Haven, Conn., 1969); Alfred D. Hirschman, *How to Divest in Latin America and Why* (Princeton, N. J., 1969).

[37]On the question of the effects of foreign aid and more generally, the relationship between economic power and political influence, see Knorr, *Power and Wealth.*

[38]Richard N. Cooper, "Trade Policy," *Foreign Policy,* Winter 1972–73.

[39]For similar views, see Michael Harrington, "American Power in the Twentieth Century," in Irving Howe (ed.), *A Dissenter's Guide to Foreign Policy* (New York, 1968), and Peter F. Drucker, "Multinationals and Developing Countries, *Foreign Affairs,* October 1974.

[40]Adalberto Pinelo, *The Multinational Corporation as a Force in Latin American Politics* (New York, 1973). For other discussions of the IPC affair see Richard Goodwin, "Letter from Peru," *New Yorker,* May 17, 1969, and Charles T. Goodsell, *American Corporations and Peruvian Politics* (Cambridge, Mass., 1974).

[41]Goodsell, *American Corporations,* pp. 8–9.

[42]Theodore H. Moran, *Multinational Corporations and the Politics of Dependence* (Princeton, N. J., 1974), p. 215.

[43]Later United States economic pressures on the Allende government and other covert efforts against it were clearly motivated primarily by general ideological disapproval of an overtly radical Marxist regime in the Western Hemisphere and concern about its potential "domino" effects elsewhere in Latin America, rather than by the relatively narrow issue of expropriation of United States corporations.

[44]For example, Moran shows that the United States copper industry never had much of a stable alliance with the Chilean "oligarchy," since even the elites resented foreign control. He concludes that "the Chilean experience suggests that foreign investors in prominent natural-resource industries in developing countries have few permanent allies." (Moran, *Multinational Corporations,* p. 247).

[45]For discussions of the shifting balance of power between multinational corporations and Third World countries see Raymond Vernon, "The Role of U.S. Enterprises Abroad," *Daedalus,* Winter 1969; C. Fred Bergsten, "Coming Investment Wars?" *Foreign Affairs,* October 1974; C. Fred Bergsten, "The Response to Third World," *Foreign Policy,* Winter 1974–75; Joseph S. Nye, Jr., "Multinational Corporations in World Politics," *Foreign Affairs,* October 1974; Moran, *Multinational Corporations;* Turner, *Multinational Companies.*

[46]Osvaldo Sunkel, in Cotler and Fagen, *Latin America and the United States,* p. 126. See below for a discussion of the overthrow of the Allende regime in Chile, which at first glance might appear to contradict the argument.

[47]Ibid., p. 61.

[48]I am indebted to Edward Kolodziej for the point about the convenience of the myth of imperialism; for discussions of the new importance of inequality per se, see Robert Tucker's recent writings, especially his "A New International Order?" *Commentary,* February 1975, and "Egalitarianism and International Politics," *Commentary,* September 1975.

2   The Case for Nonintervention

Melvin Gurtov

The unpleasant but inescapable conclusion of [a] review of American interventions in the Third World is that, on balance, they have been highly effective instruments for attaining immediate U.S. foreign-policy objectives. While U.S. administrations have sustained setbacks, as in Indonesia, the Bay of Pigs, and Bangladesh, only one—in Vietnam—has had long-term domestic and international consequences. Elsewhere, movements representing opposition to the status quo have been thwarted, friendly governments have been buttressed and unpalatable ones overturned, and U.S. economic access and political influence have been preserved or expanded. The American record is sufficiently strong to justify, in the minds of decision-makers, continuation of interventionism where circumstances abroad appear to warrant it and where other means of exerting influence seem infeasible and/or ineffective.

The motives of these interventions go beyond simple anticommunism, as was revealed with particular clarity in Lebanon, in the initial stage of the Dominican intervention, and in the opposition to Bangladesh. U.S. policy-makers assumed that social revolutionary governments and political movements were dangerous if they disturbed, or seemed prepared to disturb, a status quo favorable to U.S. political, economic, and strategic interests. Beyond the question of these movements' or governments' ideological loyalties was the threat they were believed to pose to the existing boundaries of local politics, foreign policy, economic relationships, and balance of regional power. Preventive (or pre-emptive) intervention thus aimed not simply at restoring or preserving anticommunist authority, but more broadly at maintaining or creating a dependable, advantageous "stability."

This essentially imperial foreign-policy objective* inevitably conflicts with the oft-expressed official sympathy with nationalism, self-determination, and political change. The conflict may stem from the conviction of every President from Truman to Nixon that no people would freely choose a communist form of government. Nationalism and communism therefore cannot operate in concert; and nationalism, where it takes violent expression, as in civil wars and revolutions, must be opposed, because it involves or leads to the kind of chaos that com-

---

*"Imperial" rather than "imperialistic" because the latter would mean that American interventions have been motivated mainly by the need for territory, bases, new markets, lines of communication, or corporate profits. Instead, the motivation has generally been to preserve or expand *dependency relationships* with Third World societies by insuring access to, and exerting predominant influence over, their politics, economies, and military affairs.

munist forces, local and international, are believed bound to exploit. The American "tradition" of anticolonialism and revolution thus is set aside when change is brought about by other than nonviolent, nonradical means. Indeed, counterrevolution is the more recent American tradition—preventive action, or proxy intervention behind regimes receptive to U.S. influence and hostile to leftist ideologies, programs, and parties. And with that choice, the United States becomes the enemy of the "historical process" of disruptive change characteristic of Third World politics.[1]

An imperial foreign policy gives priority to the imposition of "law and order" on the international system. American administrations have been no more willing internationally than domestically to condone or accommodate disobedience, violence, civil strife, and insurgency. In both spheres, coercion of one kind or another has been the common response.[2] Whether one chooses to explain this compulsion in political, economic, or racial terms, the outcome is the same: intervention against nationalism. Both officials and academics[3] who have argued the need for a U.S. police function abroad, usually reasoning that it is vital to act sooner rather than later and thus prevent anarchy from spreading out of control, insist that the use of force should be discrete, prudent, detached, and timely. But these qualifications have affected only the mode of intervention; that the United States has preferred acting by proxy and with minimal force to becoming directly involved scarcely reduces the American role as an imperial power.

Nationalism has not been the only victim of the American interest in "stable" societies and alignment with reactionary partners. Elementary standards of humanitarianism and international law, and respect for supranational organizations, have also suffered. When the risks and costs of intervention are weighed, human life becomes totally politicized. The achievement of political and military objectives invariably has priority in American policy-making over prospects of destructiveness—as was the case, for example, in the Congo, Vietnam, Nigeria/Biafra, and Bangladesh. ("Atrocities" and "bloodbaths" tend to be condemned in Washington only when a hostile government or movement is the alleged perpetrator—as in China, 1949–50; Cuba after Castro's takeover; and by the NLF in Vietnam.) Adherence to treaty restrictions on the exercise of power has similarly been dependent on political judgments. U.S. policy in the three Latin American interventions, which showed utter disdain for the nonintervention principle, is illustrative. In those cases, as well as in policy toward Lebanon and Bangladesh, regional (the OAS) and international (the United Nations) organizations were ignored when they failed to serve or were believed unlikely to serve U.S. interests. (When the United Nations was prepared to work on behalf of U.S. objectives in the Congo, its cooperation was welcomed.) These aspects of American behavior are not, of course, peculiar to U.S. foreign policy; they are mentioned only to emphasize that the kinds of immoral, illegal, and manipulative practices for which socialist governments are usually condemned are standard components of American interventionism.

While it will not be surprising for most readers that U.S. interventions in the Third World have been motivated by power political considerations, the basic ingredients of that motivation may be more controversial. . . . I believe that at the heart of American interventionism is an ideological consensus among postwar high-level policymakers about the necessity of an activist U.S. role, and the presumption of U.S. responsibilities, for projecting U.S. power and influence abroad. This ideology has been cloaked in a variety of strategic formulations—containment, the falling-domino principle, counterinsurgency, balance of power—all of which denote an expansionist interpretation of the national interest that has become policymaking dogma. Interventions, therefore, should be understood as resulting from the ideology's distorting effect on American officials' perception of Third World conditions.

The case studies point up a number of commonalities in the American perception that are worth recapitulating:

1. *Political or social instability in the Third World is a breeding ground for radical leftist forces.* Policy-making in Washington generally assumes the worst. Instability abroad is believed to be the result of international communist influences, to be amenable to direction by local procommunist organization (even though only a handful of communists may actually be identified), and to be detrimental to American political and economic interests. The consideration that an unstable situation abroad might enable the United States to identify with the nationalist, change-oriented objectives of those behind it, or refuse to identify with the government against which instability is directed, has been systematically ignored or downgraded. Radical nationalists like Nasser, Lumumba, Mossadegh, Castro, and Sukarno have been caricatured as communist dupes, while avowed communists (Mao, Ho) have been treated as antinationalists. Presumptions about the ultimate loyalty of these men have invariably forced them to reciprocate American hostility.

2. *History's "lessons" amply justify an imperial foreign policy.* Eisenhower's action in Lebanon, Kennedy's in the Congo, Johnson's in Vietnam—each of these, and others were prefaced by historical evaluation that "proved" the validity of concern about "another" communist takeover and "demonstrated" the wisdom of U.S. intervention. Analogies to the "loss" of China and Cuba, and to the "threat" to Greece and Korea, were useful ways for administrations to legitimize their interventions and rationalize them to the public. These experiences became models of communist behavior, distorting the intelligence community's reporting (as in the Dominican case) as well as high-level perspectives. Rarely were such manipulations of history questioned among policy-makers; since instability and the communist threat are considered constants in international politics, there apparently was every reason to regard intervention as a responsible means of dealing with them. Previous interventions thus justified later ones; interventionism was historically consistent, and if, as in the

Congo, Indochina, or Cuba, one administration succeeded to the interventionist policies of its predecessor, there was all the more justification for not reversing course and instead being prisoner to the past.

3. *Third World upheavals are foreign-policy crises having personal as well as national implications.* Not only does the ideology of national interests encourage American involvement in the domestic affairs of the developing countries, but also, for U.S. policy-makers, intervention becomes a personal test of nerve and will. The interaction of these two perspectives is well illustrated in the following statement by Walt W. Rostow:

> We must expect over the next decade recurrent turbulence in these [Third World] areas; we must expect systematic efforts by the Communists to exploit this turbulence; we must expect from time to time that crises will occur; and a great deal of skill, courage, and insight will be required to handle them in ways which do not damage—and if possible promote—the interests of the free world.[4]

A Third World crisis, from a crisis manager's viewpoint, is an expected event, since "turbulence" and communism will always be found together. The policy-making process puts a premium in such situations on toughness under fire, the ability to "see the thing through"—in other words, as in (among others) Laos, the Congo, Vietnam, and Cambodia, the attachment of higher priority to personal loyalty and strength of conviction than to intellectual sophistication and qualities of human understanding. Those persons who would make decisions on intervention hence were usually managers (of power) rather than area specialists, men who calculated costs and benefits in power-political rather than human, legal, or moral terms. They dealt with Third World problems as part of a global contest for ideological and military supremacy rather than as intractable events that are forever at the mercy of time and circumstance.*

THE CONDITIONS OF INTERVENTION

While it is not the purpose of this study to develop hypotheses about the precise circumstances and manner of American interventions in Third World countries,[5] the case studies do suggest the strategic and political factors that U.S. policy-makers did weigh when interventions were undertaken. These factors may be worth specifying because they show in another way how uninfluential considerations of Third World nationalism and principles of law and morality have been when U.S. administrations believed the national interest to be challenged.

---

*I contend that area specialists are less likely than crisis managers to abuse the power of decision on Third World policy. Area specialists have an intellectual commitment to Third World cultures that usually enables them to empathize with non-Western peoples and accept their intrinsic worth as individuals. Crisis managers, with their interest in power rivalry, systems, cost-benefit calculations, and gamesmanship, typically lack such a commitment.

There would seem to be two primary and three secondary conditions of Third World interventions:

Primary:
1. There must be a sociopolitical revolutionary milieu—either political violence in which a revolutionary movement (the so-called communist threat) is involved or radical domestic change that is being carried out by a revolutionary government.
2. The revolutionary movement's or government's policies and programs must be perceived as threatening "stability" beyond the country in which the movement or government is operating.

Secondary:
1. The risk of direct Soviet or Chinese intervention in response to U.S. involvement must be low.
2. U.S. intervention must be sanctioned by domestic (U.S.), regional, or international authority.
3. U.S. intervention must be invited by a "representative" of local political authority.

As already suggested, it is the perceived threat to stability rather than the communist threat alone that has consistently set the stage for decisions to intervene in the Third World. Radicalism must be coupled to chaos, or the likelihood of chaos. When that occurs—and it occurs quite often in Third World politics—there seems to be a visceral reaction among high U.S. policy-makers in the direction of a preventive intervention to stifle the threat before it gets out of hand.

But whether U.S. intervention in some form will actually take place seems to depend on a further condition, namely, that the American interest in stability be jeopardized beyond the specific country in which a revolutionary situation exists. There have, after all, been numerous instances of civil strife in the Third World that U.S. administrations ignored.[6] The common feature of the interventions examined in this study is that a social revolutionary movement or government was perceived from Washington to threaten a *regional* status quo. The success of the radical movement's opposition or the government's program would become infectious, in Washington's judgment, and therefore should be resisted. Recall, for instance, that the United States intervened in China mainly because a stable China under Chiang Kai-shek was deemed important to the maintenance of American predominance in postwar Asia's balance of power; intervened in Lebanon to cut short encirclement of the Middle East by radical Arab nationalist governments; intervened in Guatemala, Cuba, and the Dominican Republic to silence or prevent the spread of radical socialism in Latin America; intervened in Indochina initially to keep the "dominoes" from falling throughout Southeast Asia and later to preserve faith in America's willingness and ability to combat national liberation wars; and intervened in Bangladesh to re-establish a stable balance of power on the Indian subcontinent. *How far* the United States was prepared to pursue intervention was determined, as has been seen, by a variety of other circumstances, including domestic politics, bureaucratic bargaining, military assessments, and competing demands for attention and resources from other international problems. But the point to be emphasized here is that radicalism in Third World politics, when perceived to have more than local implications, incited the American will to intervene.

Secondary conditions of U.S. intervention are those that usually affect decisions on it but are not indispensable. Among them is the assessment of prospects for Soviet or Chinese counteraction. This consideration is considered secondary because U.S. policy-makers have, as in Laos, Vietnam, and the Congo, accepted the risk of counteraction weighed against the benefits of intervention. All the interventions discussed in this study were undertaken with great confidence, however, that such counteraction would not occur, or could be handled effectively if it unexpectedly did occur. The assessment invariably proved correct: Whereas the Americans were prepared to play for high stakes, the Russians or the Chinese were not. Had *their* evaluation of the relationship between Third World instability and their own national interests been equivalent to the Americans', one or another past "crisis" might easily have mushroomed into a direct confrontation of the major powers. Instead, the limited, hesitant, and carefully controlled character of Soviet and Chinese involvement in Third World political violence, and on behalf of Third World ideological allies, has given the United States free rein to intervene.* And the cumulative experience of these unopposed interventions has probably emboldened U.S. policy-makers to believe that the entire Third World, and not merely Latin America, is a low-risk area for applying American power.

Intervention usually has also been conditioned by sanction from various sources, most importantly from the Congress and from regional and international organizations. With the important exceptions of the Dominican, Cambodian, and Bangladesh interventions, all the others found U.S. administrations seeking, or referring to, authority for their actions from key congressmen, congressional resolutions, the United Nations, or regional associations. Sanction was rarely difficult to find, and opposition easy to avoid. Hurried "crisis" meetings with select congressional leaders almost always led to approval of interventionary actions (opposition in 1954 to U.S. involvement in Indochina being a notable exception). Public opinion could always be counted on to support the President in a time of national trial. Enabling documents such as the SEATO pact, the U.N. Charter, the OAS Charter, and the Tonkin Gulf Resolution were sufficiently ambiguous to be either stretched or distorted in order to serve the administration's purposes. But the three exceptions to these rules of procedure reduce the criticality of them. In the first case U.S. troops were landed, in the second U.S. forces invaded, and in the third aid was covertly sent and a naval

---

*The major limitation that the United States has observed in these interventions is not to escalate to the point of threatening a major adversary's most security-sensitive areas. Having paid the price in Korea of insensitivity to Chinese security interests, U.S. intervention in Laos and over North Vietnam carefully avoided provoking the P.R.C. to counteract directly. No crisis in areas adjacent to the Soviet Union has yet occurred.

task force dispatched, on each occasion without prior congressional or any other authority. The lack of domestic and supranational sanction thus will not deter administrations from using force or threat abroad if the "national interest" (incorporated in conditions 1 and 2) so dictates.

Finally, U.S. officials have also sought authorization of intervention from within the country that is the subject of intervention. Presidents value invitations for purely instrumental reasons: They lend legitimacy to the intervention by making it appear to be in response to a call for help from a lawful representative of a Third World society. On occasion, failure to find a credible local authority has played a part in preventing a U.S. intervention from occurring—for example, Eisenhower's unwillingness to intervene on behalf of Bao Dai's Vietnam in 1954, and the same administration's inability to find a suitable Cuban exile leader who would represent the Bay of Pigs invaders. But, as with the previous two conditions, this one generally has not needed to be promptly or fully satisfied to bring about intervention. Third World governments and opposition groups in whose behalf the United States intervened have clearly lacked popular credentials that would make their invitations credible (as in Laos, Vietnam, Cuba, and Guatemala). In addition, interventions have occurred where no government in fact existed (the military triumvirate that called on the U.S. Embassy in the Dominican Republic); where the national leader did not have control over his armed forces (Chamoun in Lebanon); and where no request to intervene was received or even made (Cambodia).

AN ALTERNATIVE TO INTERVENTION

The imperial persuasion in American foreign policy toward the Third World is not open to question only on moral, legal, and humanitarian grounds. In long-term perspective interventions do not serve the political, economic, and strategic interests that are usually cited to justify them. It is, in other words, in the interest of the United States, as that interest has been defined by American policy-makers, to make nonintervention the keystone of U.S. policy.

In the first place, interventions against nationalism confirm suspicions of, and hostility toward, the United States (and "U.S. imperialism"), thus limiting American access and influence in the Third World. This was or is the case, for example, in postwar China, in Sukarno's Indonesia, in Africa because of opposition to the nationalist movements in the Portuguese colonies, and throughout Latin America. American behavior in the Third World has conformed to the descriptions of it proferred by Moscow and Peking. The United States would today have far greater diplomatic latitude and economic opportunities abroad than it now enjoys had it chosen not to intervene against radical movements and governments.

Where the United States has chosen to intervene against revolutionary movements, moreover, it has often become entangled in commitments to governments that are inefficient, corrupt, lacking in popular authority, and oppressive. These regimes have been able to manipulate American commitments to acquire increased military and economic aid and to develop a U.S. interest in, and ultimate responsibility for, their very survival. U.S.-Cambodia relations after the April, 1970, invasion provide a recent illustration of this phenomenon. Should such regimes be overthrown, the American capacity to disengage its support and realign with a successor revolutionary government is weakened if not eliminated for years to come.

Intervention against radical governments does more than assure their lasting hostility toward the United States. For lack of any better alternative as much as because of ideological affinity, these governments are bound to move closer toward the socialist world, and may become politically and economically dependent on it. After U.S. interventions, the new government of China (from 1950 to 1959), Sukarno's Indonesia (from 1958 to 1965), and Cuba (after 1961) became active opponents of American foreign policy and accepted varying degrees of dependency on Soviet trade and aid. Interventions thus not only defy the concepts of state sovereignty and territorial integrity, they also weaken the capacity of radical governments to develop independent foreign and domestic policies. Had nonintervention been practiced, opportunities would probably have become available for Washington to work constructively with these governments, offering them the kind of technical help and diplomatic cushioning they needed to avoid being dependent on any one foreign power.

Intervention, often carried out in parts of the world that are as remote from the United States politically and strategically as they are geographically, makes defense of the "national interest" a world-wide responsibility. The arenas in which a direct confrontation of the major powers may occur become ever wider; the chance of war brought on by the momentum of conflict or miscalculation increases. The fact that, until now, the United States has been able to project its power into the Third World with relative impunity is no guarantee for the future, especially as both the U.S.S.R. and China are expanding their international engagements and the reach of their military power into traditionally American preserves. Nor can the United States be assured that new diplomatic understandings with those nations in the 1970's will remove Third World countries as potential points of conflict. As American conduct of the Indochina war has shown, the improvement of relations with Russia and China has not been allowed to impede the pursuit of objectives in Third World areas in which the socialist powers also have interests. The United States has proceeded with intervention at the cost of straining and setting back relations with its major international adversaries rather than abandon its minor allies.

Another long-term disadvantage of interventionism is that it confirms racial stereotypes, increases racial hatreds, and thus enhances the possibility of race conflict. American behavior broadens the global North-South conflict from an economic one (the "haves" versus the "have-nots") to a racial one (between the white and colored peoples). Rhetoric about social justice and self-determination, and technical assistance programs to Third World governments, cannot be of great

help either to the American image or to American purposes when the
U.S. Government assumes the right of intervention to ensure Third
World stability. Only when nonintervention is the rule can American
espousals of interest in assisting "have-not" peoples to be independent
and self-reliant become credible.

With the American intervention on a massive scale in Indochina,
the relationship became clear for the first time between an imperial
policy abroad and domestic division. So costly and fruitless has U.S.
policy been in Indochina since the early 1950's that widespread doubts
have arisen at home about the sanity of American foreign-policy
leadership generally, and about the usefulness of global involvement.
Resort to the most sophisticated means of violence and terror have
been seen in many quarters to have parallels at home; and the fact that,
both at home and abroad, the targets have been colored peoples ac-
centuates the sense of injustice and oppression among American
minorities that had developed before the war reached its height. Less
dramatic forms of intervention may well enable administrations to
continue to use it without fear of vigorous public opposition. But so
long as Vietnam remains recent history, interventions that previously
would have raised no eyebrows now will be subjected to public and
congressional scrutiny. At the least, the government will no longer be
able to count on the traditionally large reservoir of support (or apathy)
for foreign policies and programs that made endorsement of interventions so automatic in the past.

Noninterventionism can begin to restore confidence in the government's ability to manage foreign affairs with sense and decency. Its
axioms would essentially be the reverse of those that I have proposed
constitute U.S. foreign-policy ideology. America's domestic tranquillity
depends on the quality of life at home, not on security and stability
abroad. Security and stability abroad depend on the relationship of individual governments to their citizens, not on a moral or political
responsibility that has been unwarrantedly assumed. Finally, the
fullfillment of America's international role depends on the dynamism
and openness of American society, the opportunities for individual
growth afforded by American institutions, and the ability of the
American Government to exercise restraint in its projection of power
abroad. Refusing to become party to the domestic conflicts of other nations would not represent an abnegation of power and responsibility,
but a realization of their limits.

The mood of the public and Congress, as reflected in the 1973
War Powers Resolution that restricts the President's use of force
abroad, appears to be highly receptive to noninterventionism and the
definition of a narrower, more manageable, and more purposeful
range of foreign interests. Indeed, such a shift in over-all policy should
facilitate an administration's argument in behalf of other international
programs, including foreign economic assistance, defense budgets, and
diplomacy with the Soviet Union and China. It should be as possible to
"sell" noninterventionism today as it has been to "sell" interventionism;

much depends on whether the American Government is prepared to do away with the ideological component of foreign policy-making.

Abroad, a policy of nonintervention must include above all a receptivity to radical change, regardless of the ideology or economic philosophy of the government or movement supporting such change. This suggestion is not for a simpleminded shift from systematically resisting to systematically supporting radicalism. What counts is the quality of economic and political life that radical change promises. The United States should be identifying with those groups or governments that are devoted to promoting national independence, enhancing their capacity for self-reliant economic growth, and working toward equality of social and economic justice and personal freedom. It should not give aid or comfort to a movement or regime—such as that in white Southern Africa or Pakistan during the Bangladesh revolution—that, as a matter of policy or practice, denies its people equal opportunity and violates common standards of humanitarian treatment. The American interest should lie in the realization of long-cherished and widely accepted values rather than in a particular (Western) structure of authority, pattern of politics, or ideological tendency in the cold war.[7]

American administrations must come to accept that a stable world order in which the danger of war is receding and the urge to predominance of the major powers is checked can be promoted more surely by aligning with (but not intervening behind) the forces of change than by opposing them. Intervention can, at most, only brake temporarily the momentum of revolution; it cannot, short of prolonged military occupation (and questionably even then), eradicate those governmental deficiencies or conflicts of political interest that give rise to civil strife. The lessons for future decisions on revolution abroad should come from unsuccessful interventions; those that have achieved U.S. objectives in the short run do not advance American interests in the long run, and in fact retard them.

If this perspective were put into practice, would there not be a danger of the Third World's eventual encirclement and political absorption by the socialist world? This question, posed by those who have long and successfully argued that noninterventionism is too risky, sees communism as a singular formula for satellization rather than for what it is, a modernizing ideology.[8] Proponents of the interventionist philosophy do not see how self-fulfilling it can be—how the act of intervention promotes the very instability, anti-American hostility, and attraction to radical ideologies that it seeks to prevent. Even if a hands-off American policy toward Third World civil strife should encourage the U.S.S.R. and China to increase their efforts to benefit from it, those powers have already found, most notably in Africa and the Middle East, that there are severe limits to their ability to control events in the Third World. Third World governments, including those receptive to socialism, jealously safeguard their sovereignty, with or without an American presence or the possibility of U.S. intervention. If history is any guide, the consequences of Soviet or Chinese attempts to manipulate Third World politics are more likely to be new Vietnams for them than the establishment of a new communist imperium.

Are there nevertheless circumstances under which U.S. intervention in Third World civil wars or revolutions can be "legitimate"? Two of the African cases—the Congolese civil war, in its initial phase, and the revolutions in the Portuguese colonies—suggest exceptions to a noninterventionist policy. Where a request for intervention is made by a government whose credentials are nowhere questioned, or by a revolutionary movement whose claims to represent nationalist sentiment are not in doubt; where that request is channeled through and action is authorized by the United Nations; and where the purpose of the intervention is to weaken or remove a clearly foreign presence—in such circumstances, American involvement would be morally, politically, and legally defensible.

Such a conjunction of circumstances warranting intervention, which would be in a multilateral framework, is highly improbable. The inviting authority is seldom a single voice representative of all major political factions, and the voice itself is not likely to be universally acknowledged. For these and other reasons, the U.N. membership will rarely be in agreement on the legitimacy of the request, much less the means of acting upon it. And there will be few cases in which the "foreign" character of the intruder is obvious to all.

Intervention, however, *should be* the rare exception and no longer the practiced tool of American foreign policy. When intervention occurs, it should be universally condoned. It should not serve specifically American purposes, whether those be in pursuit of traditional imperial objectives or, as is sometimes urged, in order actively to promote the interests of revolutionary movements. If proscriptions against unilateral intervention are to have meaning, they must be enforced with respect to both "good" and "bad" governments and "progressive" and "reactionary" movements. Nor should they leave open the alternative of intervening where success is likely and U.S. interests are clearly at stake.[9] Except under the unusual conditions just mentioned, U.S. policy in the Third World should proceed from the assumption that intervention cannot be ultimately profitable and that nonintervention is the most appropriate way to promote American influence and the American example.

NOTES

[1]See the discussion in Herbert S. Dinerstein, *Intervention Against Communism* (Baltimore, Md.: Johns Hopkins University, 1967), pp. 33–37.

[2]On the domestic and international parallels of intervention to preserve order, see Bernard P. Kiernan, *The United States, Communism, and the Emergent World* (Bloomington: Indiana University Press, 1973), pp. 173–76. A recent illustration of this parallel is Richard Nixon's equation of the containment of China with the containment of "outlaw" elements in America's ghettos. See his "Asia After Viet-Nam," *Foreign Affairs,* XLVI, no. 1 (October, 1967), 123.

[3]See, for instance, George Liska, *War and Order: Reflections on Vietnam and History* (Baltimore, Md.: Johns Hopkins University, 1968), especially pp. 15–29.

[4]Walt M. Rostow, *View from the Seventh Floor* (New York: Harper & Row, 1964), p. 22.

⁵One stimulating effort in this direction is Herbert K. Tillema's *Appeal to Force: American Military Intervention in the Era of Containment* (New York: Crowell, 1973), which offers an empirical and theoretical examination of the conditions that promote and restrain U.S. military intervention abroad.

⁶See *ibid.*, chap. 5.

⁷Concerning these values, see Robert A. Packenham, *Liberal America and the Third World* (Princeton, N.J.: Princeton University Press, 1973).

⁸See Kiernan, chap. 1.

⁹These are the two criteria suggested by Hans Morgenthau, *A New Foreign Policy for the United States* (New York: Praeger, 1969), p. 128.

Race and Ethnic Nationalism

3 The Universalization of Ethnicity

Nathan Glazer

PEOPLES IN THE BOILING POT

Are there some large discernible trends in the world—political, social, economic—that are leading in general to an accentuation of ethnic conflicts?

Admittedly, there are problems involved even in the exact determination of whether there is or is not an increase in "ethnic conflicts." Thus, we have the persisting conflict between French and English speaking in Canada. Is that an "ethnic" conflict, or a "language" conflict, or the struggle of a "suppressed nation" for independence? We have the division between "Indian" and "Spanish" elements in a number of Latin American countries. Are those "ethnic conflicts"? We have the tragic conflict between Protestant and Catholic in Northern Ireland. But isn't that an essentially "religious" conflict? We have the movements for Scottish and Welsh autonomy in Great Britain; Breton and "South French" movements in France; the strain between Northern and Southern Italy. Some observers would define these as "regional" rather than "ethnic" movements. In each case an outlying section of the country has not shared in the prosperity of the centre, and this seems to have awakened some long dormant ethnic consciousness. One doesn't know whether the group pressing for autonomy or more central government funds feels deprived because of an ethnic difference, or because of regional discrimination. The group has a choice as to which basis of deprivation it will emphasise.

I will not continue this tour around the world, but if I did we would find a host of conflicts in which race, religion, region, and nationality are involved. I have just seen newspaper references to a re-emerging conflict between the Kurds of Iraq and the Iraqis (they share the same religion), and between the Muslims and the Christians of the Philippines. In both cases an international element enters into the conflict—because there are also Kurds in Iran and Turkey (and Iran and Iraq have border conflicts), while the Muslims of the Philippines are linked (by religion as well as by former political connection and culture) with North Borneo which is now part of Malaysia. Indonesia is also involved, at least distantly—because under its previous ruler Indonesia dreamed of a "greater Malay empire" which included Malaysia and the Philippines.

Let me try to clarify these varying bases of group division which seem so diverse and to justify a usage, which may seem to some to be too imperialistic, in which I label them all "ethnic." The term "ethnic" refers—and this is a usage that by now is quite common among sociologists and other social scientists—to a social group which consciously shares some aspects of a common culture and is defined primarily by descent. It is part of a family of terms of similar or related meaning, such as "minority group," "race", and "nation"; and it is not often easy to make sharp distinctions between them.

"Race" of course refers to a group that is defined by common descent and has some typical physical characteristics. Where one decides that a "race" ends and an "ethnic group" begins is not easy. Clearly, Swedes are (on the average) physically somewhat different from Frenchmen or Italians; but we normally don't use the word "race" to describe these differences. In European usage, on the other hand, at least until the time of Hitler, "race" was rather unselfconsciously used to describe what we would call "nations"—such as in the term "the genius of the French race." *Race* tends to refer to the biological aspect of group difference, *ethnic* to a combination of the cultural aspect plus a putative biological element because of the assumption of common descent. It is possible for a race not to be an ethnic group. In some descriptions, Brazilians of the predominantly Negro race do not appear as an ethnic group because they are not aware particularly of a common culture different from that of other Brazilians. This is so also because they don't have a corporate self-identity as a distinct group, even though *individuals* are aware of their physical characteristics and are aware that these physical differences tend to be associated with some common group characteristics (*viz.*, poverty). Recent accounts from Brazil seem to suggest that Blacks in Brazil may be becoming an ethnic group. This would fit in with one major theme of my article; that is, that the ethnic group is tending to become, in many countries, a more significant basis for social organisation and for individual identification.

"Race," then, refers to something more grossly physical than ethnic group. "Religion," another significant basis of human organisation, seems on the face of it a very different matter from ethnic group. Religions, in common understanding, are based on conversion and individual allegiance. The great religions—Christianity, Islam, Buddhism—include individuals and groups of every race and ethnic group. In the specific realities of social intercourse, however, religious groups very often act as, and are felt as, ethnic groups. The overwhelming majority of people, after all, are born into a religion, rather than adopt it, just as they are born into an ethnic group. In this respect both are similar. They are both groups by "ascription" rather than "achievement." They are groups in which one's status is immediately given by birth rather than gained by some activities in one's life.

Religions are generally in any given setting specifically associated with a defined ethnic group. Thus, in the Sudan and in Chad, Arabic-speaking groups in the North (which are Muslim) contrast with Negro groups in the South (which are pagan or Christian). In Nigeria, the Northern language group (or tribal, or ethnic, group) of Hausa is Muslim, while the Ibo and Yoruba are Christian. Thus, when a Hausa meets an Ibo, they assume the other's religion is Muslim and Christian, respectively. In the United States, Poles are almost all Catholic, and Swedes are almost all Lutheran—if, that is, they have any religious connection. Aside from the normal close connection between religion and ethnic group, religion in itself is culture-forming, and thus makes ethnic groups.

Thus "religion," except for periods of conversion and expansion, when members of many ethnic groups may be swept up in a religion, is in social context a category that acts very much like what we have called "ethnic group."

Perhaps the most difficult question in setting a boundary to the term ethnic group is that of its relationship to *caste*: groups defined by birth and by origin from some distant ancestors, intermarrying, traditionally fixed in a hierarchy from upper to lower, and limited to specific occupations. "Caste" is identified primarily with India, and yet there are other cases. One famous one is that of the "Eta" or "Burakumin" of Japan.[1] The Jews in medieval and in early modern Europe were treated as a caste—they had a fixed low hierarchical position, intermarried, were limited to certain occupations, and had about them (to Christians) an air of ritual impurity.

Castes (theoretically) are permanent. One cannot "convert" to another caste, as presumably Jews could convert to Christianity, and thus lose the disadvantages of being Jewish. But it should be recalled that even converted Jews were viewed with suspicion in Spain, and they were never considered really as good Christians as the others.

This fairly lengthy introduction is, I feel, necessary in view of the widespread confusions, and in view of that fact that I will be referring on occasion to religious groups, racial groups, tribal groups, language groups, and be calling them all "ethnic groups." Let me try to justify this very inclusive term by answering the obvious question: What is *not* an ethnic group? Do I set any boundaries to the term? Yes, I do. After all, distant as our studies as sociologists are from the most respectable sciences, our terms must have some clear definition, and one means of making a clear definition is to set a boundary.

There are two important social forms that are *not* ethnic groups. One of them is the political community; the State and its members.

Americans very often call a state a "nation," but in most European languages the Nation refers very specifically to the ethnic group, the State to the formal political organisation which grants citizenship. The close link between Nation and State arose because in the course of European history, and in particular in the 19th century, with the rise of nationalism, every nation demanded its own state. This led to the creation of modern Germany and Italy, the formation of ethnic European states out of the Ottoman Empire, the break-up of the Austro-Hungarian Empire into its ethnic components, each organised as a State, and the creation of ethnic Nation-States out of the Western borders of the old Czarist Empire. The United States is perhaps unique among the states of the world in using the term "nation" to refer not to an ethnic group but to all who choose to become Americans. "The American nation," a perfectly legitimate term, is not limited in its usage to those of a given heritage. Despite this, Woodrow Wilson (with his emphasis on national self-determination) insisted that every *other* ethnic group, under no-matter-what political organisation, should have its own state. The vital contrast between Nation and State was obscured in large measure between the two World Wars when so many of the independent states of the world were organised on the basis of a single dominant ethnic group. Those who remained as ethnic minorities within such states hoped for eventual reunion with the Nation-State that represented their own ethnic group.

In the post-1945 world, the close link between State and Nation, which had dominated the state-making efforts of the post-1918 peace-making (and of the politics of Europe between the two World Wars) was again broken. For most of the new states that were formed out of the colonial empires were *not* "Nation States," *i.e.* states representing a single ethnicity. And yet the world, in revulsion to war and conquest, had become strangely enough strongly attached to "old boundaries"—any boundaries, set any way. The scores of new states formed out of the colonial empires simply accepted the old accidental colonial boundaries. These new states then were faced with the problem of—as they and others saw it—becoming "nations", moulding people of different ethnic groups into "Nigerians", or "Kenyans", or some other people.

The problems of the newly-independent states of Asia were somewhat different. There were ancient cultural traditions or imperial state boundaries which did not make frontiers quite as arbitrary as they were in Africa. But even there—in Pakistan, India, Burma, Indonesia, Malaysia—the problem of creating a Single Nation became a severe one, varying in intensity from country to country. The problem in each case was: Would older identities—religious, linguistic, racial, and caste—submerge themselves in a new national identity? Or would they become (to use our problematic term again) *ethnic* identities, with some possible claim to their own kind of state existence? Would they soon be demanding political recognition of their separateness, with perhaps an ultimate claim to the right of secession?

The one social form, then, that is not an ethnic group is the State.

This is so despite the fact that in European thinking (and, to some extent, in Asian) it is generally taken for granted that the ideal form of the State is one in which there is a state for each ethnic group, and one ethnic group for each state. In the circumstances of Africa, this is almost impossible—the conflict in creating any such format would be unbearable, and it has accordingly rarely been attempted.

There is certainly a tension between ethnic groups and states. As each state tries to become a nation, it attempts to reduce the intensity of subordinate ethnic claims. The problem is that both ethnic groups and states make claims to *ultimate loyalty*. And the state inevitably comes into conflict with any social form that has a competing claim to ultimate loyalty. At one time this competing claim was most strongly put forward by religion. With the decline of religion this competing claim is most strongly put forward by *ethnicity*.

Rupert Emerson has defined the Nation as a

'terminal community—the largest community that, when the chips are down, effectively commands men's loyalty, overriding the claims of both the lesser communities within it and those that cut across it within a still greater society.'[2]

A sound definition, from a European perspective, neatly separating French loyalty from the lesser loyalty of being Gascon or Burgundian, or the larger loyalty of being European or Christian. But when applied to Nigeria or to Malaysia it simply leaves us uncertain as to what the Nation is. As Clifford Geertz writes: "[It seems] to leave such questions as whether India, Indonesia, or Nigeria are nations to the determination of some future, unspecified historical crisis."[3]

States, then, are not ethnic groups, though the linking term "nation" can be taken as one or the other. Nations are not necessarily ethnic groups, though those that are not coterminous with an ethnic group try to create a new national identity, which (if they succeed) becomes a new ethnicity.

There is one other crucial boundary limiting ethnic groups. Social classes are not ethnic groups.

One is not born an unskilled worker, a clerk, a professional. One is born into a family whose head may hold such an occupation. Some social theories insist this means, in effect, that one's future occupation and income are fixed by birth. But if this were really so, we would not be so interested in "social mobility." Social mobility refers specifically to movements between the strata of society, from one occupation, income level, education standard, to another. Social mobility is one term that cannot be used to refer to the change of one ethnic group into another. Other terms are necessary. Just as "social mobility" applies specifically to the *class* phenomena of society, so do "assimilation," "acculturation," "conversion" apply to the *ethnic* phenomena. These are rather more exceptional processes than those of social mobility. They are not accepted—or expected—processes. It is true peoples assimilate to other peoples, and do change their ethnic identity over time. But it is more or less expected that the ethnic stock remains immutable.

Thus "ethnic group," in my usage, refers basically to the vertical divisions of a society in contrast to the horizontal divisions. The horizontal divisions refer to *class;* the vertical divisions to *ethnicity.* Sometimes they coincide, as in the case of the Negroes in the American South, all of whom were by definition for a long time in the lowest class (or, in view of their inability to rise, caste). And yet the distinction was plain. As the blacks rose, socially, to become doctors, professional persons, and white-collar workers, their *class* changed. But their *ethnic group* remained the same. Even in India, the classic land of caste, one observes a similar phenomenon. The correlation between caste and class becomes somewhat weaker over time. The caste groups do become, in my definition, "ethnic groups." Perhaps the best indication of this is that they are increasingly called "communities" as the social position of their members becomes more diverse.

It is along the boundaries between Ethnic Group and State (on the one hand) and the relations of Ethnic Group and Social Class (on the other hand) that we have witnessed in the past two decades some striking new developments. It is these developments which have made *ethnicity* a new and problematic force in internal and international relations. Let me state a proposition in connection with each boundary.

Proposition Number One (on the relations between states and ethnic groups). The old hope of nationalism, accepted in the peacemaking after World War I (and to some extent after World War II)—for each Nation a state, for each State a nation—has receded into the distance. It becomes more and more difficult to grasp it effectively as a basis for international organisation. A number of developments have led to the recession of this model.

1. Too many new states have been created that are not, and cannot in the foreseeable future become, states of a given ethnic group. I refer primarily to the new states of Africa, to some extent to those of Asia. In these cases, we have seen the rise of a new concern with "Nation-Building." We have also seen the hopes for nation-building complicated or foundering on the basis of old lines of division—racial, religious, linguistic, tribal. Each division has taken the common form of ethnic group.

2. We have been surprised by the rise of new ethnic or quasi-ethnic identities and the sharpening of old ethnic identities in those states that were considered either models of contemporary modern Nation-States, or successes in having subordinated their ethnic divisions to the "terminal loyalty" of the Nation. Consider for example that model of patriotic commitment in World War I—Belgium. Look at it today: increasingly divided between groups that place their terminal loyalty more and more in the ethnic group of Fleming or Walloon. Consider Canada in World Wars I and II, with its apparently total commitment to War for the sake of the ethnic Motherland. See how delicately it now tries to reconcile the claims of French-speaking and English-speaking. Consider the remarkable, if still far from signal success, of Scottish Nationalism on the island of Great Britain, whose ethnic divisions seemed a few decades ago fully reconciled in the new identity of being "British." The United States was never a Nation-State, but certainly we have not seen as sharp a challenge in the hundred years since the Civil War of 1861–65 to the "terminal loyalty" of Americans as we saw in the rise of the militant Black Power movement (with its search for an alternative loyalty, marked even by such national symbols as a separate flag) or in the rise of new Mexican American and American Indian militant movements. Those states that are effectively single ethnic groups avoid such divisions. But few are so fortunate as, say, Sweden, or post-war Poland, made "pure" by massive population transfers. As old divisions in some states sharpen, others worry whether their old seams will rip open.

3. Many even of those older states that were ethnically homogeneous have become ethnically more heterogeneous as the economic developments of the post-War world have led to enormous migrations of labour. In West Germany, there are 2.4 million "guest workers," principally from Turkey, Yugoslavia, Italy and Greece, now forming 12 per cent of the labour force, and in some areas considerably more.[4] Germany cannot do without them; and more and more the guest workers settle down with their wives and children. Switzerland has, proportionately, even more. France has taken its foreign workers in large measure from Algeria, Spain, and Portugal. England has seen a substantial migration from the West Indies, Pakistan, and India, creating a permanent "coloured" population. In each of these countries the specific numbers and legal statuses vary; but in each of them a once remarkably high degree of ethnic homogeneity has been reduced by the introduction of new ethnic elements. The United States, from being an exception in the world because of its formation as a state out of many different elements, becomes more and more typical—as England struggles with its own colour problem, France wonders about the "integration" of the Algerians, and Germany considers how to educate the children of Turks and Yugoslavs.

4. The efforts of states, New or Old, to achieve "ethnic purity" are *not* leading to ethnically homogeneous states. Burma expels its Indians; Uganda evicts its Asian community, and other African states may do the same to theirs; Poland ejects even the pitiful remnants of its once-large Jewish community; and the Jews of other Eastern European states have migrated in large numbers to Israel. But, ironically, the attempts of some nations to become "ethnically pure" only complicate the problems of others. Britain's Asian community grows; and new Asian communities are established in other European nations, as a result of the expulsion of Asians from Africa. The Jews leaving Eastern Europe enter an ethnically mixed Israel, which is not—and never will be—without a large Arab population. There is still much debate over the origins of the Palestinian refugee problem and the causes that led Arabs to flee the emerging Jewish state. Whatever the reasons, undoubtedly many Jews believed that their problems in creating a new state would be simpler if they did *not* have a large Arab minority. But the creation of Israel as a 90% Jewish state also created a Palestinian diaspora. The Jews are now matched in their dispersion by resident

Palestinian groups in many countries, one of the developments that makes the struggle between two peoples in the Middle East a world-wide one.

Aside from the fact that each nation's ethnic purification leads to another's greater diversity, one senses that the effort at purity, for most states, is a lost cause. The divisions in Uganda between blacks of different tribes are potentially far more severe for that state than the division between all Blacks and Asians. Few black African nations are ethnically homogeneous. The attempt to create some degree of homogeneity by the expulsion of Asians seems as futile as an effort to empty the sea.

> . . . Resident aliens have been expelled from a number of African states. In November 1969, the Ghanaian government gave all resident aliens, African and non-African, two weeks to obtain residence and work permits or leave the country. The police were given broad powers to search out and arrest aliens lacking the required papers, and bands of citizens attacked alien traders in public markets. Although a few aliens died in the Ghanaian expulsion, conditions for Nigerian traders expelled from Congo-Zaire were even worse. Those who were released after a year in detention reported numerous incidents of torture and death plus confiscation of all assets. Public pressure in the Ivory Coast led to expulsion of Togolese and Dahomeyans employed in the Ivory Coast civil service since colonial days. . . .[5]

I have said enough, I hope, to give some plausibility to my first proposition. In the world as it is developing, despite tendencies to make some states "ethnically pure" (particularly in the newer states of Africa and Asia), more and more states become *multi-ethnic.* This is, in part, because of the universal commitment against boundary changes to make Ethnic Group coincide with State. (How many inter-state boundaries have, after all, been changed in the past 29 years? Fewer I would guess than in any period in history.) It is also because of the extensive international migration of labour (a migration that is almost the equal in scale of that which transformed the United States!), and because old ethnic divisions emerge in old states and new ones are created in new states.

And now to my second proposition on the relations between Ethnicity and Social Class. This, too, has developed in unexpected ways. My proposition here is that the Socialist hope for a trans-national class struggle, based on class identification, never came to pass. Instead, it has been replaced by national and ethnic conflicts to which combatants have often tried to give a "class character." The first great defeat of the Socialist hope was in World War I, when the large Socialist parties of Germany and France became patriotic, and fought on the side of their respective bourgeois governments against their national enemies (instead of, of course, together with their "class comrades" of other nations against their respective bourgeoisies). The second great defeat came with the rise of the Third International under Soviet Russian domination. Despite the heightened rhetoric of class warfare that characterised the Third International's Communist parties, it became increasingly evident that they were serving the national interests of Russia. After World War II, Communism was more and more closely integrated into a number of national movements. Chinese, Yugoslav, and Cuban Communism were clearly as "Chinese" and "Yugoslav" and "Cuban" as they were Communist. The language of international class warfare still persists. The reality however is quite different, for it masks the state interests of Russia, China, and the minor Communist powers. The antagonism of the classes and the opposition of their interests are severe in many countries (particularly the non-Communist countries of the developing world), but in most countries national interests and ethnic interests seem to dominate over class interests. India, despite its severe internal class conflicts of interest, is never so united as when it is fighting China—or Pakistan. We have witnessed some classic class warfare in recent decades, in particular in China and Cuba and in some other developing-world countries. But we have rather more frequently seen severe ethnic conflict and even bloody ethnic warfare.

Marxists try to interpret all conflict as "class conflict." Indeed in the ethnic conflicts of the post-War world there is always a class component. One group is more prosperous, owns more of the means of production, or is a more effective competitor in economic activities, than another. Economic interest undoubtedly plays a role in ethnic conflict. But this is far from saying ethnic conflict is simply "masked" class conflict. What, in the conflicts of Catholic and Protestant in Northern Ireland, of Hausa and Yoruba *versus* Ibo in Nigeria, Hutu *versus* Tutsi in Rwanda, Chinese *versus* Malay in Malaysia, Anglophone *versus* Francophone in Canada (and so on), is the "terminal community . . . that . . . effectively commands men's loyalty"? I would say it is increasingly the *ethnically*-defined community rather than any exclusively *interest*-defined group. The evidence for this is too strong to be dismissed.

In the light of these two propositions—that Ethnicity becomes less and less coincident with state boundaries, and that Ethnicity becomes a stronger basis for "terminal loyalty" than class—we can proceed to draw some consequences of importance for international relations.

Let me first recall—and put to one side—the more traditional and better-known relations between ethnicity and international relations. These relations can be described as the effort to make Ethnicity coincide with State borders. It has taken the form of *"irredentism"*—where one group, subjects of a state dominated by a different group, tries to rejoin the major part of the ethnic group in another state. Its other form is national independence movements, where an entire group is subject to a state dominated by another.

Obviously this is a real problem and still continues. But this, I would suggest, is perhaps steadily less important in the relations between Ethnicity and international conflict—because of the previously-mentioned fact that State borders have become oddly immutable. After World War II, many states became independent; some states had revolutions; some partition lines between states established after the war became international boundaries; and some states were partitioned. But even the newly-partitioned states (Viet Nam, Israel, Kashmir) in which new boundaries had to be established, have found it difficult to get those boundaries to take on the same immutability as the boundaries created by post-1918 and post-1945 settlements. Multi-ethnicity used to appear as irredentism. We can still find some classic irredentism—for example, the case of the Somalis in Ethiopia. But, increasingly, what we would once have called "irredentism" must be called simply *multi-ethnicity*. There is no easy way to make Ethnic boundaries and State boundaries coincide. Ethnic groups, owing to migrations and economic interrelationships, are less and less definable by physical boundaries.

It is these new tendencies towards *multi-ethnicity* (combined with other social developments) that, in my view, create new problematical relations between Ethnicity and the inter-State system.

One of the most important of these developments is the creation of an international system of communications. It makes the spread of ideas and ideologies from one state to another, from one troubled situation to another, ever more rapid and effective. "Ethnicity", as a part of culture, always had to be taught. But it used to be taught by parents to children, by teachers to students, by leaders to followers—*i.e.*, in traditional settings. More and more, Ethnicity and its possible implications are taught by the mass media. One group learns from another, and picks up its language, its demands, its resentments, its forms of organisation. It has become commonplace to say that the Blacks have taught through their example other ethnic groups in the United States to raise certain demands, to use a certain language, to feel resentment at exploitation and subordination in contexts which they had previously accepted. This is obviously true. What is striking to me is how much the movement of Black militancy has affected other groups in *other* countries.

In the West Indies, we have seen the emergence of "Black Power" movements—a rather unlikely term, since these movements are directed against black ruling classes as well as white economic interests in largely black societies (but the power of the American term, spread by the mass media, was evidently irresistible). In Canada, the French Canadians had their own reasons for resentment at the dominant position of the English-speaking Canadians; but one of the best known books about their situation calls them *"white niggers"!* Similarly, Northern Ireland had its own deep conflict, and it has an even longer history than that of Blacks and Whites in America. But the Catholic movement was first called the *"Civil Rights"* movement, in clear imitation of the Black "Civil Rights" struggle in the United States, even if it is arguable how much it owed to the inspiration of this struggle. The "Oriental" Jews in Israel (of lesser education, income, and power than the "Western" Jews) had their own grievances. But the actions that led to world-wide attention were initiated by "Black Panthers," again the borrowing of a term from the American struggle.[6] And, similarly, the developing colour conflict in England has been influenced, on the part of the coloured groups, by developments in the United States, and on the part of the government, by the actions taken in the United States.[7]

These examples of the international communication of ideas, slogans, demands, with one ethnic group and one ethnic struggle influencing another, also reflect of course the dominant position of the United States in the international configuration of communications. But the communication is not, I believe, all one way. One example of an ethnic struggle that has had some effect on other inter-group relations is the Israeli-Arab struggle. As I have pointed out, both groups have international diasporas. The image of the Palestinian Freedom Fighter has been as heavily imprinted on world public opinion as the images of a Martin Luther King or Angela Davis. The two diasporas internationalise the struggle. The Palestinians find their targets in many countries.

But the internationalisation also means that it is copied, and that it influences other ethnic conflicts. The Black militants in the United States and the Croatian nationalists in Sweden both borrowed the technique of "skyjacking" from the Palestinians. The Israeli-Arab struggle leads to a tension between radical groups and Jews in the United States, in France, in Germany, because the Far Left identifies with the Palestinians. The Jews of Poland, completely assimilated, are accused of "Zionism" in the wake of 1967 (and in their emigration add to the small Jewish community of Denmark). In Africa, Black states were once divided between support of Israel or of the Arabs. They were variously affected by the historical memories left by Arab conquerors, missionaries, and slave traders; by white European colonialists; by their current ideologies; and by the cash or credits one or the other party could give them. There are even reverberations of the far-away struggle in the local internal politics of African countries. President Amin of Uganda has accused the Israelis of trying to overthrow him, while Uganda's former President, Milton Obote, accuses Amin of using Palestinian liberation forces in carrying out genocide against his opponents. ("Dr Obote names both Libya and the Palestinian liberation organisations as among those assisting in killings in Uganda. . . ." "EX-UGANDAN HEAD CHARGES GENOCIDE," *New York Times*, 27 May 1973.)

The new patterns of communication are, I believe, one of the most potent forces in insuring that ethnic concerns and ethnic issues will remain serious forces and will indeed grow in seriousness. The increasing ease of air travel—combined with the existence of wide economic disparities between nations and the increasingly liberal attitude toward immigration of European states and other states with populations of European origin—guarantees that every Ethnic group can develop a Diaspora. It thus makes its problems of significance to more than one state and its neighbours. The ease of air travel also means that ethnic struggles can be fought out on a world-wide stage, involving nations that are on the surface completely removed from the struggle. The Israeli-Arab struggle has, perhaps, had the widest geographical scope. Letter-bombs explode in England, India, and Malaysia; Cypriots, Greeks, Turks, Israeli diplomats are seized in Thailand; Israeli athletes killed in Munich; Arabs are shot in the streets of Paris and Rome. The Indian-Pakistani struggle also has its international scope, as young Pakistanis are killed in the attempted seizure of Indian offices in London. Croatians, now settled in Sweden and Australia, carry on their warfare against Yugoslavia. This has led to a protest from the Australian Prime Minister to Yugoslavia because "Croatians of Australian citizenship" were executed in Yugoslavia. Within Australia, the conservative opposition has protested against government investigations of the Croatian nationalists.[8]

Thus a number of factors, it seems to me, are leading to the internationalisation of ethnic conflicts, to a "universalisation of ethnicity."

1. There is, first, the increasing difficulty, if not impossibility, of making Ethnicity and State coincide. The United States, as a nation formed of many peoples without territorial concentration in any part of the country, first demonstrated this impossibility. It had to become a multi-ethnic society. Now England, France, Germany, the nations of old Europe, the developing nations of new Africa, the ancient nations of Asia are all forced more and more to come to terms with an ethnically mixed population, whose mixture (as long as the world remains open or free to travel and settlement) must grow.

2. A second element in the growing internationalisation of Ethnicity is the rapid growth of international communications. This has made the creation of Ethnic Diasporas easier. It has created multi-ethnic societies in homogeneous ones. It has also meant that the images of identity and struggle are now spread everywhere, with significant effects in heightening ethnic consciousness and strengthening it in its conflict with other claims on terminal loyalty.

3. About a third factor leading to the internationalisation of ethnic conflict I am less certain. But I think I can at least propose as an hypothesis that we are, increasingly, refusing to accept as moral—and by "we" I mean what may be vaguely called an international community of public opinion—the exploitation or persecution of an ethnic minority by a state. We increasingly refuse to accept this as an "internal" matter. The international relations of South Africa, Rhodesia, and Portugal are decisively affected by their racial policies. Soviet Russia has been insistent that all conflicts affecting its ethnic groups are purely internal matters—but the Russian Jews have successfully challenged this position by making their demands for emigration a matter between states (in this case, the United States and Russia). The treatment of American Negroes certainly affects America's international image—the cases of Angela Davis and other Black militants

received (if possible) more attention in Western Europe than in the
U.S.A. The Developing World has tried to argue that its ethnic conflicts
should be left to itself, and that the outside world should not intervene.
Even that may be breaking down. It was impossible to keep the situation of Bengalis in Pakistan an "internal" matter (even though many
people argued that for the "peace of the world" it should be so
considered). No ethnic issue can remain simply an intra-state issue, in
part because of the growing number of diasporas, but also perhaps because of the developing world conscience which tries to reconcile state
claims with ethnic claims which are more and more felt to be legitimate.
Nigeria was, perhaps, most successful in "internalising" the civil war
against the Ibos; and the outside world has stood aside, too, from the
sanguinary conflict between Hutu and Tutsi in Rwanda. But even in
that distant and obscure struggle we have seen the United States criti-
cised (*New York Times*, 11 June 1973, "U.S. HELD REMISS IN
BURUNDI CRISIS") for not playing a larger role. Thus it is not only
international diasporas but also a globalised conscience which serve to
universalise ethnic conflict.

What I have discussed up to now—migrations, international communications, world conscience—all leave aside the initial question:
Why have ethnic identities and demands become so significant in the
first place in so many different countries, with such varied historical
backgrounds and economic and political institutions? Can we find any
general developments that have accentuated the role of the Ethnic, and
in general made it more salient?
     This is an enormously difficult problem, and various theories or
fragments of theories have been propounded. Perhaps the most ambitious general theory argues as follows. In the modern world there is a
loss of traditional and primordial identities because of the trends of
modernisation. This means: urbanisation, new occupations, mass
education transmitting general and abstract information, mass media
presenting a general and universal culture. Now all this *should* make
original ethnic identities—tribal, linguistic, regional, and the like, all
the "primordial" identities—weaker. However (as this argument runs)
in mass society there is the need in the individual for some kind of
identity—smaller than the State, larger than the family, something akin
to a "familistic allegiance." Accordingly, on the basis of the remaining
fragments of the primordial identities, new ethnic identities are
constructed. Thus, the varied tribal groups in the cities of Africa form
ethnic associations and merge into larger groups—which seems to be
the origin of the large tribes (*e.g.*, Hausa, Ibo, Yoruba). The process is
similar to that which affected the transatlantic European migrants
from East European and Southern European villages—in the U.S.A.
they developed a special Polish, Italian, Slovak, identity. The trends of
modernisation, even while they do destroy some bases of distinctive
culture and distinctive identity, create a need for a *new kind of identity*
related to the old, intimate type of village or tribal association. Thus

does the new ethnic group, as a political and social possibility, come to life.

This is one of those large social theories that seems impossible to test, to validate, or to refute. It makes sense. The world-wide scope of "ethnicisation" is matched by developments that are considered causative and are themselves of a world-wide scope. There are some other general theories that might be mentioned. Egalitarianism is the dominant social philosophy in the world, and it comes in all forms.

Egalitarianism legitimates a group's demands that its deficiencies (in income occupation, political power) be made good, and *now*. It justifies the expulsion and liquidation of trading and merchant peoples (such as Asians in Uganda). Why, however, does not the egalitarian thrust emphasise *occupational* and *class* identies more? Why does it not lead to more class conflict, and less ethnic conflict?

This is the heart of the darkness. Why *didn't* the major lines of conflict within societies become class conflicts rather than ethnic conflicts? It is of paradoxical interest to note that in the developing world the dominant ideology among students is Marxism. Yet the dominant political forces have been, first the drive for Independence, then the defence against and attack on Neo-Colonialism, then conflicts with neighbours, along with efforts to create a "national identity" at home. In most developing countries Marxism remains the ideology of the students and often of the ruling group—but *ethnicity* is the focus around which identity and loyalty have been shaped. Sometimes the two themes of class conflict and ethnic conflict are merged (as in the Chinese theory of the "Third World" as a rural world exploited by the urban developed world). It would seem that to make class conflict at all effective it must now be joined to ethnic conflict—as in the case of the revolutionary Cubans who, in liquidating their own middle class, insisted they were also fighting the North Americans (imperialistic, racist, and arrogant).

Admittedly the powerful thrust to egalitarianism *can* be attached to class conflict as well as ethnic conflict. Ethnic conflict, however, seems to have become more effective in reaching and drawing upon the more emotional layers of the human and social personality than class conflict. Class conflict is rational—it is based on the defence and expansion of interest. Ethnic conflict is rational in this sense, too—but it fuses with the rationality of class conflict a less rational, an irrational appeal, that seems to connect better with powerful emotions.

Is this because it brings to mind such primal things as the shapes of one's body, one's image and colour, one's language and religion, the earliest experiences in the home and in the family?

It would seem that the rallying cries that mobilise the classes have, in recent decades, had less power than the rallying cries that mobilise the races, tribes, religions, language-users—in short, the Ethnic Groups. Perhaps the epidemic of ethnic conflicts reflects the fact that leaders and organisers believe they can get a more potent response by appealing to *ethnicity* than they can by appealing to Class Interest. In the best of cases, the appeal is a double one, since almost every ethnic group is disadvantaged in relationship to some other; and so, by appealing to class interest and ethnic interest together, the White European (and his descendants wherever they may be) can everywhere be marked as the Enemy.

If Ethnicity is a permanent part of the modern world, and the multi-ethnic form is increasingly common within each nation (owing to the factors I have been describing), then we see the need in each country, for new approaches to the handling of multi-ethnic conflict. In the historic past, powerful and forceful assimilation was a dominant approach, combined with permanent subordination of certain groups called "inferior". Neither approach will survive long in the contemporary world. The spirit of egalitarianism assures us that each individual and each group will make its claims to just and equal treatment and will find strong support for its claims. Perhaps the answer to multi-ethnicity in each country will be a situation in which each group has guaranteed rights and guaranteed shares in the economy, the polity, in social life. It is possible to emphasise different parts of this solution: either guaranteed shares for each group, or guaranteed rights for each individual and each group. The United States in the past seemed to find the approach in terms of "guaranteed rights" more congenial than the approach in terms of guaranteed shares; but recently Americans have begun to take individual rights less seriously, and to take group shares more seriously. I think the American experience will prove to be only one of the possible ways in which a modern state deals with the problems of multi-ethnicity. Our experience—since we are the most diverse and complex of multi-ethnic societies—may serve as "a model" for some, may at least serve as a storehouse of trial-and-error experience for others who come to view what we have done and consider whether they should go and do likewise.

Yet aside from conflicts *within* nations, the world-wide spread of ethnicity as a significant basis for political action raises serious questions about the relations *between* nations. In a world in which the arrant nonsense of Marxism competed with the tepid confusions of liberalism, the problems of Ethnicity, as a source of conflict within nations and between nations, have generally appeared as simply a left-over, an embarrassment from the past. It is my conviction they must now be placed at the very centre of our concern for the human condition.

NOTES

[1]They have been described in the fascinating book by George DeVos and Hiroshi Wagatsuma, *Japan's Invisible Race*, a work that argues that one can find some remnants of caste in most East Asian countries.

[2]Rupert Emerson, *From Empire to Nation* (1960), pp. 95–6.

[3]Clifford Geertz, *Old Societies and New States* (1963), p. 108.

[4]See, in ENCOUNTER, Theo Sommer, "Der Gastarbeiter" (November 1973) and Jonathan Power, "The New Proletariat" (September 1974).

⁵Frances R. Hill, "Genesis of a New Exodus," *Harvard Political Review* (Spring 1973), p. 9.

⁶See, in ENCOUNTER, Amnon Rubinstein, "Jewish Panthers and Other Problems" (June 1972).

⁷See E. J. B. Rose et al., *Colour and Citizenship* (1969), and Anthony Lester and Geoffrey Bindman, *Race and Law in Great Britain* (1972).

⁸"AUSTRALIA PLANS CROATION INQUIRY", *New York Times,* 29 May 1973.

4 Ambush at Kamikaze Pass

Tom Engelhardt

"Westerns" may have been America's most versatile art form. For several generations of Americans, Westerns provided history lessons, entertainment and a general guide to the world. They created or re-created a flood of American heroes, filled popcorned weekends and overwhelmed untold imaginations. It's as difficult today to imagine movies without them as to think of a luncheonette without Coca-Cola. In their folksy way, they intruded on our minds. Unobtrusively they lent us a hand in grinding a lens through which we could view the whole of the non-white world. Their images were powerful; their structure was satisfying; and at their heart lay one archetypal scene which went something like this:

> White canvas-covered wagons roll forward in a column. White men, on their horses, ride easily up and down the lines of wagons. Their arms hang loosely near their guns. The walls of the buttes rise high on either side. Cakey streaks of yellow, rusty red, dried brown enclose the sun's heat boiling up on all sides. The dust settles on their nostrils, they gag and look apprehensively toward the heights, hostile and distant. Who's there? Sullenly, they ride on.
>
> Beyond the buttes, the wagon train moves centrally into the flatlands, like a spear pointed at the sunset. The wagons circle. Fires are built; guards set. From within this warm and secure circle, at the center of the plains, the white-men (-cameras) stare out. There, in the enveloping darkness, on the peripheries of human existence, at dawn or dusk, hooting and screeching, from nowhere, like maggots, swarming, naked, painted, burning and killing, for no reason, like animals, they would come. The men touch their gun handles and circle the wagons. From this strategically central position, with good cover, and better machines, today or tomorrow, or the morning after, they will simply mow them down. Wipe them out. Nothing human is involved. It's a matter of self-defense, no more. Extermination can be the only answer.

There are countless variations on this scene. Often the encircled wagon train is replaced by the surrounded fort; yet only the shape of the object has changed. The fort, like the wagon train, is the focus of the film. Its residents are made known to us. Familiarly, we take in the hate/respect struggle between the civilian scout and the garrison commander; the love relations between the commander's daughter and the young first lieutenant who-has-yet-to-prove-himself; the comic routines of the general soldiery. From this central point in our consciousness, they sally forth to victory against unknown besiegers with inexplicable customs, irrational desires, and an incomprehensible language (a mixture of pig-latin and pidgin Hollywood).

What does this sort of paradigm do to us? Mostly, it forces us to flip history on its head. It makes the intruder exchange places in our eyes with the intruded upon. (Who ever heard of a movie in which the Indians wake up one morning to find that, at the periphery of their existences, in their own country, there are new and aggressive beings ready to make war on them, incomprehensible, unwilling to share, out of murder and kill, etc.) It is the Indians, in these films, who must invade, intrude, break in upon the circle—a circle which contains all those whom the film has already certified as "human." No wonder the viewer identifies with those in the circle, not with the Indians left to patrol enigmatically the bluffs overlooking humanity. In essence, the viewer is forced behind the barrel of a repeating rifle and it is from that position, through its gun sights, that he receives a picture history of Western colonialism and imperialism. Little wonder that he feels no sympathy for the enemy as they fall before his withering fire—within this cinematic structure, the opportunity for such sympathy simply ceases to exist.

Such an approach not only transforms invasion into an act of self-defense; it also prepares its audiences for the acceptance of genocide. The theory is simple enough: We may not always be right (there are stupid commanders, etc.), but we are human. By any standards (offered in the film), "they" are not. What, then, are they? They are animate, thus they are, if not human, in some sense animals. And, for animals facing a human onslaught, the options are limited. Certain of the least menacing among them can be retained as pets. As a hunter trains his dog, these can be trained to be scouts, tracking down those of their kind who try to escape or resist, to be porters. to be servants. Those not needed as pets (who are nonetheless domesticable) can be maintained on preserves. The rest, fit neither for house training nor for cages, must be wiped out.[1]

From the acceptance of such a framework flows the ability to accept as pleasurable, a relief, satisfying, the mass slaughter of the "non-human"—the killing, mowing down of the non-white, hundreds to a film and normally in the scene which barely precedes the positive resolution of the relationships among the whites. Anyone who thinks the body count is a creation of the recent Indochinese war should look at the movies he saw as a kid. It was the implicit rule of those films that no less than ten Indian (Japanese, Chinese. . . .) warriors should fall for each white, expendable secondary character.[2]

Just as the style and substance of the Indian wars was a prototype for many later American intrusions into the third world (particularly the campaigns in the Philippines and Indochina), so movies about those wars provided the prototype from which nearly every American movie about the third world derived. That these third world movies are pale reflections of the framework, outlook, and even conventions of the cowboy movie is easy enough to demonstrate. Just a few examples, chosen almost at random from the thirty or forty films I've caught on T.V. in the last few months. Pick your country: the Mexico of toothy Pancho Villan bandits, the North Africa of encircled Foreign Legionaires, the India of embattled British Lancers, or even South Africa. One would think treatment of South Africa might be rather special, have its own unique features. But Lo! We look up and already the Boers are trekking away, in (strange to say) wagons, and, yep, there's, no . . . let's see . . . Susan Hayward. Suddenly, from nowhere, the Zulus appear, hooting and howling, to surround the third-rate wagons of this third-rate movie. And here's that unique touch we've all been waiting for. It seems to be the singular quality of the Zulus that they have no horses and so must circle the wagon train on foot, yelling at the tops of their voices and brandishing their spears . . . but wait . . . from the distance . . . it's the Transvaal cavalry to the rescue. As they swoop down, one of the Boers leaps on a wagon seat, waving his hat with joy, and calls to his friend in the cavalry, "You've got 'em running, Paul. Keep 'em running, Paul! Run 'em off the end of the earth!" (*Untamed,* 1955)

Or switch to the Pacific. In any one of a hundred World War II flicks, we see a subtle variation on the same encirclement imagery. From the deck of our flagship, amidst the fleet corraled off the Okinawa coast, we look through our binoculars. The horizon is empty; yet already the radar has picked them up. Somewhere beyond human sight, unidentified flying objects. The sirens are howling, the men pouring out of their bunks and helter-skelter into battle gear. At their guns, they look grimly towards the empty sky: the young ensign too eager for his first command, the swabby who got a date with that pretty Wave, the medic whose wife just sent him a "Dear John" letter (he's slated to die heroically). A speck on the horizon, faces tense, jokes fall away, it's the Kamikaze! Half-man, half-machine, an incomprehensible human torpedo bearing down from the peripheries of fanatical animate existence to pierce the armored defenses of the forces of Western democracy. The results? Serious damage to several ships, close calls on more, several secondary characters dead, and an incredible number of Japanese planes obliterated from the sky.[3]

That there is no feeling of loss at the obliteration of human torpedoes is hardly surprising. Even in those brief moments when you "meet" the enemy, movies like this make it immaculately clear that he is not only strange, barbarous, hostile and dangerous, but has little regard for his own life. Throwing himself on the Gatling guns of the British with only spear in hand, or on the ack-ack guns of the Americans with only bomb in portal, he is not acting out of any human emotion. It is not a desire to defend his home, his friends, or his freedom. It has no rational (i.e. "human") explanation. It is not even "bravery" as we in the West know it (though similar acts by whites are portrayed heroically). Rather, it is something innate, fanatical, perverse—an inexplicable desire for death, disorder and destruction.

When the enemy speaks a little English, he often explains this himself. Take, for instance, the captured Japanese officer in *Halls of Montezuma* (1950). The plot is already far advanced. On an island in the Pacific, hours before the big attack, Marines are pinned down by Japanese mortars whose position they cannot locate. Yet if they do not locate them, the attack will fail. The Japanese officer obstinately refuses to help them. Richard Widmark pleads with him, appealing to his life force. "You have a future—to rebuild Japan—to live for . . ." But the officer replies: "Captain, you seem to have forgotten, my people for centuries have thought not of living well but dying well. Have you not studied our Judo, our science . . . We always take the obvious and reverse it. Death is the basis of our strength." Suddenly a mortar shell explodes above the bunker. Everybody ducks. Rafters fall; dust billows; slowly the air clears; a shocked voice yells out: "My God, the Jap's committed Hari Kari!" Fortunately the idiot gave it all away. He reminded the Americans of the quirks in the non-white mind. As any schoolboy should have known, Orientals think backwards. The Japs put their rockets on the front slope of the mountain, not the protected rear slopes as an American would have done. The attack, to the tune of the Marine Hymn, moves forward, preparing to wipe the Japs off the face of the island.

If, in print, such simple idiocy makes you laugh, it probably didn't when you saw the film; nor is it in any way atypical of four decades of action films about Asia. The overwhelmingly present theme of the non-human-ness of the non-white prepares us to accept, without flinching, the extermination of our "enemies" (as John Wayne commented in *The Searchers,* 1956, there's "humans" and then there's "Comanches") and just as surely it helped prepare the ideological way for the leveling and near-obliteration of three Asian areas in the course of three decades.

It is useful, in this light, to compare the cinematic treatment of the European front in World Wars I and II with that of the Pacific front. From *The Big Parade* (a silent film) on, a common and often moving convention of movies about the wars against Germany went something like this: The allied soldier finds himself caught in a foxhole (trench, farmhouse, etc.) with a wounded German soldier. He is about to shoot when the young, begrimed soldier holds up his hand in what is now the peace symbol, but at the time meant "Do you have a cigarette?" Though speaking different languages, they exchange family pictures and common memories.[4]

The scene is meant to attest to man's sense of humanity and brotherhood over and above war and national hatred. Until very recently, such a scene simply did not appear in movies about the Japanese front. Between the American and his non-white enemy, a bond transcending enmity was hardly even considered. Instead, an analogous scene went something like this: A group of Japanese, shot down in a withering crossfire, lie on the ground either dead or severely wounded. The American soldiers approach, less from humanitarian motives than because they hope to get prisoners and information.[5] One of the Japanese, however, is just playing possum. As the American reaches down to give him water (first aid, a helping hand), he suddenly pulls out a hand grenade (pistol, knife) and, with the look of a fanatic, tries to blow them *all* to smithereens. He is quickly dispatched. (See, for instance, *In Love and War,* 1956.)

The theme of alien intruders descending on embattled humans and being obliterated from an earth they clearly are not entitled to is most straightforwardly put in Science Fiction movies; for monsters turn out to be little more than the metaphysical wing of the third world. These movies represent historical events which have taken place only in the Western imagination. Thus, the themes of the cowboy (-third world) movie come through in a more primeval way. An overlay of fear replaces the suspense. Metaphorically, the world is the wagon train; the universe, the horizon. (Or, alternately, the earth space-ship is the wagon train; an alien planet, the horizon.) From that horizon, somewhere at the peripheries of human existence, from the Arctic icecap (*The Thing,* 1951), the desert (*Them,* 1954), the distant past (*The Beast from 20,000 Fathoms,* 1954), the sky (*War of the Worlds,* 1953), at dawn or dusk, hooting and beeping come the invaders. Enveloping whole armies, they smash through human defenses, forcing the white representatives of the human race to fall back on their inner defense line (perhaps New York or Los Angeles). Imperiling the very heartland of civilized life, they provide only one option—destroy THEM before THEM can destroy us.

In this sort of a movie, the technical problems involved in presenting the extinction of a race for the enjoyment of an audience are simplifed.[6] Who would even think about saving the Pod People? (*Invasion of the Body Snatchers,* 1956) Ordinarily the question of alternatives to elimination barely comes to mind. If it does, as in that prototype "modern" Sci-Fi film *The Thing* (James Arness of Matt Dillon fame played the monster), usually the man who wants to save Them, "talk to Them," is the bad mad scientist as opposed to the good, absent-minded scientist (who probably has the pretty daughter being wooed by the cub reporter).[7]

Unfortunately for American movie-makers, Asians and others could not simply be photographed with three heads, tentacles, and gelatinaceous bodies. Consequently, other conventions had to be developed (or appropriated) that would clearly differentiate them from "humanity" at large. The first of these was invisibility. In most movies about the third world, the non-whites provide nothing more than a backdrop for all-white drama—an element of exotic and unifying dread against which to play out the tensions and problems of the white world. Sometimes, even the locales seem none-too-distinguishable, not to speak of their black, brown, or yellow inhabitants. It is not surprising, for instance, that the Gable-Harlow movie *Red Dust* (1932), set on an Indochinese rubber plantation (Gable is the foreman), could be transported to Africa without loss two decades later as the Gable-Kelly *Mogambo*. It could as well have been set in Brazil on a coffee plantation, or in Nevada with Gable a rancher.

As George Orwell commented of North Africa in 1939,

> All people who work with their hands are partly invisible, and the more important work they do, the less visible they are. Still, a white skin is always fairly conspicuous. In northern Europe, when you see a labourer plough-ing a field, you probably give him a second glance. In a hot country, anywhere south of Gibraltar or east of Suez, the chances are that you don't even see him. I have noticed this again and again. In a tropical landscape one's eye takes in everything except the human beings. It takes in the dried-up soil, the prickly pear, the palm tree and the distant mountain, but it always misses the peasant hoeing at his patch. He is the same colour as the earth, and a great deal less interesting to look at. It is only because of this that the starved countries of Asia and Africa are accepted as tourist resorts.[8]

Theoretically, it should have been somewhat more difficult since the Chinese and Vietnamese revolutions and other uprisings of the op-pressed and non-white around the world, to ignore the people for the scenery. Yet we can't fault Hollywood for its valiant attempt. Generally, American films have hewed with unsurpassed tenacity to this frame-work—reproducing the white world whole in the Orient, with Asians skittering at the edges of sets as servants or scenic menace (as in the recent horrific extravaganza, *Krakatoa, East* [sic] *of Java,* 1969, where a volcano takes over the Lassie role and the Asian female pearl divers go under in the final explosions). This is even more true in films on Africa, where for generations whites have fought off natives and lions, not necessarily in that order.

A second convention of these films concerns the pecking order of white and non-white societies when they come into conflict. It is a "united front" among whites. Often the whites portrayed are the highly romanticized third-rate flotsam and jetsam of a mythologized Amer-ican society—adventurers, prostitutes, opportunists, thieves (just as the films themselves, particularly when about Asia, tend to represent the brackish backwater of the American film industry). Yet no matter how low, no matter what their internal squabbles, no matter what their hostilities toward each other, in relation to the third world the whites stand as one: Missionary's daughter and drunken ferryboat captain ("I hate the Reds," he says to her, "because they closed a lot of Chinese ports where they have dames. Chinese, Eurasian, and White Russian. . . . Somebody pinned the bleeding heart of China on your sleeve but they never got around to me." / *Blood Alley,* 1955); soldier of fortune and adventurer-journalist, natural enemies over The-Woman-They-Both-Love (They escape Canton together, avoiding the clutches of the Reds in a stolen boat / *Soldier of Fortune,* 1955); sheriff, deputies and captured outlaws (They are surrounded by Mexican bandits / *Bandalero,* 1968); or on a national level, the British, Americans and Russians (They must deal with "the chief enemy of the Western World," Mao Tse-tung / *The Chairman,* 1970). The theme is, of course, simply a variation on a more home-grown variety—the Confederates and Yankees who bury their sectional hatreds to unite against the Indians; the convicts on their way to prison who help the wagon train fight off the Sioux, bringing the women and children to safety, etc. (See, for example, *Ambush at Cimarron Pass,* 1958, which combines everything in one laughable mess—a Yankee patrol and its prisoner team up with a Confederate rancher to fight off an Apache attack.)

The audience is expected to carry two racial lessons away from this sort of thing. The first is that the presence of the incomprehensible and non-human brings out what is "human" in every man. Individual dignity, equality, fraternity, all that on which the West theoretically places premium value, are brought sharply into focus at the expense of "alien" beings. The second is the implicit statement that, in a pinch, any white is a step up from the rest of the world. They may be murderers, rapists, and mother-snatchers, but they're ours.

When the inhabitants of these countries emerge from the ferns or mottled huts, and try to climb to the edges of the spotlight, they find the possibilities limited indeed. In this cinematic pick-up-sides, the whites already have two hands on the bat handle before the contest begins. The set hierarchy of roles is structured something like this: All roles of positive authority are reserved for white characters. Among the whites, the men stand triumphantly at the top; their women cringe, sigh and faint below; and the Asians are left to scramble for what's left, like beggars at a refuse heap.

There is only one category in which a non-white is likely to come out top dog—villain. With their stock of fanatical speeches and their propensity for odd tortures, third world villains provided the American film-maker with a handy receptacle for his audience's inchoate fears of the unknown and inhuman. Only as the repository for Evil could the non-white "triumph" in films. However, this is no small thing; for wherever there is a third world country, American scriptwriters have created villain slots to be filled by otherwise unemployable actors (though often these roles are monopolized by whites in yellow-face). From area to area, like spirits, their forms change: the Mexican bandit chief with his toothy smile, hearty false laugh, sombrero and bushy eyebrows (see, f.i., the excellent *Treasure of the Sierra Madre* 1948, or the awful *Bandalero*); the Oriental warlord with his droopy mustache and shaven head (see *The Left Hand of God,* 1955, *The General Died at Dawn,* 1936, *Shanghai Express,* 1932, *Seven Women,* 1965, etc. ad nauseam); the Indian "Khan" or prince with his little goatee and urbane manner (*Khyber Pass,* 1954, *Charge of the Light Brigade,* 1936). Yet their essence remains the same.

Set against their shiny pates or silken voices, their hard eyes and twitching mouths, no white could look anything but good. In *Left Hand of God,* Humphrey Bogart, the pilot-turned-opportunist-warlord-advisor-turned-fraudulent-priest becomes a literal saint under the leer of Lee J. Cobb's General Yang. Gregory Peck, an "uninvolved" scientist-CIA spy, becomes a boy wonder and living representative of humanity when faced with a ping-pong playing Mao Tse-tung in *The*

Chairman. How can you lose when the guy you want to double-deal represents a nation which has discovered an enzyme allowing pineapples to grow in Tibet and winter wheat in Mongolia, yet (as one of the Russian agents puts it) is holding it so that the rest of the "underdeveloped" world, "90% poor, 90% peasant . . . will crawl on their hands and knees to Peking to get it." All in all, these non-white representatives of evil provide a backboard off which white Western values can bounce in, registering one more cinematic Score for Civilization.

The other group of roles open to non-whites are roles of helplessness and dependence. At the dingy bottom of the scale of dependence crouch children. Non-white children have traditionally been a favorite for screenwriters and directors. Ingrid Bergman helped them across the mountains to safety (*The Inn of the Sixth Happiness,* 1958); Deborah Kerr taught them geography (*The King and I,* 1956); Humphrey Bogart helped them to memorize "My Old Kentucky Home" (*Left Hand of God*); Carrol Baker went with them on a great trek back to their homelands (*Cheyenne Autumn,* 1964); Richard Widmark took one (a little half-breed orphan girl—sort of the black, one-eyed Jew of the tiny tot's universe) back to the States with him (*55 Days at Peking*). And so on.

Essentially, non-white children fulfill the same function and have the same effect as non-white villains. They reflect to the white audience just another facet of their own humanity. Of course, if you ignore W. C. Fields, children have had a traditionally cloying place in American films; but in the third world movie they provide a particularly strong dose of knee-jerk sentiment, allowing their white leads to show the other side of Western civilization. It is their duty not just to exterminate the world's evil forces, but to give to those less capable (and more needy) than themselves. And who more closely fits such a description than the native child who may someday grow up to emulate us.

While it is children who demonstrate the natural impulses of the white authorities towards those who do not resist them, but are helpless before them or dependent upon them, it is women who prove the point. Even within the cinematic reflection of the white world, women have seldom held exalted positions. Normally they are daughters of missionaries, sweethearts of adventurers, daughters, nurses, daughters of missionaries, wives on safari, schoolmarms, daughters of missionaries, or prostitutes. (The exceptions usually being when women come under a "united front" ruling—that is, they confront Asian men, not white men. Then, as with Anna in *The King and I,* while their occupations may not change they face society on a somewhat different footing.) Several rungs down the social ladder, non-white women are left mainly with roles as bargirls, geishas, belly dancers, nurse's aids, missionary converts, harem girls, prostitutes. In such positions, their significance and status depend totally on the generosity (or lack of generosity) of those white men around whom the movies revolve.

However "well-intentioned" the moviemaker, the basic effect of this debased dependency is not changeable. Take that classic schmaltz of the 1950's, *The World of Suzie Wong*. William Holden, a dissatisfied architect-businessman, has taken a year's sabbatical in Hong Kong to find out if he can "make it" as an artist. (It could have been Los Angeles, but then the movie would have been a total zilch.) He meets ***Suzie Wong***, a bargirl who is cute as a Walt Disney button and speaks English with an endearing "Chinese" accent. ("Fo' goo'niss sakes" she says over and over at inappropriate moments.) He wants her to be his model. She wants to be his "permanent girlfriend." Many traumas later, the moviemakers trundle out their good intentions towards the world's ill-treated masses. They allow Holden to choose Suzie over Kay, the proper, American, upper class woman who is also chasing him. This attempt to put down the upper classes for their prejudices towards Chinese and bargirls, however, barely covers over the basic lesson of the movie: a helpless, charming Chinese bargirl *can* be saved by the right white man, purified by association with him, and elevated to dependency on him. (Her bastard child, conveniently brought out for his pity quotient, is also conveniently bumped off by a flash flood, avoiding further knotty problems for the already overtaxed sensibilities of the scriptwriters.) It all comes across as part act of God, part act of white America.

Moving upwards towards a peak of third world success and white condescension, we discover the role of "sidekick." Indispensible to the sidekick is his uncanny ability to sacrifice his life for his white companion at just the right moment. In this, he must leave the audience feeling that he has repaid the white man something intangible that was owed to him. And, in this, we find the last major characteristic of third world roles—expendability. Several classic scenes come to mind. In this skill, the otherwise pitiful Gunga Din excelled (*Gunga Din,* 1939). Up there on a craggy ledge, already dying, yet blowing that bugle like crazy to save the British troops from ambush by the fanatic Kali-worshippers. Or, just to bring up another third world group, the death of the black trainer in *Body and Soul* (1947), preventing his white World Heavyweight Champion (John Garfield) from throwing the big fight. Or even, if I remember rightly, Sidney Poitier, Mau Mau initiate, falling on the Punji sticks to save the white child of his boyhood friend Rock Hudson (*Something of Value,* 1957). The parts blend into each other: the Filipino guide to the American guerillas, the Indian pal of the white scout, that Mexican guy with the big gut and sly sense of humor. In the end, third world characters are considered expendable by both moviemakers and their audiences because they are no more a source of "light" than the moon at night. All are there but to reflect in different mirrors aspects of white humanity.

While extermination, dependency and expendability have been the steady diet of these movies over the decades, American moviemakers have not remained totally stagnant in their treatment of the third world and its inhabitants. They have over the last forty years emerged ponderously from a colonial world into a neo-colonial one. In the 1930's, the only decade when anything other than second-rate films were made about Asia, moviemakers had no hesitation about express-

ing an outright contempt for subjugated and/or powerless Asians; nor
did they feel self-conscious about proudly portraying the colonial style
in which most Westerners in Asia lived. The train in *Shanghai Express*
(1932) is shown in all its "colonial" glory: the Chinese passengers
crammed into crude compartments; the Westerners eating dinner in
their spacious and elegant dining room. Here was the striking contrast
between the rulers and the ruled and nobody saw any reason to hide it.

During this period, with the European imperial structure in Asia
still unbroken, colonial paternalism abounded. No one blinked an eye
when Shirley Temple asked her grandfather, the British Colonel (*Wee
Willie Winkie*, 1937), why he was mad at "Khoda Khan," leader of the
warlike tribes on India's northeast border; and he replied, "We're not
mad at Khoda Khan. England wants to be friends with all her peoples.
But if we don't shoot him, he'll shoot us . . . (they've been plundering
for so many years) they don't realize they'd be better off planting
crops" [a few poppy seeds maybe?]. Nor were audiences taken aback
when Cary Grant called his Indian sidekick a "beastie" (or alternately
the "regimental beastie") in *Gunga Din;* nor when Clark Gable kicked
his Indochinese workers out of a ditch (to save them from a storm, of
course), calling them similar names (*Red Dust*).

A decade later such scenes and lines would have been gaffes.[9] In
the wake of the World War and its flock of anti-Japanese propaganda
flicks (whose progeny were still alive in the early 1960's), the destruction of the British, French and Dutch empires, the success of the Communist revolution in China, the birth and death of dreaded "neutralism," and the rise of the United States to a position of preeminence
in the world, new cinematic surfaces were developed to fit over old
frames. In their new suits, during the decade of the 50's, cowboy-third
world movies flourished as never before. A vast quantity of these low-
budget (and not-so-low-budget) films burst from Hollywood to flood
the country's theatres. In the more "progressive" of them, an India in
chains was replaced by a struggling, almost "independent" country; the
"regimental beastie" by a Nehru (-Ghandi) type "rebel" leader; the
Kali-worshipping, loinclothed fanatic by Darvee, the Maoist revolutionary ("You cannot make omelettes without breaking eggs."). Yet this
sort of exercise was no more than sleight of hand. The Nehru character
looked just as ridiculously pompous and imitative as did Gunga Din
when he practised his bugle; nor did the whites any less monopolize
center stage (holding, naturally, the key military and police positions);
nor could the half-breed woman (Ava Gardner) any less choose light
(the British officer) over darkness (Darvee and his minions). Soon, all
this comes to seem about as basic a change in older forms as was the "independence" granted to many former colonies in the real world
(*Bhowani Junction*, 1956).

If any new elements were to enter these movies in the 1950's (and
early 60's), it was in the form of changes in relations within the white
world, not between the white and non-white worlds. These changes,
heralded by the "adult westerns" of the late fifties, have yet to be fully
felt in films on Asia; yet a certain early (and somewhat aborted) move

in this direction could be seen in some of the films that appeared about the Korean war (not a particularly popular subject, as might be imagined)—a certain tiredness ("Three world wars in one lifetime" / *Battle Circus,* 1953) and some doubts. The WWII flick's faith in the war against the "Japs", in a "civilian" army, and in "democracy" comes across tarnished and tired. The "professional" soldier (or flyer) takes center stage. ("We've gotta do a clean, professional job on those [North Korean] bridges." / *The Bridges at Toko-ri,* 1954). There is, for instance, no analogue in your WWII movies to the following conversation in *The Bridges at Toko-ri.* Mickey Rooney (a helicopter rescue pilot) and William Holden (a flyer) are trapped (shot down) behind the North Korean lines. Surrounded, they wait in a ditch for help to arrive. During a lull in the shooting, they begin to talk:

> Holden: I'm a lawyer from Denver, Colorado, Mike. I probably couldn't hit a thing [with this gun] . . ."
> Rooney: "Judas, how'd you ever get out here in a smelly ditch in Korea?"
> Holden: "That's just what I've been asking myself . . . the wrong war in the wrong place and that's the one you're stuck with . . . You fight simply because you are here."

Within minutes, they are both killed by the advancing Korean soldiers.

Yet though the white world might seem tarnished, its heroes bitter, tired and ridden with doubts, its relationship to the non-white world had scarcely changed. If anything, the introduction of massive air power to Asian warfare had only further reduced the tangential humanity of Asian peoples. For in a movie like *Toko-ri* (as at Danang today), you never even needed to see the enemy, only charred bodies.

This attempt, particularly in westerns, to introduce new attitudes in the white world, increasingly muddied the divisions between stock characters, brought to the fore the hero-as-cynic, and called into question the "humanity" of the whites vis-a-vis each other. Such adjustments in a relatively constant cinematic structure represented an attempt to update a form which the world's reality put in increasing danger of unbelievability. By the early 1960's, the "adult western" had reached a new stage—that of elegy (see, for instance, *The Man Who Shot Liberty Valance,* 1962). Superficially, such movies seem to be in a state of sentimental mourning for the closing of the frontier and the end of a mythical white frontier life. However, westerns as a form were originally created amidst industrial America partially to mourn just such a loss. The elegiac western of the 60's was, in fact, mourning the passing of itself. Today, this form has come to what may be its terminal fruition in America, the "hip" western—*Butch Cassidy and the Sundance Kid* (1969), which is a parody not of the western, but of the elegiac western, since not even that can be taken totally straight any more.[10]

However, even in this extension of the western, one thing has not changed—attitudes towards the third world. When, for instance, Butch and Sundance cannot make a go of it in a hemmed-in West, they naturally move on, "invading" Bolivia. In Bolivia, of course, it's the same old local color scene again, with one variation: instead of the two of them killing off hundreds of Bolivians in that old wagon train scene, hundreds of unidentified Bolivians band together to kill them. It all boils down to the same thing.

Whatever *Butch Cassidy* may be the end of, I think we stand at the edge of a not totally new, but nonetheless yawning abyss—the "sympathetic" film. The first of what I expect will be an onslaught of these are appearing now. They have at least pretensions towards changing how we see relationships not only within the white world itself, but between the white and Indian worlds. And what is appearing in westerns today may be the transmuted meat of Asian or African films within the next decade.

The recent *A Man Called Horse* (1970) is a good example. It seems to have been a sincere and painstaking attempt to make a large-scale, commercially successful movie about the Sioux (before they were overrun by the whites), to show from an Indian point of view their way of life, their rituals (recreated from Catlin's paintings) and benefits, their feelings and fears. Yet, at every turn, the film betrays the edges of older and more familiar frameworks.

It concerns an English lord hunting in the American West early in the 19th century. Captured by a Sioux raiding party, he is brought back to their village (where the rest of the film takes place). There he becomes a slave (horse) for an Indian woman (Dame Judith Anderson). Already a white "hero" has been slipped into this movie about Indians, betraying an assumption that American audiences could not sustain interest in a film without whites. Given the way we look at these films, he immediately becomes the center of our attention; thus, in the end, you are forced to relate to the Sioux village through his eyes, and to relate to the Sioux as they relate to him (aiding him or mistreating him). Second, by following the travails of this lord-turned-beast of burden as he assimilates to the tribe, the movie seems to prove that old adage, "put a white man among even the best of savages and you have a natural chief." (He kills enemy Indians, goes through the sun initiation ritual, marries the chief's daughter, teaches the tribe British infantry tactics, and, in the end, his wife and adopted mother being dead, he splits for the white world.)

His girlfriend has that Ali McGraw look which is probably supposed to allow the audience to "identify" better with the Indians, but looks about as fitting as it did among the Jews of New Jersey (*Goodby Columbus*). Even a stab at righting the wrongs westerns have done to language has a similarly dismal result. The movie's makers, reacting to the common use of pidgin-Hollywood by Indian characters in normal westerns, allow the Sioux in this movie to speak their own language. As all but two of the characters are Sioux, much of the movie is conducted in the Sioux language. If this were a French movie, there would naturally be subtitles; but as these are Sioux *au naturel,* and as there is already a conveniently English-speaking character, an alternate means is called upon. Another "prisoner" is created, an Indian who spent some time with the French and speaks broken English. At the behest of the English lord, he translates what is necessary to his and our understanding. In this way, the Indians, while retaining the dignity of their own language, are perhaps slightly less able to express themselves comprehensively in this picture than in a normal western. More important, just as if it were the normal wagon train scenario, it forces us to see everything through white eyes.[11]

And as long as the eyes through which we see the world do not change, so long as the old frameworks for movies about the third world are not thrown away, "intentions" go for little indeed. It is hard even to think of examples of films where sympathetic intentions are matched by deeds. Certainly one would have to venture beyond the bounds of the U.S. to find them—perhaps *The Battle of Algiers* (which, in reverse, does for the French colonizers what we were never willing to do for the Indians). Its view begins at least to accord with the brutal history of the third world; to tell a little what it means, from the colonized point of view, to resist, to fight back, to rebel against your occupiers.

American moviemakers, however, are at heart still in love with an era when people could accept the six year old Shirley Temple telling Khoda Khan not to make war on the British because "the Queen wants to protect her people and make them rich." Their main substitution in later movies being to replace the Queen with (American) technology— machine guns to mow em down, and band-aids to patch em up. This mood is best captured by Gene Tierney in *The Left Hand of God* when Humphrey Bogart says, "China's becoming a nightmare, Anne . . . What are we really doing here? . . . We belong back in the States, marrying, raising a family." She replies, " . . . There's too much work to do here . . . the things we're doing here are what they need; whether medicine or grace. And we can give it to them . . ." Of course, the historical joke of this being uttered in China's Sinkiang province in 1947, a time when the unmentioned communist revolution is sweeping through the central provinces, passed the scriptwriters by. Yet, on the whole, just this distance between the film's "message" and Chinese reality about sums up the American approach to the third world. In the end, no matter where the moviemakers may think their sympathy lies, their films are usually no more than embroideries on a hagiography of "pacification."

Within such a context, there is no possibility for presenting resistance, rebellion, or revolution by the intruded upon in a way that could be even comprehensibile, no less sympathetic. Quite the opposite, the moviemakers are usually hell-bent on glorifying those Asians (or other third worlders) who allied with the Western invaders, not those who at some point resisted either the invasion or its consequences. However, there is an insoluble contradiction here. The method for judging non-whites in these films is based on how dependent or independent they are of the white leads and the white world. To the degree to which they are dependent, they are seen as closer to humanity. To the degree to which they are independent (i.e. resist) they are seen as less liable to humanization or outrightly inhuman and thus open to extermination. ("Mitchell, we must stamp this out immediately." / *Gunga Din*). In other words, there is an inherent bias in these movies towards the glorification of those "natives" who have allied with us. Yet what makes the white hero so appealing is the audience's feeling that no matter how low he sinks, he retains some sense of human dignity. There is always that feeling (as Bogart and countless cowboy stars brought out so well) that despite appearances, *he is his own man.* Yet no movie Asians linked to the West can ever really be that. Though they can bask in the light of humanity, they can never be much more than imitation humans. In only one non-white role is this possibility open—that is the role of villain (he who refuses white help and actively opposes him). Only the villain, already placed outside the pale (sic) of humanity, can be his own man.

The result is a knotty problem. If those close to the whites are invariably dependent, they cannot but be viewed in some way with contempt, no matter how the movie makers go about trying to glorify them. On the other hand, if those most contemptible non-humans, the villains, are the only Asians capable of "independence" in these films, they are also the only Asians who are the cinematic equivalents of the white leads. Thus, we cannot help but have a sneaking respect for those who oppose us and a sneaking contempt for those who side with us. (How similar this is to the attitudes of many American soldiers in Vietnam towards ARVN and towards the NLF forces.) No doubt this is at least partly responsible for the extremes American moviemakers have gone to in glorifying one and despoiling the other.

What Lewis and Clark's Indian guide Sacajawea was to American history high school texts, Gunga Din was to third world movies. He makes the classic sacrifice for the white world, and in death theoretically proves he is a "better man" than his British mentors. Yet how hollow this "triumph" is for the viewing audience. No one is fooled by the words. Doing his mimic marching shuffle, around the corner from the practicing British troops, what a pitiful imitation "human" he appears to be. And even his greatest hopes—to get one toe on the lowest rung of the white regimental ladder as company bugler—leave him second best to any white who comes along. On the other hand, the leader of the Kali worshippers (read: native resistance forces) is portrayed in a paroxysm of caricature ("Rise brothers and kill . . . kill for the love of Kali, kill for the love of killing, KILL, KILL, KILL!"). He is a mad murderer, a torturer, a loin-clothed savage, a megalomaniac with bulging eyes. Yet he is the only Indian in the film who has the real ability to "love his country" like a white man. "I can die as readily for my country and my fate as you for yours," he says and voluntarily jumps into the snakepit, yelling "India farewell!"

This inability, despite pulling all the stops, to deny the enemy a certain dignity is not extraordinary. Even Mao Tse-tung, in the otherwise rabid *The Chairman* proves in some grim sense, irrepressible. On the other hand, no matter how charmingly portrayed, our allies' dependency cannot be totally overcome. They are always, in a way, trained spies in the camp of their own people.

American movies about the third world should not be given more credit than is their due. Despite the impression you might get in the theatre, American moviemakers did not invent the world, nor even the version of world history they present in their films. However, they must be given full credit for developing a highly successful and satisfying cinematic form to encapsulate an existing ideological message. With this form, they have been able to regulate the great horrors of Western expansion into the rest of the world, and present-day American hegemony over great hunks of it, to another universe of pleasure and enjoyment. They have successfully tied extermination of non-white peoples to laughable relief, and white racial superiority to the natural order of things. They have destroyed any possibility for explaining the various ways in which non-white (not to speak of white) people could resist invasion, colonization, exploitation, and even mass slaughter.

Cowboy (-third world) films are, in the end, a vast visual pacification program, ostensibly describing the rest of the world, but in fact aimed at the millions of people who for several generations have made up the American viewing audience. It's hardly a wonder that Vietnam did not sear the American consciousness. Why should it have? For years, Americans had been watching the whole scene on their screens: REV DEV, WHAM, endless My Lai's, body counts, killing of wounded enemy soldiers, aerial obliteration, etc. We had grown used to seeing it, and thrilling with pleasure while reaching for another handful of popcorn.

Such a "pacification" program is based on the inundation principle. It is not a matter of quality (probably there have been no good films on Asia since the 1930's), but quantity. So many cowboy-third world movies have rolled factory-style off the production line that the most minute change of plot is hailed as a great innovation. In the end, all the visual "choices" available to a viewer just emphasize the way in which America is strikingly a one-channel country. In fact, it might not be too far wrong to say that while pacification may have failed in Vietnam, its pilot project here in America has generally succeeded, that we are a pacified population, living unknowingly in an occupied country.

NOTES

[1]The men who historically advocated or pursued such a policy in the American West openly and unashamedly referred to it at the time as an "extermination" policy.

[2]One must at least credit John Ford, the director, with keeping the carnage down in several of his films (for example, *She Wore a Yellow Ribbon,* 1949) and with allowing the Indians (*Fort Apache,* 1948) to emerge victorious, if no more comprehensible, from at least one movie in the history of the western film.

[3]The land equivalent of the Kamikaze onslaught in the Banzai! charge (as in Fuller's *Merrill's Marauders,* 1962).

[4]While somewhat harder to find in Nazi war flicks, see *The Enemy Below* (1957) for the World War II (and naval) version of the same scene. The last shot is of the opposing American and Nazi commanders who have disabled each other's ships and saved each other's lives, standing at the stern, sharing a cigarette and looking out together over the endless sea.

[5]This is not to say that Americans are portrayed as lacking generosity. Quite the opposite, humanitarian gestures are second nature to them; however, those gestures tend to be directed towards humans. As in the scene where Merrill's Marauders, having

smashed thru a mass of Japs, are confronted with a wounded comrade. "You wouldn't leave me?" he asks. "We never leave anybody," is the reply.

[6]Extermination has, however, been spoken of quite bluntly in certain third world movies. This was particularly true of those movies made during the war against Japan. Take, for example, *The Purple Heart* (1944), about Japanese attempts to try the Doolittle flyers for "war crimes." At the trial, the leader of the American flyers tells the Japanese judge: "We'll come by night and we'll come by day. We'll blacken your skies and burn your cities to the ground until you get down on your knees and beg for mercy . . . This was your war. You asked for it. You started it . . . and now we won't stop until your crummy little empire is wiped off the face of the earth." The Japanese chief prosecutor immediately commits Hari-kiri because of loss of face in failing to break the American prisoners. Or again, *Objective Burma* (1945): the American journalist sees tortured and dead American prisoners. In anger, he says, "This was done in cold blood by a people who claim to be civilized . . . stinking little savages. Wipe em out. Wipe em off the face of the earth, I say. Wipe em off the face of the earth!"

[7]Of all the forms discussed, only Science Fiction films exhibit certain themes which run against this grain. It seems to me there are two sources for this opening towards "deviation." First, in the particularly chilly years of the fifties, anti-nuclear, anti-military freaks flocked to this form whose very fantastical nature provided an allegorical legitimacy for their questionable messages. Thus, even the monster-eradication movies often hide a plea for "peace"/deliverance from incompetent military defenders and their nuclear disasters, whose by-products are sci-fi's ubiquitous radio-active creatures. Second, a traditional tie-in with the sky, heaven, and God led to a semi-religious counter-theme of "divine intervention" and human (implicitly white) inferiority. This conception of wisdom descending from above to straighten out the stupid problems of blundering, incapable humanity is basic to *The Day the Earth Stood Still* (1951), in which "Klaatu" appears from space to tour Washington and plead for nuclear peace (and a fascist robot-police force to patrol the world); or *The Next Voice You Hear* (1950), in which God intervenes in person—via radio.

[8]George Orwell, "Marrakech," in *Essays* (Doubleday, 1954), pp. 189–190.

[9]There were, of course, some holdovers from the 30's. Particularly junk like *Khyber Pass* (1954), in which British lancer Richard Egan, getting ready to capture rebel leaders in a village, tells a fellow officer: "I don't want any of those devils to escape us."

[10]Even John Wayne, the last of the cowboy superstars still in the saddle, is forced to mourn his own passing in True Grit (1969).

[11]For another recent example, see *Tell Them Willie Boy is Coming* (1970); and I feel certain (though I have yet to see it) that *Soldier Blue* (1970) will fall in the same category.

As for the newness of "sympathetic" films—at least a couple of historical antecedents come to mind: first, *The General Died at Dawn* (1936) with Gary Cooper, and Akim Tamiroff as the warlord Yang (seems to have been a pretty popular name among warlord's mothers). This Clifford Odets script hangs heavy with the hand of the 30's Left. ("You ask me why I'm for oppressed people, because I have a background of oppression myself.") But despite its professed sympathy for the oppressed people of China, its protestations of Asian dignity and love for life, and its unbelievable murky politics, it is loaded with all the normal stuff: white-centeredness ("Mr. O'Hara, from the time you leave this room until you deliver the money, the fate of China is in your hands."); a Chinese super-evil villain; and a mass suicide scene that only could have taken place among those for whom human life meant nothing at all (In the movie's climactic scene, General Yang—who is dying at dawn—has his troops line up in two facing lines several feet apart and shoot each other), to name just a few of the more salient points.

For an example from the earlier 60's, see John Ford's "bow" to the tribulations of the Indians, *Cheyenne Autumn* (1964). Exactly the same sort of process occurs and a good book by Marie Sandoz, written from the viewpoint of the Cheyenne, is destroyed in the bargain. Even its historical ending is twisted to imply that Secretary of the Interior Schultz (Edward G. Robinson) allowed the remnants of the Cheyenne to return to their homeland—which he most definitely did not.

Haves vs. Have-nots: Upheaval Between North and South

5 The United States in Opposition

Daniel P. Moynihan

"We are far from living in a single world community," writes Edward Shils, "but the rudiments of a world society do exist." Among those rudiments, perhaps the most conspicuous, if least remarked, are the emerging views as to what kind of society it is. A measure of self-awareness has appeared, much as it did for smaller polities in earlier times. These assessments tend at the international level to be as diverse as those commonly encountered concerning national societies, or local ones. Some will think the society is good and getting better; others will see it as bad and getting worse. Some want change; some fear it. Where one sees justice, another sees wrong.

The notion of a world society is nothing new to Americans. It dominated the rhetoric of World War II, of the founding of the United Nations, of much of the cold war. It is now a received idea, and its impress may be measured by the success with which advocates have found audiences for issues defined in international terms: the world environmental problem; the world population problem; the world food problem. Not a generation ago, these were national issues at most.

Much of this internationalist rhetoric is based on things real enough. There *is* a world ecology; there *is* a world economy; and some measures important to individual countries can only be obtained through international accord. Thus the concept of interdependence has become perhaps the main element of the new consciousness of a world society. This is a valid basis on which to posit the existence of a society; it is almost a precondition of a society's coming into being.

Yet societies rarely stop at the acknowledgement of the need for cooperation which is implied by the term interdependence. The image of a society as a family is a common one, and with reason, for in both cases the idea of cooperation is frequently supplemented or even supplanted by the idea of obligation. What does one member *owe* another? This is something new in international pronouncements. If one were to characterize the discomfiture and distress with which Americans responded to the events of the 29th General Assembly of the United Nations in 1974, some measure would have to be attributed to the discovery that a vast majority of the nations of the world feel there are claims which can be made on the wealth of individual nations that are both considerable and threatening—in any event threatening to countries such as the United States which regularly finds itself in a minority (often a minority of one or two or at most a half-dozen) in an assembly of 138 members.

The tyranny of the UN's "new majority" has accordingly been deplored, and there has been much comment that whereas opposition to the United Nations was once a position of "conservatives" in the United States, it is increasingly one of "liberals" also. Yet while there have been some calls to boycott the General Assembly, or not to vote in it, there have been but few calls for withdrawal from the United Nations. It is almost as if American opinion now acknowledged that there was no escaping involvement in the emergent world society. All the more reason, then, for seeking to understand what has been going on.

I

Now, of course, a lot is going on, and no single element dominates. Yet it may be argued that what happened in the early 1970's is that for the first time the world felt the impact of what for lack of a better term I shall call the British revolution. That is the revolution which began in 1947 with the granting by socialist Britain of independence to socialist India. In slow, then rapid, order the great empires of the world—with the single major exception of the Czarist empire—broke up into independent states; the original membership of the United Nations of 51 grew to 138. These new nations naturally varied in terms of size, population, and resources. But in one respect they hardly varied at all. To a quite astonishing degree they were ideologically uniform, having fashioned their polities in terms derived from the general corpus of British socialist opinion as it developed in the period roughly 1890-1950. The Englishmen and Irishmen, Scotsmen and Welsh, who created this body of doctrine and espoused it with such enterprise— nay, genius—thought they were making a social revolution in Britain. And they were. But the spread of their ideology to the furthest reaches of the globe, with its ascent to dominance in the highest national councils everywhere, gives to the British revolution the kind of worldwide significance which the American and French, and then the Russian, revolutions possessed in earlier times.*

From the perspective of their impact on others, the American and French revolutions can be treated as a single event. They were not of course identical in themselves, and profoundly important distinctions can be made between them. But these distinctions were little noted in the political rhetoric of the century that followed, or in the forms of government fashioned in the likeness of this rhetoric, or in the goals of governments so fashioned. Men sought a constitutional regime which disestablished ancient privilege, guaranteed liberties, and promoted the general welfare through what came to be known as liberal social policies. Liberalism was at first characterized by the opposition to state intervention in economic affairs, and later by the advocacy of such intervention, but the intervention in question was a fairly mild business, it being no liberal's view that the state was an especially trustworthy servant of the citizen. The citizen, as liberals viewed the world, was a very important person, especially perhaps if he tended to clean linen.

The Russian revolution of 1917 brought into existence a regime even more dramatically different from its predecessors than had the liberal regimes of a century earlier been from theirs. Everything, it was understood, had changed. Those who would change everything, or who believed that, like it or not, everything was going to change, rallied to this rhetoric. As for the rest of the world, it came soon enough to know that a wholly extraordinary event had occurred, even that the future had occurred. For three decades, culminating in the triumph of Communist arms in China in 1948, this was quite the most vivid, and the most attended to, movement in the world.

The British revolution of the second quarter of the 20th century attracted no such attention. Everyone certainly recognized that new states were coming into existence out of former European, and indeed mostly British, colonies, but the tendency was to see them as candidates for incorporation into one or the other of the older revolutionary traditions then dominant elsewhere in the world. It was not generally perceived that they were in a sense already spoken for—that they came

---

*The term British revolution is open to objection as seeming to exclude the influence of continental socialism on the new nations, and indeed a good case could be made for calling the phenomenon I am trying to describe the revolution of the Second International. But the term British can be justified by the fact that of the 87 states to have joined the UN since its founding, more than half—47—had been part of the British empire. Even apart from the empire, British culture was in the first half of this century incomparably the most influential in the world, and that culture was increasingly suffused with socialist ideas and attitudes. I anticipate and hope for a rigorous critique of the arguments of this paper, but I also hope it will not be too much distracted by the difficulties of finding a concise term to describe what was on the whole a concise phenomenon; the development of socialist doctrine and the formation of socialist parties in Western Europe at this time. I should also note that the political ideology in the new states of the Third World of which I will be speaking was best described by the late George Lichtheim as "national socialism." This term has, of course, acquired an altogether unacceptable connotation.

to independence with a preexisting, coherent, and surprisingly stable ideological base which, while related to both the earlier traditions, was distinct from both. This most likely accounts for the almost incurious initial reaction in what would soon be known as the First and Second Worlds. In the Republic of India the United States could see democracy; the Soviets could see socialism. In truth, a certain Hegelian synthesis had occurred. On the one hand, the Minimal State of the American revolution; in response, the Total State of the Russian revolution; in synthesis, the Welfare State of the British revolution.

Samuel H. Beer describes the doctrine of British socialism as follows:

> . . . it is especially the socialist's commitment to "fellowship" that fundamentally distinguishes his approach. . . . For private ownership he would substitute public ownership; for production for profit, production for use; for competition, cooperation. A cultural and ethical revolution would also take place, and motives that had aimed at individual benefit would now aim at common benefits. Industry, which had been governed by individual decisions within the competitive system, would be subject to collective and democratic control. . . . Government would consist in comprehensive and continuous planning and administration.

Two general points may be made about this British doctrine. First, it contained a suspicion of, almost a bias against, economic development which carried over into those parts of the world where British culture held sway. The fundamental assertion of the age of the Diamond Jubilee was that there was plenty of wealth to go 'round if only it were fairly distributed. No matter what more thoughtful socialist analysts might urge, redistribution, not production, remained central to the ethos of British socialism. Profit became synonymous with exploitation. That profit might be something conceptually elegant—least-cost production—made scarcely any impress. "Production for profit" became a formulation for all that was wrong in the old ways, and Tories half-agreed. (For it was the Liberals and the Radicals who were being repudiated by such doctrine, and it was the Liberal party that went under.) This, too, was passed on. When Sir Arthur Lewis in 1974 gave the Tata lectures in India and found himself pleading, as a socialist and as a man of the Third World, but also as an economist, that profit was not a concept public-sector enterprise could afford to ignore, no less a personage than the head of the Indian Planning Commission felt called upon to rebut him.

To be sure, much of this redistributionist bias was simply innocent. British socialists, for example, proved in office to know almost nothing about how actually to redistribute income, and British income has not been significantly redistributed. Coming to power just after World War II, the socialists appeared to think they had abolished wealth by imposing a top income-tax rate of nineteen shillings six pence in the twenty-shilling pound, which is to say confiscating the rich man's pay envelope. Few seemed to note that capital gains remained exempt from income tax altogether, so that in large measure thereafter only those with property could acquire property: the very antithesis of the social condition socialism sought. (This detail perhaps did not escape the well-to-do of the developing nations when the prospect of socialism on the British model first appeared there.)

The second general point about socialist doctrine as it developed in Britain was that it was anti-American. More anti-American, surely, than it was ever anti-Soviet. The reasons for this are not that obscure. The British were not overmuch admiring of Americans in that era, nor we of them. In part their attitude began as aristocratical disdain. (An intimate of Pandit Nehru's describes once asking India's first Prime Minister why he was so anti-American. This was in 1961. Nehru's first reaction was a rather huffy denial of any such predisposition, but he then became reflective and after a moment admitted that, yes, it was true, and that probably it all dated back to his days at Harrow. There was one American boy there at the time: filthy rich, and much too pushy.) But more importantly, of course, America was seen as quintessentially capitalist.

With the Russian revolution, and then especially with the world depression of the 1930's and the onset of popular-front movements in Europe, a considerable number of British socialists, despite their party's fundamental and central attachment to democratic processes, became supporters of the Soviet regime. Russia was the future. America was the past. With the coming of the cold war this attitude became institutionalized and almost compulsory on the British Left. The *New Statesman,* a journal which tended to follow Asian and African graduates after they had left Britain and returned home, became near Stalinist in its attachment to Soviet ways with the world and its pervasive antagonism to things American.

And yet the *New Statesman* was never Communist, and neither, save in small proportions, were its readers. They were British socialists, part of a movement of opinion which spread in the course of the first half of the 20th century to the whole of the British empire, a domain which covered one-quarter of the earth's surface, and which an inspired cartographic convention had long ago decreed be colored pink. It was British civil servants who took the doctrine to the colonies. (How curious, in retrospect, are the agonizings of Harold Laski and others as to whether the civil service would carry out the policies of a socialist government. What more congenial task for persons whose status comes from the power and prestige of government? But in the Britain of that era it could be thought that class origin would somehow overcome occupational interest.)

What the civil service began, British education completed. Has there ever been a conversion as complete as that of the Malay, the Ibo, the Gujarati, the Jamaican, the Australian, the Cypriot, the Guyanan, the Yemenite, the Yoruban, the sabra, the felaheen to this distant creed? (The London School of Economics, Shils notes, was often said to be the most important institution of higher education in Asia and Africa.) In her autobiography, Beatrice Webb wrote that she and her husband felt "assured that with the School [LSE] as the teaching body, the Fabian Society as a propagandist organization, the LCC [London County Council] as object lesson in electoral success, our books as the only elaborate original work in economic fact and theory, no young man or woman who is anxious to study or to work in public affairs can fail to come under our influence." For reasons that are understandable, this was true most particularly for young men and women coming from abroad in that long and incongruously optimistic intellectual age that began amid late Victorian plumpness and ended with the austerity of postwar Britain. In 1950 the conservative Michael Oakeshott succeeded to the Fabian Harold Laski's chair in political theory at LSE and in a sense *that* party was over. But by then not Communists but Fabians could claim that the largest portion of the world's population lived in regimes of their fashioning. Before very long, the arithmetical majority and the ideological coherence of those new nations brought them to dominance in the United Nations and, indeed, in any world forum characterized by universal membership.

But if the new nations absorbed ideas about others from the doctrines of British socialism, they also absorbed ideas about themselves. The master concept, of course, is that they had the right to independence. This idea goes back to the American revolution, and even beyond to the Glorious Revolution in 17th-century Britain, but British socialism readily incorporated and even appropriated it. As the 20th century wore on and the issue of independence arose with respect to these specific peoples and places, it was most often the socialists who became the principal *political* sponsors of independence. It was a Labour government which in 1947 granted independence to India and formally commenced the vast, peaceful revolution that followed. The Indian Congress party had been founded in 1883 by a British civil servant, Alan Octavian Hume, whose politics were essentially Liberal. But by the time of independence, it was a matter to be taken for granted that the Congress was socialist and that its leaders, Gandhi and then Nehru, were socialists too.

Two further concepts triangulate and fix the imported political culture of these new nations. The first is the belief—often, of course, justified—that they have been subject to economic exploitation, exactly as the working class is said in socialist theory to have been exploited under capitalism. The second is the belief—also, of course, often justified—that they have been subject to ethnic discrimination corresponding to class distinctions in industrial society. As with the belief in the right to independence, these concepts, which now seem wholly natural, rarely occur in nature. They are learned ideas, and they were learned by the new nations mostly where they mostly originated, in the intellectual and political circles of Britain of the late 19th and early 20th century. Gandhi greatly elucidated the moral dimensions of exploitation and discrimination, but he did so in the context of a world-wide political movement that was more than receptive to his ideas, a political movement of which he was a part. At root, the ideas of exploitation and discrimination represent a transfer to colonial populations of the fundamental socialist assertions with respect to the condition of the European working class, just as the idea of independence parallels the demand that the working class break out of bondage and rise to power.

Now it is possible to imagine a country, or collection of countries, with a background similar to that of the British colonies, attaining independence and then letting bygones be bygones. The Americans did that: our political culture did not suggest any alternative. International life was thought to operate in Wordsworth's terms:

> The good old rule
> . . . The simple plan
> That they should take, who have the power.
> And they should keep who can.

So in their own terms might Marxists judge the aftermath of Marxist triumph: history was working its ineluctable way; there would be no point, no logic, in holding the past to account. Not so the heirs of the British revolution. British socialism is, was, and remains a highly moral creed. It is not a politics of revenge; it is too civil for that. But reparations? Yes: reparations. This idea was fundamental to the social hope of a movement which, it must ever be recalled, rested on the assumption that there existed vast stores of unethically accumulated wealth. On the edges of the movement there were those who saw the future not just in terms of redistribution, but of something ominously close to looting. In any event, the past was by no means to be judged over and done with. There were scores to be settled. Internally and internationally.

A final distinctive character of the British revolution concerns procedure. Wrongs are to be righted by legislation. The movement was fundamentally parliamentarian. The Labour party came to power through the ballot, and proceeded to change society by statute. This was dramatically so with respect to the empire. For the first time in the history of mankind a vast empire dismantled itself, piece by piece, of its own systematic accord. A third of the nations of the world today owe their existence to a statute of Westminster. What more profound experience could there be of the potency of parliamentary majorities in distant places, and of their enactments?

Plainly, not all the new nations of the postwar world were formerly British. There were French colonies. Belgian. Dutch. Portuguese. Political traditions in each case were different from the British. But only *slightly* different: viewed from Mars, London, Paris, and The Hague are not widely separated or disparate places. By the time of the granting of independence, all were democratic with a socialist intelligentsia and often as not a socialist government. With the exception of Algeria—which is marked by the exception—the former French and Dutch colonies came into being in very much the manner the British had laid down. For a prolonged initial period the former British possessions had pride of place in the ex-colonial world—they speak

English at the UN, not American—and pretty much set the style of politics which has become steadily more conspicuous in international affairs.

Not everyone has noticed this. Indeed, there is scarcely yet a vocabulary in which to describe it. In part, this is because the event is recent; but also because it was incomplete. As with the liberal revolution which came out of America, and the Communist revolution which came out of Russia, this socialist revolution coming mainly out of Britain carried only so much of the world in its initial period of expansion. The liberal revolution of America was not exactly a spent force by the mid-20th century, but (*pace* the Mekong Delta Development Plan) there was never any great prospect of its expanding to new territories. On the other hand, the heirs of the Russian revolution did capture China, the greatest of all the prizes, in 1948, and at least part of Indochina a bit later. But in the main the Communist revolution stopped right there, and the two older revolutions now hold sway within fairly well-defined boundaries. Since 1950 it has been not they but the heirs of the British revolution who have been expanding.

Almost the first international political act of the new states was to form the nonaligned bloc, distinguishing themselves—partially—from the two blocs into which the immediate postwar world had formed. From politics the emphasis shifted to economic affairs. In 1968 these countries, meeting at Algiers, formed the Group of 77 as a formal economic bloc. Their Joint Statement described the group as "comprising the vast majority of the human race"—and indeed it did. The B's in the list of members gave a sense of the range of nations and peoples involved: Bahrain, Barbados, Bhutan, Bolivia, Botswana, Brazil, Burma, Burundi. And yet there was—now somewhat hidden—unity to the list. Of these eight countries, five were formerly British-governed or British-directed. At its second Ministerial Meeting in Lima in 1971, the group (now numbering 96) drew up an Action Program which stated, *inter alia,* that developing countries should

> encourage and promote appropriate commodity action and, particularly, the protection of the interests of primary producers of the region through intensive consultations among producer countries in order to encourage appropriate policies, leading to the establishment of producers' associations and understandings. . . .

This was represented in the press as a major gain for the black African states who carried the point over objections from Latin Americans accustomed to working out raw-material and commodity arrangements with the United States. But the idea was fundamentally a heritage of the British revolution, and if the black Africans took the lead in proclaiming it, there is no reason to think it was any less familiar to Arabs. They had all gone to the same schools. Was it not right for those who have only their labor to sell, or only the products of their soil, to organize to confront capital? Had they not been exploited?

II

How has the United States dealt with these new nations and their distinctive ideology? Clearly we have not dealt very successfully. This past year, in the 29th General Assembly, we were frequently reduced to a voting bloc which, with variations, consisted of ourselves, Chile, and the Dominican Republic. As this "historic session" closed, the Permanent Representative of India to the United Nations declared: "The activities of the Soviet delegation at the session showed once again that the Soviet Union deeply understands and shares the aspirations of the Third World." This was not Krishna Menon, but a balanced and considerate Asian diplomat. If no equivalent pronouncement on China comes immediately to hand, this may be because the Chinese feel free to identify themselves as members of the Third World. As such, at the end of 1974 they declared that the new majority had written a "brilliant chapter" during the twelve months previous, that it was "sweeping ahead full sail as the boat of imperialism [the United States] and hegemonism [the Soviet Union] founders." "These days," the Chinese statement continued, "the United Nations often takes on the appearance of an international court with the Third World pressing the charges and conducting the trial." A statement to which many could subscribe. But no such statement could come from an American statesman, no such praise would be accorded American policy. Clearly at some level—we all but *started* the United Nations—there has been a massive failure of American diplomacy.

But why? Why has the United States dealt so unsuccessfully with these nations and their distinct ideology? A first thought is that we have not seen the ideology as distinctive. Not recognizing it, we have made no sustained effort to relate ourselves to it. The totalitarian states, from their point of view, did. They recognize ideologies. By 1971 it was clear enough that the Third World—a few exceptions here and there—was not going Communist. But it was nevertheless possible to encourage it in directions that veered very considerably from any tendency the bloc might have to establish fruitful relations with the West; and this was done. It was done, moreover, with the blind acquiescence and even agreement of the United States which kept endorsing principles for whose logical outcome it was wholly unprepared and with which it could never actually go along.

A relatively small but revealing example of this process may be seen in the development of the World Social Report, a document of the Economic and Social Council. The first volume, covering the year 1963, was directed almost exclusively to problems of the developing countries, and the United States took its advent as a promising event. The 1965 report, concentrating on "practical methods of promoting social change," might have caused some to take note, but American officials were entirely unwary: this was, after all, a report designed to help the developing world. In actual fact, it was becoming a document based on the veritably totalitarian idea that social justice means social stability and that social stability means the absence of social protest. Thus by 1970, the Soviet Union—not much social protest there!—emerges as the very embodiment of the just state, while the United States is a nation in near turmoil from the injustices it wreaks upon the poor and the protests these injustices have provoked. And Western Europe hardly comes off any better.

What happened here was that a "Finlandized" Secretariat (the official in charge of preparing the document was indeed a Finn) found that the developing countries and the Communist countries had an easy common interest in portraying their own progress, justifying the effective suppression of dissent, and in the process deprecating and indicting the seeming progress of Western societies. It is easy enough to see that this would be in the interest of the Soviet bloc. (The Chinese did not participate in the debate.) But why the developing world? First, the developing nations could ally with the totalitarians in depicting social reality in this way, in part because so many, having edged toward authoritarian regimes, faced the same problems the Communists would have encountered with a liberal analysis of civil liberties. Secondly, the developing nations had an interest in deprecating the economic achievements of capitalism, since almost none of their own managed economies was doing well. To deplore, to deride, the social effects of affluence in the United States is scarcely a recent invention. For a generation the British Left has held the patent. Further, there is an almost automatic interest on the Left in delegitimating wealth—prior to redistributing it—much as the opposite interest exists on the Right.

Small wonder that officials could describe the Social Report as the most popular document in the UN series, a statement intended as more than faint praise. Yet it has been more representative than otherwise. There are hundreds like it, suffused with a neo-totalitarian, anti-American bias.

American protests at the 26th General Assembly have evidently influenced the most recent Social Report, submitted to the 29th, but here the significant fact is that this protest—entered at the very last moment, when the document was being presented for pro-forma approval—was the first of its kind, or one of the first. In fact the United States until then did not protest. To the contrary, the United States actively participated in preparing this sustained assault on American institutions. The 1970 Social Report had been three years in the making. During those three years it made its way through layers of bureaucracies, all manner of meetings. Americans were always present, and Americans always approved. This was, after all, a Third World document; it was to be treated with tolerance and understanding. Complacency of this order could only arise from the failure to perceive that a distinctive ideology was at work, and that skill and intelligence were required to deal with it successfully.

The blindness of American diplomacy to the process persists. Two large events occurred in 1971, and a series of smaller ones were set in motion. China entered the United Nations, an event the Third World representatives saw as a decisive shift of power to their camp. In that same year the Lima conference established the nonaligned as an economic bloc intent on producer cartels. Less noticed, but perhaps no less important in its implications, a distinctive radicalization began in what might as well be termed world social policy.

This radicalization was first clearly evidenced at the United Nations Conference on the Human Environment, held at Stockholm in 1972, or more precisely at the 26th General Assembly, which was finally to authorize the conference. The conference was in considerable measure an American initiative, and while American negotiators were primarily concerned with ways to get the Russians to join (which in the end they did not), the Brazilians suddenly stormed onto the scene to denounce the whole enterprise as a conspiracy of the haves to keep the have-nots down and out. The argument was that the rich had got rich by polluting their environments and now proposed to stay that way by preventing anyone else from polluting theirs. This, among other things, would insure that the rich would continue their monopoly on the use of the raw materials of the poor. Thus was it asserted that matters originally put forward as soluble in the context of existing economic and political relations were nothing of the sort. To the contrary, they were symptomatic of economic and political exploitation and injustice which could only be resolved by the most profound transformation: to expropriate the expropriators.

At Stockholm itself, this quickly became the dominant theme—espoused by a dominant majority. "Are not poverty and need the greatest pollutors?" Prime Minister Indira Gandhi of India asked. "There are grave misgivings," she continued, "that the discussion of ecology may be designed to distract attention from the problems of war and poverty." She was wrong in this. They were not so designed. But at Stockholm the nations who feared they might be took control of the agenda. The conference declared as its first principle:

> Man has the fundamental right to freedom, equality, and adequate conditions of life, in an environment of a quality which permits a life of dignity and well being, and bears a solemn responsibility to protect and improve the environment for present and future generations. In this respect, policies promoting or perpetuating apartheid, racial segregation, discrimination, colonial and other forms of oppression and foreign domination stand condemned and must be eliminated.

The American delegates routinely voted for this resolution. It was, after all, language the new countries wanted. What wholly unwelcome meanings might be attached to "other forms of oppression and foreign domination" which stood "condemned" and had to be "eliminated" was a thought scarcely in keeping with the spirit of the occasion.

The Stockholm Conference had been turbulent. The United Nations World Population Conference, held nearly two years later, in August 1974, had an air of insurrection. This conference too was largely an American initiative, the culmination of years of State Department effort to put population on the agenda of world social policy. The Secretary General of the United Nations proclaimed the gathering would be "a turning point in the history of mankind." The centerpiece was a Draft World Population Plan of Action, which in essence set 1985 as the year crude birth rates in developing countries would be reduced to 30 per thousand (as against an anticipated 34) and when "the necessary information and education about family planning and means to practice family planning" would be available "to all persons who so desire. . . ." There can be no doubt of the social change implicit in such a conference's even meeting: in most industrialized countries, family planning has only just achieved the status of an accepted social value deserving of public support. Yet neither should there be any doubt that a disaster overtook the American position in the course of the conference, and that this disaster was wholly predictable.

To begin with, the conference was thought up by Americans to deal with a problem we consider that other people have. (In fairness, not long ago the United States itself was thought to have a problem of population size, while the provision of family-planning services is an issue of social equity as well as of population growth.) Specifically, it was considered a problem of the developing countries: countries, that is, of the British revolution who are animated by the liveliest sense that their troubles originate in capitalist and imperialist systems of which the United States all but offered itself as an exemplar. Further, the conference met in Bucharest, capital of a Communist country. At one level no great imagination would have been required to anticipate the outcome. President Nicolae Ceausescu opened the conference by declaring that "The division of the world into developed and underdeveloped countries is a result of historical evolution, and is a direct consequence of the imperialist, colonialist, and neo-colonialist policies of exploitation of many peoples." He called for "a new international economic order" and condemned "a pessimistic outlook" on population growth.

But if this was to be expected, few could have anticipated the wild energy of the Chinese assault on the Western position. China has the strictest of all population-control programs. Yet the Chinese arrived in Rumania to assail with unprecedented fury and devastating zeal the very idea of population control as fundamentally subversive of the future of the Third World. The future, the Chinese proclaimed, is infinitely bright. Only the imperialists and the hegemonists could spoil it, and population control was to be their wrecking device. A theory of "consumerism" emerged: it was excessive consumption in the developed economies which was the true source of the problems of the underdeveloped nations and not the size of the latter's population. None dared oppose the thesis. The Indians, who are thought to have a population problem, went to the conference rather disposed to endorse a Plan of Action. But they did nothing of the sort. Instead, the Maharaja of Jammu and Kashmir, who headed the Indian delegation, found himself denouncing "colonial denudation" of the East, and the "vulgar affluence" of the West. The scene grew orgiastic.

In the end, a doctrine emerged which is almost certainly more true than otherwise, namely that social and economic change is the fundamental determinant of fertility change, compared with which family planning as such has at most a residual role. There need be no difficulty with this assertion. The difficulty comes with the conclusion said to follow: that economic growth in the West should cease and the wealth of the world be redistributed. We are back to Keir Hardie, expropriating the expropriators. Not to produce wealth, but to redistribute it. As with the environment conference, the population conference turned into another occasion for reminding the West of its alleged crimes and unresolved obligations.

This tone attained to manic proportions in Population Tribune, an unofficial, American-financed parallel conference of a form that first appeared in Stockholm. Ritual recantation became the order of the day as one notable after another confessed to a class-bound past which had blinded him to the infinitely bright future. Most of the recanters were American, but it was Professor René Dumont of France who epitomized the argument in a statement, "Population and Cannibals," which was subsequently given the full front page of *Development Forum,* an official, five-language, UN publication. Professor Dumont—blaming the "Plunderers of the Third World" for world conditions—"They . . . 'under-pay' for the rare raw materials of the Third World and then squander them"—put the case with some vivacity:

> *Eating little children.* I have already had occasion to show that the rich white man, with his overconsumption of meat and his lack of generosity toward poor populations, acts like a true cannibal, albeit indirect. Last year, in over-consuming meat which wasted the cereals which could have saved them, we ate the little children of the Sahel, of Ethiopia, and of Bangladesh. And this year, we are continuing to do the same thing, with the same appetite.

Dr. Han Suyin, a sympathetic commentator on Chinese Communist affairs, summed up for others:

> You cannot cut off any talk about population, about people, from economics and politics. You cannot put in a vacuum any talk about population and world resources without relation to the present as it exists. I admire people who can talk about a noble future where there will be an equal society and where resources will be controlled by all. But, forgive me for saying so, if this is to be done, then we have to begin by sharing now everything and that would mean that a lot of people who have a lot of private property, for instance, should divest themselves immediately of it in favor of the poor. It means that at this very moment we should start to implement a very simple thing—something which we heard . . . at the United Nations at the sixth special session of the United Nations where the voice of the Third World—the majority of the world—at last formulated their demand for more equitable terms of trade, and for an end to exploitation, for an end to the real cause of poverty and backwardness, which is not population, but which is injustice and exploitation. The Third World has a word for it, it calls it imperialism and hegemony.

And the American delegation? The official view, flashed to diplomatic posts around the world, was as uncomplicated at the end as it had been at the outset: "ALL BASIC U.S. OBJECTIVES WERE ACHIEVED AND U.S. ACCOMPLISHMENTS WERE MANY. . . . U.S. DELEGATION UNANIMOUSLY PLEASED WITH FINAL RESULT."

The World Food Conference which followed in Rome in November was even more explicitly an American initiative. Yet as the American delegation somewhat sadly noted, the plenary forum was used to the fullest by LDC's (Less Developed Countries) to excoriate the United States and other developed nations as responsible for the current food crisis and the generally depressed state of their part of the world, calling for "radical adjustment in the current economic order and, in effect, reparations from developed countries" to the less developed. Such negotiations as took place were somewhat more sober since something immediately of value—wheat—was at stake and obviously only the United States and a few such countries were prepared to part with any. Even so, by the time the conference was concluded, one of the great, and truly liberal, innovations of world social policy—the American-led assertion that the hungry of the world should be fed by transfers of resources—had been utterly deprecated. Thus the Indian Food Minister's statement with respect to the needs of the developing countries:

> It is obvious that the developed nations can be held responsible for their [the developing nations'] present plight. Developed nations, therefore, have a duty to help them. Whatever help is rendered to them now should not be regarded as charity but deferred compensation for what has been done to them in the past by the developed countries.

The UN General Assembly pursued this theme with notable persistence throughout 1974, commencing with a special session in the spring which dealt with the economic crises of the underdeveloped in just such terms. Occasioned as much as anything by the devastating impact of oil price increases, the special session dwelt on every conceivable abuse of economic power save that one. At the end of the regular autumn session, the General Assembly solemnly adopted a Charter of Economic Rights and Duties of States which accords to each state the right freely to exercise full permanent sovereignty over its wealth and natural resources, to regulate and exercise authority over foreign investments, and to nationalize, expropriate, or transfer ownership of foreign property pretty much at will. The vote was 120 to 6—the United States, Belgium, Denmark, West Germany, Luxembourg, and the United Kingdom. What was being asserted was a radical discontinuity with the original, essentially liberal vision of the United Nations as a regime of international law and practice which acknowledges all manner of claims, but claims that move in all directions. Now they moved in one direction only.

In general a rhetoric of expropriation became routine. At year's end, Prime Minister Indira Gandhi, opening the 56th Conference of the International Law Association meeting in New Delhi, declared:

> Laws designed to protect the political or economic power of a few against the rights of the many, must . . . yield place to laws which enlarge the area of equality, and . . . law itself should be an ally and instrument of change.

She spoke a now-common language of resentment over population issues:

> Is it not a new form of arrogance for affluent nations to regard the poorer nations as an improvident species whose numbers are a threat to their own standard of living?

She suggested a reversal of roles had taken place as between the new nations and the old:

> An obligation rests on the haves to generate confidence among the have-nots . . . A new approach to foreign investments is indicated, in which investments abroad are regarded more as a service to the recipient community than as an enterprise where profits and their repatriation must be secured at all cost.

Now there is nothing unfamiliar in this language: only the setting is new. It is the language of British socialism applied to the international scene. American diplomacy has yet to recognize this fact and, failing to recognize it, has failed even to begin dealing intelligently with it.

III

But if the beginning of wisdom in dealing with the nations of the Third World is to recognize their essential ideological coherence, the next step is to recognize that there is every reason to welcome this ideology, and to welcome the coherence also. Because of the British revolution and its heritage, the prospect now is that the world will not go totalitarian. In the Christian sense, has there been such political "good news" in our time? But there is bad news also. The great darkness could yet consume us. The potential for absorption of these states into the totalitarian camp is there and will continue to be there. This is perhaps especially true where one-party states have been established, but even where multi-party democracy flourishes the tug of the "socialist countries," to use the UN term, persists.

The outcome will almost certainly turn on whether or not these nations, individually and in groups, succeed in establishing sufficiently productive economies. If they do not, if instead they become permanently dependent on outside assistance, that assistance is likely more and more to come from the totalitarian nations, and with it the price of internal political influence from the totalitarian camp through the local pro-Moscow, or pro-Peking, Communist party. For everywhere there are such parties. They appear able to go on indefinitely in a dormant state, and can be awakened pretty much at will. India, with a population equal to that of the whole of Africa and South America combined, is the best current example. Parliamentary democracy is vigorous enough there [*] but economic incompetence on its part and diplomatic blunders on ours have led to an increasing dependence on Soviet support, which in the space of three years has brought about an open electoral alliance between the Congress party and the Moscow-oriented Communists, an alliance we would have thought worth fighting a war to prevent two decades ago, but which we scarcely notice today.

This alliance would not have come about save for the failure of the Indian economy to prosper and the success—typical—of the argument that the cure for the damage done by leftist policies is even more leftist policies, which in practice translates into dependence on the Soviets and alliances with their internal allies. And here is the nub of the bad news: for all the attractions of this variety of socialist politics, it has proved, in almost all its versions, almost the world over, to be a distinctly poor means of producing wealth. Sharing wealth—perhaps. But not producing wealth. Who, having read British political journals over the past quarter-century, would be surprised to find that during this period (1950–73) the United Kingdom's share of the "Planetary Product" has been reduced from 5.8 to 3.1 per cent? Why then be surprised that those who have made British socialism their model have trouble taking off in the opposite direction? Yet even so, one must be surprised at the decline of economies such as those of Burma and Sri Lanka: immensely productive places not a generation ago. Sri Lanka, for example, having first got to the point where it was importing potatoes from Poland, has now got to the further point where it can no longer afford to do so. A recent survey of the Ceylonese economy in the *Far Eastern Economic Review* was entitled: "Conspiracy or Catastrophe?" For what else could explain such failure?

What else, that is, to those experiencing it (with all that implies for political instability)? The outsider can indulge a more relaxed view. The fault lies in ideas, not persons. Americans—Westerners—do not have any claim to superior wisdom on the subject of these economies. Starting in the 1950's a large number of first-rate economists began working on theories of economic growth designed to get the LDC's on a path of self-sustained growth. "To be perfectly brutal about it," Jesse Burkhead recently stated, "it hasn't worked." And yet there is no need to stand mute. Two assertions may be reasonably put forth, of which the first is that to say these economies haven't worked as well as hoped is not to say that none has worked at all. There *has* been growth. In the main, things are better than they were. For every Argentina—that "miracle" of economic nongrowth—there is a Brazil. For Ghana, Nigeria. For Calcutta, Singapore. The second assertion is that relative failure is particularly to be encountered in economies most heavily influenced by that version of late Fabian economics which compounded the Edwardian view that there was plenty to go around if

[*Editor's Note: See Introduction to Part One for changes in Indian "democracy."]

justly distributed with the 1930's view that capitalism could never produce enough to go around regardless of distributive principles.*

Still, there are gains in the relative loss of income associated with the managed economies of the Third World which need to be appreciated. An Asian economist has said of his own country, plaintively yet not without a certain defiance: "We are socialists, so we do not believe in capitalism. We are democrats, so we do not believe in terror. What, then, is our alternative save one per cent a year?" There *is* a welfare state of sorts; there is protection of industrial labor; and in some countries, at least, there is freedom to protest.

But the most distinctive gain and the least noted is that in the course of its outward journey, the managed economy was transmuted from an instrument of economic rationality to an instrument of political rationality. It is sometimes difficult to recall, but early socialist theory expounded the greater *efficiency* of production for use rather than for capital, and put much stress on capitalist wastefulness. In practice, however, the real attraction of the managed economy has been the means it provides to collect enough political power at the center to maintain national unity—almost everywhere a chancy thing in these generally multi-ethnic states.

One must still conclude, however, that these political gains are purchased at the expense of even more conspicuous economic losses. India will serve for a final example. In the year of its independence, 1947, India produced 1.2 million tons of steel and Japan only 900,000 tons. A quarter-century later, in 1972, India produced 6.8 million tons and Japan 106.8. These outcomes are the result of decisions made by the ruling party of each nation, and only an innocent child could continue to accept Indian protestations that the results were unexpected. The break in Indian growth came precisely in 1962 when the United States, which had been about to finance its largest aid project ever, a steel complex at Bokharo in Eastern India, insisted that it be managed privately. India insisted on a public-sector plant, for which read a plant that would do what the Prime Minister of India wanted done. In the manner of the Aswan Dam (and with as much political impact), the Russians stepped in to finance the public-sector plant. By 1974 this plant had yet to produce sheet steel. For the period 1962–72 Indian steel production grew by a bare 1.8 per cent, while Japanese grew 13.4 per cent.

There is no serious way to deny that India has in a very real sense desired this outcome, just as there is no way to deny that high living standards in the modern world are associated with relatively free market economies and with liberalist international trade policies.

---

*This latter idea is very much alive. On leaving my post as United States Ambassador to India, I gave a press conference in which *inter alia* I touched upon the failure of India to achieve a productive economy. The *National Herald,* the Nehru family newspaper, commented in an editorial: "Mr. Moynihan may be justified in some of his criticism of the state of the Indian economy, but what he is trying to sell is the capitalist system which can only impoverish India's millions further."

Granted that much economic policy does not have high living standards as its true objective, but is rather concerned with political stability, and granted that such a concern may be wholly legitimate in a new nation—in any event it is not anyone else's business—it nevertheless remains the case that the relative economic failure accompanying political success in regimes such as that of India sooner or later begins to undermine that very success. Promises are made and political stability, especially in the more democratic regimes, requires some measure of performance. When it is not forthcoming, regimes change. They become less democratic. They become less independent.

Neither of these developments can be welcomed by the United States. The United States in the past may have cared about the course of political events in these nations, but only in the most abstract terms. (Consider the casualness with which we armed Pakistan and incurred the bitter and enduring hostility of India, the second most populous nation in the world.) But India has now exploded a nuclear device. *That* may well prove the most important event of the turbulent year 1974. Other Third World nations are likely to follow. Hence political stability in the Third World acquires a meaning it simply has never in the past had for American strategic thinking, as well as our general view of world politics.

IV

What then is to be done? We are witnessing the emergence of a world order dominated arithmetically by the countries of the Third World. This order is already much too developed for the United States or any other nation to think of opting out. It can't be done. One may become a delinquent in this nascent world society. An outcast in it. But one remains "in" it. There is no escape from a definition of nationhood which derives primarily from the new international reality. Nor does this reality respond much to the kind of painfully impotent threats which are sometimes heard of America's "pulling out." Anyone who doubts that Dubai can pay for UNESCO, knows little of UNESCO, less of what the United States pays, and nothing whatever of Dubai.

In any event, matters of this sort aside, world society and world organization have evolved to the point where palpable interests are disposed in international forums to a degree without precedent. Witness, as an instance, the decisions of the World Court allocating the oil fields of the North Sea among the various littoral states in distinctly weighted (but no doubt proper) manner. Witness the current negotiations at the Law of the Sea Conference. Two-thirds of the world is covered by the sea, and the United Nations claims the seabed. That seabed, especially in the region around Hawaii, is rich in so-called "manganese nodules"—concentrations of ore which American technology is now able to exploit, or will be sooner than anyone else. At this moment we have, arguably, complete and perfect freedom to commence industrial use of the high seas. This freedom is being challenged, however, and almost certainly some form of international regime is about to be established.

It can be a regime that permits American technology to go forward on some kind of license-and-royalties basis. Or it can assert exclusive "internationalized" rights to exploitation in an international public corporation. The stakes are considerable. They are enormous.

And then, of course, there remains the overriding interest, a true international interest, in arms control, and here true international government has emerged in a most impressive manner. If we were to ask who is the most important international official, a persuasive case could be made for choosing the Inspector General of the International Atomic Energy Authority, the man who supervises the safeguard agreements of the world's atomic reactors. Few would know the name of this unobtrusive Swiss chemist; few, perhaps, need to. But more than a few do need to know that the post is there and that its viability derives ultimately from the international system of which it is a part. For the moment, American security derives primarily from our own armaments, and our strategic agreements with the Soviet Union and a few other powers. But the international regime of arms control is already important and certain to become more so.

If, that is, it does not go down in the general wreckage of the world system embodied now in the United Nations. But assuming that the new majority will not destroy the regime through actions that drive nations like the United States away, is it not reasonable to anticipate a quasi-parliamentary situation at the international level—the General Assembly and a dozen such forums—in which a nominally radical majority sets about legislating its presumed advantage in a world which has just come into its hands? The qualification "quasi-parliamentary" is necessary, for in fact the pronouncements of these assemblies have but limited force. So did the pronouncements of the Continental Congress. They are not on that ground to be ignored. What then does the United States do?

The United States goes into opposition. This is our circumstance. We are a minority. We are outvoted. This is neither an unprecedented nor an intolerable situation. The question is what do we make of it. So far we have made little—nothing—of what is in fact an opportunity. We go about dazed that the world has changed. We toy with the idea of stopping it and getting off. We rebound with the thought that if only we are more reasonable perhaps "they" will be. (Almost to the end, dominant opinion in the U.S. Mission to the United Nations was that the United States could not vote against the "have-nots" by opposing the Charter on the Rights and Duties of States—all rights for the Group of 77 and no duties.) But "they" do not grow reasonable. Instead, we grow unreasonable. A sterile enterprise which awaits total redefinition.

Going into opposition requires first of all that we recognize that there is a distinctive ideology at work in the Third World, and that it has a distinctive history and logic. To repeat the point once again, we have not done this, tending to see these new political cultures in our own image, or in that of the totalitarians, with a steady shift in the general perception from the former to the latter. But once we perceive the coherence in the majority, we will be in a position to reach for a certain coherence of opposition.

Three central issues commend themselves as points of systematic attack: first, the condition of international liberalism; second, the world economy; third, the state of political and civil liberties and of the general welfare. The rudiments of these arguments need only be sketched.

It is the peculiar function of "radical" political demands, such as those most recently heard in the international forums, that they bring about an exceptional deprecation of the achievements of liberal processes. Even when the radicalism is ultimately rejected, this is rarely from a sense that established processes do better and promise more. American liberalism experienced this deprecation in the 1960's; international liberalism is undergoing it in the 1970's. But the truth is that international liberalism and its processes have enormous recent achievements to their credit. It is time for the United States to start saying so.

One example is the multinational corporation which, combining modern management with liberal trade policies, is arguably the most creative international institution of the 20th century. A less controversial example is the World Health Organization. In 1966 it set out to abolish smallpox, and by the time this article is read, the job will more than likely have been successfully completed—in very significant measure with the techniques and participation of American epidemiologists. While not many Americans have been getting smallpox of late, the United States has been spending $140 million a year to keep it that way. Savings in that proportion and more will immediately follow. Here, as in a very long list, a liberal world policy has made national sense.

We should resist the temptation to designate agreeable policies as liberal merely on grounds of agreeableness. There are harder criteria. Liberal policies are limited in their undertakings, concrete in their means, representative in their mode of adoption, and definable in terms of results. These are surely the techniques appropriate to a still tentative, still emergent world society. It is time for the United States, as the new society's loyal opposition, to say this directly, loudly, forcefully.

The economic argument—which will appear inconsistent only to those who have never been much in politics—is that the world economy is not nearly bad enough to justify the measures proposed by the majority, and yet is much worse than it would otherwise be in consequence of measures the majority has already taken. The first half of this formulation will require a considerable shift in the government mind, and possibly even some movement in American elite opinion also, for we have become great producers and distributors of crisis. The world environment crisis, the world population crisis, the world food crisis are in the main American discoveries—or inventions, opinions differ. Yet the simple and direct fact is that any crisis the United States takes to an international forum in the foreseeable future will be decided to the disadvantage of the United States. (Let us hope arms control is an exception.) Ergo: skepticism, challenge.

The world economy is the most inviting case for skepticism, although it will be difficult to persuade many Americans of this during an American recession, and although the rise in oil prices is now creating a crisis in the Third World which is neither of American contrivance nor of American discovery nor of American intervention. But until the dislocations caused by OPEC, things were simply not as bad as they were typically portrayed. *Things were better than they had been.* Almost everywhere. In many places things were very good indeed. Sir Arthur Lewis summed up the evidence admirably:

> We have now had nearly three decades of rapid economic growth. . . . Output per head has been growing in the developed world twice as fast as at any time within the preceding century. In the LDC world, output per head is not growing as fast as in the developed world, but is growing faster than the developed world used to grow.

The data can be quite startling. In 1973, as Sir Arthur was speaking, the "Planetary Product," as estimated by the Bureau of Intelligence and Research of the Department of State, grew at a real rate of 6.8 per cent, an astonishing figure. The Third World product expanded by 5.75 per cent, no less astonishing.

Simultaneously it is to be asserted that these economies do less well than they ought: that the difference is of their own making and no one else's, and no claim on anyone else arises in consequence. This will be hard for us to do, but it is time we did it. It is time we commenced citing men such as Jagdish N. Bhagwati; Professor of Economics at MIT, an Indian by birth, who stated in the Lal Bahadur Shastri lectures in India in 1973:

> In the 1950's our economic programs were considered by the progressive and democratic opinion abroad to be a model of what other developing countries might aspire to and emulate. Today, many of us spend our time trying desperately to convince others that *somehow* all the success stories elsewhere are special cases and that our performance is not as unsatisfactory as it appears. And yet, we must confront the fact that, in the ultimate analysis, despite our socialist patter and our planning efforts, we have managed to show neither rapid growth nor significant reduction of income inequality and poverty.

It is time we asserted, with Sir Arthur—a socialist, a man of the Third World—that economic growth is governed not by Western or American conspiracies, but by its own laws and that it "is not an egalitarian process. It is bound to be more vigorous in some professions, or sectors, or geographical regions than in others, and even to cause some impoverishment."

A commentator in *The Statesman,* Calcutta's century-old and most prestigious journal, recently warned:

> It would be unwise for policy planners in the developing world to dismiss too easily . . . the basic premise of a society that worships success: if you

are poor, you have only yourself to blame. Development is a matter of
hard work and discipline. So if you are not developing fast, it is not because the rules of the game are stacked against you or that structural
changes are never easy to bring about, but because you are lazy and indis-
ciplined. The general disenchantment with economic aid flows from this.
It is difficult for Americans to understand why such substantial flows of
food and money have made so little impact.

Well, the time may have come when it is necessary for Americans
to say, "Yes, it *is* difficult to understand that." Not least because some
Third World economies have done so very well. For if Calcutta has the
lowest urban standard of living in the world, Singapore has in some
ways the highest. It is time we asserted that inequalities in the world
may be not so much a matter of condition as of performance. The Brazilians do well. The Israelis. The Nigerians. The Taiwanese. It is a good
argument. Far better, surely, than the repeated plea of *nolo contendere*
which we have entered, standing accused and abased before the
Tribune of the People.

Cataloguing the economic failings of other countries is something
to be done out of necessity, not choice. But speaking for political and
civil liberty, and doing so in detail and in concrete particulars, is
something that can surely be undertaken by Americans with enthusiasm and zeal. Surely it is not beyond us, when the next Social
Report comes along, to ask about conditions and events in many countries of the Third World of which almost everyone knows, but few have
thought it politic to speak. The AFL-CIO does it. Freedom House does
it. Amnesty International does it. *American* socialists do it. The time has
come for the spokesmen of the United States to do it too.

It is time, that is, that the American spokesman came to be feared
in international forums for the truths he might tell. Mexico, which has
grown increasingly competitive in Third World affairs, which took the
lead in the Declaration of the Economic Rights and Duties, preaches
international equity. Yet it preaches domestic equity also. It could not
without some cost expose itself to a repeated inquiry as to the extent of
equity within its own borders. Nor would a good many other Third
World countries welcome a sustained comparison between the liberties they provide their own peoples with those which are common and
taken for granted in the United States.

For the United States to go into opposition in this manner not only
requires a recognition of the ideology of the Third World, but a
reversal of roles for American spokesmen as well. As if to compensate
for its aggressiveness about what might be termed Security Council affairs, the United States has chosen at the UN to be extraordinarily
passive, even compliant, about the endless goings-on in the Com-
missions and Divisions and Centers and suchlike elusive enterprises
associated with the Economic and Social Council. Men and women
were assigned to these missions, but have rarely been given much support, or even much scrutiny. Rather, the scrutiny has been of just the
wrong kind, ever alert to deviation from the formula platitudes of UN

debate, and hopelessly insensitive to the history of political struggles of
the 20th century.

In Washington, three decades of habit and incentive have created
patterns of appeasement so profound as to seem wholly normal. Delegations to international conferences return from devastating defeats
proclaiming victory. In truth, these have never been thought especially
important. Taking seriously a Third World speech about, say, the right
of commodity producers to market their products in concert and to
raise their prices in the process, would have been the mark of the
quixotic or the failed. To consider the intellectual antecedents of such
propositions would not have occurred to anyone, for they were not
thought to have any.

And yet how interesting the results might be. The results, say, of
observing the occasion of an Algerian's assuming the Presidency of the
General Assembly with an informed tribute to the career of the libera-
tor Ben Bella, still presumedly rotting in an Algerian prison cell. The
results of a discourse on the disparities between the (1973) per-capita
GNP in Abu Dhabi of $43,000 and that of its neighbor, the Democratic
People's Republic of Yemen, with one-thousandth that. Again, this
need not be a uniformly scornful exercise; anything but. The Third
World has more than its share of attractive regimes, and some attractive indeed—Costa Rica, Gambia, Malaysia, to name but three. Half the
people in the world who live under a regime of civil liberties live in
India.[*] The point is to differentiate, and to turn their own standards
against regimes for the moment too much preoccupied with causing
difficulties for others, mainly the United States. If this has been in
order for some time, the oil price increase—devastating to the development hopes of half-a-hundred Asian and African and Latin American
countries—makes it urgent and opportune in a way it has never been.

Such a reversal of roles would be painful to American spokesmen,
but it could be liberating also. It is past time we ceased to apologize for
an imperfect democracy. Find its equal. It is time we grew out of our
initial—not a little condescending—supersensitivity about the feelings
of new nations. It is time we commenced to treat them as equals, a
respect to which they are entitled.

The case is formidable that there is nothing the Third World
needs less—especially now that the United States has so much withdrawn—than to lapse into a kind of cargo cult designed to bring about
our return through imprecation and threat rather than the usual in-
vocations. The Third World has achieved independence, and it needs
to assert it in a genuine manner. The condition of the developing countries is in significant measure an imported condition. In the main a distinctive body of European ideas has taken hold, not everywhere in the
same measure. Sri Lanka will be more cerebrate in its socialism than
will, say, Iraq, Brazil more given to actual economic expansion than
Syria or Egypt, Algeria considerably less libertarian than Nigeria. Still,

[*Editor's Note: See Introduction to Part One.]

there is a recognizable pattern to the economic and political postures of these countries, of which the central reality is that their anti-capitalist, anti-imperialist ideologies are in fact themselves the last stage of colonialism. These are imported ideas every bit as much as the capitalist and imperialist ideas to which they are opposed. The sooner they are succeeded by truly indigenous ideas, the better off all the former colonies will be, the United States included.

The Third World must feed itself, for example, and this will not be done by suggesting that Americans eat too much. It is one thing to stress what is consumed in the West, another to note what is produced there. In 1973, 17.8 per cent of the world's population produced 64.3 per cent of its product—and not just from taking advantage of cheap raw materials.

In the same way, the Third World has almost everywhere a constitutional heritage of individual liberty, and it needs to be as jealous of that heritage as of the heritage of national independence. It should be a source of renown that India, for one, has done that, and of infamy that so many others have not.

Not long ago, Alexander Solzhenitsyn, speaking of the case of a Soviet dissident who had been detained in a mental hospital, asked whether world opinion would ever permit South Africa to detain a black African leader in this fashion. Answering his own question, he said, "The storm of worldwide rage would have long ago swept the roof from that prison!" His point is very like the one Stephen Spender came to in the course of the Spanish Civil War. Visiting Spain, he encountered atrocities of the Right, and atrocities of the Left. But only those of the Right were being written about, and it came to him, as he later put it, that if one did not care about every murdered child indiscriminately, one did not really care about children being murdered at all. Very well. But nothing we finally know about the countries of the Third World (only in part the object of the Solzhenitsyn charge) warrants the conclusion that they will be concerned only for wrongdoing that directly affects *them*. Ethnic solidarity is not the automatic enemy of civil liberties. It has been the foundation of many. If there are any who can blow off the roof of any such prison—then all credit to them. If you can be against the wrongful imprisonment of a person anywhere, then you can be against wrongful imprisonment everywhere.

It is in precisely such terms that we can seek common cause with the new nations: granted that they, no more than we, are likely ever wholly to live up to either of our protestations. Yet there exists the strongest possibility of an accommodating relationship at the level of principle—a possibility that does not exist at all with the totalitarian powers as they are now constituted. To contemplate an oppositional role to the Soviet bloc, or the Chinese, in, say, the General Assembly would be self-deceptive. One may negotiate there as between separate political communities, but to participate as in a single community— even in opposition—would simply not be possible. We can, however, have such a relation with most Third World nations. And we can do so while speaking for and in the name of political and civil liberty.

And equality, what of it? Here an act of historical faith is required: what is the record? The record was stated most succinctly by an Israeli socialist who told William F. Buckley, Jr. that those nations which have put liberty ahead of equality have ended up doing better by equality than those with the reverse priority. This is so, and being so, it is something to be shouted to the heavens in the years now upon us. *This is our case.* We *are* of the liberty party, and it might surprise us what energies might be released were we to unfurl those banners.

In the spring of 1973, in his first address as director-designate of the London School of Economics—where Harold Laski once molded the minds of so many future leaders of the "new majority"—Ralf Dahrendorf sounded this theme. The equality party, he said, has had its day. The liberty party's time has come once more. It is a time to be shared with the new nations, and those not so new, shaped from the old European empires, and especially the British—and is the United States not one such?—whose heritage this is also. To have halted the great totalitarian advance only to be undone by the politics of resentment and the economics of envy would be a poor outcome to the promise of a world society. At the level of world affairs we have learned to deal with Communism. Our task is now to learn to deal with socialism. It will not be less difficult a task. It ought to be a profoundly more pleasant one.

6   The United States and the Third World: A Basis for Accommodation

Tom J. Farer

The United States has passed in the last decade from the United Nation's most influential state into a position of accelerating isolation as it confronts a very large proportion of the member states over a long agenda of contemporary issues. This is a truly novel development, one which threatens to poison international relations at a time that shrieks with the need for uniquely broad essays in international cooperation.

Three issues shape what may be called the North-South confrontation. One is the question of how global income and wealth and decision-making authority with respect to international economic problems should be distributed. A second issue is the attitude of the United States toward the two white-supremacist regimes in Southern Africa.

And the third is the U.S. role in the Arab-Israeli conflict. Although each issue represents a distinct axis of confrontation, they are linked by a single world view, a kind of ideology, which imparts to them an intense emotional coherence. That ideology is not, as suggested recently by Ambassador Moynihan, "socialist," unless one follows Durkheim in defining socialism not as a political program but rather as "a cry of pain." It does indeed incorporate certain themes which recur in British socialist thought, just as it patches in a number of conventionally liberal ideas such as self-determination. But socialist and liberal fragments are reshaped by a special historical experience to produce in practice a distinct amalgam which can most usefully be described as the developing states in fact describe it: "anticolonialism."

II

The paramount objective of the anticolonialist amalgam is the eradication of all the conditions and insignia of inequality and humiliation associated in the minds of the Southern elites with the epoch of European domination. This objective guides Southern positions across a broad spectrum of contemporary issues.

One vivid illustration of the adaptation of a Western liberal theme to the felt exigencies of anticolonialism is the contrasting attitude toward inequality and the deprivation of human rights in the white enclaves of Southern Africa, on the one hand, and various Third World states on the other. While the government of Burundi, for instance, was busily exterminating the entire elite of that country's majority tribe, its President received a message from the Council of Ministers of the Organization for African Unity stating that: "Thanks to your saving action, peace will be rapidly reestablished, national unity will be consolidated, and territorial integrity will be preserved." Uganda and Bangladesh could be added to the list of massacres ignored by all but a handful of Third World leaders.

The causes of immutable antagonism to South Africa and Rhodesia are evident: those societies are the residue of the European migrations which occurred during the colonial epoch, and they exemplify the racial subordination which added a special edge to colonial domination. Hence Africans everywhere participate vicariously in the travail of the suppressed black populations.

Sympathetic involvement naturally attenuates where the persecutors, as well as the victims, are non-white. But that in itself does not explain the resolute determination of the Southern bloc to ignore barbarous delinquencies committed by certain of its member governments. Something more positive than indifference is at work here. These delinquencies are, in the first place, an enormous embarrassment and a serious wound to the anticolonial movement because they seem to confirm the propaganda claims of the white racist regimes about the consequences of the loss of white supremacy. Although the wiser tactic might be to assume the lead in condemning the barbarity and proposing remedial measures, the evident instinct is to pretend it is not happening.

Perhaps that reaction stems in large measure from an inability to intervene to terminate the delinquency. Since developing states cannot intervene themselves, a call for remedial action must be addressed to the West, the homeland of colonialism. That alternative is intolerable, first for psychological reasons and secondly for the very practical one of avoiding any erosion of the barriers against intervention which the Third World has been busily constructing for the past fifteen years. The Southern elites have not forgotten that "humanitarian intervention" has been one of the favored legal and rhetorical justifications for Western interventions in the Southern Hemisphere in defense of political and economic interests. It was, for instance, one of the announced justifications for U.S. intervention in the Dominican Republic.

Fearing intervention in its own vulnerable polities, yet wanting it in South Africa, the Southern bloc has relentlessly deployed its legal and rhetorical ingenuity to impose a unique status on the southern African cases and thus to isolate the resulting precedents. Consistent with this effort was the refusal, prior to 1971, to expand the General Assembly's list of national liberation movements beyond those at work in South Africa, Rhodesia, and the Portugese Territories.

Burgeoning support in the Third World for the Arab states and the Palestine Liberation Organization (PLO) in their struggle with Israel also owes much to the anticolonialist world view. Yasir Arafat's address to the General Assembly a year ago culminated an accelerating shift in moral perception confirmed two years before by General Assembly Resolution 2787 (XVII) which for the first time included the "Palestinian people" in an authoritative enumeration of national liberation movements: i.e., those struggling "for . . . liberation from colonial and foreign domination and alien subjugation."

The PLO's legitimation could not have been accomplished without the support of the African caucus. To believe that its support for the PLO reflects simply a desperate need for petrodollars rather than any sense of moral solidarity is to practice self-deception. For some African leaders, need or greed would be enough. But not for all, not for men of such fierce moral commitment as Kaunda of Zambia and Nyerere of Tanzania.

Not many years ago, most African states, including Tanzania, enjoyed distinctly cordial relations with Israel. Israeli agricultural advisers surveyed the possibility of adapting the kibbutz to the necessities of Tanzania's rural development program. Its military advisers trained counterinsurgency forces in Ethiopia and elite paratroop units in Zaïre. Trade missions proliferated. Today, the missions and advisers, even the thinnest diplomatic relations, all are gone.

What, other than the pull of petrodollars, can explain this *volte face*? In part, there is here a certain guilt by association. At the same time that the gradual movement of European states, especially France, toward neutrality was leaving the United States as almost the only sure source of Israeli support, the United States was shuffling ostentatiously closer to colonialism and apartheid in South Africa. In this way, the issues became linked in the African mind. The Arab bloc helped along that linkage by offering heightened support for the struggle against the white regimes, a matter which, until 1973, had evoked its yawning indifference.

But that is only part of the explanation. The shift in African attitudes toward the Middle East conflict also arises, on the one hand, from the evolution of a coherent political-military organization able to incarnate a Palestinian identity and, on the other, the determined denial of that identity by Israeli officials, most notoriously by Golda Meir. This forged a second perceived link between the Israeli and South African cases. Much as South Africa sought to enhance its claims and fragment its indigenous opposition by describing its non-white population as a collection of separate nationalities, Israeli rhetoric tended to impose on the Palestinians the nationalities of the various states of their Diaspora.

Before the rise of the PLO, most non-Arab governments saw the Arab-Israeli issue as a problem of interstate relations with a refugee dimension. But after 1967, when the PLO ceased to be a passive instrument of one or another Arab state, Palestinians generally began to think of themselves as a nation rather than simply the former inhabitants of Haifa or Jerusalem or some obscure village from which they or their parents had fled years ago; then they assumed the familiar characteristics of a true national independence movement.

One of those characteristics is a distinct territory to which the PLO can lay claim. Most non-Arab states were not disposed to challenge the legitimacy of the frontiers carved out by the Israelis in 1948 in defense of rights accorded to them by the United Nations. So as long as the remainder of the West Bank of Mandate Palestine was seen to be part of Jordan, the Palestinians had difficulty associating themselves with a territory widely perceived to be legitimately theirs. Israeli occupation of the West Bank and the justifications announced by some authoritative Israelis for keeping at least a part of the seized territory helped to expose the tenuous moral and legal basis for Jordanian suzerainty. The net result was to make the occupied territory seem available for appropriation by Arab Palestinians. Thus the Palestinian people, having acquired almost simultaneously both a recognizable political personality and a potential territorial base, could be integrated into the anticolonial honor roll.

Taken seriously, anticolonialism helps to explain the moral double standard, the obsessive concern with developments in the white enclaves of Southern Africa, and the crystallization of a politicized sympathy among many Southern Hemisphere elites for non-Jewish Palestinians. But as a key to understanding it is even more useful in the economic realm which is today the main battleground for the United States and the Third World. Most dramatically, it is this sentiment that has helped greatly to glue together a solid front of Third World support for the exercise of monopoly power by the Organization of Petroleum Exporting Countries (OPEC). In comparison with its destructive impact on the majority of non-Arab developing states, the stratospheric leap of oil prices is little more than a minor inconvenience to the West. Yet when Westerners speak of military intervention to lower the price for *all* users, or even of concentrated economic pressures to that end, one listens in vain for any sign of Southern support.

The silence of some oil-poor countries may be attributable to their hope of participating in an effective producer's cartel for another Southern product. But there are at least several dozen states which have not the slightest hope of exploiting the OPEC precedent, and there are many others for whom the prospect of an effective cartel is decidedly remote. Then why the deep reservoir of sympathy for OPEC?

By describing North-South disputes concerning economic issues as a struggle over the distribution of wealth, Northern analysts assimilate them into a familiar form of social conflict. But if nothing more were at stake, one would anticipate defections from the Southern bloc particularly on an issue like oil prices. If, however, one returns to the conception of anticolonialism as an elite's deeply emotional response to a sense of humiliation, then solidarity ceases to be surprising, or at least no more surprising in its way than solidarity among classes in Western states during the two world wars. Perhaps it should be even less surprising, because while a member of the English working class could attribute particular privations to the policies of the upper classes—at a minimum, the bloody suppression of his strikes—the life-style of elites in oil-poor states is largely unaffected by the price of oil. Only the masses suffer and they do not make or seriously influence foreign policy.

It is far less surprising for yet another reason. The average Englishman had never met a Hun. His animosity was entirely vicarious. But all Southern elites have experienced immediately one or more facets of colonial behavior, if not outright domination then at least a searing patronization. They are the leaders of countries once alleged by Western scholars and diplomats to be incapable of participating in the international legal system because they were not "civilized states." They spring from peoples to whom the Laws of War did not apply according to the diktat of the West. They and their countrymen have been and remain to this day objects of study by the cultural institutions of the West. For hundreds of years they have been people to whom things happen. And that is in significant measure why all cheer when a few of their number find the strength to stand up and lash out at the source of their historical torment.

In this respect, close-to universal Southern support for OPEC is only one sign of the subordination of economic interests to ideological preoccupations. A second is the incessant campaign against the obligation, enshrined in the classical system of international law, to compensate the alien owners of expropriated property.

The very fact that most Western scholars and diplomats speak of the obligation as if its existence were unquestioned is a sign of an earlier epoch's ethnocentrism. Latin American governments and scholars consistently urged the view that international law required nothing more than equality of treatment for indigenous and foreign investors. Yet, although they pulled all the right buttons on the international legal console and pedaled vigorously, they might as well have been silent for all the effect they had on the views expounded in Western universities and chancelleries or, for that matter, on the gunboats and marines dispatched periodically to enforce the "law."

Recent changes in both theory and behavior, centering particularly on methods for evaluating expropriated enterprises, have opened the door to compromise. So far, no one has walked in. As evidenced in the debate over the Charter of Economic Rights and Duties of States, adopted in December 1974 by the U.N. General Assembly, the Southern bloc continues to demand Western acknowledgment of the death of the international standard. One is reminded of the old Welsh proverb: "The dumb will wait a long time at the door of the deaf."

George Lichtheim was right when he wrote: "No ruling class can function without a creed." One facet of the creed of the ruling class in the West is the sanctity of property. Third World elites know that. Hence they must be fairly confident that they will not secure the acknowledgment they seek. Moreover, even if through some accelerated atrophy of will the United States made the demanded concession, so far as the North-South transfer of wealth is concerned little if anything would have been gained.

What, after all, are the main restraints on confiscation? Clearly not the threat of force. That option was interred in 1956 when the Anglo-French entente flinched at Suez. Nor, in most cases, is it the threatened loss of bilateral economic assistance, the proportions of which have shrunk to the edge of insignificance for most Southern nations. Rather it is the threatened loss of private credit and private investment. And that risk cannot be affected by a formally recognized change in the legal standard. Whatever the standard, private capital will not flow to states ruled by regimes with a penchant for confiscation.

If, as suggested, the issue of compensation is at best marginally relevant to the distribution of wealth and, in any event, the Southern bloc is waging a campaign which it cannot hope to win unequivocally, its furious persistence must reflect something more than a set of shrewdly calculated economic claims. What it does reflect, I would submit, is the claim to autonomy, to insulation from appraisal, let alone intervention, by the governments of Western capitalist states. It is, in short, a collective cry of defiance.

III

Are there positions available to the United States within the confines defined by its history, its ideology and its domestic politics which, if adopted, would moderate its acerb dialogue with the developing states and thus enhance the prospects for cooperation on the global issues which will not submit to unilateral or even regional manipulation?

If anticolonialism, as defined above, is in fact the paramount source of cohesion in the Third World, one necessary consequence is the intense links it forges among all the issues which it touches. Hence, the successful accommodation of U.S.-Third World differences on some issues would necessarily enhance the prospects for accommodation all along the line. A second corollary of the main proposition is the importance of gestures. It is not only what the United States does that matters; what it says also counts. After all, some of the most damaging humiliations of the colonial relationship were a function of Western rhetoric and the patronizing and contemptuous attitudes which it embodied and to a not inconsiderable extent continues to embody. It is, for instance, still commonplace for Anglo-American "experts" on the Arab world to refer to the "Arab mind" as if it were an unchanging and slightly bizarre object of disinterested study. Yet, as Arab intellectuals wryly note, if one were to speak of a "Jewish mind" there would be an immediate outcry from organs of respectable opinion against the sort of crude stereotyping which the term implies.

The single issue most readily susceptible to accommodation is U.S. policy toward the white-supremacist regimes of Southern Africa. By its consistent behavior, the United States has managed in two decades to transform its image from that of Black Africa's best friend in the West to its most dangerous adversary. Most of the hard work was accomplished during the national stewardship of Richard Nixon and Henry Kissinger.

Early evidence of their tilt toward increased cooperation with the triumvirate of South Africa, pre-1974 Portugal and the illegal Smith regime in Rhodesia was the failure to mobilize effective opposition to the chrome amendment, which opened the doors of the U.S economy to the full range of Rhodesian mineral exports in clear violation of our obligations under the U.N. Charter. Another piece of hard evidence was Washington's loosening of the ban on the sale of military hardware to the Portuguese and the South Africans. Items clearly susceptible to military applications, including computers (for many years banned for security reasons from East-West trade), light planes, and helicopters, were treated as civilian products. In addition, large commercial planes were sold to the Portuguese with no restriction on their use as troop carriers and with the expectation that they would in fact be used for that purpose.

The tilt was magnified by the strident, largely isolated position hacked out by the United States in response to a series of General Assembly resolutions on the situation in Southern Africa. For instance, in 1973, at the 28th session of the Assembly, the Afro-Asian bloc introduced a resolution calling for the formation of a commission of inquiry concerning the reported massacres in Mozambique carried out by the Portuguese army (Res. 3114). It was passed by a vote of 104 to 4 with 12 abstentions. The United States joined Portugal, South Africa, and Spain in casting the four negative votes.

During the same session, the Afro-Asian bloc introduced three resolutions on the Rhodesian situation. The United States opposed all three, including one condemning South Africa and Portugal for violating sanctions imposed by the Security Council—violations established by incontestable evidence—and calling on all states to comply strictly with the economic embargo. On one vote it was joined by Portugal, South Africa, and the United Kingdom; on another, this group was swelled by the addition of France. And on the third, the United States could muster no company other than the pariahs of pre-revolutionary Portugal and South Africa.

The following year, with South Africa out of action and Portugal rehabilitated, the United States found itself utterly alone when it voted against a toughened iteration of the Assembly's earlier request for a comprehensive embargo on arms for South Africa (Res. 3324, Para. B). Even a plea for the release of political prisoners in South Africa could not summon U.S. support. The vote was 118 to 0, with two abstentions—the United States and Malawi (Res. 3324, Para. C).

Accommodation is possible here because Black African leaders ask so little of the United States. And much of that little is essentially rhetorical. So modest a gesture as endorsing the view championed by Kaunda and Nyerere that when all peaceful means have been exhausted, any oppressed people may turn legitimately to violence as a last recourse would transform the tone of our relations with the African caucus. And what is such a statement other than a reaffirmation of the Declaration of Independence? Yet the U.S. government continues to insist on a "peaceful solution" in such a way as to imply hostility to violence under any circumstances, thus distorting its own historical traditions while contributing nothing to the "peaceful solution."

Another modest gesture, one even more clearly within the bounds of domestic political realities, would be a determined effort by the Administration to secure repeal of the chrome amendment and to prosecute energetically any U.S.-related companies and individuals who conspire to evade the economic sanctions mandated by the Security Council. The failure of the U.S. government to meet its treaty commitments in this regard makes a mockery of its critique of procedural irregularities at the United Nations. Not only would this return to legality assuage African bitterness, but it would have the additional merit of fortifying respect for the sanctity of international agreements, a matter of some considerable importance to a powerful state preferring order over charge.

There are an array of other low-cost measures available to an American Administration which placed significant value on the amelioration of its relations with the Third World. On the material side, it could widen the ban on the sale of military goods to South Africa; this could be accomplished by employing definitions of strategic goods used in the past to restrict sales to China and the Soviet Union. It could also follow the British lead in using the country's foreign intelligence apparatus to detect violations of Rhodesian sanctions by the nationals of other states. And it could initiate special educational programs openly designed to prepare black Rhodesians, Namibians and South Africans for the assumption of political, administrative, and highly skilled technical roles in societies purged of white-supremacist conceits.

On the symbolic side, it could agree to join the United Nations Council on Namibia, it could declare its opposition to any South African-imposed solution for the Namibian problem which would fragment the country and concentrate its natural resources in minority hands, and it could not merely support but actively sponsor resolutions in the political organs of the United Nations calling on South Africa for the release of political prisoners and the progressive elimination of racial criteria for the enjoyment of social, economic, and cultural rights.

These modest steps would not commit us to a particular political solution. Nor would they be inconsistent with frank acknowledgment that the unique historical circumstances of South Africa make it difficult to safeguard the rights of all its peoples within the context of a single centralized state. We would simply be taking a stand on behalf of a fair division of that tragic country's vast resources, a result which might be achieved by a variety of electoral mechanisms and an equitable allocation of territory. Since opposition to ethnic and racial discrimination flows directly, albeit sporadically, from our central moral tradition, it should command the support of authentic conservatives as well as liberals.

Right now the question of the Palestinians stands at the other end of the spectrum of tractability. The Israeli government and almost surely a large majority of its electorate are convinced that a wholly independent Palestinian presence on the West Bank represents an intolerable threat to the security of the Israeli state.

Many Israelis cite declarations of the PLO to prove that the Palestinians categorically reject coexistence. Yet many of the same Israelis deride the PLO's claim to represent the Palestinian people. One cannot have it both ways, particularly when one has done everything in one's power to prevent the Palestinians from acquiring a political form in which they could at least speak for themselves. The Israelis some years ago dismantled an Arab nationalist party within their own state and have effectively suppressed political activities on the West Bank since the beginning of the occupation.

There is, moreover, the question of mutual recognition. While the rudimentary organs of self-expression now possessed by the Palestinians withold recognition of Israel, their mirror image is the government of Israel which, since the failure of partition, has generally denied that the Palestinians are a distinct people with a peculiar historical attachment to the villages and towns and cities of Mandate Palestine rather than an essentially indistinguishable part of the surrounding Arab world.

In private, Palestinian intellectuals often insist that official Israeli recognition that non-Jewish Palestinians also have legitimate territorial claims on the West Bank would open the door to genuine reconciliation. Yet one cannot fault the Israelis for hesitating. They accepted the original United Nations decision to divide the land. They were compelled to fight in defense of the land ceded to them. And to this day even the ablest and most morally sensitive Arabs, after alleging their grudging acceptance of Israel as an immutable fact, in the next breath wistfully imagine the ultimate "peaceful" assimilation of Israel into a larger state system in which Judaism would lose its political form.

There is every reason to take seriously the stated determination of Israel to fight yet a fifth war rather than concede on issues deemed fundamental to its long-term security. The present Israeli government may be erroneously calculating the risks of negotiating directly with the Palestinians or of recognizing in any other way their right to self-determination in the West Bank occupied territories. But so long as it hews to the view that such recognition threatens vital security interests, the ability of the United States to remove the issue of the Palestinians from its confrontation agenda with the Third World is powerfully circumscribed. Domestic political realities, moral commitments, international credibility, and the threat to Western interests immanent in any outbreak of conflict in the Middle East—all preclude the theoretical option of abandonment.

On the other hand, the United States need not act as if it were completely paralyzed by Israeli immobility. In the end, the Arab-Israeli conflict can be resolved peacefully only by agreement over the repartition of Palestine. Suppose the United States were openly to characterize the conflict in these terms while coincidentally announcing its resolve not to exercise leverage on behalf of partition until the Arabs demonstrate that they are at last reconciled to it. Such a gesture might simultaneously strengthen our relations with the major Arab states while bolstering those political forces within Israel willing, for moral and practical reasons, to explore the grounds for compromise with their fellow Palestinians. But its main virtue would be to soften our image as an intractable opponent of change by indicating that whatever we may think of their present set of leaders, we are not deaf to the appeals of the Palestinian people.

IV

There are few more contentious questions in American public life today than the possibility and desirability of accommodation with the Third World on so-called economic issues.

The anti-accommodationists, exemplified in the writings of Patrick Moynihan and Irving Kristol, argue along the following lines: The Third World is attempting to extort—through economic blackmail, moral bullying, and outright theft—a portion of the West's legitimately acquired wealth. The declared justification for redistributive claims, compensation for colonial and neocolonial exploitation, has no basis in fact. As Kristol, echoing Moynihan, has declared, Third World "economies do less well than they ought: . . . the difference is of their own making and no one else's, and no claim on anyone else arises in consequence." The West's failure to reject this justification simply encourages ever more arrogant, extortionate demands. Gestures of accommodation, both rhetorical and substantive, are construed by the Third World as evidence of a loss of will. Which, in fact, they are. And so the demands, by their nature insatiable for there is no practical limit to the "reparations" which can be justified under the theory of compensation, can only grow.

While rhetorical accommodation is said to sap our will while bolstering theirs, substantive accommodation is said to have still more serious consequences. A "New International Economic Order" designed to equalize rather than to produce wealth will undermine the incentives to efficiency, rationality, fiscal discipline and hard work which lie at the root of the First World's productivity and hence of its wealth. In absolute terms, the economic decline of the West is detrimental to the Third World as well. But that will not affect the views of Third World elites because they are essentially disinterested in productivity. What matters to them are relative shares. Now is the time to take a stand, it is claimed. If we consent to new structures which simultaneously shrink the economic pie and leave a smaller percentage in the hands of the West, it will be progressively more difficult to resist at a later date.

Implicit, sometimes explicit, in this line of argument is the claim that the developed states still deploy sufficient power to resist the Third World's redistributive efforts. The latter is portrayed largely as a paper tiger, faking it with éclat, to be sure, but still faking it. Precisely why we should regard the Southern bloc in this light has yet to be adequately explained. In the writings of Kristol and Moynihan and other such neo-conservatives one looks in vain for a serious effort to project the costs of the coercive measures required to assure continuing access to the resources and growing markets of the Third World. Seemingly buried in their subconscious is the idea that colonial rule was relinquished as an act of grace. In fact, as John Strachey and other students of imperialism have demonstrated, the colonial retreat was a grudging concession that once the Third World became infected with the virus of self-determination, the price of domination became intolerable.

For decades, France occupied Vietnam with an army of less than 20,000 men. But once the dormant idea of national independence came round again, the United States could not hold half of the country with 500,000 men and a million native auxiliaries. The proliferation of modern weapons in the Third World can only increase the costs of coercion. Moreover, the level of destruction required to reassert a Northern imperium would in many instances jeopardize the very economic ends for which the effort would be made.

Much anti-accommodationist rhetoric is unremarkably reminiscent of the haute bourgeoisie's response to working-class demands during the ascendancy of laissez-faire economics. The poor were deservedly so, the rich as well. The distribution of wealth was determined by the free market which in turn reflected an individual's net contribution to productivity. The poor were profligate, incapable of postponing consumption. Any effort to tamper with the workings of the market would reduce the wealth of the nation without any corresponding benefit to the poor who would only dissipate it in reckless consumption. To compromise with these basic principles was to threaten the whole structure of legitimacy, including private property and democratic liberties. (That the men propounding these views were often hard at work substituting their hands for the invisible one of the market seems to have affected the intensity of their belief not at all.)

The profound fear that accommodation would topple the whole structure, the concessions would simply feed an insatiable appetite, helps to explain the animosity generated by that arch American accommodationist, Franklin Delano Roosevelt. Wildly vilified as a traitor to his class, F.D.R., the supreme pragmatist, contemptuous of ideology, set about saving that class. In retrospect he seems a human analogue to Irving Kristol's vision of the State Department recently set forth in the columns of *The Wall Street Journal:* a "non-ideological institution which never fully appreciates the way in which words and ideas ultimately shape world politics and always prefers negotiation to confrontation."

What in fact happened to mitigate the class conflict which in the early decades of this century threatened to tear apart the national societies of the West and undoubtedly played a major role in the rise of fascism? What, in essence, did accommodation involve? It had, it seems to me, several elements. There was the creaming off and cooptation of the natural elite of the working class. Some members were drawn off early by opening the channels to higher education. Those who rose within the institutions of the working class, the trade unions, were welcomed into the establishment.

Their followers were pacified in very small measure by vicarious participation in the structure of power and in very large measure by receipt of slightly increased shares of a very rapidly growing pie. There is no evidence that any existing wealth was redistributed; but there was some redistribution, albeit modest, of shares in the large increments which Western economies began to produce after World War II. In addition, Western governments increased the security of the workers with measures that cushioned temporary setbacks in particular industrial sectors and in the economy as a whole.

Governmental policies effecting modest redistribution of the incremental shares and increasing security of expectation were not uniformly successful in the United States in giving the working class a vested interest in the basic institutions and ideology of the capitalist society. A quarter or more of the lower classes were left far behind the rest. In effect, those policies succeeded in creating two classes with sharply divergent interests. Members of the lower classes who worked in the key industrial and service sectors acquired a bourgeois outlook; they came to identify more closely with the upper classes than with those who were left behind.

Is the present struggle between the classes of nation-states not susceptible to mitigation by the employment of an analogous strategy of accommodation?

Some may cite the embittering experience of colonial and racial domination as a differentiating factor. For all the residual force of that experience, there is reason to question that it has been much more searing than the experience of Western working classes before they organized effectively for the ascent to political power. It is not only a question of parallel physical privation, but of humiliation. Conor Cruise O'Brien called attention some years ago to the striking similarity between racist apologetics for colonialism and the degrading descriptions of the English working class found in nineteenth-century tracts commissioned by the paladins of industry. In both cases, the exploited object is characterized as a repulsive, lower order of humanity.

In many respects, indeed, the strategy of accommodation might in fact be easier to implement in the present case than in its predecessor. Our conflict is not with huge, anonymous masses whose demands have to be aggregated through fairly uncertain representational arrangements. For the most part, Third World elites are even less committed to human equality as a general condition of humanity than are we. They are talking about greater equality between states. And in their largely authoritarian systems, the state is they.

What contemporary Brazilian statesman deplores the fact that the wealthiest 20 percent of his country's population receives over 60 percent of the national income while the lowest scrapes together three? Is there any record of a parliamentarian in the former French territories of West Africa returning part of his monthly pay because it was the equivalent of what a peasant would earn through 35 years of incessant labor, in the unexpected event that he lived so long? The central fact is that the overall number of people who have to be given a stake in the essential structures of the existing international economic system is relatively small.

That is one factor which makes accommodation seem potentially easier or at a minimum not more difficult on balance than in the prior case of class confrontation. A second is the existence of articulate, well organized representatives with whom to negotiate: the bureaucrats and political leaders of the 100-odd states which aggregate the demands of the Third World elite. There is, moreover, no reason to doubt whether the negotiators can deliver their constituents. For unlike nouveaux-riches labor leaders separated from their followers by the sheer fact of becoming negotiators, the Third World's representatives are an animate expression of the yearnings and aspirations of the elite which for the indefinite future will dominate most of the states with whom we must negotiate.

Of course the tenure of these specific negotiators may be transient. But the stability of new agreements forged in the spirit of accommodation will rest not on personal commitments but rather on their ability to reflect the class interests of which these leaders and their successors in the game of Third World musical chairs are a continuing embodiment.

A third factor facilitating accommodation is the very small number of representatives that have to be co-opted into senior decision-making roles in the management structure of the international economy. In Africa, only Nigeria. In Latin America, Brazil and Venezuela, perhaps Mexico. In the Middle East, Saudi Arabia and Iran. And in Asia, India and Indonesia.

V

If one is persuaded by the overall analogy, what programmatic conclusions might follow? What must be defended? And what can be conceded without threatening the fundamental arrangements which an accommodationist policy, as much as the hard line, is calculated to preserve?

What must be defended in the large is an economic system which rewards the capitalist virtues of investment, innovation, hard work, and sensitivity to the shifting needs and preferences of consumers. As Lincoln Gordon recently noted, this is one of the reasons why a comprehensive system of "price indexation" should be unacceptable: "If world demand is shifting away from a given commodity, . . . what is needed is a structural shift in . . . production and exports to items in stronger demand." Preservation of the incentives to practice those virtues is essential because without them the world's product will shrink. That is bad for the North, worse for the South, and absolutely destructive of any possibility of accommodation. For if anything is clear it is that the electorates of the First World will not support revisions in the economic order which intensify the transfer of *existing* wealth. It is with respect to the distribution of new increments of wealth that the "Haves" may be prepared to concede larger shares to the "Have-Nots." Hence, accommodationists must take a hard line against proposals which would reduce the prospects for growth in the global product.

Ironically, preservation of the principled foundations of the existing international capitalist system—an assemblage of values and institutions designed to reveal comparative advantage and reward economic efficiency—actually requires some practical concessions from the North rather than the South. A central plank of the latter's platform is removal of the various tariff and nontariff barriers to its present and potential exports. As investment in Southern infrastructure comes to fruition, comparative advantage in labor-intensive products shifts progressively away from the developed states. Volkswagens can already be produced more cheaply in Brazil than in Germany. For many textiles, the South's advantage has long been apparent. In addition, certain raw materials can now be refined with equal or great efficiency at their Southern sources.

So in this area, at least, all the South must yield is its rhetoric—the claim for reparations. It is we who must yield the tangibles: higher tariffs on refined raw materials, coerced textile agreements and the various other gimmicks—including restraints on the export of capital and related jobs from sectors of Northern industry that have lost their competitive edge—with which we cheat or might soon like to cheat on our own ideals.

This will be painful. If it were not, the North would have done it long ago simply in order to maximize its own growth. But if we cannot accommodate where we are asked only to bring practice into line with economic ideals, it is hard to foresee any option other than the barricades.

Consistent with its bedrock obejctive, the North also can respond affirmatively to Southern demands for tariff preferences in cases where they rest on a plausible claim to infant industry status rather than a mere appeal to equity. Nor is there any systematic objection to an affirmative response on the issue of more stable commodity prices. The North's record of economic dynamism since World War II suggests that public intervention in the market to prevent radical oscillations is perfectly compatible with and probably contributes heavily to economic growth, as well as social peace. What we cannot do, however, is guarantee a price level for any commodity in long-term opposition to powerful trends. On the other hand, following the domestic analogy, there is ample justification for accumulating funds to ease the transition out of declining economic activities.

The nub of the matter is that a considerable measure of economic security is thoroughly compatible with economic progress. That has become Holy Writ in the national societies of the North. To the extent that the South now seeks to extend the venue of this once radical notion, I see no principled grounds for resistance.

VI

Petroleum earnings have already given one bloc of Third World states a considerable material interest in preserving the basic features of the international economic system, including the prosperity of the First World. Reduced barriers to Third World exports, transitional preferences for new industries, and the unimpeded flow of capital and technology will enhance that stake and extend it to other countries that have sufficient assets and organization to grasp the resulting opportunities for accelerated growth. In theory, then, one might expect the large number of Third World countries that could benefit from such pragmatic changes to adopt in time a sort of middle-class outlook of their own and to dissociate themselves from a rhetoric of revolution and revenge. Yet even with these countries the answer will not be as easy as that, for reasons related to our earlier analysis of the attitudes that bind together all the Third World countries.

Let us look again at our recent behavior. In the first place, the transfer of wealth effected by the oil-producing OPEC states has not gone unchallenged. Official references to military action in case of "strangulation" and a drumbeat of unofficial calls for recourse to force or an economic blockade simply to roll back prices do not inspire confidence in the West's acceptance of the newly rich. Fearing an effort to reverse their gains, the oil producers naturally seek allies among the class of disadvantaged states from which they have sprung.

Secondly, given the rancorous response to this initial loss of unquestioned economic dominance, the OPEC states and others in the economic vanguard of the Third World can hardly assume that the reforms required to consolidate and expand their beachhead in the international economy will be conceded without additional struggle. The solid front and the radical rhetoric are in part designed as instruments of effective bargaining with what is seen as a tough and thoroughly unsentimental adversary. The protagonists of a hard line may convince themselves that the liberals' guilt has cost the West its will, but to the presumed beneficiaries of that loss of will it is not the "liberal" but the rigid reaction that comes across as dominant.

The radical rhetoric is not, of course, simply a bargaining ploy. It also functions to hold together the alliance of traditional "Have-Nots." There is yet another reason for the harshness of Third World rhetoric. To return to our original theme, more, much more, than economics is at stake. There is the question of dignity and respect, the redress of profound humiliations. Those humiliations continue.

Calls for action to dam the outward flow of petrodollars are often linked with vilification and crudely bigoted stereotyping of the Arab recipients. Economic coercion, so long a powerful weapon in the foreign policy armory of the United States, is transformed into "blackmail" when employed to advance the interest of other states. The clear implication is that only we have the decency of motive, the loftiness of purpose, to be entrusted with power.

The often unconscious bias which infects so much of our own rhetoric about the Third World resonates against a background of subordination to the West. Through our language, the transparent skin of our thought, we succeed only in raising the emotional barriers to pragmatic accommodation. A change in tone, possibly foreshadowed by Secretary Kissinger's more recent comments on international economic issues, is a good way to begin the process of lowering them. The small gestures enumerated earlier in our discussion of the political axes of confrontation will help. So will a formal reception of the Third World's leading states into the management group of the international economic system. Countries such as Brazil, Venezuela, Mexico, Iran, Nigeria and at least one of the major Arab states might, for instance, be invited to join the Organization for Economic Cooperation and Development and other organs of developed-country consultation.

The advocates of confrontation claim that no useful overall bargain can be struck because as soon as the Third World has devoured its benefits new demands will be made. Support for a policy of accommodation, however, does not imply support for a grand compact. Indeed, the notion of a grand compact is an illusion. The stunning diversity of problems and parties converging in this period of accelerating change simply do not admit of a single or final solution. There must be many bargains, not all of them among precisely the same parties. Some bargains will wholly resolve the issues to which they are addressed. Others will be stopgaps. Still others may prove so asymmetrical because of developments which the parties could not foresee that, just as in domestic society, the parties will have to renegotiate. No bargain is forever.

And there will remain desperately serious problems with the so-called Fourth World, for they, like the lower classes in American society, are disabled by a congeries of historical and natural forces from exploiting the opportunities for more effective participation in the competitive system. One cannot yet visualize the combination of self-help and external effort that may in time improve the lot of these poor countries. Neither the amelioration of their present agony nor the beginnings of rehabilitation can be accomplished without joing effort, free of rancor, on the part of the West *and* the more advanced Third World countries.

VII

In the years of bitter class conflict between capital and labor, before the ameliorations and compromises of the welfare state, many advocates of a hard line against the demands of labor invoked the alleged insatiability of those demands in support of a confrontational strategy. In one sense they were right, even trite. Once the myth of divinely authored shares in the social pie is fractured, no group settles willingly for less when it can, without risk, have more. Competition and struggle over the allocation of wealth and power seem endemic. But so, too, may be cooperation, which grows both out of fear of loss and the desire for absolute as well as relative gains.

One of the potential strengths of the present international system is the reality of national interdependence which creates an objective need for cooperation and consequently for accepting sharp restraints on the competitive aspects of interstate relations. The principal danger is an irrational assessment of risks and opportunities. Nothing is better calculated to promote miscalculation than the pretense that the equilibrium of power has not shifted, that we can continue to dictate to the Third World on the terms which sufficed in the epoch of the Western imperium.

Although the confrontationists indict advocates of accommodation for discounting our still-great strength, in fact, as is so often the case with those who extoll coercion, it is they who seem infected with a debilitating insecurity. To accommodate sensibly to real changes and legitimate demands is not the sign of a weak will. It is rather the essence of statesmanship.

Revolution:
The Weak Respond

7   The Strategy of Terrorism

David Fromkin

The grim events at the Athens airport on August 5, 1973, were in a sense symbolic. Dreadfully real to those who were involved, the occurrences of that day also transcended their own reality, somewhat as myths do, epitomizing an entire aspect of contemporary existence in one specific drama.

When the hand grenades were hurled into the departure lounge and the machine gunners simultaneously mowed down the passengers waiting to embark for New York City, it seemed incomprehensible that so harmless a group should be attacked. The merest glance at their hand-luggage, filled with snorkels and cameras, would have shown that they had spent their time in such peaceful pursuits as swimming, sunbathing, and snapping photos of the Parthenon.

The raid had been undertaken on behalf of an Arab Palestine. Yet the airport passengers had done the Arabs no harm. Their journey had only been to Greece. Palestine had nothing to do with them; it was another country, across the sea, and its problems were not of their making. Moreover, Athens was a capital friendly to the Arab cause—as was Paris, the scene of more recent airline attacks.

Similar incidents have occurred with terrible frequency throughout the 1960s and 1970s. The generations that have come to maturity in Europe and America since the end of the Second World War have asked only to bask in the sunshine of a summertime world; but increasingly they have been forced instead to live in the fearful shadow of other people's deadly quarrels. Gangs of politically motivated gunmen have disrupted everyday life, intruding and forcing their parochial feuds upon the unwilling attention of everbody else.

True, other ages have suffered from crime and outrage, but what we are experiencing today goes beyond such things. Too small to impose their will by military force, terrorist bands nonetheless are capable nowadays of causing enough damage to intimidate and blackmail the governments of the world. Only modern technology makes this possible—the bazooka, the plastic bomb, the submachine gun, and perhaps, over the horizon, the nuclear mini-bomb. The transformation has enabled terrorism to enter the political arena on a new scale, and to express ideological goals of an organized sort rather than mere crime, madness, or emotional derangement as in the past.

Political terrorism is a distinctive disorder of the modern world. It originated as a term and, arguably, as a practice, less than two centuries ago and has come into the spotlight of global conflict in our lifetime. Whereas both organized and irregular (or guerrilla) warfare began with the human race, political terrorism emerged as a concept only in 1793. As a political strategy, it is both new and original; and if I am correct, its nature has not yet fully been appreciated.

Of course nobody can remain unaware of the upsurge of global terrorism that has occurred in recent years. But the novelty of it has not been perceived. Force usually generates fear, and fear is usually an additional weapon. But terrorism employs the weapon of fear in a special and complicated sort of way.

II

The disassociation of fear from force in the context of organized politics emerged first in the Reign of Terror, the episode (1793–1794) during the history of revolutionary France from which the English and French words for terrorism derive. The terrorists in question were, of course, Robespierre and his satellites, St. Just and Couthon. Sitting as a faction in the Committee of Public Safety, their accusations of treason sent victims to the guillotine in droves. By the mere threat of accusation against their fellow Committee members, they used the entire Committee, thus united, in order to dominate the National Convention and the other public bodies of the French Republic.

Robespierre was overthrown when his system was used against him. His mistake was in letting Joseph Fouché know that he was the next intended victim; and Fouché, the wily intriguer who later became Napoleon's minister of police, made the best possible use of his few remaining days. He persuaded the feuding, rival politicians of his day that they had to unite against the triumvirs or else face execution one by one; fear of the regime should cause them not to serve it, but to overthrow it. On 8 Thermidor (July 26, 1794) Robespierre made another mistake when he told the Convention that he had prepared a new list of traitors in their midst—and then refused to tell them whose names were on the list. Fouché's warnings were confirmed, and his counsel was heeded. When Robespierre entered the National Convention late in the stormy summer morning of 9 Thermidor, he found a mob of delegates united by the determination to murder him before he could murder them; and that was the end of him.

Robespierre had coerced a nation of 27 million people into accepting his dictatorship. His followers sent many thousands either to jail or to their deaths; one scholar's estimate is 40,000 deaths and 300,000 arrests. Yet when retribution came and Robespierre and his group of supporters were executed, it turned out that in all there were only 22 of them.

Of course it is not meant to suggest that this is the whole story of the French Terror. Yet what emerges most strongly from any account of these events is the dramatic disparity between the objective weakness of the Robespierre faction, whose numbers were few and whose military resources were limited, and their immense subjective power, which allowed them to kill, imprison, or control so many. There was no need to fear the triumvirs other than the fact that other people feared them and therefore would execute their orders. Their power was unreal; it was an illusionist's trick. No citadels had to be stormed, no armies had to be crushed, in order to overthrow them. If the public ignored what they said, then the terrorists went back to being political nobodies. Their dictatorship vanished in an instant when Robespierre and his colleagues were prevented from reaching the speakers' platform on 9 Thermidor.

In the end, the terrorists overreached themselves, and men saw through them and stood up to them. Then—and only then—it became clear that France had never had anything to fear from them other than fear itself.

III

Perhaps the closest parallel to Robespierre's method was that followed by the late Senator Joseph McCarthy in 1950–54. Like Robespierre, McCarthy claimed to have lists of traitors whose names he would not immediately reveal, and many did his will in order to avoid being accused by him of treason or of lack of patriotism. And, like Robespierre's, his power stopped when he went too far and Joseph Welch, his Fouché, stood up to him on television. But McCarthy never seized supreme power in the country, nor did his accusations send people to the guillotine. In that sense it can be said that Robespierre has had no successors.

Since his time, in fact, political terrorism has become especially notorious in a different cause from that in which Robespierre used it. It has been used to destroy governments rather than to sustain them. This changed the way in which many people thought of it as a political strategy and how they viewed its adherents. As revolutionaries, terrorists have come to seem romantic figures to many. Their life of dangers and disguises, risks and betrayals, conspiracies and secret societies, exerted a powerful fascination. As torn and tormented characters, they provided authors with the stuff of which complex and interesting novels can be made.

Though the terrorists seemed romantic, until recently they also seemed ineffective. Until the Irish Treaty of 1921, they scored no significant political successes. The most famous of the terrorist groups up to that time was the Terrorist Brigade of the Russian Socialists-Revolutionists; and not merely did they fail to change the Tsarist government in the ways in which they desired, they also failed to pick up the pieces when it was overthrown by others. Plekhanov, Lenin, Trotsky and the other Russian disciples of Marx had seen more clearly in placing their emphasis on mass organization rather than on individual terrorism. The Bolsheviks came to power by winning the metropolitan workmen, the sailors of the Baltic fleet, and the soldiers to their side. Organization proved to be the key to victory. It was not individual gunmen but armed masses who seized power in Russia. Revolution, like war, is the strategy of the strong; terrorism is the strategy of the weak.

It is an uncertain and indirect strategy that employs the weapon of fear in a special sort of way in which to make governments react. Is fear an effective method? Is fright any kind of weapon at all? What can terrorists hope to accomplish by sowing fear? How can it help their side to vanquish its opponents? Clearly it can do so in many ways. Fright can paralyze the will, befuddle the mind, and exhaust the strength of an adversary. Moreover, it can persuade an opponent that a particular political point of view is taken with such deadly seriousness by its few adherents that it should be accommodated, rather than suffering casualties year after year in a campaign to suppress it.

All of these elements came together, for example, in the struggle that led to the independence of southern Ireland. It is difficult to disentangle the role of terrorism in this achievement from the other elements that were involved, for the Irish also had put in motion what was, in effect, a guerrilla warfare campaign. Moreover, the Liberal members of the coalition that then governed the United Kingdom had a political commitment that went back more than a quarter of a century to the cause of Irish Home Rule. Yet there can be little doubt that terrorism played a major role in causing Britain to tire of the struggle.

Terrorism can also make heroes out of gunmen, and thereby rally popular support to their cause. The problem this creates for them is that when the time comes to make the compromises necessary in order to negotiate the terms of their victory, the glamour wanes, and with it, the political support. Michael Collins was a romantic figure who captured the imagination of all Ireland as long as he was an outlaw; but when he sat down to make peace; he was seen by many in a much different light. As he signed the Irish Treaty of 1921 on Britain's behalf, Lord Birkenhead remarked to Collins, "I may have signed my political death-warrant tonight"; to which Collins replied, "I may have signed my actual death-warrant." Eight months later Michael Collins lay dead on an Irish roadway with a bullet through his head.

Just as it can make gangsters into heroes, terrorist provocations can also make policemen into villains. The Black-and-Tans who fought the Irish revolutionists were, in an objective sense, so successful at repression that Michael Collins told an English official afterwards, in regard to the July 1921 peace negotiations: "You had us dead beat. We could not have lasted another three weeks." Yet Black-and-Tan methods made the cause of repression so odious that Britain was induced to choose another course of action.

Brutality is an induced governmental response that can boomerang. It is this ability to use the strength of repression against itself, in many different ways, that has enabled terrorist strategies to succeed in many situations that have, rightly or wrongly, been described as colonialist in the modern world.

IV

Sophisticated approaches have been developed along these lines. One of these was explained to me and to others at a meeting in New York City sometime in 1945 by one of the founders of the Irgun Zvai Leumi, a tiny group of Jewish militants in what was then the British-mandated territory of Palestine. His organization had no more than 1,000 or 1,500 members, and it was at odds with the Palestinian Jewish community almost as much as it was with the mandatory regime. Yet he proposed to combat Great Britain, then a global power whose armed forces in the Second World War numbered in the millions, and to expel Great Britain from Palestine.

How could such a thousand-to-one struggle be won? To do so, as he explained it, his organization would attack property interests. After giving advance warning to evacuate them, his small band of followers would blow up buildings. This, he said, would lead the British to overreact by garrisoning the country with an immense army drawn from stations in other parts of the world. But postwar Britain could not afford financially to maintain so great an army either there or anywhere else for any extended period of time. Britain urgently needed to demobilize its armed forces. The strain would tell; and eventually economic pressure would drive the Attlee-Bevin government either to withdraw from Palestine or else to try some reckless and possibly losing gamble in an effort to retrieve the situation.

It can be argued that such is in fact what happened. Of course Britain might have withdrawn anyway, at some other time or for some other reason. But that is really beside the point, for the Irgun wanted independence then and there, in order to open up the country to refugees from Hitler's Europe. They got what they wanted when they wanted it by doing it in their own way.

There were two flaws in the Irgun strategy. It would have failed had the British not reacted to the destruction of buildings as they were expected to do. If instead they had done nothing at all, maintained only a modest military garrison, and sent for no reinforcements, all that would have happened would have been that a few more buildings would have been blown up and the owners would have collected the insurance money and would have rebuilt them; and the Irgun would have proved a failure.

In the second place, the plan of attacking property without hurting people proved to be unrealistic. Accidents inevitably occur when violence is unleashed. Almost a hundred persons were killed when the Irgun blew up the King David Hotel in Jerusalem. According to the plan, they should have been evacuated before the blast, but in actual life people misunderstand, or their telephone line is busy, or somebody forgets to give them the message in time. Moreover, terrorism generates its own momentum, and before long the killing becomes deliberate. The bloodshed caused by the Irgun isolated it politically and alienated the rest of the Palestinian Jewish community. The British failed to perceive or exploit this situation. But Ben-Gurion did; in 1948 he made use of it to crush the Irgun, for the Israeli army might have been unwilling to carry out orders to attack those unloading the Irgun ship the *Altalena,* if the Irgun had not used up its political credit before then by the taking of too many lives.

Yet despite its flaws, the strategy was sufficiently ingenious so that the Irgun played a big part in getting the British to withdraw. Its ingenuity lay in using an opponent's own strength against him. It was a sort of jujitsu. First the adversary was made to be afraid, and then, predictably, he would react to his fear by increasing the bulk of his strength, and then the sheer weight of that bulk would drag him down. Another way of saying this is that the Irgun, seeing that it was too small to defeat Great Britain, decided, as an alternative approach, that Britain was big enough to defeat itself.

V

In the 1950s, the nationalist rebel group in Algeria developed yet another method of using the strength of an occupying power against itself. Their method was to induce that strength to be used as a form of persuasion.

For, in Algeria, the whole question was one of persuasion. The problem initially faced by the miniscule band of Algerian nationalists that called itself the National Liberation Front (or, in its French initials, FLN) was that Algeria at that time had little sense of national identity. Its population was not homogeneous; and the Berbers, the Arabs, and the settlers of European descent were peoples quite different from one another. The name and separate existence of Algeria were only of recent origin. For most of recorded history, Algeria had been no more than the middle part of North Africa, with no distinct history of its own. Legally it was merely the southern part of France. The French had treated Morocco and Tunisia as protectorates, with separate identities, but not Algeria, which was absorbed into France herself. With sarcasm, Frenchmen used to reply to Americans who urged independence for Algeria by saying that, on the same basis, the United States should set Wisconsin free or give back independence to South Carolina.

It was a jibe that went to the heart of the matter. Colonial empires were coming to an end in the 1950s and 1960s. If Algeria was a nation, then inevitably it would be set free to govern itself. Only if it were genuinely a part of France could it continue to be ruled from Paris. All depended, therefore, on whether the indigenous population could be convinced by the French government that Algeria was not a separate country, or upon whether they could be persuaded by the FLN to change their minds so as to think of themselves as a nation.

The FLN strategy of terrorism addressed itself to this central and decisive issue. By itself, as has been said, terror can accomplish nothing in terms of political goals; it can only aim at obtaining a response that will achieve those goals for it. What the FLN did was to goad the French into reacting in such a way as to demonstrate the unreality of the claim that there was no distinct Algerian nation. Unlike the Irgun, the FLN did not set out to campaign merely against property; it attacked people. It used random violence, planting bombs in market places and in other crowded locations. The instinctive French reaction was to treat all persons of non-European origin as suspects; but, as Raymond Aron was to write, "As suspects, all the Muslims felt excluded from the existing community." Their feeling was confirmed when, in the middle 1950s, the authorities further reacted by transferring the French army units composed of Muslim Algerian troops out of Algeria and into mainland France, and replacing them in Algeria by European troops. By such actions they showed in the most unmistakable way that they regarded no Algerians as Frenchmen except for the European settlers. They spoke of we and us, and of they and them, and did not realize that their doing so meant the end of Algérie Française.

Thus the French conceded the issue of the war at its very outset. They threw away the potential support of Muslim Algeria because they were skeptical of the possibility that it could be obtained. From that moment the conclusion of the conflict was foregone. Once the sympathies of the population had shifted to its side, the FLN was able to outgrow mere terrorism and to organize a campaign of guerrilla warfare. It also was enabled to appeal to world sympathies on behalf of a people fighting for its freedom. From the French point of view all had become hopeless; for no amount of force can keep an unwilling population indefinitely in subjection. Even though the FLN had written the script, the French, with suicidal logic, went ahead to play the role for which they had been cast.

The FLN success was therefore a special case. It required a particular kind of opponent. It could not be duplicated in other circumstances and conditions.

VI

Revolutionist-terrorists of the last decade have failed to perceive the special characteristics of the colonialist situation that facilitated success for Irish, Irgun, and Algerian terrorists. They have tried to apply the strategy of terrorism in situations that are essentially different. This has been true, for example, of extremist groups seeking to overthrow liberal-pluralistic regimes during the 1960s. Their theory has been that their terrorist attacks would force hitherto liberal regimes to become repressive, a change which in turn would alienate the masses, thus setting the stage for revolution. But it has not worked out that way in practice. In the United States, for example, terrorist bomb attacks have not led to any change at all in the form of government, much less to a transformation of America into a police state. On the other hand, in

Uruguay, once the model democracy of Latin America, the terror of the Tupamaro bands has led to a military dictatorship that brutally destroyed the Tupamaros, but that does not seem, at least as yet, to have led to the predicted reaction by the masses in favor of revolutionary action.

Other revolutionary groups have taken a somewhat different approach. They have argued that liberal democracies are already police states. Thus, the object of revolutionary terrorist action should be to reveal this hidden reality to the population at large. Unthinking reaction by the authorities to terrorist provocation would accomplish the desired result. Thus the aim of terrorism would be to trick the government into taking off its mask.

In open societies such as Great Britain and the United States, the liberal democratic features have proved to be a face and not a mask: there is nothing to take off, and the strategy failed because its factual premise proved to be untrue.

In closed societies, the strategy has been to show that authoritarian regimes are actually impotent despite their outward show of virility. In such circumstances, supposedly, by demonstrating that the public authorities are powerless to enforce law and order, a campaign of terror can cause a government to collapse; but the flaw in the theory is that the terrorists usually are not strong enough to take its place. Either some more broadly based group will seize power, or else, as in Argentina, private groups will take the law into their own hands and retaliate in kind against murder and extortion, so that society relapses into a semi-anarchic state of reprisals and blood feuds, where terrorists are buried with their victims.

VII

It is against this background that Arab Palestinian terrorism has seized the attention of the contemporary world. It is aimed at Israel; it is aimed at the Arabs who live within Israel; and it is aimed at the world outside. It is, in other words, a mixed strategy. Each of its mixed aspects has to be considered separately. All that Arab terrorism can accomplish in the land that has been promised to so many is to frighten and to threaten the Arab inhabitants of Israel in order to keep them from cooperating with the Israeli authorities. Israel itself, however, cannot be terrorized into disappearing of its own accord; yet removing Israel from the map has long been the proclaimed goal of the Arab terrorist movement.

Terrorism can be employed more successfully in colonialist situations than in Palestine because a colonial power suffers the disadvantage of fighting the battle away from its own base, and also because a colonial power, having a country of its own to which it can withdraw, is under no compulsion to fight to the bitter end. The Israelis, though termed colonialist by the Arabs, are fighting on home territory, and they have no other country to which they can withdraw; they fight with their backs to the sea. They can be goaded into a self-defeating reaction, but unless they permit that to happen, nothing can be done to their domestic public opinion that is likely to destroy them. The Arab terrorists therefore have turned elsewhere, and have attacked the arteries of world transportation in hopes that a world indifferent to the merits of the Arab-Israeli dispute will turn against the Israelis in order to end the annoyance of a disrupted airline service.

In doing so they have strayed across a frontier and into the eerie world of Mr. McLuhan, and they have transformed terrorism into a form of mass communication—but communication aimed at the whole world and not, as in the case of Algeria, mostly at the indigenous population. Theirs is a campaign that needs publicity in order to succeed, and therefore they have come to operate within the ambit of contemporary public relations and communications arts: the world of cinema, camp fashion, and pop art, in which deadlines and prime time are the chief realities and in which shock value is the chief virtue. If audiences throughout the world react with horror, and turn against the political cause in whose name so many innocent people have been harmed and killed, the strategy will have backfired. So far they have not done so and it has not done so.

It is a corruption of the human spirit for which all political sides are responsible. The left-wing journalist Paul Johnson wrote an article some months back arguing that left-wing movements are as much at fault as anybody else for accepting the murder of the innocent as a legitimate means for the pursuit of political ends. He quoted the sixteenth-century humanist Castellio, "who was lucky to escape burning by both Catholics and Protestants, and who pointed out in his tract for toleration, *Whether Heretics Are To Be Persecuted?*, that no certitude of righteousness justifies violence: 'To kill a man is not to defend a doctrine, it is to kill a man'." Appalled at the welcome accorded by the United Nations to the leader of the Arab terrorists, Johnson wrote that, "Step by step, almost imperceptibly, without anyone being aware that a fatal watershed has been crossed, mankind has descended into the age of terror."

VIII

If this is an age of terror, then it has become all the more important for us to understand exactly what it is that terrorism means. Terrorism, as has been seen, is the weapon of those who are prepared to use violence but who believe that they would lose any contest of sheer strength. All too little understood, the uniqueness of the strategy lies in this: that it achieves its goal not through its acts but through the response to its acts. In any other such strategy, the violence is the beginning and its consequences are the end of it. For terrorism, however, the consequences of the violence are themselves merely a first step and form a stepping stone toward objectives that are more remote. Whereas military and revolutionary actions aim at a physical result, terrorist actions aim at a psychological result.

But even that psychological result is not the final goal. Terrorism is violence used in order to create fear; but it is aimed at creating fear in order that the fear, in turn, will lead somebody else—not the terrorist—to embark on some quite different program of action that will accomplish whatever it is that the terrorist really desires. Unlike the soldier, the guerrilla fighter, or the revolutionist, the terrorist therefore is always in the paradoxical position of undertaking actions the immediate physical consequences of which are not particularly desired by him. An ordinary murderer will kill somebody because he wants the person to be dead, but a terrorist will shoot somebody even though it is a matter of complete indifference to him whether that person lives or dies. He would do so, for example, in order to provoke a brutal police repression that he believes will lead to political conditions propitious to revolutionary agitation and organization aimed at overthrowing the government. The act of murder is the same in both cases, but its purpose is different, and each act plays a different role in the strategies of violence.

Only an understanding of the purpose for which such an act is undertaken can enable us to know the nature of the act. When Julius Caesar was murdered in the Roman Senate, it was an assassination of the traditional sort, intended to eliminate a specific figure from the political scene; but had he been killed there by the representative of a subversive sect, intent on plunging his dagger into the first Roman leader he encountered in order to provoke a certain political response from the Senate, it would instead have been an act of political terrorism.

It is because an action of the same sort may be undertaken by two different groups with two quite different ends in view that terrorism is so often confused with guerrilla warfare, for terrorists and guerrillas often seem to be doing the same sorts of things. Both of them, for example, often sabotage transportation facilities. When T. E. Lawrence led his classic guerrilla warfare campaign against Turkish rule in Arabia, he systematically dynamited railway tracks and bridges. Lawrence's strategy was later explained by Winston Churchill as follows: "The Turkish armies operating against Egypt depended upon the desert railway. This slender steel track ran through hundreds of miles of blistering desert. If it were permanently cut the Turkish armies must perish." And Lawrence therefore rode on camel-back across the sands to destroy the enemy army by blowing up its transportation facilities. In recent years those who say that they wish to destroy the state of Israel have also blown up transportation facilities in the Arab desert; in this case, jet airplanes belonging to civil aviation companies. Yet if thereby they were to permanently cut the airline networks of TWA or BOAC they would not cause the Israeli army to perish. Indeed the fate of such civil aviation companies is a matter of indifference to the terrorists. Lawrence the guerrilla leader attacked a railway because he wanted to destroy it, whereas Arab terrorists attack an airline even though they do not want to destroy it.

The distinction is of more than academic importance. The French lost their empire over Algeria when they mistook terrorism for guerrilla warfare. They thought that when the FLN planted a bomb in a public bus, it was in order to blow up the bus; whereas the real FLN purpose in planting the bomb was not to blow up the bus, but to lure authorities into reacting by arresting all the non-Europeans in the area as suspects.

The terrorist is like a magician who tricks you into watching his right hand while his left hand, unnoticed, makes the switch. It is understandable that the French authorities in Algeria became totally obsessed by the need to stamp out criminal attacks, but it was fatal to their policy to do so, for the violent attacks were merely a subsidiary issue. The tiny FLN band of outlaws could have blown up every bus in all of Algeria and never won a convert to their cause of independence. Failing to understand the strategy of terrorism, the French did not see that it was not the FLN's move, but rather the French countermove, that would determine whether the FLN succeeded or failed. . . .

For the Israelis, threatened by enemies outside of their society, the problem is an enormously difficult one. For societies threatened only by enemies from within, it is considerably less so. The very wickedness of terrorism makes it a vulnerable strategy in such a society. Other strategies sometimes kill the innocent by mistake. Terrorism kills the innocent deliberately; for not even the terrorist necessarily believes that the particular person who happens to become his victim deserves to be killed or injured. It is horrifying not merely because of the deed that is done but also because at first the deed seems pointless. If you want to make war on the United States on behalf of Puerto Rican independence, why blow up a historic tavern in New York's financial district? What has Fraunces Tavern got to do with Puerto Rico? Why not attack the alleged forces of occupation in Puerto Rico instead? If you opposed by force and violence the continuation of U.S. aid to South Vietnam, why threaten to destroy the Smithsonian Institution? What had its plant collections and its ichthyological specimens to do with American policy in Southeast Asia? The destruction seems so purposeless that it is a natural reaction to turn on those who perpetrate it in hatred and in anger.

The tragedies that befall great public figures can sometimes seem to have been deserved; but when a man on the street is killed at random on behalf of a cause with which he had nothing to do, it is a different matter and provokes a different reaction. In a homogeneous society, at any rate, it leads to a reaction against the terrorism, and it renders it vulnerable to a campaign that politically isolates it in order to physically destroy it, for the nature of the attacks tends to demonstrate that terrorists are enemies of the people rather than merely of the government. It is for this reason that Che Guevara, as a theoretician and practitioner of guerrilla warfare, warned against the strategy of terrorism, arguing that it hinders "contact with the masses and makes impossible unification for actions that will be necessary at a critical moment."

Even in the international arena, terrorist movements are vulnerable when their actions alienate support. . . . This is because terrorism is so much more evil than other strategies of violence that public opinion sometimes can be rallied against it.

Indeed, in view of its inherent weakness, it is remarkable how many political successes have been scored by the strategy of terrorism in the last few decades. Its success seems to be due in large part to a miscomprehension of the strategy by its opponents. They have neglected the more important of the two levels on which terrorism operates. They have failed to focus on the crucial issue of how the manner in which they, as opponents, respond affects the political goals of the terrorists. Discussion instead has centered on the criminal justice aspects of the question: prevention and punishment.

Much has been written, for example, about the technological defenses that have been developed or could be developed against terrorism in order to prevent it from occurring. This can be a highly useful line of approach, as the successful use of electronic surveillance devices at airports seems to have demonstrated. It may even be advisable to require that any new technologies that are developed from time to time should incorporate some sort of internal defense against attack, much as environmentalists argue that pollution control devices should be incorporated in equipment and its cost charged to the manufacturers. Yet no technology is perfect, and there will always be somebody who will manage to slip by any defenses that can be created.

Prevention of terrorism in non-technological ways scarcely merits discussion. Perhaps one day the social sciences will teach us how to drain the swamps of misery in which hatred and fanaticism breed, but at the moment that day seems far distant. The hollow formalism of the law offers, if anything, even less help. Ingenious schemes for new international tribunals and procedures have been proposed, and they completely miss the point. The manifest unwillingness of many governments to use existing legal remedies against terrorism shows that the real problem is the lack of a will and not the lack of a way. For example, it was only when an attack was staged at the Paris airport that the French Minister of the Interior, in January of 1975, proposed to negotiate an international convention to provide for the punishment of terrorist acts. It is not any kind of genuine solution, in any event, but it will be interesting to see if Michel Poniatowski perseveres in even so ritualistic a response as this after the fleeting memory of injured national pride fades from view. There are all too many who object to terrorism only when they are its victims.

Far more effective than the reaction of M. Poniatowski was that of the French press. There were suggestions in the newspapers that the pro-Arab policy of the French government should be reversed because it had failed to prevent the attack at Orly airport. Within days the Palestine Liberation Organization strongly condemned the attack. It also announced that it had taken measures to punish persons who engaged in the hijacking of airplanes, boats or trains. What the French journalists had correctly intuited was that the locus of the struggle was not at the Orly airport: it was at the Elysée Palace and at the Quai d'Orsay.

The overriding questions are not legal or technological; they are philosophical and political. Terrorism is the indirect strategy that wins or loses only in terms of how you respond to it. The decision as to how accommodating or how uncompromising you should be in your response to it involves questions that fall primarily within the domain of political philosophy.

IX

Those who are the targets of terrorism—and who are prepared to defend themselves by doing whatever is necessary in order to beat it—start with a major advantage. The advantage is that success or failure depends upon them alone. Terrorism wins only if you respond to it in the way that the terrorists want you to; which means that its fate is in your hands and not in theirs. If you choose not to respond at all, or else to respond in a way different from that which they desire, they will fail to achieve their objectives.

The important point is that the choice is yours. That is the ultimate weakness of terrorism as a strategy. It means that, though terrorism cannot always be prevented, it can always be defeated. You can always refuse to do what they want you to do.

Whether to pay the price of defeating terrorism is increasingly going to be a major question in our time. The answer is relatively easy in most kidnapping and ransom situations: experience has shown that blackmailers and extortionists usually are encouraged to try it again if you give in to their demands the first time. So, if you can do so, you should accept the consequences, however terrible, of standing firm in order to avoid an infinite sequence of painful events.

But the price of doing so is constantly rising, as technology increases the range and magnitude of horrible possibilities. Terrorist outrages, when they occur, are bound to become more deadly. Increasingly, we will be under pressure to abridge our laws and liberties in order to suppress the terrorists. It is a pressure that should be resisted.

In our personal lives we sometimes have to choose between these alternatives: whether to live a good life or whether to live a long life. Political society in the years to come is likely to face a similar choice. An open society such as ours is especially vulnerable to terrorist violence, which seems to threaten us with ever more dreadful and drastic fates. Have we the stoicism to endure nonetheless? Will we be tempted to abandon our political and moral values? Will we be willing to go on paying an ever higher price in order to defeat the terrorists by refusing to respond in the way they want us to?

Of course it would make things easier if terrorism simply would go away. It seems unlikely to do so. The weapons are at hand, and they probably will be used, for terrorism will never cease until the day when the Old Man of the Mountain loses his last disciple. The old man was grand master of the sect called the Assassins (hashish-ins) because of the hashish which he gave them. The old man, according to Marco Polo, used to drug his young disciples and transport them while they were asleep to his secret pleasure garden, persuading them when they awoke in it that it was paradise itself. Drugging them again, he would transport them back to the everyday world while they slept. Never afterward did they doubt that their Master could and would reward them with eternal paradise after death if they did his killing for him while they were alive. And so they did do his killing for him.

If anything, the modern world seems to breed more and more votaries of this peculiar sect. They seem to thrive and multiply everywhere in the world, bomb or machine gun in hand, motivated by political fantasies and hallucinations, fully convinced that their slaughter of the innocent will somehow usher in a political millennium for mankind. *"Voici le temps des* ASSASSINS," as Rimbaud wrote in the dawn of the industrial age; and we do indeed live in the time of the Assassins.

8   Is Peace Possible in the Middle East?

Walter Laqueur

One of the mysteries of world politics is the amount of attention being paid these days to the Arab-Israeli conflict. According to some estimates, almost half the time of the last session of the UN General Assembly was devoted to issues connected in one way or another with this conflict. A quantitative study of the uses of Henry Kissinger's energies would probably show a similar pattern, and so would an analysis of editorial comment on international affairs. Indeed, any unsuspecting newspaper reader would get the impression that the future of the Golan Heights and the West Bank are more important than all the other problems in the world put together. Yet it would be only too easy to point to at least half-a-dozen danger zones of equal or greater weight in other parts of the world, not to mention sub-acute critical trends in the political and economic sphere whose long-term effects may have the gravest results.

Of course those who put so much emphasis on the Middle East argue that it is not the future of Golan that is at stake but the general stability of the area and the securing of the oil supply. They will admit that but for these overriding considerations, the Arab-Israeli conflict would be of no greater interest than the conflict between Bolivia and Peru, or at most between North and South Korea. But unless there is some "movement" toward a "lasting peace" in the Middle East, they say, there will be another war; and a new war would trigger an oil embargo, start a worldwide depression, put at least ten million Americans out of work, destroy NATO, allow Soviet power to engulf the Straits of Gibraltar, and bring Communist ministers into coalition governments in much of Europe. If, on the other hand, Israel withdrew from the occupied territories, permanent peace would follow—Middle Eastern governments would be stable, the oil would flow, its price would go down, bankers and exporters would make profits, generals and admirals would obtain bases, and American policy-makers would be able to devote themselves to building a new and more workable world order.

Now, the resolution of the Arab-Israeli conflict would in every way be desirable. But examining recent suggestions for the settlement of this conflict, or of the hopes held out for the consequences that would follow from such a settlement, one has to cut one's way through a thicket of wishful thinking almost unique in an otherwise fairly cynical age.

To begin with, there is no cogent reason to believe that a settlement would add to the stability of the Middle East (let alone the stability of the entire world). The recent history of the Middle East is a story of conflicts: Algerian interests clash with those of Morocco and Tunisia; Libya is at loggerheads with Egypt and Sudan; there has been almost constant tension between Iraq and all her neighbors; South Yemen has a conflict of long standing with North Yemen, and is even now conducting surrogate war against Oman; Lebanon is in a state of civil war; and the survival of Jordan to this day is a miracle. The list could be extended without much difficulty. Moreover, the traditional rivalries among governments have been aggravated by the sudden influx of oil revenues.

Despite the Arab-Israeli confrontation, some of these conflicts have entered an acute phase, but thanks to the need to make common cause against the "Zionist danger," there has by and large been a truce in the Arab world. For so long as the campaign against Israel continues, Arab solidarity is the supreme necessity, and any attempt to raise other issues or press other demands is attacked as an act of treason. Once this unifying factor is removed, once the "Zionist danger" decreases, the struggles between rich countries and poor, between haves and have-nots, between pro-Soviet and pro-American regimes are bound to escalate; and so are the grave domestic tensions between "moderates" and "radicals" within each country. The Arab world would then be rent by bitter civil strife and, very probably, war; and it is the oil countries like Saudi Arabia and Kuwait which would be in the gravest danger. For while it is sometimes argued that in the absence of progress toward peace in the Middle East, moderate policies and leaders will be superseded by more radical ones, this is far more likely to happen as the *consequence* of progress toward peace between Israel and the Arab countries and the resulting increase of tension elsewhere in the Arab world.

Almost everyone believes that Israel's return to the 1967 borders and the establishment of a Palestinian state are necessary to a settlement in the Middle East. Of course the basic issue in the Arab-Israeli conflict is not the border problem or a Palestinian state—the conflict existed before there were occupied territories and before there was a demand for a Palestinian state. The real issue, as Elie Kedourie puts it, is the right of the Jews, "hitherto a subject community under Islam, to exercise political sovereignty in an area regarded as part of the Muslim domain." Why, Professor Kedourie asks, should the Arabs, who have been unwilling for twenty-eight years to grant this right to the Jews, suddenly be willing to do so just when Arab power and influence have so greatly increased?

But let us assume that the Arabs *are* willing to do so. Let us even assume that the PLO no longer regards the destruction of the State of Israel as its ultimate aim, that it is ready to accept the Jewish state, and peacefully to coexist with it in a Palestinian state of its own. What would be the nature of such a Palestinian state?

A look at the map shows that it would consist of two separate parts. One part would be the West Bank, bounded on the east by the River Jordan and including Samaria and Judaea; the western border would run west of Tulkarm and Kalkilya, east of Lod and Ramla, from there to Jerusalem, then south to Hebron and the Dead Sea—altogether some 2,165 square miles. In addition there would be the Gaza Strip. The West Bank has a population of about 600,000, the Gaza Strip of some 300,000. The two sections are not connected, and they remind one of what the late Viscount Samuel said about an earlier partition plan: it would have the effect of creating a Saar and a Polish Corridor and half-a-dozen Danzigs and Memels in a country the size of Wales. If it is argued that Israel in its 1967 borders cannot be defended, a Palestinian state would be even less defensible.

Nor would such a state be economically viable. Annual rainfall in the northern part of the West Bank is fairly high, which has favored local agriculture, but industry is all but nonexistent except for some olive-oil and soap factories in Nablus. Hebron produces glass as well as wooden and mother-of-pearl souvenirs. Bethlehem and Ramalla cater to tourists. The Gaza Strip, whose population density is one of the world's highest, has no industry either; there are citrus groves and some summer fruits such as watermelons. Given this economic situation (which has already forced many workers from the West Bank and the Gaza Strip to work in Israeli industry and on building sites), the new state would not even be able to absorb more than a token number of Palestinian refugees.

Some Arab spokesmen have recently argued that the issue of nonviability is not really a very important one, since a great many countries in the modern world are not viable either. But this, though true, is hardly a reassuring argument. Arab spokesmen also claim that the Palestinians are a hard-working people (which is correct), that they have a great deal of know-how, and that they would get support from the oil-rich countries. According to various research papers prepared by the PLO studies center in Beirut, a Palestinian state could be economically viable—provided the Saudis gave billions for an unlimited period. Past experience has shown, however, that Arab solidarity does not extend to sharing oil revenues, except perhaps for the purchase of arms. Egypt in particular, which has received no major investments from Saudi Arabia and Kuwait, has learned this lesson the hard way.

In addition to being unviable, a Palestinian state in the West Bank and Gaza would have all the makings of a permanent irredentism. If any single thought has gone into the proposals for establishing such a state (and this, unfortunately, cannot be taken for granted), it is apparently the idea that a partial fulfillment of Palestinian demands would lead to a deradicalization of the PLO. Thus it is said that once the Palestinians had to assume responsibility for a state, however small, they would have to drop their maximalist program for the conquest of Israel; nor could they afford to engage in terror any more. Yet even if one believes that there is a moderate element inside the PLO genuinely willing to coexist with Israel on the basis of the 1967 frontiers—a daring leap of faith indeed—it seems almost a foregone conclusion that the logic of events would drive those moderates toward extremism.

Once the state were founded, there would almost certainly be a struggle between the different PLO wings and, of course, the "Rejection Front" (primarily Iraq) and various Communist organizations. These groups, which stand for divergent political aims, deeply distrust one another, but the stakes are not at present sufficiently high to warrant open warfare. With control of a state in the balance, however, a bitter internal battle would begin. Units of Fatah and the PLPF stationed in the new state would regard it as a mere interim arrangement, a milestone on the road to the liberation of the entire homeland. Other Arab countries, weary of carrying the burden of Palestine, might well advise the Palestinians not to pass immediately on to the next phase of the struggle but to let a decent interval elapse. However, in the fight against Israel this would be dangerous for the Palestinians, for once the momentum were lost, it would not easily be regained. It is doubtful therefore whether they would be ready to listen to outside advice. And as to internal advice, though the merchants of Nablus and Jenin would certainly be interested in a climate conducive to business as usual, they could no more be expected to prevail against the irredentists than the bankers of Beirut have been able to do against the terrorists.

In some ways, indeed, it would be easier than in the past for the Palestinians to conduct their operations against Israel. With artillery and missile bases, physical infiltration would be largely unnecessary, while Israeli counter-shelling would be less effective since there would be fewer targets on the other side. Israeli retaliatory raids, on the other hand, would be severely condemned by world public opinion and sanctions might be taken against them.

Nevertheless, there is a limit to what the PLO could reasonably hope to achieve. The Israelis are not a minority like the Assyrians or the Kurds, nor is there any similarity between their position and that of the Maronites. Israel has a considerable military potential, and it would be unwilling to play according to rules established by the PLO. Fighting would not be limited to border skirmishes; there would be a general escalation involving other Arab armies and possibly also the Soviet Union, and the use of nonconventional weapons would not be ruled out.

In short, the moment one begins to scrutinize the practical implications of establishing a Palestinian state on the West Bank and the Gaza Strip, it becomes abundantly clear that such a state, far from contributing to a peaceful solution of the Arab-Israeli conflict, would more likely exacerbate it.

Many among those in the West who favor the establishment of a Palestinian Arab state genuinely believe that it is the only way to peace, stability, and justice in the Middle East. Others are aware of the dangers ahead but see no alternative in view of the seemingly overwhelming pressures from all quarters; they have persuaded themselves that the worst does not always happen. Then there are those who have no illusions about the outcome of this policy, who know that it will lead to a new war, or wars, but who regard this as both inevitable and desirable, on the theory that a Middle East settlement (as they see it) will be possible only after further bloodshed. Finally, there are those who, unwilling to accept these as the only alternatives, have cast about for variants on the idea of a Palestinian state.

One such variant, a way of coping with the problem of viability, is federation with either Israel or Jordan. At the present time, one cannot envisage a scheme, however ingenious, of federating Israel and a Palestinian state that has a realistic chance of working. The "Jordanian solution," which involves returning the West Bank to Jordan and which Israel now favors, might have worked in 1968, but it is unlikely at this point to break the deadlock. The Palestinians are against accepting Jordanian control in the short run, and King Hussein knows that in the long run a merger between the West Bank and the Hashemite kingdom (the majority of whose inhabitants even now are Palestinians) would make Jordan a Palestinian state.

Hussein's loss, however, would not necessarily be the Palestinians' gain. Even adding Jordan to a Palestinian state on the West Bank still would not provide sufficient scope for a large-scale resettlement of Palestinian refugees. For Jordan is a poor country. Its per-capita income is $270, lower than any other Arab country except the Sudan and Yemen; between 1965 and 1972 (the last figures available) it experienced minus economic growth. Whichever way one looks at it, a merger between the West Bank and Jordan would be no great bargain. Hussein and the Jordanians would lose, the Palestinians would not gain much, and Israel would still be threatened, only this time by one state rather than two.

Besides federation, there is of course the idea of a bi-national state. The establishment of such a state ("democratic and secular"), which was rejected for decades by the leadership of the Palestinian Arabs, is now the official aim of the PLO. The PLO formula should not be taken quite literally, for it clashes with two other Palestinian demands, namely that the character of the state must be Arab, and that the state should be integrated into the area and not remain an "outpost of the West." But a democratic and secular state could not possibly integrate itself into an area that is neither democratic nor secular. Such a state would invite envy and hostility and would be regarded as a foreign body.

With these reservations, it may be quite true that the PLO wants a bi-national state of sorts, but does not know how to achieve this aim in the present circumstances. One of its chief spokesmen in the West recently stated in an interview that if he waved a magic wand and said, "Let all the Palestinian Arabs and all the Israeli Jews live tomorrow in a democratic, secular Palestine," this would more or less immediately lead to a civil war: "All these years of conflict and tension are not a good background for the establishment of a peaceful and harmonious coexistence between two communities."* Said Hammami is of course quite right; historical experience, including some of very recent vintage, shows that bi-nationalism works only very rarely.

It will be argued that these speculations and objections are all too pessimistic, that the conflict will not necessarily escalate, that the Palestinians may well put up with the existence of Israel (and the Israelis with the existence of a Palestinian state), that there may be isolated acts of violence but no movement toward full-scale war. Yet even if an optimistic scenario for achieving a settlement is assumed, there would still remain the problem of guarantees by outside powers.

Who would these powers be? Among the various nominees who have been put forward, the United Nations and Europe can be dismissed without further comment. As for the Soviet Union, it is indeed true (as a recent Brookings Institution study group has noted) that the Russians, because of their relations with Syria and the PLO, have a considerable capacity for obstructing peace or even blocking further progress toward an overall settlement. Or to put the case even more bluntly: the Soviet Union could probably torpedo any settlement not to its liking. But is it at all certain that the Soviet Union would prefer a peace settlement to the present state of affairs? Those who argue that a new Middle Eastern war would be a disaster for the West and would greatly strengthen Soviet influence, paradoxically also maintain that it is in the interest of the Soviet Union to help make peace in the Middle East and to guarantee it. The logic underlying this argument is not readily obvious; governments seldom act for any length of time contrary to their own interests, and the Soviet government in particular is not known for excessive altruism in world politics.

This is not an abstract issue: if the Soviet Union had wanted to make a contribution to Middle Eastern peace, it could have put some pressure on the "Rejection Front" to moderate its opposition to any political solution of the conflict. This would certainly have made it

*Said Hammami, quoted in *New Outlook,* October-November 1975.

easier for Arafat to produce an ambiguous formula satisfying the State Department (though not Israel) that the PLO might be willing under certain circumstances to consider according Israel something that could be interpreted by unsuspecting third parties as *de facto* recognition. But the Soviet Union has refrained so far even from making this minor effort. It is unlikely therefore that the Soviets will extend a bona-fide guarantee to a settlement which gives their Arab friends and clients less than they want. (This is not to say that the Soviet Union might not look with favor upon the establishment of a non-viable Palestinian state, asuming with some justification that it would sooner or later gain a foothold in this state.)

American guarantees are almost equally problematical. A guarantee that does not make provisions for military intervention is worse than useless, and given the isolationist mood of Congress, this is about all that can be expected. But even if a real guarantee should be provided, it would obviously apply only in the case of an extreme violation of the agreement, such as an all-out military attack. This, however, is a less likely eventuality than the kind of shelling across the border which has been practiced in recent years from Jordan and Lebanon. Israel would find such shelling intolerable, but would the United States? And even if there were a clear case of aggression, would there not be cries of "No more Vietnams" and the like? And even if all these fears were to prove groundless, it is still true that if present trends continue, America may no longer be in a position actively to intervene even if it wanted to, simply because it is steadily falling behind the Soviet Union in military preparedness.

II

To accept the inherently unstable nature of Middle East politics and the intractability of its problems is not to preach defeatism and opt for inaction. It is, however, to ask for an end to false hopes in the West generally and in the United States in particular. For it is important to understand that even if there should be a settlement between Israel and the Arabs, major conflicts in the Middle East would persist. And so far as basic Western interests are concerned, these might be in even greater danger after a settlement were reached than in the present situation.

Yet whatever the consequences for other countries, it is certainly in Israel's interest to work for a lessening of tensions in its relations with its Arab neighbors. There are things Israel can do, but these options cannot be discussed without reference to the immobilism of Israeli policy after 1967 in which they have their roots.

Psychologically, this immobilism is easy to understand. The 1967 victory had been complete, and it seemed only reasonable to assume that the Arabs would be willing to discuss peace terms. The old borders had been a nightmare, and since Arab leaders had threatened Israel with extinction so many times, it seemed right to insist that a return to these borders was out of the question. But the Arabs refused to meet

Israel halfway, let alone to discuss a firm and lasting peace. In the circumstances, the military victors saw no reason to seize the political initiative. No Israeli leader was ready to take risks with the security of the country. It was the "safe-border" argument, not the mystique of the "Land of Israel" movement, which underlay Israeli policy between 1967 and 1973.

In retrospect, however, it is clear that this approach ignored the wider context of world politics. It underrated latent Arab power (economic and political rather than military); and giving absolute priority to security, it made the defusing of an inherently dangerous situation impossible. Again, it is easy to point to mitigating circumstances. Few countries in history have made unilateral concessions after a brilliant military victory. Psychologically, it would have been difficult to persuade the Israeli public to pursue such a course of action, especially since there was no guarantee that unilateral Israeli concessions would be reciprocated, and that the Arabs would not go to war again after a few years.

Mitigating circumstances, however, count for little in politics, and we now can see that greater risks should have been taken. Time was not working in Israel's favor, and it would have been preferable to part with at least some of the occupied territories, unilaterally if necessary, from a position of strength rather than weakness. To be sure, territorial concessions might not have prevented a new war; in that case Israel's position would have been worse. But it need not have been much worse, especially if arrangements had been made for the demilitarization of border zones. It is true that the Arab countries might still not have accepted the existence of the Jewish state. Certainly there would have been bellicose speeches and threats on the part of the Arab governments. Acts of terror would have continued and Israeli goods might not have passed through the Suez Canal. But not all the Arab governments would have felt the same overriding urgency to go to war and recover the lost territories. And since the Israeli problem was not the only one preoccupying the Arab world, the conflict might well have lost some of its acuteness. Israel would still have figured high among Arab grievances, but it might no longer have had top priority.

Israel, in other words, could not possibly have relied on Arab good will, but it could have relied on Arab disunity. It was this failure to accept anything less than peace, the insistence on a policy involving no risks, which paralyzed Israeli foreign policy between 1967 and 1973.

Some now agree that mistakes were made, but maintain that a democratically elected government could not have carried out a policy rejected by the majority of the population. Such fatalism is unfounded; public opinion would have accepted almost any policy advocated by a strong leadership, just as it accepted Ben-Gurion's decision to withdraw Israeli forces from Sinai in 1956.

Others believe that nothing Israel might have done would have made the slightest difference. They are certain that no opportunities were missed during the interwar years—which is true in the sense that the phone call General Dayan expected from King Hussein never came, and that the Arab leaders decided at Khartoum not to negotiate with Israel. But the decisive question is, of course, whether it was indeed impossible to create opportunities, thus reducing the likelihood of a new war, and whether it would not have been worthwhile to pay a price to attain this end. There are no certainties, but it seems very plausible that Israel's international position would have been considerably stronger today had it after 1967 pursued the policy it is now being forced to carry out, if it had made voluntarily and from a position of strength the concessions it has made (and is going to make) under pressure. At the very least, Israel's position would not have been worse.

Of course not even clarity about the past can produce a magic formula that will show the way out of the present impasse. This applies especially to the view that Israel should at all costs stand firm against outside pressure in the present circumstances and should not give up an inch, on the ground that the compromises suggested will lead not toward peace but to a new war under less favorable conditions.

There are serious problems with this approach, but to reject it out of hand for ethical reasons, as certain commentators do, is to apply moral standards to Israel that are not applied to any other country. After all, it was not the fault of the Israelis that the Arabs went to war against the Jewish state in 1948 and that, as a result, new realities came into being which can no longer be undone. The Arab argument that the injustice done to the Palestinians is somehow unique is based either on ignorance or on hypocrisy. All over the world many millions of people have had to leave their native countries in recent decades without hope of repatriation. Nor have the many millions of square miles of territory conquered in war over the same period been subject to demands that they be returned. As to the case for a greater Jewish state, it was put most succinctly by Jabotinsky in his evidence before a British Royal Commission on the eve of World War II:

> . . . I do not deny [that] the Arabs of Palestine will necessarily become a minority in the country of Palestine. What I do deny is that this is a hardship. That is not a hardship on any race, any nation possessing so many national states and so many more national states in the future. One fraction, one branch of that race, and not a big one, will have to live in someone else's state; well, that is the case with all the mightiest nations of the world. I could hardly mention one of the big nations, having their states, mighty and powerful, who had not one branch living in someone else's state. That is only normal and there is no "hardship" attached to that. So when we hear the Arab claim confronted with the Jewish claim—I fully understand that any minority would prefer to be a majority: It is quite understandable that the Arabs of Palestine would also prefer Palestine to be the Arab state No. 4, 5, or 6—that I quite understand—but when the Arab claim is confronted with our Jewish demand to be saved, it is like the claims of appetite versus the claims of starvation. . . .

Today a Palestinian state would not be the fourth, but the twenty-fourth Arab state. The Palestinians may reason that they are as much entitled to their own state as all other Arabs, but all Arab leaders and

political movements have solemnly declared on many occasions that the
Arabs are one nation, divided by artificial frontiers; if so, the Palestinians are at home in every Arab country. Nor is there any lack of
space in the Arab world. When it was decided to partition Palestine in
1947, less than one-sixth of one per cent of the territory inhabited by
the Arabs was set aside for Israel; one-half of one per cent of the Arabs
was to become a minority and to live in the Jewish state. This compromise was accepted by the Jews and rejected by the Arabs.

Shorn of certain dubious historical-religious arguments, then, the
case for Israel to stand firm and refuse to give an inch is not a weak case
at all. The difficulties arise on the level of reality and power, not on that
of morality and reason. For the truth is that there is not one law for
strong and weak alike. When the Soviet Union and its East European
satellites expelled many millions of Germans after World War II, world
public opinion expected the Germans tacitly to accept their fate. When
they protested, they were denounced as fascists and warmongers. But
Israel is not a power like Russia, and the Palestinians have stronger
protectors than the Germans from Poland and the Sudeten region.
The fate of the Palestinians is regarded by world public opinion as a
grave injustice, to be remedied as quickly as possible. If the Palestinians
were politically weaker, and Israel were stronger, less dependent
financially and militarily on outside help and good will, it could sit out
the storm for a few years or even a few decades. Such a policy would
find few supporters outside Israel, though; the idea frequently voiced
by Herut and its supporters that all Israel needs is *hasbara*—more effective political propaganda—is quite illusory. What really matters in the
last resort is whether Israel could get along without outside financial
support, whether it could accept the risks of political isolation, whether
it could produce at home all the arms that are and will be needed for its
defense.

But even if it could do all these things, the size of the Arab
minority in the Jewish state would still be a major problem. It is unlikely that the Arabs living in a "greater Israel" would be assimilated;
there would always be a strong pull toward the other Arab countries.
The improvement of Arab living standards in Israel would do nothing
to assuage Arab nationalism or contribute to the solution of what is
essentially a political problem. Thus a "greater Israel" would, to put the
point bluntly, either cease to be Jewish or cease to be democratic.

Except for the idea of standing firm, there is no coherent strategy
being advocated within Israel, and for a long time now there has been
no overall concept behind the government's foreign policy. This is a
general weakness of democratic societies, what with conflicting
domestic pressures and the absence of strong leadership preventing
major foreign political initiatives. There have been no such initiatives
in Israeli foreign policy for a long time, merely responses to the actions
of others. But historical experience has shown that a free society is not
doomed to impotence; a democratically elected leader, or group of

leaders, need not be unsure and indecisive, they need not be dependent in their every action on public-opinion polls and popularity contests, they can act without paying undue attention to their own political careers.

What, then, might Israel do? It would be a realistic policy on Israel's part to reaffirm unequivocally in conformity with Resolution 242 that there is no intention of incorporating Arab territories into the state. Israel could also declare that these territories will be evacuated step-by-step over a period of five to ten years within the framework of a general peace settlement involving recognition of Israel and a regulated rectification of the 1967 borders in the interest of security. Each Israeli concession would depend on Palestinian and Arab willingness to carry out the terms of the settlement. If, for instance, acts of terror were to continue, Israel would no longer be bound to fulfill its part of the bargain. (Such arrangements have been made before in history; they were used, for instance, in Central Europe after World War I.) Israel would also have to insist on transferring these territories to a representative Arab body—it would be pointless to deal with leaders whose authority is not recognized by the Palestinians. This would mean free elections, under the supervision of Israel, the Arab states, and some third parties. The PLO would of course compete in these elections, but it is obvious that there could be no dealings between Israel and the PLO unless and until the PLO were ready to accept the existence of Israel.

A procedure of this kind would not by itself solve any of the difficulties that have been mentioned. But it would to a certain extent reduce the risks, and it would make it possible in the interim period to work for a more lasting solution, either in the form of a confederation or some other framework that would safeguard the security and the political and economic viability of both states.

It is a long time since Israeli leaders have made concrete proposals to the Arabs for coexistence. This is not surprising, for such proposals would probably have fallen on deaf ears. The Arab-Israeli conflict may well have been inevitable; it is not inevitable, however, that it go on forever. It has to be recognized at long last that the Zionist attempt to "solve the Jewish question" resulted in the emergence of a Palestinian Arab question, and that Israel has to play its part in helping to solve *that* question. This does not imply that Israel has to sacrifice its own existence. Many Palestinians know quite well, and the others will learn, that speeches about the "total liquidation of Israel" will get them nowhere, for present-day armies, unlike the Crusaders, fight not with swords but with weapons of mass destruction. The PLO and the Rejection Front may want to destroy Israel, but they do not want to pay for it with the annihilation of their own people and their own future. Once they realize that the only alternative to coexistence is mutual extinction, a solution of the conflict will become possible. One hopes, though there can be no confidence, that this realization will come without recourse to yet another war.

But if one asks whether a lasting peace is possible in the Middle East at the present time, the answer must be no—whichever way one looks at it, and least of all as a result of the measures suggested so frequently these days with so little thought of the consequences. All one can hope for is the absence of war. If that can be achieved, the time gained can be used for thinking about new ways and means to find a stabler basis for coexistence between Israel and its Arab neighbors.

9   The Soviet Union, China and The West in Southern Africa

Colin Legum

Like Henry Kissinger, most American commentators have interpreted the Soviet intervention in Angola almost solely as an extension of Soviet cold war competition with the West into Africa. In this perspective the outcome in Angola has been viewed as a major gain for the Soviet Union against the West, with the Russians capitalizing on the American disadvantage in its years of support for Portugal. With the South African intervention against the Soviet-backed liberation movement, the Russians also scored an important "diplomatic triumph," as the Organization of African Unity swung around to overwhelming support for the Soviet protégé, against the Angolan leaders who had called in the South Africans. In all this the United States and the West were the big losers.

While this interpretation contains some elements of truth, it is an inadequate framework for analysis of what actually happened in Angola and what may now be in immediate prospect for Rhodesia and Namibia. For it leaves out an extremely important element—the rivalry between the Soviet Union and China for influence in Africa. Only if this rivalry is given the emphasis it deserves can one understand the true nature of the struggle that is now taking place in Rhodesia, and, prospectively, future conflicts in Namibia and South Africa.

The root of the conflict in southern Africa is of course entirely indigenous—that is, it arises from the determination of black Africans to bring an end to the white supremacist regimes there. Most African leaders would much prefer, in their own interests, to see this come about through nonviolent means, as was demonstrated by their response in 1974 to the offer to start talks by South Africa's Prime Minister Johannes Vorster. They will, nonetheless, support violence if no other way seems open, as they do presently in Rhodesia. Similarly, most influential African leaders are hostile to communism and strongly opposed to the intrusion of big-power politics in Africa; but because they see white racism in southern Africa as a bigger menace to them than communism, they will welcome anti-Western forces in the struggle against the white supremacist regimes.

Neither the Soviet Union nor China has had any conflicting interest or ideological difficulties in wholeheartedly supporting the African drive against white-minority rule. The Western position, on the other hand, has necessarily been more ambiguous, given a sizable Western economic stake in the area and strong social constraints against the risk of a race war which guerrilla tactics would unavoidably entail. At least until Secretary of State Kissinger's recent trip to Africa, this diplomatic disadvantage was reinforced for the United States by its reputed and discernible "tilt" toward the white-minority regimes.

. . .

If the Administration can quickly follow up on the promises, its ability to influence developments in southern Africa will undoubtedly be improved. Three steps are seen by Africans as an immediate test of a meaningful change in U.S. policy: repeal of the Byrd Amendment which permits chrome imports from Rhodesia; recognition of the new 18-member High Command of the Zimbabwe Liberation Army (ZILA) which is now more important than the old leadership of the African National Council (ANC); and a firm rejection of any independence for Namibia which does not have the substantial endorsement of the country's political leadership, including the South West African People's Organization (SWAPO).

But if the U.S. (and Western) posture is in fact moving closer toward African aspirations, it is more than ever vital to take full account of the deep-seated rivalry between the Soviet Union and China, and the way that rivalry interacts with the interests of black African nations, and South Africa. For the West, the Sino-Soviet struggle in Africa may hold both perils and opportunities.

II

Since the early 1960s, rivalry between the Chinese and the Russians in the Third World has grown increasingly intense. The "first front" in this struggle has been South and Southeast Asia. There the Russians, over the past decade, have more than held their own: in Vietnam and Laos they have emerged at least more influential than the Chinese, and their developing relations with Mrs. Indira Gandhi's India are, at least in the short term, a considerable achievement. In Bangladesh the rivalry is now growing keener, as the Chinese move to underpin the military regime to resist the pressures of New Delhi and Moscow.

A related part of that struggle, in Soviet strategic thinking, has undoubtedly been the competition for influence in the countries on both sides of the Red Sea, notably in the Horn of Africa. Here the Soviets were able to establish military facilities in Somalia but also suffered sharp setbacks, including the failure of the communist-led coup in the Sudan in 1971, and the erosion of their close relations with Egypt since 1972. It now also looks as if they are being eased out of the important Aden port in South Yemen.

Elsewhere in black Africa, the Soviets made determined efforts in the early 1960s, notably in Zaïre, Ghana, Guinea, and Mali, but with the failure of their efforts in the first two countries and uncertain results in the latter, the Russians became increasingly clumsy in their dealings. By 1973, Moscow had few worthwhile connections in black Africa, other than tiny Somalia and unstable Congo-Brazzaville.

The Chinese, on the other hand, having also got off to an early bad start, profited more quickly from their mistakes than the Russians, notably after their Cultural Revolution. Avoiding blatant bids for political domination, and tailoring their programs to meet the particular requests of the Africans themselves, they imparted a sense of both generosity and disinterest to their aid role which has led to their steadily widening their sphere of friendly influence on the African continent.

The Chinese had two particular successes. The first was the expansion of their friendship with Tanzania (through the building of the Freedom Railway to Zambia) and later with Zaïre: thus they established a network of relationships across the tropical waist of Africa from the Indian Ocean to the Atlantic. (At present they are considering a request from Botswana to help operate that country's section of the line recently taken over from Rhodesian Railways.) Their second success was in winning the confidence of the major liberation movements in southern Africa to a much greater extent than did the Russians, despite Moscow's arms and economic aid. With the exception of the African National Congress of South Africa (ANC-in-exile), all the major liberation movements appear to have found it easier to work with the Chinese than with the Russians. This was notably the case with the Front for the Liberation of Mozambique (FRELIMO), the Zimbabwe African National Union (ZANU) of Rhodesia, and SWAPO of Namibia.

Moscow had a particularly troubled relationship with the Angolan leadership during the liberation struggle. Although they had consistently supported the Popular Movement for the Liberation of Angola (MPLA), they had never found it easy to get along with the rather secretive and prickly Agostinho Neto. For a time in 1973 they went so far as to support one of Neto's challengers, Daniel Chipenda, and cut off all their aid to MPLA; but once it became clear that Chipenda could not win, Moscow switched its support back to Neto.

The Soviets' concern over China's successes in Africa led them, around 1972–73, to embark on a much more vigorous policy in black Africa. They became the main arms suppliers to Uganda's tyrant ruler, General Idi Amin, and they entered into an arms agreement with Libya's Colonel Qaddafi, despite his militantly anti-communist stand. While the move toward Libya was clearly aimed at President Sadat (whose relations with Qaddafi are notoriously bad), the decision to gamble on Amin gave them an apparent "gain" in East and Central Africa—in a country, moreover, hostile to Tanzania and Zambia, both of which are seen by the Russians as being "under Chinese influence." (Moscow's classification of African countries bears a strong resemblance to the simplistic views held by Western military establishments.)

This new higher priority given to Africa by Moscow enabled it to respond quickly to two major developments early in 1974. The first was the February army mutiny in Ethiopia, which marked the beginning of the end of Haile Selassie's long rule and began a new period of instability around the Horn of Africa. And the second was the Portuguese coup two months later.

The collapse of the Portuguese dictatorship in April 1974 initiated a new phase in the Sino-Soviet struggle, with the Chinese initially making far the greater gains, particularly in Mozambique, and in consolidating their relations with Tanzania and Zambia. Given the strong Chinese position already established with two of Angola's liberation movements (the Zaïre-backed Front for the Liberation of Angola [FNLA] and the National Union for the Total Independence of Angola [UNITA]) as well as with the Zaïre government, the cards were heavily stacked in the Chinese favor at the end of 1974. In this context, and within what was already emerging as a much speeded-up timetable in southern Africa generally, the Soviets made their crucial decision in Angola in 1975.

III

In terms of size and risk, the Soviet operation in Angola went a good deal beyond their previous ventures in Africa. In their all-out support of the MPLA, the Russians gambled on the success of a minority party, and for a time defied the collective policy of the Organization of African Unity (OAU), which favored government of national unity in an independent Angola. The key to these bold Soviet decisions lay above all in the Chinese factor.

In Angola, in the early months of 1975, the MPLA was facing an open challenge from the Zaïre-backed FNLA. At that time the Chinese, with their military instructors based in Zaïre, were FNLA's most effective foreign backers. U.S. aid was still small in scale. If the Russians had been primarily concerned with neutralizing U.S. aid, they could have invoked the Moscow accords to prevent the development of a situation which could lead to a military confrontation between them. But this would have meant leaving the field clear for the Chinese to spread their influence through FNLA and Zaïre.

Instead, by March 1975, the Russians were already engaged in sending substantial military supplies to the MPLA—fully six months before the first U.S. arms shipments had begun to reach FNLA through Zaïre, and only two months after Kissinger had asked Congress to approve a limited military aid program to Zaïre for this purpose. The March 1975 date is important because it explains how the MPLA could by then have become sufficiently strong to best the

FNLA forces in the continuing struggles for control of the capital in April and May. By June the MPLA was strong enough to take on UNITA as well, and to spread its forces, albeit lightly, across 12 of the 14 provinces.

It is not yet possible to fix with certainty the exact date when Moscow first began to arrange with Fidel Castro to bring in large numbers of Cubans as bearers of the communist flag on the battlefield, or when President Ngouabi of the Congo agreed that his capital, Brazzaville, should serve as the base for the buildup of Russian arms for the MPLA and the staging post for the trans-shipment of Cuban soldiers to Angola. By July, however, the Russians were almost certainly going for broke.

By September, two months before the date set for independence on November 11, the Russian and Cuban military aid was of a size that promised military supremacy to the MPLA. The scale of the Soviet/Cuban intervention increased sharply in early October, three weeks before the South African forces entered Angola in any size. (However, by September, the MPLA were very likely already convinced that such an attack was probable.) Because the Russians and Cubans had by then already established their communication lines to, and through, Brazzaville, it was a simple matter for them to increase the size of their intervention at short notice. The Russian and Cuban contention that their military intervention was the result of the South African invasion is clearly an ex post facto rationalization.

In October, the Russians openly opposed the OAU position in favor of a government of national unity. They showed their hand by a blunt demarche to the OAU Chairman, General Idi Amin, demanding that Amin, the recipient of quantities of Soviet military aid, should break with the policy of his own organization and follow the Moscow line, recognizing the MPLA as the sole legal authority. Not one to knuckle under—in any direction—Amin refused. This remarkably clumsy diplomacy was evidence of the Soviet Union's overriding determination to see its Angolan enterprise succeed.

The Chinese, on the other hand, made their decision to withdraw their instructors from the FNLA camps in Zaïre in July 1975 in response to the OAU's call for neutrality among the three rival Angolan movements. The reason they gave for this decision was that since they were not in a position to deliver aid to the MPLA, they would have been taking sides if they were left supporting only the FNLA and UNITA. Two months later the Chinese in fact withdrew all their military instructors from Zaïre. Peking was not equipped to compete with massive Soviet aid. It is also probable that the Chinese, taking a much longer historical view of their role in Africa than Moscow, believed they would be able to achieve more in the long run by proving themselves loyal to OAU decisions. (It is likely, too, that they counted on the United States not to allow itself to be ousted by the Russians from an area of traditional Western interest.)

After the South Africans invaded Angola in October, all political risk of the Soviets offending Africa was eradicated, but they were still faced with the perils inherent in their role as patron of an undeveloped and divided nation. Their willingness to commit themselves fully in the face of these uncertainties resulted largely from a desire to counter the significant Chinese influence in East Africa, particularly the Chinese involvement in the liberation struggles.

What happened in Angola suggests that in the Third World the Sino-Soviet rivalry with each other has become more important to them than either's rivalry with the West. The Chinese felt themselves to be in de facto alliance with the United States and reportedly urged U.S. intervention against the Russians and Cubans. The Russians, for their part, were willing to place détente with Washington in jeopardy at a time when opposition to détente was already growing in the United States and Western Europe.

The clearest evidence of the primary importance of the Sino-Soviet contest was provided by the propaganda circulated in the Third World by Moscow and Peking during the Angolan crisis. Both sides were concerned almost entirely with discrediting each other and only to a minor degree with attacking "U.S. and Western imperialism." Indeed, the leitmotiv of Peking's line on Angola was to accuse the "modern tsarists" of "single-handedly provoking the civil war in Angola." The Russians, on their side, insisted that:

> all the action taken by the Peking leadership shows that the Maoists, who are seeking their own hegemonic control (over the world), have not stopped subversive activity against the Angolan people for a single minute, that they gave active support to pro-imperialist groupings and organizations, pushing them to take action against the genuine representatives and vanguard of the Angolan people—the MPLA.

Each side strained to convince the Third World that the role of the other in Angola was proof of a clear design to achieve "world domination"—an obsessive refrain in the propaganda of both.

In this contest for the allegiance of the Third World, the Russians are concerned to defend themselves against what they regard as "Peking's false doctrine about the role of the two superpowers . . . a cunning trick of the Maoists who dream of dominating the world." Moscow's defensive line is typified by this kind of statement:

> The present leadership of the PRC are taking considerable pains in order to justify the so-called vanguard role of China in the world revolutionary process and to represent itself as one of the truest and most consistent allies of the Afro-Asian and Latin American peoples in their struggles for national liberation, against imperialism, colonialism and neocolonialism. But events have proved absolutely false the Maoists' representation of Peking as a factor working to cement the national liberation forces of Angola. . . .

To which the Chinese counterattacked by saying:

> People have become increasingly aware that in contending for hegemony with the other superpowers, the Soviet revisionists stoop to anything to frenziedly penetrate and expand in Africa in a vain attempt to replace the old colonialism. Their interference in the internal affairs of Angola

constitutes an important step in their scramble for hegemony in Africa, the aim being to place strategically important Angola, which is rich in natural resources, in their neocolonialist spheres of influence.

The Chinese position closely approximates that of the hawks in the West in seeing the Russian design as being concerned solely with becoming the new "colonial power in Africa." At the height of the Angolan affair, a senior Chinese diplomat remonstrated with me for questioning whether the Russians were really interested in acquiring military bases in Angola. "That," he said coldly, "may not be the wish of the Angolans; but we know how difficult it was for us to shake the Russians off our necks in China and we, after all, were in a somewhat stronger position to resist the Russians than are the Angolans."

The outcome of the Angolan affair did shift the balance of influence between the Soviets and Chinese in Africa. The Soviet Union demonstrated its willingness and capability to produce effective military support for an ally in a strategically crucial part of southern Africa. In doing so, the Russians succeeded in encouraging other liberation movements to think seriously about accepting their support. It is too early yet to know how much China's influence has suffered in Africa as a result of the Russian/Cuban/MPLA victory, but what is certain is Chinese determination to ensure that the Russians do not, if they can possibly help it, repeat their victory in Rhodesia and Namibia.

IV

The experience of Angola should not be taken as a sure guide to what will happen in Rhodesia. The Russians were able to play an effective role in Angola for a number of reasons particular to that situation, including: the peculiar nature of the power struggle among rival Angolan movements in a country without a legally recognized government; South Africa's decision to intervene militarily; the Chinese decision to opt for neutrality in the local power struggle; and the paralysis of U.S. foreign policy making in the aftermath of Vietnam, Watergate and the CIA investigations.

In Rhodesia and Namibia, the role that external powers will play is likely to be circumscribed by the active role of the leaders of the neighboring black African countries. The so-called Front-Line Presidents— Tanzania's Julius Nyerere (the chairman), Zambia's Kenneth Kaunda, Mozambique's Samora Machel, and Botswana's Sit Seretse Khama— exercise a controlling influence over what happens in the liberation struggle in Rhodesia. The effectiveness of this strong quartet depends on their ability to carry the majority of the OAU membership with them—which seems assured—and especially on their ability to retain the confidence of the new Zimbabwe Liberation Army (ZILA) high command. ZILA, whose leadership is as yet relatively unknown, has now replaced the divided leadership of the African National Council (ANC), as represented by Bishop Abel Muzorewa, and the two main guerrilla movements, the Zimbabwe African Nationalist Union (ZANU) led by the Reverend Ndabiningi Sithole and the Zimbabwe African People's Union (ZAPU) led by Joshua Nkomo.

Although Messrs. Kaunda and Khama had ended up on opposite sides from Messrs. Nyerere and Machel in the Angolan controversies, the four Presidents have remained on close and friendly terms and are agreed on a strategy for Rhodesia. They are united in their commitment to a full-scale guerrilla war in Rhodesia until a white Rhodesian leadership emerges which is willing to enter into negotiations premised on the acceptance of immediate majority rule. Although they have committed themselves to the struggle, they want to keep it as short as possible to avoid unnecessary loss of life and bitterness, and to minimize the damaging effects on the economies of Zambia and Mozambique of a war on their borders. For landlocked Zambia the disruption of its transport routes to the sea is a serious matter. Mozambique's parlous economy makes its commitment especially heroic, or reckless, depending on one's point of view.

The second point of agreement among the four Presidents is that all foreign military and economic aid for the guerrillas must be channeled through the OAU Liberation Committee in Dar es Salaam. By this measure they seek to prevent any of the major powers from backing possible rival black nationalist factions, thus repeating Angola's tragedy. The third and fourth points of agreement are also aimed at curtailing further outside intervention by insisting that the fighting itself must be done only by Zimbabweans, thereby excluding the possibility of Cuban commandos repeating their Angolan role in Rhodesia; and that no new foreign military instructors are to be admitted into the training camps of ZILA situated in Mozambique and Tanzania. This last point ensures to the Chinese a primary role in the training of the guerrillas. The Chinese already have been involved for about seven years in support of the main guerrilla group, ZANU, whose forces have now been absorbed by ZILA. The Russians have in the past given their support to ZANU's rival, ZAPU, which failed conspicuously to build up an effective guerrilla force. ZAPU is represented in the joint command, but its past military ineffectiveness makes it the subordinate partner. The ZILA military command, with only one or two notable exceptions, favors cooperation with the Chinese instructors. Continuing Russian pressures for a major training role to be given to Cuban military instructors are being vigorously resisted by the Chinese, who have described the Cuban commandos in Angola as "Russian mercenaries."

However, a small number of Cuban instructors have now been admitted as a trade-off for Russian deliveries of SAM missiles and other sophisticated weapons not yet available from China—and relations between the few Cubans and the Chinese instructors in the camps are known to be producing difficulties for the ZILA High Command.

So, in the developing Rhodesian struggle the Sino-Soviet rivalry witnessed in Angola is continued. For the Front-Line Presidents and the Zimbabwe leadership the risk of introducing the damaging rivalry between the two communist capitals into ZILA's ranks is a major concern. It is possible that, under continuing heavy Russian pressure, the Chinese might be asked to give up their present training role, but this is not immediately in prospect. The Russians, however, can be expected to exercise considerable pressures on the African leaders to un-

dercut the Chinese role. There is reason to believe that they are proving reluctant to supply arms through the OAU Liberation Committee
in protest against the present policy of the Front-Line Presidents. Because the guerrillas are particularly keen to get Russian supplies of
SAM-7 missiles, Moscow has a strong card to play.

As long as the Front-Line Presidents are able to maintain their
present unity, and to retain the confidence of the ZILA high command
(a crucial factor), they are in physical control of the strategy to be
followed in Rhodesia. It is presently no part of their strategy to allow
the Cuban commandos to repeat their Angolan role in Rhodesia. Independence and African self-determination are important ideological
goals for them. Even more important, they have no desire to see outside powers exacerbate Zimbabwean divisions by choosing sides.

However, there are a number of elements which could influence
their present strategy. If the guerrillas fail in the next several years to
crack the morale of Ian Smith's supporters, who still include the great
majority of white Rhodesians, frustration could induce an erosion of
the present policy. A prolonged struggle could change the political
situation in Mozambique (whose leadership is still engaged in implant-
ing its authority in the recently born republic) and in Zambia. Serious
economic dislocation and internal insecurity caused by the wars along
their borders could, in time, undermine the present leadership in both
countries. Unless there is an early outcome to the Rhodesian struggle,
pressure could arise for a greater input of military power against the
Smith regime; and frustration would induce a greater openness to the
involvement of outside powers.

Furthermore, if an open split were to develop within ZILA's High
Command, the Russians and Chinese could step in to support rival factions.

Another major element of uncertainty is South Africa's future role
in Rhodesia. Mr. Vorster believes majority rule in Rhodesia is both
inevitable and necessary. His present firm policy is not to become militarily involved in the Rhodesian fighting, having withdrawn his forces
from that country in 1975. His decision to withdraw his backing from
the Smith regime was made immediately after the collapse of
Portuguese colonialism, when it became clear to him that the Rhodesian position was no longer defensible in military terms without a
total commitment of South Africa's resources—an option he rejected as
not being in South Africa's best interests. Involvement in the Rhodesian struggle, he feels, would not only entail an open-ended military
commitment against the guerrillas, but would stimulate more militant
opposition from black South Africans. He also must recognize after
Angola that it could induce the African leaders to invite the communist
powers to become more directly involved in the area.

But, on the other hand, Mr. Vorster will not apply pressure on
Rhodesia by closing his border with that country, or impede the
transport of its exports and imports to South Africa's ports, even
though this action would be the quickest way of forcing white Rhodesian to accept majority rule. He will refuse to assist in "a quick kill" for

two reasons. First, in joining in the international embargo on Rhodesia he would be playing into the hands of the anti-apartheid lobby which advocates sanctions against South Africa. Second, and most important, he must take great care not to arouse the right wing of his own white electorate. Even though the majority of the ruling Afrikaner National Party's supporters appear to accept the reasons for Mr. Vorster's refusal to continue to back the Smith regime, white South Africans are, understandably enough, emotionally involved in the fate of white Rhodesians. Not only do they feel strong kinship, but they also suspect they might be watching a rehearsal for their own coming agony. The *verkrampte* (inward-looking) elements among the Afrikaners—an articulate minority—regard the abandonment by South Africa of the Smith regime as a "betrayal," and they argue that this pragmatic policy will not help South Africa to fight off the black challenge once Rhodesia has been taken over by a black government.

In the approaching denouement of the Rhodesian crisis, the big powers will be kept out of the struggle—if the African strategy works out as intended. Once the guerrillas begin to develop a more powerful thrust, it is expected that an increasing number of white Rhodesians will begin to trek southward to the South African border to settle either in the Republic or in parts of the white commonwealth. Such an exodus will then demoralize the rest of the white Rhodesians and lead to the collapse of the Smith regime, producing a new white leadership (as in the transition period in Kenya), which will be ready to negotiate acceptable terms for a settlement. That, at least, is the scenario of the Front-Line Presidents. What this picture leaves out of account is the tenacity of white Rhodesian resistance and the possibility of a white backlash in South Africa upsetting Mr. Vorster's more realistic approach to the Rhodesian crisis. It also assumes the unity of the Zimbabwean liberation movement, as well as the ability of the Front-Line Presidents to maintain their present common stand despite the competing interests of the communist powers, as well as those of the Western nations.

Faced with these considerable uncertainties it is futile to speculate about the likely course of events in Rhodesia, but it requires little prescience to suggest that what happens there will decisively affect future developments in the last stronghold of white rule in the continent—the Republic of South Africa.

V

The penultimate element in the southern African pattern—the territory of Namibia (South West Africa)—is directly controlled by South Africa. What happens there obviously depends directly on decisions taken by Pretoria.

Mr. Vorster has announced his decision to go forward with plans to grant full independence under black majority rule to Namibia within two or three years. While broad agreement has already been reached with some black Namibian leaders, headed by Chief Clemens Kapuuo,

Mr. Vorster has not been willing to negotiate with the external wing of the South West African People's Organization (SWAPO), although he is reportedly ready to talk to their leaders inside the country as well as with acceptable exile leaders. Endorsement from at least some of the recognized SWAPO leaders is essential to winning international recognition of the new state since SWAPO is recognized by both the United Nations (which holds the mandate over the territory) and by the OAU as the only representative movement of black Namibians.

SWAPO has recently been experiencing internal troubles—the first in the 15 years of its existence. There are a number of reasons for these difficulties. The recent efflux of young Namibians has produced more open criticism of some of the exile leaders in the party hierarchy and over the allegedly undemocratic way in which the exile organization is run. SWAPO has also come under pressure in recent months from the Russians, who are known to have offered the exiles' leader, Sam Nujoma, considerable military and economic support on condition that he scale down the aid his organization receives from the Chinese. After their military buildup in Angola, the Russians and the Cubans are obviously in a strong position to make an enticing offer of aid to SWAPO's leaders. So far, the organization has been remarkably successful in avoiding entanglement in the Sino-Soviet dispute; it remains to be seen whether it can continue to maintain a carefully neutral position in the present state of rivalry between Moscow and Peking in southern Africa.

If the South African government remains adamant about dealing with SWAPO, the issue of Namibia is likely to become an increasingly strong magnet for political censure of South Africa and the possibility of external intervention to aid the SWAPO guerrillas will increase. Here, as on the question of Rhodesia, protraction of the uncertainties is also likely to increase the militance of the *verkrampte* right-wing of the South African Nationalist Party and decrease the likelihood of a peaceful transition to majority rule in any of the affected areas.

With regard to South Africa's own situation, Mr. Vorster promised, well over a year ago, changes which would surprise and disarm his critics—"within six months." No one, whether within or outside the country, knew exactly what he meant by this statement, and it aroused a storm of anxiety and speculation in South Africa. The time period having long since elapsed, the most plausible conjecture is that he was referring principally to his active mediation of the Rhodesia dispute, and to his policy of "détente" with black Africa. Mr. Vorster's attempts to win the friendship of African states through offers of economic aid and cooperation have not been very fruitful: the Ivory Coast is the only important black African state to have proved at all responsive; other takers have been Malawi and the Central African Republic. None of these has been reliable political allies in the United Nations or the OAU.

Mr. Vorster may also have been referring to several parallel policies for incremental change in South Africa's domestic institutions. These include the elimination of some of the harsh racially discriminatory measures against urban black South Africans; and the launching of the Republic's ten black Homelands, or Bantustans, on the road to "independence." The first of the Homelands to achieve this form of independence [is] the one relatively sizable and integrated area, the Transkei [October 1976]. It is slated to be followed by the smaller areas of Bophutha Tswana, Venda and the Ciskei, whose territories include a number of scattered parcels of land. Two other areas, KwaZulu and Gazankulu, are headed by influential leaders, Chief Gatsha Buthelezi and Professor Ntsanwisi, who are strongly opposed to the "balkanization" of the country, and presently opposed to "independence" for their own areas.

The future of South Africa's policy of "separate development" depends on whether the partition of the republic into one state embracing two-thirds of the country, and ten black states sharing the rest will offer an acceptable basis for a peaceful settlement between the 18 million Africans and the four million whites. To outside observers this seems an extremely shaky proposition.

VI

In all this, what is the likely future role of the big powers in Africa? In general, the Soviet Union is likely to engage in the most actively aggressive pursuit of influence there, motivated both by a desire to "contain" the spread of Chinese influence and by an interest in building up the Soviet Navy's world role by establishing facilities in the littoral countries along the Indian Ocean and the Mediterranean. In broad political terms, southern Africa has probably now become the most important area of competition, but the secondary arena, the Horn of Africa, will also attract increasing attention and concern.

There the Russians, having established themselves in Somalia, may well use the opportunities presented by the difficulties of post-imperial Ethiopia to enlarge their role in the Horn. Berbera, in Somalia, in fact offers only limited facilities for the Russian Navy. Besides, the Saudi Arabians, concerned about the Russian role in the Red Sea, are known to have been using their economic power to try and persuade the Somalis to end their military reliance on the Russians, as the South Yemenis seem to be doing, and as Sadat has done in Egypt. (It is interesting, incidentally, to note that the Chinese have agreed to provide military assistance to Egypt to make up, in addition to the Americans, what they will lose through the expulsion of the Russians.) Moscow is now engaged in courting the military regime in Ethiopia, which has become uneasy in maintaining relations with its traditional ally, the United States. So far, the Ethiopians have refused to accept Moscow's offer of military aid because of their enmity toward the Russians' ally, Somalia. They have been preferring to rely on economic aid from the Chinese, and reluctantly, on military and economic aid from the United States.

Trouble is likely to come to a head in a dispute over the French Territory of the Afars and Issas (known by the name of its port,

Djibouti) which will achieve its independence from France next year. Ethiopia will strenuously resist the attempts of the neighboring territory's ethnic Somalis (who are a majority of the population) to cede the new state to Somalia. How far the United States might feel called upon to aid Ethiopia against the Soviet-backed Somalis remains to be seen.

It is in the military strategic competition to establish facilities for the Soviet Navy around the coast of Africa that the Russians are likely to offer their biggest challenge to the NATO powers, as has already become clear in the controversies over the new U.S. and British base in Diego Garcia. However, the Russians still appear to be primarily interested in the northern reaches of the Indian Ocean and the Red Sea. This is their approach route to South and Southeast Asia, which they clearly regard as vital in the context of their preoccupation with what they see as the Chinese interest in developing a world hegemony. Peking, on its side, is greatly concerned about Moscow's growing role in the Indian Ocean; they take this as seriously as the Pentagon or NATO.

It is difficult to write confidently about the long-term interests of China in Africa. Much could change in their world outlook after the death of Mao Tse-tung. Their principal short-term interest is, as already described, to increase their influence in the Third World as a means of reducing Russia's world role. Some observers (other than the Russians) believe that the Chinese, with their much longer historical perspective, are in fact engaged in building themselves up as a future superpower. If so, it is hard to establish this through observing their present behavior.

Their aid is given in an unpatronizing and low-key style that wins widespread acceptance, and most African leaders find the Chinese the most comfortable of the major powers to get along with. But in a situation which requires the ability of a superpower to deliver massive military aid the Chinese cannot compete with the Russians, as is becoming clear in southern Africa.

In this respect, exigencies and strategies for the West and the Chinese in Africa may coincide. The Angolan conflict demonstrated that no Western nation was willing to match the Russian involvement—many Europeans were secretly appalled at U.S. inaction but in no way prepared to get into the fray themselves, while the U.S. polity effectively vetoed U.S. intervention in a far-flung African civil war, despite the concern of the Administration. The reluctance of citizens in the Western democracies to spend money and lives in southern African conflicts is not likely to decrease in the near future. In Angola, the interests of the black African states which had placed their reliance on the West—namely, Zambia and Zaïre—were defeated, thus diminishing the value of alliances with the West, at least for the time being.

However, African attitudes to a future Russian role in southern Africa are bound to be affected by the part played by both the West and China in the present phase of the Rhodesian struggle and in Namibia. While China's position is one of clear-cut support for the guerrilla struggle, Western policies still remain ambiguous. It will be easier for the West, and the United States, in particular, to respond effectively to the situations in Rhodesia and Namibia to the future challenge of South Africa.

This was shown by the surprisingly favorable reaction of the Front-Line Presidents to Secretary Kissinger's Lusaka pronouncements on Rhodesian and Namibian independence during his April trip to Africa. The firm declaration of support for majority rule, coming after years of "tilt" in the other direction, was undoubtedly gratifying to the African leaders, and they do not necessarily insist on U.S. military aid for the guerrilla movements. For the time being, a firm U.S. commitment to majority rule is enough, although his could change if the guerrilla conflict drags on indefinitely. On balance, it might seem that U.S and Western policy during the transition of these two countries to majority rule should focus on economic aid and political support, including pressure on South Africa.

South Africa itself inevitably presents the United States with much more serious dilemmas, and Secretary Kissinger was careful to set apart South African whites from those in Rhodesia as "historically, an African people." U.S. and Western investment in South Africa constitutes a form of support for that country and implicitly for the status quo there. In addition the United States has functioned, with Britain and France, as the main protector of South Africa at the United Nations for the past half-decade or so.

In the long run the U.S. economic involvement may force a difficult choice. If no satisfactory way can be found to use the economic leverage to encourage internal political change in the Republic, the United States may have to choose between its interests in South Africa and in the rest of the continent. In the short run, the independence of the Homelands will create other dilemmas. The recognition of the Homelands as independent nations could enable the United States to pour in economic aid to South African blacks. On the other hand, support of what is at present a highly inequitable scheme to bulwark the policy of separate development could once again place the United States on the side of the status quo and against those seeking change and justice. At the moment the OAU is strongly opposed to official recognition of the Homelands.

The Russians and the Chinese are likely to consider this sort of issue arcane in contrast to the primacy of the revolutionary struggle, and to focus on their rivalry for influence with the liberation movements. The implicit alliance between the West and China will continue, however, in the face of their shared desire to impede Russian interests. The West could capitalize on this common interest by joining the Chinese in continuing support for a major political goal of the OAU— preventing outside powers from usurping the sovereignty of African nations. In the long run this dearly held tenet is likely to be overriding in southern Africa, but what happens in the meantime will be very important in shaping the future relations of all the great powers with the independent regimes that emerge.

10   Face-off in Panama:
U.S. Imperialists, Old and New

Penny Lernoux

Opposing camps of American imperialists face each other in Panama today, and if they do not resolve their basic dispute in the very near future, the tension they are creating will explode and seriously damage the diplomatic position and commercial interests of the United States, not only in Panama but throughout Latin America. Of these two colonies of Manifest Destiny, one occupies and operates the Canal Zone, remembering Teddy Roosevelt and an era of military expansion, while the other, a complex community of multilingual executives, lives in Panama City and relies on technology and international finance to advance its imperial goals. Although the two views still sometimes coincide in the United States, they are fast diverging in Panama, for the sort of empire to which the Pentagon and the Zonians cling is in conflict with the aims of the multinationals.

Differences over empire building might have been postponed had a new Panama Canal treaty not become a hemispheric *cause célèbre*, but now that it is a priority issue in the Third World, the argument between business and the military has become shrill. Emotional appeals to patriotism notwithstanding, the real question in the ongoing controversy over a new treaty is whether the Canal is worth the multinationals' Latin American empire.

Henry Kissinger may be accused of a good many sins, but he is one of the few officials high in government to have realized just that. A cold pragmatist, as Kissinger believes he is, has no more patience with the contention of Sen. Strom Thurmond (R., S.C.) that the Panama Canal belongs to the United States because "we paid for it" than for the Panamanians' belief that the U.S.-run Canal Zone is an outdated colonial enclave. Both arguments miss the point that the Panama Canal is not a bilateral issue between Teddy Roosevelt's admirers and a frustrated banana republic but a test case for the United States in the uses of its power.

Kissinger is not the only one to have grasped the essentials in the dispute; Panama's strongman, Gen. Omar Torrijos, knows that the stakes are political and economic, not military. Although defense of the Canal remains one of the principal stumbling blocks in the seven-year-old negotiations to replace the 1903 Hay-Bunau-Varilla Treaty governing the Panama Canal, both men are aware that there is no practical defense justification for stationing 10,000 soldiers at fourteen U.S. bases in the Canal Zone.

Since the Canal cannot be defended against nuclear attack or Panamanian guerrilla warfare, the only explanation for so many U.S. troops is that they constitute a strike force for intervention in some Latin American country. The last such invasion, of the Dominican Republic in 1965, cost the United States dearly in international good will. A repeat of that incident today would be political and economic folly, since not even the most right-wing Latin American military regime would stomach such Big-Stick tactics. Although Salvador Allende posed a far greater challenge than did the Dominican Republic's weak-willed Juan Bosch, there was never any serious question of military intervention in Chile because the State Department had come to see the wisdom of the multinationals' subtler tactics of economic pressure, propaganda and covert cooperation with the CIA.

Possibly because it is still nursing a cold-war hangover, the Pentagon has yet to comprehend this more complex form of U.S. intervention. And therein lies the danger for U.S. business. By refusing to compromise on the size and tenure of the U.S. military force in Panama, the Pentagon is jeopardizing the multinationals' Latin American operations. Saber rattling is considered unnecessary, uncouth and unwise in today's business world.

Thanks to Torrijos, what started as a bilateral dispute between a small Central American country and the hemisphere's northern giant has become the single most important issue in Latin America, with considerable potential for economic fallout. Castro's Cuba and Pinochet's Chile may agree on little, but they are as one on the question of Panamanian sovereignty over the Canal. In a rare show of hemispheric solidarity, the Latin American bloc has given Panama its seat on the U.N. Security Council for the second time in six years. The gesture is a clear signal to the United States: if Washington wants its Latin American allies to vote with the United States, Washington would be well-advised to reach a compromise with Panama.

Political solidarity may be only a short step from some form of economic solidarity. There are many ways to bring pressure on Washington through the multinationals, such as the threat of nationalization, the effectiveness of which has been demonstrated by countries as diverse as Argentina and Peru. Another commonly used, though officially disapproved, method is the bombing of U.S. subsidiaries by left-wing students. At the very least, U.S. intransigence over a new treaty will contribute to a further cooling of relations, already strained by producer cartels, economic nationalism in Latin America and by Washington's failure to develop a new policy for the region.

While assiduously and successfully wooing Latin American support during the past three years, Torrijos has been careful to restrain any violent impulses among his own left-wing students. But if the lid ever blew in Panama, the United States would be confronted by more than the sort of guerrilla warfare Kissinger says he fears there. U.S. subsidiaries might be the target of "solidarity" bombings in other Latin American countries and the object of pressure by their governments.

The local risk is high enough, Panama being the fifth largest U.S. investment in the region, but is as nothing compared to the total stake in Latin America which is the United States' second most important trading partner, after Canada, and accounts for its third largest foreign investment.

The fear of economic retaliation might never have been publicly voiced if the U.S. Congress had not thrown a spanner into the Canal talks [in June 1975] by threatening to attach a rider to the State Department appropriations bill, cutting off funds for negotiations (the threat was never carried out). Although the Pentagon's Congressional supporters have always raised a hue and cry over any concession to Panama, the State Department misjudged the extent of their power to block a new treaty. Led by Rep. Daniel Flood (D., Pa.) in the House and Thurmond in the Senate, the pro-Pentagon forces mustered the support to convince thirty-nine Senators (five more than are needed to scuttle a treaty) and 246 Representatives to go on record [in 1975] as opposed to negotiations in any form. (The House must approve a new Panama treaty because a transfer of U.S. property is involved.)

The stop-the-talks campaign was based primarily on charges that the Panamanians are incapable of running the Canal (Flood says they "are not even garbage collectors") and that the Torrijos government is "up to the hilt with the Soviets," both of which are untrue. Nevertheless, feeling over the Panama Canal, that stupendous engineering feat of our younger days, runs . . . deep among some U.S. voters . . .

Following the Congressional flap in June, the State Department hurriedly shifted its diplomatic attention from Panama to the United States. Ellsworth Bunker, former U.S. Ambassador to South Vietnam and the United States' chief negotiator in the Canal talks, was drafted to explain the historical background of the 1903 treaty to such important organizations as the World Affairs Council; the State Department has tried to do the same among influential U.S. legislators. Still, one must doubt that any of this explaining makes the least difference when so many Americans heed the misinformed viewpoint of Congressmen like Bill Alexander, (D., Ark.) who warns that "the next thing we know the Soviet Union is going to want Alaska back."

Ever since Teddy Roosevelt, the United States has ignored the fact that the Hay-Bunau-Varilla Treaty did not actually give to the United States the 533-square-mile Zone but only the rights it would exercise *as if it were* sovereign. The $10 million paid to Panama in 1903 was for treaty rights, not for territory, in contrast to the Alaska and Louisiana purchases. Nor did the treaty empower the United States to establish fourteen military bases in the Zone. Asking the public to accept these facts, which are quite unlike the facts they learned in school, is asking them to recognize another failure in the system for, here again, the United States is morally in the wrong. Who needs that sort of eyeopener after Watergate and Vietnam?

But whatever the historical interpretation of the Panama Canal, there is one argument that will be listened to—how much the controversy may cost in dollars and cents. That is why the State Department, wisely if belatedly, enlisted U.S. business to help sell a new treaty to the American public. At the invitation of Sen. Gale McGee (D., Wyo.), the Senate's leading pro-treaty advocate, representatives of more than two dozen U.S. corporations met at the State Department [in Nov. 1975] to map out a public relations campaign. The Business and Professional Committee for a New Panama Canal Treaty was founded with an intial $500,000 budget to act as a business lobby in Congress, its purpose being, in Senator McGee's words, to persuade the "wagglers, the premature commitments, the middle ground and [all those] who are not still riding up the hill with Teddy Roosevelt" that their opposition to a new treaty may have been hasty. "Too many people have committed themselves on this issue before understanding what it's all about." The business lobby "will have a good impact," says McGee, because the companies "will be taking the side of the liberals on what they consider a moral issue."

The companies, needless to say, are more concerned about what is good for business, which bombings and other anti-American demonstrations definitely are not. "The United States has raised the expectations of the Panamanians, and if we don't come up with some kind of revised treaty, we can expect an active response," said Kay R. Whitemore, first vice president and general manager of Kodak's Latin American operations. Many of the other corporations represented (Ford, Rockwell International, Bank of America, Sears, Roebuck & Co., Pan American, Chase Manhattan, Bankers Trust Co., Gulf and Shell) have been the target of violence in Latin America, usually because of some unpopular U.S. action in the hemisphere.

"If we try to maintain the *status quo,* we will face mounting hostility in both Panama and Latin America—and the possible loss of the very interest we want to preserve," warned Ambassador Bunker. Failure to reach an understanding could "start a bonfire in the continent," added Colombian President Alfonso Lopez Michelsen, one of the chief mediators in the U.S.-Panama dispute. A British-educated Bogotano who prides himself on his *sang-froid,* Lopez does not overestimate the danger. Were a bonfire to start, not only would the United States be acutely embarrassed by a nasty quarrel with its neighbors; it would also be courting the hostility of the only continent in the Third World that is still wedded to the capitalist system. And a showdown in Panama could wreck the incipient talks on world trade between First and Third Worlds, which would hardly please the Europeans or the Japanese who are much more dependent on the developing nations' raw materials than is the United States.

Unlike the Americans in the Zone, who not unnaturally relate everything to the Canal and the military bases, those employed in Panama are concerned about U.S. banking and commercial interests in Central America, the Caribbean and all of South America. Under the "Red" government of General Torrijos, Panama has replaced the Bahamas as the region's banker, its forty-five foreign banks having almost cornered the $10-billion Latindollar trade, or approximately one-tenth the total of Eurodollars. Attracted by a freely convertible currency and lax banking laws, the international banking community has developed here a tropical Swiss haven, complete with numbered accounts. But while the deposits of wealthy Latin Americans comprise a sizable chunk of the banks' business, their primary function is to serve the multinationals that use Panama as headquarters for their triangular trade with Latin America.

To circumvent the limits many Latin American countries have placed on remittance of profits to the home company, the multinationals have established holding companies in Panama, which provide free-port privileges as well as a tax shelter. Goods are shipped from the parent company in the United States or Europe to its subsidiary in Panama, where the cost of the merchandise is invoiced at a higher price before being re-exported to some Latin American country—a process popularly known as *sobrefacturación*, or over-invoicing. By sending the goods through Panama, the parent company avoids tax payments on real profits in both the country of origin and the country where the goods are finally sold.

Panamanian subsidiaries also frequently hold the patents for the multinationals' Latin American investments, which means that royalty and fee payments can be reported in Panama instead of the United States or Europe. Royalties and fees collected by Panamanian holding companies often are higher than their subsidiaries' sales profits, annual remittances on which are limited to 14 per cent of capital invested in such areas as the six Andean Pact countries. To complement its banking and trading facilities, Panama offers a haven for merchant vessels; more than 1,000 ships from the United States and Europe now fly the Panamanian flag. Although the Canal has encouraged the presence of foreign banks, multinationals and shipping companies, it is the Torrijos government's *laissez-faire* policy toward international business that has allowed these interests to thrive here at the hub of the Americas.

While Torrijos may not be every businessman's ideal ruler, foreign executives agree that no other Panamanian politician could have exacted so much patience from his people during the prolonged negotiations over a new treaty. Since seizing power in 1968, the burly, 47-year-old general has managed an admirable balancing act between Populist and pro-business policies that has succeeded in keeping all but the old, power-hungry political parties in line, and he has seriously eroded their influence. Discredited even before the Torrijos regime as the tools of a few wealthy families, the political parties have been reduced to squabbling impotence by Panama's National Guard, a combination of police and armed forces, and by the technocrats and businessmen who have put a more up-to-date gloss on Panamanian politics.

Torrijos's regime is a dictatorship, but an easygoing one by Latin American standards (torture is rare and the maximum punishment is exile). In any case, democratic ideals have never blossomed in the hothouse of Panamanian politics. Compared to the rigged elections, political corruption and constant coups that once characterized Panamanian politics, the Torrijos government appears stable and well-balanced. Torrijos has also "grown into a leader beyond the common variety of Latin American dictators," as a Panamanian university professor puts it, because of his success in uniting world opinion behind his people's aspiration to attain sovereignty over the Panama Canal.

Balancing the various interest groups in Panama is a difficult job, however, and that is something many U.S. Congressmen fail to recognize. Sweeping condemnations of Panama's military dictatorship, or its friendly relations with Cuba, do not take into account the internal situation or the eight years of stability that have allowed business to boom and treaty negotiations to progress. Torrijos is the first leader in Panamanian history to undertake some social and economic reforms for the benefit of the country's impoverished masses. He also has realized a long-standing ambition of his countrymen by buying out the banana interests of United Brands, the largest employer of agricultural labor in Panama. It may seem improbable that a government which supports the multi-nationals' triangular trade would also undertake social reforms or nationalize United Brands' holdings, but it is not far-fetched in Panama, where survival depends on a pragmatic approach to the demands of different pressure groups.

Torrijos has a very plausible reason for his friendship with Castro, since good relations with Cuba are crucial to his control over the country's left-wing students, who have been responsible for the overthrow of numerous governments in the past. He needs to avoid a clash between the students and the National Guard, for he knows from his own experience as a guardsman under previous governments how easily violence esclates in Panama, and violence would not advance the treaty talks. . . .

Not content to torpedo the Canal talks in Congress, right-wing groups in the United States are actively promoting Torrijo's overthrow. . . . As a result of this plotting, Torrijos faced the worst crisis in his eight-year-old government [in January 1975] when a group of right-wing Panamanian businessmen called a nationwide strike to set the stage for a comeback by Arnulfo Arias, a 75-year-old demagogue who has been President on three occasions and overthrown each time.
. . .

For the time being at least, Arias has no hope of returning to Panama . . . for Torrijos is still strong enough to nip any *Arnulfista* conspiracy in the bud. The January strike fizzled under the joint pressure of the National Guard, which exiled eleven of the protesters, and Panamanian workers and students who threatened to occupy any business on strike. The events of January were also a lesson to anyone who aspires to succeed Torrijos. Public opinion is now so fixed on sovereignty over the Canal that any attempt to return to the country's old political ways of accommodating the United States generates immediate opposition from some of the country's most influential sectors, including the National Guard, students and workers. The question in Panama no longer is whether the country will regain sovereignty but how—whether through negotiations or violence.

Right-wing propaganda notwithstanding, Panama is not demanding the immediate withdrawal of all U.S. troops stationed in the Zone or the retirement of a single Zonian. What it really wants, in Bunker's words, are the "appurtenances of power," or the removal of the stigma of a nation divided in half by an enclave over which it has no control.

In an eight-point communiqué signed by Kissinger and Panamanian Foreign Minister Juan Tack in 1974, it was agreed that perpetual U.S. sovereignty over the Canal Zone would be removed by a new treaty and that the two countries would review defense and administration of the Canal, the amount of land needed for Canal operations and the annual payment to Panama for the Canal's use, now a paltry $1.9 million. Contrary to charges by Representative Flood that the eight principles were "an unconstitutional giveaway by faceless wonders in striped pants," the agreement was simply a starting point for negotiations that could no longer be postponed. Kissinger, no Santa Claus, signed the agreement because he knew the State Department could no longer fob off the Panamanians with a pretense of negotiations. Indeed, Torrijos caused such an international fuss over Washington's reluctance to engage in serious talks that the U.N. Security Council agreed to meet in Panama City to study the issue in 1973. Much to Washington's embarrassment, it was forced to cast one of the United States' rare vetoes against a Council resolution that urged the controversy be promptly settled by restoring sovereignty over the Canal to Panama.

Negotiations have since progressed to the point where agreement is possible on all but four issues. Three years after a new treaty goes into effect, the current Panama Canal Co. will be replaced by a jointly owned U.S.-Panamanian Co. Panama will assume administration of Zone courts, police and postal services, and as Zonians retire Panamanians will gradually move into top technical and administrative positions. (Panamanians already occupy three-quarters of Canal-related jobs.) The two countries will also share responsibility for defense of the Canal.

Still to be settled are the number of U.S. military bases in the Zone, the duration of a new treaty, the Canal land to be returned to Panama and the amount of the annual payment. Reaching a compromise on these questions will not be easy because all four concern the Pentagon, which sees no reason why any concessions should be made.

Washington might agree to Panama's demand that the new treaty expire at the end of the century, provided Panama were willing to accept the presence of U.S. troops for at least another twenty-five years. But Panama is not willing. The U.S. troops are seen as an occupying army, and although Torrijos has warned his people that it is foolish to believe that Panama can force the hemisphere's most powerful country to decamp as soon as a treaty is signed, he also knows that he could end up in exile if he guaranteed U.S. military presence beyond the year 2000.

"No bases," which is painted on walls throughout the country, is obvious wishful thinking, as even student wall painters will admit. However, the government is demanding a reduction in the number of bases from fourteen to three and the removal of the hated School of the Americas, which has trained more than 25,000 Latin American military officers in "counterinsurgency techniques," a euphemism for the science of military dictatorship.

The Panamanians also want the return of 85 per cent of the Canal Zone lands, since much of this preserve serves no purpose but to prevent the natural growth of the country's two most important cities, Panama City and Colón, located on the Pacific and Atlantic sides of the Canal. The problem is that Zone property is considered symbolic, whether used or not. For example, when State Department officials suggested turning over two World War II airfields to the Panamanians to be used as customs sheds, they were warned not to try it since even so small a gesture to the Panamanians would be voted down as the "beginning of the giveaway" by pro-Pentagon forces in Congress.

These forces are equally adamant about any reduction of military bases although there is no strategic reason for them, and even Gen. George Brown, chairman of the Joint Chiefs of Staff, admits that a new treaty would be preferable to Panamanian sabotage. Actually, U.S. military presence in the Zone increases the likelihood of foreign attack, which is another reason why Torrijos wants U.S. troops to go home.

The Pentagon could argue that neutrality is not a deterrent to nuclear attack, but since the Canal is not neutral this is a moot point. Despite promises of "free, open and indiscriminate service," the U.S. Government stopped two merchant ships, one Russian and one Cuban, from entering the Canal after Chile's strongman, Gen. Augusto Pinochet, complained that the ships had failed to deliver cargo contracted for by the previous Allende regime. The Panamanians were outraged at such high-handedness, not so much because it irritated the Soviets as because of the principle involved. By barring a foreign ship's passage through the Canal on political grounds, the United States places Panama in the position of facing possible reprisals for a foreign policy decision on which it was never consulted.

As for local sabotage, the Panamanians know that it is unnecessary to storm the Zone in order to close the Canal. One judiciously placed plastic bomb would do it. It is inexcusable to risk sabotage by delaying a new treaty when most U.S. aircraft carriers and warships are too large to squeeze through the Canal. "We have a multiocean navy which is not dependent on passageways such as the Canal," said Senator McGee. "We rely upon massive airlifts of personnel and equipment to facilitate a prompt and effective U.S. response to crisis." Said Carlos Lopez Guevara, one of the Panamanian negotiators, "If the Canal really were vital to the United States, we would not have a chance [of a new treaty]."

This is not to deny that the military gets good value from the Canal. Aircraft carriers may have outdated its strategic importance, but the Canal still saves the Pentagon a lot of money, even though that money rightly belongs to the Panamanian people. Since the Panama Canal Co. has not increased transit rates from the time the Canal was opened, it is in effect subsidizing world shipping. According to the Economic Commission for Latin America, an agency of the U.N.'s Economic and Social Council, had tolls been adjusted to reflect world prices, the Canal would have earned an additional $2.6 billion between 1960 and 1970.

It happens that 70 per cent of the cargo passing through the Canal is en route to or from the United States and that a high percentage of this traffic is military. (Most of the supplies for the war in Vietnam were sent through the Canal.) Even the Zonians are beginning to wonder about Canal subsidies after all these decades. Having taken an $8-million loss in 1975, the Panama Canal Co. has been forced to go on an austerity budget, and now there is talk of a strike by U.S. personnel.

The Zonians' frustration is nothing compared to that of the Panamanians who believe they are entitled to a better return on the country's only natural resource—its geographical position—and the reason why Teddy Roosevelt "took" Panama in the first place. But to date they have been stymied by the United States' refusal to increase transit rates and by the Panama Canal Co.'s peculiar bookkeeping system. If the company's accounts are to be believed, the Panamanians still owe $317 million on the original $386 million spent to construct the Canal. Panamanian economists, working with different sets of figures, assert that the cost was fully amortized in 1954 and that the Panama Canal Co. has juggled the books to keep figures in the red.

Whatever the real amortization figures, there can be no doubt that the United States has cheated the Panamanians on the rental of the military bases. "The United States pays $2.3 million a year for the Canal and all the Zone lands, including fourteen military bases," said Panama's Archbishop Marcus McGrath. "Compare this with the $20 million a year the United States pays Spain for only three bases or Great Britain's annual payment of $35 million for its bases in Malta."

Although Washington realizes that Panama is entitled to a higher rental, its top offer in the negotiations has been only $25 million a year, which Panama refuses to accept.

Dependent on the Canal for 30 per cent of its gross national product and 40 per cent of its foreign earnings, Panama views the waterway as another Latin American nation would its mineral and oil resources. If these countries can demand and get better terms from the multinationals, including majority control of these resources, there is no reason why Panama should not expect similar treatment from the U.S. Government. The argument that the Canal would never have been built without U.S., money and know-how is as outdated as the multinationals' claim that but for them a region's natural resources could not have been developed. Nobody is arguing past history. What the Latin Americans say is that these companies have obtained more than good value from their investments, most of which were amortized long ago, and that goes for the Panama Canal as well as a copper mine or an oil well.

Another favorite cliché—that the Panamanians should be grateful to the United States because the Canal has given them the highest standard of living in Central America—washes no better. It is as logical as the multinationals' argument that they should be spared higher taxes and royalties because, by local standards, their workers are well paid. Both are economic *non sequiturs*. Annual per capita income in Panama is $624, and nothing to boast about. Nor is there any reason why people who live well below the U.S. definition of the poverty level should subsidize the armed forces of the richest nation in the world.

Although these and other arguments have been discussed for the past seven years, none has altered the basic position of the Pentagon or its Congressional supporters. So it is left to the multinationals to champion the Panamanian cause, a role they may not relish but one that is necessary for modern empire building, political pragmatism being a more effective sales pitch than military threats. Certainly they are in a better position than most to know that when Ambassador Bunker talks about "the possible loss of the very interest we want to protect," he is not referring solely to the Canal but to the United States' considerable economic and political stake in all of Latin America.

Were the military to take a broader view of the Canal, it would also see that its intransigence could play into the hands of the very governments the Pentagon fears most. What we cannot understand, says Venezuelan President Carlos Andrés Pérez, is how the United States could be so foolish as to create another point of conflict in Latin America when "the Soviet Union already has one base in Cuba which is generating subversive ideas and actions in the whole region." Still, it wouldn't be the first time Washington drove the Latin Americans to extremes.

PART
II
The Burden of the Strong

We turn now from the tensions between strong and weak powers and between groups of different ethnic and ideological identification to a discussion of relations among the great powers. During the Nixon-Ford-Kissinger era, American foreign policy was directed primarily toward the great powers: the Soviet Union in particular, but also China, Japan, and key western European states. This direction contrasted with the interest during the 1960s in developments within the Third World—an interest reawakened by the war in the Middle East of October 1973, the ensuing Arab oil embargo, the OPEC price rises, and escalating Third World demands for greater economic equality. The Nixon and Ford administrations seemed to believe that the creation of a balance of power among the major states would produce a more stable international order, at least on the higher levels where the United States' interests are most directly affected. But such trouble spots in the Third World as the Middle East and southern Africa have forced a progressive reorientation of U.S. interest in those areas, albeit within the perspective of our relations with the other major powers.

The first section of part two is organized in three groups. The first two articles present two different views of détente—one positive, the other negative. The next three articles deal with the Asian balance of power after the Vietnam War. Finally, we consider Europe, with emphasis on relations between the United States and its European allies.

As his title, "Appeasement and Détente," suggests, Theodore Draper asks several serious questions about the policy of détente, primarily because he distrusts the Soviet Union. He also severely criticizes the policies of Henry Kissinger. Not so Roger Morris. Although he has his criticisms, on the whole he favors détente, believing that "détente is now suffering from the fact that it was deliberately obscured as diplomacy and oversold as politics." Morris is measured in his praise and more willing than Draper to explain the weaknesses of détente by references to causes other than the policies of Henry Kissinger and the intentions of the Soviet Union. He uses explanations such as the structure of American foreign policy, the balance between the U.S. diplomacy and domestic politics, and the nature of the Soviet-American superpower relationship itself. Readers may accept either Draper's or Morris's position or, alternatively, believe that any criticism of détente is unwarranted and that accommodation with the Soviet Union should not be impeded.

We move from the question of détente with the Soviet Union to three articles devoted to the future of Asia after the Vietnam War. With the unification of Vietnam and the defeat of U.S. objectives in the conflict, most American observers (especially supporters of the war) would have expected many great changes in Asia. But in our three articles—written only a few months after North Vietnam's victory in April 1975—the message is clear: there is an altered environment but not an astonishingly different one as far as the Asian elite is concerned.

After Vietnam, American interest in Asia diminished; as a consequence, four powers now compete for influence in the area: the United States, the Soviet Union, China, and Japan. As in Africa, the fiercest competition that presently exists among powers in Asia is the Sino-Soviet rivalry. Stanley Karnow in "The Ardent Asian Suitors" analyzes the impact of the United States' defeat in Vietnam on the great-power balance, stressing in particular the Sino-Soviet confrontation. Among other topics, Karnow assesses the future of Sino-Soviet relations and their effect on American objectives (e.g., will Peking have a rapprochement with Moscow after Mao's death?). He deals with the Taiwan dispute as a factor in the Sino-Soviet-American triangle. Should the United States formalize relations with Peking at the expense of Taipei in order to solidify Sino-American détente and make improved Sino-Soviet relations more difficult? Or is the U.S. commitment to Taiwan too sacrosanct to be so easily broken? Or can the United States have it both ways (the so-called "Japanese formula") by recognizing the People's Republic of China while still maintaining close economic relations with Taiwan? Whatever the answer, U.S. policy toward Asia after the Vietnam War will require greater subtlety and perspicacity than Americans demonstrated in Vietnam.

After the Soviet Union and China, the other great power in Asia is Japan. Keyes Beech examines the "ultimate domino" and the central impact this dynamic economic power has on the fate of the United States in the area. He also demonstrates the significance of the simmering Korean issue for U.S.-Japanese relations and the Asian balance of power. Unlike the situation in Vietnam, the two Koreas have existed in uneasy armistice—each dictatorial and authoritarian, each totally opposed to the other. Given Korea's proximity to China, the Soviet Union, and Japan, both the northern and southern parts of the divided country are perceived by diplomats to possess a strategic significance for the Asian balance of power that has rarely been claimed for Vietnam.

In Southeast Asia, the site of the Indochinese conflicts which ultimately produced Communist-led, anti-American governments in Vietnam, Cambodia, and Laos, the United States remains "on a tightrope," as Donald Kirk reminds us. While less has changed in the region than might have been anticipated, countries like Thailand and the Philippines have rapidly reduced their identification with the United States. "On a tightrope" themselves, they have attempted to maintain some link with the United States while also accommodating the other powers of the area, especially China. Regional politics have remained in a state of flux, but Kirk shows us how each country's leadership has been responding to its own domestic problems—which are often chaotic. In several countries these basic problems have been only marginally affected by the "falling dominoes" of Indochina, and it is the domestic situation of the individual countries in Southeast Asia that will determine the future of the area.

By the mid-1970s Americans had switched their concern with the growth of communism from Asia to Europe. Here we see a decaying European-American alliance confronted with the irony of growing Communist party influence at the polls in countries aligned with the United States against the foremost Communist power, the Soviet Union. Richard C. Longworth discusses these "Red Votes in the Ballot Box" and identifies the many problems created by this phenomenon: the effect on NATO and the European Economic Community (Common Market), the implications for Western European democracy, and the ever-present dominoes which might "fall" if one Communist victory were to lead to others. Yet Longworth cautiously recommends a holding operation, hoping that the Western Communists may prove to be more Western than Communist, and democratic as well. Can we live with local Communist parties in power in Western Europe? Longworth carefully answers "yes." What do you answer, dear reader?

Ronald Steel continues where Longworth's analysis ends. In the context of the European-American relationship, Steel describes the lack of European reunification and the inherent weaknesses of our clients, their resentment of our hegemony, and their lessened importance in the era of détente. To Steel, Europe, has remained our economic customer, the target of our investment dollars, in return for our military protection; there is no partnership of equals. Steel is uneasy with the relationship and believes that NATO "has been a symbol of Europe's will to abdicate." He would prefer a more independent, unified Europe, but we must ask whether such a Europe would contribute to greater international stability and tranquility. What do we really want from the Europeans—reliable partners or faithful clients? Steel maintains that America's future role in Europe will depend on this assessment by policy makers. He also believes that American influence is bound to decrease whatever our preference.

Having reviewed the state of relations among great powers, we move to the next section of part two, which examines the great power balance and its relation to the rest of the world. The two articles in this section evaluate, respectively, the success of Henry Kissinger's policy on a worldwide basis and in the Middle East. Simon Head in "The Hot Deals and Cold Wars of Henry Kissinger" grapples with the paradoxes inherent in Kissinger's policy and the contradictory doctrines which seem to flow from this statesman. Is Kissinger a Cold Warrior or a seeker of détente? Critics and defenders alike are confused by the seemingly schizoid quality of his strategies. There is a strong element of containment in his maxims, and yet he does not believe opportunities for abatement of conflict should be missed. Head's analysis seems to explain these two visions of Henry Kissinger: his doctrine calls for a global view of Soviet intentions and actions but permits a flexible diplomacy to maximize negotiations when the Russians are forced to adapt to superior American capacity and will.

The paradox of Kissinger's policies is also illustrated in my article on "Dilemmas and Dead Ends: America and the Middle East Crisis." Kissinger pursued a dynamic, inventive shuttle diplomacy in the area: but as intermediary between the two parties he actually restricted opportunities for initiating direct diplomatic contacts between the Arabs and Israelis because he became the conduit through which negotiations were conducted. The two articles in this section expose the difficulties created for the United States (and, by extension, the Soviet Union) in the present international system. The competition and stalemate between the two great powers cause considerable difficulty for them in dealing with weaker nations for they must always balance policies designed for their superpower adversary and policies for allies, clients, and weaker foes.

The root cause of these difficulties is, of course, the arms race between the two superpowers. In our next section several articles examine the arms race, alternative approaches to nuclear strategy and arms control, and the problem of nuclear proliferation. Barry Blechman "handicaps the arms race" to assess the relative strengths of Soviet and U.S. forces—both conventional and nuclear. His own position is between the "minimalist" and "maximalist" perspectives.

The next two articles explore each opposing view. Paul Nitze in "Assuring Strategic Stability in an Era of Détente" masterfully reviews both strategic alternatives in the nuclear age and the progress of Soviet-U.S. arms control negotiations, which uninitiated students should find helpful; Nitze's own proposals, however, are controversial. His message is clear—the Soviet Union enjoys increasing nuclear superiority, and he doubts it will be redressed in future Strategic Arms Limitation Talks (SALT). Our very attitude toward deterrence—that nuclear war is unthinkable—permits the possibility of Soviet ascendancy. Since the 1962 Cuban confrontation, Soviet efforts have been directed to a "war-winning capability" as the best deterrent if attainable. Nitze argues that the deterrence relationship is unstable in view of increased Soviet civil defense measures, industrial decentralization, and advantages they seem to possess in effective deliverable payloads; he suggests that we must rethink our nuclear policy to aim for maximum deterrence.

John Holum, however, explicitly rejects Nitze's views in "The 'SALT' Sell: Or, Who Will Bell the Pentagon?" The key problem for Holum is not the Soviets, but the Pentagon; U.S. arms manufacturers usually win over arms controllers. While he recognizes that the Kremlin too has its hawks, he believes that unilateral American acts of restraint are the key to halting the arms race. The contrast between Nitze and Holum provides two critical views of SALT from very different perspectives; in microcosm they represent the heart of the strategic debate in the United States today.

As we noted above, the superpowers must constantly deal with each other as well as with weaker states. Their careful balancing act is becoming more complicated as the fear of nuclear proliferation threatens to become reality. Lincoln Bloomfield in "Nuclear Spread and World Order" takes an innovative approach to the issue of nuclear proliferation. He proposes a step-by-step process of internationalizing the control of plutonium reprocessing, peaceful nuclear explosions, nuclear fuel production, and eventually, uranium enrichment. His ideas are designed as a partial solution to the problem underlying proliferation: the inequality of the system resulting from the nonproliferation treaty between the nuclear haves and have-nots.

While more immediate matters at issue in international politics frequently gain the headlines, lurking barely beneath the surface is the problem of nuclear proliferation. The outcome of this issue may be the most devastating of all. Meanwhile, the great powers continue their conflict, business as usual.

Competitors and Allies: Pas de Deux

11   Appeasement & Détente

Theodore Draper

Appeasement became a dirty word in the 1930's. It had been, for centuries, a perfectly clean, even a virtuous term. How could a word that had meant peace and conciliation turn into its opposite? The transformation came when it began to be used in connection with the concessions to and deals made with the fascist dictatorships in the 1930's. The turning point was probably the speeches by Prime Minister Neville Chamberlain in the House of Commons on October 3 and 6, 1938. Just back from Munich, where he had agreed to tear off a vital part of Czechoslovakia and hand it over to Hitler's Germany, he spoke exultantly about "our policy of appeasement," of which the Munich agreement was to be only the first step. He looked forward to "the collaboration of all nations, not excluding the totalitarian states, in building up a lasting peace for Europe." The "real triumph," he said, was the execution of "a difficult and delicate operation by discussion instead of by force of arms."

A year later, force of arms instead of discussion made it almost impossible to say the word "appeasement" without shame and loathing. The word, of course, was not to blame. But why had it been misused? Why did it turn into such a ghastly mockery? Clearly—though this is not the whole story—because appeasement could not appease the unappeasable. In those circumstances it was betrayal and capitulation on the installment plan. The stench of the Munich agreement might not have been so sickening if it had not been recognized for what it was. What made it so unbearable was its glorification, such as this memorable tribute in the London *Times:* "No conqueror returning from a victory on the battlefield has come home with nobler laurels than Mr. Chamberlain from Munich yesterday."

Détente is another one of those perfectly good words that, misapplied, get a bad name. It appears to be a relatively recent importation from the French. The first citation in the Oxford English Dictionary is dated 1908. The word is usually defined as a "relaxation of tension," which may mean much or little depending on what kind of tension is being relaxed by how much. At the 1974 hearings on détente of the Senate Committee on Foreign Relations, speaker after speaker complained that the word was hard to pin down. Former Ambassador George F. Kennan said that he had "never fully understood the use of the word 'détente' in connection with" Soviet-American relations. In response, former Senator J. W. Fulbright remarked that "détente is a difficult word to have inherited in this connection, but I think we are stuck with it." Former Senator Eugene McCarthy commented that "the meaning has changed every time it is applied." Professor Marshall Shulman referred to "the ambiguities of the word 'détente,'" and Professor Herbert Dinerstein pointed out that "everyone has a different notion about what détente is." Former Secretary of State Dean Rusk said it was a "process," not a "condition." Sectaray of State Henry A. Kissinger agreed that "it is a continuing process, not a final condition."[1] An academic definition has made it into "a logical spectrum of relations along which conflict either increases or decreases."[2]

Not only is it difficult even for experts to define détente but, whatever it is, it would seem to be fluctuating and ambiguous. In theory, it has been situated somewhere between cold war and rapprochement or even entente. Since détente moves uneasily between these two poles, it occupies a purely relative position, without a definite profile of its own. This conception of détente is always moving away or moving toward something else.[3] No wonder, then, that détente according to this theory has been so hard to pin down; it is by its very nature transitory and volatile.

In practice, however, the current Soviet-American détente should have a much more positive and recognizable character. The materialization of détente was supposed to be the main achievement of the summit meeting in Moscow in May 1972 at which the new phase of Soviet-American relations was formally inaugurated. It consisted of three agreements—military, commercial, and political. The military agreement took the form of SALT I, providing in principle for quantitative parity in antiballistic missiles. The commercial agreement set up a U.S.-USSR commission to promote trade and development of economic resources. The political agreement was embodied in the "Basic Principles of Relations Between the United States of America and the Union of Soviet Socialist Republics." These three agreements gave this détente some substance and delineation. Détente could not be all that vague and ambiguous if it had "Basic Principles," no matter what they might be or whether or not they were lived up to.

Most of the debate on détente has made it appear that the only alternatives are détente and cold war. Any criticism of the current version of détente is sure to bring forth in tones of incredulity the horrified challenge: "Do you mean to say that you want to go back to the cold war?" That the cold war may not be the only alternative to détente seems to have escaped notice. It might also be asked, with equal incredulity and horror: "Do you want to go back to 'appeasement'?" In fact, an even more incredible question to some might be: "Do you realize that appeasement was built into détente?"

Let us see.

II

Détente has been so confusing not because there is a lack of definitions and interpretations but because there have been too many. There is not only an American version but different American versions. There is not only a Soviet version but different Soviet versions.

The original American theory of détente was developed, largely by Henry Kissinger, in 1972. The main concept behind it was the "linkage" of the military, the economic, and the political. The idea, as he explained it, was "to move forward on a very broad front on many issues" in order to create many "vested interests" on both sides.

After the Moscow "linkage," Kissinger was euphoric. He extolled SALT I as an "agreement without precedent in all relevant modern history." The summit meeting had been so successful, he reported, that the American side had achieved all that it had planned and had expected to achieve, "give or take 10 per cent"[4]—an extraordinary record for any diplomatic conference. For Prime Minister Chamberlain, Munich had brought "peace in our time." For President Nixon, Moscow had made possible "a new structure of peace in the world."

The second thoughts were not so ecstatic. It became increasingly clear that SALT I had been little more than a promissory note. In 1974, Secretary Kissinger himself said that, if a more far-reaching follow-up nuclear agreement were not reached "well before 1977, then I believe you will see an explosion of technology and an explosion of numbers" of fearsome proportions.[5] In that same year, Professor George B. Kistiakowsky, one of the most eminent and experienced experts in the field, testified: "The SALT I agreements do not inhibit or limit the strategic-arms race. They merely channel it into such directions as each side perceives to be militarily most advantageous to it." He characterized the antiballistic-missile treaty as "to a large degree another agreement not to do something that neither party wants to do anyway."[6] Despite the onrush of 1977, SALT II showed no signs of coming through in time to stop the technology-and-numbers explosion.

SALT I may have been oversold, and, to that extent, may have made the "linkage" with the commercial agreement even more expensive than it needed to be. But even if SALT I had been all that Kissinger had hoped for it, its linkage with the commercial agreement would still have been based on a theory that built appeasement into détente. It is this aspect of détente that should be more clearly understood.

On the American side, it was always recognized that the Soviets were mainly interested in détente for economic reasons.[7] The basic Soviet reason flowed from a declining rate of growth and productivity. According to official Soviet data, this rate fell from 10.9 per cent in 1950–58 to 7.2 per cent in 1958–67 to 6.4 per cent in 1967–73; Western recalculations of the Soviet figures show the actual decline to be from 6.4 per cent in 1950–58 to 5.3 per cent in 1958–67 to 3.7 per cent in 1967–73.[8] By 1966, the problem was already so troublesome that Prime Minister Aleksei Kosygin had called for abandonment of economic isolationism to prevent the Soviet economy from falling too far behind. A key reason for the Soviet dilemma was the failure to keep up with the advanced technology of the West. At first the Brezhnev regime had tried to overcome this weakness through earlier détentes with France and Germany. But by 1972, the American-Soviet détente made the United States the main source of scientific-technological transfer.

There was, however, a hitch. The Soviets were unable to pay for what they wanted. They demanded large-scale, long-term U.S. government credits at abnormally low interest rates. They sought most-favored-nation status without being able to reciprocate. They wanted the delivery of entire factories and plants on terms which meant that the Soviet Union would do all the owning and the Western donors would take all the risks. If anything went wrong, the Soviet Union and a few favored capitalists could not—and only the American taxpayer would—lose.*

This situation was made to order for one of Kissinger's beguiling theories—at least, enough people were beguiled to put it across. It was the theory of "incentives." According to Secretary Kissinger, the Soviets were advised in 1970 and 1971, in advance of the agreement on détente, that they could get paid off in credits and most-favored-nation treatment "if they engaged in what we considered responsible international behavior."[9] A Kissingerian formulation of the incentive-payment theory went as follows:

> We see it [economic relations] as a tool to bring about or to reinforce a more moderate orientation of foreign policy and to provide incentives for responsible international behavior and, therefore, it has to be seen in this context.[10]

An academic exponent of détente explained for popular consumption that trade, technology, and investment "would serve to offer a continuing incentive to Soviet leaders to accept the constraints of a low-tension policy." These incentives could be "regulated," he assured his readers, so that "our resources are not used to strengthen Soviet military capabilities"—as if it were possible to draw a line between the civilian and military uses of natural gas, petrochemicals, computers, and truck factories—and so that "the political competition is conducted with restraint"—as if restraint were not as much in the Soviet as in the American interest without incentive payments.[11]

The most important American incentive payments to the Soviets have been economic. This relationship has been inherently unequal. If all went well, Americans could benefit through profits and jobs. So far,

*Hedrick Smith, the former New York *Times* correspondent in Moscow, has told of a "joke" that circulated within the Soviet establishment on the eve of Brezhnev's visit to the United States in June 1973: "Brezhnev . . . asked his advisers what he should seek in America, 'Ask them to sell us cars,' suggested one. 'Ask them to build us computer factories,' said a second. 'Ask them to built atomic-power stations,' said a third. 'No,' replied Brezhnev thoughtfully. 'I'll just ask them to build us Communism' " (*Atlantic Monthly*, December 1974).

many deals have failed and a few have succeeded, so that the profits from increased Soviet-American trade have gone to a few favored or fortunate entrepreneurs. The Soviets, however, have an altogether larger stake in the relationship. They want to get out of it a structural change in their economy and a bail-out mechanism for their agriculture. This economic exchange is not an ordinary one; the Western contribution to the Soviet economy is heavy with political and military significance.

A quite recent study by Professor Marshall I. Goldman of how the economic détente has worked is not reassuring. Professor Goldman is not an enemy of détente or of Soviet-American trade—quite the contrary. Yet his cautionary analysis of what has been going on in the name of détente is most disturbing:

> The types of goods and the types of negotiating tactics the Russians tend to use in purchasing goods from the United States make it possible for the Russians to obtain high technology products for bargain prices that no other buyers could cajole. Moreover, much of the technology and sometimes the products themselves have been heavily subsidized by the American taxpayer. The initial subsidy for development and production, the bargain prices, and the subsidized interest rate of the Export-Import Bank means that the Russians are often able to obtain a triple subsidy on their American purchases.

These advantages, Professor Goldman adds, have an important political component built into them.[11a] One does not have to believe that the Soviets obtain all the benefits to see that the incentive theory works mainly in the Soviets' favor.

Curiously, the Soviets never bothered to develop a similar theory or practice vis-à-vis the United States. In fact, the Soviets have pursued a contrary course, at times most inconvenient for the United States. For example, until March 1974, months after the Arab-Israeli war was over, the Soviets urged the Arab oil producers to continue their embargo against the Western states and Japan.[12] This Soviet exhortation was not a mere peccadillo; it was a potentially deadly attack on the economic lifeline of the Western powers and Japan. The incentive theory seemed to work only one way.

Kissinger had another theory which should have made incentive payments unnecessary. It was the theory of "marginal advantages." He first produced it during the 1972 summit meeting in Moscow and kept repeating it until events proved it to be a conceptual breakdown instead of a conceptual breakthrough. In one of his clearest formulations of this embarrassing memory, he maintained that "to the extent that balance of power means constant jockeying for marginal advantages over an opponent, it no longer applies." He explained why:

> The reason is that the determination of national power has changed fundamentally in the nuclear age. Throughout history, the primary concern of most national leaders has been to accumulate geopolitical and military power. It would have seemed inconceivable even a generation ago that such power once gained could not be translated directly into advantage

over one's opponent. But now both we and the Soviet Union have begun to find that each increment of power does not necessarily represent an increment of usable political strength.[13]

This theory made the whole Kissingerian system of détente seem absurdly easy to operate. It was, in fact, a "self-regulating mechanism"—the diplomatic equivalent of perpetual motion. It ruled out "marginal advantages" and "increments of usable political strength" in the nuclear age by making them inherently "unrealistic" and catastrophically "dangerous."[14] Unfortunately, the Soviet leaders again failed to respond with a similar theory. Only a year later, their policy and actions in the Middle East were clearly based on an altogether different theory of what the nuclear age permitted in the way of struggling for "marginal advantages." Kissinger himself must have recognized that his theory, not "marginal advantages," was unrealistic and dangerous or he would not have bothered to respond to Soviet actions in the Middle East or Angola. After all, he should have reasoned, the Soviets were going after unusable and intangible "increments of power."

As if all this were not troublesome enough, Kissinger produced another, contradictory theory. In his testimony at the Senate hearings on his confirmation as Secretary of State, he delivered himself of this rule:

> But assuming the present balance holds, and granting the strategic significance of what we had both agreed upon, the increasing difficulty of conceiving a rational objective for general nuclear war makes it, therefore, less risky to engage in local adventures.[15]

One theory said that the nuclear age made "marginal advantages" unnecessary to worry about and, therefore, local adventures for such advantages less likely. Another theory said that the same nuclear age made local adventures "less risky" and, therefore, more likely.

What it all came down to in the end was an understanding of the political implications of the nuclear age. But before we get to this point, let us see what the Soviet view of détente has been.

III

In the "Basic Principles" of Soviet-American relations of May 29, 1972, the Soviets seemingly committed themselves to an interpretation of détente which fitted in with Kissinger's theory of "marginal advantages." These principles contained the following mutual restraints on engaging in "local adventures":

> Prevention of the development of situations capable of causing a dangerous exacerbation of Soviet-American relations.
> Doing the utmost to avoid military confrontations.
> Recognition that efforts to obtain unilateral advantage at the expense of the other, directly or indirectly, are inconsistent with these objectives.
> Special responsibility to do everything in their power so that conflicts or situations will not arise which would serve to increase international tensions.

These principles implied that there were two sides to détente—political and nuclear. The former was designed to prevent situations from developing which might bring on the danger of nuclear war. On ceremonial occasions, such as his speech at the Helsinki conference at the end of July 1975, Brezhnev has paid lip service to the combination of military and political détente.[16]

The "Basic Principles" also signified that détente applied not only to relations between the United States and the Soviet Union but also to the relations of each with the rest of the world. Kissinger has assured us that "we consider Soviet restraint in the Middle East an integral part of détente policy"[17] and "the principle of restraint is not confined to relations between the U.S. and the USSR, it is explicitly extended to include *all* countries."[18]

There seemed to be agreement, then, on two constituent elements of a true détente—it must apply to the political as well as to the nuclear realm, and it must apply to the relations of the United States and the Soviet Union with the rest of the world as well as to the relations between themselves.

However, there are Soviet theories underlying détente which like the American, must be taken into account to find out what it really means. For example, a basic Soviet theory is that of the "new relationship of forces." It was expressed by Brezhnev not long ago in the following formula: "International détente has become possible because a new relationship of forces now exists on the world scene."[19]

What is this "new relationship of forces"? The short answer, spelled out in all Communist propaganda, is that the "new relationship of forces" now favors the "socialist world" led by the Soviet Union. The point here is not whether the theory is right or wrong. The point is that, for the Soviet Union and its followers, détente is not an abstract, historical condition; it is the product of a concrete, historical "relationship of forces" which determines not merely what détente is but—far more important—what it does.

A second Soviet theory in this connection is that of the "two spheres." An authoritative exposition of this theory was recently given by Professor Georgi Arbatov, a high-level Soviet spokesman and present head of the Institute of the USA of the Academy of Sciences of the USSR:

> What is involved here [the policy of détente] is essentially different spheres of political life in our time (though they may influence one another in various ways). One of them is the sphere of social development, which steadily makes headway in any international conditions—whether détente, "cold" war, or even "hot" war. . . . The other is the sphere of inter-state relations, in which other extremely important questions are resolved—questions of war and peace, methods of resolving controversial foreign-policy questions, and possibilities for mutually advantageous international cooperation.
>   The drawing of a clear line between these two spheres is one of the basic premises of the Leninist foreign policy of the peaceful coexistence of states with different social systems. . . .[20]

In the pro-Soviet Communist movement, the theory of "peaceful coexistence" has been promulgated somewhat more clearly and starkly. It is now said that peaceful coexistence

> refers exclusively to the domain of inter-state relations between socialist and capitalist countries. It rules out just one form of struggle between socialism and capitalism—the form of direct military collision.[21]

Formerly, as we have seen, détente was supposed to cover anything of a political or military nature which could exacerbate Soviet-American relations, give one side unilateral advantage at the expense of the other, or serve to increase international tension. The theory of the "two spheres" eliminates a huge political area—under the trade name of "social development"—from the domain of détente. By reducing détente to the avoidance of "direct military collision" between the United States and the Soviet Union, it leaves everything else wide open.

This tendency to shunt détente out of the political sphere into a narrow military sphere has now come to a head with the need to rationalize large-scale Soviet military intervention in Angola and the use of Cuban troops as Soviet proxies. A writer in *Izvestia* of November 29, 1975 insisted that it was impossible to bring "the sphere of class and national-liberation struggle" within "peaceful coexistence."[22] On November 30, an *Izvestia* correspondent reported that détente "gave a powerful impulse to the national-liberation movement of colonial and oppressed peoples."[23] On December 2, an *Izvestia* commentator held that "the process of détente does not mean and never meant the freezing of the social-political status quo in the world" or could prevent the Soviet Union from giving "sympathy, compassion, and support" to those whom it chose to represent as "fighters for national independence."[24] On December 6, a writer in *Pravda* boasted: "Détente created favorable conditions for the new successes of the cause of national liberation."[25] On December 8, a report in *Pravda* of an "international anti-fascist conference" brought these glad tidings: "The thought that runs all through the documents of the conference and the speeches of its participants is that the strengthening process of détente creates favorable conditions for the struggles of the popular masses against imperialism and neocolonialism, against all forms of fascism and internal reaction."[26]

These thoughts were not entirely new. The Soviet Union has long claimed the right to support "national-liberation movements." In the heyday of détente, however, this motif was muted in favor of emphasis on avoiding international friction. Now almost any action which the Soviet Union chooses to take that could cause a dangerous exacerbation of Soviet-American relations, obtain direct or indirect unilateral advantage, or increase international tensions is being conveniently classified as "class and national-liberation struggle." That the Soviet political line should be turned around to provide a propaganda smoke screen for military intervention on the west coast of Africa is something new and ominous. If this sort of intervention can be justified in the name of détente, almost anything short of direct conflict with the United States can be made to fit the "Basic Principles."

There are indications, too, of a general "left turn" in the line which the Soviet Union is pressing on the world Communist movement. One telltale sign was an article in *Pravda* of August 6, 1975, by K. Zaradov, editor-in-chief of the official pro-Soviet Communist organ, *Problems of Peace and Socialism (World Marxist Review* in the English version). Zaradov's article was clearly aimed at the French and Italian Communist parties rather than at the Chinese. He called them "present-day conciliators" whose "logic is the same as that of the Mensheviks"—storm signals in Communist political meteorology. Why this sudden outburst? Because, according to Zaradov, the present-day conciliators and quasi-Mensheviks "would like to dissolve it [the proletarian party] in an ideologically amorphous organization, in any alliance created according to the formula 'unity for unity's sake.' "[27] The point was not lost on the Italian and French Communists who protested against this onslaught in the official organ of the Soviet Communist party. How high up the inspiration for Zaradov's article had come from was soon made clear by an item in *Izvestia* of September 19. This unusual social note reported that General Secretary Brezhnev had received Zaradov and had congratulated him for his fine work.

Another indication has come from the American Communist party, the most slavishly pro-Soviet of the Western Communist parties. At its recent national convention, its General Secretary discovered that "in the U.S. in the 1970's monopoly capital is preparing the climate in which fascism can come to power."[28] Various roles have already been assigned—Governor George C. Wallace as the "leading fascist demagogue"; William F. Buckley, Jr., as an "adroit exponent of 'intellectual' fascism"; a curiously promiscuous company—William B. Shockley, Arthur Jensen, Richard Herrnstein, H. J. Eysenck, Christopher Jencks, Edward C. Banfield, Robert W. Fogel and Stanley L. Engerman—as "leading exponents" of "Nazi-like poison."[29] Since everyone knows that monopoly capital rules the United States, and now we know what monopoly capital is preparing, it does not take too much foresight to see where the Communist propaganda line is heading. The Soviets may soon be saving the entire world from the menace of American fascism.

All these aspects of Soviet policy—military intervention, political theorizing, Communist propaganda—are intimately related to the changing Soviet view of détente. Fundamental to all of them is one simple rule—that what always counts most is the relationship of forces, not the arrangement of words.

IV

The Arab-Israeli war of October 1973 proved to be the first real test of the Soviet-American détente. It provided so clear a violation of the "basic principles" by the Soviet Union that even Secretary Kissinger had to admit as much, albeit in the relative obscurity of a Senate committee hearing. The violation concerned the message sent by Brezhnev to Algerian President Boumédienne and apparently to other Arab leaders telling them that it was their Arab duty to get into the war against Israel. Pressed by Senator Harry F. Byrd, Jr., Secretary Kissinger agreed, "Yes, I would say this was a violation."[30]*

Nothing more was heard of this awkward admission. All concerned would have benefited if more attention had been paid to it. Kissinger himself had testified that Soviet "restraint" in the Middle East was "an integral part of the détente policy." If it did not hold there, it was unlikely to hold wherever American and Soviet interests seriously clashed. In that case the détente relationship was relegated to taking care of relatively minor matters, leaving the major ones to a nuclear alert or rival military interventions. It can now be seen that the Middle East crisis of October 1973 was a dress rehearsal for the Angola crisis of 1975–76.

After the Middle East crisis, however, the American line on détente underwent some changes. The concept of détente is like an accordion; it can be stretched out or pulled in. It can be as broad as it seemed after the summit meeting of May 1972 or it can be as narrow as it became after October 1973. To take care of all possible contingencies, Kissinger began to stress the schizoid character of détente. It was, he explained in March 1974, "composed of both competition and cooperation" with "profound ambiguities at every stage of this relationship."[31] Later, he spoke of détente as if it were merely an improved method of communications, "a means by which a competition which is inevitable—in the nature of present circumstances—is regulated while reducing the danger of nuclear war."[32] It had become a means to an end which was contradictory and ambiguous, a regulatory system without an agency to do the regulating.

Above all, détente was now largely reduced to limiting "the risks of nuclear war," as Kissinger put it.[33] Former Senator J. William Fulbright could think of nothing better than: "Détente, in its essence, is an agreement not to let these differences [between the two superpowers] explode into nuclear war."[34] Professor Marshall Shulman instructed us that the main business of détente was "to reduce the danger of nuclear war."[35] The case for détente after October 1973 came essentially to rest on its relationship with nuclear war and on little else that was unambiguous and uncontradictory.

We have now come to the heart of the matter. It is right here—the relationship between détente and nuclear war.

---

*The exchange just before this one is worth pondering:

Senator Byrd: On the question of harrassment, which is one of the key points of the Jackson amendment, is not the entire system of government in Russia based on harassment and terror, as a practical matter?

Secretary Kissinger: Well, I think the government is more obtrusive than in our country (p. 88).

Obtrusive!

Was there a meaningful "linkage" between nuclear war, economic-incentive payments, and political restraint? The American—or Kissingerian—theory and practice of détente was fundamentally dependent on a positive answer to this question. If the answer was negative, the entire American policy rested on a dubious foundation.

For the past thirty years, during hot wars, cold wars, and détentes, nuclear weapons have not been used. They were not used by the United States when it had a nuclear monopoly, even when its forces were decimated by Chinese Communist troops in Korea, even when the United States suffered defeat in Vietnam in the longest and most humiliating war in its history. There is obviously something about nuclear warfare that has set it apart from all other forms of warfare in which we still engage. There is something about nuclear weapons which cannot be fitted into hot wars, cold wars, or détentes. The nuclear war, as much as any type of war can be, must as yet be regarded as *sui generis*. We still have no experience with it; we cannot fathom its bottomless depths of pure nihilism; we cannot imagine a rational use for it.

With the nuclear weapon we reached the *reductio ad absurdum* of all warfare—a weapon that was *too destructive*. This was already the lesson when the United States still had a monopoly of it. As soon as the Soviet Union became an atomic and then a nuclear power, we achieved a higher stage of military "absurdity"—a weapon that was *too mutually destructive*. This second stage was reached by the mid-1950's, so that we have been in it for about two decades.[36] The third stage came in the late 1960's when the United States realized that the Soviet Union would achieve rough nuclear parity. The "absurdity" had now arrived at its final destination—the power of *mutual annihilation*.

In exasperation, Secretary Kissinger once dramatically exclaimed:

> And one of the questions which we have to ask ourselves as a country is what, in the name of God, is strategic superiority? What is the significance of it, politically, militarily, operationally, at these levels of numbers? What do you do with it?[37]

It was, as the saying goes, a good question. It implied that on the level of mutual annihilation it mattered little how much more annihilating a nuclear power could or would become. It also implied that there was no political "significance" to be attached to those incomprehensibly high levels of destructiveness. Nuclear warfare cannot be weighed in political scales or translated into political terms. Politics, so to speak, is sub-nuclear. Thus Kissinger himself inferentially cut the ground from under the nuclear-political linkage.

The control of nuclear warfare, then, is of an order so different from the control of "conventional" warfare, let alone the control of political and ideological rivalries, that the former must be dealt with as something apart. Just as nuclear warfare has resisted every calculus of political or economic usefulness, so, too, it is not amenable to political blandishments or economic payoffs. The enormity of the nuclear problem defies all past human experience. This is not to say that the human race need or should resign itself to the ever-present threat of nuclear annihilation; it means that the threat must be faced on its own terms, without pretending that it can be got around through "linkages" of an altogether different order of magnitude. Economic incentives and political phrase-mongering—the tools of détente—are not in the same league as nuclear arms.

The promoters of détente sought to save it by reducing it to a hard core of avoidance of nuclear warfare. They were in fact exposing its essential hollowness. They were giving it the self-same function that the cold war of unblessed memory used to have—as an alternative to hot war. They were giving détente underserved credit for an impasse that had been brought about by the mutual destructiveness of nuclear warfare. The linkage of détente with nuclear war betrayed a misunderstanding of both.

The trouble with the narrow nuclear interpretation of détente is that it puts all the rest of the world's troubles and all the other possible forms of conflict outside détente. If détente is as schizoid as both the latest American and Soviet versions make it out to be, one must constantly ask what belongs and what does not belong to the sphere of détente. If, as the Soviet spokesman Arbatov has told us, détente belongs exclusively to the sphere of "inter-state relations" and not at all to the sphere of "social development," the question arises whether the war in the Middle East or in Angola belong to the former or the latter. In the Soviet view, the latter is decidedly the case, which tells us how broad the category of "social development" is and how narrowly détente has been confined. If, as Secretary Kissinger has told us, détente is composed of both "competition and cooperation," the question arises: What pertains to competition and what to cooperation? An even more awkward question must be asked: If cooperation is the real essence of détente, what is the nature of the competition? Isn't it the bad old "cold war"? Kissinger has also begun to talk of "moderating competition," a formula combining "accommodation and resistance."[38] Does this mean that when we get "accommodation" we have détente, and when we get "resistance" we have cold war? If we can have "accommodation and resistance" together, why not détente and cold war together? These semantic games are hopelessly muddling and contaminating all discourse on world affairs today.

How far one can go to equate détente with the avoidance of a Soviet-American nuclear war was shown by Professor Herbert Dinerstein at the 1974 Senate hearings on détente. He set out to demonstrate that "détente makes for a unique stability in the ultimate issues of war and peace, but permits, nay, encourages movement and change in all issues of lesser moment." Next, he explained that this unique stability of détente was based on the conviction that "nuclear war would be an act of mutual destruction." This line of reasoning led him to his grand climax: "Détente means that the two countries will not make war on each other."[39]

If that is all détente means, it is accomplishing exactly what the fear of "mutual destruction" was able to accomplish with or without détente. One would like to be as sure as Professor Dinerstein is that détente in this sense possesses a "unique stability." If it does, it is only because the mutual destructiveness of nuclear war possesses that same "unique stability." In any case, we have gone very far from the détente of 1972 which, according to Kissinger, had moved "on a very broad front on many issues." Those who have tried to save détente by moving it on to a very narrow front on the single issue of nuclear warfare have unwittingly been administering the last rites to it.

V

Therefore, critics of détente must answer: what is the alternative that they propose? What precise policies do they want us to change? Are they prepared for a prolonged situation of dramatically increased international danger? Do they wish to return to the constant crises and high arms budgets of the cold war? Does détente encourage repression—or is it détente that has generated the ferment and the demands for openness that we are now witnessing?[40]

Such was the angry challenge that Secretary Kissinger hurled at critics of détente [in July 1975]. He seemed to think that the answers to his questions were crushingly obvious. I, too, think that the answers were so obvious that it was a mistake to ask the questions.

1) *What is the alternative that they propose?* One alternative would be to cease and desist from the unconscionable exploitation of the word "détente," or at least to stop waving it as a banner. It has now become an obstacle to thought. It is of little or no use in relation to nuclear war. It is a mockery in relation to such wars as we have, as in the Middle East and Angola. It admittedly does not apply to ideological conflict. It has been defined and redefined virtually out of existence. If it continues to serve as a political shibboleth, it must surely suffer the same fate as "appeasement," if it has not done so already.

2) *What precise policies do they want us to change?* One policy that was misconceived from the outset and should be changed without delay is that of "incentive" payments to the Soviet Union. It is this policy more than any other which has opened the door to appeasement in the guise of détente. Arbatov and other Soviet spokesmen have stormed against the idea that the Soviets are expected to make any "payments" to the West.[41] The theory and practice of American incentive premiums are especially ruinous in connection with nuclear-weapons negotiations. If the threat of mutual annihilation is not persuasive enough to bring one or the other side to its senses, and here I do not point an accusing finger only at the Soviet Union, immeasurably lesser incentives are at best superfluous and at worst irrelevant. Advance payments to the Soviet Union for services in the common interest that may or may not be rendered have never worked and even make matters worse. They merely serve to convince the masters of the Soviet Union that the famous "relationship of forces" has so changed in their favor that payments must be made for nothing more than a piece of paper.

3) *Are they prepared for a prolonged situation of dramatically increased danger?* Let us recall that this question was flung out with much unction and indignation only a half-year ago. Since then the level of tension

and danger has increased dramatically. The question was plainly addressed to the wrong parties. The Angola crisis is hardly the work of the critics of détente. Some of them may even have seen such dramatically increased danger coming since the last Arab-Israeli war. The real question is whether the leaders and fellow-travelers of détente were prepared for a prolonged situation of dramatically increased danger.

4) *Do they wish to return to the constant crises and high arms budgets of the cold war?* To answer this question, it is useful to recall Secretary Kissinger's answer to another question put to him at the end of 1974:

> *Senator Byrd:* Is it not correct that since 1972, in a period of so-called détente, there has been a methodical improvement and expansion of nuclear and conventional power in the Soviet Union and in Eastern Europe?
> *Secretary Kissinger:* Yes, that is correct.[42]

At least we have it from Secretary Kissinger that détente, in its heyday, did nothing to discourage the Soviets from improving and expanding their military power. Whether the same can be said of the United States seems more doubtful, but let us assume that both sides have improved and expanded their nuclear and conventional power in the détente years between 1972 and 1974. It may be argued that the situation would have been worse without détente. Perhaps—but it certainly did not get better, and it is most unlikely that more intercontinental missiles and more megatonnage would have significantly changed the nature of the problem. The obvious answer, then, to this question about crises and arms budgets is: No. But what does it have to do with détente? Has détente saved us from constant crises and high arms budgets? Could Secretary Kissinger tell Senator Byrd that détente had prevailed on the Soviet Union and Eastern Europe not to improve and expand their nuclear and conventional power? More to the point, the answer, unfortunately, again is: No.

5) *Does détente encourage repression—or is it détente that has generated ferment and the demands for openness that we are now witnessing?* This is the most incredible question of all. It reveals how much Kissinger's understanding of the Soviet system has changed since he took up residence in Washington. In one of his major works, *The Necessity for Choice,* published in 1961, he discussed this very question at some length. He frowned on those who thought that "Western diplomacy should seek to influence Soviet internal developments." He scoffed at "the tendency to base policy toward the USSR on an assumed change in Soviet society." He reproached those who saw "in every change of tone a change of heart." He decried "the persistence with which it has been claimed that the economic needs of the Soviet Union would impose a more conciliatory policy on it." He severely disapproved of the fact that, "whatever aspect of the Soviet system they have considered, many in the West have sought to solve our policy dilemma by making the most favorable assumptions about Soviet trends." He instructed us sagely: "The tendency to justify negotiations by changes in Soviet at-

titude makes us vulnerable to largely formal Soviet moves." And this: "The possibility of evolution of Soviet policy in a more conciliatory direction may be jeopardized by the eagerness with which it is predicted."[43]

Nothing could illustrate more aptly the timeliness of these warnings than the connection between détente and Soviet repression. By the time Kissinger asked the question, "Does détente encourage repression?," in July 1975, repression was already in full swing. The most open period in recent Soviet history came in 1967–71, before the American-Soviet détente. The official crackdown on the underground *samizdat* movement took place in 1972, the very first year of that détente. The orchestrated vilification of Andrei Sakharov, the recent Nobel Peace Prize winner, started in August 1973. Aleksandr Solzhenitsyn was arrested and deported in February 1974. Hedrick Smith of the New York *Times* has by chance answered Kissinger's question in his new book, *The Russians,* an account of his experiences in the Soviet Union in 1971–74, dealing with precisely the years of détente, and an ideal corrective to much of what correspondents in Moscow have to send out while they are still there:

> The technology of Soviet repression had become more sophisticated and more effective as détente proceeded. The unexpected irony was that détente, instead of spawning more general ferment among the Soviet intelligentsia, as the West had hoped and the Kremlin had feared, became a reason for tighter controls and sometimes provided new techniques for quieting disaffected intellectuals.[44]

This reflex on the part of the Soviet leadership is not new. The precedent had been set by Lenin in 1920–21. At the same time that he introduced the New Economic Policy or NEP, liberalizing the Soviet economy, and as he began to make deals with Western powers, he liquidated every vestige of dissidence in both the country and the party. The two went hand in hand in order to prevent present and potential dissidents from taking advantage of "decreased tension." Stalin combined the Popular Front outside Russia with the Great Purge inside Russia. Yet Kissinger has assured us: "Changes in Soviet society have already occurred, and more will come. But they are most likely to develop through an evolution that can best go forward in an environment of decreasing international tensions."[45] The trouble with this line of reasoning is that the Soviet leadership has known what to do about it for the past fifty years. Whenever there is danger that decreasing international tensions will foster changes in Soviet society unwanted by the party, repression is increased. That is why détente has been accompanied by more rather than less repression. There may be other reasons for pursuing a policy of détente, but discouraging repression is not one of them.

One wonders why Secretary Kissinger thought that his questions were so crushing and the answers to them so self-evident. Had he forgotten so much?

VI

Secretary Kissinger, former Senator Fulbright, and others have insisted that the only alternative to détente is cold war. Since they seem to think that a return to cold war is unthinkable, or at least unbearable, that would leave us only with détente. The reality is far more confused and disagreeable. Détente, cold war, and appeasement have all been mixed up together, with appeasement given the least consideration.

One of the ways appeasement was built into détente has already been noted. The whole theory and practice of giving "incentives" to the Soviet Union to do what it should do in its own interest or not at all was the entering wedge of appeasement. We tried to buy with gratuitous and unreciprocated favors what is not for sale, especially not in the one field that is supposed to matter most in détente—nuclear warfare.

But a humiliating climate of appeasement had also been created. It was symbolized by the presidential refusal to receive Aleksandr Solzhenitsyn because the gesture might displease Leonid Brezhnev. Had Brezhnev ever refused to meet with an anti-U.S. personage in order not to displease Richard Nixon or Gerald Ford? This type of appeasement is not new and not limited to the United States. West Germany, whose détente with the Soviet Union goes back to 1970, has practiced the same kind of appeasement at the expense of one of its own foremost writers. The German incident shows that present-day appeasement takes certain characteristic forms in more than one country.

In the summer of 1973, the eminent German writer Günter Grass was invited to give a private reading from his works at the home of Ulrich Sahm, the German ambassador in Moscow. Grass made indirect contact with Sakharov and Solzhenitsyn in preparation for his visit, and Solzhenitsyn intended to give him a manuscript to take back. Meanwhile, both Sakharov and Solzhenitsyn issued statements warning against the risks of détente. This situation so frightened Ambassador Sahm that he sent a private letter to Grass withdrawing the invitation. Grass refused to let the matter remain private; he published the letter and discussed its implications on television and in the press. A former upholder of *Ostpolitik,* he now renounced it on the ground that its restrictions meant the betrayal of culture in general and Russian writers in particular. Grass was thereupon publicly and offensively rebuked by a spokesman of the German Ministry of Foreign Affairs.[46]

The Solzhenitsyn and Grass incidents were symptomatic of a moral flaccidity that always goes along with appeasement. The Soviets consider culture and ideology to be outside the boundaries of détente, but they seem to be the only ones to think so or to act on this premise. Indeed, cultural appeasement was also built into détente by virtue of how the different political systems work.

A well-known American specialist in Soviet studies has told how the systems work in the case of the scholarly-exchange program. The Soviet scholar who comes to the United States can see anything he asks for in American universities and libraries. He goes back and writes

about America's most painful contemporary problems—ethnic
conflicts, student riots, unemployment, crime, black nationalism, and
the like. The American scholar has had to accept a different set of
rules:

> Indeed, and the best illustration of that is the simple fact that for American
> scholars the most interesting subject of study in the Soviet Union is Soviet
> political history—for example Stalin and Trotsky, the history of the party,
> the relationship between party and government, the purges of the 1930's,
> Soviet foreign policy, Soviet economic policy, and so forth. We have never
> been able to send a single American scholar to the Soviet Union to look at
> any of these problems.
>
> When the exchange visits first started there were applications on our
> side for the study of these areas, but the Russians resolutely refused to
> allow for applicants into their country. Then, realizing how applications in
> these fields of study would be treated by the Russians, our young scholars
> shifted their applications to the study of less sensitive questions, such as
> local government which hardly exists in the Soviet-Union or 19th-century
> political history and problems of that kind. In others words, the Russians
> turned us away from the issues which are most central to us, and we are
> now doing their job for them, because our professors tell their young
> students not to bother with subjects that would prejudice their chances of
> being allowed into the Soviet Union. . . .
>
> Soviet control over opportunities for study in the USSR has so
> influenced some of our more timid colleagues interested in going or
> returning to Russia, that they will not join other intellectuals in protests
> against the Soviet treament of dissidents, minorities, etc. and will even
> refuse to participate in conferences that many be distasteful to the Soviet
> government. The Soviet government has in fact acquired some influence
> both over the direction of Western scholarship and over Western political
> attitudes.[47]

In effect, appeasement was built into détente whenever we
adapted ourselves to them but they did not adapt themselves to us. In
these circumstances, appeasement worked silently, automatically, almost unthinkingly. It was the most insidious kind of appeasement because the cards were stacked in the Soviets' favor without any overt effort on their part.

Such have been the acrid fruits of détente. They did not burst
forth because there was anything wrong with the ideal of détente. They
flourished because too much appeasement was built into détente. Appeasement did not work in the 1930's; it has not worked in the 1970's
and for the same reason—appeasement cannot appease the unap-
peaseable. . . .

The latest Kissingerian theory was foreshadowed by Helmut Sonnenfeldt, Counselor for the State Department, in an address on "The
Meaning of 'Détente' " at the Naval War College in the late spring of
1975. Sonnenfeldt described the Soviet Union in terms which had not
been heard previously in the era of détente:

> Its power continues to grow and its interests to expand. Indeed, it can be
> said that in the broad sweep of history, Soviet Russia is only just beginning
> its truly "imperial" phase: its military forces have acquired intercontinental

reach only fairly recently; its capacity to influence events in remote areas is of relatively recent standing; and it is only just acquiring the habit of defining its interests on a global rather than a solely continental basis. For us, therefore, the problem is that of building viable relationships with an emerging world power.

One reads these lines with astonishment. "Only just beginning"? "Only fairly recently"? "Of relatively recent standing"? Unfortunately, Sonnenfeldt did not give any clue to how recent his "recently" was. The unwary reader might imagine that all this had happened during the past three years of détente. Let us take just one of these astounding statements—that the Soviet Union "is only just acquiring the habit of defining its interests on a global rather than a solely continental basis." A quarter of a century ago, North Korea could not have carried on its war if the Soviet Union had not trained and equipped its army. Continental or global? The major supplier of North Vietnam was the Soviet Union. Continental or global? In one way or another, as Communists, the Soviet leaders have defined their interests on a global basis for almost six decades. They have had much more experience in this respect than the Americans have had. This patronizing view of the Soviet Union as a global power tells more about the Counselor's historical awareness than it does about the Soviet Union.

In any case, if this is where the broad sweep of history has taken us, it should have had some bearing on the state of détente. But Sonnenfeldt was not yet ready to go that far. Instead, he gave the fact that the Soviet Union "continues to grow in power, weight, and reach" as a reason "why we must persist in the basic policies we have been pursuing over the past several years"—incentives and all.[48]

Secretary Kissinger himself went public with the new theory in an interview with Flora Lewis which appeared in the New York *Times* of December 21, 1975. He explained that the Soviet Union had become an imperial superpower in an expansionist phase that must run its course. The Soviets, he warned, will exploit every opportunity to enlarge their dominion, unless the risks are made too great for them. The Soviet move into Angola demonstrates how far afield this expansionist momentum had carried them. Unless the United States answered in kind in Angola, the next stage of Soviet expansionism would be even more dangerous and costly.

By this time the official line had clearly gone beyond the Sonnenfeldt version of early 1975. It went even further at Secretary Kissinger's news conference on December 23. It also began with a strange history lesson:

> The basic problem in our relation with the Soviet Union is the emergence of the Soviet Union into true superpower status. That fact has become evident only in the 1970's. As late as the Cuban missile crisis, the disparity in strategic power between the United States and the Soviet Union was overwhelmingly in our favor.

In this broad sweep of history, we jump from the Cuban missile crisis of 1962 to the 1970's. This leap makes it appear as if we had to wait until December 1975 to discover what was going on. The missile crisis convinced the Soviet leadership that it was necessary to catch up with and overtake the United States in strategic arms. The Soviets caught up much more quickly than the Americans had counted on; in fact, back in 1965, the top American leaders did not think that the Soviets had any intention of catching up. By the time the SALT I talks were started in late 1969, the Soviets had made such progress that the Americans were ready to settle for freezing both sides at a level of rough strategic parity. Despite SALT I, if we may trust Paul H. Nitze, who deserves to be heard respectfully as a SALT negotiator from 1969 to 1974, the Soviets have not been satisfied with parity and have been aiming at strategic superiority, a position which Nitze thinks they began to achieve in 1973.[49]

One cannot, therefore, jump historically all the way from 1962 to the 1970's. Something was happening within two or three years of the Cuban missile crisis that brought us to the present balance in strategic power. The shift has been going on for about a decade, and its implications have been apparent throughout the course of détente. It is rather late in the game to discover that the Soviet Union possesses "true superpower status."

And what, in the name of God, is "true superpower status"? At least as long ago as 1964, Henry Kissinger referred to the Soviet Union as a "superpower."[50] In 1968, Kissinger noted that the Soviet Union was one of the two powers which possessed "the full panoply of military might."[51] Does the new status mean that the Soviet Union in 1964 was an "untrue" superpower? Or does "true superpower" mean a "super-superpower"? How much more of the full panoply of military might, *circa* 1968, was it necessary for the Soviet Union to possess to be promoted to the rank of "true superpower"? If the United States is also a "true superpower," why the special emphasis on this new classification?

This broad sweep of history is more a political than a historical operation. The new status of the Soviet Union has been discovered just in time to explain a crisis in American détente policy, as if the crisis were a result of immanent historical forces instead of a misconceived policy. That the crisis for détente may be a mortal one was made plain by Secretary Kissinger in his December 23 news conference. These were fighting words:

> We do not confuse the relaxation of tension with permitting the Soviet Union to expand its sphere by military means and that is the issue, for example, in Angola. . . .
>   If the Soviet Union continues action such as Angola, we will without any question resist. . . .
>   Unless the Soviet Union shows restraint in its foreign-policy actions, the situation in our relationship is bound to become more tense, and there is no question that the United States will not accept Soviet military expansion of any kind.

Thus Kissinger was forced to give up in fact, if not in name, one of the underlying myths of détente—the theory that the Soviet Union had become a status-quo power. This notion was actually the implied premise of the "Basic Principles" of May 1972. It has been a costly myth, made all the worse because it was implicitly fostered by official U.S. policy. . . .

It is too early to tell what the full story of Angola is. Whatever the truth may be about the various foreign interventions, the Soviets clearly outbid all the others by bringing in thousands of Cuban proxies, the nearest thing to using their own troops, and by arming their side with far more, far more costly, and far more advanced weapons. In terms of the political significance of the Angolan situation for détente, however, it matters less what each side has done than that such a faraway Soviet-American contest should have taken place at all. For if, as Secretary Kissinger has maintained, the United States must react as strongly as he has urged it to react in Angola in order to discourage the Soviet Union "from taking advantage" of favorable opportunities, we are faced with the paradox that it is necessary to wage cold and not-so-cold war in dangerous situations in order to save détente for non-dangerous situations—in short, that détente works when and where it is needed the least. If détente is so restricted, fluctuating, ambiguous, and paradoxical, it can hardly be taken as seriously as we had been led to believe.

Tactics aside, Kissinger was finally right on the strategic problem: the Soviet Union *is* in an imperial, expansionist phase. We are faced strategically with a long-term Soviet imperial pressure, now gathering momentum and based, as Soviet spokesmen like to say, on a "new relationship of forces." If the Soviets can get the world to accept their version of this "new relationship of forces," the consequences will be cumulatively disastrous.

This renewed Soviet pressure was building up while the United States was beguiled by détente. It is imprudent and implausible to conduct a foreign policy based on holding back the new Soviet expansionism while still officially enmeshed in the doctrine of détente. The new and the old theories and policies cannot coexist peacefully. One of them must go.

NOTES

[1]*Détente:* Hearings before the Committee on Foreign Relations, U.S. Senate, August-September 1974, pp. 61, 67, 102, 147, 208, 239, 301.

[2]Walter C. Clemens, Jr., "The Impact of Détente on Chinese and Soviet Communism," *Journal of International Affairs,* Vol. 28, No. 2, 1974, p. 134.

[3]"If tensions mount, the parties may move toward cold and then hot war. If tensions diminish, the parties move toward détente (whether short- or long-lived); from détente they could move further toward rapprochement or even entente" *(ibid.).*

[4]May 29, 1972.

[5]July 3, 1974.

[6]*Détente:* Hearings, pp. 161–62.

[7]Robert Ellsworth, *Department of State Bulletin,* November 23, 1970, pp. 642–43. Also: "The condition of the Soviet economy is clearly the primary determinant of present Soviet foreign policy" (Marshall Shulman, *Foreign Affairs,* October 1973, p. 43).

[8]*Détente:* Hearings, p. 32.

[9]*Emigration Amendment to the Trade Reform Act of 1974:* Hearings before the Committee on Finance, U.S. Senate, December 3, 1974, p. 106.

[10]*Ibid.,* pp. 96–97.

[11]Marshall Shulman, New York *Times,* March 10, 1974.

[11a]Marshall I. Goldman, *Détente and Dollars* (Basic Books, 1975), pp. 275–76.

[12]Marshall I. Goldman, *Daedalus,* Fall 1975, p. 137, and Note 35, p. 143.

[13]June 15, 1972.

[14]*U.S. Foreign Policy for the 1970's: A New Strategy for Peace,* A Report to the Congress by Richard Nixon, President of the United States, February 18, 1970, p. 232.

[15]*Nomination of Henry A. Kissinger:* Hearings before the Committee on Foreign Relations, U.S. Senate, September 11, 1973, Part I, p. 101.

[16]*Pravda,* August 1, 1975, p. 1 (in *The Current Digest of the Soviet Press,* Vol. XXVII, No. 31, p. 13).

[17]*Emigration Amendment to the Trade Reform Act of 1974,* p. 77.

[18]September 19, 1974.

[19]*Information Bulletin,* issued by the *World Marxist Review,* Vol. 13 (1975), Nos. 12–13, p. 14.

[20]*Izvestia,* September 4, 1975 (in *The Current Digest of the Soviet Press,* Vol. XXVII, No. 36, p. 3).

[21]*World Marxist Review,* September 1975, p. 59.

[22]N. Polyanov, *Izvestia,* November 29, 1975, p. 4.

[23]V. Kobysh, *Izvestia,* November 30, 1975, p. 2.

[24]V. Matveyev, *Izvestia,* December 2, 1975, p. 4.

[25]Oleg Skalkin, *Pravda,* December 6, 1975, p. 5.

[26]O. Kitsenko, I. Shchedrov, A. Arkhipov, *Pravda,* December 8, 1975, p. 3.

[27]K. Zaradov, *Pravda,* August 6, 1975 (in *The Current Digest of the Soviet Press,* Vol. XXVII, No. 31, pp. 15, 17).

[28]Gus Hall, *The Crisis of U.S. Capitalism and the Fight Back* (International Publishers, 1975), p. 44.

[29]*Political Affairs,* November 1975, pp. 3, 6, 16.

[30]*Emigration Amendment to the Trade Reform Act of 1974,* p. 89.

[31]March 28, 1974.

[32]Henry A. Kissinger, interview with William F. Buckley, September 13, 1975.

[33]November 12, 1973 (interview in Peking).

[34]*Congressional Record,* Senate, November 9, 1973, p. S–20136.

[35]New York *Times,* March 10, 1974.

[36]Samuel P. Huntington, *The Common Defense* (Columbia University Press, 1961), p. 88. In 1950, U.S. policy-makers had expected the second stage to be reached in 1954 (p. 60). But even if Huntington is right, and it did not come about for another two years or so, the difference is hardly significant now.

[37]July 3, 1974.

[38]Flora Lewis, New York *Times,* December 21, 1975.

[39]*Détente:* Hearings, pp. 301–302.

[40]July 15, 1975.

[41]Arbatov and Polyanov, *op. cit.*

[42]*Emigration Amendment to the Trade Reform Act of 1974,* p. 76.

[43]Henry A. Kissinger, *The Necessity for Choice* (Harper & Row, 1961), pp. 195–201.

[44]Hedrick Smith, *The Russians* (Quadrangle, 1976), p. 439.

[45]September 19, 1974.

[46]The story is told by François Bondy, *Survey,* Spring-Summer 1974, p. 43.

[47]Robert F. Byrnes, Distinguished Professor of History and Director of the Russian and East European Institute, Indiana State University, *Survey,* Autumn 1974, pp. 52–53.

[48]*Naval War College Review,* Summer 1975, pp. 3–8.

[49]*Foreign Affairs,* January 1976, p. 226.

[50]*Ibid.,* July 1964, p. 539.

[51]*Agenda for the Nation* (Brookings Institution, 1968), p. 587.

12 Détente is in the eye of the beholder

Roger Morris

In 1972 it was statesmanship, and Richard Nixon won a landslide victory running on it. In 1976, many see it as a threat, and Ronald Reagan and Jimmy Carter are running against it. Secretary of State Henry Kissinger believes it is his greatest accomplishment. Close to a majority in Congress now think it could be his worst blunder. And though recent polls show that more than 60 percent of Americans approve of it, President Ford will not let the word pass his lips. By any other name (or no name at all) it is still "détente," the elegant, suitably ambiguous French term that has come to label the complex new relationship between the United States and the Soviet Union in the 1970's.

The problem, of course, is not the word but the reality. At best, détente only describes a diplomatic climate in which two antagonistic powers have agreed to establish contact, discuss mutual interests and settle some of their difficulties. But only some. The essence of détente is its expediency; it implies an inherent contradiction between the old hostilities and the new dialogue. In that sense the concept defies any precise definition of conditions and results. Trying to define it, whether in undeserved praise or misplaced blame, has only confused the issue further.

By other names, of course, the concept has a long and checkered history, from Franklin Roosevelt's establishment of diplomatic relations and trade with the outlawed Soviet Republic in 1933, through Eisenhower's spirit of Camp David and Johnson's 1967 summit at Glassboro, N.J. Yet the Kissinger-Nixon-Ford version of détente has been unprecedented in the sheer number and importance of agreements between the two powers. It has been an effort—sometimes brilliant and in part successful—to knit together the mutual interests of Washington and Moscow in a web of specific pacts. Too often lost in the self-congratulation of it all was the fact that peace did not come in a few dramatic negotiations, however historic.

Détente is now suffering from the fact that it was deliberately obscured as diplomacy and oversold as politics. The genuine benefits for both sides over the past four years were possible largely because points of friction were left vague, and the politicians in Washington and Moscow could exaggerate the easing of tensions for purposes of their own political power and prestige at home. When the cheering stopped and the limits of the settlement were all too plain, some reckoning was inevitable. Conservative critics among both Democrats and Republicans have charged that the Russians have had the best of almost every agreement, from feeble enforcement of the strategic arms limitations to advantages in trade. Most dangerously, they argue, the Nixon and Ford Administrations have been so anxious to maintain cordial relations they have failed to keep the Kremlin from expanding its power at U.S. expense, as in Angola. Yet the current disillusionment offers no more reliable verdict on the evolving paradox of détente than those earlier champagne toasts in the Kremlin or strolls at Camp David.

Beyond the extravagant rhetoric, détente for the U.S. has been neither the deliverance its architects claim nor the fraud its critics charge. Measured against the initial diplomatic objectives of the Nixon Administration—to begin control of the arms race and fashion a new triangular diplomacy with Peking and Moscow—some results alone may have been worth the whole effort. Moreover, though many Americans believe that by pursuing a policy of détente, we have permitted ourselves to be deceived by the fearsomely cunning Russians, the deception they perceive may actually be more the result of our own weaknesses in the organization of American foreign policy.

At the same time, the flaws and dangers in détente are real enough, and are likely to be with us for the foreseeable future. Diplomacy and domestic politics are so entangled in the relationship between the superpowers that volatile competition between them is the price of their accommodation. The challenge to our statesmanship and public good sense is to manage the fine, frustrating balance between clash and cooperation without surrendering the national interest to the pull of either. In all this, though, détente seems nothing more nor less than an emblem of the untidy new era of international relations facing American foreign policy after the relative certainties of the cold war. It is a world of unpredictable resource politics, shifting alliances and strife and schism within national boundaries. The most shrewd diplomatic arrangements are likely to be ambiguous, paradoxical and rarely final. By coming to terms with détente, we can begin the larger task of learning to cope with that world.

It is difficult, if not impossible, to draw a precise balance sheet on the assets and liabilities of détente for the U.S. The best achievements of diplomacy often lie in what did *not* happen—the disaster quietly deflected—as much as in the tangible trend of events. By any standard, however, some of the returns have been historic. Perhaps least appreciated is the role U.S.-Soviet détente played in the American opening to China. Both Washington and Moscow hoped to balance off Peking as they began their diplomatic minuet in the SALT talks and other negotiations in 1969. Those American contacts with the Russians no doubt heightened China's already acute sense of isolation and insecurity, and that, in turn, hastened the ensuing Ping-Pong diplomacy and Henry Kissinger's clandestine flight over the Himalayas to arrange President Nixon's 1972 visit to Peking.

On the other hand, had Nixon gone to Peking without trying to break the chill in U.S.-Soviet relations, he might well have provoked the U.S.S.R. further toward a military solution to its bitter schism with China. Four years ago, as today, the Russians and Chinese saw each other, not the United States, as their most immediate and dangerous adversary. Those calculations were very much the stuff of U.S. diplomacy. In the winter of 1970, for example, Kissinger thought a Sino-Soviet war so plausible that he secretly ordered his National Security Council staff to prepare detailed contingency plans for the U.S. response; before the summits of 1972, the possibilities had been dangerously limited.

Such a war—likely to have included the first use of nuclear weapons since 1945, a Chinese strike on European Russia conceivably triggering Soviet retaliation elsewhere, or even a Soviet military move in Europe to secure the Western flank—would clearly have been the worst crisis of the last three decades, threatening the ultimate catastrophe. There is no proof, of course, that the Nixon-Kissinger three-cornered strategy helped deter a Soviet nuclear strike on China, or that fear of a U.S.-Soviet condominium was a decisive motive in Chinese foreign policy. But it is equally hard to imagine—as 8-year-old Chinese children now drill to fight an expected Russian invasion and Soviet troops remain massed on the Far Eastern borders—that these influences were not felt, and are not still. In the twists of *Realpolitik,* the United States owed the success of its China policy in some measure to its willingness to negotiate on mutual interests with the U.S.S.R.

The SALT agreements and negotiations have been a more direct and controversial product of détente. Here, too, even in the province of strategic hardware, it is hard to quantify what détente has provided or sacrificed. However limited or lax the first Moscow Treaty of May 1972, even ardent critics like Senator Henry Jackson agree that the signing saved a generation of weapons unbuilt and billions unspent. Secretary Kissinger recently warned that if a new arms limitation were not concluded with the Soviets soon, Congress would be asked for an added $20 billion in strategic weapons over the next five years. Probably conservative, Kissinger's figure should be seen against Administration proposals to increase military spending by billions apart from the outcome of SALT II, or next to the "major savings" of $5 billion in the Pentagon budget trumpeted by Democratic candidate Jimmy Carter.

The most important long-run advantage of SALT, however, transcends specific dollar figures. In the course of those often tortuous negotiations, Washington (and, much evidence suggests, the Politburo, too) conducted the first systematic examination of the costs and benefits of the vast nuclear arsenals piled up since 1945. The bargaining for SALT—between the delegations in Helsinki and between Kissinger and the Joint Chiefs in the West Basement of the White House—threw desperately needed light on the bureaucratic inertia of the Pentagon on these fateful issues and in a real sense changed how we are governed in matters of national security.

Ironically, it may be a new inertia of vested interest growing out of détente itself that threatens to become the fatal flaw in SALT. A reformer for arms control in 1969–72, Henry Kissinger by 1976 is the beleaguered defender of his own record and orthodoxy in strategic issues. To gain the Moscow accords, he used hard facts to battle the generals and admirals with slanted intelligence and stubborn rationalizations. Now he seems loath to re-examine, on the basis of other, equally hard facts, either his misjudgments or his methods.

There are thus three main questions of possible Soviet violation of SALT I to which Mr. Kissinger's response has been evasive at best. Though the treaty explicitly prohibits new land-based missile launchers, the Soviets have since 1972 built some 200 new III-X concrete silos. Mr. Kissinger has accounted for the new silos as "command and control centers," though he did not explain why they should then have "blowaway" lids, the sort used to cap missile silos. Similarly, the 1972 ABM treaty provided that new test facilities would be within existing ranges. Yet the Soviets have now built a new ABM radar complex in Kamchatka, more than 3,000 miles from their known test range in Central Asia. The Kamchatka radar is readily convertible into a full-fledged ABM site of the sort that SALT was precisely designed to rule out; like the peculiar "command" silos, it is a breach of the spirit of the treaty if not, as Mr. Kissinger argues, its technical letter. Finally, and perhaps most seriously, since 1972 the Russians have steadily deployed the new SS-19 missile, which according to C.I.A. analysts, can carry more than double the payload SALT I was supposed to have frozen by limiting the number of "heavy" SS-9 missiles. But since the Soviets never themselves defined "light" and "heavy" in the negotiations and now claim the SS-19 is "light," Mr. Kissinger has called the SS-19 an issue of "interpretation." The American position has been to accept the deployment and try to limit the new missiles in SALT II. So far the effort has not been successful.

Added to these questions of Soviet compliance are related doubts about the singular Kissinger style in arms negotiations. Retired Adm. Elmo Zumwalt and others have complained that one-man diplomacy put Kissinger alone at the table with Soviet experts at critical moments in SALT I when the U.S. side needed its own technical specialists to judge the give and take. Critics also blame Mr. Kissinger's legendary secretiveness (matched, it should be noted, by Richard Nixon's) for blinding U.S. intelligence analysts to important data flowing in the personal negotiations. The practice put Mr. Kissinger in an "interesting position," as Zumwalt testified recently to the Senate Select Committee on Intelligence. "He had to review intelligence estimates prepared without access to data he had withheld," said Zumwalt. "He then had to judge, if he could without being an expert intelligence analyst, how to compensate for these flaws, having in mind the information he had withheld." Even allowing for the Admiral's own biases and political ambitions as well as for Mr. Kissinger's intellectual virtuosity, the charge has merit. It traces not only to Mr. Kissinger's arrogance, but also to a style of government, particularly in the Nixon years, in which the White House often regarded the Pentagon or the seventh floor of the State Department as a more troublesome foe than either Moscow or Hanoi. The compulsive secrecy that limited leaks and gave Mr. Kissinger negotiating freedom also placed the SALT bargaining on a precariously narrow base.

The SALT negotiations, the heart of détente, began in 1969 with Mr. Kissinger's insistence within the U.S. Government on the most rigorous scrutiny of the issues, including his founding of the Verification Panel to monitor compliance and his own special systems-analysis staff at the National Security Council to check the Pentagon's figures as well as the Soviets'. As détente became a reality and very much Kissinger's personal achievement, however, those critical groups have atrophied; the Verification Panel is a rubber stamp for the Secretary of State and the once independent systems-analysis staff is a largely forgotten appendage. "There is a real danger," says one aide close to Kissinger, "that we are not asking the right questions because we have such a stake in the answers." Or as another official puts it, "SALT is being devoured by its own success." Again, Mr. Kissinger's motives here are not based on mere vanity. He has obviously made the calculation that some Soviet shiftiness is minor compared to the larger goal of keeping the talks going. But such winking at violations may now endanger the negotiations as much as demands for harsh enforcement.
None of this should obscure the authentic accomplishments of SALT, or the opposite dangers of yielding mindlessly to the criticism of a military establishment with its own continuing stake in fat weapons budgets and Soviet perfidy. The larger point is that these strains in détente lie not in the concept of negotiation and relaxation of tensions, but in the structure of American foreign policy. We seem to have passed, as one cynical high official characterized the last seven years, "from a Pentagon oligarchy to King Henry's monarchy" without experiencing the balanced, self-critical government necessary to deal on the intricate issues of arms control with a still insecure, distrustful and aggressive adversary. Yet that task requires far-reaching reform of people and institutions in Washington—of which there has been no hint in the shallow campaign rhetoric about "selling out" or "staying number one."
There are other cases where the apparent failures of détente have not been the fault of the policy itself. The 1972 wheat deal is a telling example. Months before Kissinger went to Moscow in the summer of 1972, the Agriculture Department had considerable intelligence pointing to a worldwide decline in food reserves and the resulting unprecedented demand for American grain. Yet the department decided to withhold from production some 62 million acres of farmland (about

equal to the total acreage of the United Kingdom). After Kissinger's negotiations encouraging expanded trade, the Russians purchased 18 million tons of U.S. grain for $1.1 billion, and the deal set off a buying panic in Europe and Japan. When it was over, U.S. agricultural reserves were exhausted and exports rose by nearly $5 billion, yet taxpayers subsidized one-third of the purchases and all of us paid an incalculable cost in grocery stores. Why had the Administration ignored the intelligence of shortages and the likely effect of the Russian sale? "Butz didn't want to be known as a cheap-food man in an election year," an Agriculture official said of the Secretary. Others contend that a good deal of the telltale intelligence was buried in the Agriculture Department. But neither explanation had anything to do with Soviet scheming. In a system where intelligence is so easily bungled and the Agriculture Secretary sees himself as a champion of high prices, bureaucratic advocacy can have the same disastrous consequences as conspiracy.

Nor did détente account for the disarray of the American domestic food market and skyrocketing grocery prices. There the governing powers were the huge American grain companies that command the food industry from seed to shipping. Dominating the commodity exchanges in Chicago, New York and other cities, only lightly policed by public regulation, the food barons largely shape American agricultural policy toward consumers both abroad and at home. The system is attacked periodically, both by Congress and private groups, such as the Federation of American Scientists, which recently described U.S. food policy as "disingenuous." But it goes on. And critics of détente—with their simpler myth of shrewd Russians stealthily robbing our granaries—have seldom appreciated how much the problem has to do with the exploitation of Americans by Americans.

Détente has exposed with stark clarity a number of problems in American foreign policy, but it did not create them. Next to the food scandal there is no more depressing evidence of this than the debate over human rights in the Soviet Union. Have we, in fact, ignored our principles in this area simply to preserve the diplomatic niceties of détente? U.S. pressure did cause some progress on Jewish emigration and occasional Kremlin restraint in the persecution of dissidents. On the other hand, the Americans have indulged in a notorious reticence on the subject, as well as in petty acts like the symbolic snub of Aleksandr Solzhenitsyn by President Ford last summer. Again, it is more relevant to recognize that the record of U.S. diplomacy on behalf of human rights has been almost uniformly miserable, with no particular obeisance to the tyrants in Moscow.

Since 1972, Washington for the most part has looked the other way when confronted with the genocide of a quarter-million in Burundi, ethnic slaughters in Iraq, Ethiopia and Uganda, torture in Chile and Indonesia, not to mention South Vietnam and several other cases. The motives for these policies varied from a reluctance to offend established clients to sheer neglect. Some of the atrocities, most notably the torture in Chile, have finally come under U.S. censure at the U.N. and in bilateral relations. Actually, the record reveals that U.S. official

attention to human rights in the U.S.S.R., by dint of powerful public
pressure from Jewish groups and several members of Congress, has, if
anything, been greater than to similar outrages elsewhere. That comparison scarcely vindicates Washington's on-again, off-again concern
with the human costs of the Soviet system; it does suggest, once more,
that the surrender of principle or responsibility in foreign policy goes
well beyond détente.

In all these areas, to be sure, the costs of détente itself have been
real. The noble but seductive vision of a new arms agreement that has
drawn Mr. Kissinger past probable Soviet cheating is implicit in
détente. So, in a way, was the rush to conclude the 1972 agreements
before the Nixon-Brezhnev summit, which only added to the usual
neglect of food policy. And there can be no doubt that Washington has
cynically weighed each action on behalf of Soviet human rights against
the prospect of a penalty in some other province of the relationship.
Yet the worst costs of détente, like its best achievements, may be still
more political and intangible. The sum of our diplomatic compromise
and internal disarray has probably given Moscow a clearer sense of
American weakness and division than ever before. For similar reasons,
the policy has no doubt left uncertainty among allies in Europe and
elsewhere who alternately fear a U.S.-Soviet condominium or an
American withdrawal, and worry that we cannot manage to balance the
two. Finally, the heaviest price of détente has been that it has aggravated the large problem of public distrust of foreign policy. The eva-
sions of the SALT debate, the fiasco in Angola, the cryptic defensive-
ness about a policy that can stand open debate—all this and more have
further eroded the public faith that is essential not only to détente but
to every element of foreign relations.

The tendency to inflate and oversimplify both the rewards and
costs of détente seems inherent in the Soviet-American relationship.
The affliction has a long history. From Woodrow Wilson and Lenin
to Gerald Ford and Brezhnev, the rivalry of ideology and power has
been a sure-fire issue in both countries, now in hostility, now in
statesmanlike dialogue. No single development so caught the paradox
as the career of Richard Nixon. From the postwar Red scare to the
summitry of the 1970's, he swung from anti-Communist zealot to
ardent negotiator, winning votes all the while from the alternating
public mood. Still, behind the politics remains the basic fact that is both
the necessity and risk of détente: The two countries have the power to
obliterate each other many times over, and their present political values
are in fundamental contradiction.

Conflict and competition in the relationship appear inevitable.
Both sides began détente with limited motives. Both wanted some relief
from the arms burden and some relaxation of tensions. But the
original aims were deliberately vague because there were powerful
voices in each Government skeptical or opposed, and the skeptics and
opponents are still very much there, inside the councils of Moscow and
Washington as well as on the outside. The Politburo still has its periodic

tests of manliness, its military constituents, its own politics of insecurity and chauvinism—no less (and perhaps more) than Mr. Ford had Ronald Reagan foraging for votes in the Panama Canal or the defense budget. There will always be the temptation, moreover, to disarm the domestic skeptics by some demonstration of fearsomeness that, one presumes, certifies the legitimacy of other dealings in the relationship.

The peril of this tactic, however, is that it may trap the practitioner, as it ensnared Kissinger in Angola, in a diplomatic conundrum in which the convoluted strategy only makes the most feared prospect come true. Of the various motives spurring secret U.S. intervention in Angola in 1975, the involved officials are unanimous that the most crucial was Kissinger's sometimes venomous rivalry with then Defense Secretary James Schlesinger.

In the raging debate with Schlesinger and the Joint Chiefs over force levels and SALT II positions, it was inevitable that the Secretary of State would be accused of being "soft" on the Russians. In that unsavory battle of leaks and backstairs maneuvering at the White House, Angola provided an opportunity, as one official put it, for "Henry to refurbish his toughness." Otherwise oblivious to Southern Africa, Kissinger first approved new covert U.S. support for one of the warring guerrilla groups in January 1975, in a meeting of the Forty Committee, that small group of officials who oversee covert U.S. intelligence operations abroad. State Department intelligence reports show, however that the first major Soviet arms shipments to Angola came in February, *following* the conspicuous U.S. subsidies. By June, the Angolan war was widening, and the Kissinger-Schlesinger feud over SALT II had also escalated. The Forty Committee under Kissinger approved another clandestine subsidy for Angola in July, and events moved toward the familiar climax last winter. In the end, aiming his policy more at opponents in Washington than at African realities, Kissinger had backed the losing side, perhaps provoked Moscow to a greater involvement than it had planned and enraged the Congress with what seemed another secret entanglement less than a year after the end of the Vietnam agony. In the process, he had also demonstrated the relative impotence of American policy to the Russians and to others. The lesson of the debacle seems clear—if the U.S. is to prove its resolve to Moscow in such marginal precincts (as it sometimes may have to) its policy must be carried out candidly with public support and not as some arcane bureaucratic gambit.

The same rule should apply to the resolution of the fateful issues bearing on nuclear arms control. Given the natural domestic political distortions of détente, we should debate questions of Soviet compliance as fully and as clearly as possible in public, where we can be sure, at least, that the issues have substance and are not merely surrogates for some hidden skirmish of institutions or personalities. However the Kremlin conducts its side, détente is not likely to survive in American foreign policy unless this takes place. Like fighters groping in the dark, the executive and Congress are now too prone to mistake some lesser confrontation as a make-or-break issue for the larger U.S.-Soviet dialogue, or to let an issue pass that does indeed encourage Russian recklessness.

Détente is now a political football—its meaning lost—because both supporters and critics have insisted on distorting it for domestic purposes. It belongs to public debate for what it is: a complex foreign-policy problem whose pros and cons should be aired without the critics' ritual resort to national-security machismo or the Administration's furtive if only-you-knew-what-we-know approach.

If Washington can make that leap of faith and sophistication, the future of détente will probably resemble its past—uneven, contradictory, a major factor in the survival of the planet. The motives of Soviet policy are likely to remain much the same over the next decade, from fear of China to an effort to stress consumer, as well as defense, production in order to buy off a politically stifled society. By 1986, the two sides will probably look back on a list of accomplishments that one hopes would include:

□SALT III and IV agreements controlling a whole new generation of weapons, from unmanned bombers to giant missile submarines to laser weapons.

□Increased trade opening the U.S.S.R. more and more to American consumer goods, and increasing U.S. dependence on Soviet oil and natural gas.

□The deterrence of a major Sino-Soviet war.

As important to understanding détente, though, is an equally clear expectation of what it will *not* achieve. As Vietnam demonstrated, it will not prevent folly or bloody sacrifice by either power in the world. Nor will it determine the fate of Communist parties and their pro-Western opponents from Europe to Latin America; their fortunes will be determined by local politics and economics. Détente will not stem the tide of population that threatens to swamp the developing world, or prevent the squandering of environment and resources that mortgages the future of the industrial countries. And it will not correct the weaknesses of our own institutions, from the bureaucratic distortions of foreign policy to the costs of monopoly in food. To many of the challenges of the next decade it is simply irrelevant.

The beginning of wisdom may be to recognize that détente, with all its limits and paradoxes, is not a unique problem for American diplomacy in the final quarter of the century. In a world where decisions behind mud walls on the Persian Gulf can darken houses and halt machines in Oklahoma or New Jersey, power is truly multiple, and countries that are allies on one issue are adversaries on the next. More than ever, our security and economic welfare everywhere will depend on the kind of delicate balancing of cooperation and friction that characterizes our relations with the Soviet Union.

There is scarcely any major part of our foreign relations in which the lessons of détente could not apply—with the poor countries, who see themselves as our opponents in their commodity bargaining or at the U.N., but remain eager for our economic aid, our weapons, our investments and our political backing on other issues; with the Arabs and Israelis who each must treat the United States as a subtle combination of patron and mediator; with Europe and Japan, who share our military security and yet vigorously assert their economic and political independence; with the Latin Americans, ever caught between the benefits of our enormous power and their deep drive to be free of it. Détente in that respect reflects the politics of a new equality in the world. It is a mode of dealing with conflicting interests long obscured by an American omnipotence that has ended, in myth and in fact. In many cases, there is simply no longer any choice but to accept the incongruity détente represents.

Such uneasy collaboration will never be comfortable for Americans; we have preferred a more finely drawn view of international affairs. Most of our confusion with détente stems from the abiding dilemma that arises from having to choose between making the world fit our policy or making a policy to fit the world. In that sense, the hardest bargain we have to strike is not with the Russians, but with ourselves.

13   The Ardent Asian Suitors

Stanley Karnow

A generation ago, when the Korean War erupted, the United States believed itself to be confronted by an enormous challenge. The Soviet Union and China, which had lately been conquered by Mao Tse-tung's legions, represented a formidable Communist monolith that stretched from the banks of the Elbe to the shores of the Pacific, and it not only seemed to menace Western Europe but also appeared to threaten Japan and the states of Southeast Asia. Alarmed by this apparent danger, the Truman administration acted urgently to bulwark America's defenses in the Far East. It pledged military assistance to France, which was then fighting to save its Indochinese possessions, and it rapidly signed a series of bilateral pacts designed to protect Japan, South Korea, Taiwan, and the Philippines. The result was an American commitment to the area that still largely stands despite the disasters in Vietnam and Cambodia, the imminence of a Communist takeover in Laos, and Thailand's shift away from reliance on the United States.

A key question for the future, however, is whether the United States will continue its involvement in the parts of Asia to which it is committed—or whether, with the balance of forces changing in the region, American policy will undergo a drastic revision. For the multipolarity that has overtaken the world has affected Asia as well. The dispute between Moscow and Peking, combined with the rise of Japan to economic gianthood, has vastly complicated the Far Eastern equation. Within this new framework, therefore, the United States must shape a role far more sophisticated than the mere "containment" of communism.

There is a present tendency, in the wake of the dramatic debacles in Saigon and Phnom Penh, to consider that the United States has been ejected from the Far East. This view is not entirely valid. The United States has plainly lost its foothold on the mainland of Asia; yet its influence is still significant through the arc that reaches from South Korea through Japan, Taiwan, and the Philippines to Indonesia. In short, the United States remains a Pacific power even if it is no longer an Asian power.

Although the diplomacy of the Japanese has become increasingly flexible, they regard their relationship to the United States to be the keystone of their international strategy, partly because their economy would crumble without American trade and partly because, through a mutual-defense arrangement, America assures their security. The South Koreans are similarly dependent on the United States, and the link is symbolized by the presence of a division of American troops on their soil. President Ferdinand Marcos of the Philippines, despite his recent decision to establish formal diplomatic relations with Communist China, has no intention of loosening his ties to the United States, which provides his country with military and economic aid and, by maintaining bases there, also guarantees its defense. Thailand is also seeking to maintain relations with the United States even though Bangkok, too, has recognized Peking. The Chinese Nationalist regime on Taiwan leans on the United States for its security. . . . Indeed, the United States will have to maneuver more adroitly than it has in the past, for the conflict between the Soviet Union and China is likely to inject uncertainties into the Asian situation, and these could face American policy in the region with both hazards and opportunities.

One arena in which the Russians and Chinese have been struggling against each other for years to exert influence is Hanoi, and this contention has worked to the benefit of the North Vietnamese as they manipulated their rival supporters. But the Communist victory in Vietnam may change the attitudes of Moscow and Peking. For if both were devoted to the triumph of Vietnamese communism over American "imperialism," neither really wants the North Vietnamese to extend their domination over the rest of Southeast Asia. The Russians fear that the dynamic North Vietnamese, whose revolutionary zeal is still fervent, may subvert Soviet efforts to reach accommodations with bourgeois governments in such countries as Thailand, Malaysia, and Indonesia, and thereby undermine Moscow's grand design of creating a cordon of sympathetic states around the rim of China. The Chinese are equally anxious to restrain Hanoi, largely because they traditionally perceive Southeast Asia to be a region subordinate to Peking's sway, and as a consequence, they would prefer to see the area Balkanized rather than remaining under North Vietnamese control.

Attempts by both the Russians and Chinese to curb North Vietnamese ambitions are welcomed by the United States. But the prospect that the area will become a cockpit of Sino-Soviet squabbling is undesirable, because it would perpetuate the instability that has made the region explosive for decades. Some specialists, notably Doak Barnett of The Brookings Institution, accordingly suggest that the time may soon be ripe for the United States, the Soviet Union, and China to revive the idea of an international agreement which would "neutralize" Southeast Asia. The United States could begin to set this process in motion by recognizing Hanoi . . . and by initiating economic aid programs. . . . President Ford has spurned requests by the Vietnamese Communists for diplomatic relations, presumably because he is concerned about the opposition that such a gesture would provoke among his conservative political opponents at home. . . . But unless the United States moves in this direction, some experts submit, it may lose a chance to contribute to peace in Southeast Asia.

Another arena in which the triangular jockeying for influence offers both advantages and risks is Korea, where North Korean dictator Kim Il Sung, inspired by Hanoi's success in Vietnam, has recently hinted that he, too, would like to reunify the peninsula. Kim Il Sung's posturing aroused worries in Washington that another Korean War might lie ahead, and Ford administration officials, eager to seize a pretext to emphasize the need for a big defense budget, added to the apprehensions by inflating the danger of conflict. Here again, however, the Sino-Soviet dispute is serving as a deterrent to the Korean Communists—but, at the same time, it is preventing the possibility of a reconciliation between Kim Il Sung and South Korean President Park Chung Hee.

The Chinese are in no mood for a repetition of the Korean War, for several reasons. They bitterly remember the conflict of 25 years ago, which cost them a million casualties, set back their domestic economic development, and increased their dependence on Moscow—which, despite proclamations of "proletarian brotherhood," made them reimburse every ruble of Soviet military aid. The Chinese also realize that another war would mean a collision with the United States, thereby eliminating the lever they have been able to use in their argument with the Russians. A war in Korea would break China's bond with Japan, which the Chinese have carefully been trying to tighten within the past few years. And, to add a human element, Mao Tse-tung recalls sadly that his son, a fighter pilot, died in the last Korean conflagration. So, when Kim Il Sung went to Peking not long ago in quest of help for an offensive against South Korea, the Chinese politely brushed him off by stressing that they were partial to "peaceful" reunification of the peninsula.

There is no evidence that Kim turned to the Russians as an alternative, but it is virtually certain that if he had, they, too, would have treated him coolly. For the Soviet leaders are determined to avert a war that would torpedo détente with the United States, wreck their maneuvers to woo Japan, and, among other things, saddle them with additional military expenditures at a time when their resources are already being strained by the arms race as well as by aid programs to Eastern Europe and to their Middle East clients.

Ideally, both the Russians and the Chinese would favor the kind of co-existence between North and South Korea that has developed between East and West Germany. But their hopes in this respect are being thwarted by their rivalry, because neither can appear to show softness toward the Korean situation without seeming, to radical extremists both at home and abroad, to have abandoned the revolutionary cause. Thus they have rebuffed South Korean overtures made with American encouragement.

Some American officials believe nonetheless that a deal regarding Korea can be reached with the Communist superpowers. One notion that has been advanced is that the United States may be able to use the 34,000 American troops in South Korea as a bargaining chip by offering to withdraw them in exchange for Communist recognition of South Korea's integrity as a separate state. Such an arrangement would be given international sanction if both Koreas were admitted into the United Nations. So far, though, this idea has made little headway, in part because Kim Il Sung regards himself as the legitimate ruler of all Korea and partly because of resistance in Washington—especially among military men and their political backers—to pulling out the American contingent in the peninsula.

Yet another arena that will be crucial in the period ahead is Japan, which is striving to improve its relations with both Communist China and the Soviet Union while it maintains its close ties with the United States. The Japanese are optimistic that they can play this three-way game, and judging from their diplomatic performance until now, they have good reason to feel confident.

Although Japan's ties with Peking were somewhat tangled at first, the Japanese have managed within the past year to strengthen their Chinese connection, largely because the Chinese have been eager to block any substantive improvement in Japan's relations with the Soviet Union. Sensitive to the Japanese thirst for oil, for instance, China last year sent Japan some 4 million tons, nearly all the Chinese petroleum available for export, and its shipments this year may be triple that amount. Moreover, the Chinese are selling this oil to Japan at slightly less than world prices. Even though satisfying only a tiny fraction of Japan's immense requirements, these shipments are calculated by Peking to signal the future means of helping Japanese industry. In contrast, an ambitious Soviet plan for developing Siberian oil and natural-gas resources jointly with Japan has faltered, primarily as a result of Russian wrangling over contractual arrangements. Moscow has also annoyed the Japanese by refusing to return four inconsequential islands captured by the Soviet forces during World War II.

The islands are a matter of national pride to the Japanese, but the Russians evidently fear that their return would weaken the Soviet Union's territorial haggling with China. Consequently, the Russians seem to be lagging behind the Chinese in the race to win Japanese sympathies. The Chinese have also scored points with the Japanese by encouraging them, in elliptical but unmistakable terms, to maintain their defense pact with the United States.

The security treaty with the United States not only is the main pillar of Japan's foreign policy but also is vital to the Japanese for other reasons. With the American nuclear umbrella above them, the Japanese need not contemplate the manufacture of their own advanced weapons, and thus they are freed from the internal political turmoil that such a program would trigger. In addition, American protection makes it unnecessary for the Japanese to engage in large defense expenditures, thus relieving their economy of a tremendous economic burden.

Realizing that opposition to Japan's treaty with the United States would alienate significant segments of the Japanese population, the Chinese have let it be known that they are not hostile to its continuation. And they further perceive that the Japanese bond with America serves their own purposes. As long as Japan is shielded by America, the Chinese estimate, its own militarist factions will remain subdued and the danger of the Japanese returning to their belligerence of the Thirties will be reduced. And, the Chinese also figure, a Japan intimately associated with the United States should logically resist the temptation of closer ties with the Soviet Union.

How long the Chinese represent a force of stability in Asia depends on a variety of factors. One question is whether the Peking leadership group centered around Mao Tse-tung and Chou En-lai, who have stood for moderation within recent years, will be succeeded by an equally temperate faction or by the raving radicals who surfaced during the Cultural Revolution. Another question is whether the heirs to Mao and Chou, whatever their complexion, will try to edge back toward the Soviet Union in order to strengthen their diplomatic leverage with the United States. Still another question is whether the United States, taking advantage of the desire of the current Communist Chinese leaders for a reconciliation, can plausibly put Sino-American relations on a more solid footing before they disappear. These questions are intertwined, because China's domestic and foreign policies tend to run along parallel lines.

The big problem challenging the United States as it seeks to cement its bonds with Peking is the Taiwan issue, which President Nixon skillfully side-stepped during his visit to China in February 1972. The Chinese now say that they cannot entertain the idea of official Sino-American relations until the United States declares unequivocally that Taiwan is part of China, and that there is only one China. The United States would take this step if the Communists, by way of compromise, would pledge not to employ force to "liberate" the island, because, as American officials point out, that move would compel Washington to invoke its defense treaty with the Chinese Nationalists. The Communists refuse to make such a pledge, contending that the Taiwan question is an internal Chinese matter. But, they privately submit, Peking would be willing to consider a formula that could carry both the United States and China over this hurdle without excessive loss of face. President Ford and Secretary of State Kissinger are at present searching for the magic formula, but their room for maneuvering is limited. The fall of Indochina has inhibited them in the sense that they cannot bargain away Taiwan, and so a fuller Sino-American rapprochement may be delayed.

Asia, then, is in transition. The Chinese and Russians are vying for influence, and the Japanese are trying to make the best of their rivalry. The United States, meanwhile, is navigating to maintain its diminished position. In the meantime, the powers involved in the Far East can do little beyond watch and wait, and attempt, in their assorted ways, to assure the fragile equilibrium of forces that now exists. The only certainty that lies ahead in these circumstances is that Asia will not be the domain of a single authority but, in all likelihood, will be the scene of complex and often confused maneuvers by the four major states concerned with its future. The situation will surely be more difficult to understand than it was in the days when the United States was committed to its crusade against monolithic communism, but it may be a good deal safer.

14   Japan—The Ultimate Domino?

Keyes Beech

Years ago, long before détente became fashionable, an American correspondent asked a Japanese foreign minister what Japan was going to do about China. The question seemed to amuse the minister. "You tell me what the United States is going to do," he chuckled, "and I'll tell you what Japan is going to do."

When President Nixon got around to deciding what the United States was going to do about China, he did not tell Japan. Instead, he announced to an astonished world that he was going to visit Peking. Then, enormously pleased with himself, he went off to dinner at an expensive Los Angeles restaurant with his advance man, Henry Kissinger.

Three months ago, in a speech before the Japan Society in New York, four years after the Nixon bombshell, Secretary of State Kissinger finally apologized for that omission: "Adjustments in U.S. economic policies and a new policy toward China in 1971 led to painful but transitory misunderstanding to which—let us be frank—our own tactics contributed. We have learned from experience. . . ."

This rare display of humility by the Lone Ranger of American diplomacy went down well with the Japanese, who do not especially like him. More important, the Kissinger speech was the first of a series of carefully prepared steps agreed upon by the two governments toward forging a new "special relationship" between Washington and Tokyo.

Significantly, many of the thoughts incorporated in Kissinger's speech were suggested by the Japanese. After 30 years of fumbling and groping, it seemed that U.S.-Japan relations were on the right track. After a disastrous detour to Southeast Asia, the thrust of U.S. Asia policy had returned to Northeast Asia—where it belonged.

Unlike the British, with whom Washington has a "special relationship" of diminishing importance, the Japanese do not share with Americans the bond of a common language. But there are other relationships that transcend the language barrier. Taken together, Japan and the United States account for more than 50 percent of the world's trade. They also happen to be the two greatest overseas trading partners in history. In the non-Communist world they rank first and second as economic powers. Politically, both are vigorous democracies whose people share common problems and common aspirations despite cultural differences.

Therefore, it should be clear that the United States cannot afford to withdraw from Asia, militarily or otherwise, unless it is willing to abdicate its role as a world power. Without Japan, the United States has no Asia policy. Moreover, despite the Japanese mass media's gloating over the American humiliation in Vietnam, the last thing Japan wants is an American withdrawal.

What is open to debate is whether the United States should be an "Asian" power or a "Pacific" power. The latter role is far more attractive, because it would mean withdrawal from the Asian mainland to an island defense chain—including Japan—thus ruling out the possibility that the United States may become involved in another Asian land war.

The only problem with this argument is that the United States, committed by treaty to the defense of South Korea, has 34,000 troops there whose presence, as was intended, would automatically guarantee American involvement in the event of a North Korean invasion. Interestingly, there is every indication that another Korean War would have strong public and congressional support. A recent Harris poll showed that 43 percent of Americans would favor using American land, sea, and air forces to defend South Korea; 37 percent voted no, and 20 percent weren't sure. Thus, only six weeks after the ignominious United States exit from Vietnam, many Americans were ready to commit themselves to another land war in Asia.

The full impact of the American failure in Vietnam has yet to be assessed. That American credibility suffered a horrendous blow cannot be disputed. On the other hand, it seems clear that Japan preferred the United States out of Vietnam rather than in it. Like a good many Americans, most Japanese could never understand what we were doing in Vietnam anyway. Although the Vietnam War sometimes stirred leftist passions in Japan, most Japanese couldn't have cared less what happened in such a remote and, to them, uncivilized place. It should never be forgotten that the Japanese identify more readily with Americans than they do with other Asians.

Refusing to go along with the conventional wisdom of Marxist-oriented Japanese intellectuals, one prominent Tokyo political scientist challenged the view that America was no longer to be trusted because it had "betrayed" the old Saigon regime. What, he asked tartly, did the critics want the United States to do? Become militarily involved in Vietnam a second time? Personally, he added, he had gained, rather than lost, trust in the United States, because of its refusal to make the same mistake twice.

Many Japanese commentators were not so charitable. But, as one Japanese press critic observed, the major newspapers refrained from fully celebrating the Communist victory, possibly out of fear that the United States might not react in case North Korean President Kim Il Sung tried to make good his renewed cry for "reunification" of the Korean peninsula.

Just what Japan would do if the United States decides to abandon its forward bases in the western Pacific is something most Japanese would prefer not to think about. But in the wake of the Vietnam juggernaut, they have begun to think about the possibility.

Michita Sakata, director general of the defense agency, has ordered a defense white paper . . . to stimulate a national consensus on the state of Japan's defenses. (According to Sakata, Japan's defense rests on three principles: the will of all Japanese to defend the nation, an adequate defence force, and the mutual security treaty with the United States. All three principles will be examined.) In addition, the national defense council, which is headed by the prime minister, has been revived and strengthened. And a supply group of leading civilians has been formed to advise the defense agency.

Renewed concern with the nation's security is reflected in the number of articles about that subject appearing in the newspapers. The same can be said of television panel discussions.

Apart from the anticipated results of the white paper, it is entirely possible that Japan will decide to do nothing much about changing its defense posture. Nor, it would seem, is there any reason to think that all this talk about defense will mean a revival of the aggressive, jack-booted militarism of the Thirties and Forties.

Few aspects of life in Japan are watched more closely than this one, not only by foreign observers and Japan's neighbors but even by the Japanese themselves. Robert S. Ingersoll, a former ambassador to

Tokyo . . . summed up the American view in testimony before Congress last year: "If ever Japan were judged to be returning to an earlier militarism, tensions would rise throughout Asia, countries would arm, and China in particular would react strongly. The situation would be thrown into more serious relief were Japan to acquire a nuclear capability."

Implicit in Ingersoll's statement is the belief that the United States, rather than Japan, should be responsible for Japan's security, and the Japanese would whole-heartedly agree with that view. Not even leftist Japanese intellectuals want to tamper with the U.S.-Japan security treaty, which provides Japan with a nuclear umbrella at no cost and without the risks inherent in being a nuclear power. Even China had endorsed the treaty as part of its campaign to block Soviet "encirclement."

Quite clearly, if Japan wished to do so, it could become a major military power simply by diverting to rearmament the tremendous energy and resources that have made it the world's third largest economic power. Experts say Japan could produce a nuclear bomb similar to India's within two to six months.

But the weight of evidence against Japan's embarking on a major defense buildup or a return to militarism is overwhelming. In the first place, no other major power is so dependent on raw materials to feed its industrial machine as is Japan, which was sharply reminded of this dependency by the 1973 Arab oil squeeze. No amount of military power could guarantee the passage of Japanese tankers from the Persian Gulf through the Strait of Malacca.

Politically, there is no national consensus for such a buildup in this consensus-oriented country. No political party reading from right to left advocates a return to the old militarism, although some conservatives would like to see Japan have a bigger and better defense establishment within its present political framework.

Support for the no-war clause of the nation's Constitution—according to legend, written by General MacArthur's own hand—is overwhelming. The Constitution is a kind of judicial chastity belt preventing a return to militarism. Strictly interpreting the no-war clause, a Japanese court has ruled Japan's existing armed forces, officially called self-defense forces, unconstitutional. The government has appealed.

So strict are the bounds of the defense forces that Japan can't even send a military man overseas with a U.N. peace-keeping mission. This restriction not only keeps Japan out of international brouhahas but even has the added advantage of contributing to Japan's peaceful image and saving money.

Japan's existing armed forces are hardly of the kind to cause alarm, nor is its defense budget. Japan spends less than 1 percent of its GNP on defense, an amount that is said to be lower than that spent by any other developed country except Denmark. Comparable figures are 8 percent for the United States, 18 percent for Israel, and 20 percent for the Soviet Union. To put it another way, Japan spends only $33 per person on defense compared with $404 in the United States, $468 in Israel, and $352 in the Soviet Union.

Two reasons cause the defense forces to be chronically short of manpower: Japan has attained a new affluence, and Japanese soldiers are still second-class citizens. The authorized strength of the combined forces is 266,000, but they actually number 232,000. This is less than half the armed strength of three much smaller neighbors—South Korea, North Korea, and Taiwan. American military scenarists, conjuring up a war with the Soviet Union, say that Japan's air force would last for four hours; the navy, for perhaps four days; and the army, maybe four weeks.

But perhaps the best argument for a peace-loving Japan is its awful vulnerability to attack. "The biggest non-floating target in the world," one State Department official called Japan in pointing to the density of its population and industry. Scoffing at an American futurologist's prediction that Japan would "go nuclear," a Japanese defense analyst said: "To be an effective nuclear power, you must have a second-strike capability. But after the first strike on Japan, there wouldn't be anything left of Japan."

If Japan was threatened, the situation could well be different. But Japan does not feel threatened. It cherishes its image as a superpower without guns. When it is pointed out that both China and the Soviet Union have nuclear weapons while Japan has none, a Japanese is likely to shrug and say, "So what? They would be crazy to drop a bomb on us, and there is nothing you can do about a crazy man anyway."

For the present, then, Japan will try to come to terms with its Communist neighbors through diplomatic and economic channels. This process was under way long before the conquest of South Vietnam. Tokyo had already established diplomatic relations with Hanoi and was quick to recognize the new Provisional Revolutionary Government in Saigon.

But an upset in the balance of power on the Korean peninsula could change this situation radically overnight, for next to the Middle East this area is potentially the most explosive spot in the world. The last American helicopter had barely left the embassy roof in Saigon before Korea became the focal point of U.S. strategic planning because, as Washington sees it, that is where the interests of China, the Soviet Union, Japan, and the United States converge.

Korea owes its newly acquired prominence in large measure to North Korea's bellicose President Kim Il Sung, who, while Indochina was falling to the Communists, paid his first visit to China in 14 years. His battle cry was "reunification" of the Korean peninsula, and to underline his point, Kim was accompanied by an entourage of generals.

"War may break out at any moment," Kim kept saying during his trip to China and, later, through friendly capitals in Europe and North Africa. The American response to this kind of talk was predictable, especially as the Ford administration sought to restore shaken confidence in American power and resolve after the Indochina debacle. A stream of declarations by President Ford, Secretary Kissinger, and Defense Secretary James Schlesinger began flowing from Washington, reiterating American resolve and warning North Korea against "miscalculations." Ford refused to rule out the use of nuclear weapons if North Korea should invade the South.

There is, of course, more than a little irony in the fact that American security interests should return to Korea 25 years after we fought an indecisive war there at a cost of more than 33,000 American lives. Korea had, in many ways, led a strong and confident America into Vietnam. And now Vietnam, having sapped American strength and resolve after more than a decade of war, was leading us back to Korea like a yo-yo being reeled in to its starting point. To make the prospect even more distasteful, the United States was once again aligned with an unsavory Asian dictator, South Korean president Park Chung Hee, who refused to pay even lip service to democracy.

Yet, for the present there seems to be no sensible alternative to a strong American military presence in South Korea. To withdraw or even to reduce the number of American troops there at this stage would do more to provoke a war than to prevent it, for Kim would doubtless interpret such a move as an invitation to invasion.

Recent history tends to support this view. After four years of occupation after World War II, the United States had withdrawn its combat troops from South Korea, leaving only a military advisory team. After that came Secretary of State Dean Acheson's much-discussed speech in January 1950, suggesting that South Korea lay outside the "defense perimeter" of the United States. Acheson was only reflecting what was American military doctrine at that time.

But that policy changed with the North Korean attack on June 25, 1950. Suddenly, the policy of "containment of communism," which had up to then applied mainly to Europe, was extended to Asia. The United States proceeded to fight the Communists to a draw in Korea. It was later assumed as a matter of course that the same thing could be done in Southeast Asia.

If keeping American troops in South Korea makes sense for the short haul, there is doubt about the long haul. President Ford, in one of his post-Vietnam "forward movements" in foreign policy, has said that he aims to "tie more closely together South Korea with the United States."

What he really means by this remark is that by keeping an anti-Communist beachhead in South Korea, the United States is casting itself in the role of an Asian power instead of a Pacific power. A majority of the American people, shaken by the defeat in Indochina, may support this policy now. There is less reason to think that they will support it a year or two from now.

It is entirely possible that so much talk of war in Korea is nothing more than bombast—that the risk, while always present when two hostile armies are facing each other, is much less than it appears to be if we listen to Kim and his counterpart, President Park, in Seoul. Park has made convenient use of North Korean truculence to pressure the United States for more military aid and to stamp out the slightest show of dissent in the South—so much so that it is becoming increasingly difficult to distinguish between his regime and the one in Pyongyang, which is his mortal enemy.

Kim's bellicose rhetoric can easily be read as part of his continuing war of nerves against the South, as a testing of American will in the wake of Vietnam, or as both. American intelligence, which keeps a watchful eye on the Korean peninsula, has found no evidence that North Korea is planning another invasion. There is one exception, however: the construction of two tunnels between the two-and-one-half-mile demilitarized zone, one of them big enough to move a division through in a few hours, according to military judgment.

Much as Kim would like to annex the South, there are some powerful deterrents to anything like the 1950 invasion. One is the American reaction. So long as American troops remain in South Korea, the United States would inevitably be drawn into any conflict. While the presence of American troops might not be decisive, that of a bristling array of nuclear tactical weapons could be.

Fear of failure is another element that should give Kim pause. The 600,000-man South Korean army is said to be the finest non-Communist fighting force in Asia. Equally important, there is no doubt where the South Korean people stand. Many of them would like to bring President Park down, but they aren't ready to trade President Park for President Kim.

Nor is there any sign that North Korea would get the backing it needs for a full-scale war. In contrast to Kim's strident cry for "reunification" during his visit to China, the Chinese were mild. They favored peaceful reunification. Nor has Kim received any known support from his 1950 backer, the Soviet Union.

Both major Communist powers have a vested interest in restraining North Korea from doing something rash. In the first place, a war in Korea would almost certainly finish off détente between Washington and Peking and Moscow. Besides, it would alienate Japan at a time when the two Communist rivals are wooing Japanese affection for their own political and military ends.

Although nobody can predict with certainty how the Japanese would react, if anything could remilitarize Japan it would be a Communist Korea. The cliché "Korea is a dagger pointed at the heart of Japan," which this reporter first heard more than 25 years ago, has been dusted off and given new currency. The validity of the cliché depends upon who holds the dagger. It is easy for the Japanese to accept a Communist Indochina; it would be considerably more difficult for them to accept a Communist Korea so close to home.

The Japanese have made it clear they are counting on the United States to keep the peace in Korea by keeping troops there. But they also are aware that this status quo cannot go on indefinitely. Therefore, Japan has expressed a willingness to undertake new diplomatic initiatives that it would not have attempted before.

Some indications suggest that Japan had a hand in persuading the Ford administration not to slam the door all the way shut on the possibility of diplomatic relations with the new Communist regimes in Indochina. Japan may also be in a position to stimulate a meaningful dialogue between Pyongyang and Seoul in the hope of persuading North Korea to soften its warlike posture toward the South. Conceivably, such diplomacy could make possible the withdrawal of American troops from Korea without upsetting the apple cart.

Meanwhile, the Japanese worry that the Americans will do something rash and precipitous without telling them. Assurances that the United States will live up to its defense commitment in Korea do not wholly satisfy the Japanese. For example, they can easily imagine a situation where American intervention might bring in the Chinese or the Russians and make Japan an inviting target.

To an American who has in mind that his country and his dollars are helping pay for Japan's defense as well as South Korea's, the Japanese attitude may seem unreasonable. On the other hand, the Japanese got where they are by looking out for their own best interests.

The United States might do well to take the same pragmatic approach to its post-Vietnam policy in East Asia. And after all else is said, it seems the best policy that we can have toward Japan is the one we have now. The alternative is to cut Japan adrift from its Western ties. That could be an extremely dangerous thing to do. "Japan," observed a onetime Japan-watcher, "is nobody's domino."

15   On a Tightrope in Southeast Asia

Donald Kirk

Top Southeast Asian leaders, diplomats, and businessmen may talk of the need for "self-reliance" and "non-alignment" and "adjustment," but they still look to the United States as they always have for aid, trade, investment, and expertise. Startling though this judgment may seem after the debacle in Indochina, the relevance of certain old realities clearly re-emerged once the first shock of disaster had slowly receded. "There is a great jilted-lover syndrome," said an American scholar with specific reference to Thailand. "All the equations are changing in Southeast Asia." Yet real change may not occur soon—and then only after a period of civil strife and internal coups.

At the moment, while weighing American reassurances, Southeast Asian leaders would like to temporize with other great powers, notably the Soviet Union and China. Beneath a superficial veneer of serious change, they appear more interested in maintaining or improving on the status quo, "the system," than in adopting a radically new approach. All of them pay lip service to the Association of Southeast Asian Nations (ASEAN), which was formed [in 1967] as a nucleus for regional cooperation beyond any great-power alliance. ASEAN members— Indonesia, Singapore, the Philippines, Malaysia, and Thailand—would theoretically welcome Vietnam . . . to membership.

Yet this outlook, enlightened though it may seem, is essentially another manifestation of the desire for maintenance of the old post-colonial order. It is a measure of considerably more than residual American influence that Philip Habib, assistant secretary of state for East Asian and Pacific affairs, was a welcome guest in ASEAN capitals in late May and June [1975]. Seemingly desperate in his pleas for more aid for Vietnam and Cambodia before the final collapse, he had recovered sufficiently to adopt an almost euphoric tone in tête-à-têtes, dinners, receptions, and press conferences from Jakarta to Singapore, Kuala Lumpur, Manila, and Bangkok.

"For those people who thought at the outset that there was going to be some kind of, you know, total hand-wringing and despair and consternation on the part of the Asian leaders," said Habib in Manila, "they're made of more resilient fabric than that." While no one was happy with what happened, he conceded, Asian leaders understand now that "the United States is not just simply walking out and leaving Asia," is "not turning isolationist," "will sustain its obligations," "understands its responsibilities in this part of the world and seeks to work with, in a cooperative spirit, the Asian countries." Unconvincing though such words may have initially sounded, they fit in with the prevailing mood of most, if not all, of the national leaders whom Habib met on his trip.

Nowhere was this response more evident than in the Philippines. True, President Ferdinand Marcos, ruling under martial law since September 1972, has called for "adjustments in our domestic and foreign policies" and underlined this plea by flying to Peking and opening diplomatic relations with China on June 9 [1975]. In fact, however, Marcos had initiated the process toward recognition of Peking last year, when his wife, Imelda, visited the mainland on an official mission. At this juncture, China, of all major powers seeking influence in Southeast Asia, views the American presence as a check on Soviet strength. Much more relevant in the Philippine-American relationship than China's position is 2 billion dollars' worth of annual trade, 2 billion dollars' worth of American investment, and U.S. military spending that accounts for a tenth of the Gross National Product of nearly $14 billion a year.

Does Marcos, who considered forming a "revolutionary" government before he proclaimed martial law instead, really wish to cast off such neo-colonial ties with the Philippines' former ruler? "It is not my intention to wave a placard saying, 'Americans, Go Home,'" he remarked after the fall of the Saigon regime. "Americans will always be welcome in the Philippines." He did vaguely suggest the return of the bases—perhaps a "Philippinization" scheme enabling both governments to agree to canceling the leases by which the United States legally holds the land rent-free until 1991. The feeling, however, is that American naval ships will continue to put in at Subic, which is vital to the Seventh Fleet, while airmen remain at Clark, the headquarters of the U.S. Thirteenth Air Force, regardless of who actually holds the turf. One factor in the equation is the annual military-aid dole, $21 million proposed for the current fiscal year, proffered by the United States as de facto "rent" for the right to retain men and matériel on Philippine soil.

It is in the economic area, though, that figures are most impressive and clearly negate highly publicized indications of real "change." The Laurel-Langley agreement, under which the Philippines and the United States granted each other trade preferences, expired in 1974, but American and Filipino diplomats are still negotiating for preferential treatment. Specifically, the Philippines is asking the United States to reduce tariffs, and the United States wants American businessmen to have the same rights and privileges accorded to Filipinos for investing and operating there. "We're going through an evolutionary process," said an American diplomat, "but the essential thing about the Philippines is that they want us."

Much more genuinely ambivalent than the position of the Philippines is that of Thailand. The reasons for the contrast are obvious. Thailand provided the bases from which American planes bombed Vietnam, Laos, and Cambodia until August 15, 1973. One fear in Bangkok is that Hanoi, after consolidating its position in Indochina, may adopt a revanchist attitude; that is, it may demand some form of "punishment," particularly for the December 1972 "Christmas" B-52ing of the Hanoi-Haiphong region. Already Vietnam may have increased its support for several thousand insurgent troops ensconced in the low-lying mountains of Thailand's barren northeastern provinces, across the Mekong River from Laos, itself almost entirely governed by Pathet Lao forces indirectly controlled by Hanoi. China, in the meantime, goes on providing rifles and bullets for rebellious mountain tribesmen in the northern Thai provinces closest to the Chinese frontier.

"We got away with murder in Thailand for years," remarked an American official with extensive experience in Bangkok. "People in Washington seemed to think that all you had to do was snap your fingers, and the Thais would jump through the hoop. We take our most trusted ally for granted." The official accused both the State Department and the Pentagon of having "failed to recognize the fundamental changes that occurred after the October 1973 revolution," in which an entrenched military regime was overthrown and replaced by civilian rule. One seeming manifestation of Washington's incomprehension occurred at the beginning of 1974, when a conservative academician, William Kintner, director of the Foreign Policy Research Institute, was assigned as ambassador to Thailand in place of career diplomat Leonard Unger, who was partially responsible for manipulating Thai leaders into permitting the United States to use Thai bases as it wished.

Contrary to expectations, however, the outspoken, sometimes tactless Kintner proved a realistic analyst rather than a right-wing advocate; he was recalled earlier this year after he had objected strenuously to State Department and Pentagon demands that he apply further pressure for the free use of Thai bases. From his vantage on the ground floor of the State Department, he was not in the least surprised by the outraged Thai response to the American use of the base in U Taphao in the *Mayaguez* incident. It was from U Taphao that a combined marine—air force operation rescued the merchant ship, seized by a Cambodian Communist patrol boat in May [1975]. "It was a direct infringement on Thai sovereignty," said one nonplussed American. "The Thais told us not to use it, and our attitude was 'Here's this stupid Asian country. Who the hell do the Thais think they are?' "

The Thai Prime Minister, Kukrit Pramoj, a complex, intellectual editor, commentator, and politician related to the royal family, not only protested the incident but even recalled his ambassador from Washington. Then, on July 1, Kukrit and Chinese Premier Chou En-lai signed a joint communiqué in Peking, agreeing to open diplomatic relations while Thailand broke with the Kuomingtang regime on Taiwan. The questions remain, however, How much of the Thai response was show, and how deeply will it cut into the Thai-American alliance? The United States, at the "request" of Thailand, had already begun withdrawing its 27,000 troops* from Thai bases, a sensible move under any circumstances since they were no longer needed for Indochina. Despite all semblance of change, the generals and colonels still rule Thailand behind the scenes, and none of them has suggested curtailing American military aid averaging $30 million a year for the highly corrupt, woefully laggard, 200,000-man Thai military establishment.

In fact, the expectation is that the generals and colonels will prevail upon Kukrit to permit the Americans to retain minimal communications and logistics facilities on at least one of the bases, Udon in the northeast or U Taphao on the coast. (Kukrit's warily phrased declaration, in March, that foreign troops must withdraw "within one year through friendly negotiations," considering "the situation in this region," shrewdly left the way clear for compromise.) "The Thais don't want to be American stooges," said a diplomatic source. "At the same time, they don't want us to go away completely," particularly because the United States contributed directly to the rise of the ruling elite by pouring in more than $600 million in base-construction projects, most of them built by companies owned by Thai military officers. According to Jeffrey Race, an academic specialist in Thai politics who now lives in Bangkok, national-assembly elections in January [1975] revealed increasing discontent over economic inequity but reconfirmed "the

*Editor's note: Reduced to 270 military assistance personnel by mid-1976.

essential conservatism" of Thai voters, since right-wing military and civilian candidates won most of the seats.

Someday the problems cited by Race—"inflation, land alienation, income inequality, agricultural backwardness"—may conspire with armed revolt to bring about genuine revolution. In the meantime, following the historic pattern by which the kingdom of Siam avoided colonization, the Bangkok regime perceives that the survival of Thailand as a thoroughly capitalist, royalist, benevolent autarchy lies in its ability to play off great powers against each other.

Although the American position is necessarily reduced in Thailand, however, it remains strong in Indonesia, the only other country in Southeast Asia that is still dependent on Washington for both military and economic aid. Several basic reasons account for the ostensible difference between attitudes in Indonesia and those in Thailand and the Philippines. "The Communist Party is still a threat to the survival of our country," remarked a member of the Indonesian embassy here, reflecting a lingering fear of the Partai Kommunis Indonesia (PKI), all but obliterated after an abortive Communist coup in 1965. Second, as a result of Chinese support of the old PKI, Indonesia, unlike the Philippines and Thailand, is not disposed to restore diplomatic relations with Peking. "Anti-Chinese feeling still prevails," said the diplomat. "We cannot risk immediate disturbances."

Then, as a concomitant of the response to the failed coup, Indonesia has formed an extremely close relationship with the United States, one not posited on American use of military bases or necessarily on the outcome of the Indochinese War. Rather, the United States, as the leading member of the 16-nation International Government Group on Indonesia, has provided as much as $233 million in economic aid in a single year and furnishes an annual average of approximately $90 million. American companies have invested some $2 billion in Indonesia, half of it in oil exploration and drilling, the rest in exploitation of other resources ranging from rubber to copper. And U.S. military aid for Indonesia's 300,000-man army—an internal peacekeeping force that props up the military-dominated regime of General Suharto—averages $15 million a year.

American officials sometimes refer to Indonesia, rather crassly, as "the only bright spot for American policy in Southeast Asia" and as "a triumph for American diplomacy." Despite the heavy-handed self-interest apparent in such remarks, the reversal of Indonesia's leftist, virulently anti-American policy of a decade ago under Suharto's flamboyant predecessor, Sukarno, is indeed remarkable. Less remarkable, however, is the use to which Indonesia has put its new investment and aid funds. "There is a very high population growth rate, very high urban unemployment, and a growing shift in population to the cities," said an Indonesian specialist. "The result is that many people in Indonesia are worse off than they were under Sukarno, and the gap between the rich and the poor has widened."

Lest such concern with democratic egalitarianism seem rather irrelevant, American diplomats also point out that the Indonesian government is in danger of falling into the same dire financial condition that characterized its affairs under Sukarno. Indonesia has just begun to pay back some $2.1 billion in foreign debts, including $1 billion owed to the Soviet Union since the Sukarno era, but the government-owned oil company, Pertamina, has piled up bills totaling some $3 billion. "The company borrowed large sums on a short-term basis, and the debts are falling due," explained one expert observer. "There was a big hue and cry; so the government assumed Pertamina's foreign obligations. This is a striking development, since Pertamina is the aorta of the 'new order' under Suharto."

One common conclusion is that much of Pertamina's earnings was siphoned off for the benefit of its own president-director, Lt. Gen. Ibnu Sutowo, other company officials, and government and political figures. A direct connection may exist between visible evidence of lavish life-styles and the financing of a range of projects over which inexperienced managers could hardly maintain close supervision. "They're into all kinds of things that won't be productive for a long time," said an economics analyst, citing "a steel plant that will cost $2 billion and won't pay for another 20 years." Then, aside from overextending, Pertamina has begun to underproduce. Crude-oil production, from which Indonesia, the world's eleventh largest oil producer, derives 70 percent of its foreign exchange, has slipped from 1.5 to 1.25 million barrels a day.

How long, then, can Indonesia, a land that has 130 million people and a Gross National Product of only $20 billion, go on before another cataclysmic reversal in policy—a shift possibly exacerbated by its close ties with Washington and the failure of American policy in Indochina? "The stability of this regime is open to some question," responded a diplomatic source, "but things should creak along for a couple of years while the regime gets more repressive, closes more newspapers, and puts more people in jail." One side effect of the new oil prosperity has been the emergence of a "sub-upper class"—the importing of more foreign cars and the opening of five luxury hotels, bars and massage parlors, an indoor skating rink, and gambling casinos, all in the capital. "They hide the poverty," said the diplomat. "To most observers, Indonesia is in great shape, but because of the socioeconomic problems, things are changing fast. What had seemed stable is far from that now."

Indicative of the insecurity of the government has been a campaign to silence intellectuals—the very same ones who once railed privately against Sukarno. Indonesian authorities hold these critics, notably Sudjatmoko, a scholar and a former ambassador to Washington, responsible for inspiring riots against the government during the visit of the former Japanese prime minister, Kakuei Tanaka, in January of last year. Officials are also angry with the view, often expressed in Jakarta, that the American-supported Saigon regime collapsed as a result of "corruption" and "lack of contact with the people"—and that the same problems exist in Indonesia. "There is no connection," reply military leaders, conjuring "national resilency" as the latest in a series of slogans by which first Sukarno and then Suharto have attempted to buoy the masses.

In the meantime, the perspicacious foreign minister, Adam Malik, views ASEAN as the possible salvation of this country, at least in foreign policy. "ASEAN today is not only a viable, but also a vigorous, reality, and its presence and personality is an accepted fact of international life," said Malik in a speech before the parliamentary assembly of the Council of Europe in Strasbourg, shortly before the final Communist victory in Saigon. "In economic cooperation, progress, though still modest, has been steady and quite encouraging," he went on. Critics may charge that ASEAN lacked real substance beyond pro forma committees, but Malik indicated Indonesia's own enthusiasm by noting that it would soon open its first permanent secretariat—in, of all places, Indonesia's capital city, Jakarta.

The choice of the Indonesian capital for ASEAN headquarters may not have been altogether fortuitous. The very anti-communism of Indonesia, the anti-Chinese, anti-Soviet, pro-American policy of the Suharto regime, could automatically render ASEAN suspect in its dealings with Communist states. Better as a site might have been the Malaysian capital of Kuala Lumpur or the port city-state of Singapore, ruled by the peripatetic Lee Kuan Yew, one of the most eloquent, effective spokesman for Southeast Asian regionalism. The fact that neither Malaysia nor Singapore, alone among ASEAN members, receives one cent in military aid, advice, or assistance from the United States would seem to rule heavily in their favor as a potential ASEAN headquarters. Despite both nations' lack of dependence on foreign aid, however, their leaders share the regional sense of shock over the results of the war.

It is because Singapore occupies a unique, pivotal position in Southeast Asia that Lee is so anxious to apprise the United States of regional concerns, and yet the city is also strangely isolated from the rest of the region. The fact that its 2.2 million populace is 75 percent Chinese renders it a potential menace to every other ASEAN nation, all of them traditionally fearful of economic domination by overseas Chinese minorities. Indeed, the expulsion of Singapore from the Malaysian federation in 1965 reflected underlying Malaysian concern that Singapore would challenge Kuala Lumpur for supremacy. The fact that an ethnic Malay minority comprising 45 percent of the Malaysian population rules politically while a Chinese minority of 35 percent controls most of the money has led periodically to riots and demonstrations, even without the influence of Singapore.

Now, however, Malaysia also faces the real threat of renewed Communist revolt. Defeated by the British after World War II, some 1,800 "CTs," or "Communist Terrorists," as they are still termed, have been based ever since in jungles just north of the Thai border. During the past six months, they have sharply increased the level of "incidents"— the most serious of them an ambush killing 17 members of a joint Thai-Malaysian survey team—in a declared seven-year campaign to gain power by 1982. Divided into three main factions, each of them competing with the other for leadership, the Malay Communist Party still draws most of its support from poor Chinese villagers. CTs have little or no following among Malays or bourgeois Chinese except for the odd "radical" intellectual. Clearly, however, the Communist success in Indochina has encouraged the MCP to reassert itself, possibly with arms provided by the Vietnamese Communists.

Thus Malaysian Prime Minister Tun Abdul Razak unhesitatingly hosted a conference of ASEAN foreign ministers in Kuala Lumpur, in May, to discuss the impact of Indochina. If Kuala Lumpur did not seem important enough in comparison with Jakarta as the locale for the ASEAN secretariat, it at least provided a graceful setting for the ministers to exchange views and apprehensions—and to try to solidify a common economic and diplomatic front. As often has been the case, however, Lee Kuan Yew indicated the greatest understanding of realities when he noted the dependency of the region on external factors. "The future of all these five countries will be influenced most of all by the economic health of the industrial world, by their own capacities to attract capital and investment, their access to markets for commodities, agricultural and mineral, and exports of their simpler manufactured goods to America, Japan, and Western Europe," he said before the conference.

Lee's observations captured the essence of the Southeast Asian response to Vietnam. *"Plus ça change, plus c'est la même chose,"* to cite Voltaire. "The more things change, the more they stay the same."

16 Red Votes in the Ballot Box

Richard C. Longworth

"We are," says a French Communist Party leader, "the party of individual modesty, goodness, generosity, fraternity, and love of life." Enrico Berlinguer, head of Italy's Communist Party, has said, "We favor membership in NATO and friendship with the United States." Santiago Carrillo, the Spanish Communist Party leader, told an interviewer that a communist government in Spain "would be viewed with concern in Moscow."

Are they kidding? Do they mean it? Can they be trusted? And what should we do about it? For the first time, these questions are not academic; the odds are rather better than even that communist parties, operating legally through democratic means, will win a share of power (although not a monopoly) in one, maybe more, of America's Western

European allies. Indeed, general elections in Italy this month could easily make Berlinguer's communists the nation's strongest party, with some 35 percent of the vote.* In France parliamentary elections two years hence may give a majority to the Socialist-Communist Popular Front, which won 56 percent of the vote in recent local elections. In the tense and evolving Spanish situation, the still-illegal Communist Party appears to be the nation's best-organized political force. (Portugal's Communist Party, the only one of the four that makes no bow to democratic principles, appears discredited because a left-wing coup failed last year.)

The prospect, in short, is both immediate and crucial: communists in power would change the entire context of European—hence Western—politics. As such, this must be considered the most serious problem facing the West since the mid-1950s because it threatens to alter patterns on which the postwar world is based—the patterns not only of America's relationship with Europe but of the Common Market, of Europe's relations with Russia, of the European position between two superpowers, of democracy on the Continent.

But the interesting thing is that any potential upheaval would probably result not from the fact of communist participation in Western European governments but from the reaction of others—particularly the United States. Even in an election year, a contingency so freighted with peril for American policy normally would demand careful thought. Not so: the American response so far appears designed to alienate the maximum number of Europeans, to damage America's allies, to bolster its detractors, and to assure that any communist-influenced government in Western Europe will automatically be hostile to Washington.

President Ford, between trips to Moscow and Peking, has said that "any communist government would thoroughly undercut, undermine, the aims and objective of NATO. If there is a communist government in any one of the NATO countries, it would have a seriously adverse effect on the justification and reason for NATO. We vigorously oppose any government in NATO that would have a communist head or control." Secretary of State Kissinger has said that any communist power-sharing in Europe would be "unacceptable," would erode the American public's support for NATO, and would probably lead to the folding of the American nuclear umbrella and to the recalling of the 300,000 GI's stationed there. The commander of NATO forces, Gen. Alexander Haig—a sort of military remittance man foisted on the Europeans to get him out of the Ford White House—tells European audiences that he is "very uneasy" about the prospect of communists in NATO governments and that "death can be as fatal from within as from across existing borders." John Volpe, a serviceable right-wing Massachusetts pol miscast as ambassador to Italy, lectures Italian journalists that "we cannot afford to come to the aid of those who

*Editor's Note: In the Italian elections of June 1976, the Christian Democratic Party won by its most narrow margin thus far (38.7 percent to 34.8 percent) and maintained control of the Italian government by acquiesence of the Communists.

might find themselves in a different position from our own." In Paris American diplomats warn the French socialists that the United States will "not tolerate" communist participation in a French government and caution them to be "very prudent" in their dealings with communists. In Stockholm American Ambassador (since appointed U.S. representative to NATO) Robert Strausz-Hupe, who once wrote a book advocating war with Russia, urges Swedish Premier Olof Palme to use his influence in the world socialist movement to discourage cooperation with communists.

The reaction to these injunctions has been predictably negative. An aide to Palme said Europeans were big enough to handle their own affairs. Gaston Defferre, leader of the French parliamentary Socialist Party, accused the American embassy of "absolutely unacceptable meddling"; the anticommunist French Gaullists noted that "it is a bit much when General Haig gives lessons on domestic politics"; and François Mitterrand, the French socialists' presidential candidate, said that "the Americans will have to accommodate themselves to the evolution of French politics. They will adapt, believe me, to the new terrain, and it will be for us to define the terrain." *The Times* of London saw "a woeful lack of proportion in the highest-level discussion in Washington" and said that Kissinger, "for someone born in Europe, shows little appreciation of the level of resistance which Europeans might exhibit against actually 'going Communist.' "

American policy so far toward the possibility of communist participation in European governments begs all the important questions:

- If this participation is unacceptable to us, precisely what are we going to do about it?
- How damaging would such governments be to American policy and the alliance, how hostile to our interests?
- To what degree would they be under Moscow's thumb?
- Is it the American purpose to deny Europeans the right to elect any government they wish, even if that government includes communists?

To most of these questions, much of the evidence, let alone the answers, is not yet in. It is a situation distinguished by its uncertainty. Europe is changing, particularly around the Mediterranean, where the communist prospects are brightest. The results will, alas, be clear only after the dread deed happens, after the communists move into a government or two. Any policy, therefore, must be a gamble. But at least the right questions can be asked now and the available evidence studied. This is exactly what the United States is not doing. The American reaction has been a knee-jerk response worthy of John Foster Dulles—a sort of reflex anticommunism heedless of the fact that not all strings are pulled by Moscow. This is the kind of thinking that got us into so much trouble in China, Cuba, and (need it be said?) Vietnam.

Let us, then, ask some questions and consider some evidence to see if a more balanced policy emerges.

First, if a European nation wishes to elect a communist government, there is probably not a thing we can do about it (short of sending in troops, an American Brezhnev Doctrine, which one trusts is not under consideration). Second, if it happened, we would have to live with it. Threats to punish the offending nation, through NATO or the International Monetary Fund or some other institution in which American influence is strong, would only drive that nation into the arms of Moscow, as did our embargo against Cuba. Sub-rosa financing of anti-communist factions abroad has its limits: the $65 million that the CIA slipped under Italian tables over the years was, at best, ineffective and, at worst, responsible for the present chaos in which communists can pose convincingly as the party of good government. We would have to stop pretending that the communists don't exist. At the moment, the State Department orders American embassies in Europe to ignore communist parties. No American ambassador in Europe ever meets a local communist official. In Rome the embassy's political section is deputed to meet regularly with a middle-ranking official of the Italian Communist Party, but Volpe never sees Berlinguer, and no other American embassy in Europe has any official contact at all—"although we read L'Humanité [the French Communist Party newspaper] every day," an American diplomat in Paris says proudly. Since an important task of embassies is to watch local political trends and to strengthen American ties to all shades of local opinion, this policy, dating back to the days of Dulles, simply keeps the embassies from doing their job. It would be cheaper and just as effective if the State Department closed the embassies and used the money saved to subscribe to L'Humanité and its Italian counterpart, L'Unità. As it is, if communists come to power, the United States will be without personal knowledge of and influence with the new governors of one of its allies.

Washington should remember that it has company in its concern. The communist thrust is a problem for everybody. It's a problem for the Russians, who doubt they can control any Western communist governments and who have learned from their experience with China that a hostile communist government is more trouble any day than a barrel of capitalists. It's a problem for all 15 NATO nations: how many military secrets do you tell a communist, even if he's an ally? It's a problem for the rest of Europe, which has been moving recently toward the Right, and for the Common Market, which is a capitalist organization to which both France and Italy belong. It's a problem for noncommunist politicians, who wonder whether communists, once in power, would ever give that power up.

Would communists in a Western government be controlled by Moscow? The Western communists deny it, and Moscow, judging by its scowls, seems to believe them. Berlinguer's Italian party probably has won the right to be taken seriously on this. Its postwar leader, Palmiro Togliatti, criticized repression in Russia, talked about "an Italian road to socialism," and invented the theory of "communist polycentrism," which still distresses the Soviets. At the recent Soviet party congress in Moscow, Berlinguer rose in the Kremlin to proclaim that "the recognition and respect of the full independence of each country, progressive movement, and communist and workers' party are matters of decisive importance in principle and practice." For more than 20 years, the Italian communists have been more political party than revolutionary cabal and have competed, with increasing success, for the Italians' votes; to do this, they have had to demonstrate independence from Moscow. Most of their economic policies are reformist, in the Social Democratic tradition, rather than Marxist or millennial. This has frequently enraged the Russians: Mikhail Suslov, Moscow's leading theoretician, hinted recently that the Italians are "enemies of Marxism." There are those, of course, who see this as a hoax, a shadow show cooked up by the Italians and Russians to sucker a gullible West. But there are also those who said the same thing about the Sino-Soviet split, even after Chinese and Soviet soldiers began shooting at one another across the Amur River.

Berlinguer says he would keep Italy in NATO and do nothing to upset the East-West balance of power. Eugenio Peggio, the Italian party's leading economist, says that "we do not have any prejudice against any foreign capital and, in particular, American capital." And at any rate, the Italian party, as *The Guardian* of Britain notes, "is certainly more autonomous than Italy's Christian Democrats with their chains to the Vatican and Washington."

The independence of the French party merits more skepticism. Over the years, the French communists have been more pro-Moscow, more doctrinaire, more rigid. Only in the past year has Georges Marchais led his party into a new stance that rejects the "dictatorship of the proletariat" and criticizes concentration camps in Russia. Some of this—like the replacement of the clenched-fist salute with the outstretched hand of friendship—is cosmetic. Much of it seems opportunistic, inspired by the realization that the Italian party's independent line is winning more votes than the French party's subservient posture. Marchais, who likes to say, "I drink wine, not vodka," has promised that "decisions made by the French Communist Party cannot be made in Moscow, Washington, Bonn, or anywhere else." The Russians take all this seriously enough. They sent Andrei Kirilenko, Leonid Brezhnev's heir apparent, to Paris to criticize "all this noise over the 'defense of the rights of man' in socialist countries."

Both parties keep close formal relations with the Soviet party, and many people wonder how independent they could be in practice. But this is not 1948, Italy is not Czechoslovakia, and France is not Poland. The Soviet Union has never been able to impose its will on an ally without tanks. Italy and France have no common border with Russia, and anyone who doubts the importance of such a border as a factor in Soviet control should consult the Hungarians or Latvians. If Portugal were contiguous to Russia, it would be communist today.

It's possible that Russia's empire may be about to spread westward. But it seems more likely that what is happening constitutes the third great schism in world communism, after Tito's breakaway in 1948 and the Sino-Soviet Split 12 years later.

If Europe's communists want to stay in NATO, should NATO accept them? The question applies only to Italy; Spain is not in NATO, and de Gaulle pulled France out of the military part of the alliance in 1966, doing as much damage to it as Marchais could ever hope to. Italy is a member in good standing and the headquarters of NATO's Mediterranean command. As the Sixth Fleet finds fewer and fewer Mediterranean harbors, Italy's strategic importance grows. But could Italian communist ministers be trusted to sit in NATO's inner circles, plan NATO strategy, take part in NATO's Nuclear Planning Group, in which the allies get a peep at American nuclear thinking? Portugal allowed itself to be squeezed out of the NPG, but what if Italy insisted on staying in? Would the United States then stop sharing its secrets with NATO? The answers are not necessarily obvious, despite the warnings of Ford and Kissinger. To assume that communism in Italy would "undermine" NATO is to accept that a political event in one nation should be allowed to destroy the entire edifice of Western collective security. This over-reaction would only compound the problem. Before it happens, the United States should consider whether Italy's communists, if sincerely anxious to remain independent of Moscow, might find their NATO membership a useful shield. If so, why drive them out? What is the alliance for, if not to protect its members from the Russians?

There is no such thing as European unity. But the Common Market has succeeded in creating a customs union and an agricultural market that bring real benefits to Italy and France—particularly France. The other seven nations of the European Economic Community cannot keep communists from coming to power in those nations, but they have plenty of financial weapons to ensure communist cooperation in the Western economic and political world. It is possible that the prospect of a communist government would cause such a flight of capital from France or Italy that severe exchange controls—anathema to the EEC concept—would be inevitable. In that event, financial statesmanship would be required that is equal to the diplomacy needed to keep NATO together, but, as with NATO, the mutual benefits would be worth the effort.

The dangers which Western-style communism poses to European democracy are perhaps the most serious problem of all and cause concern not only in Washington but also among Europeans, especially the anticommunist socialists of Northern Europe. The communist record on democracy is unrelievedly terrible. There are 17 nations in the world that have gone communist, and not one is democratic today (although only one, Czechoslovakia, had solid experience with democracy, none was democratic in the years before the communists took over, and none chose communism by ballot). Communist theory holds that only Marxists understand both history and the future and so have a duty to wield power, democratic scruples notwithstanding.

Against this, the Italian and French communists say, in effect, "We're different." Both have pledged to protect the basic freedoms of speech, dissent, press, and religion. In the face of doubts that they would ever yield power after once gaining it, both have promised to go gracefully if the voters so command. Unlike the parties in communist nations, both have been competing in democratic societies for years and have learned the rules.

Most important, no European communist party stands any chance of governing alone. The French communists are the junior partner in a popular front dominated by the socialists, who are convinced they can keep control. Berlinguer insists on a left-right "historic compromise" with the Christian Democrats, to avoid polarizing Italy and igniting the kind of right-wing military coup that toppled Allende in Chile. (The fate of Allende, as well as the American role in destroying his regime, haunts the European Left and has created a suspicion of Washington, amounting almost to paranoia, that may be impossible to eradicate.) Berlinguer calls the Christian Democrats a "great popular force" that must stay in the government "to save democracy and achieve a general renewal of society and public life in Italy." Certainly, the communists' record in governing many Italian and French cities is good, especially by comparison with the graft and inefficiency in other cities.

To present these arguments is not to contend that the United States should welcome the possibility of communists in power; any way you look at it, the prospect presents more problems than opportunities. But neither should we treat it automatically as an unbelted disaster. As noted earlier, there probably is nothing we can do about it. Our support over the years for the self-serving gerontocracy that has misruled Italy since the war (38 governments in 33 years) has had a lot to do with the communists' success. To order Italians and Frenchmen to beware of their communists is pointless. To reject in advance any collaboration with them is self-defeating because it will force them to seek their support from Russia and guarantee that what opportunities exist will be missed. For there *are* opportunities—not the least the possibility that Western communists may prove more Western than communist and, encouraged and protected by their nations' allies, may be absorbed into the democratic mainstream, becoming no more revolutionary than the socialists who were similarly absorbed in the first quarter of this century. Wouldn't *that* be a prize worth winning?

Finally, it comes down to one question: why have we been in Europe these past 30 years? Is our task to defend the West against all communists, domestic and foreign? Or is it to defend the Western democratic way of life—a way of life that includes free elections and, by extension, the Europeans' right to elect communists to office? Put this way, the question answers itself; given the stakes involved, however, it is not that pat. It *is* a terrible risk that Italy and France—and the rest of us—may be taking. But to reject that risk would invite even greater hazards, from the rot of disillusion to the rage of unrest, and we can do better than that.

17   The Abdication of Europe

Ronald Steel

It is quite "unacceptable," Henry Kissinger has warned our European
allies, to allow Communists into the governing coalitions. This is not because the French or Italian parties would be dominated by Moscow, he
explained, but because they would ostensibly threaten the "democratic
processes," and, more explicitly, make it difficult for the United States
to keep troops on the continent. Whatever the threat to the "democratic processes"—something with which the Secretary of State has not
been noticeably concerned in other parts of the world—the prospect of
Communist participation would throw into question the very purpose
of the Atlantic Alliance, which has always been conceived as an anti-
Communist as well as an anti-Soviet organization. With the acquiescence of the Europeans themselves, it has helped keep Western
Europe firmly within an American sphere of influence. To change the
internal European political balance is to question not only the premises
of NATO, but of the entire relationship between America and Europe.

The Atlantic alliance was built on a reality and marketed on an illusion. The reality was that the United States could not let Western
Europe fall under Russian dominance, and that the Europeans wanted
American protection. The illusion was that the alliance would lead to a
true partnership of equals with virtually identical interests. The illusion
has dissipated. The reality remains.

Despite striking achievements in economic cooperation and expansion, Western Europe remains a congeries of independent nation-
states with different, and often conflicting, foreign policies. There is no
single European will, unless it be a will to prosperity. Political union
seems more elusive today than it was a decade, or even a generation,
ago. Unable to achieve a common currency, a common defense or even
a common policy on such crucial matters as energy, Western Europe
remains in a state of military and political dependence.

If Europe has not achieved unity, neither has it attained com-
munion with America. Because Europe is neither unified nor strong,
the relationship is not one of equals, but of clients and their protector.
To speak of "partnership" in such a relationship is to engage in euphemisms. Europe's role in the alliance is to keep its house in order, to
be a good customer for American products, and a safe haven for investment dollars.

The decisions over war and peace are made elsewhere. This may
be the basis for a convenient political relationship. But the proper word
to describe it is not "partnership," nor perhaps even "alliance." As
Walter Lippmann wrote in the early days of NATO, "As between a
global power and a regional power, a complete two-way alliance is im-

possible—that is to say, if the regional power is not a dependency or a satellite."

For the United States the Atlantic relationship has been strikingly successful. It has held the line against the expansion of communism beyond Eastern Europe, provided an economic trading bloc that financed American investments abroad, and confirmed for Americans a global sense of mission. That it has simultaneously been able to achieve all of these objectives has greatly enhanced its desirability and, until recently, made it virtually sacrosanct.

There are good reasons for this. First, the alliance seemed an inspired response to a military necessity. To American leaders, and to many Europeans as well, Stalinist Russia appeared bent on dominating the entire continent, whether by conquest or by penetration and subversion. This perception was strengthened by the extinction of democracy in Czechoslovakia and confirmed by the Korean war. By the 1950s it took on global dimensions.

Through a straight line of development a foreign policy consensus was created in America: first the Truman Doctrine, then NATO, and finally global "containment." By its possession of the atomic bomb, by a vast rearmament program launched by Truman and Acheson, and by forging an integrated military alliance with Western Europe, the United States would meet its new "responsibilities" to hold back communism. NATO became the indispensable finger in the dike.

The second virtue of the alliance was that it provided a vast protected market for the products of America's farms and factories. Indeed it was virtually the only market from which America would receive hard currency in exchange for its products. From the late 1940s until the early 1960s the United States exported twice the value of goods to Western Europe as it imported from those nations. Even though the creation of the Common Market reduced this surplus, a favorable trade balance continued through the 1960s and helped defray the cost of maintaining American troops in Europe.

Because they were willing to underwrite the American balance of payments deficit by accepting unlimited amounts of dollars minted lavishly by the US Treasury, the Europeans helped finance such costly adventures as the Vietnam war. In the same way they also facilitated, much to their eventual dismay, the takeover by American firms of a good many European industries. This condition of "monetary hegemony" was the price that Europeans were expected to pay for American protection, as Washington made clear in the unilateral dollar devaluation of August 1971.

Third, the alliance, in addition to its military and economic virtues, was flattering to American pride. It confirmed that the mantle of Western leadership had passed from the Old World to the New. The child of Europe and for nearly two centuries its dependent, the United States had become the protector of its parents. This was not only an American perception. The British, particularly, but also the French, urged the United States to assume the imperial responsibilities they found increasingly difficult to manage: Greece, the Middle East,

Indochina. After the Truman Doctrine, to be sure, Washington needed little prodding. But even those who questioned the self-assumed global "responsibilities" found a flattering sense of power in the American protectorship of Western Europe.

That all of these conditions have now changed is obvious. Restored to prosperity, if not to full self-reliance, Western Europe feels less threatened by the Russians and less acquiescent under American protectorship. The themes first sounded by De Gaulle have now been picked up as a generalized European litany. There is resentment at the takeover of European industries with inflated American dollars, irritation at pronouncements from Washington over political and economic matters affecting Europe no less than the United States, and mounting anxiety over a superpower entente that seems to involve the denuclearization and political impotence of Europe.

From an American perspective the changes are no less striking. It is no longer "international communism" that is seen as the enemy, but rather, in Kissinger's Metternichean world view, political instability. Thus there has been a new flexibility, and a new uncertainty, in American foreign policy. Not only has the Sino-Soviet rivalry finally been officially noticed, but it has been the precondition of the triangular balancing act undertaken by Kissinger with the blessing of Nixon and then of Ford. Soviet Russia remains an adversary, but also an accomplice in the effort to maintain a global status quo that is congenial to the interests of both superpowers.

Now that the cold war has been transformed from a life-or-death struggle into an old-fashioned contest for influence in the hinterlands, it is difficult to generate public or congressional enthusiasm for the old line alliances. With security being more narrowly defined than in the past, the cost of maintaining foreign garrisons and a global network of military bases is beginning to seem a dubious luxury. After Vietnam it will be a long time before any President can send American soldiers to fight a protracted land war. Given this revision of military strategies, the cost of maintaining the American garrison in Europe is increasingly hard to justify.

Even more important than cost in the new equation is the change in the relationship between America and Western Europe. Throughout most of the cold war, Europe was an acquiescent political partner of the United States and a profitable commercial one. With only minor misgivings, the allies, except for Gaullist France, accepted the military strategy that was chosen for them and provided a profitable market for American exports.

But when the allies demanded a voice in how and where American nuclear weapons would be used in the defense of Europe, they treaded on ground that directly involved America's own security interests. Deterrence, in Washington's view, depended upon absolute control by the United States over these weapons. To share control with the Europeans could force the United States against its will into nuclear war with Russia. The Europeans, congenitally fearful that they might be abandoned, wanted the United States to leave the tactical atomic weapons in place as a guarantee of involvement. This is not so much because they fear a Russian attack, or even less because they could conceive surviving a "tactical" nuclear war fought on their own soil, but because of its symbolic value as collateral against a pledge. American strategists, on the other hand, favor a conventional strategy for European defense and now want to withdraw some of the tactical atomic weapons. This has left Europeans in a quandary. They know the weapons mean instant death if ever used, but they don't want to see them removed. They want the Americans to provide atomic protection, but they want control over the protection. They demand an equal voice, but don't marshal equal power, nor are they willing to pay for acquiring it. Thus, the strategy for European defense has changed over the years, but the anxieties remain. They are built into a system resting on an inequality of power and decision-making.

Together with these differences over strategy has come a change in the economic relationship. By the end of the 1960s America's trade surplus with Europe had shrunk by 80 percent. The very success of the European Economic Community—with its booming exports and its demands for controls on the inflated dollar—transformed Europe into a powerful economic competitor. The Marshall Plan worked brilliantly in restoring Europe as a market for American products. But the process went too far when it resulted in European attacks on American "monetary hegemony."

In the early 1970s all these factors came together: the détente with Russia, the opening to China, the disenchantment with cold war alliances, European resistance to American nuclear strategy, and the growth of economic competition among the Atlantic allies. The result was a fundamental change in American foreign policy. The United States would emphasize its military security through a policy of nuclear deterrence based on intercontinental strategic weapons, and seek to contain the weapons race by arms-control negotiations with Russia. This new policy sharply reduced the military importance of allies, who were informed that they would be helped in proportion to their willingness to help themselves.

This, of course, was the so-called Nixon Doctrine. While it was originally thought to include only such client states as South Vietnam, Cambodia and South Korea, its logic applies to Europe as well. Its purpose was to assuage domestic opposition to costly interventionist wars through a limited military retrenchment, yet at the same time remaining politically engaged throughout the globe. The United States would retain its dominant world role by maintaining bases and by providing military equipment for client regimes. But it would intervene far more selectively, leaving the fighting of peripheral wars to its allies and clients.

The Nixon-Kissinger "structure of peace" was based on three assumptions: that after Vietnam the American public would no longer support direct military interventions, that China and America had a mutual interest in the containment of Soviet power and influence, and that a *modus vivendi* could be reached with Moscow based on mutual restraint and respect for spheres of influence.

The effect of this new strategy on America's cold war allies is only now beginning to be felt. In Southeast Asia it means the gradual neutralization of the area, as De Gaulle had urged in the early 1960s. In the Middle East it means recognizing that a settlement between Israel and the Arabs can be achieved only with the cooperation of Moscow. The contest for influence between America and Russia has fed the Arab-Israeli quarrel and hardened positions on both sides. Inheriting Britain's classic role, the United States has sought to exclude Russian influence from the Middle East. But this policy long ago became obsolete with Russia's rise to superpower status. However evenhanded the United States may be in its efforts to bring about an Arab-Israeli settlement, it cannot hope to succeed without Soviet acquiescence. Such a settlement will be difficult at best; but it is virtually impossible so long as the superpowers see the Middle East as a staging area for their own competition.

In Europe the new strategy means providing a nuclear cover, but insisting that the major share of the conventional defense of the continent be assumed by the Europeans themselves. An American garrison would remain in Germany, both as a symbol of American involvement and as an element in the conventional defense of Europe. But its primary purpose would not be to serve as a nuclear trip-wire, as it had been explained to many Europeans and as they prefer to believe. American strategy precludes such a role since it seeks, in the event of conflict, to confine the defense of Europe to conventional weapons for as long as possible. The role of the American forces thus becomes both symbolic and political: a symbol of the American nuclear guarantee, a manifestation of the political influence that America exerts over Europe through NATO. Such a role could be satisfied by retaining American forces on the continent at only a fraction of their current level. A reduction of these forces can be delayed, however, so long as this method of assuaging European anxieties does not become unduly costly.

Inherent in the concept of the Russo-American détente is the determination that the dialogue between the superpowers will be conducted directly and not by proxy or through intermediaries. Each, of course, will remain dominant within its own alliance. The United States would no more allow Russian interference in NATO decisions than Moscow would allow Americans to interfere in the Warsaw Pact. The détente nonetheless affects relations within the alliance as much as between the superpowers. The European allies will be informed, and even consulted. But the critical issues will be decided by those with the power to do so. Insofar as the Europeans complicate or impede an agreement, they will be circumvented. This was dramatized by the Soviet-American weapons accord of June 1973 on mutual force reductions, which was worked out between Washington and Moscow without a European voice being heard.

With the replacement of containment by a policy of guarded engagement between the superpowers, it is essential that allies be kept in line and Third World crises defused. In the new Washington-Moscow entente, allies play a distinctly subsidiary role. They can impede or even sabotage détente. But their contribution to America's physical security is greatly reduced. From a military prespective the cold war alliances are becoming a historical anachronism.

This does not mean, to be sure, that they are unimportant. To the contrary, they are militarily useful, for the bases they offer—although the European allies, as the last Middle East crisis revealed, are resistant to allowing them to be used for anything but their own defense. They also serve a political purpose as levers for political influence and the exercise of economic power. On a psychological level they serve as confirmation that a great power has attained the global status to which it aspires. Since security is rarely defined in military terms alone, alliances provide for the extension of influence and the creation of an orbit congenial to the perceived interests of the dominant power. So long as America and Russia remain great powers, each will feel compelled to keep the other locked out of its sphere of influence.

While allies have not become irrelevant, the alliances forged during the cold war have lost much of their original *raison d'être*. They were the product of a bipolar world, a stage of military technology, and an Armageddon psychology that no longer exist. As America's key alliance, NATO has been profoundly affected by these developments. Yet its structure remains rooted in an earlier world. That it is in a state of confusion is axiomatic. That it cannot persist in a form consistent with its rhetoric has now become unavoidable.

There are four possible routes the Atlantic alliance could take. First, it could be transformed into a true political community linking America and Western Europe. This is the dream of the old Atlanticists, and it is an inspiring vision. But the price would be higher than either America or Western Europe is now willing to accept. For the United States it means giving Europeans a share in the nuclear deterrent and subjecting America's global military and economic policies to European control. For Europe it means abandoning any hope of reuniting the continent or of protecting Europe's economy from disappearance into an Atlantic trading bloc under American direction. If such an Atlantic union did not occur during the worst days of the cold war, it is highly unlikely today.

Second, the alliance could simply disintegrate. Whether it would be formally dissolved, whether various states would exercise their exit option and leave one by one, or whether it would remain a decorative object housed in a Brussels suburb is not really important. Yet such a disintegration is unlikely for the simple reason that it would leave the Europeans dangerously exposed to Russian power. While they complain about American dominance of the alliance, it is infinitely preferable to being left alone with Russia while still militarily weak. If NATO simply collapsed without a European organization to replace it, the individual members would go scurrying for cover. Most would seek refuge under an American umbrella, a few might even try to bargain an accommodation with Russia. In either case their position would be weak and their dependency intensified. That none of the Europeans want this, and that they have labored over the past three decades to prevent it from happening, is the best argument against it.

Third, NATO could split in two as the divergence of interests intensifies. As Henry Kissinger observed, in reminding the Europeans of their proper place in the alliance: "The United States has global interests and responsibilities. Our European allies have regional interests." This was an accurate, if blunt, assessment of the situation. Should the Europeans choose to act on it, they could decide to reduce their military dependence on the United States. This would require the creation of a strong conventional army subject to a single European command. It would also mean building a credible European nuclear deterrent, based on the French and British forces. Such a nuclear force is clearly within Europe's economic capabilities, but at the moment it remains far beyond Europe's political capacities. Except for a handful of Gaullists on both sides of the Channel and the Rhine, few Europeans care deeply about the ability to stand alone—particularly when the benefits of a benevolent American hegemony are so obvious and so relatively cheap.

Finally, the alliance could settle into an institutionalized American hegemony over Western Europe. This would be the simplest alternative, since it would require no significant changes in the present state of affairs. The Europeans would have to acknowledge that the price of American military protection is economic dependency. This would mean refraining from building a monetary union, for such a union would likely diminish the role of the US dollar and the ability of the United States to dominate economic policy in the West. The Europeans would have to maintain a liberal, rather than a mercantilist, economy and subordinate their own internal needs to those of a trans-Atlantic economy dominated by the United States. On a practical level, the Europeans would be expected to pay the cost of maintaining a garrison of GIs on the continent, although at considerably lower force levels than at present, and to cover, if necessary, the deficit in the US balance of payments by the purchase of military equipment and Treasury notes.

These alternatives may seem stark, but they cannot indefinitely be avoided. If Europeans want to change the balance of forces, they must choose a path of action. The United States does not have to choose, for the current situation is quite favorable to its interests. Europe is dependent upon America for security and prosperity, for protection against the Russians, and for access to Arab oil. America is not dependent on Europe in that sense, even though the two economies are tightly interwoven. There is a reason why Europeans complain, but Americans make declarations. It is all a function of power.

Washington can remain impervious to the complaints of its allies about its economic policy, or its military strategy, or its private deals with Moscow, because it knows that there is little the Europeans can do about it. Whenever the complaints become unduly shrill, the Europeans are reminded that the piper calls the tune. Nixon made the links quite clear in the spring of 1974 when he warned the Europeans that they could not have "cooperation on the security front and then proceed to have confrontation and even hostility on the economic and political front."

However heavy-handed such a statement may be, it is an accurate assessment of the balance of forces within the alliance. The choice is clear for the Europeans. Either they forge a political union capable of providing for their own defense, or they come to terms with the fact that America's economic and political hegemony is the unavoidable price of military protection. They cannot have it both ways.

Even sympathetic Americans find it tiresome when Europeans complain about Washington's domination of the alliance, but shrink from undertaking the steps that would be necessary to end it. Choices are made by default as much as by design. So far the Europeans have chosen abdication and grumbling rather than initiative and resistance.

The United States, to be sure, is not making the road to independence easy for its allies. Washington periodically declares its support for a self-reliant European Community. But what it means by that is a Europe that will pay for its own defense yet continue to allow the key decisions to be made across the Atlantic. Whenever the Europeans have tried to act independently, as in the oil crisis of 1974, American officials reacted indignantly and even issued guarded threats. As it turned out, the EEC cracked under the Arab oil boycott, as each nation tried to save its own skin. It was a performance that showed not only how divided the Europeans were, but that the real decisions over their energy sources lay outside their control.

Although Washington claims to favor a politically unified Western Europe, the rhetoric need deceive no one. By its own actions the United States has consistently sought to impede the creation of any European entity that would not be fully integrated into an American-directed Atlantic system. "We cannot be indifferent to the tendency to justify European identity as facilitating separateness from the United States," Henry Kissinger scoldingly declared in 1973. The Secretary of State presumably assumed that his listeners would not remember his pleas, before he entered the US government, for a greater American understanding of European sensibilities. "A separate identity has been established by opposition to a dominant power," he had written only a few years before. "A united Europe is likely to insist on a specially European view of world affairs—which is another way of saying that it will challenge American hegemony in Atlantic policy."

What was true then is true now. But the pleasures of hegemony are such that the view is rather different from the top. American policy-makers are not necessarily insincere when they call for a strong Europe. It is just that they suffer from mixed motives. This is the built-in paradox of Atlanticism. The United States is verbally committed to

the creation of an independent Europe that can be built only in opposition to American hegemony. This independence Washington has
sought to block whenever it has become manifest.

There is, to be sure, a good case for "devolution," the gradual
turning over to Europeans of military decisions hitherto held exclusively in American hands. This could provide a much-needed spur to
European unification, and relieve the United States of responsibilities
that the Europeans are perfectly capable of bearing. But it would also
reduce American influence over Europe. To a greater degree than we
have been generally willing to admit, our definition of security has been
based on our ability to influence and to serve as an example to others.
Without these psychological factors much of American postwar foreign
policy makes little sense. Viewed narrowly, neither economic influence
nor military security dictated either of the two major wars of intervention: Korea and Vietnam. It was only in the wider perspective of
maintaining the perimeters of an American sphere of influence, and of
behaving as a superpower is presumably expected to behave (as Kissinger later explained of Angola), that these were justified by their advocates.

Thus, to concentrate on the security aspect alone—or at least to
define security exclusively in military terms—is to miss what much of
NATO is about. For this reason American policy-makers find good
reasons to maintain the alliance indefinitely in its present form. Even
though NATO may be militarily outmoded or even superfluous, it is
extremely useful for the exercise of American influence over Europe.
In addition, the troop contingent keeps the American army brass
happy, provides jobs for untrained youth in a time of high unemployment, and flatters the nation's self-image as the guardian of Mother
Europe.

Paradoxically, considering the present balance of forces within the
alliance, it can be said that while the plight of NATO seems to be hopeless, it is not particularly serious so far as the United States is
concerned. Washington currently has all the options, since Europe is
too weak and too divided to make a clear stand.

In the absence of any real European initiative, which seems unlikely anytime soon, there are three possible courses of action open to
the United States. First, it can continue present policies. Most of the
GIs would remain in Europe and a good part of their cost would
continue to be covered by offset arrangements. The Europeans would
complain about changes in American strategy over which they have no
control, or about nuclear and political arrangements reached between
Washington and Moscow. But they also insist that they want troops as a
symbol of America's willingness to become involved in nuclear war on
their behalf. The price of these hostages is a hegemony they find
distasteful, but apparently not yet intolerable.

Second, the United States could dramatically reverse field, seize
the standard of NATO's most acerbic European critics, and actively encourage the creation of a politically unified Western Europe with its
own nuclear deterrent. This would, presumably, reduce complaints of

US dominance and eventually eliminate the conditions that Europeans have so resented and Americans have found so profitable. In the long run, such a course may be unavoidable. It is far from certain, however, that a nuclear-armed Western Europe with a territorial grievance against the Russians would be a source of stability in the world. Nor is it clear that the virtues of equality would exceed for the United States the pleasures of hegemony over Europe. Why relinquish unnecessarily a position that provides such benefits? An abdication of such proportions is usually imposed by circumstances; rarely is it offered gratuitously. In any case, the situation has not reached a state of crisis grave enough to make such an American offer necessary.

Third, Washington could downgrade the alliance without ending it. This would mean pulling out its forces, rather as was done in France and Greece, while still maintaining a political commitment. The purpose of this would be to reduce the danger of America's being drawn into a European war against its will. Some have seen this as the ulterior meaning of the 1973 Russo-American treaty on nuclear weapons and believe that accord implies the denuclearization of Europe. There are some 7000 tactical nuclear weapons in Europe. Many of them are only nominally controlled by the United States and pose a considerable political danger.

Were they deprived of American hostages and the tactical nuclear weapons, Europeans might well fear that the American guarantee would not be fully honored in time of crises—or that Washington would prefer to confine any future war to European soil. But since the United States has compelling reasons to prevent Western Europe from falling into Russian hands, any rational Soviet diplomacy would have to assume that the guarantee might well be invoked in the event of attack.

Nonetheless, it is possible that a formally denuclearized Europe would feel cast adrift and might try to establish some form of *modus vivendi* with the Russians. For many this evokes fears of "Finlandization," that is, independence subject to Soviet scrutiny and goodwill. Naturally most Europeans find this unacceptable. For this reason alone they might be driven to build their own nuclear force, thus spurring the political integration that has so far been blocked by their dependence on the United States.

A nuclear or self-reliant Europe would, to some degree, mean a more neutralist Europe. This need pose no threat to American security. But the economic and political hegemony that Washington has exercised over the continent would be greatly reduced. Many Americans, particularly those who associate the nation's well-being with the national security apparatus, would find it hard to adjust to this situation. It would mean the loss not only of material advantages, but of psychological satisfaction. Having found a flattering identity in the role of Europe's spokesman and protector, many would resent the "loss" of our richest dependency. This may be the most important factor of all. It is the fear of losing influence, of playing a diminished role in the world stage that lies at the heart of America's imperial diplomacy.

In the long run this loss of influence is unavoidable—at least the kind of influence that has been exerted during the cold war. It is a product of détente with Russia and the accommodation with China. It has been powerfully affected by events over which the United States has no effective control: the recovery of Europe, nuclear proliferation, the oil crisis, the disintegration of the world monetary system, world-wide inflation and depression, and the inability to prevent the Soviet Union from playing a political role in areas traditionally considered to be under Western influence—such as the Middle East and Angola.

For America the path is clear, though not always straight. It will pursue détente with its adversaries—despite pitfalls, detours and set-backs—because it is clearly to its advantage to do so. Toward allies it will continue to exert hegemony—which it will define as "cooperation" and "interdependence"—until it is forced to abandon this by drastically changed circumstances.

Those circumstances could take one of two forms: first, from a European withdrawal into neutralism and an accommodation with Moscow; second, from the creation by Europeans of a political union that would permit them economic and military dependence. In either case the United States would find that it had lost its role as Europe's protector, along with the economic and political advantages that have gone along with that role. Should Europe choose independence and power, rather than subservience and accommodation, this would also dramatically transform the world balance of power—as would Japan's decision to acquire nuclear weapons.

In any case, the writing is on the wall, although there is a good deal of time in which to indulge in hegemonic privileges. Interdependence may be an illusion, and alliances may be of declining military im-portance for the United States. But the prerogatives of hegemony are real. They are institutionalized in the structure of the Atlantic alliance. They are likely to persist so long as the Europeans continue to fear in equal measure the Soviet Union and an independent power role for themselves.

All in all, too much has been made of NATO. It is neither a prison nor a partnership. It is only a symbol of Europe's will to abdicate. This abdication is what De Gaulle threatened a dozen years ago, and why he was so ritualistically denounced by Washington. It is again being raised by the prospect of a "historic compromise" in Italy and perhaps elsewhere—which is what Kissinger finds so "unacceptable."

The Global Balance of Power: Can the Great Powers Rule the World?

18 The Hot Deals and Cold Wars of Henry Kissinger

Simon Head

. . . In the past, Americans have been able to understand the broad themes of American foreign policy by studying the grandiose and sweeping doctrines proclaimed by successive American Presidents. These doctrines accurately described the policies the United States was following. The Truman Doctrine, the Eisenhower Doctrine, the foreign-policy ideology of John F. Kennedy, even the crude, inchoate nationalism of Lyndon B. Johnson, all set forth the propositions of containment—the belief that there exists a legitimate world order composed of states aligned or friendly with the United States; the belief that the major Communist powers, whether collectively or individually, are intent upon undermining this order, and the belief that it is the duty of the United States to resist these attempts whenever and wherever they are made.

When Richard Nixon and Henry Kissinger came to power, it was natural that they too should proclaim doctrines, and equally natural, given the habit of 20 years, that the American people should regard these doctrines as reliable indicators of what the new Administration proposed to do. Kissinger, a former theorist of international relations, was particularly adept in the art of constructing doctrines; "the structure of peace," "the multipolar world," "the new world order"—these are characteristic phrases of the Kissinger years, and to each of them there cling fragments of doctrine. Yet the more one studies the Kissinger record, the clearer it becomes that proclaimed doctrine has ceased to be a reliable guide to how the United States behaves in the world.

The problem is not simply that the neat correspondence between words and actions, which existed during the cold-war era, has broken down; it is also that there no longer exists any coherent body of doctrine at all. While the Kissinger image is one of great intellectual discipline and control, the truth is that during the past six and a half years doctrines have flowed from the smooth Kissinger tongue with promiscuous abandon. Doctrines have been put together and discarded according to the needs of the hour. Contradictory doctrines are proclaimed almost simultaneously. A crisis evokes one kind of doctrine; a negotiation successfully concluded, another. The haze of uncertainty and doubt that surrounds so much of what Kissinger has done is in part a reflection of this chaos.

The events of the past seven months provide ample evidence of this doctrinal prolixity. During the weeks when Vietnam was collapsing and an American policy of 30 years lay in ruins, Kissinger behaved like the generalissimo of a global army whose defense line had just been broken. Where would the enemy strike next on the global battlefield? How could the American side deter him from attacking again? How could the wavering allies be reassured? The acute anxiety felt by Kissinger and others after the loss of Vietnam stemmed not only from the fact that the United States had lost, but that it had lost without putting up a fight. It had fled headlong from the battlefield. Thus, the danger of some new enemy move somewhere else on the global battlefield was particularly great, for might not the enemy conclude that the United States had lost the will to resist altogether? It is in the context of this militaristic thinking that such an obscure incident as the Mayaguez affair can take on an enormous significance. By providing the opportunity for a ferocious resort to force, the Mayagüez incident proved, in Kissinger's view, that the American will to resist was still very much alive.

Thoughts and actions such as these place Kissinger firmly in the mainstream of the cold-war tradition. Yet there are other sides of the Kissinger diplomatic personality that convey a very different message. The seven-month period that saw Kissinger prophesying doom over Indochina also saw him preparing for President Ford's visit to Peking, traveling around the country defending the Russians as worthy partners in détente, hobnobbing with Brezhnev at the European Security Conference, and keeping Aleksandr Solzhenitsyn away from Ford lest the touchy Soviet leader take offense. If the stress of crisis brings to the surface a Kissinger vision of a world community scarcely emancipated from the habits of the Stone Age, the practice of détente finds Kissinger describing a world order that takes on the characteristics of a bourgeois society: The behavior of one state toward another comes to be governed by a generally accepted code of rules; negotiation takes the place of confrontation; solutions are found for longstanding disagreements; former rivals begin to trade profitably with one another; rivalry itself, if it still exists, is muted in the interests of retaining the other partner's goodwill.

The Kissinger-watcher who attempts to penetrate this ideological fog, looking for some clear and consistent pattern of action that would reveal the true nature of the Kissinger grand design, will find only more confusion. Nowhere is this more apparent than in Kissinger's approach to the Soviet Union. At times, Kissinger seems to be more of a revisionist vis-à-vis the orthodox cold-war view of the U.S.S.R. than practically anyone else in Washington. During the Middle East war of October, 1973, he was one of the few who claimed that the Russians had been "moderate" in their behavior. A year later, he suggested that there were many other "incipient crises with the Soviet Union" that had been "contained or settled without ever reaching the point of public disagreement." He was willing to lend the Soviet Union $7-billion, on extremely favorable terms, for the development of its natural gas and oil deposits, and opposed the notion of demanding explicit concessions in return. And in playing the SALT numbers game with Senator Henry Jackson and the Pentagon, he has more often than not given the Soviets the benefit of the doubt. All this suggests a liberal and progressive Kissinger, a Kissinger who has shed the dogmas of the cold war.

Yet while Kissinger often seems ready to go to extreme lengths to conciliate and even appease the U.S.S.R., he is also ready to go to extreme lengths to contain it. Again and again, Kissinger's diagnosis and management of crises have been governed by the maxims of containment: the assumption that a Soviet presence in some third-world country is often sufficient reason to conclude that the country is well on the way to becoming a Soviet satellite; the assumption that the Soviet Union can freely manipulate such "satellites" in order to further its expansionist ambitions, and the belief that if the American response to any Soviet-manufactured crisis is "feeble" and "half-hearted," the Russians will conclude that the American "will to resist" has decayed, and will be bolder and more reckless in provoking future crises.

Perceptions such as these determine how Kissinger analyzes the meaning of a crisis and how he reacts to it; they account for the militancy that often grips him in the heat of a crisis; they account for his infatuation with military power and his willingness frequently to use it. They largely determined his reaction to the Indo-Pakistani war of 1971, the crisis over the Syrian invasion of Jordan in 1970, the crisis the same year over the alleged Soviet plan to build a nuclear submarine base in Cuba, the Cyprus crisis of 1974, and the Mayagüez affair. They account for "destabilization" in Chile, and for the worldwide nuclear alert during the Middle East war of October, 1973. Above all, they account for the violence and brinkmanship that marked every stage of the American withdrawal from Indochina.

In these crises and confrontations, Kissinger, acting together with Nixon and Ford, moved drastically and often dangerously to head off threats from the Communist world the evidence of whose existence was and still is very slender. These actions are examples of what can happen when Kissinger's principles of containment are applied in the real world. They show how the Kissinger philosophy can involve the United States in the kind of global interventionism that the Indochina experience supposedly taught it to avoid. During the Indo-Pakistani war of 1971, for instance, Kissinger and Nixon sent a part of the Seventh Fleet into the Bay of Bengal and threatened to abort the whole course of East-West diplomacy in order to deter the Russians from "unleashing" the Indians against West Pakistan. But neither during that war nor since then has there existed any convincing evidence that the Indians intended to follow up their intervention on behalf of the Bengalis with an invasion or annexation of West Pakistan, or that the Russians were encouraging them to do so. During the Jordan crisis of 1970, Nixon and Kissinger alerted five American divisions in Germany, formed five carrier task forces in the eastern Mediterranean, and threatened to intervene militarily in Jordan—all on the assumption that it was the Russians who had ordered the Syrians into Jordan and the Russians who had to be frightened into calling them back. Here Kissinger simply took it for granted that the Russians control the radical nationalist regimes of the Arab world in much the same way that they control their Eastern-European satellites.

The strategy of intimidation practiced during the Indo-Pakistani war and the Jordan crisis involved straightforward acts of containment; it was assumed that there existed a potential or actual Soviet threat to the stability of the Middle East and the Indian subcontinent, and that the United States was, therefore, obliged to act in order to preserve the status quo. The Kissinger-Nixon policy in Indochina was also, from start to finish, an act of containment, undertaken to preserve the regional balance of power between the United States and China and the global balance between the United States and the Soviet Union—and, beyond that, to demonstrate the credibility of American power to America's allies in every part of the world. In Indochina, Nixon and Kissinger were aiming for what might be called a "Korean solution." They hoped to strengthen the South Vietnamese Army to the point where it could hold off the North indefinitely; then, after years, perhaps even decades, of military stalemate, the North would acknowledge the hopelessness of the task, abandon the war and accept the division of the country.

From the end of 1969 onward, Nixon and Kissinger were obliged by American public opinion to withdraw the United States expeditionary force from Indochina, but their "Korean strategy" required all along that American military involvement there, employing every form of military power short of the actual use of ground troops, had to continue for years afterward. This basic requirement became clear at the beginning of 1973; Kissinger had managed to negotiate a final agreement with Hanoi that secured the release of American prisoners and made possible the withdrawal of the last American ground troops. The South Vietnamese were now thought to be "on their own." But were they?

Within weeks of the agreement's being signed, Nixon and Kissinger were informing the American people and warning the North Vietnamese that, in the event of any further Communist offensives like those of Tet, 1968, or March, 1972, the United States would be obliged to resume the bombing. We now know that at about this time Nixon wrote privately to President Thieu giving him the same assurance. The haste with which these threats and commitments were made reflected the leading role that air power was to play in the second phase of the strategy. The threat to resume the bombing was intended to deter Hanoi from launching any more large-scale offensives; *actual* resumption of the bombing, were deterrence to fail, was to have weakened the North Vietnamese army to the point where the Saigon army could deal with it. Meanwhile, behind this shield of American air power, the long and arduous task of turning the Saigon army into a replica of the United States Army could continue; more American tanks and guns, more American advisers and technicians, more American money, were to have been committed to the Thieu regime.

By the beginning of 1973, Nixon and Kissinger had every reason to believe that this strategy was going to work. The threat to resume the bombing, around which the whole second phase of the strategy was built, was a very credible threat. This becomes clear if we look at the situation from the point of view of the North Vietnamese. By March, 1973, Kissinger and Nixon had skillfully demonstrated to Hanoi that there was no longer anything to restrain them from bombing North Vietnam as savagely as they wanted. In theory, they might have been restrained by fear of Soviet or Chinese retaliation, but the failure of China or the U.S.S.R. to do anything on Hanoi's behalf during the May, 1972, mining of Haiphong harbor or during the Christmas terror bombing of Hanoi and Haiphong the same year proved conclusively that neither power was willing to jeopardize its developing relationship with the United States in the interests of North Vietnam. In theory, again, Nixon and Kissinger might have been restrained by American public opinion, but the North Vietnamese had seen how public opinion had tolerated the attacks of May and December; besides, by early 1973, Nixon was serving his last term in the White House and could afford to defy public opinion in the interests of his "place in history" (*i.e.,* to avoid being the first President to lose a war). As for the other major requirement of the "Korean strategy," the need for gigantic quantities of heavy armaments to keep the Saigon army fighting in the American style, only the United States Congress could frustrate Nixon and Kissinger—and, as a President with one of the greatest electoral mandates in American history, Nixon had every reason to believe that he could get what he wanted from Congress.

What undermined and eventually destroyed this strategy was, of course, Watergate. Nixon and Kissinger were forced to retreat, step by step, just as they were on the point of bringing off one of the great diplomatic coups of the age. What monumental frustration they must have felt as Watergate deprived them of one essential power after another! In the summer of 1973, they lost the power to bomb in Cambodia and resume the bombing of North and South Vietnam. During 1974 and 1975, they saw the level of military and economic assistance to the Saigon regime progressively reduced by a Watergate-inspired Congress, and they saw Thieu's authority decline with it. As the level of aid fell, the South Vietnamese Army could no longer afford to fight in its accustomed manner. It became transformed into an army whose fortunes in battle depended ultimately on the willingness of the infantryman to face death rather than allow the enemy to pass. Once that happened, the game was lost.

Henry Kissinger may be the last major American statesman whose view of the world has been fundamentally shaped by the ethos of the cold war. Far from infusing the conduct of American foreign policy with the spirit of the diplomacy of 19th-century Europe, Kissinger operates on beliefs and prejudices firmly rooted in the recent American past. If one strips the pronouncements of John Foster Dulles, that Archbishop of Containment, of their doomsday rhetoric and self-righteous moralizing, there turns out to be a strong resemblance between many of the beliefs that guided Dulles two decades ago and those that guide Kissinger today. For both, the Russians have always been the main enemy: Dulles saw them presiding over a monolithic Communist bloc that threatened American interests everywhere; Kissinger sees them following an ambitious and expansionist global strategy that has retained its dynamism even in the face of such setbacks as the Sino-Soviet split and the Sino-American rapprochement. Both have believed that Soviet aggressiveness and expansionism are characteristics deeply rooted in the nature of the Soviet system, and that the Soviet leaders are driven to expand the territory under their control or influence by the nature of their Marxist-Leninist convictions. Both, therefore, have rejected the revisionist view that Soviet intentions toward the West can be transformed by changes in the international environment or in the Soviet system itself.

In contrast to the typical American view that a rigid attachment to ideology can be a source of political weakness, both Kissinger and Dulles have regarded Soviet ideology as a formidable weapon in the Soviet conduct of foreign policy. The quasi-scientific character of Marxism-Leninism, Kissinger has argued, leads the Soviet oligarchs to view the outside world in much the same way that an astronomer might view some exploding galaxy; a given diplomatic situation reflects only "a temporary relation of forces" that is "inherently unstable" and can be maintained "only until the power balance shifts." Led by their most fundamental beliefs to see the world as being always in a state of flux, the Soviet leaders, in Kissinger's view, become endowed with an uncanny ability to detect the point when the "global balance of forces" inclines in their favor—an ability to "manage the inevitable flow of history . . . to bring about the attrition of the enemy by gradual increments . . . to tilt the scales by constant if imperceptible pressure." Both Kissinger and Dulles, therefore, have regarded the Russian leaders as the most talented of opportunists, and this explains why both of them have had a peculiar horror of any display of American weakness, however trivial the situation and however obscure the territory in which it might occur. For both have been obsessed with the idea that the men in Moscow are constantly scanning the world from their

Kremlin control tower, watching for the slightest sign of American weakness, ready to take immediate advantage of it with some probe or foray of their own. "We certainly have to keep in mind," Kissinger warned in 1970, "that the Russians will judge us by the general purposefulness of our performance everywhere."

There is also a striking similarity between the operating tactics preferred by Dulles and Kissinger in dealing with concrete acts of Soviet aggression. Dulles, whose early years of power coincided with the years of American nuclear supremacy, was able to threaten to escalate any confrontation with the Russians to the level of general nuclear war because he knew the Russians did not yet have the wherewithal to respond in kind. According to this doctrine of "massive retaliation," the penalty the Russians would have to pay for an attack on, say, Persia or Turkey, was total annihilation. Kissinger, operating in the age of nuclear equality, has been deprived of this most persuasive of deterrents, and he has had, instead, to base his deterrence on a threat to retaliate with conventional rather than nuclear force; yet he has managed to come up with an amended version of the doctrine of massive retaliation that preserves much of the spirit of the original. Just as deterrence Dulles-style depended on the threat to escalate the level of conflict to the point where America's nuclear supremacy would come into play and where the U.S.S.R. could no longer compete, deterrence Kissinger-style has depended on a willingness to escalate to a level where the superior nerve and willpower of the American leadership would come into play and the Russians would not *dare* to compete, even though they possessed the resources to do so. In Kissinger's words, "deterrence is greatest when military strength is coupled with the willingness to employ it. It is achieved when one side's readiness to run risks in relation to the other is high; it is least effective when the willingness to run risks is low, however powerful the military capability."

But how could Kissinger actually go about proving that the United States was willing to take greater risks than the U.S.S.R.? During the course of the various confrontations with the Russians in which he has been directly involved, Kissinger has made many extravagant threats. During the Jordan crisis, he threatened, in effect, to transform an intra-Arab struggle into a general Middle East war involving a risk of armed confrontation between the United States and the Soviet Union. During the Indo-Pakistani war, there was a hint of military intervention and a more explicit threat of diplomatic escalation: Unless the Russians called off the Indians, Nixon would not visit Moscow. During the Cuban submarine-base crisis of 1970, Kissinger threatened the Soviet Ambassador with a crisis on the scale of the Cuban missile crisis of 1962. The mere fact, however, that Kissinger uttered these threats did not in itself guarantee that they would be taken seriously, for the basic problem that confronts any practitioner of the art of deterrence is the problem of credibility—will his threats be believed?

Kissinger's problem of credibility was solved in Vietnam; Vietnam was the testing ground where the United States proved what Kissinger and Nixon have called its "unpredictability," thereby establishing the authenticity of its threats against the Russians. The Russians had to take seriously the American threats to intervene in the Middle East or the Caribbean because the United States just months before had intervened so decisively in, say, Laos or Cambodia. "We believe," Kissinger said in 1970, "that the action in Cambodia where the President did what he said he would do if the war would be spread, and if the other side escalated its action, did help establish the credibility of his action in Jordan." Other such linkages can no doubt be inferred; the bombing of Hanoi and Haiphong in December, 1972, could be seen as having enhanced the credibility of the global nuclear alert declared by the Nixon Administration during the 1973 Mideast war; and if the invasion of Cambodia established the credibility of the Administration's threats in regard to Jordan, why not also the credibility of its threats during the Cuban submarine-base crisis (which occurred within days of the Jordan crisis), or, for that matter, its threats during the Indo-Pakistani crisis, which occurred a year later? And might not the passivity of Soviet diplomacy during Kissinger's most recent foray in the Middle East be related in some way to the Ford Administration's handling of the Mayagüez affair last spring? The possible combinations are endless.

The ultimate objective of any strategy of containment is to arrive at a point where deterrence is so effective and the credibility of American power is so great that no Soviet leader considers it worthwhile to embark upon any new foreign adventure; in his own mind, the odds against success are too great. Something approaching a global equilibrium is then established, and it rests upon the supremacy of American power. It is on the issue of how the United States ought to exploit such superiority, if and when it is achieved, that Kissinger's opinions begin to diverge sharply from those of Dulles. It has long been Kissinger's view, a view that predates détente by many years, that the moment when the United States has the advantage in the global struggle for power is also the moment when it should enter into serious negotiations with the Russians on the main questions dividing the two nations.

This point of view once again reflects Kissinger's conviction that ideology plays a crucial role in the practical formulation of Soviet foreign policy: The ruthless Leninist opportunism that supposedly makes the Soviet leaders so adept in exploiting any strategic opportunity that comes their way may also lead them to act with flexibility and realism once they see that events are flowing against them. If there is no longer any possible advantage to be gained from a strategy of provocation and confrontation, the Soviet leaders may be willing to turn to diplomacy instead. None of this means that there has been any Soviet "change of heart" or that the Russians might have abandoned their efforts to expand their sphere of influence at the expense of the West, and in his writings Kissinger never tires of warning Western statesmen against such dangerous illusions. What has occurred is simply a change of tactics, but it is a change the West can seek to exploit for its own ends. For if the Russians decide to use diplomacy to achieve by peaceful means what they can no longer achieve through intimidation, the West can, by the same token, try to use diplomacy to freeze a status quo slanted in its own favor.

In Kissinger's view, there have been three occasions during the cold war when the West enjoyed such an advantage over the Russians and ought, therefore, to have engaged in serious negotiations. The first opportunity arose after World War II, when the United States possessed the atomic bomb and the U.S.S.R. did not. It was then, when "our relative military position would never be better . . . that we should have taken advantage of the bargaining power inherent in our industrial potential and our nuclear superiority." The second opportunity arose after Stalin's death, "the period of maximum confusion in the Kremlin," when "the possibility was greatest that the new Soviet leadership might break with its past, if only to consolidate itself." The third arose during the two-year period that elapsed between the Cuban missile crisis of 1962 and Khrushchev's fall two years later.

The Western failure to negotiate on the first two occasions was, in Kissinger's opinion, largely the result of the pigheadedness of the American leaders then in charge. Because they believed that worthwhile negotiations with the Communists could only take place some time in the far-distant future, when the Communists might have cleansed themselves of their aggressiveness and become respectable members of the international community, they were completely blind to the potential of negotiations that might be held in the here and now. Only on the third occasion, in Kissinger's view, did the West begin to do the right thing: President Kennedy followed up his success in Cuba with the conciliatory American University speech of June, 1963, and negotiated the nuclear-test-ban treaty later the same year. But this promising start was doomed once Kennedy was assassinated and Lyndon Johnson became bogged down in Indochina.

Luckily for Kissinger, there arose a fourth occasion when the time was right for serious negotiations with the Russians, and this time Kissinger himself was in a position to take advantage of it. The conventional wisdom is that the willingness of the Russians to negotiate and reach agreements with the West from the late nineteen-sixties onward has been a response to events that had nothing to do with the foreign policy of the United States, the most important of these being the intensification of the Sino-Soviet dispute and the failure of the Soviet economy to sustain an adequate rate of growth. But Kissinger has argued that these events were not sufficient in themselves to bring about détente; the Sino-Soviet split, for instance, might have led the Soviet Union to adopt a "more aggressive attitude toward the capitalist world in order to assert its militant vigilance." Kissinger's own explanation of how and why détente came about is extraordinarily Americocentric, even Kissinger-centric, but one that is fully consistent with his doctrine of the relationship between diplomacy and détente.

From Kissinger's own account of what happened during the crucial years of 1970–71, one gets the strong impression that the Soviet leaders played a completely passive role; that the steps they took toward détente during that period were always in reaction to some American move, orchestrated by Henry Kissinger himself. In 1969–70, Kissinger saw the Russians, guided as usual by the principles of Leninist opportunism, embarking on a worldwide effort to take advantage of America's apparent weakness. These years were, by any standard, Nixon's and Kissinger's worst. They were the years of Cambodia and the great antiwar demonstrations in Washington, years when impatience with the slow pace of withdrawal from Indochina was steadily mounting and it was not yet clear how Nixon and Kissinger intended to deal with that impatience. Expecting Soviet perfidy, Kissinger saw every Soviet "move" everywhere as part of a grand subversive strategy aimed at the United States; and there were at this time enough incidents which, when viewed from Kissinger's perspective, appeared to confirm this thesis. Along with the Russians' "dangerous forays" in Jordan and Cuba, there was their regular "harassment" of the land and air access routes to West Berlin, their "intransigence" at the negotiations on SALT and Berlin, their attempted negotiating strategy of "divide and rule" in Central Europe ("Soviet policy seemed directed toward fashioning a détente in bilateral relations with our Western allies, while challenging the United States") and their "conspiracy" to violate the Middle East cease-fire of 1970 by allowing the Egyptians to move their SAM missiles right up to the Suez Canal. "By the fall of 1970," Kissinger wrote in the President's 1972 foreign-policy report, "we seemed to be on the verge of a new, perhaps prolonged and certainly fruitless and dangerous period of tension."

But within a matter of months the atmosphere was radically transformed—and in Kissinger's view it was American policy that was almost exclusively responsible for this change. As he saw it, he and Nixon had stood firm during months of Soviet adventurism; and just as President Kennedy's actions during the Cuban missile crisis proved to the Soviet leaders that, in Kissinger's words, "the balance of forces was not in fact favorable," so the qualities of toughness and will power the American leadership exhibited anew eight years later conveyed the same message. As Kissinger saw it, he and Nixon held the line in Jordan, beat back the Russians in Cuba, flexed their military muscle in Cambodia, rallied the silent majority in the United States, refused to budge an inch in the negotiations on SALT and Berlin, and avoided the Russian trap of divide-and-rule in Central Europe. With the credibility of American power thus fully established, the moment had come when, according to the Kissinger doctrine, serious negotiations with the Communists had to be undertaken. Just as President Kennedy followed up his Cuba success with the American University speech, so Nixon and Kissinger followed up their "victories" with Nixon's United Nations speech of Oct. 22, 1970. "In the world today," Nixon said, "we are at a crossroads. We can follow the old way, playing the traditional games of international relations, but at ever-increasing risks. Everyone will lose. No one will gain. Or we can take a new road. I invite the leaders of the Soviet Union to join us in taking that new road."

Suitably awed by this demonstration of the credibility of American power and by Nixon's great magnanimity in proferring the olive branch at his moment of triumph, the Soviet leaders in Kissinger's view, were only too ready to "join in taking that new road." Led by his own theoretical beliefs to expect that, as a direct result of his own skillful and sophisticated strategy, some major change in the Soviet line ought now to take place, Kissinger interpreted every subsequent Russian move toward détente as proof that this was indeed happening. What endowed the Kissinger theory with a certain plausibility was the fact that several important changes in the Soviet-American relationship did take place during the winter of 1970–1971. But these changes, which from the Soviet point of view were part of a long-term strategy of détente—a strategy that had been launched during the Khrushchev period and that had already involved a Franco-Soviet détente during the mid-nineteen-sixties and a Soviet-German détente during the late sixties—were now interpreted by Kissinger as more or less *ad hoc* responses to an American strategy worked out by Kissinger himself. Thus, when the impasse at the SALT negotiations was broken and the same thing happened with the negotiations on Berlin; when, at the 24th Congress of the Soviet Communist party, Brezhnev committed himself to a policy of improved relations with the United States; when, in the spring of 1971, agreement was reached on American participation in the construction of the huge Kama River truck plant in the U.S.S.R., by far the most important economic agreement between the two countries since World War II—when these things happened, it was a unilateral American strategy that was being vindicated.

Kissinger's estimate of the Soviet leaders is a highly flattering one: They are alert, inventive, flexible and daring, all in the tradition of Stalin and Khrushchev. Without such an assumption of Soviet dynamism, a great many of the things Kissinger has done do not make sense; indeed, it may be precisely because the threat posed by a supposedly dynamic Soviet leadership provides the best rationale for an activist American strategy that an activist like Kissinger can be motivated, consciously or subconsciously to keep alive as alarming an image of the Soviet leaders as he possibly can. But regardless of whether Kissinger's views are primarily a product of subconscious motivation or rational thought, the gap between Soviet reality and the Kissinger image of it is wide indeed. During the Khrushchev period, Soviet foreign policy had a genuine dynamism that was a reflection of Khrushchev himself—of his great personal power, of his buoyant and reckless personality, formed in the years before the party was shattered by Stalin, of his conviction that the economic and political systems of the newly independent third-world countries would come more and more to conform to the Soviet model, of his optimism about the future of the Soviet system itself.

With the advent of the Brezhnev-Kosygin regime, these great political and psychological assets disappeared. Tactical flexibility and ingenuity were lost when power became diffused among a collective leadership; the dullness and caution of the new leaders, men who in their formative years had known nothing but the Stalinist terror, sapped Soviet ideology of whatever external appeal it had had under Khrushchev. More and more, the Soviet leaders found themselves bogged down in monumental problems for which there was no solution—with domestic economic problems, which had become acute only toward the end of Khrushchev's reign; with the dispute with China, barely manageable under Khrushchev, now escalated into a full-blooded power struggle. In the third world, the area where Kissinger worries most about Soviet "penetration," Russian power and influence have been diminished both by the declining appeal of the Soviet system as a possible model to be emulated, and by the rising strength, confidence and intractability of third-world nationalism.

This last development has weakened the Soviet Union much more than the United States because of the difference between the third-world constituencies to which each tries to appeal. America's natural constituency in the third world is composed predominantly of aristocratic or bourgeois regimes, whose nationalism is often softened by the existence of close economic and cultural ties with the West. The natural Soviet constituency, on the other hand, comprises strongly nationalist regimes whose leaders have usually spent their formative years fighting European colonial powers. However much power and status they may have acquired since independence, these leaders still react angrily against attempts by the Russians or anybody else to meddle in their domestic politics—witness Sadat's expulsion of the Soviets in July, 1972. The ambitious superpower can do more with the Philippines, Thailand, South Korea, Brazil or post-Allende Chile than with Iraq, Syria, Somalia, India or North Vietnam. This is a simple truth that Kissinger has consistently failed to grasp.

Yet, however obsolete Kissinger's private vision of Soviet reality, however much it may be rooted in the age of Stalin and Khrushchev, it is still the vision that counts. Once it is understood, détente itself becomes intelligible. The fact that détente has "happened," that agreements have been reached, that Soviet and American leaders now regularly visit one another—for Kissinger, none of this has meant for a moment that the United States can relax its global posture of constant vigilance. Instead, such qualities are as necessary during periods of détente as during periods of confrontation. For if the "sudden and dramatic" shift of Soviet policy that took place in the winter of 1970–71 was essentially an accommodation to demonstrations of superior American power, then, by the same token, an American failure to maintain this strength could bring about as dramatic a shift in the opposite direction. In the face of opportunities to advance at the expense of the West, the Russians would pay no attention to the treaties and agreements of détente. "We have always assumed," Kissinger explained in 1970, "that as Marxists they would keep an agreement only so long as it serves their interest; as Marxists, they have almost no mechanisms by which they would keep an agreement that is against their interests."

This kind of reasoning explains why, in spite of détente, the psychology of the cold war still grips Kissinger as firmly as ever; it explains why Kissinger felt it necessary, to the bitter end, to try to salvage the Vietnam commitment and to avoid at all costs the humiliation of American defeat. It explains why the Mayagüez incident can be thought of as an American victory of global significance.

This reasoning also accounts for the paradox described at the beginning of this essay—the great contrast between the Kissinger who is always flexible, always ready to understand the Russian point of view, and the Kissinger who is striving constantly to keep his global front intact. This is a contrast that infuriates Kissinger's enemies and baffles many of his admirers; but seen in the context of the Kissinger doctrine, there is no paradox at all. The two Kissingers are performing two separate but complementary functions. Kissinger the general must maintain the basic balance of power that underlies détente and makes negotiations possible. Kissinger the diplomat must be ingenious enough to conclude the agreements that reflect this balance.

19 Dilemmas and Dead Ends: America and the Middle East Crisis

Steven L. Spiegel

American efforts to resolve the Arab-Israeli conflict are infinitely complicated because the contestants have vastly opposing views on the nature of a settlement. As the lowest common denominator, the Arabs seek complete Israeli withdrawal from all territories captured in 1967. In response, they are offering under the most generous interpretation some form of international guarantee of Israel's existence secured by the great powers—probably through the United Nations Security Council.

The net effect of such a condition would be to maintain Israel's total isolation in the Middle East, to increase her dependence on outside parties, and to weaken her ability to take independent military initiatives in the name of her security. Most important, a settlement maintained and supported by outside parties would leave open an option of renewed Arab-Israeli hostilities because there would be no process of commitment by the two sides themselves to mutual reconciliation and a new order for the area. The radical Arabs' vision, on the other hand, is both starker and more precise than the moderates'; it foresees an end to Jewish sovereignty in any part of the former area of Palestine.

The Israelis, by contrast, seek complete normalization of relations with their neighbors; their model resembles the transformation of Franco-German relations rather than the frequent ceasefires between Greece and Turkey. In the absence of total denouement, security remains their preoccupation, thereby diminishing the prospects for territorial withdrawal.

In theoretical terms, the United States identifies with the Israeli vision of the future of the area, but in practical terms and in the short run, the Arab vision appears easier to achieve. Since 1948 there has been constant tension in United States policy between the long-range aims embodied in Israeli policy and the need to demonstrate immediate diplomatic results. The Israeli position was upheld when negotiations for a permanent settlement seemed distant. Whenever opportunities seemed to arise, American policy makers leaned toward the Arab vision, which has seemed more attainable because it is more limited.

Since the war of October 1973 the pressures of the energy crisis have demanded some kind of resolution of the conflict; hence the attractiveness of any advances toward any sort of settlement has been greater than ever. On the other hand, the Arab League Rabat conference of October 1974 annointed the Palestine Liberation Organization (PLO) as the sole representative for receiving any Palestinian territory. This decision impeded movement toward a settlement because the PLO has been careful to clarify its conception of the future, one which no Israeli government could accept. Progress was hindered even more by the escalating partisanship of United Nations resolutions and activities and then by the Lebanese civil war, which created disarray in the Arab world and severely weakened the PLO. Therefore pressure for action has continually confronted obstacles.

By a twist of history Henry Kissinger became secretary of state on the very eve of the 1973 war. Kissinger—in background, politics, and style a bundle of contradictions—seemed peculiarly suited to deal with the complications and vagaries of the Arab-Israeli issue. At first he appeared to be a man for every culture and political preference. To conservative Arabs and their American sympathizers, the secretary offered hope for reversal of the losses of 1967 by U.S. diplomacy; in other words, that Kissinger was a chubby Eisenhower with glasses and a German accent. To Israel and her supporters, his diplomacy offered hope for the beginning of progress toward peace; was Kissinger a modern version of the legendary Queen Esther, a Jew in the royal court, who at the crucial moment rises to protect his people? Despite the cynics and skeptics both at home and abroad, Kissinger's unique acceptance by Jerusalem, Damascus, Cairo, and Amman at first dazzled many observers. Yet he was caught between warring parties abroad, feuding factions at home, and contradictions in his own approach. Over time these became more difficult to reconcile.

In the felicitous phrase of *New York Times* columnist William Safire, Henry Kissinger is the first secretary of state whom two presidents have served. His stewardship at Foggy Bottom coincides with Richard Nixon's rendezvous with resignation and Gerald Ford's presidential education. Thus Kissinger, during the very period when the Arab-Israeli dispute became the center of American interest in international affairs, had an even wider authority than John Foster Dulles over the conduct of foreign policy. Never a Zionist, always fascinated with displacing the Russians, Kissinger's experiences in office can be summarized in three phases: (1) 1969 to mid-1973, (2) mid-1973 to March 1975, and (3) March 1975 to January 1977.

Until mid-1973 Kissinger was not at the center of Middle East policy making, for Secretary of State William Rogers carried the burden in this one area while Kissinger, as National Security Council advisor, dealt with the Chinese, the Russians, and the Vietnamese. But Kissinger was not totally removed from the concerns of the Middle East, especially after the Jordanian crisis in September 1970, when U.S. policy was coordinated at the White House and he worked closely with Israeli Ambassador Yitzhak Rabin. There were several subtle differences between Kissinger and Rogers. Rogers viewed the Arab-Israeli dispute in regional terms, while Kissinger was more tempted to see the conflict within the context of the Soviet-American balance of power. Rogers sought to gain leverage over the Israelis by limiting the amount of arms they received; Kissinger believed a strong Israeli position would help deter the Arabs and ultimately enable the Israelis to make concessions. Kissinger was closer to the president in these views than was Rogers, who reflected the thinking in the bowels of Foggy Bottom. While the first Nixon term drifted on, the president's initial inclination to give Rogers's ideas a chance changed into an increasing tendency to bolster the Israelis. The Israelis, in turn, assumed that the resulting U.S. military and economic aid meant unstinting support. Though Nixon admired the Israelis' "moxie," both his and Kissinger's goals were similar to Rogers's, even though their tactics differed "at this point in time."

By the spring of 1973 Kissinger had begun to pursue the diplomatic initiatives in the Middle East which Nixon had promised during the 1972 presidential campaign. Unbeknownst to Rogers, he initiated abortive secret talks with the Egyptians; at the United Nations on the eve of the Yom Kippur War he was already beginning to shuttle between the two sides. A crisis, like an illness, never occurs at an easy moment, but for the Nixon administration the timing was especially inappropriate. Henry Kissinger had just become secretary of state—and Richard Nixon was in the throes of a political virus called Watergate, which was in the end to prove terminal. Inauspiciously, Spiro Agnew resigned as vice-president of the United States on the fifth day of the Middle East war; Gerald Ford was named to succeed him just hours before the decision was reached to begin a massive airlift of military equipment to the Israelis.

The response of the Nixon-Kissinger team to the crisis was

consistent with its previous experiences in dealing with the Vietnam War and with the Soviet Union and China. Highly personalized and centralized diplomacy was combined with an effort to achieve dramatic breakthroughs, maintain momentum, and achieve the support of as many parties as possible—especially former adversaries. In short, Nixon and Kissinger decided to aid Israel after the Arab attack but they saw the Arab military initiative as an opportunity—not as an act of aggression. Out of the military stalemate engineered by Kissinger's maneuvering, much activity—perhaps even achievement—might flow. Arms to Israel were at first delayed, then generously furnished, but in the end Israel was denied victory through American maneuvering. U.S. policy sought to guarantee that the Yom Kippur War would not be another 1967, when stalemate and diplomatic paralysis, rather than movement and momentum, followed hostilities.

Kissinger's style predisposed an attempt to resolve outstanding problems by resort to diplomatic finesse. With regard to the energy crisis created by the Arab oil embargo, limited conservation measures were announced in the United States, but the major thrust of Kissinger's diplomacy was to improve relations with the Arab world and to achieve sufficient progress in resolving the Arab-Israeli dispute so that the embargo would be lifted and not repeated. His policy thus embraced regional foes abroad and opposing constituencies at home. The Israelis were encouraged by continuing military supplies and verbal assurances. The Egyptians were reassured by appeals to the newly revealed Arab strength, by the opportunity to gain leverage vis-à-vis the Soviet Union and Israel, and by the hope of American economic and diplomatic assistance. Leaders of the pro-Israeli constituency in the United States were treated to an unprecedented campaign of private meetings, appeals, and other attentions. The pro-Arab constituency was won over by the attention and care pursued in relations with the Arab world; for once the U.S. government appeared to be following the injunctions of those most against the pro-Israeli leanings of earlier years.

In the first few months after the October War, few objected to Kissinger's approach. The results of his activities were a disengagement accord between Egypt and Israel in January 1974 and another between Syria and Israel that May after thirty-three days of shuttle diplomacy. At the time, both accords were hailed as unprecedented achievements heralding a new era in Arab-Israeli relations. A more accurate description is "much ado about little." The two accords did bring some abatement of Middle East tensions and demonstrated a method for achieving an Arab-Israeli settlement. Yet, there were a number of weaknesses. First, the accords themselves were necessitated by the U.S.-Soviet agreement to a ceasefire even though the war had not actually ended. The crazy-quilt pattern of ground forces, especially on the Sinai front, demanded some sort of resolution. Yet because these accomplishments were tied to the consequences of the war, it became more difficult to cross the threshold to future negotiations. Second, by interposing himself between the Arabs and Israelis, Kissinger could demonstrate his skill as a diplomatic superstar, but this meant that the sides were negotiating with him rather than with each other—an inauspicious omen for ultimate Arab-Israeli reconciliation. And finally, step-by-step diplomacy had the advantage of isolating issues short of complete settlement, and thereby making each easier to handle. The problem was that so much effort had to be devoted to fitting together comparatively small pieces of the puzzle that little energy remained for solving the wider issues of the dispute.

Nevertheless, in 1973 and 1974 it looked as if Arabs and Israelis alike admired the American Lone Ranger diplomat, whose true identity seemed as mysterious as that of Tonto's partner. Kissinger, with his entourage of aides and reporters and the ever-present "senior official" aboard his aircraft, pursued peace and tranquillity on seemingly endless journeys. For months it appeared as if the state department were a traveling road show, a combination of electronic gadgetry and journalistic glitter serving one man. American policy in the Middle East seemed merely to reflect the achievements and beliefs of a lone hero on his gallant air force charger.

Meanwhile on the domestic front, efforts to use quick diplomatic achievements in the Middle East as a prescription for Watergate therapy were unsuccessful and were eaten away by a major complication ("tapeworm"?). President Nixon's trip of June 1974 to the Middle East was a largely unrecognized but significant failure. Nixon was fascinated with Kissinger's opening to the Arab world; more people cheered the president in Egypt than live in Israel. At a dinner in Jerusalem, Golda Meir, in praise of Nixon, declared (to the delight of the American press corps), "Your President; he is capable of anything." But behind the scenes, Israelis began to worry about the painful decisions Kissinger was implying for them.

Into this carefully balanced but fragile stalemate between competing domestic foes and Middle East adversaries appeared a new central figure—Gerald R. Ford, who succeeded Nixon as president in August 1974. The new president was distinguished by his pro-Israeli statements in the past, his inexperience in foreign affairs, and his unproven executive ability.

In old Michigan style, Ford centered the ball to Kissinger. But where was he to run with it? Jordan seemed the most likely place for the next disengagement, but before agreement could be reached, the Arab League appointed the PLO as the negotiator for the area including the West Bank. Now Kissinger moved toward a second disengagement in the Sinai, but when his efforts failed in March 1975, he blamed the Israelis.

The failure of the spring talks marked a crucial turning point in Kissinger's approach to the Middle East. Previously he had posed as an objective observer and had gained the support of both sides. He had thus become the first effective mediator acceptable to both opponents since Ralph Bunche. But Kissinger was playing too many roles—friend of the Arabs, partisan of the Israelis, evenhanded arbitrator. In March 1975 the contradictions caught up with him. He thereby sacrificed a measurable share of Israeli and pro-Israeli opinion by faulting Jerusalem for the breakdown. Previously, he had favored increasing arms sales to Israel; now he reassessed his position.

Kissinger had thus come full circle; in the end he had assumed more than Rogers's office as secretary of state. The centerpiece of Kissinger's policy in the Middle East now emerged; it was to be found in Cairo. For almost a quarter of a century American diplomats had been fascinated with the idea of capturing the allegiance of the Arab world through support of Egypt. Presidents Eisenhower, Kennedy, and Nixon had all failed in major efforts to deal with the mercurial Egyptian leader Gamal Abdel Nasser. But Anwar Sadat, Nasser's successor, appeared to be more receptive to U.S. overtures, and he continually portrayed himself both privately and publicly as disillusioned with the Soviets. When Kissinger visited him the American secretary of state was treated with urbanity and with the rapid decisions possible in an authoritarian regime. From the Israelis he had to suffer the hesitations and internal squabblings that often characterize democratic societies. Besides, only the Egyptians could offer a reversal of the Soviet position in the Middle East. In this sense, Sadat was the real author of Kissinger's policy, for without the temptations and inducements he presented to the Americans, there would have been no shuttle and no step-by-step diplomacy.

Thus Kissinger could hardly blame the Egyptians for the March 1975 breakdown. To have faulted them would have been to endanger his only real trump card in the Middle East. Sadat reciprocated by reopening the Suez Canal, and the first steps were taken toward a second Egyptian-Israeli disengagement. When the disengagement came in September, pro-Arab supporters cried foul, while many of Israel's friends staunchly defended the document and the accompanying confidential agreements, which were gradually leaked to the press. Superficially, the Israelis were the victors in the agreement. In return for a comparatively minor withdrawal from the Sinai, they gained an unprecedented commitment from an Arab country to refrain from warfare against them for at least three years so long as they did not launch a preemptive attack against any Arab country; Sadat also agreed that nonmilitary cargo to and from Israel could pass through the Suez Canal in non-Israeli ships. From the United States Israel gained a host of commitments, including a major economic and military aid package, advanced weapons, assurances of consultation if a Soviet-American confrontation developed over the Middle East, a promise not to deal with the PLO unless it recognized Israel in some form, and a further promise by the United States to concert with Israel its strategy at Geneva.

The balance sheet of the agreement was quite different. Egypt regained the Abu Rudeis oil fields and, more importantly, thereby deprived Israel of over half her source of petroleum—making her more dependent on the United States. Israel had gained a degree of recognition from an Arab state, but after three years this could easily be abrogated. Israel's arrangements with the United States were just as elusive. American aid commitments to Israel had been delayed several months during the "reassessment." They were not organically linked to the agreement. Was it credible that the United States would weaken Israel's deterrent and allow her economy to be ruined, especially with Congress calling for aid to Israel? Similarly, American promises of consultation on the Soviets and the PLO were nothing less and nothing more. The limited value of these promises would be seen by the Israelis during the next several months, when they would receive one rude shock after another.

The one major new commitment in the accord was the stationing of 200 American civilian observers in the Sinai. Although the Israelis ineptly managed to have themselves regarded as the sponsors, the idea was originally Sadat's. Through the observers, the Israelis gained added assurance of Egyptian compliance with the accord, but Sadat acquired further American involvement in Middle East diplomacy and he further decreased the possibility of direct Israeli-Egyptian contact.

Considered as a package, high-ranking American diplomats regarded the commitments to Israel as "mind-boggling,"* but that was because of their loathing for increased American identification of any sort with Israel. Actually, as later events were to show, the agreement did not contain mandatory constraints on American diplomacy. It could serve to strengthen Israeli-American ties or to whitewash the relationship as the ties were loosened.

To the apparent surprise of Sadat and Kissinger, the accord was condemned by Syria, leading to the dead end of step-by-step diplomacy. But Sadat's apparent isolation in the Arab world fueled his desire to improve relations with the United States. Because he had accepted Washington's accord despite widespread Arab opposition and because he continued to defy the Soviets, he would have to be rewarded. First, he received a cordial welcome in the United States. He was invited to address Congress, and occasional anti–Semitic lapses during his trip were ignored. When the Egyptians supported a UN General Assembly resolution declaring Zionism as racism, this act was overlooked by the United States. President Ford even suggested that the United States might punish some of the countries that voted with the majority, but not the Arab states. Second, the United States began to take tentative steps on the Palestinian question which would indicate its flexibility in the absence of substantial progress. At least Sadat could demonstrate to his fellow Arabs that his actions were leading to improvements in the American diplomatic posture. Controversial statements by Ford administration officials on various aspects of the Arab-Israeli conflict, implicit acceptance of a PLO presence at the UN Security Council, and contacts with the PLO during periodic American evacuations from Lebanon suggested that Sadat's policies were bearing fruit. Third, U.S. aid to Israel was diminished in the proposed 1977 budget, and it was only partially increased after heated protests by pro-

*Edward R. F. Sheehan, "How Kissinger Did It: Step-By-Step In The Middle East," *Foreign Policy*, 22 (Spring 1976), 63.

Israeli forces on Capitol Hill. Fourth, the embargo on arms to Egypt was lifted through the initial sale of six C-130 transports. The deal was clearly intended as the beginning of a new military assistance program to be instituted after the presidential election.

Furthermore, American backing of Syrian intervention in Lebanon during the civil war there served as an opportunity to build bridges back to Damascus and to prevent a radical regime from emerging in Beirut. Though American camaraderie with Cairo and Damascus did not prevent the disintegration of Lebanon or ease Syrian-Egyptian tensions, the administration continued to pursue its diplomacy as if the Arab world were divided solely between pro-American and pro-Soviet governments, or moderates and radicals.

Kissinger's policy, as it ultimately evolved, turned Israel into a burden rather than an asset to the United States. Israel's main value was as bait to attract the Arabs, for only the United States could successfully pressure Israel to make concessions. Although coherent and cogent, the policy was not the only alternative that might have been pursued by a U.S. government in line with U.S. interests, but it was the only policy which the Ford administration adopted. As a consequence, the measure of Arab moderation was judged *not* by Arab actions toward Israel, but by the Arabs' relations with the United States. Improved Arab-American relations were designed to prevent an oil embargo and war at all costs. The oil weapon has therefore proved effective. In this context, Israel must be compromising without expecting normalization of relations with the Arabs or even nonbelligerence.

Kissinger's policy can be summarized as follows:

1. Prevent a fifth Arab-Israeli war, which might precipitate another oil embargo or lead to Soviet-American confrontation.

2. As part of this strategy, decrease the incentive of either side to attack. Therefore, maintain diplomatic "momentum," giving the Arab side hope of progress toward attainment of its objective (defined as regaining the territories Israel captured in 1967). Maintain sufficient Israeli strength for deterrence but do not allow Israel to become so strong economically and militarily that she can consider preemption or can ignore American diplomatic initiatives.

3. Take advantage of Egyptian and Syrian willingness to consider an opening to the United States. Grant Egypt economic aid, diplomatic honors (e.g. Nixon, Sadat visits), begin a program of military aid. However possible take advantage of Syria's new flexibility vis-à-vis the Soviet Union.

4. As part of this effort, seek a Palestinian formula even in the wake of the Lebanese conflict which would accomplish the following aims: ease the Egyptian position in the Arab world after the September 1975 Israeli-Egyptian Sinai accords, demonstrate U.S. attractiveness to the Syrians, maintain diplomatic momentum, and cover Israel's minimum requirements, thereby justifying American insistence that Jerusalem accept the formula's terms. Until the Palestinians cooperate, staunchly oppose them at the United Nations while indicating a willingness to alter American policy if they revise their posture.

   5. Embrace Israel at the United Nations and in a generous foreign aid program, but maintain a distance in the diplomatic context.

   6. Pursue diplomatic negotiations in the absence of direct Arab-Israeli contacts; demonstrate the American belief that Israel must adjust to a settlement short of normalization—with supplementary guarantees to compensate her.

   7. Increase commercial contacts and trade and sell large quantities of sophisticated arms to Saudi Arabia and Kuwait to maintain their close relations with the United States, to upgrade their "moderate" Arab governments, and to correct the imbalance of trade caused by the rise in oil prices.

   8. Involve the Soviets in the peace settlement process, but only on U.S. terms. Otherwise, keep them out.

   9. Stand up to the Third World at the United Nations, while indicating American willingness to engage in discussions for moderate stakes.

   10. Use the time gained from Arab-Israeli diplomatic momentum to arrange a new era of stability in the international oil industry—thereby preventing future embargoes and precipitous price hikes.

The policy thus devised was a complex enterprise with tradeoffs designed to satisfy various constituencies at home and abroad. In addition, the effort sought to resolve the Sisyphean problems raised by the issues themselves. But differences at home over future directions and the intensity of the Lebanese conflict made Kissinger's task in the area even more difficult. Step-by-step diplomacy was running out of steps; momentum had run out. In the end Kissinger floated off into new fertile areas for his considerable talents—especially southern Africa. The Middle East was left to simmer, leaving the question, What next?

A Middle East settlement can be meaningful only if it breaks down the barriers presently dividing Arabs from Israelis. It cannot endure without concrete acts of reconciliation: an end to belligerent propaganda and boycotts; the creation of telephone, postal, and telegraph links; the establishment of transportation routes between countries; the encouragement of cultural and diplomatic exchanges leading to full-scale diplomatic relations.

Normalization is closest to American conceptions of how international relations should be organized; it is therefore the popular objective. However, for practical reasons, U.S. policy has frequently been closer to the first approach as it has seemed more attainable because of its limited nature. In the crunch, successive administrations have succumbed to the perennial need to demonstrate immediate results. It seemed better to achieve something rather than nothing.

Here lies one of the great tragedies of our diplomacy in the Middle East over the last several years. Because the U.S. government has not made completely clear its commitment to normalization between Arabs and Israelis, we have thereby encouraged the Arabs to assume they could gain a more limited arrangement as they did in 1957. We have in turn led the Israelis to fear that they would be denied authentic acceptance by their Arab neighbors. We have served our own interests poorly as well, for a settlement can bring the tranquillity and stability to the area that our interests demand only if the process of reconciliation between the two sides has been set in motion. Otherwise the United States faces the risk of increased responsibility in a context of greater danger should a settlement which we have sponsored and guaranteed break down.

When considering the details of a settlement, some authorities believe that the Palestinian problem is the heart of the conflict; others, that Israeli occupation of Arab territories captured in 1967 is the central issue; still others that Arab refusal to accept the sovereignty of a non-Arab state in their midst is the primary problem. The latter view is the most compelling, for before 1967 there was no occupied territory and the Arab governments, had they desired, could have created a Palestinian state on the West Bank of the Gaza Strip. Even though the Arab states controlled these territories, Arab-Israeli hostilities persisted. Yet times change and today the territories *are* occupied by Israel and the Palestinian issue *has* become far more pressing than it was in 1967.

The issue we face today is not whether to satisfy Palestinian aspirations, but *how* to satisfy them and *who* should satisfy them. The tragedy of Palestinian history since World War I has been the plague of internal Palestinian division and the absence of responsible, unified, moderate leadership. This description is as applicable today as it was in the 1920s. It is also applicable to most of the Arab world. Many observers suggest that the PLO represents a basic alteration in the traditional pattern of Palestinian political history, but the warfare in Lebanon, the contrasting ideological perspectives of competing groups within the PLO, and the frequent resort to acts of terrorism suggest that the Palestinian extremists are as influential, and as divided, as ever. Therefore it would be foolhardy to support the establishment of a PLO state which would likely be politically unstable and would maintain irredentist claims against both Jordan and Israel. The PLO has demonstrated that if granted power, it would not refrain from acts of aggression against its neighbors. We have the right to ask the Israelis to take risks in the cause of peace, but we do not have the right to ask Israel to risk self-destruction to satisfy a hunch that the PLO might be content with half a loaf.

Fortunately, other routes besides reliance on the PLO might satisfy Palestinian aspirations, for it is erroneous to equate all Palestinians with the warring factions of the Palestine Liberation Organization. First, an autonomous Palestinian province within the Jordanian kingdom is a possible outcome of negotiations. Second, the Palestinians on the West Bank may serve as a leadership pool for a future state or autonomous entity. The Israelis have received little credit for their courage and foresight in conducting elections with a broadened franchise on the West Bank in the spring of 1976. When these elections produced a younger, more nationalist leadership, the Israelis accepted the results even though they were likely to complicate their task of occupation. From the ranks of these new officials may come nationalists who are nonetheless prepared to deal with Israel. The dramatic Israeli "open fences" policy on her northern borders with Lebanon in the wake of civil war there is another reminder that this type of conflict can be healed only by personal contacts. Israeli aid to Lebanese survivors in 1976 suggested the kind of new Middle East that could one day come into existence.

Whatever the consequences, fear of short-term diplomatic set-backs should not allow us to accept any Arab entity as a negotiating partner which does not explicitly recognize the existence and legiti-macy of Israel and does not explicitly indicate its willingness to live in peace with the Jewish state. On the other hand, if a representative Pal-estinian group comes forward which explicitly accepts normalization of relations with Israel and renounces terrorism, we should insist that this body be included in any Middle East negotiations.

In addition to the Palestinian question, any general settlement in the Middle East must necessarily involve Israeli territorial withdrawals. The Arabs seek at a minimum the return of all their lands captured in 1967, while the Israelis seek secure and defensible boundaries on each of their frontiers (which may not mean the return of all territories cap-tured in the Six-Day War). The precise delineation of boundaries must be determined by the parties to the dispute themselves, for it is they who must live with the settlement. To press for a particular resolution against the preferences of one side is to assure resentment and possible irredentism. Therefore, we should not adopt the negotiating posture of either side against the other toward the issue of territories.

We should, however, promote normalization as the only means of achieving a genuine reconciliation. As part of this process, we should encourage the following stages toward reaching a general settlement.

The parties should agree either bilaterally or multilaterally on the end point of their relations. These negotiations may take years, but each party has the right to know what it will receive from a settlement. It should be clear to the Arabs how far Israel will withdraw from oc-cupied territories and it should be clear to Israel how far the Arabs are prepared to move toward normalization. The further the Arabs proceed toward normalization, the easier it should be for Israel to risk more extensive territorial withdrawals. It is often argued that Israel is being asked to grant concrete concessions in the form of territories, while the Arab concessions are vaguer and composed of intentions and sentiments. But the Arabs can demonstrate their intentions and make concrete their concessions through specific acts of denouement in-volved in trade, tourism, and transportation—a process we have al-ready witnessed in "ping pong diplomacy," which began the process of Sino-American détente.

Once the parties have agreed on the substance of a settlement, it should be implemented in previously arranged phases. Israeli withdrawal would be matched by specific acts of normalization on the part of individual Arab states. The two sides would not proceed to the next stage until all aspects of the previous phase had been completed and were mutually acceptable.

The major accomplishment of the Nixon and Ford administrations in the Middle East was to engage several key Arab states in a dialogue with the United States while we maintained close relations with Israel. If our efforts are to succeed in this area, we must be careful not to equate Arab friendship toward the United States with Arab moderation toward Israel.

Whenever Arab-Israeli diplomacy is discussed, some suggest perpetuation of Kissinger's step-by-step approach; others advocate a Geneva conference. But the two are actually complementary. Even if a conference is convened, individual steps taken by one or more parties may contribute to a receptive diplomatic atmosphere. American diplomacy can play a role in encouraging such actions as the suspension of all acts of terrorism and retaliatory raids; the suspension of all boycotts, hostile propaganda and antagonistic acts in international organizations; an agreement to maintain all UN forces in place as long as the conference lasts; the suspension of new settlements in occupied territories. The United States may sponsor such a conference, but our role should be limited to convener, organizer, and "cheerleader." The actual negotiations must be engaged directly between the parties themselves.

It is essential that the United States maintain the closest relations with the state of Israel. It is more important than ever that generous amounts of aid continue to Jerusalem, that American opposition to the Arab boycott be made absolutely clear, and that our support for Israel at the United Nations be vociferous. If Jerusalem and Washington are frequently caught in fraternal but public bickering, Arab governments will conclude that an advantage of their new relationship with the United States is Israeli-American tension. This condition will reduce their willingness to make concessions to Israel because they will conclude American pressure is bound to be forthcoming on the Jewish state. In the end these optimistic Arab assumptions would likely be dashed, with very negative consequences for the policies we will be pursuing.

We need to aim for a situation wherein the Arabs understand our support for Israel and our commitment to Arab-Israeli normalization and nevertheless accept our involvement and mediation. Only this kind of Arab acceptance will enable us to contribute positively to a settlement of the Arab-Israeli dispute. We can reach this goal if we serve as lubricant rather than motor for peace negotiations, if we encourage a peace process without interposing ourselves between the parties. We must maintain our contacts with both sides and support their moves toward settlement. In the final analysis it is the Arabs and Israelis themselves who must achieve reconciliation, and they must be judged by their actions toward each other rather than by their professions of comradeship with the United States.

Arms: The Crisis Imposed by Technology

20   Handicapping the Arms Race

Barry M. Blechman

The United States will spend almost twice as much for defense in the current fiscal year, 1976, as it did in 1964. But the increase is more apparent than real. After inflation is taken account of, and if parts of the budget (like pensions for retired military personnel) that contribute little to military capabilities are taken out of the calculation, quite a different trend emerges: real military spending has declined by about 20 percent in the past 12 years. This decline represents a major change in the nation's priorities. During the same 12-year period, US defense expenditures fell from 8.3 percent of the gross national product and 43 percent of federal outlays, to about 5.8 percent of GNP and 25 percent of the federal budget.

Conversely US intelligence agencies estimate that Soviet military spending has been increasing steadily. Assessments vary, but a good guess seems to be that Soviet defense spending has risen between three and four percent each year, for a cumulative real increase of perhaps 40 percent between 1964 and 1976. As a result there has been a marked change in relative US-Soviet military spending. US defense expenditures, which exceeded those of the Soviet Union by about 20 percent in 1964, are now only about 70 percent of the Soviet total.

The specific extent of the change in relative spending is a matter of dispute. The accuracy of the estimates and the methodology employed to get them have been challenged. But there is no doubt about the direction of the trend: the United States is spending less, and the Soviet Union is spending more; and that has been going on for about a dozen years.

Have these contrasting budgetary trends resulted in important changes in the military balance, or will they soon? And if the balance has been seriously affected does that imply adverse consequences for US foreign policy and for maintaining a relatively stable international political system in the years ahead? On the first question, the facts are clear. There have been important changes—adverse ones. It is true that much of the additional Soviet spending was made necessary by the build-up on the Chinese border. While the United States shifted its military planning from buying forces sufficient to fight two major wars simultaneously to forces adequate for one war, the USSR saw a need to move in the opposite direction. Nonetheless, over the past 12 years, Soviet military capabilities, relative to those of the United States, have improved markedly in three important arenas.

The most dramatic change has occurred in the *strategic nuclear balance,* where the Soviet Union has moved from gross inferiority to rough parity. For example, in 1965, the US held roughly 7-to-1 edge in total equivalent megatonnage—the best static measure of the destructive potential of nuclear weapons. The ratio is now about 1.3-to-1 in favor of the Soviet Union and is likely to increase in the years ahead. The United States still retains a number of advantages in strategic nuclear capabilities. For example, the US lead in the number of independently targetable warheads is still about 3.5-to 1. But Soviet mastery of multiple warhead technology and other advances now emerging from its research program promise to close these remaining gaps during the next decade.

In Europe additional Soviet military spending has been used mainly to improve the quality of the forces deployed there. (The Soviet Union did add five divisions to its Eastern European deployment at the time of the Czech invasion, and has kept them there.) The Soviet military has introduced new kinds of weaponry, such as self-propelled artillery and mobile air defenses. It has increased the number of armored fighting vehicles assigned to each division, and generally has modernized its equipment. In the near future it seems likely that the main area for improvement will be the Soviet tactical air forces—the newest aircraft now entering the Soviet inventory are far more capable than their predecessors. Overall, while there has not been any sudden or dramatic shift in the military balance in Europe, many US and West European defense planners fear that NATO's conventional force posture is becoming increasingly less credible. Should these concerns be transmitted to political leaders—and there are some signs that such a process may be underway—it could raise serious problems for the alliance over time. At the recent NATO meetings, the Socialist governments of Western Europe seemed particularly apprehensive that a diminished American military presence might encourage the Soviets and further strain détente.

Finally *the naval balance.* Here the Soviets have been pursuing a steady program to improve the quality of their fleet. The Soviet navy does seem to have been designed mainly to counter the threats posed to the USSR by Western sea-based strike forces—aircraft carriers and strategic submarines. Moreover the United States retains significant advantages in naval power, notably in sea-based aviation. Nonetheless there has been a marked change in relative naval capabilities over the past 12 years that may have important implications for the future success of US foreign policy. While the USSR has not yet developed a large marine corps with amphibious ships and sea-based air power to back it up, the Soviets have the missile-equipped aircraft and submarines in some regions, like the Eastern Mediterranean, to make the United States think twice before intervening with its own forces.

Of what political significance is all this? Two schools of thought have developed. A "minimalist" discounts the political significance of these changes in the military balance, stressing three factors:

1.) The overriding deterrent effect of the risk of nuclear war. Awareness of the devastation that would accompany a major nuclear exchange has had a sobering effect on the behavior of the super-powers. The fear of nuclear war (even the fear of precipitating a situation in which the likelihood of nuclear war might increase) has caused both superpowers to behave prudently . . . most of the time. Insofar as nothing has happened that promises to end either superpower's ability to destroy the other, should the worst occur, a "minimalist" believes that this restraint is likely to continue. He thus can discount changes in the military balance—*and particularly those in the sector in which change has been most dramatic: the strategic nuclear balance.*

2.) Accommodation in Europe. Here the "minimalist" points mainly to the settlement of past disputes. So what if Soviet military capabilities in Europe are improving, what is there to fight about? The USSR has its buffer zone in Eastern Europe, legitimized at Helsinki this past summer. Germany has apparently given up any thoughts of unification. The Soviet Union has access to the West's capital, technology and food. Risk all that, and more? For what? Certainly not for the fulfillment of an old ideological dream.

3.) The relative insignificance of the superpowers' policies generally, and their armed forces specifically, in determining the course of world affairs. On this point, the "minimalist" emphasizes that for many reasons—nationalism, the global revolution in communications, economic interdependence, the nuclear standoff—crises come and go in world affairs with relatively little effective intervention by the superpowers. In effect, and with few exceptions, the outcomes of local conflicts seem to depend mainly on the relative strengths of local actors. Vietnam demonstrated that conclusively, the "minimalist" says. And if the proposition is not true, how then, for example, does one explain the erosion of the Soviet position in Egypt at precisely the time when Soviet military power in the region was most on the upswing? To the degree that the superpowers do have influence, this view continues, it is likely to depend far more on economic policies, on diplomacy, and on intangible factors like the personalities of their leaders and the wisdom of their policies, than on changes in the military balance.

A "maximalist," one who sees grave political significance in the shift in the military balance, probably finds little to quarrel with in these three points. He is far less sanguine about the future, however, believing as he does that the present fairly equable state of world affairs depends on deliberate policy choices by the USSR. In short, he believes that if things appear calm now, they are only so because the Soviet Union has chosen to keep them that way. And he believes that should the past 10-year trend in the military balance continue for much longer, there will be less restraint in Soviet behavior. The Soviet role in the October 1973 war in the Middle East may be a case in point, he argues. The lack of progress in the negotiations to formally control the military balance in Europe—the MBFR talks—may be another, and the blatant Soviet intervention in Angola a third.

Moreover the "maximalist" is more skeptical about nuclear restraint. If sufficient advantage accrues to the USSR in strategic power, he believes, it will be used, maybe not in a physical sense, but at least in direct support of Soviet policy through nuclear blackmail. Most of all, the "maximalist" sees the changing military balance as a symbol of changing wills. He interprets the United States' reluctance to spend more on defense as a sign of its weariness, its growing isolationism, its overriding preoccupation with individual pursuits. And he believes that military and political leaders in the Soviet Union interpret it in the same way. Conversely he views continuing increases in Soviet military spending as tangible evidence of ominous Soviet intentions, of the very restrictive interpretation that the Soviets place on détente, and of their continuing belief in the inevitability of conflict.

My own view falls somewhere between these two obviously caricatured extremes. Aggregate budgetary comparisons are not very meaningful; for one thing the approach rewards inefficiency. If both nations had precisely the same military capability, the less efficient military establishment would have the larger budget. Nor do I believe that the competition in strategic nuclear weapons is very significant. So long as our secure retaliatory capability is not in question, the maintenance of rough overall parity is quite sufficient to ensure that nuclear weapons do not play a role in the resolution of international conflict. Finally there is little reason to match Soviet involvement in remote corners of the globe. Neither Soviet adventures in Angola, nor the establishment of Soviet bases in Somalia, threaten important US interests. And in all likelihood, just as we so painfully learned in Southeast Asia, the cost of these forays to the Russians will soon exceed any possible benefit.

On the other hand there is nothing to be gained, and potentially much to be lost, by ignoring changes in the military balance. The Soviet military build-up has now passed the point where it could be attributed solely to their quest for equality. Nor can it any longer be lightly passed off as the price the political leadership has had to pay to the Soviet military for a relatively restrained foreign policy. And even if it could, one wonders how long the now expanded military would remain content.

The time has come to expect a sign from the USSR of its seriousness about reaching accommodations with the West—a tangible sign in the form of unilateral restraint in its military expansion. To the degree that there is a US-Soviet arms race today, the pace is set by the USSR. If the Soviets abhor such competition, as they say they do, it is up to Soviet leaders to give meaning to their words. In the absence of such a sign, I think that prudence alone would call for a response from the United

States; a demonstration of willingness to compete in those areas most important to US-Soviet relations: Europe and the Middle East. It is not the United States' capacity to match pertinent advances in Soviet military capabilities that is in question; it is our will to do so. In light of the strident internal discord over Southeast Asia, the continuing imbroglio between Congress and the executive over foreign policy, the virtual paralysis of the presidency within the past few years, questioning should not be unexpected. Changes in the military balance in Europe and the Middle East only heighten these concerns, however. Pointed changes in the US defense budget and military posture might go a long way toward dispelling doubts.

Such a move need not imply an increase in the defense budget. There are sectors of US military spending in which further cuts could be made, sectors that still operate inefficiently or that still fund forces inappropriate for conflicts that are likely to be faced in the years ahead. Yet other sectors, *particularly those that finance conventional forces appropriate for European and Middle Eastern contingencies,* deserve new emphasis. Such moves should include a continuance, and an elaboration, of the changes in the US military posture in Europe prompted by the Nunn amendment and instituted by former Secretary of Defense James R. Schlesinger. And they should also include accelerated modernization schedules for certain kinds of military hardware, as well as far-reaching reforms in the structure of some components of the armed forces.

It is only by demonstrating our ability to match *pertinent* advances in Soviet military capabilities within *realistic* budget ceilings, that Soviet leaders will come to understand the futility, and the dangers, of the present competition. And we can only attain that objective by reordering our military priorities so as to emphasize those forces that would be applicable in the contingencies likely to be encountered in the years ahead.

21 Assuring Strategic Stability in an Era of Détente

Paul H. Nitze

Even though the translation of the Vladivostok Accord on strategic arms into a SALT II Treaty has not yet been resolved, I believe it is now timely to take stock of the strategic arms balance toward which the United States and the Soviet Union would be headed under the terms of such a treaty. To that end it is necessary to raise certain basic questions about the maintenance of strategic stability—in terms of minimizing both the possibility of nuclear war and the possibility that nuclear arms may be used by either side as a means of decisive pressure in key areas of the world.

It appears to be the general belief that while such strategic stability may not be assured by the SALT agreements, it is not and will not be substantially endangered—that on the contrary it has been furthered by the SALT negotiations and agreements since 1969—and that in any event the best hope of stability lies in further pursuit of negotiations with the aim of reducing the level of strategic weapons and delivery systems on both sides. Unfortunately—and to the profound regret of one who has participated both in the SALT negotiations and in a series of earlier U.S. decisions designed to stabilize the nuclear balance—I believe that each of these conclusions is today without adequate foundation.

On the contrary, there is every prospect that under the terms of the SALT agreements the Soviet Union will continue to pursue a nuclear superiority that is not merely quantitative but designed to produce a theoretical war-winning capability. Further, there is a major risk that, if such a condition were achieved, the Soviet Union would adjust its policies and actions in ways that would undermine the present détente situation, with results that could only resurrect the danger of nuclear confrontation or, alternatively, increase the prospect of Soviet expansion through other means of pressure.

While this highly disturbing prospect does not mean that strategic arms limitation should for a moment be abandoned as a U.S. (and world) goal, the practical fact we now face is that a SALT II treaty based on the Vladivostok Accord would *not* provide a sound foundation for follow-on negotiations under present trends. If, and only if, the United States now takes action to redress the impending strategic imbalance, can the Soviet Union be persuaded to abandon its quest for superiority and to resume the path of meaningful limitations and reductions through negotiation.

Finally, I believe that such corrective action *can* be taken: (a) within the framework of the Vladivostok Accord; (b) with costs that would increase the strategic arms budget marginally above present levels (themselves less than half the strategic arms budget we supported from 1956 through 1962, if the dollar values are made comparable); (c) with results that would encourage the diversion of the Soviet effort from its present thrust and in directions compatible with long-range strategic stability. At the close of this article I shall outline the key elements in such a corrective program.

II

Let us start with a brief review of the overall state of Soviet-American relations. The use of the word "détente," in its current sense, began in

1971. U.S. efforts to improve its relations with the Soviet Union go back to 1933. They dominated the War and the immediate postwar period, and the early years of the Eisenhower Administration. They formed an important strand of U.S. foreign policy in both the Kennedy and Johnson Administrations. The word "détente" as currently used implies something different from these efforts; it implies that their goal has now been achieved and that all that remains to be done is to make détente "irreversible."

The chain of events leading to the present situation goes back to the Sino-Soviet split and the great buildup of Soviet forces facing China. There were about 15 Soviet divisions facing China in the mid-1960s; between 1968 and 1972 the number grew to at least 45 divisions. This caused the Chinese Communists to be deeply concerned about the danger of an attack by the Soviet Union on China. The Chinese turned to the one power that could help deter such an attack; they opened the ping-pong diplomacy that resulted in the so-called normalization of U.S. relations with China.

Mr. Nixon was, I think, correct in taking the position that he wished good relations with both China and the U.S.S.R. and did not want an alliance with either. Moscow, however, wanted to be sure that the new relationship between China and ourselves did not deepen into something closer to an alliance and thus impede Soviet policy toward China. For this and other reasons the Russians began to go out of their way to be friendly to Mr. Nixon and Mr. Kissinger. They opened up a vista of relaxation of tensions and of a growing collaboration between the United States and the Soviet Union. In 1972 not only were the SALT I agreements—the Anti-Ballistic Missile (ABM) Treaty and the Interim Agreement—entered into, but also there was signed at Moscow a document called Basic Principles of Relations Between the United States and the Soviet Union. Together with a subsequent agreement signed in Washington in 1973, this laid out what appeared to be a good basis for continuing relations between the U.S.S.R. and ourselves. Among other things, these agreements called for collaboration to see to it that crisis situations in other parts of the world did not build up into confrontations which could increase the risk of war between the two countries. It was understood that this collaboration was to have special reference to Southeast Asia and to the Middle East. These bilateral agreements were accompanied by the Paris Agreements with respect to Vietnam, and the Soviet Union was among those guaranteeing that the Paris Agreements would be implemented and abided by.

These understandings, however, produced no positive Soviet actions. With respect to the final North Vietnamese takeover in Southeast Asia, the Soviets actually took actions to help the North Vietnamese violate the agreements. With respect to the Middle East, it is hard to sustain the argument that is often made that the Soviets exercised restraint in the October 1973 crisis. There appears to have been little that they refrained from doing to encourage and make possible the attack by Egypt and Syria on Israel and the OPEC action on oil prices and the embargo. The Soviets not only trained and equipped the Egyptians and the Syrians for their surprise attack, but also failed to warn us when they knew that an attack was imminent. When the battle turned against the attackers, they threatened to intervene with their forces.

These two experiences in Southeast Asia and in the Middle East are bound to make us skeptical that the Soviet leaders are in fact moving toward any lasting reduction in tensions, or any abandonment of expansionist aims. A further ground for skepticism comes from what Soviet leaders are saying to their own people, and especially what they are saying in authoritative pronouncements aimed at leadership circles. Here readings of the past year are all too clear. To take but one example, there were published in January 1975 companion articles, one by Boris Ponomarev, a deputy member of the Politburo, the other by Aleksandr Sobolev, a leading theoretician, each arguing that the evolution of the correlation of forces—in which they include not only military but economic and social forces—has moved very favorably from the standpoint of the Soviet Union over recent years.[1] Hence, they say, it is now possible to shift the target of communist action from the formerly colonial world to the developed world—particularly Europe. This shift in target is made possible by two things: one of them is "détente" and the other is "nuclear parity" (as they interpret the term, in a way we shall examine shortly).

In the sum total there are strong grounds for concluding that in Soviet eyes "détente" is not that different from what we used to call the "cold war." When we talked about the "cold war" we were in part emphasizing the fact that despite the deep hostility of the U.S.S.R. to the West in general and to the United States in particular, it would be a terrible thing if there were to be a "hot war" with the Soviet Union. When the Soviets use the word "détente" in their internal writings, they make it clear that they intend "détente" to mean the same thing as "peaceful coexistence." Peaceful coexistence, they make it clear, implies no change in their basic objectives, while they expect that current tactics will weaken the West and strengthen the socialist states.[2]

III

However one reads these broader signs of present Soviet behavior, a prime touchstone of the reality of détente—not only now but for the future—must lie in the area of strategic arms. If the Soviets are acting (and negotiating) in a way that gives promise of a stable nuclear balance (with meaningful reduction in due course), then the future of détente is clearly much brighter. If they are not, however, then the disturbing signs must be taken more seriously, and the long-term dangers are great indeed.

Let us begin by discussing the similarities and contrasts between Soviet and American views on certain strategic questions.

"Is the avoidance of war—particularly a nuclear war—between the two countries desirable?" On this question I think both sides are in agreement. However, there is a certain difference of approach. Clausewitz once said that the aggressor never wants war; he would prefer to achieve his objectives without having to fight for them. The Soviets take seriously their doctrine that the eventual worldwide triumph of socialism is inevitable; that they are duty bound to assist this process; and that, as the process progresses, the potential losers may stand at some point and feel impelled to fight back. On the U.S. side some say that there is no alternative to peace and therefore to détente. This attitude misses two points. The first is that capitulation is too high a price for free men. The second is that high-quality deterrence, not unilateral restraint to the point of eroding deterrence, is the surest way of avoiding a nuclear war.

This thus leads to a second pair of questions: "Is nuclear war unthinkable? Would it mean the end of civilization as we know it?" We in the United States tend to think that it is, and this view prevailed (except for a small group of believers in preventive war, who never had strong policy influence) even in the periods when the United States enjoyed a nuclear monopoly and, at a later time, a clear theoretical war-winning capability.[3] When the effort was made in the late 1950s and early 1960s to create a significant civil defense capability, public resistance soon aborted the effort, so that today the United States has only the most minute preparations in this area. Rather, Americans have thought throughout the last 30 years in terms of deterring nuclear war, with the debate centering on how much effort is necessary to maintain deterrence, to keep nuclear war unthinkable.

In the Soviet Union, the view has been quite different. Perhaps initially because of the U.S. monopoly, Soviet leaders from the outset discounted the impact of nuclear weapons to their people. But as the Soviet nuclear capability grew, the Soviet leaders still declined to depict nuclear war as unthinkable or the end of civilization. On the contrary, they directed, and still direct, a massive and meticulously planned civil defense effort, with expenditures that run at approximately a billion dollars a year (compared to U.S. civil defense expenditures of approximately $80 million a year).[4] The average Soviet citizen is necessarily drawn into this effort, and the thinking it represents appears to permeate the Soviet leadership. In the Soviet Civil Defense Manual issued in large numbers beginning in 1969 and 1970, the estimate is made that implementation of the prescribed evacuation and civil defense procedures would limit the civilian casualties to five to eight percent of urban population or three to four percent of the total population—even after a direct U.S. attack on Soviet cities. The Soviets may well overestimate the effectiveness of their civil defense program, but what is plain is that they have made, for 20 years or more, an approach to the problem of nuclear war that does assume, to a degree incomprehensible to Americans (or other Westerners), that nuclear war could happen, and that the Soviet Union could survive.

These differences in approach and attitude appear to be basic and deeply rooted. In essence, Americans think in terms of deterring nuclear war almost exclusively. The Soviet leaders think much more of what might happen in such a war. To the extent that humanitarian and moral objections to the use of nuclear weapons exist in the Soviet

Union—as of course they do—such objections are subordinated for practical planning purposes to what Soviet leaders believe to be a realistic view.

It may be argued that these differences are more apparent than real, and that with the passage of time and the emergence of near-equality in the respective nuclear capabilities the differences are today less significant. Unfortunately, as the civil defense picture suggests, the trend in comparative nuclear weapons capabilities has if anything accentuated them.

That this is so can be seen in the more concrete realm of nuclear strategic concepts, and the postures that result from them. Often over-refined or expressed in terms hard for the layman to grasp, the range of strategic nuclear concepts available to any nuclear-weapons nation in fact boils down roughly to five:

1. *Minimum Deterrence.* This means a capacity to destroy a few key cities with little if any counterforce capacity to attack a hostile nation's military forces. In essence, it relies on the threat alone to deter. As between the Soviet Union and the United States, in the event deterrence failed, this level of American capacity would concede to the Soviet Union the potential for a military and political victory. The Soviets would risk U.S. retaliation against a portion of their industry and population, if our action policy in the event deterrence failed turned out to be the same as our declaratory policy before deterence failed. To reduce this risk of retaliation, the Soviets could limit their attack to U.S. forces and continue to hold the U.S. population as hostage. In sum, the effect of this level of deterrence would be to provide limited deterrence of a full-scale attack on the U.S. population. It would have less strength in deterring a Soviet attack on U.S. forces or on allies whose security is essential to our own.

2. *Massive Urban/Industrial Retaliation.* As the name implies, this posture is designed to destroy many cities, many millions of people and much productive capacity, and to do so on an assured second-strike basis. This level of deterrence, sometimes called "Assured Destruction," would concede to the Soviet Union the potential for a military victory if deterrence failed, but (it would be anticipated) would make any such victory worthless in political terms. This form of deterrence differs from minimum deterrence largely in the degree of damage to Soviet industry and population it would threaten.

3. *Flexible Response.* In this form of deterrence the United States would have the capability to react to a Soviet counterforce attack without going immediately to a counter-city attack. It would thus increase the credibility of deterrence. The question of military or political victory if deterrence fails would depend upon the net surviving destructive capacity of the two sides after the initial counterforce exchanges. If the net surviving capacity after such a flexible response were grossly to favor the Soviet Union, or if each limited exchange placed the United States in a progressively weaker relative position, we are back to the minimum deterrence or massive urban/industrial retaliation situation, depending on the amount of surviving effective nuclear capability on the U.S. side.

4. *Denial of a Nuclear-War-Winning Capability to the Other Side.* This means a nuclear posture such that, even if the other side attacked first and sought to destroy one's own strategic striking power, the result of such a counterforce exchange would be sufficiently even and inconclusive that the duel would be extremely unattractive to the other side. This level of deterrence, in addition to deterring an attack on U.S. population centers, should also deter a Soviet attack on U.S. forces or those of its allies. In practice, against any major nuclear nation, the posture would also include a capacity for effective massive urban/industrial retaliation if such a strategy were called for.

5. *A Nuclear-War-Winning Capability.* This would be a position so superior that, whatever the initial forms of nuclear exchange, one's own surviving capacity would be enough to destroy the war-making ability of the other nation without comparable return damage. Such a U.S. posture would deter any Soviet attack on the United States and could also limit other serious Soviet military initiatives contrary to U.S. and allied interests. However, Soviet weapons technology and program momentum are such that the United States probably could not obtain this capability.

A review of the choices made by the United States and the Soviet Union among these five concepts goes, I believe, further than any other form of analysis in explaining and clarifying the changes in the strategic balance since 1945. Until roughly 1954, the United States retained nuclear superiority without extraordinary effort. By the late 1950s, the vulnerability of American bomber bases (bombers then being the only effective delivery method) emerged as a serious weakness in the American posture.[5] This weakness, and the rapid advances in missile technology of the period, led the United States between 1956 and 1962 to place great emphasis on ensuring the survivability of its nuclear striking power; average strategic obligational authority during these years was about $18 billion a year in 1974 dollars.[6] As a result the feared intercontinental ballistic missile (ICBM) "gap" of the 1960 presidential campaign never in fact became reality, but on the contrary the United States re-established a clearly superior nuclear capability by 1961–62. This was the situation at the time of the only true nuclear confrontation of the postwar period, the Cuban missile crisis of the fall of 1962.

Up to that point something approaching a war-winning capability seemed to most Americans the best possible form of deterrence, and thus desirable. However, as it became clear that the Soviet Union, too, was developing massive and survivable missile delivery capabilities, this view changed to the belief that even though a nuclear war might be won in a purely military sense, it could not be won in a political sense. That led to the further view that mutual deterrence through mutually assured destruction was the best feasible objective.

I have explained elsewhere at greater length the decisions of the early 1960s, in which I was one of those who participated with Robert McNamara, then Secretary of Defense.[7] In essence, the United States opted at that point to stress technological improvement rather than expanded force levels. While numerical comparisons were not ignored, the basic aim was an underlying condition of what may be called "crisis stability," a situation where neither side could gain from a first strike, and of "mutual assured destruction," where each side would have a fully adequate second-strike capability to deter the other. In such a condition it was believed that neither could realistically threaten the other in the area of strategic weapons, and that the result would be much greater stability and higher chances of the peaceful resolution of crises if they did occur. While nuclear weapons would always be a major deterrent, the conventional arms balance at any point of confrontation would remain important (as it had been in the Berlin crisis of 1958–62 and also in the Cuban missile crisis itself). In short, the aim was to downgrade nuclear weapons as an element in U.S.-Soviet competition and to prepare the way for systematic reductions in nuclear arms. If both sides were to adopt such a concept, it should be possible, over time, to move from what might be called a "high deterrent" posture to a "low deterrent" posture, with the deterrent remaining essentially equivalent on both sides but at successively lower levels.

As the United States thus adjusted its posture, the invitation for the Soviet Union likewise to seek a similar posture—and stop there—was patent both from statements of American policy and from the always-visible American actions. Unfortunately, however, the Soviet Union chose to pursue a course that was ambiguous: it could be interpreted as being aimed at overtaking the United States but then stopping at parity; it could, however, be interpreted as being aimed at establishing superiority in numbers of launchers and in throw-weight[8] and, perhaps ultimately, a nuclear-war-winning capability on the Soviet side.

It is important to consider the reasons that may have entered into this choice. In part, the Soviet leaders may have been motivated by technological factors—that they had already moved to heavy rockets but were behind in other areas, such as solid propellant technology, accuracy and MIRVing (the development of multiple, independently targetable reentry vehicles). In part, there may have been an element of traditional Soviet emphasis on mass and size. But it is hard to avoid the conclusion that an important factor was the reading the Soviet leaders gave to the Cuban missile crisis and, to a lesser extent, the Berlin crisis. In the latter case, Khrushchev had briefly sought to exploit the first Soviet rocket firings of 1957—by a series of threats to Berlin beginning in late 1958—but then found that the West stood firm and that the United States quickly moved to reestablish its strategic superiority beyond doubt. And in the Cuban missile case, the very introduction of the missiles into Cuba in the fall of 1962 must have reflected a desire to redress the balance by quick and drastic action, while the actual outcome of the crisis seemed to the Soviet leaders to spell out that nuclear superiority in a crunch would be an important factor in determining who prevailed.

Harking back to the Soviet penchant for actually visualizing what would happen in the event of nuclear war, it seems highly likely that the Soviet leaders, in those hectic October days of 1962, did something that U.S. leaders, as I know from my participation, did only in more general terms—that is, ask their military just how a nuclear exchange would come out. They must have been told that the United States would be able to achieve what they construed as victory, that the U.S. nuclear posture was such as to be able to destroy a major portion of Soviet striking power and still itself survive in a greatly superior condition for further strikes if needed. And they must have concluded that such a superior capability provided a unique and vital tool for pressure in a confrontation situation. It was a reading markedly different from the American internal one, which laid much less stress on American nuclear superiority and much more on the fact that the United States controlled the sea lanes to Cuba and could also have expected to prevail in any conflict over Cuba waged with conventional arms.[9]

One cannot prove that this was the Soviet reasoning. But the programs they set under way about 1962—above all the new family of weapons systems, embodying not only numbers and size but also greatly advanced technology, the development and deployment of which began to be evident beginning in 1971 but which must have been decided upon some years earlier—seem to reflect a fundamental state of mind on the Soviet side that contains no doubt as to the desirability of a war-winning capability, *if feasible*. Believing that evacuation, civil defense and recuperation measures can minimize the amount of damage sustained in a war, they conclude that they should be prepared if necessary to accept the unavoidable casualties. On the other hand, the loss of a war would be irretrievable. Therefore, the best deterrent is a war-winning capability, if that is attainable.

There have been, and I believe still are, divisions of opinion on the Soviet side as to whether such a capability *is* feasible. There are those who have argued that the United States is a tough opponent with great technical expertise and that the United States can be expected to do whatever is necessary to deny such a war-winning capability to the Soviet side. Others have taken the view that the developing correlation of forces—social, economic and political as well as military and what they call the deepening crisis of capitalism—may prevent the United States and its allies from taking the necessary countermeasures and that the target of a war-winning capability, therefore, is both desirable and feasible. Again, this is not to say that Soviet leaders would desire to initiate a nuclear war even if they had a war-winning capability. They would, however, consider themselves duty bound by Soviet doctrine to exploit fully that strategic advantage through political or limited military means.

IV

The SALT negotiations got under way in late 1969. As a participant in those talks from then until mid-1974, I have described elsewhere some of the difficulties that attended the U.S. side.[10] What was most fundamental was that the U.S. delegation sought at every level and through every form of contact to bring home to the Soviet delegation, and the leaders behind it, the desirability of limitations which would assure "crisis stability" and "essential equivalence"—and that the Soviet side stoutly resisted these efforts.

Indeed, the negotiations very early revealed other major stumbling blocks. One, in particular, revolved around the Soviet conception of "strategic parity." In the SALT negotiations the U.S. delegation consistently argued for the acceptance by both sides of the concept of "essential equivalence." By that we meant that both sides did not have to be exactly equal in each component of their nuclear capabilities but that overall the nuclear strategic capability of each side should be essentially equal to that of the other and at a level, one could hope, lower than that programmed by the United States. The Soviets have never accepted this concept, but have argued instead for the concept of "equal security taking into account geographic and other considerations." In explaining what they meant by "geographic and other considerations," they said that, "The U.S. is surrounded by friendly countries. You have friends all around the oceans. We, the U.S.S.R., are surrounded by enemies. China is an enemy and Europe is a potential enemy. What we are asking for is that our security be equal to yours taking into account these considerations." They never went so far as to say that this really amounts to a requirement for Soviet superiority in capabilities over the United States, the U.K., France and China simultaneously, but watching the way they added things up and how they justified their position, this is what it boiled down to.

Yet the two sides were able to reach agreement in May of 1972 on stringent limitations on the deployment of ABM interceptor missiles ABM launchers and ABM radars and on an Interim Agreement temporarily freezing new offensive missile-launcher starts.

After the May 1972 signing of the ABM Treaty and the Interim Agreement, it turned out that the two sides had quite different views as to how the negotiating situation had been left. On the U.S. side, we told the Congress that the Interim Agreement was intended to be merely a short-term freeze on new missile-launcher starts, and that this, together with the ABM Treaty, should create favorable conditions for the prompt negotiation of a more complete and balanced long-term agreement on offensive strategic arms to replace the Interim Agreement and be a complement to the ABM Treaty. Both sides had agreed promptly to negotiate a more complete agreement to replace the Interim Agreement. And the Interim Agreement specifically provided that its provisions were not to prejudice the scope or terms of such a replacement agreement. We thought such a replacement agreement should be based, as was the ABM Treaty, on the principles of equality in capabilities, greater stability in the nuclear relationship between the two sides, and a mutual desire to reduce the resources committed to strategic arms.

However, the Soviet Union had a quite different view. Its negotiators held that in accepting the Interim Agreement we had conceded that the Soviet Union was entitled to an advantage for an indefinite time of some 40 percent in the number of missile launchers and something better than double the average effective size, or throw-weight, of their missiles over ours. In working out a more complete and longer term agreement, in their view, all that was necessary was to add strict and equal limits on bombers and their armaments, provide for the withdrawal of our nuclear forces deployed in support of our allies capable of striking Soviet territory, and half our B-1 and Trident programs but not the "modernization" of their systems. The difference of position between the two sides was such that it was difficult to see how agreement could be reached.

In the Vladivostok Accord of December 1974 the Soviets did make concessions from their past extremely one-sided negotiating demands. Those concessions were greater than many in the U.S. executive branch expected. However, does the Accord promise to result in achieving the objectives which the United States has for many years thought should be achieved by a long-term agreement on offensive forces? Those objectives were parity, or essential equivalence, between the offensive capabilities on the two sides, the maintenance of high-quality mutual deterrence and a basis for reducing strategic arms expenditures. I believe it does not.

The Vladivostok Accord, in essence, limits the total number of strategic launchers—ICBMs, submarine-launched ballistic missiles (SLBMs) and heavy strategic bombers, to 2,400 on both sides, and the number of MIRVed missile launchers to 1,320 on both sides. It limits the Soviet Union to the number of modern large ballistic launchers (MLBMs) that they now have, while prohibiting the United States from deploying any modern launchers in this category.[11] The Accord calls for air-to-surface missiles with a range greater than 600 kilometers, carried by heavy bombers, to be counted against the 2,400 ceiling. The treaty would allow freedom to mix between the various systems subject to these limitations.

As this article goes to press, there still remain some things to be cleared up: Secretary Kissinger has said that there was a misunderstanding concerning air-to-surface missiles (ASMs), that our understanding was that only *ballistic* air-to-surface missiles of greater than 600-kilometer range are to be included in the 2,400 launcher limit, not *cruise* missiles.[12] That is being argued between the two sides at the present time. There is also a question about mobile missiles, particularly land-mobile missiles: Should they be banned or should they be permitted and counted against the 1,320 and 2,400 ceilings? And there is the open question of what constitutes a "heavy bomber." The Soviets are building a plane called the "Backfire" whose gross take-off weight is three-quarters that of the B-1 and which is two and a half times as big as our FB-III. It is a very competent plane, more competent than some of the planes they now agree should be defined to be heavy bombers. The Soviets say the Backfire should not be included in the category of heavy bombers because "we don't intend to use it in that role." However, it can in fact carry, even without refueling (and it is equipped to be refueled), a significant payload to intercontinental distances if the aircraft is recovered in a third country. The way the Vladivostok Accord reads, air-to-surface missiles in excess of 600 kilometers in range, if not carried on a heavy bomber, are not required to be counted at all. So Backfires and FB-111s with long-range missiles would not count in any way against anything. These problems must be resolved in order to have a meaningful agreement.

Then there are the problems of verification. Messrs. Kissinger and Gromyko have been trying to work out a compromise on the verification issue. I personally take the verification issue less seriously than most because the limits are so high that what could be gained by cheating against them would not appear to be strategically significant.[13] However, we should be careful not to establish a precedent which would cause trouble if more meaningful limitations were agreed upon.

A notable feature of the Vladivostok Accord is that it does not deal with throw-weight. The agreement would not effectively check the deployment of the new Soviet family of large, technically improved and MIRVed offensive missiles. While both sides are permitted equal numbers of MIRVed missiles, the new Soviet SS-19s have three times the throw-weight of the U.S. Minuteman III, and the new SS-18s, seven times. What this comes down to is that under the Accord the Soviets can be expected to have a total of about 15 million pounds of missile throw-weight and bomber throw-weight equivalent. If the Congress goes forward with the B-1 and the Trident system but the United States does not add further strategic programs, the Soviets can be expected to end up with an advantage of at least three-to-one in missile throw-weight and of at least two-to-one in overall throw-weight, including a generous allowance for the throw-weight equivalent of heavy bombers, and two-to-one or three-to-one in MIRVed missile throw-weight. This disparity leaves out of consideration the Backfire, the FB-111, and the highly asymmetrical advantage in air defenses that the Soviet Union enjoys.[14]

Thus, the Vladivostok Accord, while a considerable improvement upon the prior negotiating positions presented by the Soviet Union, continues to codify a potentially unstable situation caused by the large disparity in throw-weight, now being exploited by Soviet technological improvements.

V

The prospects for SALT III center on reductions in the strategic forces on both sides, an aim of the SALT talks since their inception. My personal view is that meaningful reductions are highly desirable, and that the aim of reductions should be to increase strategic stability. But this aim is not served by reducing numbers of launchers, unless throw-weight is also reduced and made more equal.[15]

The agreed reduction of the throw-weight of large, land-based MIRVed missiles, however, would increase stability. I see no reason why the Soviet Union needs to replace its SS-9s with SS-18s, nor why it needs to replace a large number of its SS-11s with SS-19s. Although it is perfectly feasible and permissible under the Vladivostok Accord for us to develop missiles of equally large or even greater throw-weight than the SS-19s and fit them in Minuteman III silos, would it not be far better for both sides if there were sub-limits of, say, 50 on the number of SS-18s the Soviets were permitted to deploy and 500 or less on the number of SS-19 and SS-17 class ICBMs that either side was permitted to deploy? Even in a context of no other changes in the postures of the two countries, the reduction in missiles to these numbers would change the missile throw-weight asymmetry to one-and-a-half to one.

It might then be more feasible to work out subsequent reductions in numbers of vehicles which would include the Soviet older unMIRVed missiles, such as the SS-9, along with our Minuteman II and Titan. But in the absence of throw-weight limitations of some sort, reduction per se will not improve stability.

However, the Russians are opposed to considering throw-weight limitations and have also taken the position that a future negotiation for reductions has to take into account all forward-based systems—all the systems we have in Europe and in East Asia, and on aircraft carriers. Thus, it is hard to see how we can have high hopes of getting anything in SALT III that will provide relief for the anticipated strain on the U.S. strategic posture as the Soviet deployments proceed and as their accuracy improves.

VI

The country as a whole has looked at strategic nuclear problems during the last six years in the context of SALT, hoping to make the maintenance of our national security easier through negotiations. It now appears, however, for the reasons outlined above, that we are not likely to get relief from our nuclear strategic problems through this route. Therefore, we have to look at our strategic nuclear posture in much the way we used to look at it before the SALT negotiations began and determine what is needed in the way of a nuclear strategy for the United States and what kind of posture is needed to support it. A fundamental aim of nuclear strategy and the military posture to back it up must be deterrence: the failure to deter would be of enormous cost to the United States and to the world.

Once again, two important distinctions should be borne in mind: the distinction between the concept of "deterrence" and the concept of "military strategy," and the accompanying distinction between "declaratory policy" and "action policy." Deterrence is a political concept; it deals with attempts by indications of capability and will to dissuade the potential enemy from taking certain actions. Military strategy deals with the military actions one would, in fact, take if deterrence fails. A responsible objective of military strategy in this event would be to bring the war to an end in circumstances least damaging to the future of our society.

From the U.S. standpoint, just to level a number of Soviet cities with the anticipation that most of our cities would then be destroyed would not necessarily be the implementation of a rational military strategy. Deterrence through the threat of such destruction thus rests on the belief that in that kind of crisis the United States would act irrationally and in revenge. Yet serious dangers can arise if there is such a disparity between declaratory deterrence policy and the actual military strategy a nation's leaders would adopt if deterrence fails—*or* if there is a belief by the other side that such a disparity would be likely. I think former Secretary James Schlesinger's flexible response program was, in effect, an attempt to get our declaratory policy closer to a credible action policy and thus improve deterrence.

Ultimately, the quality of that deterrence depends importantly on the character and strength of the U.S. nuclear posture versus that of the Soviet Union. In assessing its adequacy, one may start by considering our ability to hold Soviet population and industry as hostages, in the face of Soviet measures to deter or hedge against U.S. retaliation directed at such targets.

In 1970 and 1971—when the focus was almost exclusively on "mutual assured destruction"—the congressional debates on whether or not to deploy a U.S. anti-ballistic missile system recognized clearly the importance to deterrence of hostage populations. Critics of the ABM argued—and with decisive impact on the outcome of the debate—that an effective ABM defense of urban/industrial centers could be destabilizing to the nuclear balance: if side *A* (whether the United States or the U.S.S.R) deployed an ABM defense of its cities, side *B* could no longer hold side *A*'s population as a hostage to deter an attack by *A* on *B*. And in 1972 the same argument carried weight in the negotiation and ratification of the ABM limits in the SALT I agreements.

Yet today the Soviet Union has adopted programs that have much the same effect on the situation as an ABM program would have. And as the Soviet civil defense program becomes more effective it tends to destabilize the deterrent relationship for the same reason: the United States can then no longer hold as significant a proportion of the Soviet population as a hostage to deter a Soviet attack. Concurrently, Soviet industrial vulnerability has been reduced by deliberate policies, apparently adopted largely for military reasons, of locating three-quarters of new Soviet industry in small and medium-sized towns. The civil defense program also provides for evacuation of some industry and materials in time of crisis.

In sum, the ability of U.S. nuclear power to destroy without question the bulk of Soviet industry and a large proportion of the Soviet population is by no means as clear as it once was, even if one assumes most of U.S. striking power to be available and directed to this end.

A more crucial test, however, is to consider the possible results of a large-scale nuclear exchange in which one side sought to destroy as much of the other side's striking power as possible, in order to leave itself in the strongest possible position after the exchange. As already noted, such a counterforce strategy appears to fit with Soviet ways of thinking and planning; it is a strategy we must take into account.

Tables I and II, located on page 291, apply this test over a period of years running from 1960 to (as it happens) 1984. For past periods,

TABLE I: Soviet-U.S. Throw-Weight Ratios

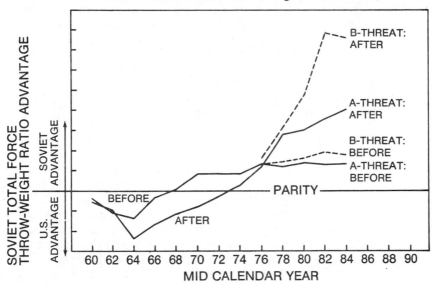

TABLE II: Soviet-U.S. Throw-Weight Differentials

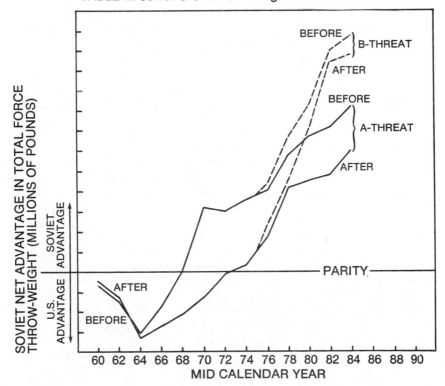

fairly assured estimates are available for both sides. For future years, a median estimate of U.S. programs, based on published data, has been used, while on the Soviet side there are two alternative projections—an "A-threat" based on a representative estimate of Soviet force deployments and accuracy capabilities, and a "B-threat" reflecting the possibility of increased Soviet emphasis on accuracy and other strategic force factors. Both forces are assessed in terms of total available throw-weight, measuring this directly for assumed missile inventories and making full allowance for the bomber equivalent of missile throw-weight for both sides.[16]

The Tables assume an exchange in which the Soviet Union has attacked U.S. forces, and the United States has retaliated by trying to reduce Soviet strategic throw-weight to the greatest extent possible. To assess the opposing forces *before* attack in terms of their relative throw-weight is of course only a partial measure of their comparative original capability. In working out what would actually happen in the assumed exchange, full account has been taken of all relevant factors—in particular the number, yield, accuracy and reliability of the reentry vehicles associated with that throw-weight, and the hardness of the targets against which they are assumed to have been targeted.

It is the situation *after* attack, of course, that is most important. And here, since the targets remaining after the exchange would almost all be soft ones, missile accuracy and other refinements in the original postures no longer have the same significance. Surviving throw-weight thus becomes an appropriate *total* measure of the residual capability on both sides.

As worked out by Mr. T. K. Jones, who served as my senior technical advisor when I was a member of the U.S. SALT delegation, the results of such an assessment are shown in Table I, expressed in terms of the ratios, and Table II, expressed in terms of the absolute units of weight—by which one side exceeds the other before and after attack in the various periods and alternative cases examined.[17]

Based on this method of assessment, the United States in 1960 held a slight but increasing advantage over the Soviet Union, and this advantage became greatest in about mid-1964. Thereafter, however, Soviet programs—greatly accelerated, as earlier noted, after the Cuban missile crisis—started to reverse the trend, so that by mid-1968 the total deployed throw-weights on both sides, before a hypothetical nuclear exchange, were roughly equal. However, as the "after" curve shows, the U.S. operational military advantage persisted for some time thereafter, offsetting the Soviet superiority in deployed throw-weight. For example, if in 1970 the Soviets had attacked U.S. forces, their entire prewar advantage would have been eliminated, leaving the United States with substantial superiority at the end of the exchange. However, this situation began to be reversed in 1973, with the Soviets gaining the military capability to end an exchange with an advantage in their favor. Moreover, in 1976 the "before" and "after" curves of Table I cross, signifying that the Soviets could, by initiating such an exchange, increase the ratio of advantage they held at the start of the exchange.

By 1977, after a Soviet-initiated counterforce strike against the United States to which the United States responded with a counterforce strike, the Soviet Union would have remaining forces sufficient to destroy Chinese and European NATO nuclear capability, attack U.S. population and conventional military targets, and still have a remaining force throw-weight in excess of that of the United States. And after 1977 the Soviet advantage after the assumed attack mounts rapidly.

In addition to the ratios and absolute differences that apply to the remaining throw-weights of the two sides, there is a third factor which should be borne in mind. That factor is the absolute level of the forces remaining to the weaker side. If that absolute level is high, continues under effective command and control, and is comprised of a number of reentry vehicles (RVs) adequate to threaten a major portion of the other side's military and urban/industrial targets, this will be conducive to continued effective deterrence even if the ratios are unfavorable. These considerations reinforce the desirability of survivable systems and methods of deployment.

VII

In sum, the trends in relative military strength are such that, unless we move promptly to reverse them, the United States is moving toward a posture of minimum deterrence in which we would be conceding to the Soviet Union the potential for a military and political victory if deterrence failed. While it is probably not possible and may not be politically desirable for the United States to strive for a nuclear-war-winning capability, there are courses of action available to the United States whereby we could deny to the Soviets such a capability and remove the one-sided instability caused by their throw-weight advantage and by their civil defense program.

To restore stability and the effectiveness of the U.S. deterrent: (1) the survivability and capability of the U.S. strategic forces must be such that the Soviet Union could not foresee a military advantage in attacking our forces, and (2) we must eliminate or compensate for the one-sided instability caused by the Soviet civil defense program. Specifically, we must remove the possibility that the Soviet Union could profitably attack U.S. forces with a fraction of their forces and still maintain reserves adequate for other contingencies.

As to the civil-defense aspect, the absence of a U.S. capability to protect its own population gives the Soviet Union an asymmetrical possibility of holding the U.S. population as a hostage to deter retaliation following a Soviet attack on U.S. forces. Although the most economical and rapidly implementable approach to removing this one-sided instability would be for the United States to pursue a more active civil defense program of its own, such a program does not appear to be politically possible at this time. Its future political acceptability will be a function of the emerging threat and its appreciation by U.S. leadership and by the public.

Two more practicable avenues of action suggest themselves. First, all of the options which would be effective in diminishing the one-sided Soviet advantage involve some improvement in the *accuracy* of U.S. missiles. Differential accuracy improvements can, at least temporarily, compensate for throw-weight inequality.

This is a controversial issue which has been studied extensively. The results of one such study by a member of Congress are shown in the *Congressional Record* of May 20, 1975. According to that study the United States presently holds a 4:1 superiority in the hard-target kill capability of missile forces. The Congressman notes in his opposition to a U.S. high-accuracy maneuvering reentry vehicle (MaRV) program that MaRV would by the late 1980s improve U.S. accuracy to .02 n.m. (120 feet), incorrectly estimating that this would increase the U.S. advantage to 7:1 over the U.S.S.R.—assuming the latter was unable to develop MaRV by that time. However, the Congressman's data also predict that the hard-target kill capability of the Soviet missile force will by the 1980s have increased 100-fold, so that if the United States took no action to improve the accuracy of its missiles, the Soviet Union would have an advantage of 25:1. While it is unnecessary to equip more than a portion of U.S. missiles with high-accuracy RVs, it is clear that substantial accuracy improvements are essential to avoid major Soviet superiority in a critical respect.

Others argue that improvements in U.S. missile accuracy would be "destabilizing." More specifically, such programs "could spur Soviet countermeasures such as new programs to increase their second-strike capabilities by going to (1) more sea-launched strategic missiles, (2) air- and sea-launched cruise missiles, (3) expanded strategic bomber forces, and (4) mobile ICBMs."[18] These arguments ignore the central fact that deterrence is already being seriously undermined by unilateral actions of the Soviet Union. Hence, further self-restraint by the United States cannot but worsen this condition.

Moreover, the Soviet programs cited as consequences of U.S. accuracy improvement are in fact stabilizing rather than destabilizing. Under the SALT agreements on force ceilings, such reactions would compel offsetting reductions in the Soviet silo-based ICBM force, thereby reducing their total force throw-weight. Moreover, the replacement ICBM systems are not likely to achieve accuracy equal to that of the silo-based ICBMs, while throw-weight moved to bombers and cruise missiles, because of the long flight time to targets, cannot be effectively used in a first-strike counterforce role.

In sum, even on the information furnished by those generally opposing improved accuracy of U.S. missiles, improvement *is* necessary to avoid a major Soviet advantage, and the logical Soviet counter to such improvements would move the Soviets in a direction which would stabilize the strategic relationship and reduce the Soviet throw-weight advantage.

Second, the prospective Soviet advantage could be offset by measures to decrease the *vulnerability* of U.S. strategic nuclear forces. Here there are several ongoing programs already under way, notably the development of the Trident submarine and the B-1 bomber; both these delivery systems will be inherently less vulnerable to a counterforce attack than fixed ICBM installations, the submarine by reason of its mobility at sea and the B-1 by virtue of its mobility and escape speed as well as the potential capacity to maintain a portion of the B-1 force airborne in time of crisis. In addition, programs to increase the pre-launch survivability of U.S. bomber forces generally, as well as programs to increase air defense capability through the so-called AWACS system, operate to reduce vulnerability of the total U.S. force. To a considerable extent, however, these programs are already taken into account in the calculations shown on Tables I and II—if they were to be delayed, the effect would be negative, and the contrary if they were to be stepped up and accelerated.

I believe, however, that these measures do not go far enough. The most vulnerable U.S. delivery system today is that of our fixed and hardened ICBM installations, including Minuteman silos. Under present trends, it is only a question of time until a combination of the large throw-weight available to the Soviets and improved accuracy will threaten the destruction of a high percentage of these installations—so that today there is considerable talk in some quarters of actually phasing out U.S. ICBM installations.

I believe such action would be unwise, and that it is entirely feasible, at not excessive cost, to adopt a new system of deployment that would not only permit the retention of our ICBMs—which contribute heavily to the total U.S. throw-weight—but would actually make these a more critical and effective component of the U.S. striking force. The system that would accomplish these ends would be a proliferation of low-cost shelters for what is called a multiple launch-point system. The essence of such a system would be to construct a large number of shelter installations, so that the smaller number of actual missile launchers could be readily moved and deployed among these installations on a random pattern deliberately varied at adequate intervals of time.

The ingredients for such a system are, I believe, already in existence, notably through the availability of sufficiently large areas of western desert land now owned by the Department of Defense. On this land there could be created a large number of hardened shelters, or alternatively the missiles themselves could be encased in hardened capsules redeployable among a large number of "soft" shelters. Preliminary study indicates that the research, development and procurement costs of a system along these lines would average approximately $1.5 billion a year in 1975 dollars over the next eight to ten years. Inasmuch as the current level of obligational authority for strategic weapons systems is on the order of $7 billion per year—much less, as already noted, than the comparable amounts obligated annually in 1956–62—I believe this is a cost we should be prepared to accept.

The objective of creating such a new system of deployment would be to greatly increase the throw-weight costs to the Soviets of destroying a substantial portion of our deterrent forces. This is achieved with a multiple launch-point system, since in order to destroy the system virtually all of the relevant shelter installations would need to be destroyed. There would be many more hardened shelters or encapsulated missiles than the present number of fixed installations, so that the Soviets would be required to commit a larger portion of their throw-weight to this task than they would to the task of attacking fixed installations—the trade-off of U.S. throw-weight destroyed to Soviet throw-weight used would greatly favor the United States. Thus the Soviet advantage in a counterforce exchange would be drastically reduced or eliminated.

Furthermore, I believe that such a U.S. move would be likely to lead to Soviet countermoves that would have a constructive impact on the overall balance. The logical answer to such a U.S. move would be for the Soviet side to substitute either multiple launch-point missiles or SLBMs for a portion of their large fixed ICBMs. They would thereby increase the survivability of their systems, but at the cost of substantially reducing their throw-weight advantage. Such moves by both sides would greatly improve crisis stability and thus significantly reduce the risk of a nuclear war.

In essence, the multiple launch-point idea is a method of preserving and increasing the effectiveness of land-based systems by making them partially mobile. It is, however, necessary to take account of the usual argument advanced for banning land-based mobile missile systems. This argument is that it is more difficult to verify with confidence the number of mobile and thus redeployable launchers deployed by either side than it is to verify the number of fixed silos. The merit of this argument fades in a situation where up to 10 or 12 million pounds of MIRVed throw-weight can be expected to be available to the Soviet side under the limits contemplated by the Vladivostok Accord. With improved accuracy, less than four million pounds of MIRVed throw-weight could threaten the destruction of a high percentage of the fixed silos on the U.S. side. No practicable addition through unverified mobile launchers to the 10 to 12 million pounds of throw-weight permitted the Soviet side would compensate strategically for the additional throw-weight requirement that a U.S. multiple launch-point system would impose. A significant portion of a U.S. multiple launch-point system should survive even if the Soviet Union were to devote to the task of attacking it double the four million pounds of MIRVed throw-weight it would have to allocate to the destruction of our Minuteman silos.[19]

Undoubtedly, there are other programs which would also be necessary. In particular, it would seem to be essential, if the Soviet Union is to be permitted an unlimited number of Backfires, that we not grant them a free ride for their bomber forces. This would require a reversal of congressional action limiting support for the AWACS program. But taking everything into consideration, the magnitude of the U.S. effort required would be far less than that which we undertook in the 1957–1962 period in response to Sputnik and the then-threatened vulnerability of our bomber force.

VIII

Some of my friends argue that those knowledgeable about such matters should bear in mind the horrors of a nuclear war, and should call for U.S. restraint in the hope the U.S.S.R. will follow our lead. Having been in charge of the U.S. Strategic Bombing Survey team of 500 physicists and engineers who measured the detailed effects of the two nuclear weapons used at Nagasaki and Hiroshima, the only two such weapons ever used in anger, and having been associated with many of the subsequent studies of the probable effects of the more modern weapons, I am fully sensitive to the first point. But to minimize the risks of nuclear war, it would seem to me wise to assure that no enemy could believe he could profit from such a war.

As to the second point, Helmut Sonnenfeldt, Counselor for the State Department, recently described the preconditions for the U.S. détente policy in the following terms:

> The course on which we embarked requires toughness of mind and steadfastness of purpose. It demands a sober view not only of Soviet strengths but of our own. It is an attempt to evolve a balance of incentives for positive behavior and penalties for belligerence; the objective being to instill in the minds of our potential adversaries an appreciation of the benefits of cooperation rather than conflict and thus lessen the threat of war . . . . Interests will be respected only if it is clear that they can be defended. Restraint will prevail only if its absence is known to carry heavy risks.[20]

Unfortunately, I believe the record shows that neither negotiations nor unilateral restraint have operated to dissuade Soviet leaders from seeking a nuclear-war-winning capability—or from the view that with such a capability they could effectively use pressure tactics to get their way in crisis situations.

Hence it is urgent that the United States take positive steps to maintain strategic stability and high-quality deterrence. If the trends in Soviet thinking continue to evolve in the manner indicated by the internal statements of Soviet leaders, and if the trends in relative military capability continue to evolve in the fashion suggested by the prior analysis, the foundations for hope in the evolution of a true relaxation of tensions between the U.S.S.R. and much of the rest of the world will be seriously in doubt.

NOTES

[1]B. N. Ponomarev, "The Role of Socialism in Modern World Development," *Problemy Mira i Sotsializma* (Problems of Peace and Socialism), January 1975, pp. 4–13; A. I. Sobolev, "Questions of the Strategy and Tactics of the Class Struggle at the Present Stage of the General Crisis of Capitalism," *Rabochiy Klass in Sovremennyy Mir* (The Working Class and the Contemporary World), January 1975, pp. 3–20.

[2]See comments by Aleksey Rumiantsev, at a conference sponsored by *Problemy Mira i Sotsializma,* Summer 1975.

[3]To see how top officials viewed American nuclear power even in the period of American monopoly, one can now consult the recently declassified text of the NSC 68 policy paper dated in the spring of 1950. Even though Soviet nuclear capacity (after the

first Soviet test of August 1949) was assessed as small for some years to come, that paper rejected any idea of reliance on American nuclear power for the defense of key areas. To be sure, in the 1950s under John Foster Dulles, the United States had a declaratory policy of "massive retaliation." But in the actual confrontations of that period, this declaratory policy was not in fact followed; instead, conventional force was used, for example in the Lebanon crisis of 1958 and, less directly, in the Offshore Islands crisis of the same year. After 1961 massive retaliation was abandoned.

[4] Eugene Wigner, "The Atom and the Bomb," *Christian Science Monitor,* November 13, 1974, p. 4.

[5] See Albert Wohlstetter, "The Delicate Balance of Terror," *Foreign Affairs,* January 1959, pp. 211–234.

[6] It should be noted that this figure refers to the amounts obligated annually for equipment, materiel, and personnel that can be directly attributed to the program mission, including all support costs that follow directly from the number of combat units. It does not include allocable costs of such related activities as communications, general support, and intelligence.

[7] See Paul H. Nitze, "The Vladivostok Accord and SALT II," *The Review of Politics* (University of Notre Dame), April 1975, pp. 147–60, especially pp. 149–50.

[8] "Throw-weight" is a measure of the weight of effective payload that can be delivered to an intended distance. In the case of intercontinental ballistic missiles (ICBMs) and submarine-launched ballistic missiles (SLBMs), the throw-weight is a direct measure of such a payload in terms of the potential power of the missiles' boosters. In view of the more variable loads carried by heavy bombers, a formula for equivalence is needed to take account of all factors including explosive power. This point is addressed in footnote 16.

[9] See Maxwell D. Taylor, "The Legitimate Claims of National Security," *Foreign Affairs,* April 1974, p. 582.

[10] Paul H. Nitze, "The Strategic Balance Between Hope and Skepticism," *Foreign Policy,* Winter 1974–75, pp. 136–56.

[11] There has been no agreed definition of a heavy ballistic missile. However, both sides acknowledge that the SS-9 and the SS-18 are MLBMs and that the U.S. Titan missile, while it is considered heavy, does not fall within the definition of "modern." The U.S. has no launchers for MLBMs and is prohibited from converting any of its silos to such launchers. The Soviets are estimated to have had 308 launchers for MLBMs and are permitted to convert the SS-9 launchers into launchers for the even larger and much more capable SS-18s.

[12] There are several relevant points on the 600-km. range and cruise vs. ballistic ASM questions. The inclusion of cruise missiles as well as ballistic missiles in the aggregate would offer a distinct advantage to the U.S.S.R. In the first place, cruise missiles with a range greater than 600 km. would significantly contribute to U.S. bomber penetration in the face of the strong Soviet antiaircraft defenses. Furthermore, the United States needs longer range cruise missiles to reach meaningful targets within the opponent's interior than does the Soviet Union. Secondly, the Soviets now have cruise missiles of large size with large conventional warheads having a range close to 600 km. With smaller nuclear warheads their range could be more than doubled. It is not possible to verify the substitution of nuclear warheads for conventional ones, or to tell armed cruise missiles from unarmed ones. In any case, a single cruise missile cannot be equated with a Soviet ICBM carrying 50 times as much warhead weight.

[13] The significance of verifiability is a function not only of the confidence one can have in verifying a particular number but of the strategic significance of the number being verified. Fixed ICBM silos are large and the number deployed is therefore readily verifiable; however, the throw-weight of the missiles which can be launched from such silos can vary by a factor of ten.

The provision in the SALT I Interim Agreement that the interior dimensions of silos not be increased by more than 15 percent was an attempt to get at this problem. However, the volume of a missile which can be launched from a silo of given interior dimensions can still vary by a factor of two or three, and the throw-weight of a missile with a given volume can vary by a factor of two. Even if the probable error in directly verifying a throw-weight limitation were 20 percent, such a limitation would be strategically far more significant than any of the preceding limitations.

In addition to throw-weight, there are other significant strategic factors, such as the survivability of the launcher through mobility or hardening, and the accuracy, reliability, and number of RVs (reentry vehicles) carried by a MIRVed missile. None of these other factors is limited under the Vladivostok Accord and, in any case, they are inherently difficult to verify.

[14]In mid-1973 the United States had 602 fighter interceptors and 481 surface-to-air missiles, compared to the Soviet Union's 3,000 fighter interceptors and 10,000 surface-to-air missiles. Edward Luttwak, *The U.S.-U.S.S.R. Nuclear Weapons Balance,* The Washington Papers, Beverly Hills: Sage Publications, 1974.

[15]Indeed, if total throw-weight is not reduced while the number of launchers is, the fewer launchers become more vulnerable and critical to each side and crisis stability is actually lessened. See Lt. Gen. (then Col.) Glenn A. Kent, "On the Interaction of Opposing Forces under Possible Arms Agreements," Occasional Papers in International Affairs, No. 5, Center for International Affairs, Harvard University, March 1963.

[16]A B-52 has been assigned an equivalent throw-weight of 10,000 lbs. and a B-1 about 19,000 lbs. The SRAM air-to-surface missile has a yield about equal to that of a Minuteman III warhead; hence, for every three SRAMs carried by a bomber, that bomber is given a throw-weight equivalent equal to the throw-weight of one Minuteman III. Laydown bombs are assumed to have roughly the yield of Minuteman II; hence, for each laydown bomb carried by a bomber it is given a throw-weight equivalent equal to the throw-weight of a Minuteman II. The alert bomber force is assumed to be 40 percent of the B-52 inventory and 60 percent of the B-1 inventory, degraded to incorporate penetration factors.

[17]I regret that, even if space permitted, the full assumptions used in Mr. Jones' study cannot be spelled out here. Security considerations necessarily enter in for some of the underlying data. I have myself gone over Mr. Jones' data and assumptions with care and believe that they represent a careful and objective analysis of the relevant factors. Above all, since his methods are self-consistent from one period to the next, they show a valid trend-line and pace of change—which I believe the more expert readers of this article will find conform to their more general judgments.

[18]Additional views of Representative Schroeder, "Alternative Defense Posture Statement," Report 94–199 of House Armed Services Committee, May 10, 1975, p. 130.

[19]Under the Vladivostok Accord, both sides are permitted 1,320 MIRVed missile launchers. The maximum MIRVed throw-weight the Soviets could obtain within this limit with the missiles they are currently testing and beginning to deploy is:

> 4,500,000 pounds on 308 SS-19s (about 15,000 pounds each)
> 7,100,000 pounds on 1,012 SS-19s (about 7,000 pounds each)

for a total MIRVed throw-weight of 11.6 million pounds. However, it is unlikely that the Soviets will reach this maximum, as they are currently deploying some SS-17s, which will have a throw-weight of about 5,000 pounds, and they may choose not to MIRV all of their SS-18s. A more likely figure is less than ten million pounds of MIRVed throw-weight.

A reliable megaton-range RV with a CEP (circular error probable, a measure of accuracy) of 0.125 nautical miles has a probability of damage of 85 percent against a silo of 1,500 psi (pounds per square inch) hardness. The targeting of two such RVs on the silo would give a probability of damage of about 92 percent taking into account both reliability and accuracy. An SS-18 missile may have up to eight megaton-range RVs (International Institute for Strategic Studies, *The Military Balance, 1974–75*); thus a megaton-range RV may require around 2,000 pounds of throw-weight. The net throw-weight required, then, to threaten 92 percent destruction of 1,000 hard silos would be approximately four million pounds, assuming the Soviets achieve CEPs averaging an eighth of a mile.

A multiple launch-point ICBM system with 600-psi hard shelters or encapsulated missiles in soft shelters would require considerably more throw-weight for its destruction. To barrage attack such a mobile system deployed on 6,000 square nautical miles of land as an area target would require about 19,000 megaton-range RVs to achieve a 92 percent damage level. The throw-weight required for this force would be considerably above the Soviet available force. Even as low a damage level as 20 percent would require almost 4,000 megaton-range RVs, a throw-weight of at least eight million pounds.

Assuming the same factors for accuracy and reliability as used above in calculating the potential results of an attack on silo-based ICBMs, an equal probability of damage (85 percent for a single reliable RV) can be achieved against a 600-psi shelter with a 290-kiloton weapon. Since a Minuteman III, with a total of three RVs of less than 200-kt yield, has a throw-weight of about 2,000 pounds, an RV of 290-kt yield might require about 800 pounds of throw-weight. Thus a U.S. deployment of some 10,000 shelters would require eight million pounds of Soviet MIRVed throw-weight to threaten destruction of 72 percent of the multiple launch-point system. The entire ten million pound force would raise the level of destruction to only 77 percent. The cost of adding RVs to the Soviet attack force should be substantially greater than the cost to the United States of adding shelters. In any case, it would appear technologically infeasible to reduce the throw-weight required per RV to less than 300 pounds, even if accuracies were eventually to approach zero CEP.

[20]Helmut Sonnenfeldt, "The Meaning of Détente," *Naval War College Review*, July-August 1975, pp. 3–8.

22   The 'SALT' Sell Or, Who Will Bell the Pentagon?

John Holum

. . . In a 1962 speech at Ann Arbor, then Defense Secretary Robert McNamara began the search for flexibility in nuclear war. He outlined a "no cities" policy, under which it was assumed that the two sides would first fire at each other's weapons (counterforce), and that a nuclear war could then be stopped before the ultimate holocaust occurred.

The trouble was that counterforce weapons are inherently ambiguous. Weapons accurate enough for a retaliatory second strike at Russian missiles would also be accurate enough for a disarming first strike. Until then the central purpose of our nuclear arsenal had been deterrence—to notify the other side that if it struck first, we could inflict unacceptable damage in return. It was a relatively stable situation, with the debate focused not so much on the essentials of strategy as on the question, "how much is enough" to deter nuclear war. But McNamara opened something new. If we were not explicitly talking about a first-strike strategy, we were, under a humanitarian-sounding "no cities" rubric, beginning to talk about weapons that could deny to the Soviet Union the minimum safety we demanded for ourselves—a secure deterrent force.

But in 1962 it was only talk. By the late 1960s it was becoming a threat. The Army was pushing anti-ballistic missiles (ABM), which were supposed to intercept incoming warheads from the other side. At the same time, we were preparing to test multiple independently targetable re-entry vehicles, or MIRVs, which are a method of multiplying each missile into several warheads—up to twelve or fourteen on Poseidon submarine-launched missiles—and to send each warhead to a separate target. In combination, those two developments made it possible to conceive of someone actually winning a nuclear war. With the benefit of surprise, one side could send highly accurate and numerous MIRVs to knock out the other side's land-based missiles in their silos, then catch their sub-launched missiles with the ABM, and limit damage to acceptable levels.

It still would not be something to undertake lightly, of course, since there would be enormous damage to the attacker—the incineration of New York City or Moscow, for example—if even a few retaliatory missiles got through. But nuclear scenario builders make fine distinctions. In the January issue of *Foreign Affairs,* Paul Nitze measures the adequacy of our posture by calculating how much nuclear force each side would have left after each had fired two or three salvos at the other. In the real world that has no relevance except to people who plan to be ensconced far underground, pushing buttons when it all takes place. But if both sides had MIRVs and ABMs, those same people, in both Washington and Moscow, would certainly see a great advantage to the side striking first. In any crisis it would be vastly easier to slip into nuclear war. Instead of both losing, one—the side attacking first—would chalk up a relative win.

SALT I is widely credited with averting that ominous prospect, because an ABM was thought essential to a plausible first-strike strategy and the agreement ruled out ABMs. But look again. When the SALT talks got underway, the Soviet Union had long since left off construction of its own primitive ABM System—the GALOSH—around Moscow. And in the United States, by 1969, there was enough doubt about whether the thing would work, and enough concern about the arms race implications, to produce a tie vote in the U.S. Senate on our ABM. And that vote came on the concept of a "hard point" ABM, designed to protect only missile sites, not population centers; the Nixon administration knew it was hopeless to try to get the whole system past Congress. So the ABM was about to be defeated anyway. The main contribution to SALT I was to keep it alive for two more years as a "bargaining chip." (After spending something between $5 billion and $6 billion, Congress finally voted last November to mothball the Grand Forks, N.D. ABM site, to save at least the operating costs of a system which had never made any military sense.)

This has been the pattern of SALT. The hard bargaining has been not with the Russians but with the Pentagon. The arms controllers have lost every bureaucratic fight, and the military has not had to give up anything on arms-control grounds that it otherwise would have had.

The point is better illustrated by what was left out of SALT I. With the advent of MIRV, the quantitative race, which was covered by SALT I, had lost much of its relevance. Anyone can build more missiles. The real excitement, and the best chance to stay ahead, was in the qualitative race, which was not controlled.

In 1969, when our MIRV program had reached the flight testing stage, Senators Case, Brooke and others pleaded for at least a postponement of the tests, pending discussions in SALT. There was no military need to go ahead, since we already had the capacity to destroy any adversary several times over, several different ways—with bombers, with missiles based on land (ICBMs), and missiles on submarines (SLBMs). The Soviet Union was years away from testing a similar program. Further, MIRV raised the first-strike threat outlined above, and it also posed enormous problems for unilateral policing of any arms-control agreement. Sponsors of amendments to delay MIRV pointed out that each side's satellites can count how many missiles the other side has, but that even the most sensitive camera cannot look inside the cover and count how many warheads are there. Once ours was tested, they said, the Soviet Union would have to assume it had been mounted everywhere it would fit. Then they would build the same thing, costs would go up, risks would rise, and arms control would be harder—all for no net gain.

But those warnings went unheeded. Despite the fact that SALT negotiations were underway—and in part because of it, because MIRV, in turn, became a "bargaining chip"—amendments to postpone the tests were defeated. Since then, twenty-seven of our forty-one ballistic missile submarines, each with sixteen missiles, have been loaded with MIRVs, as have 550 of our Minuteman ICBMs. The total number of individual weapons—bomber loadings and independently targetable warheads—is now projected at 8,900, climbing toward almost 10,000. That's more than twice what it was in 1970. It is enough to hit every major urban or industrial center in the Soviet Union fifty times over, with warheads roughly the size of the one that blasted Hiroshima.

At the same time, under Secretary of Defense James Schlesinger, the McNamara counterforce theory was broadened and hardened into policy. If we have been spared the ABM, today's targeting doctrines, no matter how implausible, conveniently build the case for more and more accuracy and for mountains of costly overkill. If we want to aim at weapons and military installations as well as at cities, then no matter how big the arsenal, the Pentagon can always claim it isn't enough. The doctrine itself is wrong, but if they can keep the debate within the doctrine, the Pentagon can make a military case for rising budgets forever. In the process they can argue that any arms-control agreement, almost by definition, is strategically bad.

Now, five years later, as predicted, the Russians are beginning to build MIRVs of their own. Pentagon spokesmen point to that development to justify a jump of more than $2 billion next year in spending to design, buy and operate nuclear weapons. They do not acknowledge that Soviet MIRVs probably could have been avoided, if only we had been willing to show some restraint. But because of our quantum jump, the best that could be achieved at SALT II was a limit of 1,320 MIRVed missiles per side.

It should have said "none"—no MIRV deployments, and no flight tests, to make sure there would be no deployment. But the arms builders won the day over the arms controllers. The agreement is designed not to limit arms but to fit around Pentagon plans to build them.

Secretary of State Kissinger has complained of this around Washington, particularly in the context of his discussions preliminary to President Ford's Vladivostok trip in November 1974. Columnists were writing then about the State-Defense split over SALT. Kissinger was embarrassed in Moscow because he had to incorporate in his conversations these Pentagon claims that the Russians are ahead in missile throw-weights. They do have bigger missiles. But they responded, quite correctly, that missiles don't kill people; warheads kill people, and in that category the United States, with its early MIRV, had an overwhelming lead.

But if he complained to columnists and Congressmen, Kissinger apparently did not complain with much effect to President Nixon or President Ford. For now something even more unsettling than MIRV has virtually been excluded from SALT. This spring both the Navy and Air Force are slated to test advanced strategic cruise missiles—systems which make MIRV look like a piker's arms-control problem.

The cruise missile is not a new concept; it is as old as the V-1 rockets used by the Germans in World War II. But advances in technology have transformed it into an extremely formidable carrier for nuclear weapons—advances which are, for the present, exclusively ours.

Cruise missiles are essentially pilotless aircraft with either a conventional or nuclear nose. They could be launched from airplanes, from attack submarines, from surface ships or even from land. They would fly just above the terrain to avoid radar detection. New terminal guidance systems can give them near pinpoint accuracy. And, if you discount the cost of the launch platform, they are comparatively cheap—under $1 million per copy, even allowing for overruns and inflation.

The arms-control problems are obvious. With MIRVs one can at least count launchers and calculate the maximum force. But cruise missiles—especially the sea-launched version, SLCM (for acronym buffs, that's pronounced "slick-em")—could be literally anywhere and everywhere, and there would be no way to know.

Yet the Pentagon wants to go ahead now. Harking back to Senator Case's 1969 attack on MIRV, Senator McGovern tried late last year to amend the Pentagon's money bill so as to postpone cruise missile flight tests until a total SALT ban had been tried. The Pentagon lobby cranked up to defeat it, and did. Secretary Kissinger went to Moscow in January to argue dutifully that cruise missiles must be allowed. Any State-Pentagon difference on this one somehow disappeared.

Of course there is the 1,500 mile limit on range in SALT II. But if it has some engineering effects, that figure has virtually no practical political meaning. For enforcement purposes in SALT, each side must assume that the other wants to cheat. A side bent on doing so could limit its cruise missile tests to 1,500 miles and still deploy longer-range versions, with high confidence that all aspects would work. As with MIRV, the only way to stop the cruise missile is in the testing stage. Instead, SALT II legitimized cruise missiles—ours and ultimately the Russians'—and effectively excluded them from enforceable limits.

That may be the final blow for SALT. (The negotiations have left out most of the race, and it is too late to restrain it that way.) Perhaps the discussions are not entirely useless. But neither are they terribly relevant. At least, given the current U.S. approach, there is very little they can affect—only what the Pentagon does not want or cannot get anyway.

The problem is that in practice we have repudiated the one workable foundation for arms control—the starting conviction that both sides share an interest in curbs and eventual cutbacks in their costly, deadly strategic arsenals. Our posture has been dictated instead by a view that the negotiations are but another way to continue the competition, to jockey for advantage.

It came home to me in a recent discussion with a nuclear arms specialist from the Pentagon. I ventured the assertion that SALT had been almost wholly a bust—that nothing had been sacrificed that otherwise would have been built; that, at home, the process had only added another justification—the "bargaining chip"—for building every new weapon that comes down the pike, off the drawing board, whether we need it or not. I suggested further that the whole process can only be discredited by agreements that leave gaping loopholes—loopholes that are designed to suit Pentagon plans now, but which will open suspicions that the Russians are cheating later on (how would Kissinger prove to Senator Jackson or Admiral Zumwalt five years from now that the Russians are not deploying cruise missiles with a 3,000-mile range?).

I was told rather impatiently that these observations amounted to a simple-minded misunderstanding of the very reasons why we talk: "The purpose of these discussions is not to cut our defense budget. The best SALT agreement would be one in which we were allowed to build everything we wanted, and the Russians were required to give up everything they had."

So that has been our controlling doctrine. No mutual interest is involved. The negotiating table is nothing more than another cold-war battlefield. That is the way SALT has been played. And that is why SALT is about played out.

On balance, then, the SALT II agreement deserves neither opposition nor support. If we are serious about controlling weapons, then it mostly deserves to be dismissed as unimportant. President Ford and Secretary Kissinger should be told to defend their performance themselves.

That means arms controllers must think about, and responsible candidates must address, a posture which goes well beyond a general sympathy for SALT negotiations. It could be something like this:

For the present, *de jure* limits would be de-emphasized, and we would concentrate on holding unilaterally to a nuclear position that is truly limited to national security needs.

It should excise the exotic counterforce and limited nuclear war doctrines developed under Secretary Schlesinger, and should concentrate instead on the single sane and achievable mission of nuclear weapons—to deter war—by maintaining the forces needed to convince any adversary that we can answer any first strike with a society-destroying blow in return.

It should drop spurious references to "superiority" and even "parity." Those terms have no military meaning in a realm where each side can totally destroy the other with only a fraction of its forces. They have political meaning only to the extent that we say they do. The theory is that third countries will be inclined toward the Soviet Union, or our allies will feel less secure, if the Russians can destroy us, say, sixty times over, and we can destroy them but forty. Every country in the world can muster more sense than that.

Our position should freeze the deployment and flight testing of all new weapons. With the redundant insurance already in force, we would have far more than an ample deterrent if additional weapons and new systems were stopped right now. In 1967 then Secretary of Defense Robert McNamara quantified an adequate deterrent as the assured ability to land 400 one-megaton equivalents on separate Soviet targets. Our MIRV warheads are considerably smaller than one megaton. But, essentially because explosions are spherical and targets are flat, smaller warheads are more efficient. Increases in numbers more than make up for reductions in size. At nearly 9,000 warheads now, almost anyone should agree that we are some distance beyond a borderline case.

The responsibility for further arms race initiatives should be placed on the Soviet Union. We should make a clear declaration of intent: that instead of unilaterally running ahead in the competition, we are unilaterally calling a halt; that we are continuing reasonable research and development programs on a wholly defensive basis, to guard against technical breakthroughs which might threaten us; that we do not intend to add anything more until or unless the Soviet Union moves to undermine our deterrent; that we will welcome and are watching for reciprocal steps.

There is no guaranteeing that this attempt at *de facto* arms control would produce such results. Perhaps the Politburo, too, is peopled by Strangeloves who exult in the game. But there is precedent for such an approach. The 1962 Nuclear Test Ban Treaty flowed from President Eisenhower's unilateral suspension of tests, and President Kennedy's patient maintenance of the same approach. And most Kremlinologists recognize that there are also hawks and doves in Soviet ruling circles. The old approach has strengthened the hawks. Why not play to the doves for a time?

Finally, in this context there is an especially poignant application of the standard argument for anything new—it's bound to be better than what we have now. . . .

Most polls show widespread impatience with overkill and Pentagon waste. Arms spending boosts inflation and distorts the economy. Nuclear weapons are still the quickest way going, assorted environmental threats notwithstanding, to make the planet uninhabitable; the electorate has a right to know in some detail what kind of thinking guides aspiring hands on the trigger.

But now it is not enough for candidates to tell us how they will negotiate with the Russians. They must first tell us where, how and how often they'll say "no" to the generals and admirals—in the arena here at home where the real arms-control battles are fought.

23 Nuclear Spread and World Order

Lincoln P. Bloomfield

Until a year or two ago we were entitled to believe that the Nuclear Nonproliferation Treaty (NPT) could successfully hold the line at five nuclear weapons powers, if only a few holdout countries would sign or ratify it. Two events have thrown into serious doubt the ability of present policies to stem the further proliferation of nuclear weapon capabilities among additional nations.

The first event was the Indian "peaceful" nuclear explosion in May 1974, which jumped the firebreak between the five permanent members of the U.N. Security Council—who are also the nuclear weapons powers— and all other nations. That barrier had held for ten years since the first Chinese detonation in 1964.

What seemed to undermine the earlier mild optimism that the NPT could do the job was not that "nuclear-weapons-capable" countries such as Sweden, Canada, Switzerland, Australia, Netherlands, Italy, Poland, Argentina, Brazil, Japan, and West Germany, or even nations in conflict like Pakistan, Taiwan, South Africa, South Korea, Israel, or Egypt were on the verge of exploding their own nuclear devices (though many think Israel is in fact the "seventh" nuclear weapons power). It was rather that the general climate of expectation about what was likely to take place had changed significantly. Many now believe that there *will* be Nuclear Weapons Power numbers 7, 8, 9, ad infinitum. Members of the international professional strategic community have already been discounting the future and shifting their planning to ways of living in a world of many nuclear weapons powers. The crucial new reality is thus not merely the existence of a sixth (or seventh) such power; it is above all the altered prediction that influential people around the world are making as a consequence.[1]

Having one more "nuclear-capable" power does not change the world. But what could change it would be a snowballing, fatalistic belief that becomes a self-fulfilling prophecy unless it is countered by a different belief that is equally potent.

The second event was the worldwide energy crisis. Predictions of numbers of future nuclear power plants now far exceed the figure planners had been using prior to the Arab oil embargo of 1973–74. The amount of plutonium to be produced over the next decade will be enough to put a major dent in the energy shortage—*and* to make thousands of atomic bombs.

These two portentous shifts in perception and planning came at a time when 55 of the 90 or so countries that have signed the 1970 Nuclear Nonproliferation Treaty attended its May 1975 five-year Review Conference in Geneva. Just prior to the conference, and doubtless in anticipation of it, ratification had been completed by five West European states and South Korea.

The conference concentrated on tightening up technical controls and safeguards over the rapidly growing worldwide nuclear power-generating industry as well as the flow of nuclear fuels, uranium and plutonium, that go in and out of peaceful atomic reactors. The hair-raising specter of nuclear blackmail by hijacking and sabotage sharpened the delegates' concern for better means of guarding against capture of nuclear materials by terrorist groups.

The International Atomic Energy Agency (IAEA) is even now doing a competent, though limited, job of inspecting peaceful reactors to catch (or at least discourage) clandestine diversion of plutonium or enriched uranium. Most of the countries that are able to supply nuclear fuels and reactor technology, notably the United States and the Soviet Union, have agreed among themselves to export only to recipient countries that adopt IAEA safeguards (though last year's U.S. offer to Israel and Egypt showed Washington still unwilling to require inspection of older facilities as the price for new help).

All in all, many laudable efforts are going into strengthening the NPT "regime," which is clearly the best answer so far to limiting the further spread of nuclear weaponry. The great majority of nations, and certainly of human beings, clearly support its goal. A few people may remain comfortable with the scenario of dozens of countries, some at war with one another, newly enabled to destroy humankind by the millions, even to trigger the apocalypse of superpower strategic war. But overwhelmingly the rest of us cling to the conviction that, as someone put it, "when you have five, or even six, idiot children, it's time to practice birth control." Certainly no one can quarrel with this concentration on the contingent problem of clandestine nuclear activities, aimed at preventing cheating as well as making peaceful nuclear technology more readily available under safeguards.

But now that the Review Conference is out of the way, it is time to raise the sobering possibility that all this activity, while essential, will not be enough. For what has never been adequately dealt with, probably because it seemed politically insuperable, is the inherently discriminatory nature of the present system.

II

In our epoch, the evidence is everywhere of the dominant role of national status-seeking and the drive to "feel equal." An entire philosophy of resentful Third World economics bears the telltale name "dependency theory." Third World proposals for a "New Economic and Social Order" reflect a veritable obsession with eradicating the stigmata of inferiority. The walls of every international conference room, from OPEC to the U.N. General Assembly, resound with strident demands for equal status. At the symbolic level (which Harold Isaacs reminds us is anything but trivial[2]) there are few nations, however poor or tiny, that cannot boast of a flag airline, diplomatic limousines (usually longer than that of the U.S. Ambassador), international hotels, supersonic jets—and nuclear power reactors.

Even at the superpower level, no serious negotiation with the Soviets on strategic nuclear arms was possible until Moscow felt it had acquired "parity." And if final proof were needed, even those Indians most critical of their government for other deeds or misdeeds unanimously express pride over its achievement in exploding a "peaceful" nuclear device.

It is against this backdrop that the NPT regime has to be assessed. The cold fact is that, without exception, every single aspect of the nuclear nonproliferation system is discriminatory. Indeed, the more successful the NPT system, the more absolute the distinction between those who have nuclear weapons and those who do not.

The most obvious distinction is of course that between five (or six) nations possessing the means of mass nuclear destruction, and the remaining hundred and forty or so which do not and, according to the proposed rules of the game, never will.

This distinction carries the further division between openness to verification by the Vienna agency's inspectors (for all nonweapons' countries) and secrecy for all the great powers' reactors, even their peaceful ones. The exception is the United States, which has offered to open its peaceful reactors, though of course not its military ones, to IAEA inspection. Conversations in Moscow in the spring of 1975 confirm the insistence of the other nuclear superpower on increased controls for everyone *but* the great powers.

Article VI of the Nonproliferation Treaty commits the superpowers to good-faith efforts toward nuclear disarmament, but few outside Moscow and Washington believe the process was seriously begun with the 2,400-launcher agreement of Vladivostok in 1974.

Brazil for one (and India before it) apparently believes that some of its economic development projects could benefit from peaceful nuclear explosions (PNEs). The United States now argues that peaceful nuclear explosions are bad for others, since we don't find them cost-effective for us. If other countries still want PNEs they are free to come, hat in hand, to Washington, Moscow, London, Paris, or presumably Peking, as supplicants for Big Brother's technical fix.

Security guarantees were offered in 1968, but they are subject to the veto, and moreover it seems absurd to guarantee only against nuclear attack when countries can be devastated by nuclear powers using conventional weapons.

As for the spent fuel rods coming out of nuclear reactors and requiring reprocessing in expensive plants to recover the residual plutonium, the position Washington has taken is that we will do the reprocessing for our clients. But of course India, once deciding to acquire a nuclear explosion capability, built her own chemical separation plant and thus bypassed the controls the donor—Canada—had put on the power reactor that produced the used fuel rods.

In all of these ways the system provides that the "first-class" nuclear states not only have a monopoly on the weapons, but also on the international decision-making about peaceful uses.

In the same vein, it is a fact that all current anti-proliferation policies, however worthy, are in the realm of denial. More than that, except for the inspection performed by IAEA inspectors, these policies are overwhelmingly on a nation-to-nation rather than a multilateral basis. Both of these features—denial and nation-based action—may actually reinforce the possible trend toward proliferation to the extent that the trend arises from a sense of inequality, resentment against what is perceived as discrimination, and a desire for equivalent rights and status.

The irony is that while we live, *pace* Marx, in an age of international class struggle, the international "ruling class" of nuclear weapons states (led, *pace* Lenin, by the U.S.S.R.) demands its right to exclusive status unto perpetuity. In an era dominated by demands for identity, respect, equity, and participation, it seems reasonable to ask whether, with the best will in the world, the present NPT system of discrimination, denial, and second-class citizenship will in fact achieve its aim of preventing the further spread of nuclear weapons. For if my reasoning is correct, it is considerations of prestige and nondiscrimination that in an age of rampant nationalism stand as the chief obstacles to universal agreement on nonproliferation.

III

It follows that the chief danger in the years ahead is not that any given country will secretly cheat in its nuclear bookkeeping—which is what the present international system seeks to inhibit. It is that a country will *openly* decide to acquire a nuclear weapons capability, for reasons which since time immemorial, and today as never before, drive nations to seek prestige, influence, and above all equality.[3]

Of course, if all countries were to sign and ratify the Nonproliferation Treaty, and the Treaty regime were greatly strengthened, the
problem would presumably be solved. But this is a tautology: in fact, a
dozen key "threshold countries" have *not* fully joined, countries such as
Brazil, Argentina, Israel, Japan, Pakistan, Egypt, Spain, and South
Africa, whose importance to international peace and stability is obvious. India may not actually fabricate a bomb; but neither is she likely
to take a "morning-after" pill that will return her to pre-1974 nuclear
innocence. Each new nuclear weapons country tends to stay that way.
Even the present safeguard procedures may become inadequate as new
technical options, such as the breeder reactor and high-temperature
gas reactor, call for much more intrusive inspection.

Yet if the conclusion is correct that the problem of proliferation is
as much psychological as it is technical, political, or military, current
incentives to take the pledge are insufficient. No matter what the
rhetoric, a world in which five or six nations control the weapons
technology is by definition discriminatory; a system which leaves all the
decision-making in their hands is by definition paternalistic. Clearly
there is an unfilled need for a more attractive option than either accepting the monopolistic position of the "nuclear OPEC," or going it
alone.

It follows that to provide not just negative but also positive incentives to the principal holdouts, additional measures need to be
developed that go beyond technical safeguards, important as these are.
In the classic language of criminology, efforts at nonproliferation
need to aim not only at means and opportunity—means which are universally increasing while opportunity for open violation of the spirit of
the treaty remains unhindered—but also at the motives for going nuclear as a political act.

Such measures would have to confront directly the political and
psychological foundations of the potential drive toward further nuclear spread. Perhaps no steps even in this direction would deflect
leaders determined to acquire weaponry they believe will give them an
edge, even if strategic analysis proves them overwhelmingly wrong.
But to the extent the drive is primarily motivated—as I believe it to
be—by nonstrategic and to that extent non-"rational" feelings and perceptions, the countries that presently hold the power and the institutional leadership will now have to open their minds to some hitherto
"unrealistic" answers to the central question: What policies by those
who favor the Nonproliferation Treaty are most likely to change the
climate surrounding nuclear spread back to one in which the normal
expectation is continued nonproliferation?

A comprehensive answer to this question must be two-tracked. On
the first track it is still essential to pursue the goals of effective controls
and safeguards—"disincentives" to going nuclear.

But the second track, to which little attention has been given, is to
reduce the political and psychological incentive to become a nuclear
weapons power.

How is this to be done?

IV

The logic of the situation requires that an expanded nonproliferation strategy focus on tangible ways to give the outsiders a far more genuine sense of participation in the system. It is obviously not enough to say to them, with the late President Kennedy, "Life is unfair." Deep-rooted feelings of political alienation and resentment can be overcome only by greater true equality. There must be shared opportunities to gain prestige through participation in decision-making, which in turn requires that responsibilities be much more broadly allocated than under the present two-class system. The operative hypothesis is that a seat at the top table of nuclear institutional diplomacy is the price the "monopolists" must pay to others who agree to forgo a seat at the top table of nuclear weaponry.

When we speak of "participation" we are no longer dealing in symbols but in the hard currency of political power. And if the number of those becoming involved in decision-making about international nuclear activities is to grow to include at least the "near-nuclear" countries, here too we come to the end of abstractions, and into the creation, design, and operation of political forms and structures appropriate to the problem.

Are we then talking about a new Baruch Plan? Nuclear disarmament? World government?

The Baruch Plan of 1946 (based on the so-called Acheson-Lilienthal Report) called for "managerial control of ownership of all atomic energy activities potentially dangerous to world security," along with "power to control, inspect, and license all other atomic activities." That program entailed internationalization of the whole vertical structure starting with uranium ore, through isotope-separation plants, processing of fuel, and, *a fortiori,* the making of nuclear weapons, which were to be totally banned without national veto.

Soviet antagonism to supranational schemes in a U.S.-led world, the weakness of the United Nations in an era of cold war, and despair at the prospects of nuclear disarmament, all made a dead letter of the Baruch Plan approach. Even apart from political unreality, international ownership of the entire vertical industrial nuclear structure, from mine to power generator, is inconceivable today given the enormity and complexity of that structure compared with 1946. Uranium is everywhere in the ground, and soon nuclear reactors will be in virtually every country in the world. In addition, to link progress toward nonproliferation to effective nuclear disarmament (as the Baruch Plan did) would ensure the former's automatic failure. It was hard enough to negotiate SALT I and II over a five-year period, and these leave enough weapons in superpower hands to destroy the planet many times over. Our puzzle is how to change the system enough to get a better political-psychological base under nonproliferation *without* having to work a total transformation in man or in the basic geometry of his political world.

What *can* be done is to turn the 1946 Plan on its head, so to speak, and, while candidly admitting the possibility of indefinite possession of nuclear weapons in national hands, to concentrate on internationalizing, to the extent necessary, the nonweapons aspects of the fuel cycle that represent key avenues to further weapons proliferation. The text could well be Henry Kissinger's comments that a "new international structure" has to be built "not on the sense of preeminence of two power centers, but on the sense of participation of those who are part of the global environment."[4] It is a mark of our recent loss of confidence in international institution-building that neither Secretary Kissinger nor many of those concerned with nuclear spread . . . seriously tried to implement such insights with the kind of thinking that made the mid-1940s a relatively Golden Age of international political inventiveness and institution-building.

Even in this age of limited vision, the NATO Nuclear Planning Group, for instance, went a good distance toward draining tension from the two-class Atlantic Alliance structure by the device of sharing in planning on a matter vital to all. Similarly, a partial approach to nonproliferation would seek to create a changed political environment in which some key elements of peaceful nuclear activities were actually regulated by the international community, and in which important nonweapons countries were full participants in international decision-making. If this were achieved, the political motive to go nuclear arising from resentment at discrimination would be significantly diminished. And so also would the technical means to do so.

V

Four things can be done within the framework of a partial approach. None of them requires nuclear disarmament, a working collective security system, or total international ownership à la Baruch—all of which seem far-fetched in the present world of nationalism. But the partial approach would call for some degree of change in the operating international political and economic ground rules. Starting with the least threatening or "revolutionary" steps, candidates for significantly greater international control are: (1) the reprocessing of plutonium from reactors; (2) peaceful nuclear explosions; (3) nuclear fuels, notably those based on plutonium and highly enriched uranium; and (4) more distantly, the uranium enrichment processes. Success with the first steps would generate momentum toward next steps. But each step taken, beginning with the first, would have enormous significance for nonproliferation.

First, plutonium which is sufficiently pure to be used in a light-water reactor—or a bomb—requires in most cases processing in a chemical separation plant that separates it from unspent uranium and other materials contained in fuel rods which have been irradiated in a reactor. For most of the reactors being built, where the spent fuel rods are reprocessed is where weapons-grade plutonium could also be produced.

The number of spent fuel rods that will be moving about in the years to come is staggering. The Stockholm International Peace Research Institute (SIPRI) estimates there will soon be between 7,000 and 12,000 shipments annually between reactors and reprocessing plants. By the early 1980s this will mean that the present nonweapons countries will have available to them annually 26,000 or so kilograms of plutonium 239—enough to make 50 atomic bombs a week if they choose to. Thus plutonium need only be extracted from the spent fuel rods through reprocessing techniques which, as India has shown, can be readily built at least on a small scale.

This seems an excellent candidate for immediate internationalization. Not many reprocessing plants have yet been built, thanks to the expense, which runs to the hundreds of millions of dollars. The United States has arranged to have recipients of U.S. nuclear fuels send their spent fuel rods for reprocessing to the United States (or in some cases a third country). Little of this is actually being done yet, and the present is thus a good time to rethink the system. For current arrangements simply perpetuate the politically pernicious system of patronage and multiclass citizenship.

A series of internationally controlled facilities, along with internationally regulated and protected transport of this lethal material to and from plants, would represent "community" control of a process that is crucial to all, but is currently held by the "nuclear monopolists." It would upgrade vital safety and ecological considerations by standardizing the process. And it would ensure economies of scale by means of consolidated facilities, located on economically rational rather than political-nationalistic grounds. This is clearly a case where a planned regional approach makes sense (as on a regional scale Eurochemique, an agency of the OECD, today reprocesses the spent fuel rods of OECD members in Europe). Regionalization also reduces the danger of domination or capture and, more positively, spreads control facilities and thus participation.

A second candidate for genuine international management is peaceful nuclear explosions (PNEs). As I suggested earlier, the value of PNEs for engineering purposes is highly controversial. Various groups of U.S. scientists have tried hard in recent months to persuade their Soviet counterparts that on the basis of the American "Plowshare" experiments, PNEs are uneconomic, dangerous—and a spur to proliferation. Moscow today seems as divided as Washington was a decade ago between skeptics and enthusiasts, and may still want to use PNEs to reroute rivers, dredge canals, and move mountains.

Both India and Brazil have talked of the need to retain the "PNE option," given that their only choice was between asking for great-power help or going nuclear themselves. Recognizing this incentive, some modest efforts have been made to implement the NPT's promise of international procedures to ensure the benefits of peaceful nuclear explosions. The current U.S. position calls for "internationally approved facilities," national in nature although sprinkled lightly with U.N. or IAEA holy water. In fact the Mexican government—a pioneer in innovative NPT thinking—seven years ago proposed internationalization of the PNE program. Officials of the Agency for the Prohibition of Nuclear Weapons in Latin America (OPANAL) justifiably point out that both Argentina and Brazil—two current NPT holdouts—supported that 1968 initiative; perhaps even India would have found it hard to justify her unilateral explosion if the Mexican initiative had been followed up.

Proposals to internationalize PNEs have usually foundered on military security grounds reflected by the question, "Would you want to give an atomic bomb to Waldheim?" There are, as always, pros and cons to this question, including the danger that creation of a new facility for peaceful nuclear explosions might persuade countries to believe it to be a good idea and thus encourage them to acquire the capability nationally. Against this is the more likely contingency of other countries doing what India did: acquiring a nuclear capability on the pretext—or genuine belief—that peaceful nuclear explosions may contribute to their economic development.

Given the great importance of creating a new political-psychological climate for nuclear power, it would seem more important to move to internationalize these peaceful capabilities than to temporize further on debatable technical and engineering grounds. Even if such explosions prove to be uneconomic, the purpose of designing a truly international facility will have been served if, through its symbolism, it contributes to the belief on the part of nations that there is a real promise of a new and fairer international order involving nuclear power, in which all will be assured of receiving benefits.

But a changed approach would also have to be for real. An "international PNE facility" would not affect the stockpiles of nuclear weapons in the hands of the big powers. But it must give to countries that hold back from the NPT on grounds of status and autonomy a greater sense of participation in a far less discriminatory system.

The technical and security issues in a joint international PNE service are complex but not insurmountable. The challenge would be to find a political-technical mix between the extremes of "giving a bomb to Waldheim" and continuing to require proud nations to come to Washington or Moscow to appeal for the technology for peaceful explosions. As a first approximation, the technology for a reasonably clean and efficient nuclear device could be set at the lowest level of common technical knowledge between the United States and the Soviet Union, a level that is probably fairly sophisticated. To reach that point, a joint research project could be undertaken to define and engineer such a "state of the art" device.

Security precautions would of course be required to ensure against risks of theft or sabotage. Some of the means already in existence include making explosive devices unwieldy, utilizing multiple electronic "keys," and applying such proven measures as the warhead security procedures of the U.S. Air Force.

By keeping the technology simple, it seems plausible that the facility could operate at the threshold of common technical knowledge and still be genuinely multinational in comparison, security, and decision-making. This is the chief point—that the essentially political decisions about rendering PNE services, including policy questions of cost, personnel, priorities, timing, and the like would be made by an international board consisting of all the nuclear weapons powers plus the principal near-nuclear powers.

Already some countries such as Australia and Canada have endorsed proposals for international arrangements for peaceful explosions. This is a case where leadership could best come from those states most affected by the problem rather than from Washington. But what needs to come from Washington (and Moscow and London and Paris and Peking) is a willingness to implement their words about equality and world order.

This brings us to the third point. Looking ahead to a climate in which steps have been taken to share at least some important peaceful nuclear responsibilities and privileges, it may become possible to consider the means by which the international community could get a handle on the basic element of the process—the uranium itself.

Given the widespread existence of uranium in natural local formations in many parts of the world, it is out of the question to transfer title of uranium ore, even of high (say one percent to two percent) concentration, to the international community. But a partial plan might in its later stage provide for international title over all processed uranium-based nuclear fuels, which would include all enriched uranium and all plutonium. All such fuels would be defined as "public goods." Compensation to present owners for fuels now in process would be made through a bond issue to be amortized over a period of years from the proceeds of future sales to power and research plants. Licenses would be issued for extraction and primary processing and shipping, and efficient surveillance and record-keeping would be maintained to ensure that shipments went to their intended destinations. The control process would be supported by fees from licensing.

The legal principle for plutonium, and for high-grade uranium, would be that these "goods" have the same international legal standing as the seabed beyond the likely 200-mile economic resources zone. Under international rules the seabed and the seas above it represent "the common heritage of mankind" whose exploration will, with any luck, be licensed and regulated by an international authority. Similarly, an international authority would license and regulate national or private production of enriched uranium. The international community would also prescribe standards for the handling of enriched uranium and its insertion into the power reactor network. IAEA inspection would be performed at *all* nuclear power reactors using both U-238 and U-235.

One reason for deferring this step is that historically some weapons-grade fissionable material is produced by power reactors and some by military reactors. This kind of complication would be bypassed by taking the larger arms-control step of ending production of all fissionable material for military purposes. We should return to the

1966 U.S. proposal for a cut-off in the production of all weapons-grade material and the transfer of substantial military stocks of U-235 and plutonium to peaceful uses.

The final element of the scheme is to bring under international control the means of enriching uranium. The expensive and complex isotope-separation method of gaseous diffusion may in time be replaced by much less expensive and complex techniques such as gas centrifuge technology, lasers, and the South African nozzle process. The last stages of an agreed partial plan would require that all means for generating enriched uranium be regarded as a public utility. Private or national ownership under licensed international supervision would continue in the first stage, but by the final stages such plants would be publicly owned and operated either directly or under international license. Compensation would be as above.

VI

Each step in the suggested plan entails empowering an international authority to do an increasingly complex job. Where to start?

One approach would be to start with the principal nations willing to proceed now rather than to await universal agreement. For instance, China and France might not join at the outset, but agreement might be reached among a substantial number of nations to designate international reprocessing facilities and outline a workable system of control and management under the IAEA—or as a separate agency.

If a "coalition of the willing" could be formed by the United States, the Soviet Union, Britain, and India, plus most of the key "threshold powers," a partial community with embryonic common institutions could be set up among them, creating a standard to which the unwise could be encouraged to repair. Whether the new authority is a specialized agency of the U.N. family, or a new agency, or attached to the IAEA, is far less important than that the membership in the first instance include most of the present nuclear supplier powers and, above all, most of the crucial *potential* nuclear powers.

Alternatively, the proposal could be put to the United Nations and to the IAEA to be adopted and implemented by the existing organizations. The IAEA, the U.N., or the parties to the Treaty could decide to create blue-ribbon panels of experts to study and report, by a specified deadline, recommendations which a reconvened NPT Review Conference might consider.

In proceeding to increase the power of the international community, a step-by-step process is essential, with a final stage that does not put the entire plan in jeopardy because of its obvious absurdity or its failure to take into account persistent characteristics of the human condition. Such a phased plan could specify one function on which work should begin without delay, e.g., international reprocessing facilities; the urgency of this step is underlined by the proposal of Iran—a full party to the Treaty—to build its own separation plant. Stage Two could create an international facility for PNEs. Stage Three, control over refined fuels of a specified type. And Stage Four, international control or ownership of uranium enrichment facilities. Or steps could be taken on each of these fronts in each stage, with modest steps in Stage One, and completion across the board in Stage Three or Four.

To begin with, however, in the spirit of the proposal, consultations should begin with others so the plan can become theirs as much as it would be ours. Those others must include the present nuclear weapons powers. But above all it must involve those whose decisions, both on capabilities *and* intentions, will be the fateful ones. For all parties, even the partial approach calls for a leap of imagination. But so does living in a world of proliferated nuclear weapons where every minor international quarrel could become genocidal.

NOTES

[1] An informal poll of leading U.S. nonproliferation experts meeting privately in March 1975 showed 14 out of 21 anticipating the existence of one to four additional nuclear weapons powers in the next decade. Four experts expected seven to ten more "bomb powers," and none predicted that the line would be held at six.

[2] Harold Isaacs, "Nationality: End of the Road?" *Foreign Affairs*, April 1975.

[3] On April 1, 1975, in introducing a bill calling on the Argentine government to build a nuclear bomb, one legislator declared: "Recent events have demonstrated that nations gain increasing recognition in the international arena in accordance with their power." The example he cited was China, deliberately ignored by the great powers until she went nuclear.

[4] See *The New York Times*, October 13, 1974.

PART III

The Crises of Institutions

In part three we deal with a variety of institutions: international and domestic, political and economic. We also examine the role of individuals in these organizations, as bureaucrats and as leaders.

The first section deals with the future of international institutions. What will the new world order be like? We have already discussed the concept of a balance of power. Those guided by this philosophy view the future as a world very much like our own, in which order evolves from a stalemate of forces between the great powers, with the nation-state still the central institution. Many who believe in international integration argue that greater political or economic interdependence would discourage countries from going to war. Economic integration, following the model of the European Economic Community (Common Market), would mean that nations of a particular region would become so dependent on each other that they could not conceive of preparing for war against each other. Those who favor a balance of power among the great powers have also argued that increased interdependence will restrict conflict. Such a notion was at the heart of the effort to pursue the SALT agreements.

Many authorities believe that political union is a more effective means of restricting the ability of nations to wage war than either increased economic interdependence or the balance of power. The successful federations within the United States, Canada, and Australia are often cited as examples of effective political integration, despite the internal problems present in each country. One of the original goals of the European unity movement was to limit conflict among Western European states, an objective which seemed particularly pressing after World War II. Today many Europeans have other reasons for participating in the Common Market, including their desire to benefit from its economic strength, technological development, and political influence with respect to the rest of the world. It is still not clear whether the new European Economic Community consisting of nine states (the six original members—France, West Germany, Italy, Belgium, the Netherlands, and Luxembourg—and three later additions—Great Britain, Ireland, and Denmark) will remain an economic union, disintegrate, or evolve into some form of political federation.

319

Daniel Yergin in "Europe's Identity Crisis" discusses this question and relates the future of Europe to the crisis of confidence triggered by the economic recession of the mid-1970s.

Many who have been concerned with ways of bringing order to the tension-ridden sphere of world politics have been intrigued with the possibility of world government—a global union in which a United States of the World would provide the supervision and restraint in managing relations among nations which have hitherto been lacking. Presumably, through an international parliament with binding powers on its members, conflict would be restricted. Others have viewed this solution either as unachievable or undesirable; they have pursued instead the concept of collective security embodied in both the League of Nations and the United Nations. Although the organizational differences between these two institutions are many, both held out the hope that international politics could be partially ordered by agreement among states to deter and control their conflicts. The League of Nations ended in dismal failure; by 1975, its thirtieth anniversary, the United Nations seemed to have grown moribund through its failure to deal effectively, or often to deal at all, with the major crises of our times.

Many have become disillusioned with the United Nations; Abraham Yeselson and Anthony Gaglione are clearly among them. In their article "The Use of the United Nations in World Politics" they argue that the international institution is simply a tool of national interests, its organs a weapon in the hands of those who can muster a majority in a given dispute. Far from being a viable peacekeeping organization, they see the United Nations as a frequently dangerous impediment to conflict reduction. These controversial propositions should arouse much debate, with the key questions being whether their position is realistic or whether they have misunderstood the limited uses for which the United Nations was originally designed. The authors' challenge to past American policies on this issue cannot be ignored for they question the very basis of American support for collective security efforts.

The notions of world order discussed thus far all rely on the continued existence of the nation-state in some form. The multinational corporation, however, presents an alternate type of institution in world politics. The growth and increasing role of multinational corporations in world affairs has made it possible to conceive of a world in which the major units would no longer be nation-states but economic conglomerates composed of directors from a variety of countries. Conceivably, multinational corporations could overcome cultural differences among peoples because individuals from a variety of backgrounds would work together in a common global operation. In the resulting world order, economic rather than political institutions would prevail, and dollars, francs, or pounds might replace missiles and tanks as "weapons," with a corresponding diminution of violence. Yet, as Robert Heilbroner suggests in his article "The Multinational Corporations and the Nation-State," it is still not clear precisely what role this comparatively novel institution will play in future international politics. Multinational corporations are still run by individuals based in, and citizens of, a particular nation, and it is not clear whether these corporations are simply extensions of the most powerful nation-states or whether they represent a new kind of institution entirely.

Although the articles in the second section of part three focus explicitly upon the United States, they deal with problems of bureaucracy and authority that affect the actions of all governments and hence the degree of tranquillity and stability in international relations.

In "The Ten Commandments of the Foreign Affairs Bureaucracy," Leslie Gelb and Morton Halperin demonstrate the importance of bureaucratic interests in the conduct of American foreign policy, and they refer to a variety of historical examples to substantiate their position. Showing that the interests of lower echelon personnel may be quite different from the goals of the national leadership, Gelb and Halperin caution against the patterns which emerged in the Johnson and Nixon administrations. In the former, the bureaucracy succeeded in hiding the diversity of views in a makeshift consensus which they called "option B"; in the latter, the Kissinger apparatus was used to bypass the bureaucracy completely. Gelb and Halperin suggest a third alternative in which conflicts between competing bureaucracies would be used to maintain morale of individual agencies but at the same time keep the president better informed.

Sanford J. Ungar's "The Intelligence Tangle" deals more specifically with the dangers of a foreign policy based on an "ends justifies the means" philosophy within the bureaucracy and at the White House as well. In the light of revelations involving the CIA and the FBI, Ungar demonstrates that the danger to basic American liberties can be acute when public servants conclude they are above the law in formulating and implementing policy. Ungar addresses himself to the agonizing questions raised by the misdeeds of the intelligence community. Are there occasions when covert operations are necessary and justifiable? Can national policies be articulated to give adequate guidance to spies, analysts, and operatives? How much should the public, and public officials, be told? The key question is deciding how to reform the intelligence agencies. In February 1976 President Ford announced several changes in government procedures, including the creation of an independent three-man oversight board, the expansion of the CIA director's authority over the entire intelligence community, and the renaming and reorganization of the Forty Committee, which became infamous for its supervision of covert operations. As Ungar's article suggests, the reforms have not stemmed the tide of criticism of the executive branch's approach to the intelligence issue in Washington.

In "How Could Vietnam Happen? An Autopsy," James Thomson examines the most notorious instance of the application of bureaucratic methods to a particular area of U.S. foreign policy. U.S. involvement in Vietnam resulted from a variety of misconceptions, as well as policy errors; but the Vietnam debacle might have been averted had not the bureaucratic procedures intended to produce careful consideration of all possible options become highly convoluted. Thomson, who was personally involved in the early stages of the Vietnam imbroglio under both Presidents Kennedy and Johnson, attempts to show how the Vietnam War came about. He presents us with an extraordinary case history of a government making incremental decisions based on misleading information and false conceptions. The perils of the bureaucratic crisis in the U.S. government, the risks of bureaucratic entanglement for all governments, and the threat to world order created by bureaucratic procedures are thus graphically presented.

In the past, turmoil or crisis has sometimes brought forth the dramatic emergence of individuals capable of rallying those who sought radical change. As did Lincoln and Churchill, such leaders have brought their countries through great crises and led them to a new era. A "great man" usually emerges in a crisis, often a war, and is recognized beyond his actual political acumen and achievements for the philosophy of life or ideology he represents. He is often a scholar or a literary figure. In the first edition of this book we examined the achievements of two of the most controversial and intriguing figures of our time, Mao Tse-tung and Charles de Gaulle. We thereby provided a useful balance to any examination of the crisis of institutions, for it is not only bureaucracies which control governments and the course of international affairs. The individual values, objectives, style, and effectiveness of a determined and vigorous leader at the pinnacle of a governmental hierarchy may in certain circumstances affect greatly that government's policies as well as the international order. Whereas it may be that the course of international and domestic institutions will be the primary determinants of the future global system, the role of individual leaders in positions of great authority cannot be ignored.

In this edition, we chose not to include specific articles about great men, having decided that no individual in recent years has dominated international politics in the manner of a Lenin or a Wilson. Richard Nixon or Indira Gandhi might be chosen for their misdeeds; Henry Kissinger for his diplomatic acrobatics and finesse; Mao might have been chosen again for his monumental effect on international politics and American foreign policy. But, since the death of such figures as Mao and de Gaulle, ours is generally an age of leadership by technocrats. We suffer the tyranny of the bureaucratic personality. Charisma is largely lacking among national leaders, except in the very new nations, and many of these leaders are either dying out or being overthrown. The significance of leadership should be remembered; the absence of a "great men" section in this edition symbolizes the poverty of present statesmanship.

Internationalism: The Crisis of International Institutions and Unity Movements

24 Europe's Identity Crisis

Daniel Yergin

United Europe, the Europe of the Nine, is in crisis—"a crisis of confidence, a crisis of will, a crisis of lucidity," in the words of Commission President François-Xavier Ortoli. But when was the Community not in crisis? For crisis is the inevitable companion for a venture of such unclear boundaries—the attempt to create a new political and economic system on the back of six or nine old ones, to do so without the sanction of force or disaster, but rather by consensus and conscious will, all in the direction of a goal that is uncertain in outline and legitimacy.

Still, just as the current world recession is deeper and different from other postwar recessions, so this crisis in the Community is more intense, and unlike previous crises. Indeed, Gaston Thorn, the new president of its Council, recently announced that the Community's only achievement in 1975 was that it did not fall apart. The Nine are like kin, arguing ever more sharply about how they are related, and what obligations they bear to each other and to the entire family, and whether they should do anything about any of it, in any event.

One senses around the Berlaymont, the triangular glass skyscraper in Brussels that is the Community's headquarters, the frustrations of those who want to feel themselves a part of a government, but realize they are not, and begin to feel they may never be. The resulting discouragement only makes matters worse, for the fuel of European integration is political will.

To help sort out the mess, the Community more than a year ago commissioned the Belgian Prime Minister Leo Tindemans to undertake a vast survey of the state of the Community. Last month, he finally produced his report. Considering that it is supposed to be a landmark, it was greeted with muted fanfare, but then it is a muted report, concentrating on procedural matters, leaving the grand vision for another day—if there is still a grand vision.

The refrain of those committed to the European idea is that there is no choice; integration must proceed; the will must be found. But there are alternatives, three alternatives. One, not very palatable to the "Europeans," is for the Community to remain what it is today— essentially, a common market with agricultural policy and some antitrust procedures. The second alternative involves a change of character, with a redirection away from the creation of an "automatic" community, to a less-reassuring voluntary community, a bloc, a con- federation, an affiliation of like-minded states that continue to insist upon the trappings of sovereignty. The third is for the Community to fall apart, an occurrence that, despite all the discouragement, must be discounted, in the face of 19 years of association and institutional inter- weaving.

Whatever the course, it will be shaped by the European response to a number of pressing problems.

Coping with Contraction. The first decade-and-a-half of the Com- munity's lifetime was also a period of prosperity and rapid growth. In the early 1970s, instability began to interfere with economic processes, culminating in the present slump of unprecedented severity in postwar experience. This slump has placed considerable pressure on the Com- munity, which has been bereft of effective cooperation. Each nation is waiting for another's recovery. There is a lack of common prescrip- tions, a lack of common outlook among the Nine as to what is tolerable in inflation and unemployment. In some ways the countries have been working against each other. Contraction eliminates the margins that normally exist in government budgets and in sectors of the economy that can cushion painful readjustments; it increases the sensitivity of pressure groups, reduces the time horizons of governments, and thus puts them in a position of having to choose between their communi- tarian values and constituent interests. They can no longer calm those interests by promising that integration will promote overall growth. It gets increasingly difficult to resist demands of domestic groups, even demands that run counter to the concept of a free trade Community: France slaps a border tax on Italian wines, Britain institutes selective import controls, and it gets harder for other countries to say no to their constituents.

Germany, whose wealth has put it in the position of Community paymaster but which in the face of rising budget deficits is trying to practice austerity at home, has become critical of the growth of the Community's budget, especially that of the common agriculture policy. Discord feeds upon itself. "What we feel in the German attitude is a kind of intolerance of everybody else," observed one senior Italian official. "They feel they can do everything better by themselves. Of course, they are wealthy, they export, they have a strong balance of payments and low inflation, they are well organized. But they underestimate the advantages of one European market—they benefit almost as much as French agriculture."

Contraction also causes the Community international complications. Reduction of trade barriers, or even the maintenance of present barriers, depends upon a certain finessing, again, on that margin to cushion shock. The margin has shrunk between the United States and the Community, resulting, since the middle of 1975, in a trade skirmish, principally over automobiles and steel.

The best solution to this challenge would, of course, be economic recovery. Prospects for recovery, unfortunately, remain uncertain. A good deal of the power to affect it is not in European hands, although the Germans could do more. The Nine are left with the less than satisfying program of merely coping—realizing that such pressures will mount, working to minimize them, and remembering that they do not mean that dissolution is imminent.

Establishing Legitimacy. The European Community involves nine democratic countries but is itself only indirectly democratic. In recent years, it has come to resemble more and more a confederation of associated states, an entente with a secretariat, rather than an entirely new political entity. The Commission, the civil service in Brussels, has suffered a relative loss of independent authority since the middle 1960s, and it has become more clearly subordinated to national governments, rather than an alternative to them. The Council, the forum for the individual governments, has become more visible and active; the heads of government meet at least three times a year. The foreign ministers are expanding their supervisory role. Such a development of course satisfies the desire of the national governments to maintain their own positions. The French have seen this as an alternative to economic integration. The reconfirmation of British membership has contributed to this direction.

European purists object to this "nationalization" of the Community. They remain attracted by the concept of "spill-over," in which—according to theory—the extension of authority in one area automatically creates other problems, which in turn demand a further extension of authority. Such, so the theory went, would inevitably bring about the desired goal, the withering away of the national state.

Developments have not followed theory; and, in fact, there is much to recommend the alternative of nationalization. After all, here is where habit does change reality; this very orientation indicates a commitment of the nine governments to act together in a Community, and it promotes continuously close contacts at functional levels among the countries' political leaders and foreign and civil services. Bureaucracies move closer in such a confederal process. But at the same time, it does tend to freeze the Community at a certain level and emphasizes the consensual rather than "organic" character of the Community. It is also a potentially reversible process, especially if one of the three major countries should be led by a would-be De Gaulle.

This last possibility points up the importance of the further development of the European Parliament. Now that the United

Nations has turned into a confrontation between "producers" and "consumers" (as though the consumers were not also producers), interrupted only occasionally by dialogues between producers and consumers and by efforts of dictatorships to denounce or expel democracies, the European Parliament may well have become the most interesting multinational assembly in the world. Despite the awkward and somewhat playful names of the parties (*e.g.* European Progressive Democrats, European Conservative party), it is a far more serious organization than one might think. Many of the 198 legislators, who are selected from the membership of their national parliaments, easily spend 150 days a year in the sessions (in Luxembourg and Strasbourg) and committee meetings (in Brussels) of the European Parliament. It has limited but growing budget powers, the right to force the Commission and the Council to reconsider matters, and the influence to spotlight positions and issues.

Today the parliament is an assembly of Europeans, not Europe's parliament. Its real importance is that it can become the latter and thus gain legitimacy for itself and for the Community. The current proposals provide for direct elections to be held in May 1978 to an enlarged parliament of 355 people. These elections raise a number of problems with important consequences. For instance, can candidates continue to be members of national parliaments as well? If not, will participation in the European Parliament, as one German official put it, "be worthwhile not just for third rate experts on milk prices?" Low turnout and lack of attention would certainly diminish the "will" towards integration. But if elections are taken seriously, then there will be opposing candidates, and they will have to find issues to separate them from their opponents, and the Community's affairs will become politicized, a subject of contention at mass levels, and not merely that of elites and specific interest groups at specific times.

The national governments have endorsed direct elections with varying degrees of reservation, for as H. R. Nord, the secretary-general of the European Parliament, pointed out, "You cannot have a Community without stepping on the toes of national sovereignty." Direct elections will increase the power of the European Parliament *vis-à-vis* national parliaments, and some interesting constitutional clashes are inevitable. But the fact cannot be escaped; the Community makes decisions affecting people's lives, and that is the stuff of politics and elections.

Speaking With One Voice. At the end of 1969, the year De Gaulle left power, the heads of government began to move toward a political role for the Community in world affairs, that Europe start "to speak with one voice." There were a number of reasons for this effort. Economics was indeed becoming high politics, and the Community itself, as primarily an economic institution, would be involved in more controversial issues. The very existence of the Community with the magnetic attraction of its economic power, made it a factor in international politics. Enlargement, by involving Britain, the third major state of

Western Europe, would automatically add an extra foreign policy dimension; and the Nine could certainly have more influence speaking in one voice in world affairs than in nine voices. "In foreign affairs, sovereignty is the ability to influence the external world," explained one Italian official. "If you can't do that, what does sovereignty mean? If we Europeans want to establish a presence in foreign affairs, the way to do it is to unite."

The Political Cooperation Effort is essentially intergovernmental, without legal treaty foundation, running parallel to the Commission's work. It works on consensus, and any one government can wield a veto, but knowing that a veto threatens the whole effort. All the governments currently seem to find an interest in maintaining the momentum. The effort involves a coordination of viewpoints through regular consultations, three times a year for the heads of government, more frequently for foreign ministers, and even more frequently for political directors and specialists from the various foreign offices.

Its most notable achievement to date has been the coordination of policy on Portugal (belatedly) and in the European Security Conference, where the Nine worked out, in the first instance, the Western policy positions. They also worked up a European position at the seventh special session of the United Nations General Assembly last September. Though not political cooperation strictly speaking, the Europeans managed to establish a foreign policy presence through the so-called Lomé Convention, which provides tariff advantages and export income stabilization to 46 developing nations. Less promising is the Euro-Arab dialogue, stalled because of the all-consuming Arab interest in pushing the Europeans to an anti-Israel position.

This political cooperation effort is going to face even more challenging tests in framing a specifically European effort, which is what is necessary, to deal with the new Spain and also with the succession crisis that is near in Yugoslavia. The US has not welcomed the development of this cooperation, which is a pity since it does add a strong force committed to common values; but that opposition is likely to be temporary, the product of the now receding monopoly over policy enjoyed by a virtuoso Secretary of State.

Structure. With what kind of structure shall the Community seek unity? There is still some question as to whether Britain is committed to further integration; no doubt it will take at least another year or two to know whether Britain's membership is serious. Even before Britain is completely digested, more nations are trying to serve themselves up. The most eager is Greece, an associate member since 1961, which applied for full membership in June, 1975. The Nine have formally approved. The reasons for agreement on both sides are the same—participation in the Community will help underwrite continued democracy in Greece. Yet Greek participation would raise many problems. There is reason to question whether Greek industry and agriculture and its civil service could cope with the pressures of membership. Greek membership would dilute the political force of the Community, and add another economic "sick man" to the list that currently includes Britain, Italy and Ireland, putting further strains on the agricultural and regional funds. Similar considerations will be involved with future applications from Turkey, Portugal and Spain. Such a prospect certainly makes the integration process more difficult and runs the risk instead of turning the Community into a more neutral extended free trade area. The answer may be a new intermediate status between full and associate membership.

It is ironic that European leaders should be talking about integrating nations into a larger polity when the nation-states themselves are under pressure, not merely from the new forces of transnationalism, but also from a revival of old forces, nationalism, or, more properly, subnationalism. If the Community is eroding national sovereignty on one side, then these subnationalisms—reflecting a renewal of old conflicts that, as so often is the case, are tied to language—are doing much the same on the other, most noticeably in the United Kingdom, France, Belgium and perhaps Italy. The sanction of force cannot be easily applied, as it can be in Eastern Europe. The separatist movements in turn see the European Community as their ally and talk about a "Europe of Regions." That may be a possibility in the longer term, but it is hard to see how it can be achieved, for if the national governments perceive the Community as an ally of the separatists, then they will step back from participation in it.

Integration. The heart of the effort to create not merely an affiliation of nine sovereign countries, a kinship community, but a supranational entity is the process of integration—of economies, laws and institutions. The work still goes on, chipping away at non-tariff barriers, harmonizing company laws and taxes, making it possible for a lawyer in one country to practice in another. But it is a slow process, and the very slowness causes despair. A small example. The largest Dutch brewer, Heineken, has for years included in its home division not merely the Netherlands but also the rest of the European Community countries. But the company has recently concluded that the "harmonization" of duties, laws and standards is still so far away that it is reorganizing; now the other eight countries will become part of the company's international division. The explanation of the managing director might sound like an epitaph: "The problem of managing our interests in the EEC countries apart from Holland are much more similar to those of territories outside Europe than the problems we meet in the Netherlands." The integration process has one success to its recent credit, the establishment of the Regional Development Fund, which is intended to help modernize backward and retarded areas (primarily Ireland, Southern Italy and the north of Britain) as a counterweight to the Community's tendency to accentuate differences between rich and poor regions.

Against this achievement must be matched two large and prominent failures. In 1972 Andrew Shonfeld speculated: "The problem of how to reinforce the Community's capacity for decisive action remains. No doubt, a manifest crisis, requiring a joint policy in a hurry, would be a good help—a military threat, or the prospect of a world slump or perhaps some critical shortage of a commodity like oil putting our whole economic system at risk." Slump aside, the shortage occurred, but the opposite has happened. The energy crisis has emphasized differences in outlooks and problems of the members, and promoted fragmentation rather than concert. European energy policy means primarily parallel, but still individual, policies of individual countries, while coordination goes on within the 18-nation International Energy Agency, in which the United States plays a leading role. Finally at the December 1975 summit, the leaders of the Nine did, belatedly, agree in principle to an emergency oil sharing scheme and to a floor price for oil. But, in terms both of Community action, and strengthening the Community this is still little and late.

The great failure has been on the question of fundamental forward movement—toward what has been called Economic and Monetary Union. As outlined in the years 1969–71, it was to be achieved in three steps by 1980. What was to be achieved beyond the first step of monetary unification was never clearly delineated. And that's just as well, for that first step of monetary unification collapsed quickly enough. Inflation and slump provided a bad era for attempting to mate currencies. Moreover currency is both a symbolic and practical demonstration of sovereignty. The governments were unwilling to surrender it, especially when other aspects of economic life remain unintegrated. This failure has resulted in a widespread feeling that future integration is impossible. On the contrary, small steps toward integration, though with realistic expectations of their overall impact, remain an important part of the process towards the European goal. There remains the task of identifying areas in which the Community's competence can be extended. Terrorism, for example, provides room for Commission action, for coordination among interior ministries, and for the Community to take a foreign policy position toward countries that on the one hand want preferred access to Europe but on the other provide succor and support for groups carrying out terrorist activities in Europe.

In his year of peregrinating from city to city in Europe, in effect taking depositions, Belgian Prime Minister Tindemans had ample opportunity to hear the complaints that arise from all these problems, and his proposals are meant as a response. Instead of a grand blueprint for Europe United, decorated with dates and pious declarations, he has offered up a series of smaller, but still significant goals, of a practical and procedural nature: closer integration of foreign policies, including the removal of the veto; Community responsibility for crises in the "region" of Europe; expanded powers for the European Parliament; the appointment of one spokesman to deal with the United States in a "dialogue based on equality"; joint weapons buying; closer links among all Community currencies.

His most controversial proposal is for a kind of two-tier Community, in which those with stronger economies like France and Germany march quickly towards further integration, while countries with weaker economies like Britain and Italy are left behind, to catch up when and as best they can. Such a proposal could be ultimately self-defeating; for it could create an Inner Market very much different from an Outer Market, the latter in effect nothing more than a customs union adjunct.

But whether this report actually leads to a stronger Community depends upon another factor, to which Tindemans alluded when he criticized the "lack of political will" on the part of Europe's leaders. For finally it is only conscious political will that can bridge problems. "Will" means a commitment to the ideology of unity, to the European Idea, and that in turn raises the fundamental problem—that the European Idea may be exhausted, in part by its own successes.

The impetus behind this idea was a desire to reform Europe, in particular to resolve the conflict between France and Germany. Here the Community succeeded. The other reasons? To create a counterweight against Soviet power in the East—another goal achieved. And the economic reasons? That an expanded market would promote prosperity and prevent return to the autarkic economic policies of the 1930s. Another success, the current recession notwithstanding. All three reasons are still valid, though less clearly obvious.

Another strong impetus was the fact that the United States wanted a united Europe. Indeed, the best "Europeans" were the Americans, and European integration was a major policy goal, vigorously pursued from the first post-World War II days.

In the past several years, however, it has no longer been clear that current US leaders still want a united Europe that could become an unmanageable ally and a new rival. Certainly such suspicion is rife in Europe. "The basic problem is that the United States did good work after the war to help establish a kind of community in Europe," observed a German diplomat. "But the Europeans now feel that the Americans are astounded by the result and are saying 'we didn't mean it this way'. They had a love affair with the idea, but they won't acknowledge the child. Now we're grown up, nearly an equal."

Hard as it may be for some Americans and even Europeans to believe, the United States is far less central to the entire enterprise, and its wishes will increasingly count for less, especially now that Britain is part of the Community and the "special relationship" fades into the past. "I often think," speculated a British official assigned to Brussels, "that the best way to get the Nine to agree on a position today is for the United States to oppose it."

The European generations that, from their own adult experience, were deeply committed to the European Idea are passing from the scene; the gains from further integration are not altogether obvious to their successors. But there are cogent new arguments. The range and scale of emerging problems like energy can best be met in a European framework. Acting in concert, the Europeans can establish a foreign policy presence of major benefit to the individual countries.

"I keep thinking we did take on quite a lot, trying to change course from a thousand years of history," observed H. R. Nord, of the European Parliament, whose own conversion to the European Idea occurred during World War II. "I'm not too frustrated after 19 years." But it should also be said that the easier things were done first, in easier times. It does no good to predict on the basis of logic or trends that there will be a united Europe. If there is any rule, it is otherwise: whether Europe is ready for unity, whatever the methods, depends upon only one factor—whether the Europeans want it.

25 The Use of the United Nations in World Politics

Abraham Yeselson and Anthony Gaglione

Hope, disappointment, indifference, anger, and resentment blend to form the contemporary American view of the United Nations. Throughout the Western world, criticism is mounting against the irresponsibility of General Assembly majorities which elevate the status of the Palestine Liberation Organization, arbitrarily deny a voice to the Republic of South Africa, and pass unenforceable resolutions affecting the economic interests of the capitalist world.[1] Furthermore, hypocrisy reigns when the Assembly condemns white supremacy in South Africa or Rhodesia while ignoring the most brutal violations of human rights in Uganda or the Soviet Union. Idealists lament the wreckage of dreams and aspirations which were incorporated into the UN Charter 30 years ago. Confusion about the UN is compounded by a generation of academicians who have consistently perceived special benefits for mankind resulting from the continued existence of the organization. Starting from the ideals in the Charter, they develop theories consistent with those principles. They find that the injection of the UN into world politics alters the international system and promotes more positive behavior patterns by national actors. Some even insist that there is a comparable relationship between structural development within the UN and the growth of parliamentary democracy.[2] Others argue that the UN contributes to a consensus concerning such general problems as colonialism and economic underdevelopment.[3] There are those who claim that debate at the UN is a healthy form of catharsis which reduces the potential for physical violence.[4] They explain failures in terms of structural defects or maverick behavior by one or a few member states.

Actually, laymen and experts have been deceived. In a world characterized by nationalism and sovereignty, the proper starting point of analysis must be the motivation of those who use the UN to advance selfish interests. The most crucial question is: "Who brings what issues into the United Nations and why?" If the intention were to solve disputes peacefully, there would be prior agreement concerning the site for negotiations, procedures, and the definition of the issues in conflict. These vital preliminary steps are nearly always missing in respect to questions before the UN. At least one of the parties usually vehemently opposes having an issue discussed in the organization. Thus, it becomes clear that initiating member states are consciously seeking national advantage through the exercise of conflict diplomacy at the UN. The opponent correctly perceives this step as a hostile act. When this observation is buttressed by the fact that states enjoying good relations *never* air their differences in the world forum, it can be concluded that the use of the UN provides both a barometer of the level of interstate hostility and a weapon in world politics.

As is true for any other weapon, the United Nations is not available to all. Certain nations—*e.g.*, Israel and the Republic of South Africa—can never hope to achieve national ends through the UN. During the first 20 years of the Cold War, the Western allies dominated debate and actions in the organization. However, as a result of the membership explosion, the world body has become increasingly less useful for the U.S. and other Western countries. On the other hand, developing countries and the socialist bloc are presently the beneficiaries of whatever advantages may be secured in the organization. Although issues and targets change, the strategic objectives of initiating states remain fairly constant because their possibilities are determined by the unique qualities of the UN as a weapon.

STRATEGIES IN THE UNITED NATIONS

An analysis of political issues brought to the General Assembly and the Security Council suggests that the UN is most effective in relation to four general strategies—embarrassment, status, legitimization, and socialization. All of these are conflict strategies, and sometimes initiating states will employ more than one of them simultaneously. Estimates of success or failure must relate to these purposes, and not to those based on assumptions that the UN is an independent actor. To illustrate, the Hungarian issue was raised in the UN in order to embarrass the Soviet Union and the government of Janos Kadar.[5] The intent was precisely the same as that of the Soviet Union in bringing American intervention in the Dominican Republic to the Security Council nine years later.[6] In both instances, the initiating state was unwilling to commit its military forces to the side of the victim of Great Power intervention. The UN provided a convenient forum for the expression of frustration and rage. This is characteristic of embarrassment politics. It explains, in part, the supposed ineffectiveness of the UN because analysts fail to appreciate that the states seeking to embarrass opponents are disinterested in a solution.

The politics of status has been used consistently by anti-colonialist states. A normal first step is to have an area defined as a non-self-governing territory as a prelude to demands for independence for indigenous populations. This process is now being followed in respect to Puerto Rico. By insisting that the correct name for Southwest Africa is Namibia, the General Assembly confers added status to the natives of that place. A recent, dramatic use of this strategy involved the use of the General Assembly to improve the bargaining position of the Palestine Liberation Organization.[7] At the same time, an unsuccessful effort was made to confer status on Prince Sihanouk of Cambodia by having his authority recognized over that of Lon Nol in the General Assembly.[8] This strategy is hardly of recent origin. Status politics was at the root of early disagreements concerning the admission of new member states. During the Cold War, the West actively promoted the status of South Korea, South Vietnam, and the Federal Republic of Germany by acquiring observer status for these states. Although the U.S. denounced the China-led attempt to displace Lon Nol in the General Assembly, it might be recalled that the U.S. was successful in 1960 in having a delegation led by Pres. Joseph Kasavubu recognized as the legitimate government of the Congo, rather than one headed by Premier Patrice Lumumba.[9] For new states, admission into the UN confers a final seal of respectability.

Legitimization is a strategy used by states which wish to reenforce ongoing policies. These policies include preparation and use of war. Thus, the American decision to fight in Korea was backed by the legitimizing function of the UN. Other examples of this strategy would include use of the organization during the Berlin air-lift, the Cuban missile crisis, and the Vietnam war. In all cases, the UN was a support for policies determined elsewhere. A prerequisite for legitimization politics is that states using the strategy be able to control debate or the passage of resolutions in the organization. It is not surprising, therefore, that early uses would be made by the West against the communist states, and that present uses would involve developing countries and Arab states. By defining colonialism and Zionism as "permanent aggression," these countries have laid the foundation for the legitimization of any actions—including use of war—against Israel or colonial territories.

Finally, we define the strategy of socialization as efforts by one side—usually the weaker—to change the balance of forces. The very first conflict brought to the Security Council—the complaint of Iran against the Soviet Union—illustrated this objective.[10] Since then, there have been numerous other examples of this strategy. The same basic purpose motivated Panama to complain in 1973 about American occupation of the Canal Zone.[11] An obvious reason for Arab use of the UN against Israel is to modify American support of the Jewish state by forcing the U.S. to use its veto and, thus, be otherwise isolated in the organization. In the Arab-Israeli dispute, too, it is obvious that Arab-dictated cease-fires are a more potent weapon than Soviet-supplied missiles. The apparent ability to end a war at will permits one side to escape defeat on the battlefield and provides the military, geographical, and psychological bases for the next war.

IMPACT ON CONFLICTS

Having identified national strategies, it becomes easier to understand the impact of conflict diplomacy on the actual disputes. As is true for any other weapon, the introduction of the UN into a dispute changes the nature of the dispute and has as a normal effect the exacerbation of international relations. Contrary to the opinion of some publicists, neither moral nor legal restraints flow from the invocation of Charter principles at the UN. National interest creates the necessary rationalizations. In the world forum, all states defend all policies by reference to the Charter. Appropriate clauses are selected to support policies on each issue, and states exchange positions easily. Thus, the Soviet Union objected bitterly when Jan Papanek, former chief delegate to the UN from Czechoslovakia, addressed the Security Council in 1948.[12] The Russians argued that the organization could hear only bona-fide representatives of governments. Later, of course, the Soviets supported the appearances of Archbishop Makarios of Cyprus and Yasir Arafat of the P.L.O. As noted above, the U.S. objected that the General Assembly had no business deciding between the claims of Lon Nol and Prince Sihanouk in Cambodia, but urged precisely that action in support of Pres. Kasavubu over Premier Lumumba in the Congo. States which insist that Israel may not retaliate against Arab states which base, arm, and encourage guerrilla incursions have themselves used the same "right." Charter principles are clearly convenient pegs on which to hang any foreign policy. This debasement of the principles causes them to lose whatever moral authority they might otherwise exert. Furthermore, victorious states are emboldened by the vindication of their policies, and losers are embittered by injustice.

CONFLICT VS. PEACE

Debate in the UN can now be seen accurately. It has nothing to do with peace, and everything to do with conflict. Real negotiations require that the parties define differences as narrowly as possible, avoid recrimination, and exclude extremists from the discussions. At the UN, issues are widened, insults are common, and the most violent spokesmen frequently dominate the debate. The effect of such deliberately provocative discussions is to contaminate efforts to achieve peaceful settlements. Furthermore, it is nonsense to claim that verbal assaults reduce chances for war because of the cathartic effect on the speakers.

When Jews are described as Nazis at the UN, Israelis become more than ever convinced that war is the only means of dealing with their enemies. Verbal abuse of the Chinese or the Russians by Westerners must be overcome when the West seeks an accommodation with the communist states. South Africans who are constantly reminded at the UN that their words are unworthy of being heard by more civilized ears become even more hardened in their positions. When nations desire peace, they follow the path of quiet diplomacy and avoid name-calling.

The decision-making process in the UN creates further impediments to peace. Resolutions won in support of national objectives widen differences and harden positions. Winners have difficulty abandoning the high ground which has been backed by "the opinion of mankind," and losers interpret the extreme positions as evidence that compromise is impossible. For both sides, the path to the negotiating table becomes more treacherous. When Arab states do not want to negotiate with Israel, they go to the UN and win resolutions concerning the Palestinian refugees or Jerusalem. Since the resolutions are not part of a negotiating process with Israel, they simply create new obstacles which must somehow be overcome during serious talks. Similarly, normalization of relations between the two Koreas requires the abandonment of pro-South Korean resolutions which have been adopted at the UN for a quarter of a century. India and Pakistan have been unable to go beyond a 1948 Security Council resolution which endorsed the principle of self-determination in Kashmir.[13] If relations between these two great Asian states are to improve, they must ignore that resolution and, finally, after three wars and 25 years of ill-feeling, negotiate a realistic settlement.

A further consequence of public diplomacy is that it reduces the potential for constructive third-party intervention in a dispute. Initiating states do their best to maximize support by involving as many other states in behalf of their causes as possible. Votes are traded off. Thus, when the Black African states were frustrated by Western vetoes in their effort to have the Republic of South Africa expelled from the UN, they turned to the General Assembly. There, they struck a deal with the Arab states who were simultaneously promoting the status of the Palestine Liberation Organization.[14] With Arab support, the General Assembly voted to silence the South African delegation. In return, the Black Africans supported the P.L.O. This process which constantly forces states to take sides has the effect of reducing the number of countries uninvolved in disputes. As a result, fewer and fewer statesmen are available for mediating or other helpful roles. The international arena becomes more inflexible.

There is still another unappreciated threat to peace resulting from uses made of the UN. It was assumed during the writing of the Charter in 1945 that cooperation among the Great Powers was the key to world peace. Whether or not this aspiration was realistic, it is clear that American-Soviet differences threatened to erupt into World War III in the period which culminated in the Cuban Missile Crisis of 1962. Now that there is at least the prospect of a limited détente among the U.S., the Soviet Union, and China, it can be seen that the superpowers cannot make the UN an effective means of preserving international peace. The world is too complex. Even during détente, there are areas where the Big Three compete for influence. To the extent that the appearance of harmony threatens the interests of other, smaller states, the latter do everything they can to exploit that competition and to disrupt relations among the powerful. The UN is a useful weapon for accomplishing this purpose. In addition to other objectives, the General Assembly debate on the Palestine Liberation Organization forced the U.S. to stand against the communist states. Even if it is granted that the Soviet Union wished to minimize conflicts with the U.S., its competition with China for influence in the developing world would compel the Russians to back the Arabs. Similarly, should developing countries press the Puerto Rican issue, communist countries, despite minimal real interest in that commonwealth, could well feel obligated to support the anti-colonialist majority and, thereby, exacerbate relations with the U.S. In short, not only does Great Power agreement fail to convert the UN into a viable peacekeeping organization, the availability of the organization for conflict purposes directly threatens their attempts to cooperate with one another.

CONCLUSIONS

The perspective underlying the discussion above squarely places the role of the UN within the context of world politics. Deliberate decisions to raise issues in the organization must be compared to equally conscious decisions to keep conflicts out of the UN. It is observed that, when states are seeking peaceful solutions to problems, they always avoid the UN. When Arab states raise the issue of status for the P.L.O., they deliberately advance a conflict position at the expense of negotiations in Geneva or anywhere else. Normalization of relations between the two Koreas can occur only by direct talks which abandon 25 years of rhetoric and resolutions in the UN. If Communist China does *not* raise the Taiwan issue at the UN, it is because that country still expects to achieve a satisfactory settlement of the problem. When "friendly" states bring issues into the organization, it is a sure sign of the deterioration of their relations. The Greco-Turkish conflicts over Cyprus is an obvious example. Most disputes among allies are resolved by quiet negotiations, because they are unwilling to jeopardize common interests by dramatizing their differences.

The implications for students of the UN are apparent. They must concentrate on national motivations in order to explain initiatives and other uses of the UN. When surrogates speak for particular causes—*e.g.,* the rights of blacks in the Republic of South Africa—it is essential that the interests of the surrogates be analyzed. Comparisons must be made between use and non-use of the UN in order to perceive the limitations of the organization in conflict politics. The impact of UN involvement on a dispute must be reassessed. It becomes irrelevant to consider so-called successes or failures for the UN when, in fact, the important questions relate to the strategies of those who are employing this weapon.

Those who would "reform" the UN must reexamine their thinking. It should be appreciated that the organization has already been amended, both formally and informally. In 1950, the Uniting for Peace Resolution was an attempt by the West to convert the General Assembly into a reserve Security Council.[15] By 1956, at least Britain and France had cause to regret the change when the new procedure was used against them during the Suez Canal crisis. By the 1970's, the chief sponsor, the U.S., had completely reversed its attitude towards the General Assembly. Although academic analysts spoke in terms of loose versus strict interpretation of the Charter, it has become obvious that support for one organ over another is no more than a tactical decision to be changed when conditions warrant. In 1965, a formal amendment of the Charter increased the membership of the Security Council to 15, thereby increasing the representation of Afro-Asian countries. They have used this additional leverage to apply greater pressure against Israel and colonialist powers. When reformers propose that the UN be strengthened, they must ask: "stronger for whom?" Other idealists searching for answers to the problem of war on this planet must abandon the UN model in developing their theories.

In the interests of world peace, the political role of the UN should be abandoned. Unfortunately, it is unlikely that this will occur precisely because the organization is considered a potent weapon in the pursuit of national interests. Although its diminished utility has caused the U.S. and other Western nations to reduce their support for the world body, Third World and communist countries will follow an opposite policy. In these circumstances, the best that can be recommended is that the dangers be recognized by statesmen, and that they adjust their policies accordingly.

NOTES

[1]Speech by U.S. Delegate John Scali to the General Assembly, quoted in *The New York Times,* Dec. 7, 1974, p. 15.

[2]See, for example, Herbert J. Spiro, *World Politics: The Global System* (Homewood, Ill.: Dorsey Press, 1966), p. 129.

[3]See Inis Claude, *The Changing United Nations* (New York: Random House, 1967), *passim.*

[4]See Keith S. Petersen, "The Uses of the United Nations," *Southwestern Social Science Quarterly,* June, 1963, p. 59.

[5]Security Council Official Records Meetings, 752–754, Oct. 28-Nov. 4, 1956.

[6]UN Document S/6316, May 1, 1965.

[7]*The New York Times,* Nov. 23, 1974, p. 6.

[8]*The New York Times,* Nov. 25, 1974, p. 6.

[9]General Assembly Resolution 1498 (XV), Nov. 22, 1960.

[10]*Yearbook of the United Nations,* 1946, p. 332.

[11]*The New York Times,* Nov. 12, 1972.

[12]Security Council Official Records Meeting 268, March 17, 1948.

[13]UN Document S/726, April 21, 1948.

[14]*The New York Times,* Nov. 13, 1974, p. 14.

[15]General Assembly Resolution 377 (V), Nov. 3, 1950.

26 The Multinational Corporation and the Nation-State

Robert L. Heilbroner

Of all the problems we call "economic," few have so baffled the expert and the nonexpert alike as those that involve the relations between nation-states. Indeed, one might even go so far as to say that economics, as a "science," got its start from efforts to explain how gold and goods traveled from nation to nation, working their various effects on the countries they left and those they entered. In particular, that ill-associated group of seventeenth- and early eighteenth-century pamphleteers we call the mercantilists deserve their place in the history of economic thought if only because they annoyed people like Hume and Adam Smith (among others) sufficiently to get economic inquiry started along its present lines.

The basic theme of mercantilist doctrine had, at first glance, a certain logic. The mercantilists believed that a nation's self-interest lay in the accumulation of a national treasure—gold. Gold was to be gained by selling goods to foreigners and was lost by buying goods from them. Therefore the pursuit of national self-interest resided in policies that would encourage exports and discourage imports, thereby increasing the stock of precious bullion by which the national wealth has to be measured.

To describe this underlying belief is enough to reveal that the philosophy of mercantilism is by no means dead. But at least in its original crude form, the mercantilist theory of international economic relations received its *coup de grâce* from the cool analysis of the classical economists. For the central message of Smith's *Wealth of Nations* (1776) was that the proper measure of national wealth was not its stock of gold bullion but its annual flow of production. The road to maximizing wealth lay therefore in the pursuit of policies that would encourage the increase in that annual flow—in particular, policies that would augment production by encouraging the division of labor.

Smith, accordingly, envisaged the basic objective of international economic relations as one of bringing about a world-wide division of labor, a point of view that clearly required a willingness to buy abroad as well as an eagerness to sell abroad. Under his great successor, David Ricardo, this doctrine received its first keen analytical treatment, as Ricardo demonstrated that one nation, such as England, would benefit by trading with another, such as Portugal, even though England might be able to produce *both* cloth and wine more effectively than Portugal.[1]

From this genuinely stunning insight of the classical economists there followed an obvious prescription regarding the economic relationships between nations. That was that the well-being, not merely of one nation but of *all* nations, would be achieved by a willing surrender to the international division of labor, in which each did the work for which its climate, soil, skills, etc., best suited it. As a corollary, of course, each would thereafter trade its own products for the products of other nations, with no effort to block this exchange by tariffs or other impediments (except in very special cases, such as the infant industries of emerging nations). Thus emerged the doctrine of free trade, a doctrine under which most economists still march, fortified by a century of theoretical buttressing of Ricardo's work which culminates, in our own time, in contributions by such major figures as Paul Samuelson and others.

Alas for economics, from the beginning this grand and logically impeccable doctrine has ruled the theory of international economic relations rather than its reality. The reasons are not difficult to find. First, there was the fact that the flows of trade between nations often failed to "balance," giving rise to complicated problems that had to be resolved by an international settlement of accounts. But this in turn was rendered difficult by the stubborn refusal of nation-states to adopt a single universal money-of-account, so that monetary bottlenecks of all kinds constantly prevented the smooth settlement of international obligations. (These so-called balance of payments problems also arose—and still do arise—from the fact that international financial transactions are not limited to the payment for international flows of goods and services, but are also used to transfer capital from one nation to another, to wage war overseas, to find a haven in numbered bank accounts in Switzerland, etc.) As a result, some nations have had trouble "financing" the imports they would have otherwise been willing to buy, while other nations have had trouble "selling" goods they were eager to get rid of because they were not willing to accept payment in another country's currency.

Second, the doctrine of free trade has from the beginning encountered the stubborn resistance of the very workmen and employers whose ultimate well-being it was supposed to promote. No doubt part of the appeal of Ricardo's theory lay in the fact that there were, in fact, no wine-makers in England who were being asked to shift to sheepshearing. But the advice is more difficult to follow for the wine-makers of California who might be advised to take up automobile making, or for the French auto worker who is urged into champagne-bottling, so that the international output of both wine and automobiles might thus be maximized.

Last, the classical doctrine of the international specialization of labor and free trade has received its most crushing rejection from those nations on whom the theory was imposed most ruthlessly. Among the underdeveloped nations of the world a genuine specialization of labor did take place, accompanied by a more or less free importation of their products. But the emergence of banana-economies and coffee-economies and copper-economies did not bring with it the gradual convergence of living standards that was implicit in the theories of both Ricardo and Samuelson. Instead, the mono-economies discovered to their dismay that the ruling doctrine worked to widen rather than to narrow the disparity between themselves and their rich customers—a state of affairs for which standard theory had no explanation at all.[2]

II

I trust that the reader, especially if he or she is an economist, will forgive this capsule resumé of the theory of international economic relations. I offer it not to attack current theory, large portions of which are relevant to and indispensable for an understanding of these relations. My purpose, rather, is to set the stage for an exposition of the most important change in both the conception and practice of international economic affairs since Hume and Smith and Ricardo first promulgated the notion of international *trade* as the paradigm for the economic intercourse of nations. This change is the emergence of a new form of international economic relationship, based not so much on the exchange of goods as on the *internationalization of production itself*—an internationalization arising from the startlingly rapid growth of what are called multinational corporations.

Perhaps the best way to illustrate the nature of the change is to examine the multinational operation in action. Let me begin with a description of his own company offered by Donald M. Kendall, president of PepsiCo:

> PepsiCo [operates] in 114 countries. Its most familiar product is bottled in 512 plants outside the United States. Production and distribution facilities in almost every country are owned by nationals of those countries. Regional managers may come from the area in question—or from some other part of the world—Frenchmen, Englishmen, Latin Americans—not necessarily from the United States. In the Philippines, where PepsiCo is about the twelfth largest taxpayer, the whole operation has only two persons from the home office. The company is multinational as far as employment, operations, manufacturing and marketing are concerned, and a good part of the operating management and plant ownership abroad is also multinational.[3]

We will come back to certain aspects of this multinational operation—one suspects, for example, that the two Americans in the Philippine office are not office boys. But the essence of the matter is that PepsiCo no longer exports Pepsi-Cola to, say, Mexico. *It produces it there.* And precisely this same internationalization of production is to be found in IBM, General Motors, Ford, Standard Oil, and so on down the hierarchy of American corporate enterprise. I do not wish to imply that every big company is multinational. But we do know that sixty-two of the top one hundred firms have production facilities in at least six foreign countries, and Kenneth Simmonds has shown that seventy-one of the top 126 industrial corporations (for which data could be obtained) averaged one-third of their employment abroad.[4] . . .

Meanwhile, on a broader canvas, there is little doubt about the importance of US international production taken as a whole. In 1966 . . . the United States exported $43 billion of goods and services to various parts of the world. In that same year, the value of United States overseas production—that is, of goods and services made in US-owned factories or establishments abroad—came to $110 billion, or two and a half times as much.

Another way of establishing the importance of international production is to trace the rise in the value of US foreign "direct" investment (that is, investment in real assets rather than in securities). In 1950 the size of our foreign direct investment was roughly $11 billion. In 1969 it was something over $70 billion, or about one-fifth of the total assets (domestic as well as foreign) of the top 500 industrials. Moreover this figure for foreign direct investment represents only the value of the American dollars invested abroad, and not the additional value of foreign capital that is controlled by these American enterprises (for instance by their command over subsidiaries).[5] If we add these assets to the purely American ones, the value of the American business empire abroad comes to considerably more than $100 billion.[6]

This is still, however, only part of the changing picture of international economic relations. The expansion of American corporate production abroad, especially in Europe, has given rise to a general awareness of The American Challenge, best expressed in Servan-Schreiber's book of that name. But as economists Stephen Hymer and Robert Rowthorn point out, what seems to Europeans like an American challenge can be seen from another vantage point as a challenge *to* American corporations.[7] For whereas it is true that American companies in Europe have been expanding faster than their European rivals, thereby scaring the daylights out of many Europeans, it is also true that European corporations have been expanding their total production, in Europe and abroad, as fast as or faster than the growth in *total* sales (at home and abroad) of the US giants.[8] Thus while we challenge Europe in Europe, the Europeans challenge us elsewhere in the world, including within our own borders (think of the invasion of the American automobile market by European models).

The dynamics of this challenge and counterchallenge are complex, depending in part on the general tendency of larger companies to grow *less* rapidly than not-quite-so-large ones (hence the slower average rate of growth of the American giant); in part on the effect of the environment on corporate effort (the American companies in Europe were operating in a very fast-expanding market); and partly again on the relative technological capabilities of different countries and companies.

But Hymer and Rowthorn's critical point is that the change in international economic relations is not an American, but a truly multinational phenomenon. If we take the ten leading capital exporting nations together, for example, we find that for 1967 their combined exports came to over $130 billion, whereas their combined overseas production amounted to at least $240 billion. Estimates by Professor Sidney Rolfe, by Judd Polk of the International Chamber of Commerce, and by Professor Howard Perlmutter (among others) indicate that the rate of capital outflow from the industrialized European nations and from Japan bears roughly the same proportion to their GNPs as does our own.

On the basis of such data, one can estimate that the value of international production of all kinds is now roughly equal to about a fourth of world output of the commodities produced, and that if the rate of expansion of overseas production continues as it has in the recent past, the internationals will account for half or more of world industrial output by the year 2000. Indeed, Professor Perlmutter has argued that some 300 corporations (200 of them American) will soon dominate the world economy in much the way that the fifty or one hundred top American corporations dominate our economy.[9]

But enough of these figures. The essential point is that the rise of the multinational corporation signals a new era in international economic relationships, an era in which the international shipment of domestically produced goods is giving way to one in which nations affect one another by directly producing "foreign" goods within each other's economies.

III

It must be apparent that the rise of the multinationals poses a bewildering array of questions. Why did they come into being? What is likely to be the outcome of the struggle among them? How does the rise of the vast international company affect the underdeveloped nations? How can a corporation simultaneously abide by the often conflicting laws and policies of a dozen countries? Is the multinational company a new source of potential international friction or an embryonic form of a new world order?

One asks such questions more to introduce some semblance of order into a sprawling problem than in the hope of providing crisp answers. As we shall see, much concerning the future of the multinationals remains obscure and unpredictable. But we can at least begin with some facts, for thanks to the work of Mira Wilkins, we now have a picture of the evolution of the overseas thrust of corporations, comparable to their domestic evolution from single-plant, single-product firms to multidivisional enterprises.[10] For the reason why a corporation should *produce* abroad is, on reflection, not self-evident. It is expensive for a corporation to run facilities overseas. Inevitably, it leads to the kinds of economic and political tangles that our initial set of questions suggests. If the profit drive is the impelling force behind corporate expansion, as most economists and businessmen tell us it is, we must explain why at one stage a corporation is perfectly content to export its wares, at another point to license their production overseas, and then finally to assume the responsibility for their actual foreign production.

As Miss Wilkins points out, the involvement of American business with foreign production has a considerable history. Samuel Colt, the inventor and successful producer of automatic pistols on an "assembly line" basis in America, transplanted his equipment and key workmen to

London in the mid-1850s, and promptly failed. On the other hand, in those same years a group of American capitalists and engineers pushed the first railway across the Panama isthmus; and by the 1870s, Singer Sewing Machine was successfully producing abroad (in Scotland) and was in fact selling half its total output overseas. Moreover the degree of penetration (by export as well as production) continued until by 1914 a British writer could already speak on an "American challenge" in these terms:

> The most serious aspect of the American industrial invasion lies in the fact that these newcomers have acquired control of almost every new industry created during the past fifteen years. . . . What are the chief new features of London life? They are, I take it, the telephone, the portable camera, the phonograph, the electric street car, the automobile, the typewriter, passenger lifts in houses, and the multiplication of machine tools. In every one of these, save the petroleum automobile, the American maker is supreme; in several, he is the monopolist.[11]

Miss Wilkins's work allows us to see a certain organizational logic behind the quantum leaps overseas. It lies (if I may read certain conclusions into her work) in the existence of critical thresholds of size, domestic market saturation, and technology—thresholds that may differ from industry to industry, but that provide for each one, at some stage in its development, a point at which it is "natural" (i.e., more profitable) to take the leap.[12]

What is it, then, that marks the recent surge of international investment? If my speculations are justified, the answer must lie in the arrival of more and more industries at their critical thresholds, powerfully aided in our day by the development of a new technology for transferring information that makes it not markedly more difficult to supervise a plant in Hong Kong than one in Indianapolis. In a general way we can trace the influence of the improvement in the technology of supervision by noting the long-term shift of investment away from "next door" to more distant areas. In 1897, 56 percent of our direct foreign investment was in Canada and Mexico; in 1914 it had fallen to 46 percent; in 1968 to 32 percent.[13]

A second part of the difference (I am here again speculating beyond the bounds of Miss Wilkins's work) can be traced to the gradual shift of corporate interest toward "high technology," as contrasted with heavy capital, products, and activities. In 1897, 59 percent of American foreign direct investment was in agriculture (plantations), mining, or railways; by 1969 this figure had dropped to 11 percent. Conversely, in 1897 only 15 percent of our overseas direct investment was in manufacturing; this has jumped to over 40 percent today.

This shift to high technology has redirected the marketing concentration of international direct investment. In 1897, 54 percent of our overseas direct investment was in the underdeveloped parts of the world, the remainder in the European-Canadian developed areas. Today the balance has swung the other way. Sixty-four percent of our foreign direct investment is now in Canada, Europe, and Oceania and only 36 percent in Asia, Africa, and Latin America. More striking, of the increase in American foreign direct investment during the last decade, almost three-quarters was located in the developed world.

Thus behind the rise of the interlocking, interpenetrating webs of overseas production there lies a certain logic of technology and organization—a logic that no doubt applies in much the same fashion to the expansion of European or Japanese investment as it does to our own. The gradual "saturation" of national markets (which occurred, needless to say, earlier in the small European nations than in our continental-sized one) provided the initial stimulus for a shift from mere export-orientation to true international production, and accounts for the fact that in 1914 European foreign investments (both direct and portfolio) were ten times larger than American; whereas in 1966 American direct investments were a third larger than European.[14]

Simultaneously, the explosion of high technology vastly altered the character of international enterprise in a direction favorable to American-dominated industries: the annual growth rate of IBM alone at home and abroad for the past decade has been sufficiently great so that, if it continues uninterrupted for another generation, IBM will be the largest single economic entity in the world, including the entities of nation-states. This proliferation of high technology in turn has redirected the areas in which international investment was profitable, turning it away from the banana groves of Honduras, whose market was relatively slow-growing, to the developed world where the demand for high technology products was expanding with extraordinary speed.

IV

What is apt to be the outcome of this shift in the nature of international economic relations? Here we move from the domain of fact, however shadowy, to that of findings, however speculative. Let us postpone the most tenuous of these to the end and deal initially with a few things that we know.

The first of these is that—despite the claim made on behalf of PepsiCo by Mr. Kendall—the great international producers are not "truly" multinational. With very few exceptions (one thinks of Unilever or Shell, whose ownership is genuinely divided between different national interests) most of the multi-corps, PepsiCo included, are essentially extensions of national enterprises, controlled by a single national center, in so far as the location of investment and (more important) the international remission of profits are concerned.

To be sure, the multinationals have learned to break away from what Howard Perlmutter calls an ethnocentric attitude, in which the number of calls made per day by a salesman in Hoboken becomes the standard for operations in Brazzaville or Buenos Aires, toward a more "polycentric" and even geocentric (world-oriented) perspective.[15] Moreover a few harbingers of true internationalism are visible in the presence of a Canadian as president of Standard Oil of New Jersey, a Venezuelan on its board, and a Frenchman as president of the IBM World Trade Corporation.[16]

But these are, I think it can safely be said, exceptions to the general rule of the tight retention of *national control* over the operations of the international corporation. As Kenneth Simmonds has pointed out (in the study we previously cited), foreigners constituted only 1.6 percent of the 1,851 top managers in those US companies with substantial employment overseas. Simmonds has not matched his findings with similar studies of Belgian, British, Swiss, Swedish, Japanese, etc., firms, but one has the strong suspicion that a similar conclusion would emerge. Simmonds, with his eye on the rise of American economic power in Europe, fears that an American "master race" of executives will come to control much of the international production of the globe, unless American corporations allow other nationals into the top echelons of power. On the other hand, if Hymer and Rowthorn are correct in stressing the genuinely multinational character of international production, we are more apt to have a master "race" of executives of different nationalities.

Whichever view is right, the problem brings us to the next question: What of the relationship between these corporations, which, whatever their "nationalities," are organized for private ends, and the nation-states within whose territories they operate? Here we begin to arrive at the critical areas in which politics and economics collide or coincide, and in which the "logic" of this new kind of international economic relations must make its peace with the "logic" of national interests as they now exist.

On one side of this complex issue is the fact that the multinational corporations are often in the same position in dealing with governments as were the railroad builders of the West in dealing with the various municipalities that competed for their services. A considerable competition exists among European nations for the location of high technology investment within their national borders, a competition that takes the form of capital grants, tax privileges, and, not least, an "acquiescence" in a growing American presence. As Kenneth Waltz points out, in 1962 the French government refused to permit General Electric to buy 20 percent of the ownership of Machines Bull, a large manufacturer of computers and other electronic products. By 1964, unable to find another buyer and unhappily aware that Machines Bull could not begin to develop the R & D needed to stay abreast in its field (IBM spends more on R & D than the sales of its largest English competitor), the government capitulated to a 50 percent GE ownership.[17]

To an even greater degree, the multinationals can dictate to the governments of the underdeveloped nations. For all the talk (and the reality) of imperialist domination, most of the underdeveloped nations want domestic foreign investment, European and/or American, for a variety of reasons. The multinationals pay higher wages, keep more honest books, pay more taxes, and provide more managerial know-how and training than do local industries. Moreover, they usually provide better social services for their workers, and certainly provide fancy career opportunities for a favored few of the elite. They are, in addition, a main channel through which technology, developed in the West, can filter into the backward nations. To be sure, the corporations typically send home more profits than the capital that they originally introduce into the "host" country; but meanwhile that capital grows, providing jobs, improving productivity, and often contributing to export earnings.[18]

This is, however, only one side of the story—the side that stresses the ability of the multinationals to drive hard bargains, to win strategic geographic positions, and to exercise a powerful voice in the economic policy of the countries in which they deign to operate. There is another side as well. For if the multinationals are bases for the exercise of economic power, they are also hostages within the nations in which they have settled. In the backward nations, the threat—and, more and more, the practice—of nationalization hangs over the heads of the multinational corporations, partly as an act of revenge against an often grossly exploitative past history, but more and more, simply because countries that are beginning to plan for development cannot allow critical decision-making powers to escape their control. As George Ball, in an essay highly sympathetic to the "cosmocorp," candidly puts it: "How can a national government make an economic plan with any confidence if a board of directors meeting 5,000 miles away can by altering its pattern of purchasing and production affect in a major way the country's economic life?"[19]

Ball and others think that the answer lies in the gradual "denationalization" of the international company, a view to which we will revert at the end of this essay. But let me first emphasize that the balance of power between the corporation's ability to allocate its technical expertise and its production, and the nation's ability to force a plant, once located, to abide by its will, is by no means one-sided in Europe or the developed areas, any more than it is in the underdeveloped countries. Here too, the economic benefits provided by foreign capital are often overwhelmed by the sentiments of nationalism to which the plusses and minuses of the balance sheet simply do not apply.

For example, the Canadians may be grateful in their moments of economic reflection for the enormous boost to productivity that has resulted from the inflow of American investments, but in their political moments they are bitterly resentful of a situation in which US residents own at least 44 percent of *all* capital invested in Canada, and in which foreigners (mainly Americans) own 54 percent of all Canadian manufacturing, 64 percent of all Canadian oil, and virtually 100 percent of its auto industry. Hence, in Canada, France, and elsewhere, the multinationals face actual or prospective legislation limiting the degree to which they can invade or dominate the domestic economy. As a case in point in 1969 France refused to allow Westinghouse Electric Corporation to buy a controlling interest in the Jeumont-Schneider group (producers of heavy electrical equipment), insisting that the company remain French.

In this tension between the corporate drive for logistical coherence and the national drive for economic independence, the "proper" role for the multinational is far from clear. Even if we assume that the directing management is of "neutral" national composition, what should be its guiding policy with respect to the international location of research and development facilities, the expansion or contraction of production in plants located in different countries, the remission of profits from one unit to another? It is not enough to say that the rule of profitability must hold sway, for in obeying that rule the multinationals are also affecting the growth rates, the employment, and the balance of payments problems of nation-states who put *their* national well-being far ahead of the profits of any international enterprise.

There is, in fact or theory, no answer to such questions, for they pose problems entirely outside the present legal and juridical arrangements of nation-states and international organizations. Henry de Vries notes for example that no consistent pattern can even be discerned for such a basic question as where the "home office" of a corporation exists. In the United States and the United Kingdom, it is the place of incorporation. In Morocco, it is the location of the registered head office. In France, Belgium, and Germany it is the center of management. In Italy and Egypt it is the locus of principal business activity. This and innumerable other legal problems bestrew the path of international production and are far from being close to solution.[20]

V

What, then, are the ultimate implications of this new form of international economic relationship? If the question leaves us groping, the reason lies in the fact that we have not yet developed a coherent picture in our minds—a "model"—with which to organize the confusions and conflicts introduced by the rise of the multinational company. We lack, in other words, a theory of international production (even a wrong theory) that would introduce into the disarray of facts the possibility for systematic analysis that the theory of free trade gave us for an earlier epoch.

Already, however, we can see some of the elements with which such a model will have to come to grips. First, a theory of international production must explain whether or not the interpenetration of national territories by foreign producers will lead to a stable "division of the market" or not. If, as Perlmutter and others hypothesize, the industrial core of world production and trade is moving in the direction of global ogligopoly, will the outcome be a more or less peaceful coexistence of giants, such as we see in the American automobile or steel or electrical equipment industries, or a struggle *à outrance,* such as characterized the cut-throat competitive race of the late nineteenth century?

The answer to this question lies partly in the habits and attitudes of business managers, who are now mainly accustomed to the non-price-cutting "competition" of gadgetry and style. But it will also be powerfully influenced by the national elements that are inextricably intermingled with the economic ones. That is, the degree of ferocity and effectiveness of the "European" response to le *défi americain* depends to a large extent on whether European governments overcome their parochial nationalisms enough to allow the formation of truly Pan-European corporations whose strength and penetrative power could then be matched against American enterprise *on American soil.*

Thus, unlike the theory of international trade, which rested its case solely on the economic consequences of the division of labor, there is no theory of "the division of the market" unless we introduce political variables into the picture. Lacking a knowledge of this political element, we cannot yet place limits on the degree of interpenetration that will occur, or on the probability of an "equilibrium" being reached on a global scale.

Second, there arises the question of whether the rise of international production can be viewed as a force making for world integration and betterment, or for world divisiveness and disruption. The classical theory of international trade promised that the international division of labor would in fact unify the world, both with regard to living standards and (implicitly) with regard to political stability because of the increased interdependence of nation-states. That noble image proved to be delusive. But what image does the rise of international production project?

Two views are currently propounded. One, advanced by George Ball, sees in the emergence of the "denationalized" multinational corporation the first appearance of a supranational world order—an order in which the terrible and violent rule of competitive nationalism would gradually be superseded by an international organization of production, regulated by the impersonal constraints of profit (which even the socialist countries concede is the single best indicator of efficiency). What is envisaged is a "businessman's peace" in which pragmatism and production take precedence over national pride and vainglory.

The proponents of this view have very little trouble demonstrating that the multinationals are much less interested in the cold war than are the members of the political elites; that "co-production" between capitalist and socialist countries is already in existence; and that, all stereotypes (and some examples) to the contrary, businessmen usually have preferred to do business with governments, even revolutionary governments, than to call in the Marines.[21]

There is undoubtedly an element of truth in this view: one thinks of Henry Ford seeking to build tractor plants for the Soviets; of the recent Fiat contract to build Russian autos; of the chafing of American companies at the idiocy of State Department constraints on their investment in communist countries, etc. It is one thing, however, to point to the presumably less bellicose disposition of businessmen (a point that was first made by Herbert Spencer) and another to ask what sort of "world order" the multinationals could create.

Ball's view assumes that the internationalization of production would bring about a more rational world than that in which we now live. But such a view begs the question as to whether a world order that is rational for the multinational corporation is necessarily also rational for a backward nation seeking to escape from the shackles of its heritage. For the assumption that the multinational company can become a major vehicle for development ignores a major aspect of under-development itself—the gulf between the "Western" metropolises of the backward world and their "Eastern" countrysides. This is a gulf that the presence of the multinationals is more likely to widen than to bridge. Ball's view overlooks as well the certainty that the multina-tionals will powerfully oppose the kinds of revolutionary upheavals that in many backward areas are probably the essential precondition for a genuine modernization.

This conflict between the demands of the nation-state and those of the corporation forms the core of the Hymer-Rowthorn view, which stands opposed to that of Ball and his like-minded business interna-tionalists. Hymer and Rowthorn do not doubt that the momentum be-hind the internationalization of enterprise is very strong, but they see this as leading to an exacerbation of world conflict rather than to a resolution of it. For they do not see the economic imperative asserting itself easily over that of the national entity, either in the developed world or in its backward regions. "Nation-states are powerful and are not likely to die easily," they write. "Merely to ask which institution one expects to be around 100 years from now, France or General Motors, shows the nature of the problem."[22]

I should say, rather, that this question reveals the tensions of the problem but does not fully analyze its outcome. There are some things that nation-states can do that international corporations cannot, but there are other things, of increasing importance, in which the corpora-tion is the more effective instrument of social action. If Hymer and Rowthorn had posed the question of long-term survival as between Costa Rica and IBM, another answer might have suggested itself; and if they had asked which was likely to be here a century hence, the French national state or some transnational production unit that had evolved from IBM, the answer would not be so unambiguously clear; it is probable that both will be here.

Thus what we seem to be witnessing at the moment is a conflict between two modes of organizing human affairs—a "vertical" mode that finds its ultimate expression in the pan-national flows of produc-tion of the giant international corporation, and a "horizontal" mode expressed in the jealously guarded boundaries of the nation-state.

Hymer and Rowthorn conceptualize this conflict in two "ideal-types"—a capitalist ideal-type in which the global production of a single commodity is organized under the unified direction of a single cor-poration; and a socialist ideal-type in which the production of all com-modities in a single state is organized under the control of a single plan-ning agency. In a word, they see the trend of capitalism toward the vertical unification of production and the trend of socialism toward its horizontal unification. In this conflict of ideals, they clearly believe that the socialist mode of organization will, in the end, prove the more resilient and enduring.

Perhaps. And perhaps not. At least in my belief, their dichotomy underestimates the adaptive capabilities of both systems. Hymer and Rowthorn do not ask what might be the role of a vertical organization of production among *socialist* states—whether, for example, a Russian ministry of computers might not play the same role, within a bloc of planned economies, as IBM might play within the bloc of capitalist economies. Nor do they inquire into the possibilities of capitalist economies adopting "socialist" modes of control through the agencies of conglomerate corporations.

In the mid 1960s, for example, at the very time that the Ford Motor Company was investing American dollars in the purchase of Ford in England, a British syndicate was investing pounds in the Pan Am Building. Why did not Ford build Pan Am and the British investors put their money into cars? If the full-blown conglomerate corporation comes into existence, where the top management serves only as a (private) planning board for the allocation of capital, precisely this sort of thing may take place. Indeed it already has: International Telephone now bakes bread, rents cars, runs hotels, builds houses, lends money, and manages a mutual fund, in addition to providing communication service. At this level of organization, the "fundamental" conflict between the ideal-types of socialist and capitalist planning begins to melt away.

Indeed, to my way of thinking, it is quite the wrong way of seeking to understand the problem of the nation-state and the multinational corporation. Both nation-states and corporations are crude instrumentalities by which we deal with the state of humankind today. Governments, no matter how socialist, still depend on patriotism which remains the last refuge of scoundrels; and international corporations, no matter how purified of national taint, are still run by motives that glorify propensities of mankind that should be, at most, tolerated. Both forms are ill-suited to the long-run development of humanist societies. It is only because we do not know how else to organize large masses of people to perform those tasks essential for society that we have to depend on the nation-state with its vicious force and shameful irrationality, and the corporation with its bureaucratic hierarchies and its reliance on greed and carefully inculcated dissatisfaction.

This is emphatically not to claim that other organizational means do not exist. From the study of primitive societies we know that people can order their lives without the commands and incentives of modern society, by building them around the great supportive principle of tradition. What we have not learned is how to reintroduce this mode of societal organization in a civilization dedicated to the accumulation of knowledge, to experiment, to change, to accumulation. Perhaps it is impossible, at least until the period of accumulation has come to an end.

In our present-day conflict between the organizational capabilities of the state and the corporation, it is difficult to state with certitude on which side "progress" lies, when both modes of social control are freighted with the capacity for human degradation and even destruction. All that one can say is that at this moment in history both seem necessary. I suspect that the interaction of the international corporation and the nation-state is less comprehensible as a conflict between "capitalism" (Sweden? Japan? South Africa? The US?) and "socialism" (USSR? Yugoslavia? Cuba? China?) than as part of the ignorant and often desperate process by which we seek to contain the demon of technology and to organize the collective endeavors of men at a time when the level of human understanding is still pitiably low, even in the most "advanced" countries.

NOTES

[1] The point of this doctrine of comparative advantage can be summed up in the homely analogy of the banker who is also the best carpenter in town. Will it pay him to build his own house? Clearly not, for he will make more money by devoting all his hours to banking, even though he has to pay for a carpenter less skillful than himself. In the same manner, classicists explained that one country will gain from another if it devotes all its resources to those activities in which it is relatively advantaged, allowing less well-endowed or less skilled nations to supply those goods which it has relinquished in order (like the banker) to concentrate its efforts where their productivity is greatest.

[2] It should be mentioned that in recent years the idea of the benign effect of an international specialization of labor has come under increasingly critical scrutiny, stemming mainly from the work of Gunnar Myrdal. Myrdal pointed out that in international relations (as also in the interregional relationships within a given country), free trade does not always lead to an equalization of wages, etc. Rather, an initial center of industrial strength attracts supporting skills and services, public as well as private, whereas an initial center of weakness loses them. (E.g., an industrialized center has a rich tax base that provides schools, roads, etc., while a rural backwater stagnates.)

These so-called "spread" and "backwash" effects can override the pull of market forces that supposedly act as a great equalizer between the high-priced city and the low-priced country. Instead, as Myrdal has shown, the advantages of developed areas or countries attract skills and resources away from the hinterland, with the result that strong nations or regions grow stronger, and weak ones weaker. See his *Rich Lands and Poor* (Harpers, 1957).

[3] In *World Business*, edited by Courtney Brown, pp. 258–9.

[4] *Interplay* (November, 1968), p. 17; Simmonds in *World Business*, p. 49.

[5] Much of these assets may also be grossly undervalued. The entire book value of the US private investment in Middle Eastern petroleum for 1969 is carried at $1.65 billion. Earnings from petroleum from that area amount to over $1.1 billion for the same year. (*Survey of Current Business*, October, 1970, pp. 28–9.)

[6] Kenneth Waltz in *The International Corporation*, edited by Kindleberger, p. 219.

[7] In Kindleberger, *The International Corporation*, pp. 57–91.

[8] In Kindleberger, *The International Corporation*, p. 72.

[9] *Interplay* (November, 1968); also Louis Turner, *Invisible Empires*, p. 191.

[10] Wilkins, *The Emergence of Multinational Enterprise*. For the most impressive exposition of the changing structure of domestic enterprise, see Alfred Chandler, *Strategy and Structures* (MIT, 1962).

[11] Wilkins, pp. 216–7.

[12] It is interesting to note that the degree of international production (as contrasted with export) varies widely from one industry to another. There is a considerable amount of international production in glass and very little in steel; a huge amount in computers but virtually none in machine tools; a great deal in automobiles but not (so far as I am aware) in shipbuilding. The reasons for this variation are not altogether clear. The answer may lie in specifics affecting the technologies of different industries, or in the characteristics of the markets they serve, or simply in their "outlooks," for I believe there is a discernible variation in the "character" of industries, much as there is in that of nations.

[13] See Wilkins, p. 110; *Survey of Current Business* (October, 1970), pp. 28–9.

[14]Wilkins, p. 201; *Interplay* (November, 1968), p. 16.

The destruction or forced sale of European foreign assets during World War II was also an immense factor in this striking turnabout. But the shift since the war seems to indicate that the US has reached a domestic "saturation threshold" comparable to that which England or Germany experienced long before.

[15]In Brown, pp. 66–82.

[16]Kindleberger, *American Business Abroad*, p. 208.

[17]In Kindleberger, *The International Corporation*, p. 216.

[18]See essays by Emile Benoit in Brown, p. 22; and by Carlos Alejandro, in Kindleberger, *The International Corporation*, p. 329.

[19]In Brown, p. 334.

[20]In Brown, pp. 281–303.

[21]Wilkins, pp. 154–72; Brown, pp. 6–7, 122.

[22]In Kindleberger, *The International Corporation*, pp. 88–9.

The United States:
The Crisis of Government

27 The Ten Commandments of the Foreign Affairs Bureaucracy

Leslie H. Gelb and Morton H. Halperin

The average reader of *The New York Times* in the 1950s must have asked: why don't we take some of our troops out of Europe? Ike himself said we didn't need them all there. Later, in 1961, after the tragi-comic Bay of Pigs invasion, the reader asked: how did President Kennedy ever decide to do such a damn fool thing? Or later about Vietnam: why docs President Johnson keep on bombing North Vietnam when the bombing prevents negotiations and doesn't get Hanoi to stop the fighting?

Sometimes the answer to these questions is simple. It can be attributed squarely to the President. He thinks it's right. Or he believes he has no choice. As often as not, though, the answer lies elsewhere—in the special interests and procedures of the bureaucracy and the convictions of the bureaucrats.

If you look at foreign policy as a largely rational process of gathering information, setting the alternatives, defining the national interest and making decisions, then much of what the President does will not make sense. But if you look at foreign policy as bureaucrats pursuing organizational, personal, and domestic political interests, as well as their own beliefs about what is right, you can explain much of the inexplicable.

In pursuing these interests and beliefs, bureaucrats (and that means everyone from Cabinet officials to political appointees to career civil servants) usually follow their own version of the Ten Commandments.

I

On May 11, 1948, President Harry Truman held a meeting in the White House to discuss recognition of the new state of Israel. Secretary of State George Marshall and State Undersecretary Robert Lovett spoke first. They were against it. It would unnecessarily alienate forty million Arabs. Truman next asked Clark Clifford, then Special Counsel to the President, to speak. Arguing for the moral element of U.S. policy and the need to contain Communism in the Middle East, Clifford favored recognition. As related by Dan Kurzman in *Genesis 1948*, Marshall exploded: "Mr. President, this is not a matter to be determined on the basis of politics. Unless politics were involved, Mr. Clifford would not even be at this conference. This is a serious matter of foreign policy determination . . . " Clifford remained at the meeting, and after some hesitation, the U.S. recognized Israel.

The moral merits of U.S. support of Israel notwithstanding, no one doubts Jewish influence on Washington's policy toward the Middle East. And yet, years later, in their memoirs, both Truman and Dean Acheson denied at great length that the decision to recognize the state of Israel was in any way affected by U.S. domestic politics.

A powerful myth is at work here. It holds that national security is too important, too sacred, to be tainted by crass domestic political considerations. It is a matter of lives and the safety of the nation. Votes and influence at home should count for nothing. Right? Wrong. National security and domestic reactions are inseparable. What could be clearer than the fact that President Nixon's Vietnam troop reductions [were] geared more to American public opinion than to the readiness of the Saigon forces to defend themselves? Yet the myth makes it bad form for government officials to talk about domestic politics (except to friends and to reporters off the record) or even to write about politics later in their memoirs.

And what is bad form on the inside would be politically disastrous if it were leaked to the outside. Imagine the press getting hold of a secret government document that said: "President Nixon has decided to visit China to capture the peace issue for the '72 elections. He does not intend or expect anything of substance to be achieved by his trip—except to scare the Russians a little." Few things are more serious than the charge of playing politics with security.

Nevertheless, the President pays a price for the silence imposed by the myth. One cost is that the President's assumptions about what public opinion will and will not support are never questioned. No official, for example, ever dared to write a scenario for President Johnson showing him how to forestall the right-wing McCarthyite reaction he feared if the U.S. pulled out of Vietnam. Another cost is that bureaucrats, in their ignorance of Presidential views, will use their own notions of domestic politics to screen information from the President or to eliminate options from his consideration.

II

In the early months of the Kennedy Administration, CIA officials responsible for covert operations faced a difficult challenge. President Eisenhower had permitted them to begin training a group of Cuban refugees for an American-supported invasion of Castro's Cuba. In order to carry out the plan, they then had to win approval from a skeptical new President whose entourage included some "liberals" likely to oppose it. The CIA director, Allen Dulles, and his assistant, Richard Bissell, both veteran bureaucrats, moved effectively to isolate the opposition. By highlighting the extreme sensitivity of the operation, they persuaded Kennedy to exclude from deliberations most of the experts in State and the CIA itself, and many of the Kennedy men in the White House. They reduced the effectiveness of others by refusing to leave any papers behind to be analyzed; they swept in, presented their case, and swept out, taking everything with them. But there remained the problem of the skeptical President. Kennedy feared that if the operation was a complete failure he would look very bad. Dulles and Bissell assured him that complete failure was impossible. If the invasion force could not establish a beachhead, the refugees, well-trained in guerrilla warfare, would head for the nearby mountains. The assurances were persuasive, the only difficulty being that they were false. Less than a third of the force had had any guerrilla training; the nearby mountains were separated from the landing beach by an almost impenetrable swamp; and none of the invasion leaders was instructed to head for the hills if the invasion failed (the CIA had promised them American intervention).

Kennedy was told what would persuade him, not the truth or even what the CIA believed to be true. Bureaucrats like Dulles and Bissell are confident that they know what the national security requires. The problem is to convince an uninformed and busy President. To do that you do not carefully explain the reasoning that leads to your position, nor do you reveal any doubts you may have. Rather you seek to figure out what the President's problem is as he sees it and to convince him that what you want to do will solve it.

III

Vietnam policy under President Johnson exemplified the concept of Option B. The papers to the President went something like this: Option A—Use maximum force (bomb Hanoi and Haiphong and invade North Vietnam, Laos, and Cambodia). Recommend rejection on the ground that the Soviets and the Chinese might respond. Option C— Immediate unilateral American withdrawal. Recommend rejection because it will lead to a Communist victory in Vietnam. Option B—Bomb a little more each time and seek negotiations (even though the bombing was preventing negotiations). Turn more of the fighting over to the Saigon forces and send more U.S. troops (even though the American buildup obviated the need for the South Vietnamese to shoulder more of the burden). Press Saigon for reforms and give them all they want for the war effort (even though aid without conditions gave Saigon no incentive to reform). Option B triumphed.

Option B solves a lot of problems for the bureaucrat. Bureaucrats do not like to fight with each other. Option B makes everybody a winner (by letting everyone do the essence of what he wants), preserves the policy consensus, and provides ultimate comfort to the bureaucrat—deference to his expertise and direct responsibility. Very few will be so dissatisfied as to take their case to the public.

Unfortunately, while this process allows the President to keep his house happy, it also robs him of choice. The alternatives he is given are often phony, two ridiculous extremes and a jumbled, inconsistent "middle course." Unless a President knows enough and has the time to peel off the real alternatives from within Option B, he ends up being trapped by the unanimity of advice.

IV

Former Secretary of State Dean Acheson, summoned by President Kennedy to join the Executive Committee of the National Security Council debate on Soviet missiles in Cuba, favored a "surgical strike," a limited air attack designed simply to destroy the missiles before they could become operational. Each time the military was asked to come in with a plan for a surgical strike, they asserted that a limited air strike could not destroy all the missiles—despite their having the capability to do so. Instead, they produced a plan for their favored option—an all-out air assault on Cuba climaxed by a ground invasion. Their plan had something in it for each service—the Air Force and Navy would pound the island by sea and air, the Marines would storm ashore as the Army paratroopers descended—and the military would be left free to act as they chose. The military insisted that a surgical strike was "infeasible" in part because they assumed that Soviet missiles were "mobile" (i.e., capable of being moved in a few hours) rather than "movable" (i.e., their actual capability of being moved in a few days). Kennedy was intrigued by the surgical-strike option and met with the commander of the Tactical Air Command. When the commander solemnly assured the President face-to-face that the option was "infeasible," Kennedy with great reluctance abandoned it.

"Infeasibility" is one technique to disqualify an option; demanding full authority is another. Early in his administration, Kennedy confronted a deteriorating situation in Laos. He was reluctant to commit any American forces, but neither was he prepared to have Laos overrun. At a critical White House meeting he asked the military what could be done with various levels of force. The Joint Chiefs' answer was clear. They would not recommend any landing of American forces and could guarantee nothing unless the President was prepared to authorize the use of nuclear weapons whenever, in their judgment, that use was required. Kennedy reluctantly decided not to send any forces to Laos.

V

With the Chinese Communist guns firing at the tiny island of Quemoy three miles from the mainland and an invasion expected momentarily, President Eisenhower's principal advisers met to frame a recommendation. The problem, as they saw it, was to formulate an argument that would persuade the President that the U.S. must defend Quemoy. The advisers resorted to the prediction of dire consequences, recognizing that only if the alternative could be shown to be very adverse to American interests would Eisenhower agree to the use of force. They warned the President that in their unanimous judgment, if he permitted Quemoy to be captured, "the consequences in the Far East would be more far-reaching and catastrophic than those which followed when the United States allowed the Chinese mainland to be taken over by the Chinese Communists."

Did Eisenhower reject this prediction as absurd? On the contrary, he accepted it and defended Quemoy.

The uncertainties of international politics are so great that it is difficult to disprove any prediction. This puts the President in a bind. If he fails to act and things go badly, the overruled advisers are likely to leak their warnings. In fact, much of the dialogue within the government is in terms of worst cases. An advocate who does not warn of extreme consequences is often viewed as not seriously supporting his prediction.

VI

Although the advocates of the Bay of Pigs landing had convinced President Kennedy that the invasion of Cuba was worth a try, they recognized that they were not yet in the clear: they still had to persuade the President to act immediately. Presidents are, in the eyes of bureaucrats, notorious for putting off decisions or changing their minds. They have enough decisions to make without looking for additional ones. In many cases, all the options look bad and they prefer to wait. The Bay of Pigs plan called for an effective "now or never" argument, and the CIA rose to the occasion. The agency told Kennedy that the invasion force was at the peak of its effectiveness; any delay, and it would decline in morale and capability. More important, it warned the President that a vast shipment of Soviet arms was on the way to Cuba; the Castro forces would soon have such superior weapons that substantial American combat involvement would be necessary to bail out the anti-Castro Cuban invaders. Faced with these arguments, Kennedy gave the order to proceed.

Conversely, when a President wants to act, bureaucrats can stymie him by arguing that "now is not the time." President Eisenhower reported in his memoirs that he came into office believing, after having served as commander of the allied forces in Europe, that the United States should withdraw most of its forces there; he left office eight years later still believing that the U.S. had far too many troops assigned to NATO. Secretary of State John Foster Dulles knew better than to argue with the military substance of General Eisenhower's position. Instead he argued timing. Each time Eisenhower raised the issue, Dulles pointed to some current NATO difficulty. This was, he would argue, a critical moment in the life of the alliance in which one or another NATO country was experiencing a domestic crisis. For the U.S. to withdraw troops would be to risk political disintegration. The moment for troop withdrawals never arrived. To this day, pressures for some American withdrawals from Europe have been headed off by the same ploy.

VII

We had a glimpse of this phenomenon with the publication of the Anderson Papers, in which we read about Henry Kissinger warning his State, Defense, and CIA colleagues: "The President does not believe we are carrying out his wishes. He wants to tilt in favor of Pakistan. He feels everything we do comes out otherwise." And, "The President is under the 'illusion' that he is giving instructions; not that he is merely being kept apprised of affairs as they progress." The President's subordinates disagreed with the President's policy toward the India-Pakistan crisis. They were undermining him by resisting his orders and then by leaking his policy. He knew it and did not like it; but apparently could not do much about it.

Although leaking the texts of many documents, à la Pentagon and Anderson papers, is relatively rare, much classified information regularly makes its way into the press. Presidents are surprised not when something leaks but rather when any hot item remains out of the press for even a few days. Providing information to the press—whether in press conferences, backgrounders, or leaks—is the main route by which officials within the executive branch bring their supporters in the Congress and the interested public into action. Only bureaucrats with potential outside support are tempted to leak. In some cases, it is sufficient to leak the fact that an issue is up for decision; in others, what is leaked is information on the positions of key participants. In many instances sufficient factual material must be leaked to convince Congressmen and others to join the fray.

Presidents don't like leaks by others and complain about them whenever they occur, often asking the FBI to run down the culprit. Such efforts almost always fail.

VIII

On March 20, 1948, President Harry Truman rose from bed early, as was his custom, and began scanning the morning newspapers. He was astonished to read that his ambassador to the United Nations, Warren Austin, had told the Security Council the previous day that "there seems to be general agreement that the plan [for the partition of Palestine] cannot now be implemented by peaceful means." Truman had agreed to no such thing. He was firmly committed to partition and on the previous day had reiterated his support in a private meeting with Chaim Weizmann, the leader of worldwide Zionism. Austin and the Arabists in the State Department did not know about the meeting with Weizmann, but they knew the President wanted partition and believed that it could be carried out peacefully. Austin and his associates had no doubts about what the President wanted; they simply felt no obligation to do what he wanted them to do.

At the end of his term in office, Truman was acutely conscious of the limited ability of Presidents to have their orders obeyed, and he worried about his successor. "Poor Ike," he was heard to muse, "he'll sit here and say do this and do that and nothing will happen." And so it continues.

During the first week of the Cuban missile crisis, in October 1962, an adviser warned Kennedy that the Russians were likely to demand that the United States withdraw its missiles from Turkey in return for the Soviet withdrawal of its missiles from Cuba. Kennedy was astonished. Months before, he had ordered the missiles removed from Turkey and could not believe they were still there.

Most students of the Cuban missile crisis have emphasized the degree to which Kennedy controlled every detail of what the American Government did. However, a closer look by Graham Allison, in his book on the crisis, *Essence of Decision,* has shown that the bureaucracy was behaving otherwise, choosing to obey the orders it liked and ignore or stretch others. Thus, after a tense argument with the Navy, Kennedy ordered the blockade line moved closer to Cuba so that the Russians might have more time to draw back. Having lost the argument with the President, the Navy simply ignored his order. Unbeknownst to Kennedy, the Navy was also at work forcing Soviet submarines to surface long before Kennedy authorized any contact with Soviet ships. And despite the President's order to halt all provocative intelligence, an American U-2 plane entered Soviet airspace at the height of the crisis. When Kennedy began to realize that he was not in full control, he asked his Secretary of Defense to see if he could find out just what the Navy was doing. McNamara then made his first visit to the Navy command post in the Pentagon. In a heated exchange, the Chief of Naval Operations suggested that McNamara return to his office and let the Navy run the blockade.

Bureaucrats know that the President and his principal associates do not have the time or the information to monitor compliance with all Presidential orders. Often, the bureaucrats can simply delay or do nothing, and no one will notice. If the President is actively involved, they may find it necessary to obey the letter, but not the spirit, of his orders. As Henry Kissinger observed to a journalist recently, the problem is not to know what to do, but rather to figure out how to get the bureaucracy to do it.

IX

The commandments discussed thus far have all dealt with relations between the Departments and the White House. When issues get that far, one of the fundamental rules has already been violated: keep issues away from the President. Bureaucrats prefer to be left alone to do their own thing. They will not voluntarily bring issues to the attention of the President (or senior officials) unless they conclude that he is likely to rule in their favor in a conflict with another agency. Consider the case of surplus and long supply arms transfers to other countries.

One of Secretary McNamara's goals in the Pentagon was to reduce the level of military assistance, particularly to countries that did not need the weapons and could afford to pay for what they needed. A prime objective was Taiwan. McNamara and his office of International Security Affairs engaged in a yearly battle with the State Department and the military over the level of aid to Taiwan. The White House was drawn in because a number of influential Congressmen were strong supporters of aid to Taiwan. One year in the late 1960s a battle raged over whether Taiwan would get $30 million or $40 million in military assistance. During the same year, the military quietly shipped to Taiwan more than $40 million worth of military equipment, which the Pentagon had labeled "excess or long supply." No senior civilian official was aware of the fact that these transfers were taking place, and no junior official aware of what was going on felt obliged to report up. Thus while senior officials argued over irrelevant ceilings on expenditures, Taiwan got more aid than anyone realized.

Observers sometimes assume that the bureaucracy bucks the hard choices to the President. Nothing could be further from the truth. Left alone, the bureaucracy will settle as many issues as it can by leaving each organization free to act as it chooses. When and if the President learns of an issue, bureaucrats will try to incorporate current behavior into "Option B."

X

If an official strongly disagrees with a consensus or dislikes a key man behind the consensus, he might chance a leak to the press. But frontal assaults on a consensus happen only rarely. In the summer of 1965, Undersecretary of State George Ball was among the first to confirm this fact with respect to the policy of bombing North Vietnam. Ball thought U.S. bombing of the North was folly—and worse than that, would only stiffen Hanoi's will. But he did not propose a unilateral cessation. In a TV interview last year, Ball explained himself as follows: "What I was proposing was something which I thought had a fair chance of being persuasive . . . if I had said let's pull out overnight or do something of this kind, I obviously wouldn't have been persuasive at all. They'd have said, 'the man's mad.' "

Ball's remarks express at once the futility of resisting agreed policy and the bureacrat's concern for his personal effectiveness. Ball knew he could not convince anyone if he revealed his true beliefs. He knew he would have been dismissed as "mad" and would not have been in a position to argue another day. So, he tempered his arguments and went along. Like all other bureaucrats, he hoped to preserve his effectiveness.

As it turned out, Ball's more moderate arguments were not persuasive either, but he did not resign over Vietnam and did not take his case to the public. No one resigned over Vietnam policy. Indeed, there seems to be no evidence that any civilian official has resigned over any foreign-policy matter since World War II.

The only officials with a record for resigning are the professional military. Generals Ridgway, Taylor, and Powers are notable examples. What is more, they tour the hustings, write books, and complain out loud. Military officers feel strongly about the interests of their military organization and often believe that if the people of the country only knew "the truth," they would support the military's position. With this record on resigning and going to the public, it is no wonder the military has been so influential in Presidential decisions.

But again, it is the President and the nation who ultimately suffer. If the President remains confident that none of his civilian advisers will resign and take their case to the public, he has little incentive ever to question his own assumptions.

The Ten Commandments pose a serious problem for a President, who is after all the one who got elected and has the responsibility. Truman understood the problem but feared that Eisenhower would not. But evidence abounds that President Eisenhower, precisely because of his background in Army politics and international military negotiations, was far from a novice. President Kennedy was quite expert and attuned to the ways of the bureaucracy—especially after the Bay of Pigs fiasco. His famous calls to State Department desk officials made the point well. President Johnson was a master of such maneuvering. Even as he stepped up the bombing of North Vietnam he would say, "I won't let those Air Force generals bomb the smallest outhouse north of the 17th parallel without checking with me. The generals know only two words—spend and bomb."

The Nixon-Kissinger team [was] second to none in its sensitivity to bureacratic behavior. The elaborate National Security Council decision-making apparatus they established is predicated on tight White House control of the bureaucracy. Their system is designed to neutralize narrow organizational interests (meaning the viewpoints of State and Defense), force the bureaucracy to suggest real alternatives and provide more accurate information (meaning, as has been done, to centralize the intelligence functions around Kissinger).

While this new system has been an improvement in some respects over the past, it has decisive costs and limitations. It has totally demoralized the State Department. The Department's expertise has been for naught, and its exclusion has led to a rash of pointless leaks from disgruntled Foreign Service Officers. With all its reins on the bureaucrat, the new system did not prevent part of the bureaucracy from tilting the "wrong way" (meaning against the President, as revealed in the Anderson papers) in the India-Pakistan crisis.

The problem, then, boils down to this: given the fact that the President cannot either chain the system or entirely work around it without serious costs, and given the judgment that a President strong enough to collar the bureaucracy would be too strong for the good of the nation, is there a better way to make foreign policy?

The answer is yes—probably. The President, we think, should make a determined effort to use the system. The personal and organizational interests of the bureaucrat are a reality. So are the different viewpoints on what is good policy. The President's main theme of operation should be to force bureaucratic differences out into the open. Pick strong and able men to lead State and Defense. Let them use their judgment and be advocates for their organizations. Encourage debate and contention rather than asking for agreed upon recommendations. Such tactics may be the only way for the President to ferret out hidden or conflicting information and to leave himself with real choices.

Perhaps, in the end, neither this suggested system nor any system will produce better decisions. Perhaps better decisions really depend on beliefs and events and guesses. But a fuller, more honest and open treatment of the bureaucracy might make for more honest and open treatment of the American people. Presidents might be less inclined to spend a good deal of their time denying differences and hiding policy. This would mean less deception and less manipulation. What better reason for trying it?

28 The Intelligence Tangle

Sanford J. Ungar

I. WHAT WE HAVE LEARNED

It seemed at times the cruelest kind of juxtaposition. Crises were breaking nearly everywhere, at home and abroad, demanding official attention and perhaps action. Terrorism: a siege at the headquarters of the Organization of Petroleum Exporting Countries in Vienna; a bomb explosion at a baggage claim area of La Guardia Airport in New York. International tension: a civil war in the newly independent African nation of Angola between factions loyal to the communists and the "free world"; a situation that threatened to reach the same point in Angola's former colonial parent, Portugal, a NATO ally. A United Nations increasingly unfriendly toward and uncomfortable for its American hosts. A virtually complete underground society in the United States that permits fugitives to evade the authorities for years without serious threat of capture. Religious and ethnic strife: in Lebanon, where it could explode a fragile Middle Eastern peace; and in Northern Ireland, where many of the arms were paid for by American partisans.

Doubts about détente; curiosity about the Chinese; ominous-looking antennas on the roof of the Soviet Embassy on Sixteenth Street in Washington, which may be intercepting the most sensitive deliberations of the American government. In an ever more complex world, full of trouble and danger, the need, obviously, was for information, for good "intelligence"—a loaded and often undefinable word—and for some formula that would permit the country to cope and to calculate its roles carefully, to avoid the prospect and the appearance of becoming a helpless giant.

At the same moment, the nation was steeped in self-doubt, painfully examining events in the recent past that raised questions about the society's commitment to its own most fundamental principles. In the post-Watergate era, when nothing is any longer sacred, men and women once considered the ultimate patriots who could do no wrong—the likes of J. Edgar Hoover—are put under a microscope, and the enlargement is not pretty. The misbehavior of those responsible for gathering this commodity called intelligence has been so severe, says Senator Gary Hart of Colorado, that at one point "the possibility existed of destroying freedom in order to save it." A black congressman from Detroit, Charles Diggs, travels to Addis Ababa, where the Organization of African Unity is meeting, to denounce his own government's policy in Angola as "the biggest blunder in the history of [American] relations with Africa." The international image of the United States has been severely damaged. Once regarded as the bulwark of freedom—and as the country which saved Western Europe from successive totalitarian threats in the 1940s—it has come to be widely identified with the torturers in Chile, the racial separatists of South Africa, and assorted minor anticommunist despots. Richard Welch, the station chief for the Central Intelligence Agency in Athens, is murdered, setting off a new round of recrimination about who is revealing too much and who concealing too much. Is Welch's death a result of American policies and practices, or of their disclosure? Or of sloppy "cover"? Or is it a coincidence shamelessly played upon by an agency seeking relief from its pain?

At the center of this affair of state is, naturally enough, the United States Congress, itself dizzy with dreams of renewal and enhanced power at a time when the presidency stands discredited. The accusations are a bit overdrawn at times, the personalities flawed, and the exultation over disclosure sometimes extreme. There is an air of examining yesterday's events with today's morality and an oh-so-much-wiser perspective than that of the last generation. One of the ironies is that many of the examiners—the bright young professors and lawyers on the congressional committee staffs—are out of the same mold and tradition and education as those who once went into the CIA with notions of saving the world.

The political climate is typical, suggests Attorney General Edward H. Levi, of a country that has just come through a war, this time an especially unpopular war which left wounds not yet healed. William E. Colby, the career spy in reformist clothes whose term as director of central intelligence was cut short by the uproar, says the situation reminds him of the 1920s, when the Western world was inclined to ignore realities because it was tired, disgusted with war, economically depressed, and myopic about better days on the horizon. Yet the intelligence-spying debate of 1975–1976 has also renewed some of the most encouraging qualities of a self-conscious democratic government. The country has been forced to evaluate itself, discuss some very embarrassing facts in public, and pick up the pieces and move on—while much of the world watches with a mixture of amazement and horror. It is an all-American adventure.

For Congressman Morgan F. Murphy, an old-line Democrat from Chicago who seemed at once honored and pained by the opportunity to participate, the congressional inquiries were a matter of "getting into the bowels of the FBI and the CIA." Senator Richard S. Schweiker of Pennsylvania, a liberal Republican who had been quiet through most of his first term in the Senate, discovered in himself a sense of outrage and found an exciting issue to apply it to: the need to re-examine President John F. Kennedy's assassination. To Democratic Congressman Ronald V. Dellums, a black man from Berkeley who has been the target of official surveillance now and again, there was a genuine danger that the congressional investigations would turn out to be a charade: "We are working with people who have been trained to disinform, to lie, and to falsify," he warned. Senator Barry M. Goldwater of Arizona, guardian of the conservative Republican faith, could not be bothered to attend many of the hearings; he took every occasion to proclaim that "enough is enough," and he advocated suspending the investigations in midstream before they damaged national security and "prove[d] harmful to the United States and to freedom everywhere." Henry Kissinger, the aggrieved secretary of state whose world view was challenged by the nature and substance of the inquiries as by other contemporaneous developments, saw it all as one more case of American "self-flagellation," the kind of exercise that, he believes, makes it impossible for the country to deal confidently and confidentially in international affairs.

Frank Church of Idaho was selected as chairman of the Senate Select Committee precisely because he was not among the many Democratic candidates for President; but soon the national exposure and opportunity for center-stage performing inherent in his role as chief inquisitor aroused old dreams and aspirations. He showed genuine concern over and insight into the intelligence business, but he began indulging in routine pronunciamentos. Church's tendency to speak slowly and sanctimoniously, in near-perfect syntax, brought on the accusation that he was converting the hearing room into a campaign platform. Otis Pike, a Democratic congressman from Long Island with half an eye on a New York Senate seat, became chairman of the House Select Committee when it was reorganized and sent belatedly into the fray. Sassy and sarcastic, Pike aimed for the jugular and the headlines.

His pyrotechnics, including staged personal confrontations with Kissinger over access to classified documents (at one point he tried to obtain a contempt-of-Congress citation against the Secretary of State), tended to obscure the real substance of his committee's inquiry. He was accused of rank showboating.

It was, at best, a confusing and chaotic effort, this congressional surge to investigate, expose, and, presumably, improve the intelligence community. There were moments when the investigating legislators appeared to be shouting, "Here, look! We have discovered a corner of the executive branch that has been misbehaving all these years. Let us tell you about it." What they were not saying, but were dramatically demonstrating, is that Congress is a reactive institution, moving clumsily now to unravel a web and to expose a subculture that it had itself been weaving, creating—and, at least on paper, overseeing—for decades.

Congress was reacting this time, as in other recent crises of public conscience, to newspaper stories: the revelation by the New York *Times* that the Central Intelligence Agency had, probably in contravention of its legal mandate, conducted extensive domestic intelligence investigations and kept improper files on American citizens; and the timely reminder by the Washington *Post* (repeating what the Chicago *Tribune* and others had said previously) that the Federal Bureau of Investigation had extensively wiretapped and bugged the Reverend Martin Luther King, Jr., most notably at the 1964 Democratic national convention in Atlantic City where it was also doing other political chores for Lyndon B. Johnson. . . .

Some of the congressional revelations were not so new or, by the time they came, devastating. Press stories based on leaks, many from within the Ford Administration or from CIA alumni, told most of the details about Agency involvement in assassination plots against foreign leaders whose philosophies and policies put them on the hit-lists of successive Presidents and secretaries of state: Fidel Castro in Cuba, Patrice Lumumba in the Congo (now Zaire), Rafael Trujillo in the Dominican Republic, Ngo Dinh Diem in South Vietnam, and Rene Schneider in Chile. It was known that American intelligence had failed to predict international crises like the 1968 Tet offensive in Vietnam, the 1973 Yom Kippur War in the Middle East, and the 1974 Greek and Turkish moves on Cyprus. The Justice Department and regularly constituted congressional committees had been revealing bits and pieces of the FBI's counterintelligence programs (COINTELPROs) since late 1973. Attorney General Edward Levi had already provided an unusually extensive accounting of some of J. Edgar Hoover's secret personal files.

Yet when the investigating committees addressed these subjects, they lent additional credibility, an official imprimatur, and a certain drama to the information. And much of the detail was fresh and sordid: back-room mail-openings; COINTELPRO actions, justified on the basis of preventing violence, but used to frighten people and to destroy their family life and livelihood, even when there was no sign of violence or illegal activity on their part. The FBI, it emerged, was handy at the impersonation of newsmen; at "DO NOT FILE" procedures to prevent the uncovering of illegal "black bag jobs"; at looking the other way while local police wiretapped illegally and then shared the catch with their friends the Feds. Frederick A. O. Schwarz and Curtis R. Smothers, majority and minority counsel respectively for the Church committee, one white and one black, scored a theatrical coup when, sitting before the senators and the television cameras, they testified in grotesquely specific detail about Hoover's vengeful pursuit of Martin Luther King, Jr. Church's controversial report on the assassination plots, perhaps the most significant document to emerge from the entire process, drew a stark portrait of the well-bred gentlemen in the CIA and the White House scheming to take the lives of foreign statesmen who posed no actual threat to the United States—a secret government at its worst that had flourished in an atmosphere of euphemism, subterfuge, and cynicism.

The committees also shed new light on the intelligence activities of the Internal Revenue Service, and the fact that its reservoir of personal information on individuals had long been exploited for political purposes, converted into, as Church put it, "a lending library of tax information." And there was a first public glance into the National Security Agency, ostensibly responsible to the secretary of defense, exposed as a sort of electronic gun for hire that does little thinking about who its targets will be, but stands ready to zero in on one or another "watchlist" when so ordered by its superiors, listening for evidence of everything from travel to Cuba to international drug trafficking and "possible foreign support or influence on civil disturbances." It became clear how easily the NSA made the transition from matters of foreign concern to domestic ones. And all of these findings came in the context of a General Accounting Office report to the Senate's Permanent Subcommittee on Investigations that the federal government spends $2.6 billion a year on police, investigative, and intelligence-gathering activities (including $482 million for the FBI, but not including the budgets of the CIA, NSA, and "certain sensitive activities of the Defense Department"). Piecing evidence together, the Pike committee estimated that the United States spends $10 billion on all intelligence activities, more than three times what is acknowledged in the annual appropriations budget.

II. HOW THE JUNGLE GREW

The real importance of the congressional probes lies less in headlines about assassinations or statistics than in the investigations' long-range impact: the universalization of concern about federal agencies that have slipped out of control and strayed from their original purpose; the lessons they teach about the past; and, with any luck, the creation of a climate for thorough-going reform of the system and the structures that led to the abuses.

The investigations also had a subtler lesson: that the "intelligence community" has indeed become a genuine community within the government, a special-interest group that lobbies for its own positions, struggles for influence and authority in policy-making circles, and becomes haughty or defensive when it is challenged.

This community consists largely of intelligent, well-educated, well-motivated, and patriotic men and women. But they—especially those whose attitudes are formed during assignment to CIA and FBI headquarters in Washington—are inclined to act as if they are above the public dialogue, forced to deal with politicians and other petty men who do not share their wisdom.

Where did this intelligence community come from, and how did it evolve into a many-headed monster? The clumsiness and heavy-handedness may be explained in part by the fact that Americans are new to the intelligence business. Unlike the European powers that had empires and a wide range of vested interests to protect, and thus have intelligence establishments dating back centuries, the United States used to view intelligence, both offensive and defensive, as it did armies and armaments: something to build up in wartime and dismantle in peace. As a result, the country was an easy target for spies and terrorists; indeed, German agents had a field day here in the years leading up to both world wars, and the Soviets were suspected of doing the same during the 1930s. It was out of concern over that situation that Franklin D. Roosevelt ordered the FBI back into the intelligence field in 1936 (it had been ordered out more than a decade earlier, when Hoover was appointed director by Attorney General Harlan Fiske Stone, because of the abuses of its authority during the post-World War I "red scare" and the Harding Administration scandals). The threats from foreign agents and from their domestic allies—in such organizations as the German-American Bund and the American Communist party—were seen as one.

Only as actual American involvement in the European hostilities became a prospect did the United States contemplate setting up its own apparatus to conduct espionage. Espionage was not a part of American tradition; it involved exhorting foreign citizens to commit treason and otherwise to violate their own countries' laws and standards of behavior. But various government agencies clamored for the job, and Roosevelt, in a Solomonlike solution, split it up among them: the FBI won jurisdiction over all of the Western Hemisphere except Panama; the Navy over the Pacific; and the Army over Europe, Africa, and the Canal Zone. The derring-do of the Bureau's Special Intelligence Service in Latin America, mostly unheralded at the time, was soon to be overshadowed by the newly created, quasi-military Office of Strategic Services, which operated mostly in Europe, including behind enemy lines.

Thus began a competition that has continued to this day. Hoover and the chief of the OSS, General William J. "Wild Bill" Donovan, were old rivals—dating back to the 1920s, when they were both in the Justice Department—and their organizations tried to match each other in currying favor with the British (whose secret intelligence service, MI-6, had trained most of the OSS teams) and with the White House. After the war, Donovan's successor, Allen Dulles, and his regiment of well-bred Ivy League spies beat out Hoover's corps of law-enforcement types for the ongoing foreign intelligence assignment. They became the Central Intelligence Agency and were given responsibility by the Truman Administration and its successors for a major piece of the American action abroad. Still, Hoover did not give up or forgive easily. He kept some of his men overseas as "legal attachés"; they were billed (and still are today) strictly as liaison officers with foreign police, but they also collected (and still collect) intelligence. And the Bureau held on to its growing domestic role in the fields of counterintelligence and internal security.

The charters of the CIA and the FBI that emerged from World War II were designed to be open-ended, and were fitted out with loopholes. Roosevelt's dispatch of the Bureau into the security field had been accomplished through executive orders and press statements. As Hoover wrote to Roosevelt and Attorney General Homer Cummings on October 20, 1938:

> In considering the steps to be taken for the expansion of the present structure of intelligence work, it is believed imperative that it be proceeded with the utmost degree of secrecy in order to avoid criticism or objections which might be raised to such an expansion by either ill-informed persons or individuals having some ulterior motive . . . it would seem undesirable to seek only special legislation which would draw attention to the fact that it was proposed to develop a special counterespionage drive of any great magnitude.

And there, in bureaucratic ambiguity, the matter would stand; the FBI had a splendid reputation, and the country seemed prepared to trust it with virtually any job. Similarly, the National Security Act of 1947, which formally created the CIA, was deliberately written to be vague. Because the drafters "were dealing with a new subject with practically no precedents," says one of them, Clark Clifford, a Truman adviser and later secretary of defense under Lyndon Johnson, "it was decided that the Act . . . should contain a 'catch-all' clause to provide for unforeseen contingencies." So it was that the CIA would be asked to "perform such other functions and duties related to intelligence affecting the national security as the National Security Council may from time to time direct." Within the framework of Cold War policies, the United States would be vigilant against the communists abroad and, in the name of "internal security," against the Left at home.

"A desperate struggle [was] going on in the back alleys of world politics," is how former Secretary of State Dean Rusk perceived the situation, and the United States would have to meet the challenge. In order to measure up, said a special committee that reported to President Eisenhower in 1954, the country might have to reconsider "long-standing American concepts of fair play" and adopt tactics "more ruthless than those employed by the enemy." Out of this philosophy came a heavy reliance on "covert actions," in which the Agency moved beyond its reporting and evaluation roles to try to influence the course of events more directly. As William Colby puts it, "You were asked to go do the job, without anybody telling you what it was or being willing to share the responsibility for it." The CIA's covert operatives had advanced technology and brilliant technicians available to them, they had the confidence of the rest of the government, and they had to report to no one outside the Agency about how they spent their money.

There was another complicating—and, for the intelligence community, liberating—factor: a double standard in international affairs between the pretense of official behavior and the reality of what went on behind the scenes. Looking back on the crisis in 1959 when Francis Gary Powers was shot down and captured by the Soviets during his aerial reconnaissance mission for the CIA, Colby recalls that "the Soviets knew for some years that we were flying U-2s over. When we used the cover story that it was a weather plane, they weren't going to do much about it." It was only after a controversy developed within the United States over the fact that the intelligence collectors were responsible, and after Eisenhower admitted that this was true, Colby says, that "Khrushchev went up the wall," not because of that specific flight but because the Americans were, in effect, breaking the unwritten rules by publicly asserting the right to violate the Soviet borders and airspace. Nikita Khrushchev and John F. Kennedy went on to sign the Vienna Convention of 1962, which stressed, among other points, the inviolate nature of each other's embassies. But as one source close to the CIA puts it, "The embassies are to the intelligence agencies as the bank was to Willie Sutton—where the money is. That agreement was never intended to be respected, and it never was."

Other treaties and agreements paid ritual lip service to the sanctity of the mails and of other international communications; but each side seemed to assume that they were written to be mutually broken. "Oh, *that* mail—yes, that mail was opened," CIA officials would acknowledge discreetly, when pressed to say whether the agreements, not to mention domestic laws, had been honored. Little wonder, then, that Nathan Gordon, a CIA scientist, could not fathom a presidential order to destroy the Agency's precious reserve of shellfish toxin, so powerful that 11 grams (a couple of teaspoons), if properly administered, could kill 55,000 people. Gordon had spent much of his career developing the potion; to destroy it must have seemed tantamount to destroying himself. Yes, the United States had signed a treaty outlawing chemical and biological warfare, and yes, CIA Director Richard Helms had issued a directive implementing it; but nobody bothered to tell Gordon whether this was one of those things we *really* meant to do.

The CIA's daring and profligacy was reinforced by a certainty that its Soviet counterpart, the KGB, was far more ruthless about its covert activities. Everyone knew, or assumed, how nasty the KGB could be and how often the Kremlin sent it to the ramparts to implement its needs and desires. At times, the conception of the threat posed by the KGB was based less on actual evidence than on an assumption that *they* must be playing the same subversive games abroad that *we* were playing, and that even if they were not we had to keep the game going lest they join in. The logic became a conundrum that could only have the effect of strengthening both the CIA and the KGB, throwing them into a symbiotic relationship. They became an international community of interest, probably more similar than either would ever admit. Each needed the threat of the other to justify its own existence.

There was a home-front parallel to overseas covert action, something the FBI came to call "preventive action" and to justify under the rubric of "counterintelligence programs." Domestically, too, the threat was ill-defined and the development of tactics left in the hands of the implementers. Although the Bill of Rights officially guarantees certain basic freedoms to every citizen, political hysteria made some people less equal than others under the Bill of Rights provisions. First communists, then fringe Marxist groups, and eventually others—the Ku Klux Klan, the "New Left," and "black extremists"—came in for special treatment. Unchecked, unmonitored, that treatment included disruption of personal lives and maneuvers that seemed to be intended more to foment violence than to prevent it. As with the CIA, intelligence came to mean both investigation and action. The two activities seemed inseparable. The world had to be set right.

The community was not only doing what it perceived to be its duty, but after a time it was also having fun. As times grew more tense and complicated, business got better. Presidents, secretaries of state, attorneys general, aroused politicians, and editorial writers fulminated in the most general terms over the need to "do something" about the likes of Fidel Castro, the Klan, or the Black Panthers. The agencies did something: they developed exploding cigars and poisoned diving suits. They ordered Klansmen informants to sleep with the wives of other Klansmen. They wiretapped and bugged beyond the most energetic agents' ability to read and digest the product. The CIA, ever ambitious and sensitive to presidential whims, got more into the FBI's line of work, and the FBI, ever defensive and the best of bureaucratic infighters, got into the CIA's. The Bureau reached out further for targets, finding among ecologists and women's liberation groups and other purveyors of discontent sure signs that the revolution was at hand. The CIA zeroed in on the Grove Press and the American Indian Movement, among other purely domestic targets. The higher authorities winked and went about their work, taking refuge in "plausible deniability," express or implied. Congress saw clear enough hints of what was going on to have set off alarms, but none came from Capitol Hill. The secret war in Laos was funded time and again; J. Edgar Hoover's quite public lists of targets for special attention were perused regularly in the course of annual congressional appropriations testimony.

III. WHAT CAN BE DONE?

Those congressmen who expected some degree of contriteness from the agencies under investigation were in for a disappointment. The first level of reaction was more on the order of anger, coupled with a warning that the committees might be doing grave harm to the FBI and the CIA, not to say the national security.

Old rules of the game and standards of behavior, a sense of politesse and stoicism in the service of a noble cause, prevent the community from expressing publicly the full outrage it feels over being dragged ungratefully through the mud. But there is plenty of complaining in private. "The whole ambience these days, the increase in the decibel count . . . is damaging," said one CIA man; "you begin to wish that something harmless would come along, like a typhoon, to distract attention." FBI Director Clarence M. Kelley, who had the delicate problem of trying to renounce the abuses of the past without damaging the morale and pride of old-timers still in powerful positions, was fuming. "Some of the charges people have made against us are absolutely ridiculous," he said, "but we're just going to sit here and take it. We're not going to fight back." "Fight back" is exactly what the FBI would have done in the old Hoover days—with a public relations offensive, even to the point of seeking to undermine the reputations of the congressmen and journalists who were the bearers of bad tidings about the Bureau.

But the best revenge, the proof of the community's strength, may be business as usual. Even while the congressional committees were conducting their investigations, the CIA set out on new secret and controversial projects—about $50 million worth of aid to pro-Western factions in Angola (the exact amount of the assistance was unknown, because the Agency undervalued some of the arms it shipped to Angola via Zaire) and an infusion of $6 million to the noncommunist centrist political parties in Italy, to bolster their effort in that country's next parliamentary elections. Both initiatives were dear to the heart of Kissinger, who was determined to prevent the Italian Communists from joining a coalition government in Rome, notwithstanding their well-known differences with Moscow, and who wanted to use Angola to score points with critics of his policy of détente with the Soviets. The only reason the American public found out about these two involvements was that Congress passed a law in 1974 requiring the director of central intelligence to brief six congressional subcommittees on any plans for covert actions; Angola leaked through the Senate and Italy through the House. The leaks, rather than their substance, gave the agencies a new ground for crying foul. But beyond the charges and countercharges the leaks gave proof, if any was needed, that for all the CIA's humiliations and consequent internal reforms, the basic process had not changed a bit: the Agency could be sent off on chores that bore little clear relationship to any national policy known to the public.

There were modest reforms at the FBI too, aimed at avoiding repetition of past abuses, beginning with Acting Director L. Patrick Gray's 1972 order that every "security" case state some formal basis for the Bureau's jurisdiction, and continuing through to Attorney General Levi's decision in the last days of 1975 to scrap the "administrative index" (ADEX), a catalogue of people who would come in for intensive investigation in time of national emergency. (Under the old "security index," predecessor to the ADEX, they could have been put in detention camps.) FBI Director Kelley, while defending some of the Bureau's excesses in the 1960s on grounds of the "temper of the times" then, swore that they could not happen again. No more professors getting fired because of their political views and associations; no more agents flying from Washington to Atlanta to mail poison-pen letters. And yet the FBI was still conducting voluminous domestic intelligence investigations against targets of its own choice, coordinated out of the Internal Security Section of its Intelligence Division at Washington headquarters. A study by the General Accounting Office showed that barely 3 percent of these actually led to federal prosecutions.

Both agencies invited—in effect, dared—Congress and the executive branch to go beyond fighting the last war and to write new rules that would be appropriate for this and future seasons, that would respect civil liberties without neglecting the genuine dangers of the real world. It is not an easy job, especially if one wants to do something more than tinker (an extra deputy director here and strengthened powers for an inspector general there), but stop short of dismantling the intelligence community entirely.

A fundamental problem is how to define, and perhaps realistically limit, modern-day American intelligence needs. The United States does not confront the threat of invasion by a foreign power. With new electronic and photographic capabilities, fewer and fewer people are directly involved in the collection of tactical military intelligence. What nations want to know about each other, and need live bodies to collect and analyze, is more in the nature of political, economic, and social information, the kind of knowledge that helps governments to perceive the intentions and understand the motives of both their friends and their potential enemies. Much of that can be learned through the press, especially in the Western world, or through normal diplomatic channels. But dealing with closed societies may require some use of clandestine sources and methods.

There is strong sentiment in Washington in favor of new ground rules that would be based more squarely than ever on American concepts of fair play and due process. Senator James Abourezk, Democrat of South Dakota, for example, has repeatedly proposed legislation that would, in its broadest application, prevent the United States from doing anything in its overseas intelligence operations that would be a violation of the law if done at home, and he has a small but solid bloc of votes on his side. Bur Walter Mondale, Abourezk's colleague from Minnesota, no unreconstructed cold warrior himself, criticizes this as a "simple answer" that ignores crucial realities. The United States might gain something in self-righteousness and moral certitude if it stops listening in on private conversations overseas and no longer urges foreign nationals to commit espionage and treason against their own governments, even if most other powers continue to do these things with impunity, but would it not at the same time lose in other very important ways?

In the same vein, the American Civil Liberties Union has proposed that the FBI give up "all foreign and domestic intelligence investigations of groups or individuals unrelated to a specific criminal offense," without suggesting anyone else who could take over the Bureau's counterintelligence function. The intent is pure, but does the proposed remedy go too far when, according to Colby, every year sixty to eighty Americans are approached overseas and asked to spy for the Soviet Union, and when there is evidence of a substantial network of illegal foreign agents operating in this country? Should the government not be looking for those agents well in advance of any hard probable cause to believe that specific acts of espionage have been committed? Even Mondale, disturbed as he is over FBI abuses, thinks that it should. "We have to be able to keep track [of foreign agents] without abiding by all of the requirements of due process," he concedes. But then what about the "agents of influence," the American citizens, fully protected by the Constitution, upon whom the foreign agents depend? And the "dormant assets," the potential spies who are in place and waiting to be activated? Where to stop?

The best solution, obviously, would be to achieve some measure of détente in those back alleys of the world, as well as in the official channels. Indeed, during the closing days of World War II, when Soviet-American cooperation against the Axis was still operative, "Wild Bill" Donovan proposed an exchange of security delegations in Moscow and Washington between the OSS and the NKVD (forerunner of the KGB). The intended purpose was to trade information about sabotage operations behind German lines, but the cooperation presumably would have continued after the war. At the time, Hoover interceded to shoot down Donovan's plan; and the CIA and KGB agents in the embassies in Moscow and Washington today are hardly there on a formal exchange basis. Even if Kissinger and Leonid Brezhnev were to startle the world by swapping lists of secret agents, as some seriously propose, each would suspect the other of a nasty trick, and they would probably both be right.

Failing that, where can and should the United States draw the lines? Much of the recent dialogue has focused on the red herring of the intelligence investigations, covert actions. The Abourezk proposal, in a somewhat milder form, and recommendations of the Center for National Security Studies, among others, would ban them completely. Morton Halperin, a former official of the Defense Department and the National Security Council, and now director of the center's "Project on National Security and Civil Liberties," told the Church committee that "covert operations are incompatible with our democratic institutions." But Cyrus Vance, who was himself concerned with national security issues as deputy secretary of defense and in other government positions, argues, "It is too difficult to see that clearly in the future. . . . I believe it should be the policy of the United States to engage in covert actions only when they are absolutely essential to the national security."

The real question is whether the United States wants, and considers it to be in the interests of national security, to influence events in other nations. If the answer is yes, as it probably is, then some of that influence may have to be exercised secretly, because sovereign governments are not likely to welcome open interference in their affairs. Ironically, a democratic system like the American one has a problem the Soviets do not. Our government cannot funnel its aid through an organization like the Communist party and say that it is simply helping kindred political spirits.

Certain hypothetical dilemmas are easily solved: the United States almost surely would have liked to be able to assassinate Hitler before or during World War II; that act might have saved millions of lives and earned the gratitude of people the world over. In drawing up standards for peacetime, however, it is easier to delineate what should be prohibited than what should be permitted. No assassinations or even peripheral involvement in plots that might lead to them; no interference in the electoral processes of other countries; no more secret wars; no misleading propaganda that distorts the truth about the world situation; no drug-dealing or other activity that affects the health, livelihood, and well-being of people at home or abroad. But what about secret support for an underground publishing network in the Soviet Union which advances freedom of expression by making the writings of dissidents available to Soviet citizens who want to read them? And what about continuing the postwar tradition of American help to democratic parties in Western Europe that might otherwise be swamped, and eventually repressed, by minority parties that are heavily endowed by Moscow? Or help even to the Western Communist parties that have broken from the Soviet Union and are committed to working for Marxist principles through free elections? Those are tougher cases.

Mitchell Rogovin, a liberal Washington attorney who has represented the CIA through its recent trials and tribulations, proposes a three-part standard for evaluating future proposals for covert action: "Does it advance the legitimate interest of the country [the United States]? Is the means [of carrying out the action] acceptable in a moral sense? If it is revealed, would it hurt more than it would help?" But even that kind of standard would make sense, Rogovin acknowledges, only within the context of basic, well-defined and -articulated national policies—which are nonexistent right now. If those policies were openly debated and established (along with reformed and strengthened procedures for review and accountability), then even if the actions themselves remained secret, the public could know the fundamental attitudes being implemented.

As for "preventive action," the FBI's equivalent of the CIA's "covert operation," it is only a little easier to decide. Again, there is no trouble drawing up a list of prohibited activities: no character assassination; no interference with freedom of speech and association and travel; no indiscriminate electronic surveillance; no provocation to violence. Tentative guidelines drawn up by a Justice Department–FBI committee named by Levi would permit some official preventive actions—at times when violence threatens, on the condition that the attorney general authorize the action in advance and later report on it to

Congress—but Senator Mondale, for one, feels that this might set a dangerous precedent. He argues for use of the arrest power, when necessary under the conspiracy laws, in such circumstances. (People who share his view contend that even an occasional "bad" arrest, which is thrown out of court later, would be preferable to an express government policy of disruption.)

Whatever the standard, all police and intelligence work is bound to continue to include a certain number of unofficial counterintelligence techniques; any smart policeman or agent will make a pretext phone call to try to determine whether a fugitive is home before he goes out to arrest him. And doesn't society want and expect its protectors to find out about terrorist plans in advance and then prevent occurrences such as the bomb explosion at La Guardia?

How much reform and restructuring is really necessary? Levi insists that however many fail-safes are built in, "you have to trust someone at some point." Otis Pike believes that if "more people have to sign off" on controversial policies and actions (that is, if more of the agencies' superiors in the executive branch have to record their approval of such steps) and share responsibility for the outcome, they are likelier to foster and enforce caution and care. But the recent sorry record of abuse of trust and sheer neglect by government officials at all levels provides little basis for relying on the human instincts and personal judgments of those to whom the FBI and CIA must answer. Nor can the solutions be left to the courts; their arbitration of such matters generally comes after it is too late to protect the innocent victims of government excesses.

Proposals for assuring greater accountability and better behavior are now as numerous as the past abuses, but general agreement is crystallizing around a few basic propositions:

■ A new apparatus—either a single special assistant or a small committee—reporting directly to the President on intelligence matters. As envisioned by Ralph Dungan, who was ambassador to Chile when the CIA launched its program of covert activity as a parallel to official American policy there, the new chain of command would assure that all controversial activities could ultimately be said to be carried out in the President's name, and would make the decision-making process on covert actions less casual and informal.

■ A new system of congressional oversight of and participation in intelligence decisions. Although it would mean offending both the powerful apologists for the intelligence community and some of the more effective existing units, the wisest course would probably be to establish a new Joint Committee on Intelligence or, preferably, a separate committee in each house, with exclusive jurisdiction in the area. The members would be selected to represent a cross-section of the Congress, and they and their staffs would automatically rotate off the committee after fixed terms to prevent the kind of cozy buddy system and protection of the agencies that has characterized congressional oversight in the past.

Once a reasonable system is developed for protecting that narrow category of confidential information that legitimately deserves to be kept confidential, Congress could begin to be consulted in advance on any covert actions. (The threat of fines or even suspension from Congress might be necessary to assure adequate security. As matters stand now, a single member of Congress can effectively sabotage or even veto delicate Administration plans with a clever leak.) Some procedure might ultimately be devised for the legislative branch to overrule plans that it considers to be in clear violation of the public interest. The committees could weigh the question of whether the CIA's budget should continue to be kept secret, in apparent violation of the Constitution.

■ The writing of detailed charters for both the FBI and CIA, so that they no longer have to rely upon loopholes, outdated executive orders, and secret communications from the White House for major areas of their jurisdiction. Enacted into statutes, the charters should be specific enough to make it clear what the agencies are forbidden to do. (The GAO has privately told the Church committee that Levi's draft guidelines for the FBI would permit a repetition of virtually all the questionable activities it discovered in its audit of the Bureau's domestic intelligence operations.) But they should not become so specific as to eliminate executive discretion altogether. (Levi has pointed out that once rulemakers get into the business of proscribing certain areas of investigation—for example, personal sexual preference or drinking habits—they may also change their minds and require just such areas of investigation later.)

In all of these areas, Congress, the Executive, and, for that matter, the public must realize that a durable solution will not come overnight. Exact definition of terms and the ability to forecast all hypothetical situations may well elude the drafters, just as they did in 1947. The intelligence community will probably require frequent checkups and routine re-examination of its ground rules. And other problems lie ahead: one is the issue of what Senator Mondale calls "idle hands," large bureaucracies within the bureaucracies whose job it is to spot subversion or dream up covert actions.

Many people, including Dungan and former CIA covert operator David Phillips, suggest taking covert actions out of the Agency and attaching them instead to the Department of State or Defense. A similar solution might be necessary for the Internal Security Section of the FBI. One problem is that when reform of the FBI and the CIA is complete, the old ways of doing business might crop up in the NSA and other lesser-known dark corners of the intelligence community. (Exact numbers vary, depending on whom you talk to about what figures, but an informed estimate is that even now the CIA's budget of approximately $1.5 billion accounts for only 15 percent of the total intelligence community's budget, compared to the NSA's 25 percent.) As Senator Gary Hart puts it, "The danger is not so much the assassin or the black bag job as the Orwellian electronic capacity. . . . It outruns the human ability to control it."

Little can be accomplished, however, until public confidence in the intelligence community is restored. That will take time, and the appointment of a politician like George Bush to be director of central intelligence does not help. One of the most tangible effects of the congressional investigations was indeed to lower this confidence still further, to reinforce and legitimize the fears of dirty tricks that were so widespread in the 1960s and early 1970s. For all the assurances that the FBI and the CIA have changed, that they are no longer misbehaving, many people remain skeptical. They are still not sure whether they are getting the truth. Washington reporters working on sensitive stories still retreat to pay phones for their most delicate calls, and controversial politicians worry about the privacy of files in their offices and homes. (Indeed, when the homes of two members of the Church committee, Howard Baker and Charles Mathias, were burglarized, valuables were ignored but documents were gone through. Police were unable to solve the crimes.) Otis Pike asked the Capitol police to sweep the offices of all members of his committee for wiretaps and bugging devices.

Some executive branch officials agree that it is always a good idea to be careful—one never knows to what lengths the spies of the Soviets, the Chinese, and other potentially hostile foreign powers might go. But it was not those spies whom the journalists, senators, and congressmen feared; it was the ones who work for their own government.

29 How Could Vietnam Happen? An Autopsy

James C. Thomson, Jr.

As a case study in the making of foreign policy, the Vietnam War will fascinate historians and social scientists for many decades to come. One question that will certainly be asked: How did men of superior ability, sound training, and high ideals—American policy-makers of the 1960s—create such costly and divisive policy?

As one who watched the decision-making process in Washington from 1961 to 1966 under Presidents Kennedy and Johnson, I can suggest a preliminary answer. I can do so by briefly listing some of the factors that seemed to me to shape our Vietnam policy during my years as an East Asia specialist at the State Department and the White House. I shall deal largely with Washington as I saw or sensed it, and not with

Saigon, where I have spent but a scant three days, in the entourage of
the Vice President, or with other decision centers, the capitals of
interested parties. Nor will I deal with other important parts of the
record: Vietnam's history prior to 1961, for instance, or the overall
course of America's relations with Vietnam.

Yet a first and central ingredient in these years of Vietnam decisions does involve history. The ingredient was *the legacy of the 1950s*—by
which I mean the so-called "loss of China," the Korean War, and the
Far East policy of Secretary of State Dulles.

This legacy had an institutional by-product for the Kennedy
Administration: in 1961 the U.S. government's East Asian establishment was undoubtedly the most rigid and doctrinaire of Washington's
regional divisions in foreign affairs. This was especially true at the Department of State, where the incoming Administration found the Bureau of Far Eastern Affairs the hardest nut to crack. It was a bureau
that had been purged of its best China expertise, and of farsighted, dis-
passionate men, as a result of McCarthyism. Its members were generally committed to one policy line: the close containment and isolation
of mainland China, the harassment of "neutralist" nations which
sought to avoid alignment with either Washington or Peking, and the
maintenance of a network of alliances with anti-Communist client
states on China's periphery.

Another aspect of the legacy was the special vulnerability and
sensitivity of the new Democratic Administration on Far East policy
issues. The memory of the McCarthy era was still very sharp, and Kennedy's margin of victory was too thin. The 1960 Offshore Islands TV
debate between Kennedy and Nixon had shown the President-elect the
perils of "fresh thinking." The Administration was inherently leery of
moving too fast on Asia. As a result, the Far East Bureau (now the Bureau of East Asian and Pacific Affairs) was the last one to be over-
hauled. Not until Averell Harriman was brought in as Assistant
Secretary in December, 1961, were significant personnel changes attempted, and it took Harriman several months to make a deep imprint
on the bureau because of his necessary preoccupation with the Laos
settlement. Once he did so, there was virtually no effort to bring back
the purged or exiled East Asia experts.

There were other important by-products of this "legacy of the
fifties":

The new Administration inherited and somewhat shared *a general
perception of China-on-the-march*—a sense of China's vastness, its numbers, its belligerence; a revived sense, perhaps, of the Golden Horde.
This was a perception fed by Chinese intervention in the Korean War
(an intervention actually based on appallingly bad communications and
mutual miscalculation on the part of Washington and Peking; but the
careful unraveling of that tragedy, which scholars have accomplished,
had not yet become part of the conventional wisdom).

The new Administration inherited and briefly accepted *a monolithic
conception of the Communist bloc*. Despite much earlier predictions and
reports by outside analysts, policy-makers did not begin to accept the

reality and possible finality of the Sino-Soviet split until the first weeks of 1962. The inevitably corrosive impact of competing nationalisms on Communism was largely ignored.

The new Administration inherited and to some extent shared *the "domino theory" about Asia*. This theory resulted from profound ignorance of Asian history and hence ignorance of the radical differences among Asian nations and societies. It resulted from a blindness to the power and resilience of Asian nationalisms. (It may also have resulted from a subconscious sense that, since "all Asians look alike," all Asian nations will act alike.) As a theory, the domino fallacy was not merely inaccurate but also insulting to Asian nations; yet it has continued to this day to beguile men who should know better.

Finally, the legacy of the fifties was apparently compounded by an uneasy sense of a worldwide Communist challenge to the new Administration after the Bay of Pigs fiasco. A first manifestation was the President's traumatic Vienna meeting with Khrushchev in June, 1961; then came the Berlin crisis of the summer. All this created an atmosphere in which President Kennedy undoubtedly felt under special pressure to show his nation's mettle in Vietnam—if the Vietnamese, unlike the people of Laos, were willing to fight.

In general, the legacy of the fifties shaped such early moves of the new Administration as the decisions to maintain a high-visibility SEATO (by sending the Secretary of State himself instead of some underling to its first meeting in 1961), to back away from diplomatic recognition of Mongolia in the summer of 1961, and most important, to expand U.S. military assistance to South Vietnam that winter on the basis of the much more tentative Eisenhower commitment. It should be added that the increased commitment to Vietnam was also fueled by a new breed of military strategists and academic social scientists (some of whom had entered the new Administration) who had developed theories of counterguerrilla warfare and were eager to see them put to the test. To some, "counterinsurgency" seemed a new panacea for coping with the world's instability.

So much for the legacy and the history. Any new Administration inherits both complicated problems and simplistic views of the world. But surely among the policy-makers of the Kennedy and Johnson Administrations there were men who would warn of the dangers of an open-ended commitment to the Vietnam quagmire?

This raises a central question, at the heart of the policy process: Where were the experts, the doubters, and the dissenters? Were they there at all, and if so, what happened to them?

The answer is complex but instructive.

In the first place, the American government was sorely *lacking in real Vietnam or Indochina expertise*. Originally treated as an adjunct of Embassy Paris, our Saigon embassy and the Vietnam Desk at State were largely staffed from 1954 onward by French-speaking Foreign Service personnel of narrowly European experience. Such diplomats were even more closely restricted than the normal embassy officer—by cast of mind as well as language—to contacts with Vietnam's French-speaking urban elites. For instance, Foreign Service linguists in Portugal are able to speak with the peasantry if they get out of Lisbon and choose to do so; not so the French speakers of Embassy Saigon.

In addition, the *shadow of the "loss of China"* distorted Vietnam reporting. Career officers in the Department, and especially those in the field, had not forgotten the fate of their World War II colleagues who wrote in frankness from China and were later pilloried by Senate committees for critical comments on the Chinese Nationalists. Candid reporting on the strengths of the Viet Cong and the weaknesses of the Diem government was inhibited by the memory. It was also inhibited by some higher officials, notably Ambassador Nolting in Saigon, who refused to sign off on such cables.

In due course, to be sure, some Vietnam talent was discovered or developed. But a recurrent and increasingly important factor in the decision-making process was *the banishment of real expertise.* Here the underlying cause was the "closed politics" of policy-making as issues become hot: the more sensitive the issue, and the higher it rises in the bureaucracy, the more completely the experts are excluded while the harassed senior generalists take over (that is, the Secretaries, Undersecretaries, and Presidential Assistants). The frantic skimming of briefing papers in the back seats of limousines is no substitute for the presence of specialists; furthermore, in times of crisis such papers are deemed "too sensitive" even for review by the specialists. Another underlying cause of this banishment, as Vietnam became more critical, was the replacement of the experts, who were generally and increasingly pessimistic, by men described as "can-do guys," loyal and energetic fixers unsoured by expertise. In early 1965, when I confided my growing policy doubts to an older colleague on the NSC staff, he assured me that the smartest thing both of us could do was to "steer clear of the whole Vietnam mess"; the gentleman in question had the misfortune to be a "can-do guy," however, and is now highly placed in Vietnam, under orders to solve the mess.

Despite the banishment of the experts, internal doubters and dissenters did indeed appear and persist. Yet as I watched the process, such men were effectively neutralized by a subtle dynamic: *the domestication of dissenters.* Such "domestication" arose out of a twofold clubbish need: on the one hand, the dissenter's desire to stay aboard; and on the other hand, the nondissenter's conscience. Simply stated, dissent, when recognized, was made to feel at home. On the lowest possible scale of importance, I must confess my own considerable sense of dignity and acceptance (both vital) when my senior White House employer would refer to me as his "favorite dove." Far more significant was the case of the former Undersecretary of State, George Ball. Once Mr. Ball began to express doubts, he was warmly institutionalized: he was encouraged to become the inhouse devil's advocate on Vietnam. The upshot was inevitable: the process of escalation allowed for periodic requests to Mr. Ball to speak his piece; Ball felt good, I assume (he had fought for righteousness); the others felt good (they had given a full hearing to the dovish option); and there was minimal unpleasantness. The club remained intact; and it is of course possible that matters would have gotten worse faster if Mr. Ball had kept silent, or left before his final departure in the fall of 1966. There was also, of course, the case of the last institutionalized doubter, Bill Moyers. The President is said to have greeted his arrival at meetings with an affectionate; "Well, here comes Mr. Stop-the-Bombing . . ." Here again the dynamics of domesticated dissent sustained the relationship for a while.

A related point—and crucial, I suppose, to government at all times—was *the "effective" trap,* the trap that keeps men from speaking out, as clearly or often as they might, within the government. And it is the trap that keeps men from resigning in protest and airing their dissent outside the government. The most important asset that a man brings to bureaucratic life is his "effectiveness," a mysterious combination of training, style, and connections. The most ominous complaint that can be whispered of a bureaucrat is: "I'm afraid Charlie's beginning to lose his effectiveness." To preserve your effectiveness, you must decide where and when to fight the mainstream of policy; the opportunities range from pillow talk with your wife, to private drinks with your friends, to meetings with the Secretary of State or the President. The inclination to remain silent or to acquiesce in the presence of the great men—to live to fight another day, to give on this issue so that you can be "effective" on later issues—is overwhelming. Nor is it the tendency of youth alone; some of our most senior officials, men of wealth and fame, whose place in history is secure, have remained silent lest their connection with power be terminated. As for the disinclination to resign in protest: while not necessarily a Washington or even American specialty, it seems more true of a government in which ministers have no parliamentary backbench to which to retreat. In the absence of such a refuge, it is easy to rationalize the decision to stay aboard. By doing so, one may be able to prevent a few bad things from happening and perhaps even make a few good things happen. To exit is to lose even those marginal chances for "effectiveness."

Another factor must be noted: as the Vietnam controversy escalated at home, there developed *a preoccupation with Vietnam public relations as opposed to Vietnam policy-making.* And here, ironically, internal doubters and dissenters were heavily employed. For such men, by virtue of their own doubts, were often deemed best able to "massage" the doubting intelligentsia. My senior East Asia colleague at the White House, a brilliant and humane doubter who had dealt with Indochina since 1954, spent three quarters of his working days on Vietnam public relations: drafting presidential responses to letters from important critics, writing conciliatory language for presidential speeches, and meeting quite interminably with delegations of outraged Quakers, clergymen, academics, and housewives. His regular callers were the late A. J. Muste and Norman Thomas; mine were members of the Women's Strike for Peace. Our orders from above: keep them off the backs of busy policy-makers (who usually happened to be non-doubters). Incidentally, my most discouraging assignment in the realm of public relations was the preparation of a White House

pamphlet entitled *Why Vietnam*, in September, 1965; in a gesture
toward my conscience, I fought—and lost—a battle to have the title
followed by a question mark.

Through a variety of procedures, both institutional and personal,
doubt, dissent, and expertise were effectively neutralized in the making
of policy. But what can be said of the men "in charge"? It is patently absurd to suggest that they produced such tragedy by intention and calculation. But it is neither absurd nor difficult to discern certain forces
at work that caused decent and honorable men to do great harm.

Here I would stress the paramount role of *executive fatigue*. No factor seems to me more crucial and underrated in the making of foreign
policy. The physical and emotional toll of executive responsibility in
State, the Pentagon, the White House, and other executive agencies is
enormous; that toll is of course compounded by extended service.
Many of today's Vietnam policy-makers have been on the job for from
four to seven years. Complaints may be few, and physical health may
remain unimpaired, though emotional health is far harder to gauge.
But what is most seriously eroded in the deadening process of fatigue is
freshness of thought, imagination, a sense of possibility, a sense of
priorities and perspective—those rare assets of a new Administration
in its first year or two of office. The tired policy-maker becomes a
prisoner of his own narrowed view of the world and his own clichéd
rhetoric. He becomes irritable and defensive—short on sleep, short on
family ties, short on patience. Such men make bad policy and then
compound it. They have neither the time nor the temperament for
new ideas or preventive diplomacy.

Below the level of the fatigued executives in the making of
Vietnam policy was a widespread phenomenon: *the curator mentality* in
the Department of State. By this I mean the collective inertia produced
by the bureaucrat's view of his job. At State, the average "desk officer"
inherits from his predecessor our policy toward Country X; he regards
it as his function to keep that policy intact—under glass, untampered
with, and dusted—so that he may pass it on in two to four years to his
successor. And such curatorial service generally merits promotion
within the system. (Maintain the status quo, and you will stay out of
trouble.) In some circumstances, the inertia bred by such an outlook
can act as a brake against rash innovation. But on many issues, this
inertia sustains the momentum of bad policy and unwise commitments—momentum that might otherwise have been resisted within the
ranks. Clearly, Vietnam is such an issue.

To fatigue and inertia must be added the factor of internal confusion. Even among the "architects" of our Vietnam commitment, there
has been persistent *confusion as to what type of war we were fighting* and, as
a direct consequence, *confusion as to how to end that war*. (The "credibility
gap" is, in part, a reflection of such internal confusion.) Was it, for
instance, a civil war, in which case counterinsurgency might suffice? Or
was it a war of international aggression? (This might invoke SEATO or
UN commitment.) Who was the aggressor—and the "real enemy"? The
Viet Cong? Hanoi? Peking? Moscow? International Communism? Or

maybe "Asian Communism"? Differing enemies dictated differing strategies and tactics. And confused throughout, in like fashion, was the question of American objectives; your objectives depended on whom you were fighting and why. I shall not forget my assignment from an Assistant Secretary of State in March, 1964: to draft a speech for Secretary McNamara which would, *inter alia,* once and for all dispose of the canard that the Vietnam conflict was a civil war. "But in some ways, of course," I mused, "it *is* a civil war." "Don't play word games with me!" snapped the Assistant Secretary.

Similar confusion beset the concept of "negotiations"—anathema to much of official Washington from 1961 to 1965. Not until April, 1965, did "unconditional discussions" become respectable, via a presidential speech; even then the Secretary of State stressed privately to newsmen that nothing had changed, since "discussions" were by no means the same as "negotiations." Months later that issue was resolved. But it took even longer to obtain a fragile internal agreement that negotiations might include the Viet Cong as something other than an appendage to Hanoi's delegation. Given such confusion as to the whos and whys of our Vietnam commitment, it is not surprising, as Theodore Draper has written, that policy-makers find it so difficult to agree on how to end the war.

Of course, one force—a constant in the vortex of commitment— was that of *wishful thinking.* I partook of it myself at many times. I did so especially during Washington's struggle with Diem in the autumn of 1963 when some of us at State believed that for once, in dealing with a difficult client state, the U.S. government could use the leverage of our economic and military assistance to make good things happen, instead of being led around by the nose by men like Chiang Kai-shek and Syngman Rhee (and, in that particular instance, by Diem). If we could prove that point, I thought, and move into a new day, with or without Diem, then Vietnam was well worth the effort. Later came the wishful thinking of the air-strike planners in the late autumn of 1964; there were those who actually thought that after six weeks of air strikes, the North Vietnamese would come crawling to us to ask for peace talks. And what, someone asked in one of the meetings of the time, if they don't? The answer was that we would bomb for another four weeks, and that would do the trick. And a few weeks later came one instance of wishful thinking that was symptomatic of good men misled: in January, 1965, I encountered one of the very highest figures in the Administration at a dinner, drew him aside, and told him of my worries about the air-strike option. He told me that I really shouldn't worry; it was his conviction that before any such plans could be put into effect, a neutralist government would come to power in Saigon that would politely invite us out. And finally, there was the recurrent wishful thinking that sustained many of us through the trying months of 1965–1966 after the air strikes had begun: that surely, somehow, one way or another, we would "be in a conference in six months," and the escalatory spiral would be suspended. The basis of our hope: "It simply can't go on."

As a further influence on policy-matters I would cite the factor of *bureaucratic detachment.* By this I mean what at best might be termed the professional callousness of the surgeon (and indeed, medical lingo— the "surgical strike" for instance—seemed to crop up in the euphemisms of the time). In Washington the semantics of the military muted the reality of war for the civilian policy-makers. In quiet, air-conditioned, thick-carpeted rooms, such terms as "systematic pressure," "armed reconnaissance," "targets of opportunity," and even "body count" seemed to breed a sort of games-theory detachment. Most memorable to me was a moment in the late 1964 target planning when the question under discussion was how heavy our bombing should be, and how extensive our strafing, at some midpoint in the projected pattern of systematic pressure. An Assistant Secretary of State resolved the point in the following words: "It seems to me that our orchestration should be mainly violins, but with periodic touches of brass." Perhaps the biggest shock of my return to Cambridge, Massachusetts, was the realization that the young men, the flesh and blood I taught and saw on these university streets, were potentially some of the numbers on the charts of those faraway planners. In a curious sense, Cambridge is closer to this war than Washington.

There is an unprovable factor that relates to bureaucratic detachment: the ingredient of *cryptoracism.* I do not mean to imply any conscious contempt for Asian loss of life on the part of Washington officials. But I do mean to imply that bureaucratic detachment may well be compounded by a traditional Western sense that there are so many Asians, after all; that Asians have a fatalism about life and a disregard for its loss; that they are cruel and barbaric to their own people; and that they are very different from us (and all look alike?). And I *do* mean to imply that the upshot of such subliminal views is a subliminal question whether Asians, and particularly Asian peasants, and most particularly Asian Communists, are really people—like you and me. To put the matter another way: would we have pursued quite such policies—and quite such military tactics—if the Vietnamese were white?

It is impossible to write of Vietnam decision-making without writing about language. Throughout the conflict, words have been of paramount importance. I refer here to the impact of *rhetorical escalation* and to the *problem of oversell.* In an important sense, Vietnam has become of crucial significance to us *because we have said that it is of crucial significance.* (The issue obviously relates to the public relations preoccupation described earlier.)

The key here is domestic politics: the need to sell the American people, press, and Congress on support for an unpopular and costly war in which the objectives themselves have been in flux. To sell means to persuade, and to persuade means rhetoric. As the difficulties and costs have mounted, so has the definition of the stakes. This is not to say that rhetorical escalation is an orderly process; executive prose is the product of many writers, and some concepts—North Vietnamese infiltration, America's "national honor," Red China as the chief enemy—have entered the rhetoric only gradually and even sporadically. But there is an upward spiral nonetheless. And once you have *said* that the American Experiment itself stands or falls on the Vietnam outcome, you have thereby created a national stake far beyond any earlier stakes.

Crucial throughout the process of Vietnam decision-making was a conviction among many policy-makers: that Vietnam posed a *fundamental test of America's national will.* Time and again I was told by men reared in the tradition of Henry L. Stimson that all we needed was the will, and we would then prevail. Implicit in such a view, it seemed to me, was a curious assumption that Asians lacked will, or at least that in a contest between Asian and Anglo-Saxon wills, the non-Asians must prevail. A corollary to the persistent belief in will was a *fascination with power* and an awe in the face of the power America possessed as no nation or civilization ever before. Those who doubted our role in Vietnam were said to shrink from the burdens of power, the obligations of power, the uses of power, the responsibility of power. By implication, such men were soft-headed and effete.

Finally, no discussion of the factors and forces at work on Vietnam policy-makers can ignore the central fact of *human ego investment.* Men who have participated in a decision develop a stake in that decision. As they participate in further, related decisions, their stake increases. It might have been possible to dissuade a man of strong self-confidence at an early stage of the ladder of decision; but it is infinitely harder at later stages since a change of mind there usually involves implicit or explicit repudiation of a chain of previous decisions.

To put it bluntly: at the heart of the Vietnam calamity is a group of able, dedicated men who have been regularly and repeatedly wrong— and whose standing with their contemporaries, and more important, with history, depends, as they see it, on being proven right. These are not men who can be asked to extricate themselves from error.

The various ingredients I have cited in the making of Vietnam policy have created a variety of results, most of them fairly obvious. Here are some that seem to me most central:

Throughout the conflict, there has been *persistent and repeated miscalculation* by virtually all the actors, in high echelons and low, whether dove, hawk, or something else. To cite one simple example among many: in late 1964 and early 1965, some peace-seeking planners at State who strongly opposed the projected bombing of the North urged that, instead, American ground forces be sent to South Vietnam; this would, they said, increase our bargaining leverage against the North— our "chips"—and would give us something to negotiate about (the withdrawal of our forces) at an early peace conference. Simultaneously, the air-strike option was urged by many in the military who were dead set against American participation in "another land war in Asia"; they were joined by other civilian peace-seekers who wanted to bomb Hanoi into early negotiations. By late 1965, we had ended up with the worst of all worlds: ineffective and costly air strikes against the North, spiraling ground forces in the South, and no negotiations in sight.

Throughout the conflict as well, there has been *a steady give-in to pressures for a military solution* and only minimal and sporadic efforts at a diplomatic and political solution. In part this resulted from the confusion (earlier cited) among the civilians—confusion regarding objectives and strategy. And in part this resulted from the self-enlarging nature of military investment. Once air strikes and particularly ground forces were introduced, our investment itself had transformed the original stakes. More air power was needed to protect the ground forces; and then more ground forces to protect the ground forces. And needless to say, the military mind develops its own momentum in the absence of clear guidelines from the civilians. Once asked to save South Vietnam, rather than to "advise" it, the American military could not but press for escalation. In addition, sad to report, assorted military constituencies, once involved in Vietnam, have had a series of cases to prove: for instance, the utility not only of air power (the Air Force) but of super-carrier-based air power (the Navy). Also, Vietnam policy has suffered from one ironic by-product of Secretary McNamara's establishment of civilian control at the Pentagon: in the face of such control, interservice rivalry has given way to a united front among the military reflected in the new but recurrent phenomenon of JCS unanimity. In conjunction with traditional congressional allies (mostly Southern senators and representatives) such a united front would pose a formidable problem for any President.

Throughout the conflict, there have been *missed opportunities, large and small, to disengage ourselves from Vietnam on increasingly unpleasant but still acceptable terms.* Of the many moments from 1961 onward, I shall cite only one, the last and most important opportunity that was lost: in the summer of 1964 the President instructed his chief advisers to prepare for him as wide a range of Vietnam options as possible for postelection consideration and decision. He explicitly asked that all options be laid out. What happened next was, in effect, Lyndon Johnson's slow-motion Bay of Pigs. For the advisers so effectively converged on one single option—juxtaposed against two other, phony options (in effect, blowing up the world, or scuttle-and-run)—that the President was confronted with unanimity for bombing the North from all his trusted counselors. Had he been more confident in foreign affairs, had he been deeply informed on Vietnam and Southeast Asia, and had he raised some hard questions that unanimity had submerged, this President could have used the largest electoral mandate in history to de-escalate in Vietnam, in the clear expectation that at the worst a neutralist government would come to power in Saigon and politely invite us out. Today, many lives and dollars later, such an alternative has become an elusive and infinitely more expensive possibility.

In the course of these years, another result of Vietnam decision-making has been *the abuse and distortion of history.* Vietnamese, Southeast Asian, and Far Eastern history has been rewritten by our policy-makers, and their spokesmen, to conform with the alleged necessity of our presence in Vietnam. Highly dubious analogies from our experience elsewhere—the "Munich" sellout and "containment" from Europe, the Malayan insurgency and the Korean War from Asia—have been imported in order to justify our actions. And more recent events have been fitted to the Procrustean bed of Vietnam. Most notably, the change of power in Indonesia in 1965–1966 has been ascribed to our Vietnam presence; and virtually all progress in the Pacific region—the rise of regionalism, new forms of cooperation, and mounting growth rates—has been similarly explained. The Indonesian allegation is undoubtedly false (I tried to prove it, during six months of careful investigation at the White House, and had to confess failure); the regional allegation is patently unprovable in either direction (except, of course, for the clear fact that the economies of both Japan and Korea have profited enormously from our Vietnam-related procurement in these countries; but that is a costly and highly dubious form of foreign aid).

There is a final result of Vietnam policy I would cite that holds potential danger for the future of American foreign policy: *the rise of a new breed of American ideologues who see Vietnam as the ultimate test of their doctrine.* I have in mind those men in Washington who have given a new life to the missionary impulse in American foreign relations: who believe that this nation, in this era, has received a threefold endowment that can transform the world. As they see it, that endowment is composed of, first, our unsurpassed military might; second, our clear technological supremacy; and third, our allegedly invincible benevolence (our "altruism," our affluence, our lack of territorial aspirations). Together, it is argued, this threefold endowment provides us with the opportunity and the obligation to ease the nations of the earth toward modernization and stability: toward a full-fledged *Pax Americana Technocratica.* In reaching toward this goal, Vietnam is viewed as the last and crucial test. Once we have succeeded there, the road ahead is clear. In a sense, these men are our counterpart to the visionaries of Communism's radical left: they are technocracy's own Maoists. They do not govern Washington today. But their doctrine rides high.

Long before I went into government, I was told a story about Henry L. Stimson that seemed to me pertinent during the years that I watched the Vietnam tragedy unfold—and participated in that tragedy. It seems to me more pertinent than ever as we move toward the election of 1968.

In his waning years Stimson was asked by an anxious questioner, "Mr. Secretary, how on earth can we ever bring peace to the world?" Stimson is said to have answered: "You begin by bringing to Washington a small handful of able men who believe that the achievement of peace is possible.

"You work them to the bone until they no longer believe that it is possible.

"And then you throw them out—and bring in a new bunch who believe that it is possible."

PART
IV

The Problems of the Future: Will the World As We Know It Survive?

It has become commonplace to evaluate the problems of the future. Discussions of the year 2000, "future shock," the "energy crisis," the "food crisis," the "environmental crisis," and the "population bomb" have become prevalent. Many view postindustrial society as an emerging scientific utopia in which many of our pressing material problems will have been solved. Others see the new society as plagued by the poisonous fruits of that same science and technology. Pessimism about the effects of scientific progress and economic growth has intensified among intellectual and professional elites. Indeed, to many observers preoccupation with such issues as the balance of power appears trivial at a time when our future existence seems imperiled by environmental conditions rather than atomic Armageddon.

During the past several years the "future" seems to have arrived in the form of crisis rather than utopia, and the pessimists appear to have won the day. In part four we discuss the problems of population, energy, and food. Barry Commoner begins with a stimulating essay arguing that "poverty breeds overpopulation and not the other way around." He discusses several methods recommended in recent years for controlling population growth—family planning, legally restricting reproduction, imposed starvation. His answer is to limit poverty rather than population, for he believes that as the standard of living rises in a society, economic incentives for bearing children diminish and population eventually decreases. Commoner is even more controversial later in his essay: he states that the root of the problem lies in inequitable distribution of resources created by colonial exploitation, which has limited the economic growth of have-not nations. "The poor countries have high birthrates because they are extremely poor, and they are extremely poor because other countries are extremely rich." Commoner's proposals that some of the world's wealth should be redistributed to developing countries ought to provide us with ample food for thought.

In relation to the energy crisis, Josiah Auspitz takes a very different position from Commoner, for Auspitz favors protection of the interests of the industrialized West. Auspitz charges U.S. oil diplomacy with shortsightedness which results from viewing oil as a commodity rather than a "strategic utility that fuels the entire postwar economic system." The Arabs, he says, have constantly reneged on promises to stabilize oil prices, and the United States has retaliated only verbally. Such shortsightedness may result in a few years of prosperity brought on, for example, by the arms trade, and it may cause an "artificial spurt" in the economy because of petrodollar purchases. However, he believes we will have to pay in the future for many undesirable consequences of our diplomacy with OPEC. These include among other woes "a stop-go economy, a weakening strategic position, a reverse Marshall Plan for Europe and Japan, an effective collusion with the cartel, a distortion of capital allocation, an inequitable redistribution of income both internationally and within the United States, a reinforcement of the worst habits of our two-tier industrial system, a rise in populist demagoguery at home, a shift in the locus of real economic authority to unrepresentative and ill-prepared banking institutions, an increasingly unstable level of armaments in the Persian Gulf." In Auspitz's view, then, we must be more aware of the economic threats which the oil producers and, in particular, the Arabs pose to the Western economic system.

Paul Seabury takes a concern about the energy crisis to its ultimate conclusion, for he is prepared to entertain the possibility of an "oil war" if other avenues fail to alleviate the problems caused Western societies by the OPEC oil price rise and increased Arab economic power. Touma Arida, an Arab journalist, responds to Seabury with the argument that the international monetary and energy crisis caused the petroleum price increase and not the reverse; and he claims that the West's economic difficulties are largely unrelated to oil price rises. Noting that OPEC membership is not exclusively Arab, Arida sees the petropower revolution as the justifiable culmination of oil producer efforts to undo their domination by oil corporations. He argues that revenues which oil producers have at their disposal will either be "recycled" for use by the industrial states or will be used for development projects at home; therefore, petrobillions in the hands of OPEC countries need not disrupt the world economy. Arida concludes by reminding Seabury of the perils of oil war: confrontation with the Soviet Union, alienation of the Arabs, a protracted guerrilla war in reaction to a new Western occupation. Seabury responds by reviewing the negative consequences of OPEC's quintupling the price of oil. The reader is left to ponder the implications of this dialogue for the future of American foreign policy in terms of the direction in which energy policy should proceed and the degree to which the United States should consider resort to force when particularly painful problems arise.

Dan Morgan turns to an area where America is the country with resources aplenty: food. He regards the United States as "the world's only agricultural superpower, and there are not even any close challengers." This position creates "both political opportunities and moral dilemmas," as the United States gains the power through the instrument of food to affect political and economic stability in countries around the world and the ability to determine who shall go hungry in periods of famine. Morgan believes that U.S. policymakers have failed to face up to the implications of this growing American strength. He spells out the dangers and proposes some initial steps to alleviate what he sees as an American grain monopoly which is reaching "unhealthy proportions." His message applies to energy and population problems as well: "What is lacking are creative solutions and the political will to avert a potential global catastrophe."

The crises these five authors identify must give us pause in thinking about the course of future society and the tasks we must face. Some people speak optimistically about quiet new advances in science and industry and about "progress in general," while these authors worry for different reasons about social and economic decline. Whether the issues are balance of power and nuclear proliferation or energy and food crises, the problems of tomorrow are inextricably involved with justice and equality, scientific achievement, and political wisdom. The future, whether it brings a new age of rare achievement or a turbulent era of escalating crises, may make our thermonuclear era appear tranquil by comparison.

Edmund Burke once wrote,

> Society is indeed a contract. . . . It is a partnership in all science; a partnership in all art; a partnership in every virtue, and in all perfection. As the ends of such a partnership cannot be obtained in many generations, it becomes a partnership not only between those who are living, but between those who are living, those who are dead, and those who are to be born.

In a new society of pain or plenty the links between generations may seem broken as technology or turmoil makes it increasingly difficult for us to identify with the ways in which people have lived before us. Perhaps the greatest challenge of all in this future environment will be to maintain our links with tradition and preserve the best of human values as society continues to change. In the world arena a search for links to the past may become central to the quest for a form of order that will maintain what Burke called "the great primeval contract of eternal society."

30 How Poverty Breeds Overpopulation

Barry Commoner

The world population problem is a bewildering mixture of the simple and the complex, the clear and the confused.

What is relatively simple and clear is that the population of the world is getting larger, and that this process cannot go on indefinitely because there are, after all, limits to the resources, such as food, that are needed to sustain human life. Like all living things, people have an inherent tendency to multiply geometrically—that is, the more people there are the more people they tend to produce. In contrast, the supply of food rises more slowly, for unlike people it does not increase in proportion to the existing rate of food production. This is, of course, the familiar Malthusian relationship and leads to the conclusion that the population is certain eventually to outgrow the food supply (and other needed resources), leading to famine and mass death unless some other countervailing force intervenes to limit population growth. One can argue about the details, but taken as a general summary of the population problem, the foregoing statement is one which no environmentalist can successfully dispute.

When we turn from merely stating the problem to analyzing and attempting to solve it, the issue becomes much more complex. The simple statement that there is a limit to the growth of the human population, imposed on it by the inherent limits of the earth's resources, is a useful but abstract idea. In order to reduce it to the level of reality in which the problem must be solved, what is required is that we find the *cause* of the discrepancy between population growth and the available resources. Current views on this question are neither simple nor unanimous.

One view is that the cause of the population problem is uncontrolled fertility, the countervailing force—the death rate—having been weakened by medical advances. According to this view, given the freedom to do so people will inevitably produce children faster than the goods needed to support them. It follows, then, that the birthrate must be deliberately reduced to the point of "zero population growth".

The methods that have been proposed to achieve this kind of direct reduction in birthrate vary considerably. Among the ones advanced in the past are: (a) providing people with effective contraception and access to abortion facilities and with education about the value of using them (i.e., family planning); (b) enforcing legal means to prevent couples from producing more than some standard number of children ("coercion"); (c) withholding of food from the people of starving developing countries which, having failed to limit their birthrate sufficiently, are deemed to be too far gone or too unworthy to be saved (the so-called "lifeboat ethic").

It is appropriate here to illustrate these diverse approaches with examples. The family planning approach is so well known as to need no further exemplification. As to the second of these approaches, one might cite the following description of it by Kingsley Davis, a prominent demographer, which is quoted approvingly in a recent statement by "The Environmental Fund" that is directed against the family planning position: "If people want to control population, it can be done with knowledge already available . . . For instance, a nation seeking to stabilize its population could shut off immigration and permit each couple a maximum of two children, with possible license for a third. Accidental pregnancies beyond the limit would be interrupted by abortion. If a third child were born without a license, or a fourth, the mother would be sterilized." (Quoted from the Environmental Fund's Statement "Declaration on Population and Food"; original in *Daedalus,* Fall, 1973).

The author of the "lifeboat ethic" is Garrett Hardin, who stated in a recent paper (presented in San Francisco at the 1974 annual meeting of the American Association for the Advancement of Science) that: "So long as nations multiply at different rates, survival requires that we adopt the ethic of the lifeboat. A lifeboat can hold only so many people. There are more than two billion wretched people in the world—ten times as many as in the United States. It is literally beyond our ability to save them all . . . Both international granaries and lax immigration policies must be rejected if we are to save something for our grandchildren."

Actually, this recent statement only cloaks, in the rubric of an "ethic," a more frankly political position taken earlier by Hardin: "Every day we [i.e., Americans] are a smaller minority. We are increasing at only one percent a year; the rest of the world increases twice as fast. By the year 2000, one person in 24 will be an American; in one hundred years only one in 46 . . . If the world is one great commons, in which all food is shared equally, then we are lost. Those who breed faster will replace the rest . . . In the absence of breeding control a policy of 'one mouth one meal' ultimately produces one totally miserable world. In a less than perfect world, the allocation of rights based on territory must be defended if a ruinous breeding race is to be avoided. It is unlikely that civilization and dignity can survive everywhere; but better in a few places than in none. Fortunate minorities must act as the trustees of a civilization that is threatened by uninformed good intentions." (*Science,* Vol. 172, p. 1297; 1971).

THE QUALITY OF LIFE

But there is another view of population which is much more complex. It is based on the evidence, amassed by demographers, that the birthrate is not only affected by biological factors, such as fertility and contraception, but by equally powerful *social* factors.

Demographers have delineated a complex network of interactions among these social factors. This shows that population growth is not the consequence of a simple arithmetic relationship between birthrate and death rate. Instead, there are circular relationships in which, as in an ecological cycle, every step is connected to several others.

Thus, while a reduced death rate does, of course, increase the rate of population growth, it can also have the opposite effect—since families usually respond to a reduced rate of infant mortality by opting for fewer children. This negative feedback modulates the effect of a decreased death rate on population size. Similarly, although a rising population increases the demand on resources and thereby worsens the population problem, it also stimulates economic activity. This, in turn, improves educational levels. As a result the average age at marriage tends to increase, culminating in a reduced birthrate—which mitigates the pressure on resources.

In these processes, there is a powerful social force which, paradoxically, both reduces the death rate (and thereby stimulates population growth) and also leads people voluntarily to restrict the production of children (and thereby reduces population growth). That force, simply stated, is the quality of life—a high standard of living, a sense of well-being and of security in the future. When and how the two opposite effects of this force are felt differs with the stages in a country's economic development. In a pre-modern society, such as England before the industrial revolution or India before the advent of the English, both death rates and birthrates were high. But they were in balance and population size was stable. Then, as agricultural and industrial production began to increase and living conditions improved, the death rate began to fall. With the birthrate remaining high the population rapidly increased in size. However, later, as living standards continued to improve, the decline in death rate persisted but the birthrate began to decline as well, reducing the rate of population growth.

For example, at around 1800, Sweden had a high birthrate (about 33/1000), but since the death rate was equally high, the population was in balance. Then as agriculture and, later, industrial production advanced, the death rate dropped until, by the mid-nineteenth century, it stood at about 20/1000. Since the birthrate remained constant during that period of time, there was a large excess of births over deaths and the population increased rapidly. Then, however, the birthrate began to drop, gradually narrowing the gap until in the mid-twentieth century it reached about 14/1000, when the death rate was about 10/1000.* Thus, under the influence of a constantly rising standard of living the population moved, with time, from a position of balance *at a high death rate* to a new position of near-balance *at a low death rate*. But in between the population increased considerably.

*This and subsequent demographic information is from: Agency for International Development. *Population Program Assistance*, December, 1971).

This process, *the demographic transition,* is clearly characteristic of all western countries. In most of them, the birthrate does not begin to fall appreciably until the death rate is reduced below about 20/1000. However, then the drop in birthrate is rapid. A similar transition also appears to be under way in countries like India. Thus in the mid-nineteenth century, India had equally high birth and death rates (about 50/1000) and the population was in approximate balance. Then, as living standards improved, the death rate dropped to its present level of about 15/1000 and the birthrate dropped, at first slowly and recently more rapidly, to its present level of 42/1000. India is at a critical point; now that death rate has reached the turning point of about 20/1000, we can expect the birthrate to fall rapidly—provided that the death rate is further reduced by improved living conditions.

One indicator of the quality of life—infant mortality—is especially decisive in this process. And again there is a critical point—a rate of infant mortality below which birthrate begins to drop sharply and, approaching the death rate, creates the conditions for a balanced population. The reason is that couples are interested in the number of *surviving* children and respond to a low rate of infant mortality by realizing that they no longer need to have more children to replace the ones that die. Birth control is, of course, a necessary adjunct to this process; but it can succeed—barring compulsion—only in the presence of a rising standard of living, which of itself generates the necessary motivation.

This process appears to be just as characteristic of developing countries as of developed ones. This can be seen by plotting the present birthrates against the present rates of infant mortality for all available national data. The highest rates of infant mortality are in African countries; they are in the range of 53-175/1000 live births and birthrates are about 27-52/1000. In those countries where infant mortality has improved somewhat (for example, in a number of Latin American and Asian countries) the drop in birthrate is slight (to about 45/1000) until the infant mortality reaches about 80/1000. Then, as infant mortality drops from 80/1000 to about 25/1000 (the figure characteristic of most developed countries), the birthrate drops sharply from 45 to about 15-18/1000. Thus a rate of infant mortality of 80/1000 is a critical turning point which can lead to a very rapid decline in birthrate in response to a further reduction in infant mortality. The latter, in turn, is always very responsive to improved living conditions, especially with respect to nutrition. Consequently, there is a kind of critical standard of living which, if achieved, can lead to a rapid reduction in birthrate and an approach to a balanced population.

Thus, in human societies, there is a built-in control on population size: If the standard of living, which initiates the rise in population, *continues* to increase, the population eventually begins to level off. This self-regulating process begins with a population in balance, but at a high death rate and low standard of living. It then progresses toward a population which is larger, but once more in balance, at a low death rate and a high standard of living.

DEMOGRAPHIC PARASITES

The chief reason for the rapid rise in population in developing countries is that this basic condition has not been met. The explanation is a fact about developing countries which is often forgotten—that they were recently, and in the economic sense often still remain, colonies of more developed countries. In the colonial period, western nations introduced improved living conditions (roads, communications, engineering, agricultural and medical services) as part of their campaign to increase the labor force needed to exploit the colony's natural resources. This increase in living standards initiated the first phase of the demographic transition.

But most of the resultant wealth did not remain in the colony. As a result, the second (or population-balancing) phase of the demographic transition could not take place. Instead the wealth produced in the colony was largely diverted to the advanced nation—where it helped *that* country achieve for itself the second phase of the demographic transition. Thus colonialism involves a kind of demographic parasitism: The second, population-balancing phase of the demographic transition in the advanced country is fed by the suppression of that same phase in the colony.

It has long been known that the accelerating curve of wealth and power of Western Europe, and later of the United States and Japan, has been heavily based on exploitation of resources taken from the less powerful nations: colonies, whether governed legally, or—as in the case of the U.S. control of certain Latin American countries—by extra-legal and economic means. The result has been a grossly inequitable rate of development among the nations of the world. As the wealth of the exploited nations was diverted to the more powerful ones, their power, and with it their capacity to exploit, increased. The gap between the wealth of nations grew, as the rich were fed by the poor.

What is evident from the above considerations is that this process of international exploitation has had another very powerful but unanticipated effect: rapid growth of the population in the former colonies. An analysis by the demographer Nathan Keyfitz leads him to conclude that the growth of industrial capitalism in the western nations in the period 1800–1950 resulted in the development of a one-billion excess in the world population, largely in the tropics. Thus the present world population crisis—the rapid growth of population in developing countries (the former colonies)—is the result not so much of policies promulgated by these countries but of a policy, colonial exploitation, forced on them by developed countries.

A VILLAGE IN INDIA

Given this background, what can be said about the various alternative methods of achieving a balanced world population? In India, there has been an interesting, if partially inadvertent, comparative test of two of the possible approaches: family planning programs and efforts (also on a family basis), to elevate the living standard. The results of this test show that while the family planning effort itself failed to reduce the birthrate, improved living standards succeeded.

In 1954, a Harvard team undertook the first major field study of birth control in India. The population of a number of test villages was provided with contraceptives and suitable educational programs; birthrates, death rates and health status in this population were compared with the comparable values in an equivalent population in control villages. The study covered the six-year period 1954–1960.

A follow-up in 1969 showed that the study was a failure. Although in the test population the crude birthrate dropped from 40 per 1,000 in 1957 to 35 per 1,000 in 1968, a similar reduction also occurred in the control population. The birth control effort had no measurable effect on birthrate.

We now know *why* the study failed, thanks to a remarkable book by Mahmood Mamdani (*The Myth of Population Control*, Monthly Review Press, New York, 1972). He investigated in detail the impact of the study on one of the test villages, Manupur. What Mamdani discovered is a total confirmation of the view that population control in a country like India depends on the economically motivated desire to limit fertility. Talking with the Manupur villagers he discovered why, despite the study's statistics regarding ready "acceptance" of the offered contraceptives, the birthrate was not affected:

"One such 'acceptance' case was Asa Singh, a sometime land laborer who is now a watchman at the village high school. I questioned him as to whether he used the tablets or not: 'Certainly I did. You can read it in their books—From 1957 to 1960, I never failed.' Asa Singh, however, had a son who had been born sometime in 'late 1958 or 1959.' At our third meeting I pointed this out to him . . . Finally he looked at me and responded. 'Babuji, someday you'll understand. It is sometimes better to lie. It stops you from hurting people, does no harm, and might even help them.' The next day Asa Singh took me to a friend's house . . . and I saw small rectangular boxes and bottles, one piled on top of the other, all arranged as a tiny sculpture in a corner of the room. This man had made a sculpture of birth control devices. Asa Singh said: 'Most of us threw the tablets away. But my brother here, he makes use of everything.' "

Such stories have been reported before and are often taken to indicate how much "ignorance" has to be overcome before birth control can be effective in countries like India. But Mamdani takes us much further into the problem, by finding out why the villagers preferred not to use the contraceptives. In one interview after another he discovered a simple, decisive fact: that in order to advance their economic condition, to take advantage of the opportunities newly created by the development of independent India, *children were essential.* Mamdani makes this very explicit:

"To begin with, most families have either little or no savings, and they can earn too little to be able to finance the education of *any* children, even through high school. Another source of income must be found, and the only solution is, as one tailor told me, 'to have enough children so that there are at least three or four sons in the family.' Then each son can finish high school by spending part of the afternoon working . . . After high school, one son is sent on to college while the others work to save and pay the necessary fees . . . Once his education is completed, he will use his increased earnings to put his brother through college. He will not marry until the second brother has finished his college education and can carry the burden of educating the third brother . . . What is of interest is that, as the Khanna Study pointed out, it was the rise in the age of marriage—from 17.5 years in 1956 to 20 in 1969—and not the birth control program that was responsible for the decrease in the birthrate in the village from 40 per 1,000 in 1957 to 35 per 1,000 in 1968. While the birth control program was a failure, the net result of the technological and social change in Manupur was to bring down the birth rate."

Here, then, in the simple realities of the village of Manupur are the principles of the demographic transition at work. There *is* a way to control the rapid growth of populations in developing countries. It is to help them develop—and more rapidly achieve the level of welfare that everywhere in the world is the real motivation for a balanced population.

ENOUGH TO GO AROUND

Against this success, the proponents of the "lifeboat ethic" would argue that it is too slow, and they would take steps to *force* developing nations to reduce their birthrate even though the incentive for reduced fertility—the standard of living and its most meaningful index, infant mortality—is still far inferior to the levels which have motivated the demographic transition in the western countries. And where, in their view, it is too late to save a poor, overpopulated country the proponents of this so-called "ethic" would withdraw support (in the manner of the hopelessly wounded in military "triage") and allow it to perish.

This argument is based (at least in the realm of logic) on the view, to quote Hardin, that "It is literally beyond our ability to save them all". Hardin's assertion, if not the resulting "ethic," reflects a commonly held view that there is simply insufficient food and other resources in the world to support the present world population at the standard of living required to motivate the demographic transition. It is commonly pointed out, for example, that the U.S. consumes about one-third of the world's resources to support only six percent of the world's population, the inference being that there are simply not enough resources in the world to permit the rest of the world to achieve the standard of living and low birthrate characteristic of the U.S.

The fault in this reasoning is readily apparent if one examines the actual relationship between the birthrates and living standards of different countries. The only available comparative measure of standard of living is GNP per capita. Neglecting for a moment the faults inherent in GNP as a measure of the quality of life, a plot of birthrate against GNP per capita is very revealing. The poorest countries (GNP per capita less than $500 per year*) have the highest birthrates, 40–50 per 1,000 population per year. When GNP per capita per year exceeds $500 the birthrate drops sharply, reaching about 20/1,000 at $750–$1,000. Most of the nations in North America, Oceania, Europe and the USSR have about the same low birthrates—15–18/1,000—but their GNP's per capita per year range all the way from Greece ($941 per capita per year; birthrate 17/1,000) through Japan ($1,626 per capita per year; birthrate 18/1,000) to the richest country of all, the U.S. ($4,538 per capita per year; birthrate 18/1,000). What this means is that in order to bring the birthrates of the poor countries down to the low levels characteristic of the rich ones, the poor countries do not need to become as affluent (at least as measured, poorly, by GNP per capita) as the U.S. Achieving a per capita GNP only, let us say, one-fifth of that of the U.S.—$900 per capita per year—these countries could, according to the above relationship, reach birthrates almost as low as that of the European and North American countries.

The world average value for birthrate is 34/1,000, which is indicative of the overall rate of growth of the world population (the world average crude death rate is about 13/1,000). However, the world average per capita GNP is about $803 per year—a level of affluence which is characteristic of a number of nations with birthrates of 20/1,000. What this discrepancy tells us is that if the wealth of the world (at least as measured by GNP) were in fact evenly distributed among the people of the world, the entire world population should have a low birthrate—about 20/1,000—which would approach that characteristic of most European and North American countries (15–18/1,000).

Simply stated, the world has enough wealth to support the entire world population at a level that appears to convince most people that they need not have excessive numbers of children. The trouble is that the world's wealth is *not* evenly distributed, but sharply divided among moderately well-off and rich countries on the one hand and a much larger number of people that are very poor. The poor countries have high birthrates because they are extremely poor, and they are extremely poor because other countries are extremely rich.

THE ROOTS OF HUNGER

In a sense the demographic transition is a means of translating the availability of a decent level of resources, especially food, into a voluntary reduction in birthrate. It is a striking fact that the efficiency with which such resources can be converted into a reduced birthrate is much higher in the developing countries than in the advanced ones. Thus an improvement in GNP per capita per year from let us say $682 (as in Uruguay) to $4,538 (U.S.) reduces birthrate from 22/1,000 to 18/1,000. In contrast, according to the above relationships if the GNP per capita per year characteristic of India (about $88) were increased to only

*These and subsequent values are computed as U.S. 1969 dollars. The data relate to the 1969–70 period.

about $750, the Indian birthrate should fall from its actual value of about 42/1,000 to about 20/1,000. To put the matter more simply, the per capita cost of bringing the standard of living of poor countries with rapidly growing populations to the level which—based on the behavior of peoples all over the world—would motivate voluntary reduction of fertility is very small, compared to the per capita wealth of developed countries.

Food plays a critical role in these relationships. Hunger is widespread in the world and those who believe that the world's resources are already insufficient to support the world population cite this fact as the most powerful evidence that the world is overpopulated. Conversely, those who are concerned with relieving hunger and preventing future famines often assert that the basic solution to that problem is to control the growth of the world population.

Once more it is revealing to examine actual data regarding the incidence of malnutrition. From a detailed study of nutritional levels among various populations in India by Revelle & Frisch (Vol. III, "The World Food Problem", A report of the President's Science Advisory Committee, Washington, 1967) we learn, for example, that in Madras State more than one-half the population consumes significantly less than the physiologically required number of calories and of protein in their diet. However, the *average* values for all residents of the state represents 99 percent of the calorie requirement and 98 percent of the protein requirement. What this means, of course, is that a significant part of the population receives *more* than the required dietary intake. About one-third of the population receives 106 percent of the required calories and 104 percent of the required protein; about 8 percent of the population receives 122 percent or more of the calorie requirement and 117 percent or more of the protein requirement. These dietary differences are determined by income. The more than one-half of the population that is significantly below the physiologically required diet earn less than $21 per capita per year, as compared with the state-wide average of $33.40.

What these data indicate is that hunger in Madras State, defined simply in terms of a significantly inadequate intake of calories and protein, is not the result of a biological factor—the inadequate production of food. Rather, in the strict sense, it results from the *social* factors that govern the *distribution* of available food among the population.

In the last year, newspaper stories of actual famines in various parts of the world have also supported the view that starvation is usually not caused by the insufficient production of food in the world, but by social factors that prevent the required distribution of food. Thus, in Ethiopia many people suffered from starvation because government officials failed to mobilize readily available supplies of foreign grain. In India, according to a recent *New York Times* report, inadequate food supplies were due in part to a government policy which "resulted in a booming black market, angry resentment among farmers and traders, and a breakdown in supplies." The report asserts further that "The central problem of India—rooted poverty—remains unchecked and seems to be getting worse. For the third year out of four per capita income is expected to drop. Nearly 80 percent of the children are malnourished . . . The economic torpor seems symptomatic of deeper problems. Cynicism is rampant: the Government's socialist slogans and calls for austerity are mocked in view of bribes and corruption, luxury construction and virtually open illegal contributions by businessmen to the Congress party." (*New York Times,* Apr. 17, 1974)

Given these observations and the overall fact that the amount of food crop produced in the world at present is sufficient to provide an adequate diet to about eight billion people—more than twice the world population—it appears to me that the present, tragically widespread hunger in the world cannot be regarded as evidence that the size of the world population has outrun the world's capacity to produce food. I have already pointed out that we can regard the rapid growth of population in developing countries and the grinding poverty which engenders it as the distant outcome of colonial exploitation—a policy imposed on the antecedents of the developing countries by the more advanced ones. This policy has forcefully determined both the distribution of the world's wealth and of its different populations, accumulating most of the wealth in the western countries and most of the people in the remaining, largely tropical, ones.

Thus there is a grave imbalance between the world's wealth and the world's people. But the imbalance is not the supposed disparity between the world's *total* wealth and *total* population. Rather, it is due to the gross *distributive* imbalance among the nations of the world. What the problem calls for, I believe, is a process that now figures strongly in the thinking of the peoples of the Third World: a return of some of the world's wealth to the countries whose resources and peoples have borne so much of the burden of producing it—the developing nations.

WEALTH AMONG NATIONS

There is no denying that this proposal would involve exceedingly difficult economic, social and political problems, especially for the rich countries. But the alternative solutions thus far advanced are at least as difficult and socially stressful.

A major source of confusion is that these diverse proposed solutions to the population problem, which differ so sharply in their moral postulates and their political effects, appear to have a common base in scientific fact. It is, after all, equally true, scientifically, that the birthrate can be reduced by promulgating contraceptive practices (providing they are used), by elevating living standards, or by withholding food from starving nations.

But what I find particularly disturbing is that behind this screen of confusion between scientific fact and political intent there has developed an escalating series of what can be only regarded, in my opinion, as inhumane, abhorrent political schemes put forward in the guise of science. First we had Paddock's "triage" proposal, which would condemn whole nations to death through some species of global "benign neglect". Then we have schemes for coercing people to curtail their fertility, by physical and legal means which are ominously left unspecified. Now we are told (for example, in the statement of "The Environmental Fund") that we must curtail rather than extend our efforts to feed the hungry peoples of the world. Where will it end? Is it conceivable that the proponents of coercive population control will be guided by one of Garrett Hardin's earlier, astonishing proposals:

> How can we help a foreign country to escape over-population? Clearly the worst thing we can do is send food . . . Atomic bombs would be kinder. For a few moments the misery would be acute, but it would soon come to an end for most of the people, leaving a very few survivors to suffer thereafter ("The Immorality of Being Softhearted", Stanford Alumni Almanac, Jan., 1969).

There has been a long-standing alliance between psuedo-science and political repression; the Nazis' genetic theories, it will be recalled, were to be tested in the ovens at Dachau. This evil alliance feeds on confusion.

The present confusion can be removed by recognizing *all* of the current population proposals for what they are—not scientific observations but value judgments that reflect sharply differing ethical views and political intentions. The family planning approach, if applied as the exclusive solution to the problem, would put the burden of remedying a fault created by a social and political evil—colonialism—voluntarily on the individual victims of the evil. The so-called "lifeboat ethic" would compound the original evil of colonialism by forcing its victims to forego the humane course toward a balanced population, improvement of living standards, or if they refuse, to abandon them to destruction, or even to thrust them toward it.

My own purely personal conclusion is, like all of these, not scientific but political: that the world population crisis, which is the ultimate outcome of the exploitation of poor nations by rich ones, ought to be remedied by returning to the poor countries enough of the wealth taken from them to give their peoples both the reason and the resources voluntarily to limit their own fertility.

In sum, I believe that if the root cause of the world population crisis is poverty, then to end it we must abolish poverty. And if the cause of poverty is the grossly unequal distribution of world's wealth, then to end poverty, and with it the population crisis, we must redistribute that wealth, among nations and within them.

3 1 Oil: The Strategic Utility

Josiah Lee Auspitz

In a November 14, 1974 speech that has become the central document for US oil diplomacy, Henry Kissinger compared the energy crisis to the "economic chaos and political upheaval" that threatened the world in the Truman years. And he called for a creative spirit comparable to that which made possible NATO, the Bretton Woods agreement and the reconstruction of Germany and Japan. The analogy struck most observers as excessive even for Dr. Kissinger, whose public rhetoric has always been Spenglerian. How, an influential columnist asked, can one weigh a rise in gasoline prices on the same scale as the formation of the entire postwar era? Oil, like sugar, now costs more but surely this does not mean the decline of the West.

On this issue, however, Dr. Kissinger's lugubriousness was much closer to the truth than the pundit's good cheer. The low and stable price of oil can be compared to the achievements of the Marshall Plan years because it was in fact one of the most important of those achievements. Its demise threatens the very economic foundations of the postwar world because the oil pricing system has itself been an invisible underpinning of the postwar political economy. As long as the public fails to face this, it cannot understand the conditions of its long period of prosperity or the forces that have set the broad terms of the energy policy over which the President and the Congress will be quibbling for the next few months.

In 1946 when the price of Arabian crude was $1.05 a barrel, it was evident that this cheap new source of fuel would revolutionize the world economy. It had been discovered by American firms in unpopulated desert sands where British geologists doubted anything would be found. It was developed with high technology in ways that contrasted dramatically with the usual pattern of imperial exploitation: its extraction involved no plantations, no coolies, almost no native labor. If one believes, with Algeria's Marxist theoreticians, in a labor theory of value, one must recognize that it was American labor and technology that gave this fuel its worth. Once the initial investment in exploration was made, it cost only pennies a barrel to take the oil out of the ground— and there was enough of it, had it been fully exploited, to drive Texas oil, Venezuelan oil and even Iraqi oil off the market.

The cheapness and abundance of Arabian crude posed a dilemma for the United States: if America accepted a free market for oil, it would put its own industry out of business and depend increasingly on a remote and precarious source of supply. If, on the other hand, the US protected inefficient production at home, it would have higher fuel costs than Europe or Japan and deplete its own resources more rapidly.

In the years 1945–49 a tacit policy emerged from bargaining among the major oil companies, the US and British governments, and the European Cooperation Administration. The price of Arabian crude was propped up at over two dollars a barrel—a level that would subsidize new exploration in the Western hemisphere. The price was then allowed to recede to $1.75 a barrel in 1949, at which level the Western hemisphere would be a net exporter, with Britain a midpoint where Eastern and Western hemisphere oil were equally competitive. With remarkably few fluctuations, a uniform international price was held in the $1.75—$2.25 range through most of the 1950s and 1960s.

This pricing system was managed by a cartel of American, Dutch and British firms with cooperation and regulation from their governments, and military protection from the US and Britain to prevent Soviet reentry into Iran. The United States gave its firms extraordinary tax advantages to assure that the profits from oil would be plowed back into further exploration. The result was that oil became a preponderantly American industry.

The US government and oil industry functioned like an international utility, on the whole a reliable one. The partnership kept prices low and stable; it kept the flow of oil free from Soviet interference; it enabled Europe to follow America into the automotive age. And in the unpopulated Arabian peninsula, it involved no neocolonial exploitation. On the contrary it almost singlehandedly made possible the flowering of a desert country like Kuwait.

As one might expect of a private utility whose rates had been stable for 20 years, the oil companies wanted an increase in the 1970s. They argued that rising world demand required more exploration and hence higher profit; that a quantum jump in price was again necessary to make the Western hemisphere self-sufficient; and that they had, on the whole, exercised reasonably well a quasi-governmental function that was necessary to a free and vigorous world economy.

Arguments like these became political liabilities, however. The role of oil as a strategic utility had been treated as a dirty secret by the publicists of US foreign policy. Only radical assistant professors of sociology liked to talk about it—and only in the most lurid terms. No one bothered to tell the American people that their postwar safety and comfort rested on some very hardheaded decisions about maintaining a stable international price of oil. To reopen this question in the Nixon years proved politically impossible.

Further, in their preoccupation with Vietnam, government planners did not take adequate steps to assume the military responsibilities that the British were relinquishing in the Persian Gulf or to cultivate friendly relations with the army officers who deposed the King of Libya in late 1969 and promptly ordered the Americans out of Wheelus Air Base. Finally the oil-producing countries were becoming more assertive: they had had a generation to educate and hire technocrats and to learn some bargaining tricks of their own, the first of which was the foundation of OPEC in 1960.

The oil companies, hardly philanthropic organizations, saw the writing on the wall. The 25-year harmony of corporate and government interests was coming to an end. The Anglo-American military presence was less reliable, public opinion was dead set against them, the oil producers were getting restive, and the US position on the Arab-Israeli conflict could only work against them. If their position was untenable, they might as well get out comfortably. Hence they did nothing to oppose measures by OPEC to jack up the price of oil to a level that now makes it possible for them to sell their foreign holdings on lucrative terms. And the US Departments of State and Treasury, accustomed to taking cues from oil company officials, responded to the most outrageous moves by the OPEC countries only with admonitions.

From 1970 to 1973 first Libya then the other OPEC countries as a group tested American responses. They set terms for the purchase of Western firms, and then reneged, pushing up the timetables and raising the percentage of the share they demanded. Acting collectively, they doubled the price of oil and promised not to change it again soon. On this too they reneged repeatedly. Their actions provoked only verbal rebukes from the US followed by a quiet adjustment to the new demands almost as if they had been decreed by the Supreme Court. In 1973–74 OPEC, breaking its word with impunity, quadrupled the price of oil: the industrial world is now trying to adjust to this too, revising its entire financial structure to deal with every new OPEC demand. The Algerians who have read both Lenin and oil drilling manuals, doubtless have a slogan for it: "When you hit mush, push."
If oil were a commodity like peanuts or palm oil this might be a minor annoyance. Were it even a strategic commodity like uranium or titanium, it might be tolerable. But oil, as we have seen, does not function as a commodity but as a *strategic utility.* The regularity and predictability of its flow are as essential to an industrial economy as the flow of clean water to the city of Washington. The chief flaw in the world's economy today is that the management of an essential utility— the international oil supply—has been left in irresponsible hands by the inattention of the US government and cold indifference of the oil companies.
In a civilized society there are certain things utilities are not allowed to do. They are not allowed to change rates without notice, to renege on published notice, or to alter rates without hearings and deliberation. More important, they are not allowed to play politics with the service they provide, to discriminate among customers or arbitrarily to deny service. And they are expected to plow their profits back into improving service. This writer once worked as a volunteer in a Third World nation in which the minister of power regularly cut off the electricity of businesses from which he wanted to extract bribes or political favors, gave cut rates to his friends and spent surplus funds on real estate speculation and bodyguards. Similar practices, as the film *Chinatown* should remind us, also occur in some American localities. But here, as in the Third World, when such practices are exposed they are treated as crimes.

It is precisely this kind of economic criminality with which OPEC has run the utility it has taken over from the previous and more responsible private cartel. Whereas the oil companies, for all their faults, kept a stable price and a steady supply, the OPEC countries have changed prices without notice or consultation, repudiated published pledges, played politics with the provision of services and interrupted the oil flow arbitrarily. And they have used their monetary surplus in short-term financial manipulations and arms purchases. Their price rises during [1974–75] have, by the most conservative estimates, accounted for one-third of the US rate of inflation—or precisely that portion for the removal of which we are accepting an eight percent unemployment rate.

After all this we are told that we should not get alarmed, because the king of Saudi Arabia and the shah of Iran do not want to see the Western economy collapse. But there is a big difference between not wanting capitalism to collapse and wanting to see it thrive. When the Western powers decided not to internationalize the Arabian oilfields after the war, they assumed that Anglo-American officials and businessmen were competent to be entrusted with the economic health of the West. Does anyone believe OPEC is worthy of this trust?

The past three years have made it clear that however honorable the OPEC finance ministers may be in their private lives, their word on oil policy is worthless. The central reality that the American public has yet to face is the need to replace the informal, regional management of the oil price by OPEC ministers with a formal, truly international system of agreements. OPEC can be part of such a system only if it divests itself of all claims to the unilateral rights to raise or lower prices, to discriminate in pricing either directly or through bilateral deals, to impose embargoes or restrict sales to specific countries. These procedural questions must be settled before bargaining over price begins, for until they are resolved there can be no long-term economic planning anywhere.

Suppose, for example, that OPEC were to cut its price $8.40, and pledge to keep this price for five years. What is to stop OPEC members from changing their minds? And even if they didn't, what is to stop them from cutting the price at the end of the period, thus bankrupting the new high-priced energy industries? Or what is to stop the Saudis, for example, from offering oil at a discriminatory rate of two dollars a barrel to the Japanese in exchange for a joint agreement to monopolize petrochemicals? And how at the end of five years could Western industrial countries expect to have any influence on OPEC's richest members, who by then will have spent billions of dollars, possibly on nuclear armaments, to make themselves immune to military threats? And if we agree to political concessions now to get more oil (for example, permitting Iran to occupy the Arab Emirates, or sacrificing Israel's safety) what is to stop the OPEC countries from extracting new concessions later?

Surplus oil profits present another problem. The Arabian peninsula surplus—by which is meant not all oil revenues but only those that cannot be absorbed in arms purchases or economic development—is conservatively estimated at between $150–$200 billion in constant dollars [between 1975 and 1980]. This represents only a fraction of the world's income, but in economics it is always the discretionary money at the margin that counts. Raymond Vernon of the Harvard business school estimates that US overseas firms have accumulated $200 billion in assets during the postwar period. Thus the Arabian oil producers will have discretionary holdings equivalent to the entire worth of US multinational firms overseas, and since they will garner this wealth in five years rather than 30, the leverage it represents will be far greater than that wielded by US multinationals. The investment of so much money in so short a time will require that the bulk of it be allocated by international money managers, officials of central banks and governments. In the US the big New York banks and the Treasury will do most of the work. This allocation of capital by a central authority can be efficiently used by nations whose economies are dominated by major firms and an efficient central banking system. The Japanese are particularly good at steering money to the most productive giant enterprises. In the United States, however, such quasi-governmental funds are commonly used to strengthen not the most vigorous firms but the weakest—the Penn Central, for example, or Chrysler, Westinghouse, the City of New York and numerous real estate investment trusts. Those entwined in loans to such inefficient entities may be complacent about the petrodollar crisis, but for the country as a whole this attitude only postpones the day of reckoning—a day that two devaluations of the dollar should have warned us is long overdue. The centralized disbursal of petrodollars will have the effect of exaggerating the worst aspects of the two-tier American economy by propping up the weakest entities in the subsidized tier and leaving competitive private enterprise. starved for capital.

It has been argued (notably by Hollis Chenery of the World Bank in the January [1975] issue of *Foreign Affairs* and by David Rockefeller, president of the Chase Manhattan Bank, in a February lecture at the Harvard business school) that the petrodollar surplus is a blessing in disguise, since it amounts to a form of "forced savings." It is said that, at a time when private markets are not providing adequate capital, the oil price hike, by increasing energy company profits and by putting new surplus funds at the disposal of the banks, will make it possible to finance a new spurt of industrial growth. But the reason we have a capital squeeze today is that the average consumer, at least as he expresses himself in the polls and pressures on Congress, has become cynical about the value of economic growth. While he recognizes that Chrysler needs a high volume of sales to survive, he no longer believes that increased productivity benefits him personally. To chortle that this unsatisfactory state of affairs will be remedied by collecting artifical "savings"—and remember that the average consumer must pay for these savings through higher fuel prices—is cynical and dangerous. It makes the entire economy dependent on bonanza oil capital, the benefits of which will not be felt by those who are making the sacrifice.

It will further embitter the small man. The corrosive aftereffects will be an increase both in managerial smugness and populist resentment, and a polarization of politics between these two attitudes.

The moral consequences of using "forced savings" also deserve serious attention. Bear in mind that they will be extracted less from American consumers than from the Japanese and West Europeans. If America uses its political leverage, as it shows every sign of doing, not in bargaining over price, but in assuring that petrodollar investments come disproportionately to New York, and that bilateral trade deals are channeled through Washington, we shall in effect be using the "forced savings" of our allies to bolster our own economy. In diplomacy where the effect is often identified with the intent, the US will increasingly appear to be using its military preponderance in the Middle East to extract a form of material tribute from its allies. Moreover as its economy becomes dependent on such unearned capital, there will be less incentive to follow prudent habits of capital formation at home. Already in the past decade the United States has fallen below Britain among major industrial countries devoting the smallest percentage of their output to new capital formation. In the period 1960–73 the percentage of US output invested in capital was exactly half the proportion of Japan, 70 percent of that for Germany and France and 85 percent of that for Italy. Extracting money from these countries by way of petrodollar recycling will rot the moral foundations of our own economy just as forced tribute has done for other empires.

There are those who say cheerfully that Britain thrived for decades on such tricks of finance, and that as long as the OPEC money surplus is held in dollars the United States will benefit from it, much as Britain benefited from Commonwealth balances held in sterling after World War II. Reasoning of this kind seems to underlie Secretary Kissinger's easy assumption in his interview with *Business Week* that the United States will be in a position to "bail out" and "discipline" the economies of Europe. But there is another important fact to bear in mind about Britain's golden age of financial manipulation: she always had America to rescue her. If the US system of capital allocation becomes distorted and top-heavy, if public attitudes toward productivity become cynical, if the US locks itself into an energy system that's more costly than Russia's, who will come to *our* rescue? Will we have to beg the Japanese to "discipline" and "bail out" our effete economy?

There is, needless to say, a coalition of interest groups—representing energy corporations, financiers, arms makers and even opponents of economic growth—that welcomes a permanently high price for oil and views the petrodollar surplus as a benign growth. If this coalition is allowed to gain ascendancy. . . . it may be politically difficult to unseat it or to lower the price of oil even if a glut of energy develops. In Britain, for example, North Sea developers and London financial brokers, who processed 37 percent of all 1974 petrodollar investments, have been exulting over high oil prices, even as the position of the country deteriorates because of its severe debt to OPEC.

As a practical matter, if the United States does not break the cartel, it will have to join it. Speeches by Henry Kissinger and Assistant Secretary of State Thomas Enders to the International Energy Agency in early February have already proposed a world price floor at the $7.00 to $8.40-a-barrel price thought adequate to make the US self-sufficient in energy by 1985.

There is, indeed, a widespread American notion that a high price is a shrewd way to make the US self-sufficient in energy. This confuses free market and national security arguments. As a matter of national security, it may be important to subsidize inefficient energy sources like oil shale and coal liquefaction. But to use the price mechanism for this national defense aim is like quadrupling hospital costs to give physicians an "incentive" to cure cancer. A high price is an efficient incentive only if it can be maintained over the indefinite future. Moreover there is now great leakage from a high price, since most of the windfall surplus accrues to foreign governments that have no incentive to plow back their earnings into energy supply. The main effect of the high price, then, is to redistribute income from Europe and Japan to the unpopulated Arabian peninsula, to distort capital allocation, and to redistribute income within the US from consumers of energy to producers of old oil and managers of petrodollar investments. Politically, the high price has the effect of a reverse Marshall Plan in which European economic and social stability is sacrificed to pay for American self-sufficiency. The damaging effects of high prices for Europeans and Japanese are not compensated for by the offers to let them "invest" in American energy technology.

The use of the price system to create self-sufficiency is not even intelligent from a point of view that considers protection of national security the first priority. The traditional argument for energy independence dates from World War II, when we could not protect the sea lanes from submarine attack. Even if this concern were still valid in the nuclear age, it would argue for standby oil capacity, not autarky. If an artificially high price makes it profitable for private enterprise to drain US oil reserves first, we decrease our ability to be self-sufficient in an emergency. It is not only cheaper but strategically more prudent to consume Arabian reserves at the lowest possible price, while subsidizing directly the early development of technologies in the US that will make it possible to switch to alternative fuel sources later. The current plan to set the price high enough to drain the more remote US oil reserves, and to continue to encourage Sunday drivers to tank up on American gas is the very opposite of sound strategic thinking. The only industrial country that will really benefit from a high price is the Soviet Union, which according to a CIA study now made public, ran a significant hard currency balance of trade surplus in 1974, thanks to a 250 percent increase in oil and related exports. Russia is the world's largest producer of petroleum: a high oil price will make her independent of American economic pressures through 1980, enable her to consolidate her economic hold over the Warsaw bloc nations and perhaps tempt her to use cheap oil and Polish coal to replace Western sources as Germany's main supplies of energy. The Chinese will also be encouraged by the high price to give Japan an alternative to Persian Gulf supplies.

A price-linked program of energy independence also has anomalous effects on our own economy in times of recession. It requires simultaneous programs of economic expansion and oil conservation. Taken together these reinforce a sense of uncertainty among consumers and investors alike. This lack of confidence may be masked temporarily (as it was a year ago) by setting interest rates below the perceived rate of inflation. An appearance of prosperity results as people borrow money to invest in goods, commodities and inventories. But once interest rates move back up, as they inevitably do, the drop in confidence is drastic (as it was six months ago). Professional economists, who analyze such developments in terms of long-term propensities to save, consume and invest, are predictably bewildered when the interaction of foreign and domestic factors creates discontinuities and sudden lurches in economic behavior. Short-term stimulants may fob off the auto industry and other powerful opponents of the high-price strategy, but they do not build long-term confidence in the economy.

A stop-go economy, a weakening strategic position, a reverse Marshall Plan for Europe and Japan, an effective collusion with the cartel, a distortion of capital allocation, an inequitable redistribution of income both internationally and within the United States, a reinforcement of the worst habits of our two-tier industrial system, a rise in populist demagoguery at home, a shift in the locus of real economic authority to unrepresentative and ill-prepared banking institutions, an increasingly unstable level of armaments in the Persian Gulf—these are all undesirable and unintended consequences of the shortsighted view of oil as a commodity rather than as a strategic utility that fuels the entire postwar economic system. Yet because it is a shortsighted view, its effects may well be pleasant enough in the short term: we may see a bustling arms trade, a thriving domestic energy industry, a few golden years for the big banks, an artificial spurt in the economy primed by petrodollar purchases, loans and investments.

During the past 18 months American policy, for all its conflicting signals, appears to have settled on maximizing these favorable effects. Two American Presidents have now given low priority to the pricing and regulation of oil, high priority to attracting OPEC funds; low priority to standby fuel reserves for an emergency, high priority to a price-linked program of self-sufficiency. As if by an invisible hand, the interaction between Presidents and Congress has thus far weeded out initiatives inconsistent with the high price option. While the press has been occupied with Watergate, shuttle diplomacy and Vietnam, America has been moving unobtrusively toward arrangements reminiscent of the 1950s and 1960s when a high price for Arabian crude permitted Western hemisphere self-sufficiency in oil.

Unfortunately this time around the rules of the game have changed. The United States, not the Western hemisphere, is the new locus of self-sufficiency. Britain, once an active partner, is now a passive beneficiary hoping that her North Sea holdings will make her a member of the cartel by 1980. Saudi Arabia and Iran, once little more than puppet regimes, are now able to make significant political demands in any new collusory arrangements. Western Europe and Japan, having prospered under the old arrangements, can look forward to a period when Russia and China offer them the main alternatives to stagnation.

Since there is much in the current drift of American policy that is not attractive to talk about, the prospect of engaging public support for such a program is small among a people used to earning their way in the world. All this suggests an urgent need for a public airing of issues in our oil diplomacy before we take the current arrangements as inalterable, or are tempted to wait for the outbreak of a new Middle Eastern war as a smokescreen for reversing matters. As Dr. Kissinger is doubtless aware, the way in which America has debated the oil problem thus far fits nicely one of Spengler's prophecies: "Parliamentarism . . . is tending rapidly toward taking up itself the role it once assigned to kingship. It is becoming an impressive spectacle for the multitude of the Orthodox, while the center of gravity of big policy . . . is passing de facto . . . to unofficial groups and the will of unofficial personnages . . . And as for America, hitherto lying apart . . . the parallelism of President and Congress . . . has with her entry into world politics become untenable and must . . . make way for formless powers, such as those with which Mexico and South America have long been familiar."

32 An Exchange of Views: Oil and Power Politics

Thinking About an Oil War

Paul Seabury

I sometimes wonder whether . . . a democracy is not uncomfortably similar to one of those prehistoric monsters with a body as long as this room and a brain the size of a pin. He lies there in his comfortable primeval mud and pays little attention to his environment; he is slow to wrath—in fact, you practically have to whack his tail off to make him aware that his interests are being disturbed; but, once he grasps this he lays about him with such blind determination that he not only destroys his adversary but largely wrecks his native habitat.

—GEORGE F. KENNAN,
American Diplomacy 1900–1950

Perhaps because of the difficulty of establishing a plausible chain of causation there so far has not been an extreme public reaction in Europe, Japan and the United States to the implications of the oil price rise, the energy crisis and the monetary squeeze. Inflation, for instance, cannot simply be explained by the drastic oil price increase—it was well under way before the Organization of Petroleum Exporting Countries (OPEC) acted. Similarly, the energy crisis cannot be placed exclusively at the door of the energy-exporting nations—it was bound to come some day in any event, and, as the Shah of Iran is pleased to point out, it is due to the notoriously high consumer habits of Western nations.

But the course of developments on the international monetary scene promises to drastically alter the current climate of opinion. As OPEC members accumulate wealth in astronomical amounts, as the political power of Arab states grows in seemingly inordinate fashion, as industry falters, unemployment rises, depression spreads, and one after another industrial nation goes bankrupt, a systemic crisis the likes of which have not been known in this generation appears inevitable. Unless some change occurs, the merciless chain of events will drive countries to acts they thus far have refrained from considering openly. Indeed, when words like "the fate of civilization" slip from the tongues of statesmen, and are echoed even by politicians, something already is afoot.

This will be no ordinary crisis, for short of threat of force the major democratic powers will not be able to resolve it. No amount of resource-pooling, no concerted crash programs to develop alternative energy sources, no wage-price controls, no public appeals for "belt-tightening" will change the reality of an oil cartel of unprecedented power endangering the vital interests of the advanced world. That this cartel is made up principally of so-called fourth-world non-Western nations, that its spokesmen will cry foul when its actions are opposed, that it may appeal to the Communist bloc and to underdeveloped nations— all this may be assumed. The measures of the Western countries will also undoubtedly expose them to charges that the imperialists are again commencing their depredations against the non-Western world; that the chief victims of today's oil piracy are poor and non-Western will be forgotten with the first ultimatum.

A moment of historical reflection will suffice to explain how the Western world happens to find itself in its present peculiar condition. Would this kind of piracy have been conceivable 40 years ago? Obviously not. Ten years ago? No. But why?

Forty years ago the Middle East was for the most part the property of Europe. Except for Persia, it was composed of principalities created by British and French diplomacy, with European and American oil companies jostling among themselves for concessions. Boundaries had been established by Europeans during World War I. The Hashemite Kingdom of Jordan was actually constructed from the bottom up by the British, who furnished an unknown Bedouin chieftain with an army, deposited him in Amman and drew a line around his arid domains. Those parts of the Middle East not explicitly under European control were Europe's dependencies.

It is not necessary for us to reflect too long on the iniquities of such a situation: For the inhabitants of the region, the end of Ottoman domination meant the beginning of European rule. But the main point here is simply that any Arab uprising threatening the vital interests of Europe would have been unthinkable. Divided, discordant and beset with many fundamental problems, the Europe of the pre-World War II period was nevertheless the *center* of the society of nations. It no longer is. And though its very survival depends upon access to Mideast oil, it lacks the authority and the institutions for a collective foreign policy that would guarantee this. The October War amply demonstrated its impotence.

Today the Continent is at the mercy of princes who preside over less than 1 per cent of the earth's population and seem determined to possess all of the world's monetary wealth. These rulers have shown their ability to use oil as a political weapon; they have the capacity as well, and perhaps even the will, to use it as a deterrent by threatening to destroy it. Through actions taken wholly within their borders, they can bring an end to industrial Europe. This is not science fiction. (That they, with lesser OPEC countries, have had the temerity to concert their designs at meetings in Vienna is an irony that ought not go unnoticed.)

Would a situation of this kind have been possible 10 years ago? Probably not. At that time, too, the regional balances of power were markedly different than they now are. The United States, with others, had the ability, if not to dictate the affairs of the Middle East, at least to influence the flow of events and contain the more dire tendencies of the troubled region. For example, a nimble exercise of the Sixth Fleet in the Eastern Mediterranean, by order of President Johnson, may have discouraged Soviet Intervention in the Six-Day War of 1967. But much has changed since then: In any eventuality other than the worst conceivable one, U.S. naval supremacy in the Eastern Mediterranean is currently nonexistent. Moreover, should there be a new Mideast war, the Arabs may be able to purchase their allies. Such are the grim realities.

An Arab oil producer, or an OPEC devotee, will argue that oil is a commodity, to be sold or not sold, and that it is hardly a grievance under either equity or law for the producer to determine his price. Historic wrongs further intensify the Arabs' conviction of Western hypocrisy—and strengthen the temptation both to expose it and to bask in the warm sun of reverse exploitation. Although feelings of this sort could have disastrous consequences for everyone concerned, the danger is obscured by chimeric prospects of gathering in $1 trillion or more from a compliant world each decade.

Thus the oil-importing nations face a prospect of choosing between bankruptcy and the risks of using force, unless OPEC reverses course and cuts prices. And the United States, while less affected than the Europeans and the Japanese because of its higher degree of self-sufficiency, is nonetheless confronted with the same urgent problem. For in contrast to all postwar crises, what distinguishes this one is the ubiquity of the objects it directly and simultaneously erodes. It is genuinely systemic. It permeates and could profoundly derange the entire world.

In addition, where some crises intensify and subside according to sequences of decisions, the present one is the result basically of only the oil price hijack. Everything else ensues from this, including the central political concern—the ability of Western democratic institutions to handle the profound domestic stresses imposed on them. Most advanced democratic societies, plagued by pre-oil-price-rise inflation, have already been experiencing internal commotion about distributive justice. The oil-energy-monetary crisis does not merely exacerbate this struggle; in many countries it appears to destroy the possibility for any solution.

In an expanding economy, the question is: How should a constantly growing pie be sliced? In a static economy, the question is: From whom should be taken, to give to whom? In a disrupted economy where gigantic sums are trundled off yearly to vaults of small emirates and their allies, the question becomes: Who should bear the brunt of the severe loss of income—the increased unemployment, the gravely accentuated inflation, the reduced social services, the growing incapacity to buy essentials abroad, the termination of many civilized amenities?

To be sure, arrangements have been made for some Arab states to invest their capital in the U.S. and Europe. But this could give rise to a state of affairs in which key sectors of the Western infrastructure are controlled by foreign powers on an unsettling scale. The swiftness of the change of ownership as well as the fact that the policies of Arab nations are incongruent with those of the industrial democracies pose untold difficulties of instability and conflict.

The cartelization of economic power in the hands of a few Middle Eastern states would make earlier Western plutocrats—the Krugers, Rockefellers, Sassoons, Rothschilds—fade into paltry insignificance. To their credit, Western societies tamed the activities of the original "robber barons" by subjecting their enterprises to regulation. But the modern robber barons lie outside the reach of legal structures. Under the guise of international law they claim immunity from control and demand their sovereign rights. What is more, they have a strong case. The West has long respected private property, protecting foreign investments from nationalization and extortive taxation.

That tradition, though, should not blind us to the peculiarity of our present predicament. It hardly can be said that the *results* of Western investment in underdeveloped countries were patently extortive and punitive. Whatever the social side-effects, in general that investment was devoted to the economic development of those lands. This is not true of Arab investment imperialism, which entails stripping the West of its own capital, either to withhold it or to feed it back into the same societies. Whatever it is, Arab money is not productive. It involves only a transfer of power and control, with no possibility of anything significant being added.

Oil-producing states are essentially misnomered. They do not produce oil; rather, they remove it from the ground. Western industry provides the technology, the pumps, the refineries, the shipping facilities. No toiling masses sweat in subterranean mines, adding the value of their harsh, demeaning labor to the product (as is true for the coal industry).

Could the Arab rulers, emulating robber barons of the past, acquire a humane streak allowing them to alleviate the plight of their victims? If we take the Shah at his word, the predicament of the West leaves him indifferent. We are the ones who have supposedly despoiled and plundered. We now shall pay, so that others, a tiny minority of historically less fortunate persons, may cheaply reap the benefits of gigantic wealth. The Shah carefully identifies his targets as giant corporations and ignores ordinary citizens. Yet his meaning is clear.

To further understand the effects of the oil crisis, let us imagine that the enormous flow of riches and power from energy-consumers to energy-exporters hypothetically had gone to a congregation of small nations resembling Switzerland. Staggering questions of equity, and of the domestic effects of this transfer, would remain. Still, Switzerland is Switzerland. The wealth would have entered a country characterized by prudent politics, relative tranquility, a reasonably fortunate geographic location, and a benign albeit selfish foreign policy.

Unfortunately, none of the OPEC members—except possibly Venezuela—can begin to claim Switzerland's attributes. The Arab countries pursue policies pointing to a revision, by great violence if necessary, of the Arab-Israeli status quo. Persian Gulf states have generally been more restrained in their actions toward Israel than Syria and Egypt, yet time and again they have shown their willingness to wage war. That the capacity of all these countries to indulge their belligerency has now grown to truly astonishing heights must be observed with meticulous care.

Nor should it be forgotten that these feudal regimes—out of pace with modern political developments, either Communist or Western—rest on precarious bases. Lacking a tradition of democratic civility, they are remnants of dominions that, elsewhere in the Middle East, have been overthrown by revolutionary movements. Ironically, in the recent past they owed their survival, in large measure, to aid from their current victims, especially from the United States. (It was the 1953 Anglo-American intervention in Iran, remember, that ousted Mossadegh and restored the popular Shah to control.)

Proximity to the Soviet Union, combined with fragile domestic conditions, should be a reminder to the leaders of these governments of the need for prudence. One might even reasonably expect that they would regulate their hubris in their own self-interest, but they have not done so. Consequently, Europe, the United States and Japan must begin exploring, in the most realistic and careful terms, the use of force—whether to employ it at all, or under what circumstances it might be employed. This subject requires examination immediately, before we advance much further down the road.

Admittedly, to raise this prospect, even in a reflective article of this kind, is to risk an uncertain reception, since Western-style political communities today recoil from the idea of using force in their international relations. How they have been led to this pacific stance differs greatly. Europe, an American strategic dependency for more than a quarter-century, has quietly relinquished the reins of its overseas responsibilities, at the same time rising to unparalleled heights of prosperity. The majority of Europeans have chosen to disregard the fact that their culture (often viewed as the direction in which *all* societies should move) has developed in an ambivalent global environment outside their control. Otherwise, they might earlier have attempted to safeguard themselves.

To be sure, in NATO most European nations have grown used to forms of cooperation against the enormous power of the Soviet Union—although as détente proceeds they are becoming less concerned about their safety from the East, too. The new threat, however, comes from another direction, and this quintessentially civilian society is simply unaccustomed to thinking about security, tranquility and prosperity as things that have to be vigilantly defended.

America's recent experience has been different, but the results have been remarkably similar. No matter how divided they were on the Vietnam war, both the Left and the Right in this country were happy to be out of it. Moreover, the former President's words were warmly received by all segments of society when, in enunciating the Nixon Doctrine, he proclaimed that an era of "negotiation" was replacing an era of "confrontation."

Congress, for its part, has abetted this disposition by weaving constraints around the White House; and the military, mindful of its public ordeal during the '60s, no doubt fears being called upon in the existing atmosphere. Haunted by the immediate past, tormented by the ravages of Watergate, no Administration—including the one we happen now to have—would eagerly choose a course of action entailing the use of force *except* in the most desperate circumstances.

Yet it is precisely such circumstances that prudent policy has to prevent, by appearing credibly committed to protecting vital interests. We should make clear, for instance, that the political collapse of one, or more, of our most necessary and valued allies because of the monetary-foreign-exchange crisis would be intolerable. It must be universally understood that any menace to the delicate network of commercial relations linking advanced Western societies would not be permitted.

But as things stand, we see a reversal of Theodore Roosevelt's axiom: If the U.S. through its President speaks loudly today, it carries a small stick. What seems evident to the world is an absence of will and authority. Tamed American leaders, aware of their predecessors' destinies and wishing to avoid similar fates, conceivably could choose to wait until affairs deteriorated to a point where it would be *politically* feasible for them to act. Catastrophe might be necessary to cope with a gloomy sequence of events. The only question then would be whether we had passed a point of no return.

In America, the realities are especially clouded by a growing myth of potential self-sufficiency. Many believe that the nation can withstand the shocks of the oil crisis, that serious political and social dislocations in Europe and Japan would not have parallels here. This makes it possible to imagine a less-than-catastrophic scenario—in fact, one where the U.S. economy might ultimately profit.

Such an inference of insulation, though it might be argued abstractly, ignores the incalculable psychological stresses that would inevitably radiate from Asia and Europe as the crisis deepened. The possibility of Western democracies collapsing would unquestionably have vast impact within the United States, and would surely be mirrored in American politics.

Besides, it should be remembered that the closed Communist states—with a high record of massive repression—will be better able to retain their authority in economically troubled times. Whatever political moves the Kremlin might decide to make, the inner disruption of Western Europe would decisively tilt the balance of power eastward, possibly irreparably.

Within official circles, these considerations must be familiar. Yet governments are understandably loath to express such ideas; to do so would be to risk further angering the oil-producing countries. Doubtless quiet diplomacy is already at work, seeking to impress upon adversaries the long-term cataclysmic consequences that would result from a continuation of existing policy.

It is important in all political affairs carefully to distinguish what one would wish to do from what circumstances might compel. In dealing with the Middle Eastern OPEC countries, this distinction must be made particularly clear. Their own viability, after all, depends upon a viable international system—indeed, the very one their policies are now shaking the foundations of. This is true irrespective of what policies the Western nations may devise.

It is also important that the people of the Western democracies ponder the unpleasant scenarios that now lie ahead. George Kennan's dinosaur need not metaphorically apply to a public able realistically to prepare in advance for future adversities and hard choices. But it should be cautioned that ostriches cannot easily transform themselves into competent dinosaurs. When their heads come out of the sand, their protection is only to be found in their ability to run at great speed from their predators. This talent is not appropriate to present circumstances.

Oil and Power Politics

Touma Arida

In his article "Thinking About an Oil War" Paul Seabury concedes that inflation and the energy crisis cannot simply be explained by the drastic oil price increase." Yet his argument as a whole implies the contrary, to the extent that later, stirred by his campaign against "Arab investment imperialism," he flatly contradicts himself and states: "The present crisis is the result basically of only the oil price hijack."

This view is common to many Western politicians, commentators, oil executives, economists, and even university professors. An examination of the facts, however, suggests that not only didn't the oil price increase cause the international monetary and energy crises, but the very opposite is true.

The current situation is no more than a logical stage in a series of events that started in 1971 with the American decision to suspend convertibility of the dollar and was followed by devaluations of currency around the world. These actions, together with mounting costs for industrial goods and raw materials, led the oil producers to raise the price of their resource gradually through 1971 and 1972. In reality, we are experiencing an unfortunate war of price increases by the exporters of industrial equipment and the exporters of oil.

Moreover, one should remember that only after October 1973 did the control of oil prices finally pass from foreign concessionaires to national authorities in the oil-producing countries. Until then the "big seven" companies (five American, one British and one Anglo-Dutch) dominated the industry, both by their ownership of most of the world's low-cost oil and by their vertical expansion into refining, transportation and marketing. The economic might of these concerns was backed by the weight of their home governments. Evidently, Seabury's analysis is swayed by nostalgia for this fundamentally inequitable state of affairs.

In the ten years from 1960–70, a combination of enormous untapped fuel supplies and competition from profit-maximizing newcomers to the international oil industry led to a steady decline in the market price of petroleum. In the case of Arabian light crude, to cite one typical example, prices fell from about $2.00 per barrel in the early '60s to nearly $1.15 per barrel at the end of the decade. U.S. experts were confidently predicting a further drop.

In December 1969, though, Colonel Muammar el-Qaddafi siezed power in Libya, pulling one of the oil producers with the greatest bargaining leverage into the radical camp; and after a seven-month struggle in 1970, he succeeded in forcing a price rise from the companies. Encouraged in no small part by Qaddafi's fiercely nationalistic policies, other producers proceeded to negotiate price hikes in 1971 and ownership participation agreements one year later, thus overcoming at long last the monopolistic domination by the oil corporations. All of this, of course, was closely connected with the decline of America's global hegemony.

But the most drastic alterations in the structure of the oil industry occurred in the wake of the October War, when the production cutback and the embargo imposed by the Arab oil-producing nations had the effect of increasing oil prices. The Organization of Petroleum Exporting Countries (OPEC)—which, it should be noted *en passant,* is not exclusively Arab—then stepped in to formalize this rise. The new situation destroyed as well the carefully worked-out timetable for handing over ownership of the oil fields to the governments.

Two essential facts related to these changes must be recognized. First, the oil companies have all gained tremendously from the higher prices; second, the U.S. economy has itself reaped sizeable benefits.

During the first half of 1974, the oil enterprises realized quite unprecedented profits, averaging 68.3 per cent over the corresponding period of 1973. This was largely due to the imposition of an exceptionally wide margin between market prices and tax-paid costs in the major OPEC countries.

As for the United States, its considerable degree of energy self-sufficiency has placed its products in an advantageous competitive position now on the world market, since the European and Japanese economies are dependent on imports from OPEC. Not surprisingly, pressure was exerted by the U.S. through its traditional Middle Eastern ally, Saudi Arabia, to prevent or delay the lifting of the Arab embargo on the Netherlands, Rotterdam being Europe's largest center for oil transport and refining.

The exporters, in short, are hardly alone in profiting from the new oil rates. Nor can they be held responsible for international financial and economic difficulties. The problem of oil prices must be analyzed in a general trading framework that takes into account the cost and availability of other vital raw materials and industrial commodities.

Another matter of misunderstanding is the projected threat to the economies of the West, and hence to the world of the vast funds flowing into the treasuries of the producers. Here, some basic points require explaining:

1. Although precise figures are not available, it is generally accepted that oil revenues cannot be spent in their entirety, and that the surpluses will have to be "recycled." But the whole surplus notion must be treated with caution. A number of Arab producers, including Algeria, Iraq and Egypt, suffer from capital shortages, not income gluts. Within the Arab world, in fact, only Saudi Arabia, Kuwait, the Gulf states, and Libya enjoy the much-vaunted excesses; and in those countries many major projects remain to be realized, or even commenced, because the necessary funds have only become available in the last year and the infrastructures necessary to absorb them efficiently and

economically have not yet been developed. (This latter draw-back can in great measure be laid at the door of the Western world: It is, after, all of some significance that in over half a century of oil exploitation in the Middle East, no large company ever saw fit to establish a single institute of petroleum instruction or research in the area.)

2. In the light of their overall requirements, the Arab oil producers, far from looking forward to decades of financial surpluses, will have innumerable opportunities to spend their income on their own development and the development of other less wealthy states in the region. A study by the World Health Organization has estimated the minimum cost for a health program in the Arab world at $35 billion. The number of doctors in these countries, for instance, averages 2.7 per 10,000 inhabitants, compared with 15.6 in the United States and 17.2 in West Germany. Similar or greater amounts are urgently needed in other fields—$25 billion per year for education, and more than $100 billion for the construction of a modern road network between the Gulf countries and the Mediterranean, to give but two examples.

   Indeed, in the long run, any revenue surpluses will be self-liquidating: The OPEC nations will assess their needs, deploy their resources and ultimately undertake an accelerating industrialization program for their own and their neighbors' economies—thereby gradually absorbing the funds resident in the West.

3. Finally, it must be borne in mind that oil is not the only traded material ever to be in short supply. Periodically, there have been restrictions in steel, cement and foodstuffs. The Food and Agriculture Organization of the United Nations recently predicted that by the end of this century about 1 billion human beings will have died from hunger. One must ask why the countries that export the particular commodities needed to prevent this tragedy do not feel as obliged to increase their output for the international good as they believe the oil products should be.

But if Seabury has failed to think through the economic side of the oil crisis, he is no less misguided in his interpretation of its political aspect. Specifying the dangers he perceives from the emergence of the oil "barons," he declares that the "Arab countries pursue policies pointing to a revision, by great violence if necessary, of the Arab-Israeli status quo." Yet what is sacrosanct about a status quo based on Israel's arrogant refusal to carry out the numerous resolutions passed by the United Nations? Until he recognizes that the Arabs have a legitimate case, Seabury is unlikely to understand the politics of the oil comfrontation.

As might be expected, his conclusions make depressing reading. "Consequently," he writes, "Europe, the United States and Japan must begin exploring, in the most realistic and careful terms, the use of force—whether to employ it at all, or under what circumstances it might be employed. This subject requires examination immediately, before we advance much further down the road." In other words, Seabury is blithely recommending that the West seriously contemplate armed intervention—occupying the oil fields should this be thought necessary—to bring the oil exporters to heel.

Such a development, though, is highly improbable. Seabury fails to consider the danger of confrontation with the Soviet Union, or the prospect of a prolonged guerrilla war. In addition, any power attempting something as foolhardy as occupation would inevitably lose whatever standing it had with the Arabs. The simple truth is that a military action would not solve the energy crisis and recession in the West. If Europe and the United States are passing through a period of profound economic difficulty, the reasons are mainly unrelated to the price of oil and the level of imports from the Middle East.

What is really required is a scheme for cooperation between the industrial nations and the oil producers that encompasses all fields of activity relevant to both groups. The West should be assured of an adequate supply of crude oil at fair prices and the exporters should be permitted to utilize their decreasing resources to speed up social and economic development. The OPEC countries, and particularly the Arabs, have shown considerable willingness to move in just this direction. Unfortunately, the response from the West has all too often been along the lines of Paul Seabury's article.

The Moral Issue

Paul Seabury

Touma Arida's reply to my article seems chiefly designed to assert the notion that OPEC price policies are no more damaging to, or blameworthy for, current international energy and monetary problems than the practices of other nations, now or in the past. But this appears credible only because it omits governing facts that are quickly becoming common knowledge. I hesitate to consume newsprint repeating them; even less do I wish to tax the attention of reasonably informed readers. However . . .

First, to the matter of magnitude. The world price of oil, in December 1970, was $1.80 per barrel. In August 1973, it suddenly jumped to $3.07. And in October of that year, it surged to $11.65. Since then, the whole globe has shared, with peaceable acquiescence, the agony of adjusting to the decision of a tiny group of men, made for the enrichment of their families or their small nations. Hardly anyone anymore contests the proposition that the present transfer of wealth from the industrial nations to the OPEC lands, most of them unproductive members of the international community, is one of the largest in human history.

Arida languidly suggests that the oil price hike is merely one of many Stations-of-the-Cross marking the consumer countries' procession to Golgotha. Or, to switch Holy Land metaphors, it is to him only one more straw on an overburdened camel's back. But what a straw! Its impact, both primary and secondary, is being felt everywhere—beginning with the monetary world—in ways Arida does not take pains to describe.

The cost of oil to the principal consuming nations has risen, in the one year *after* the price hike, from a known $46.2 billion in 1973 to an estimated $120 billion in 1974. The chief burden of this gigantic increase has been borne by Western Europe. But the cost to America has also catapulted, from $8.5 billion in 1973 to approximately $25 billion in 1974.

This is not the whole story, for the OPEC action has inspired severe price rises in other (higher-cost) fuel and energy sources. Thus, as economist Walter Levy notes, "nearly unmanageable problems are posed for all the oil-importing countries." It has been calculated that West Europe, Canada, Japan, and the United States will suffer a deficit ranging from $25–$40 billion in 1974 alone, as a result of tribute.

The muted cries inspired by these heavy injuries have mainly come, so far, from persons in countries relatively less grievously afflicted, where there is a certain freedom of expression not present in poorer and far more vulnerable lands. Yet the effect of the price rise on less-developed and authoritarian societies—nations Arida neglects to mention—has been devastating. In at least 40 countries of Africa, Asia and Latin America, catastrophic prospects—including the collapse of the agricultural sector—loom large. If the West faces unemployment and general deprivation, the Third World faces widespread death.

In particular, one might consider black Africa. There, only two countries have any significant oil fields. Seventeen have neither production or refining facilities. Their recent pleas to the Arab oil exporters for special treatment have been coldly ignored. The Indian subcontinent, including Bangladesh, which suffers the oil crisis silently and subserviently but is predictably loud and strident when it complains to the West, likewise deserves sympathetic mention.

Nor is this all Arida fails to discuss. While lamenting the pitiable difficulty the Gulf states and Libya are having in digesting their immense revenues (a difficulty that, for some reason, he blames upon the West), Arida might have noted what informed observers suggest as a likely possibility: Should the torrent of money become wholly unmanageable, even for Arab graduates of the Harvard Business School, they always have the option of drastically cutting production back—an option whose consequences the prospective victims would do well to carefully contemplate.

We might also wonder how Arida concludes that *(mirabile dictu!)* the United States is profiting from the remarkable oil swindle facilitated, as he tells us, by "the decline of America's global hegemony." "The U.S. economy," he declares, "has itself reaped sizable benefits," since other Western nations have found themselves undercut in world markets by more competitive U.S. exports. Were this so, it would presumably show in balance-of-payments figures. Yet in fact the downward spiral of U.S. trade balances commences in October 1973— the precise date of the price hijack. (For September 1973, U.S. trade produced an $800 million surplus; by August 1974 it resulted in a $1.2 billion deficit.)

The force of Arida's strange assertion about America's "sizeable benefits" depends primarily upon his seeing the United States as synonomous with the oil companies. Even this proposition, though, cannot fly. I do not wish to contest his figures on the industry's profits for the first half of 1974; these have been widely reported. But if we were to say that the price-hike profits to the companies and to the OPEC nations constitute 100 per cent, then OPEC has taken 95 per cent and the companies only 5 per cent.

In any case America is not a disembodied aggregation of businesses, as some simplistic neo-Marxists avow; it is a nation of live persons. Citizens have many means available for regulating the domestic oil companies' take in this enormous depredation. There are no means available, other than suasion or force, for the popular will to reach into distant sovereign states. As for Arida's *ex cathedra* contention that the United States connived with Saudi Arabia after the October War to prolong the Arab strangulation of the Netherlands and its international refineries for gain, it deserves no reply.

Elsewhere Arida seeks to play down the Arabs' undigestible new wealth because, had he bothered to quantify it, he would have reached conclusions opposite to those he announces. "The whole surplus notion," he says, "must be treated with caution." Then he observes that oil-exporting countries—Algeria, Iraq and Egypt—suffer from capital shortages; "only Saudi Arabia, Kuwait, the Gulf states, and Libya enjoy the much-vaunted excesses."

These desolate and largely uninhabited nations, however, *are* the major exporters. In 1973 their combined production was 15.5 million barrels per day, compared with a mere 3.1 million barrels from Morocco, Algeria, Tunisia, Egypt and Iraq. Egypt, the Arab world's most populous land, produces a tiny amount—equivalent to only 2.5 per cent of Saudi Arabia's output. Lebanon produces none.

Conservative estimates now project 1975 oil earnings for the Gulf states (minus Iraq) and Libya in the neighborhood of $50 billion. On the other hand, Iraq and Algeria—the two countries Arida says are best able to absorb immense funds for immediate and profitable domestic purposes—will take in $11.4 billion.

Perhaps most stimulating, though, is Arida's concluding rhetorical question. He wonders why "the countries that export [steel, cement and food] do not feel as obliged to increase their output for the international good as they believe the oil producers should be." Precisely because of the astronomical increases in energy costs, these producing countries are less able to do this than they were a year-and-a-half ago.

Moreover, several supplementary questions might be raised: What would have happened if the United States (which now accounts for far more than 50 per cent of the world's grain exports) had chosen to enrich itself by suddenly quintupling the price of grain on the world market in collusion with the other suppliers, Canada and Australia? What would America's reputation in the world be, had it embargoed its food exports for political purposes? Going a bit further, what would America's reputation be today if the world's available petroleum reserves were chiefly located in the United States, and Washington had abruptly decided to quintuple the price of oil, and/or to cease all oil exports for political purposes?

There is, in addition, a deep moral issue that Arida's loaded question inspires. He equates the American producers of foodstuffs, steel and cement with OPEC "producers" of oil. That equation cannot be honestly made.

To produce is to manufacture; to manufacture is, ultimately, to make something by hand and effort of hand. Manufacturing entails labor, skill, and intelligence. That technological innovation reduces the immediate presence of labor in no way affects the central issue: It takes very little production to obtain petroleum. Oil is simply pumped from the ground, and that is accomplished by Western technology. Those now garnering enormous riches from this activity in fact neither sow nor reap.

I emphasize this moral point with deliberate intensity. For it lays open a grave matter that to date has not been candidly discussed because the advanced nations have been courteous. But the hundreds of millions of persons in developed countries—whose jobs, incomes and good temperaments depend upon guaranteed access to energy—will not long accept a policy that daily, monthly and yearly drains and saps them. Protracted deprivation brought about by a transfer of their earned wealth (acquired through labor, skill and intelligence) to those already inordinately rich and becoming more so with each day, who contribute nothing of themselves to what they claim and sell as their own, is not a condition likely to produce either friendship or peace.

Finally, with regard to the question of force, I must confess to being a poor armchair strategist. But when I wrote "Thinking About an Oil War" (which has gained me a small reputation as a premature anti-OPECer), I had no intention of making "blithe" and adventurist proposals. As I said then, "no one would eagerly choose a course of action entailing the use of force, except in the most desperate circumstances." Yet, as I also said, "it is precisely such circumstances that prudent policy has to prevent, by appearing credibly committed to protecting vital interests." And, to repeat myself a bit more, "it is important in all political affairs carefully to distinguish what one would wish to do from what circumstances might compel."

The issue of intervention, after all, is one that must be treated as an available option, its merits considered in terms of the damage to the U.S. and other nations resulting from a man-made situation imposed upon us. Already the damage has been very heavy. And because of OPEC pricing policies, it is continuing and increasing. At some point the risks entailed in passively continuing to accept this damage may greatly outweigh the risks entailed in intervention. Other nations have vital interests; is Providence so kind to us as to exempt us from having to care about our own basic needs?

33 American Agripower and the Future of a Hungry World

Dan Morgan

Geopolitical fantasy, Act I. It is the summer of 1977 and Panama's President Omar Torrijos has provoked an unexpected international crisis by seizing control of the Panama Canal. The American President and his advisers meet in emergency session at the White House to plan a response. The options are not promising. Military action seems inadvisable, for the canal is vulnerable to sabotage, American forces are badly outnumbered by tens of thousands of rampaging Panamanians, and the mood in Congress is hostile to committing more U.S. troops.

After examining the alternatives carefully, the President decides to employ an untested weapon. That weapon is food.

Act II. American wheat shipments to Panama have stopped, and after a month there is not a grain of wheat or a sack of flour left in the country. Torrijos's economists remind him that his country's wheat dependence on the United States had been total. All 53,000 tons consumed there in 1976 as bread, pasta, and cake came from America. Food inflation is rampant. When Torrijos quietly contacts France about buying wheat, grain-trade sources tip off friends in the U.S. Department of Agriculture. The White House informs France that if it breaks the wheat embargo, Washington will cut off corn deliveries to the European Common Market—the 11-million-tons-a-year pipeline on which Western Europe depends for its animal feed. France backs off. Australia and Canada also withdraw their discreet overtures to Panama. American agricultural attachés in those countries pass the word that if Torrijos gets help, the United States will dump wheat at cut-rate prices into favorite Australian and Canadian wheat markets in the Middle East and in communist China.

Act III. Torrijos caves in and sends his negotiators back to the bargaining table to continue interminable talks with the United States on the future of the canal.

Is such a scenario actually plausible? Yes, very much so. It is, in fact, likely that a highly detailed plan along these lines even now reposes in the vaults where the CIA squirrels away its various "contingency" schemes.

This is not to say, however, that the government is not fully aware of the politcal, moral, and technical reasons why such a deployment of American food power might well backfire. In fact, Don Paarlberg, director of economics at the Department of Agriculture, describes America's alleged food power as a "myth," saying that the use of food as a weapon would be "an error on diplomatic as well as on moral grounds."

Then, too, U.S. policymakers must keep in mind the powerful domestic and political constraints against grain embargoes—as witness the grain shipments to the Soviet Union in 1975.

The world grain trade is, moreover, a leaky business. It is operated by a handful of multinational corporations that know better than any government where grain is and how to get it from one place to another. They operate vast global shipping and communications networks that enable them to trade grain outside the purview of government bureaucrats. In the global grain trade, the 53,000 tons of wheat that Panama gets from us is a raindrop in a deluge, a mere two-freighter cargo. Mexico alone could supply such a paltry amount to Panama without anybody's being the wiser.

Given the volume of the world's grain trade, now running at 157 million tons a year, only a few huge importers, such as Japan, Western Europe, the Soviet Union, and (in poor harvest years) India, could be crippled by an American food curtailment.

Nevertheless, American food power is a reality. It is, so to speak, there, though its manifestations are, as a former cabinet official described them, "very, very subtle." The Central Intelligence Agency concluded in a study that the world's increasing dependence on American surpluses "portends an increase in U.S. power and influence, particularly vis-á-vis the food-deficit poor countries." Soviet officials have sometimes hinted at their concern about the growing American grain hegemony, warning their U.S. counterparts not to act as if "you have your boots on our necks." Yet how else could the Soviet grain dependency on America be described? Since the summer of 1975, 8 percent of *all* the grain used to feed people and animals in the Soviet Union has been American. Food "kept the Russians on the sidelines" while Secretary of State Henry A. Kissinger negotiated a Middle East peace agreement in 1975, in the view of our then Secretary of Agriculture Earl L. Butz.

The United States is the world's only agricultural superpower, and there are not even any close challengers. As the United States has lost its monopoly in nuclear technology and economic know-how, its food monopoly has grown apace. The country now produces half of all the world's corn, and its share of the corn and wheat trade is still greater. Most of the growth in the world grain trade since 1972 has been accounted for by the growth in American exports, from 34 million tons then to 82 million tons in 1975.

Iowa alone produces about 10 percent of all the corn grown in the *world,* and Kansas and North Dakota produce almost as much wheat as Canada (the world's third largest producer) and more than Australia (the fourth largest). Poor weather in those three states can wreak havoc in world markets, push up food prices from Seattle to Singapore, and increase the level of global malnutrition. The United States is a major force in the world rice trade, too, even though rice is a minor American crop. In fact, with its exports of 1.4 million tons, the United States is the world's leading rice-trading nation.

The patterns of an American-centered global grain trade are clearly established. The American grain pipeline, as it now exists, criss-crosses the world without regard to the borders of either geography or ideology.

East Germany, an implacable ideological adversary of the United States, has become almost totally dependent on corn from the American Midwest to feed its growing hog, poultry, and beef populations. Virtually all of the 1.3 million tons of corn that East Germany consumed in 1975 and 1976 came from the United States.

The same pattern of dependency is true of America's closest allies. Japan, which lacks adequate farmland to support its population, receives from the United States about 11 million tons out of the 19.2 million tons of the grain it uses. (The dependence of Asian rice-eating countries such as Japan, Taiwan, South Korea, and the Philippines on American wheat is a postwar phenomenon, spurred in part by efforts of the American government, wheat-farmer organizations, and grain companies to change Asian diets.)

In Western Europe only France could do without American grain for an extended period of time without disruptions in the economy. (In that sense, French bread, which is made almost entirely from indigenous soft-wheat flour, is a proud symbol of French independence, as well as a tribute to Gallic culinary superiority.)

The level of grain dependence is also high in many countries in which the United States has a vital economic or security interest. In 1975 and 1976 oil producer Venezuela bought almost all its wheat from the United States. In the same period three-fourths of all the grain used by Israel was American. More recently, the regime in Chile is importing most of its wheat from the United States.

Tropical countries whose soil and weather are unfavorable for growing cereal grains are particularly reliant on the United States as a supplier. Jamaica (which has led efforts to form a cartel of bauxite-producing countries) gets almost all of its annual requirement of 200,000 tons of grain from the United States.

To suggest that these patterns do not pose both political opportunities and moral dilemmas for the United States seems naive. The country's food monopoly gives it the power to affect diets, nutrition, and economies around the world—perhaps even to decide who starves and who lives in times of famine and periods of poor harvest. In many countries food imports from the United States have become a major factor in political stability.

In cities that have recently been swelled by an influx of former peasants, farmers, and rural dwellers no longer able to feed themselves, food imports are crucial. Faced with hungry urban populations, many governments have chosen the politically easier option of importing food rather than trying to increase their countries' own food production. Providing food at reasonable prices is often a priority matter in the political survival of governments. Food-price increases (resulting from poor harvests and skimping on imports) led to bloody rioting and to the overthrow of the regime of Wladyslaw Gomulka in Poland in 1970.

Food, therefore, is not only a resource that is basic to human civilization. It is also a prominent factor today in the political stability of countries around the world. Yet U.S. policymakers have been slow to acknowledge the grave responsibilities that the country's food monopoly have created.

America's enormous food exports today are not primarily feeding the hungry; they are feeding those who can afford to pay for grain that is about twice as costly as it was four years ago. For the most part, the United States distributes its food abroad according to the purchasing power of buyers rather than need. Last year, the country gave away only 1.3 million tons of its total production of 240 million tons. And the country's largest *cash* buyer of wheat was India.

Other countries are well aware of the significance of the American grain dominion. "You Americans have something more powerful than the atomic bomb—you have protein!" said a Rumanian agriculture official to former Secretary Butz last year. Butz himself was fond of saying that "corn is helping maintain the peace of the world."

Yet beyond such vague acknowledgements as these, policymakers in Washington tend to hide behind the ideology of "free trade" in discussing the implications of the food monopoly. Any suggestion that the American government has profound responsibility for seeing to it that the available food is distributed equitably is met with arguments that the government should not interfere in the grain marketplace. U.S. food policy under Presidents Nixon and Ford can best be described as mercantilist. The government has only the loosest kind of surveillance of the grain trade itself. For the most part, large privately owned grain companies allocate American grain to buyers abroad according to the laws of supply and demand. Rich countries and poor countries alike pay the same price for the grain they buy in the wide-open American supermarket—though poor countries sometimes end up paying more if they are unfortunate enough to make their purchases after heavy buyers such as the Soviet Union have completed transactions in this country.

American leadership in creating new institutions to deal with the new reality of a continuing global grain shortage has been timid, uncertain, and reluctant. In the 1950s and 1960s the country could hardly give away its enormous surpluses. Today demand for American food is strong all around the world. But Washington seems to have been unprepared for the country's transition from major food producer to major food power. In the situation that has existed since 1973, the policy of the Department of Agriculture has been a narrow one: to get farmers to produce as much as they can and to sell the surplus abroad for the highest possible price. In a real sense, the United States has been the main beneficiary of the world food crisis.

The record food exports from the United States have apparently not made a dent in the problem of world hunger. Malnutrition is more widespread than it was four years ago. The U.N. Food and Agriculture Organization says there are still 500 million inadequately fed people in the world. In many countries where large numbers of people live at the edge of starvation, food imports from abroad are not allocated to the hungry but are resold to those who can pay. Honduras imports 110,000 tons of wheat a year from the United States, but a British journalist recently witnessed, in a rural hospital in that country, the death of an infant suffering from malnutrition.

The growing dependence of the world on American food is, in fact, a symptom of a global crisis that is getting worse, even though it has dropped out of the headlines recently. The world has a bountiful supply of rice and wheat this year for those who can pay for it, thanks to good harvests. Yet the world has not been able to return to the upward trend in overall grain production that it held to until 1971. The expected grain production for 1976 (wheat, corn, barley, oats, rye, and millet) is expected to be slightly above a billion tons, about the same as in 1973. The International Food Policy Research Institute (IFPRI), in Washington, predicts that the world's poorest countries will have grain deficits of between 42 million tons and 48 million tons by 1985 unless they sharply increase their own food production—something that has not been happening.

Much more will be required to reach those targets than more injections of money and technology from rich, developed countries. Political leadership and courage will be required, not only in the poor countries, in which agriculture has had a low priority for too long, but also in rich countries, which have certainly contributed to the food crisis by catering to narrow political and national interests of their own.

Officials at the U.N. World Food Council, in Rome, throw up their hands in frustration when they talk about the monumental apathy they confront. "The politics on both sides, rich and poor, has got to be changed," said one such official "But there isn't a single political leader in the world who wants to focus on this problem."

Studies by the U.S government, private organizations, and the United Nations have all pinpointed an array of policies in developing countries that impede rather than encourage agricultural production. Lack of credit for farmers, low prices for farm products, export taxes, and "outmoded agrarian structures" in which big landlords prosper at the expense of small tenant farmers are all part of the problem. (In the

Philippines 98 percent of loans to farmers go to the one-fourth of the farmers with the largest holding.)

But the policies of wealthy countries such as the United States also pose obstacles to a solution. Studies by the General Accounting Office, in Washington, fault the United States for dumping its food surpluses abroad and discouraging countries to produce more of their own food. In wealthy nations the problem often is not too little political influence on the farm sector but too much.

Lack of information about how the global food system works and about why it is failing to respond quickly enough now is no longer the problem it once was. We know a great deal about the interaction of domestic and international agricultural policy. Policymakers clearly understand that there is a link between the tariff policies of wealthy nations and the food production of poorer ones and that there is no isolating domestic decisions from their international consequences.

What is lacking are creative solutions and the political will to avert a potential global catastrophe. As the only agricultural superpower, the United States has the responsibility for at least making sure that its policies don't adversely affect countries least able to pay for the consequences.

Yet Dale E. Hathaway, director of IFPRI, notes that "there has been very little effort here to use food in a positive way." Within the Ford administration, responsibility for making agricultural policy has seesawed back and forth between the State Department and the Department of Agriculture, coming to rest finally with Butz just before the Illinois Republican primary, when Ford was trying to appease farm-state voters.

Only Kissinger has continued to speak out publicly about the need for international institutions to stabilize prices and to provide access to adequate supplies at reasonable prices, within the context of a new global economic order. But he has been a lonely voice in an administration that, by and large, is ideologically inclined toward free trade, noninterference in the markets, and latter-day mercantilism. At the Agriculture Department, Kissinger's overtures have been attacked as the utopian dreaming of "striped-pants amateurs."

Yet it is obvious that the old laissez-faire policies have left much to be desired. As one White House official said, "Agriculture has become too important to be left to the Department of Agriculture."

Three times since 1973, the White House has been forced to impose embargoes on soybeans or grain in a highly charged emergency atmosphere. Given the importance of agriculture in the American economy and the dependence of other nations on U.S. grain, these actions have sent shock waves through the American Midwest and around the globe.

Some legislators, such as Democratic Congressman James Weaver, of Oregon, have called for the creation of a national grain board along the lines of the Canadian Wheat Board to allocate grain to customers abroad and to dispense food aid as necessary. Weaver would have sporadic customers such as the Soviet Union pay premium prices, sell grain cheaply to poor countries, and block food shipments to countries that withhold vital raw materials from the United States.

Such a plan, which would vest control of half the world grain trade in a government agency subject to political and diplomatic pressures, seems fraught with pitfalls and the potential for abuse. On the other hand, the emergency embargoes and wildly fluctuating prices of the past three years clearly show that some government management of grain supplies is urgently needed.

The only alternative to this confusion is a broad American food policy that would balance the interest of American farmers and consumers, cash-paying customers abroad, and poor nations. So far, talks aimed at creating an international food-reserve system have gone nowhere at the International Wheat Council, in London, partly because the U.S. government is itself divided on the issue. Two years after the World Food Conference, in Rome, wealthy countries and the major oil-producing nations are still wrangling over the size of their contributions to a fund to finance agricultural production in poor countries. The United States has agreed to put up $200 million, but only if others put up their share.

In Congress, only Senator Hubert H. Humphrey has a comprehensive food-policy plan. It envisions government controls on grain exports as a last resort. But under his plan the likelihood of such a drastic step would be greatly lessened. The plan would contribute to more stability of grain prices, which would help poor nations abroad as well as U.S. livestock men, who have been hard hit by the oscillating prices of grain.

Adequate stocks of wheat and feed grains—perhaps 15 million tons of both—are the basis of the Humphrey plan. The bulk of the stocks would be held by farmers and the grain trade, but the government would also hold some. As long as prices stayed within a fairly wide band, the government would keep its hands off. But if prices rose past the ceiling, the government would sell off some of its stocks and caution buyers abroad to pare down their imports. If prices dipped below the floor, the government would buy grain, and if they kept dropping, the Secretary of Agriculture could announce that he would order farmers to plant less the next year—unless other countries increased their buying for the purpose of building up reserve stocks of their own.

If nothing else, the plan would announce to the world that the United States acknowledges its responsibility for safeguarding a more stable global grain economy. It would recognize that, where food is concerned, there are much larger issues at stake than the interests of private grain companies or even the U.S. balance of payments. It would be a step toward rationing food in an orderly way as the world enters a time of inevitable shortages.

The American grain monopoly has reached unhealthy proportions. And it has been fostered by a myth in the Department of Agriculture that U.S. technology and U.S. production are the answer to the world food problem. The real answer is enlightened policies, which need to begin in the United States itself.